ROUTLEDGE LIBRARY EDITIONS:
JEWISH HISTORY AND IDENTITY

Volume 3

THE SEPHARDIM OF ENGLAND

THE SEPHARDIM OF ENGLAND

A History of the Spanish and Portuguese Jewish Community 1492–1951

ALBERT M. HYAMSON

Routledge
Taylor & Francis Group
LONDON AND NEW YORK

First published in 1951 by Methuen & Co. Ltd

This edition first published in 2020
by Routledge
2 Park Square, Milton Park, Abingdon, Oxon OX14 4RN

and by Routledge
52 Vanderbilt Avenue, New York, NY 10017

Routledge is an imprint of the Taylor & Francis Group, an informa business

© 1951 Albert M. Hyamson

All rights reserved. No part of this book may be reprinted or reproduced or utilised in any form or by any electronic, mechanical, or other means, now known or hereafter invented, including photocopying and recording, or in any information storage or retrieval system, without permission in writing from the publishers.

Trademark notice: Product or corporate names may be trademarks or registered trademarks, and are used only for identification and explanation without intent to infringe.

British Library Cataloguing in Publication Data
A catalogue record for this book is available from the British Library

ISBN: 978-0-367-44247-7 (Set)
ISBN: 978-1-00-300850-7 (Set) (ebk)
ISBN: 978-0-367-46176-8 (Volume 3) (hbk)
ISBN: 978-0-367-46179-9 (Volume 3) (pbk)
ISBN: 978-1-00-302742-3 (Volume 3) (ebk)

Publisher's Note
The publisher has gone to great lengths to ensure the quality of this reprint but points out that some imperfections in the original copies may be apparent.

Disclaimer
The publisher has made every effort to trace copyright holders and would welcome correspondence from those they have been unable to trace.

INTERIOR OF THE SYNAGOGUE
From a water-colour by Isaac Mendes Belisario

THE SEPHARDIM OF ENGLAND

A HISTORY OF THE SPANISH
AND PORTUGUESE JEWISH COMMUNITY
1492–1951

by

ALBERT M. HYAMSON

METHUEN & CO. LTD., LONDON
36 Essex Street, Strand, W.C.2

*Published by Authority of the
Wardens of the Spanish and Portuguese Synagogue,
Bevis Marks, London, on the Occasion of the
250th Anniversary of the Opening
of the Bevis Marks Synagogue,*
1701 : 5461

First published in 1951

CATALOGUE NO. 3844/U

PRINTED IN GREAT BRITAIN BY
JARROLD AND SONS LTD., NORWICH

PREFACE

FEW WORDS ARE necessary as a preface to the chapters that follow. If the intention with which they were written is fulfilled they will tell their own story, that of the development in England of the Sephardi branch of the Jewish community, the co-heirs, with their kinsmen in Holland, in Italy, in North America and in the Moslem lands, of the far distant, but still remembered, Golden Age of Jewish history in Spain. To me has been given the great privilege of telling this story. There have been many difficulties in the way, and I am the first to realize that my ideal has not been attained. Can any ideal ever be attained? If, however, the past has to some extent been brought back to life, the lives and interests, pictured and interpreted, of the predecessors and ancestors of those with whom the responsibility for the guidance and maintenance of that which is still known as Bevis Marks rests today, then my work has not been in vain. As for myself, I am very conscious of the privilege that has been conferred on me by entrusting me with the work, and I am proud and grateful for it.

Although the first to write a full-length history of the Sephardi Community in England, I am not the pioneer in the field. The first to turn his attention to this corner of Jewish history was James Picciotto, whose fascinating *Sketches of Anglo-Jewish History*, published three-quarters of a century ago, are as readable and interesting today as they were when they first appeared. He was the first to open the archives of the Community and to bring to the light many an interesting incident, until then buried deep in dust. He did not write a history of the Community nor did he claim to do so. Yet he is the literary father of all who followed him along this road.

A quarter of a century later, just fifty years ago, the two hundredth anniversary of the opening of the synagogue in Bevis Marks was celebrated, and the occasion was marked by a handsome volume from the pen of the then Haham, Moses Gaster—*History of the Ancient Synagogue of the Spanish and Portuguese Jews*. This work, although also not in the full sense a history of the Community, was also based on the original documents in the archives. Gaster's work was indeed a *tour de force* for, as the author points out in his preface, just five months elapsed between the day on which he was asked to write the book and that on which he completed his task. When one realizes the magnitude of this task, with no available printed material beyond Picciotto's *Sketches* and scattered items in the Anglo-Jewish periodical press, one feels astounded at the work that resulted. This book, even if it stood alone, would be a not unworthy monument to the intellectual breadth and versatility of its author.

The third historian of Anglo-Sephardi Jewry whose work joined with that of his two predecessors to provide the solid foundations on which the following chapters stand is Dr. Lionel Barnett. Of his two books on the subject one is a careful, well-documented literal translation from the Spanish and Portuguese of the earliest Minute Book of the Mahamad or governing committee of the Community, *El Libro de los Acuerdos*. This contains the skeleton of the history of the Community from 1663 to 1681. Later, Dr. Barnett followed with another volume, *Bevis Marks Records* (Part I) being, as he puts it, 'Contributions to the History of the Spanish and Portuguese Congregation of London . . . from the Beginning until 1800.'

These four books, together with a few monographs on phases of Anglo-Sephardi history for which Paul Goodman, the secretary of the Congregation, found leisure in the course of his busy life, may be said to exhaust the printed material which should form the basis on which a history of the Community can be built up. But the Sephardim of England have not only a history: they have also a prehistory. In this region the ground has been well and scientifically tilled, and anyone who follows the pioneers there will find his work facilitated at almost every turn. The two scholars who stand out as lighting up the darkness of this earlier period and also of the first years after the establishment of a formal Sephardi Community in London are Lucien Wolf and Mr. Cecil Roth. Mr. Wilfred Samuel also, by his researches into the records contemporary with the first years of the organized community, has turned light into recesses that had hitherto been unexplored and has provided material for a chapter which would otherwise have been almost blank. The writer of the present volume realizes his great indebtedness to these historians of Anglo-Jewry, who have not only made his path easier but have directed his attention to sources that would otherwise probably have been overlooked. The historian of the Sephardim of England must never forget his debt to them.

Despite all the assistance made readily available by these pioneers there remained and remains the rich mine contained in the scores of volumes of archives of the Community. These had hardly been touched. Their pages may have been turned over: an occasional fruit has been plucked here and there. Many still awaited the gleaner. Some more have been gathered on this occasion, but it cannot be claimed that the harvest is yet complete.

Finally I must record my debt to the willing and generous assistance given me by friends in the work I undertook. Dr. Lionel Barnett was always at my disposal with his wealth of knowledge and sage advice. Among the other debts I owe him is the use of the note-books which he filled in preparation for his two works on the same subject. His son, Mr. Richard Barnett, is the Honorary Archivist of the Congregation. There was never an occasion on which he was not ready, nay anxious, to assist when appeal was made to him. Mr. Neville Laski, K.C., generously placed at my disposal the documents copied by his father-in-law, Moses Gaster, for a second edition of his *History* which, however, he never published. Mr. Owen E. Mocatta, the president and chairman of the Council, and Mr. R. Galan, the secretary, of the West London Synagogue of British Jews, readily and generously placed at my disposal the early records of their Congregation which relate to the withdrawal of most of their founders from the Parent Synagogue in Bevis Marks. The Very Reverend the Haham, Dr. Solomon Gaon, Mr. Richard Barnett, and Mr. Felix Nabarro kindly read this book in manuscript and gave valuable advice whenever this seemed to them to be called for. Other friends also rendered me assistance in greater and less degree. These are too numerous to mention, but two of them, members of the office staff of the Community, I cannot pass over in silence. Mr. Frank Hassan's knowledge of the Portuguese language and of the dialect, neither classical nor colloquial, in which many of the records are written, elucidated many a passage that would otherwise have been a closed book; Mr. I. D. Duque, having spent a lifetime among the archives, knows them almost as intimately as he does the ritual and personnel of the Community. Miss S. M. Levy also placed her leisure at my disposal in helping to elucidate many a passage in Portuguese. Without the assistance of these three friends my task would have been far more difficult than I found it—perhaps insuperable.

Many of the illustrations are from originals in the possession of the Congregation. For others, Mr. Alfred Rubens has generously placed at my disposal his unique collection of Anglo-Jewish portraits. To him I am also indebted for calling my attention to the trade card of Abraham Delvalle in the Print Room of the British Museum. From the authorities of that institution I received permission to reproduce this card and also the plans of the cemetery and synagogue districts of London. The portrait of Jacob Quixano Henriques is from one in the Council Room of the West London

Synagogue, and that of Naphtali Basevi from a painting that belonged to his descendant, the late Colonel W. H. Basevi. Mr. Owen Mocatta kindly lent me the pastel portraits of his great-grandfather and of the latter's uncle, and Mr. John Sebag-Montefiore those of two of the earlier members of his distinguished family. The illustration of Coppeed Hall, Totteridge, is from a photograph of an engraving supplied by the Jewish Theological Seminary of America, that of the Silver Salver presented to the Lord Mayor from one received from the Jewish Museum of New York, and that of the House of Joseph Salvador from one in the possession of Mr. Edgar Roy Samuel.

A.M.H.

15 *August* 1951

SEAL OF THE CONGREGATION

CONTENTS

		PAGE
PREFACE		v
LIST OF ILLUSTRATIONS		xi

CHAPTER

I.	THE EARLIEST SEPHARDIM IN ENGLAND	1
II.	THE ORIGINS OF THE PRESENT COMMUNITY	10
III.	THE ORGANIZATION OF THE COMMUNITY	24
IV.	SET-BACKS AND ADVANCES	36
V.	THE ENLARGEMENT OF THE SYNAGOGUE	53
VI.	A NEW HAHAM AND A NEW SYNAGOGUE	74
VII.	SOME EIGHTEENTH-CENTURY PERSONALITIES	98
VIII.	EXTERNAL AFFAIRS	123
IX.	THE SEPHARDIM BEYOND THE SEAS	145
X.	THE GREAT PERIOD IN SEPHARDI HISTORY	163
XI.	THE INTERNAL LIFE OF THE SEPHARDIM	182
XII.	MORE PERSONALITIES	199
XIII.	THE TURN OF THE CENTURY	220
XIV.	THE FIRST DECADES OF THE NINETEENTH CENTURY	240
XV.	THE GREAT SECESSION	269
XVI.	THE SEPHARDIM AND THE ASHKENAZIM	296
XVII.	SIR MOSES MONTEFIORE	332
XVIII.	A THREAT TO BEVIS MARKS	357
XIX.	THE PENULTIMATE HALF-CENTURY	378
XX.	THE LAST FIFTY YEARS	403

Appendices

I.	CHANGES IN THE SYNAGOGUE SERVICE (1664–1950) by the Very Rev. The Haham	416
II.	THE FOUNDERS OF THE CONGREGATION	422
III.	SEATHOLDERS IN 1682	423
IV.	THE EARLIEST LIST OF ELDERS	425
V.	THE MEMBERS OF THE MAHAMAD—1663–1951	426
VI.	GLOSSARY	455
	INDEX	459

PLATES

*INTERIOR OF THE SYNAGOGUE	*Frontispiece*
	FACING PAGE
PETITION OF THE MARRANOS TO CROMWELL, 1655–6	16
LAST PAGE OF THE FIRST CODE OF ASCAMOT, 1663	17
*HAHAM JACOB SASPORTAS (1610–98)	32
*HAHAM DAVID NIETO (NETTO) (1654–1728)	32
*DR. FERNANDO MENDES (1647–1724)	33
TABLETS OF THE LAW, 1674	64
CHAIRMAN'S MALLET	64
*DON JOSÉ CORTISSOS (1656–1742)	65
†THE JERUSALEM INFIRMARY	80
*DR. JACOB DE CASTRO SARMENTO, F.R.S. (1691–1762)	81
COPPEED HALL, TOTTERIDGE	96
SILVER SALVER PRESENTED TO THE LORD MAYOR	97
*THE OLD MAHAMAD CHAMBER	112
THE OLD BETH HAIM, SHOWING TOMBS OF HAHAM DAVID NIETO AND HIS WIFE	112
*HAHAM MOSES COHEN D'AZEVEDO (1720–84)	113
*HAZAN DAVID ISAAC DE CRASTO (CASTRO) (D. 1784)	113
THE TOWN HOUSE OF JOSEPH SALVADOR	128
†CARICATURE OF SAMPSON GIDEON (1699–1762)	129
TRADE CARD OF ABRAHAM DELVALLE	144
*DAVID ALVES REBELLO (1741–96)	145
NAPHTALI BASEVI (1738–1808)	145
†DAVID ABARBANEL LINDO (1765–1851)	208
†JOHN KING (JACOB REY) (1753–1824)	208
†PELLEGRINE TREVES (1733–1817)	209
†EPHRAIM LOPES PEREIRA, SECOND BARON D'AGUILAR (1739–1802) (From *New Wonderful Museum and Extraordinary Magazine*)	209
†DANIEL MENDOZA (1763–1836)	224
†JACOB DE CASTRO (1758–1824)	224
*HAZAN DAVID AARON DE SOLA (1796–1860)	225
*HAHAM RAPHAEL MELDOLA (1754–1828)	225

	FACING PAGE
*JOSEPH D'ALMEIDA (1716–88)	240
*HANANEL DE CASTRO (1794–1849)	241
*ISAAC D'ISRAELI (1766–1848)	241
†MOSES EDREHI (1771–1840)	256
†JACOB KIMHI (1739–1820)	256
KETUBA OR MARRIAGE CONTRACT	257
DANIEL MOCATTA (1774–1865)	272
ABRAHAM MOCATTA (1797–1880)	272
THE BETH HOLIM, 1851	273
SIR MOSES MONTEFIORE, BART., F.R.S. (1784–1885)	336
*SOLOMON ALMOSNINO (1792–1878)	337
*HAHAM BENJAMIN ARTOM (1835–79)	337
JACOB QUIXANO HENRIQUES (1811–98)	352
SIR JOSEPH SEBAG-MONTEFIORE (1822–1903)	352
*HAHAM MOSES GASTER (1856–1939)	353

* *From portraits, etc., in the possession of the Congregation.*
† *From portraits in the collection of Mr. Alfred Rubens.*

TEXT ILLUSTRATIONS

	PAGE
SEAL OF THE CONGREGATION	viii
CEMETERY INSCRIPTION, 1684	25
PLAN OF SYNAGOGUE DISTRICT, 1756	77
INSCRIPTIONS ON CHAIRMAN'S MALLET	97
CEMETERY INSCRIPTION, 1733	321
PLAN OF CEMETERIES, 1786	323
CEMETERY INSCRIPTION, 1855	325

CHAPTER I
THE EARLIEST SEPHARDIM IN ENGLAND

THE TWO GREAT groups into which Jews are divided are called Sephardim and Ashkenazim. In essentials their differences are in liturgy and in pronunciation of Hebrew. The Sephardi and Ashkenazi liturgies—their teachings are identical—derive, it is said, in the one case from the great Jewish centre that was set up in Babylonia by the exiles settled there by Nebuchadnezzar after the fall of the Kingdom of Judah in 586 B.C., and in the other from the revived community established in Palestine by the returning exiles who accompanied or followed Ezra and Nehemiah. The development of Judaism or rather of the liturgy thus followed two separate courses, and as communications between Spain, where the Sephardim originated, and Babylonia seem to have been closer than those between Spain and Palestine, the influence of the Babylonian prevailed among the Sephardim. The pronunciation of Hebrew, the language widely used in prayer and otherwise by both communities, also developed differences, but never sufficient to make language of the one group unintelligible to the other. The Sephardim in their travels moreover came into contact with more widely scattered Jewish communities than did the Ashkenazim, who until comparatively recent times were never established outside of Europe. The Sephardim and these smaller communities were originally distinct from one another, but when the Sephardim found new homes in other parts, they assimilated as a rule with the local communities. In northern Africa, in Turkey proper, and in Italy, where the Sephardi settlement was relatively considerable, it seems on the other hand to have absorbed the local communities, so that, for instance in Italy, where the Jews originally adhered to the Ashkenazi rite, the whole community in the end became Sephardi. Thus today all Italian Jews are Sephardim, but their origins to an appreciable extent do not derive from either Spain or Portugal.

The separation of the Sephardim from the other principal group in Jewry, the Ashkenazim or Jews of central and eastern Europe, goes back for a very long period, probably to the beginning of the present era, possibly even earlier. The Jews, who left Spain in 1492 and Portugal five years later, settled for the most part in North Africa, Italy, and the Ottoman Empire. After them for two centuries and even longer came the Marranos, Jews and the descendants of Jews, sometimes of mixed ancestry, who had adopted Christianity more or less voluntarily, often under great pressure, and had remained in their homes, only to find sooner or later that, despite their submission to circumstances, life in supportable conditions in their old homes was impossible and that the choice lay no longer between partial conversion and exile, but between complete renunciation and death at the stake; often the latter fate was imposed without an alternative. The new emigration of the Marranos to some extent followed the course of the earlier one, but it entered also new fields. Marranos settled in increasing numbers in South and Central America and the West Indies where, although still under Spanish and Portuguese rule, they thought that the hand of the Inquisition and of its secular supporters would be lighter. From the Spanish and Portuguese territories in the New World a number of these refugees from martyrdom spread into North America and those islands of the West Indies in which under the English or the Dutch flag they were safe from persecution. Other Marrano refugees remained in Europe, overflowing into southern France or taking ship and settling in the ports of the North Sea with some of which they already had commercial relations. It was Marranos such as these who founded the English Sephardi community, indeed the Anglo-Jewish community as a whole, the first Jewish communities in England after the expulsion of the Jews from the Kingdom in 1290 being established in London and Bristol.

The last day on which an unbaptized Jew was free, according to the decision of the King, Edward I, to reside in England was 10 October 1290, and that may be taken as the date of the expulsion of the Jews from England. Practically every Jew left the country, and it was not until the middle of the seventeenth century that the lawyers gave the opinion that there was no bar to the residence of Jews in England. A few of the exiles found their way to Spain and Italy, where the surname Ingles, denoting an English origin, occasionally appeared, and it may be that when a new Jewish community was formed in England some centuries later, a few of the new-comers were returning unknowingly to the land of their ancestors. Although from October 1290 until early in 1657 no open Jewish community existed in England, during almost the whole of the intervening period individual professing Jews from time to time were to be found in the country. Most of these came from the neighbouring France, but a few came from farther afield, in some cases, Spain. The House of Converts in Chancery Lane

THE EARLIEST SEPHARDIM IN ENGLAND 3

was active—with intervals in the later years—throughout this period, and residence in England and the profession of Judaism were conditions for admission to this institution. Among the earliest of the inmates of this House after the Expulsion was Janathus (? Jonathan) of Spain. In 1348 Theobald, a convert from Turkey, was admitted. A few years later, in 1356, John of Castile was an inmate. At the end of the fourteenth century most of the not very numerous inmates had come to England from Spain, and Jews from Spain and Portugal and other southern lands continued to appear until the beginning of the reign of James I. Prominent among these was Sir Edward Brampton (né Brandão or Brandon), who after baptism, with King Edward IV as his godfather, became a prominent Yorkist general, Governor of Guernsey, and knight. After the fall of the Yorkists he retired to his native Portugal, after an interlude in Flanders. Brampton's entrancing story has been told by Mr. Cecil Roth.[1] There was also Rabbi Solomon haLevi, far more famous after his baptism as Paul of Burgos, Chancellor of Castile, Bishop of Cartagena and of Burgos, Archbishop Primate of Toledo and persecutor of the kinsmen he had deserted. He was also known as Paul de Santa Maria, taking this name as a tribute to his membership of the same tribe in Israel as that of the Mother of Jesus, whom he claimed as a collateral ancestress. He was in London late in the fourteenth century, and a letter from him complaining of his consequent lack of opportunity for the celebration of Purim,[2] written to Don Meir Alguadez, a rabbi and physician of Castile, is extant.

With the expulsion from Spain in 1492, however, a few of the fugitives seem to have come at once to London, where possibly before their exile they had had business correspondents who may themselves have been Marranos. The presence of this small group soon became known in Spain and protests against the harbouring of its members were made by his Most Catholic Majesty. The marriage of the Prince of Wales and Catherine of Aragon was then being negotiated, and as a part of the agreement Henry VII undertook to break up the small community to whose existence his attention had been directed. No particular action seems, however, to have been taken, but the group was too small to take root and was either absorbed into the surrounding population or left the country. In fact it was from the exiles from Portugal of 1496 more than from those from Spain four years earlier that the new Sephardi settlements in England and elsewhere were drawn. The Jews of

[1] See *Transactions of the Jewish Historical Society of England*, vols. IX and XVI.
[2] The festival ordained in the Book of Esther.

Portugal had been especially prominent in international commerce, and in the course of their activities, especially after the Expulsion, had appointed agents in foreign centres, in particular on the coasts of the North Sea. These agents were, as a rule, relatives or close associates of the heads of the firms in Portugal, and were in consequence not avowed Jews, but Marranos. The greatest of all these Jewish or Marrano commercial, and by a natural development, financial organizations was that of Francisco and Diogo Mendes,[1] with headquarters in Lisbon and branches or agents in all the principal commercial centres of western Europe, in London as elsewhere. Through this last-mentioned agency the firm was concerned with English Government loans and finance, and seems to have given the English authorities such satisfaction that when, in 1532, Diogo Mendes, the head of the important Antwerp branch, was threatened with prosecution on a charge of Judaizing, the King of England, Henry VIII, himself intervened and helped to free Mendes from the threat. Three years later Francisco, Diogo Mendes' brother and head of the firm in Portugal, died, and his widow, Beatrice de Luna, better known as Dona Gracia, perhaps the most distinguished of Jewish women of all time, left Portugal with her daughter and other relatives, intending to settle in Antwerp. The security of the Marranos in the Low Countries at that time suffered frequent variations, and it was the custom for vessels carrying Marranos from Portugal to call at Southampton or Plymouth, to learn there whether it was safe for them to proceed farther. At these ports one of the Mendes agents used to advise the Marranos on board the vessels whether to continue their journeys or to await in England a more favourable opportunity for proceeding. Dona Gracia received such a warning and she and her party, which included her nephew and future son-in-law João Miguez, to become in later years Joseph Nasi, Duke of Naxos, the trusted adviser of Ottoman sultans and the prospective King of Cyprus, in consequence landed in England and for a time enjoyed English hospitality. This was in 1536. By then there was already a small secret Jewish community in England. It centred in London round the agents of the firm of Mendes, of whom passing mention has already been made. That it was continuous with the small Sephardi immigration on the morrow of the Expulsion from Spain is improbable, especially as the members whose names survive seem to have been not Spanish Jews but Portuguese Marranos.

---

[1] There is much about the commercial activities of this firm in Cecil Roth's *The House of Nasi: Dona Gracia* (Philadelphia, 1947), but a full-length account of Marrano commerce has still to be written.

One of the new group was Jorge Añes or Ames, the head of a family that attained to some distinction in English public life.[1] Jorge Añes settled in London at the latest in 1521. They were encouraged by the business relations between the financial house of Mendes of Antwerp and Henry VIII of England which gave the Marranos some feeling of security. This community was somewhat fluid, for members were continually leaving to settle in Antwerp, but there was a core of permanent residents who, like the Añes family, were ultimately absorbed into the surrounding population. Gaspar Lopes was a cousin of Diogo Mendes and his agent, Antonio della Rogna, another agent of Mendes, acted as financial adviser to the Marranos who reached England and provided them with bills of exchange on Antwerp. The names of four members of the Pinto family, including the wife of Antonio della Rogna, have survived. There were three or four physicians, but otherwise most of the members of this group were merchants. That this was not merely a group of individuals but a community is clear, for one of them, Alvares Lopes, had a secret synagogue in his house, and was himself the spiritual head, in effect if not by title, of the small community. One or two names seem to connect with later times when there was an open Jewish community in London. Christopher Garcia was a prominent merchant trading in Antwerp and London before 1550. Antonio Rodrigues Andrada (Andrade), his wife and two children were living in London ten years earlier. There were at least four members of the Lopes family in London about this period. James Casseres bore a name that appeared again among the founders of the existing Sephardi community in the middle of the seventeenth century. Anthony de Marchina had a namesake in Moses Mocatta, the first of the family to settle in England, who was known as Marchena in his earlier years. The Jewish community of London of this period probably numbered about a hundred. Sixty-nine names have survived, but in only ten instances are the names of both husband and wife given. It is improbable that only ten of the thirty-seven men mentioned were married.

Even in those days London Jewry was concerned not only with its own affairs. The situation of Jewry, then as always, was precarious in one quarter or another. The position of the Marranos on the Continent, outside the Iberian Peninsula, was threatened

[1] One of the sons of Jorge, Francis, was a secret agent of Drake in the Azores and later commanded the English garrison at Youghal in Ireland, which town he successfully defended against the rebels. Another son, Dunstan, a merchant and importer, supplied the Royal Household—in modern parlance held the Royal Warrant. A sister of Jorge Añes was the wife of the far better known Dr. Rodrigo Lopes, Queen Elizabeth's physician.

in 1540 and a sort of international Jewish conference was convened at Antwerp to consider the situation. The London community was represented at this conference by one of its members and made its contribution to the fund that was raised for the help of the Marranos who were in danger. Moreover, events on the Continent had their reaction in England. The attention of the English Government was drawn to the discovery by the Holy Inquisition of a community of secret Jews settled in London, and King Henry VIII felt compelled to act. This community was broken up and most of its members left the country. Those who remained seem very successfully to have concealed their Judaism.

The interval before the reappearance of Jews did not, however, last long, for within a very few years a new community, very much smaller than its predecessor, appeared in London, and, still more surprisingly, a larger one in Bristol, then one of the principal ports of the kingdom. The London community now centred round the Añes family, which had not been active in its predecessor. The Añes do not seem to have been connected with the firm of Mendes as were the pillars of the earlier Jewish community. In addition to this family there was a Simão Anriques (? Henriques), a native of Italy and an observant Jew, Manuel Serrão and Rodrigo da Veiga, agents of their fathers who were still in Portugal, and Dr. Hector Nunez. The small community in Bristol was perhaps more distinguished in its membership. Its centre was a physician named Henrique Nunez and his wife (Beatriz Fernandes) in whose house divine service was regularly held. The Jewish ritual was observed as closely as possible, for it is known that the Jews of Bristol were kept informed of the dates of the festivals and in touch with contemporary Sephardi Jewish literature. The inspiration of the little secret community was, however, Beatriz Fernandes, several of whose near relatives were also resident in Bristol. She taught Jewish observance and Jewish prayers to the succession of newly arrived Marranos, and so strict was she herself in her observance that, when she occasionally travelled to London, she arranged with the innkeepers on the way to provide new cooking utensils so that she should not run the risk of having to eat forbidden food. The *seder*[1] was observed in her house every year, and she herself baked the unleavened bread for the whole community. Apart from the physicians[2] the Jews of Bristol seem to have been engaged in the export of cloth, still one of the staple English businesses. In this

[1] Passover eve service.
[2] One of these was Antonio Brandão or Brandon, a nephew of the famous Papal Marrano physician and medical writer, Amatus Lusitanus, who mentions his nephew several times.

they were no new-comers, for as early as the beginning of the fifteenth century, ninety years before the Expulsion of the Jews from Spain, Spanish Jewish merchants in this trade were connected with correspondents in Bristol, some of whom may have been secret Jews. Whether or not these communities were known to be Jewish, they passed generally as groups of Protestant refugees from Spain and Portugal and as such were given shelter. However, the position of Protestant Christians in England had not yet at this time been stabilized and, with the accession of the Catholic Queen Mary in 1553, it was threatened. Among the first victims of the new régime were the two small Jewish communities which were broken up. That of Bristol seems to have been completely dispersed, and Henrique Nunez and his wife left for France. In London, however, some of the Marranos—the Añes family, Dr. Hector Nunez and Simon Ruiz—went still further underground, to come to the surface and to do valuable service to the English queen and her ministers later, when the Roman Catholic interlude had passed.

In the new Marrano community that arose in the reign of Elizabeth the centre was Dr. Hector Nunez, a survivor from the earlier one, who was not only a physician but also a foreign trader on a considerable scale, whose connexions provided him with information on events and conditions abroad, especially in the dominions of the King of Spain, then England's 'divinely appointed enemy'. This information was of outstanding value to Queen Elizabeth's government, and his services earned him the complete confidence of Walsingham and Burleigh, Elizabeth's trusted statesmen. It was Nunez who gave Walsingham the earliest news of the sailing of the Great Armada. Nunez and his associates occupied under Elizabeth the position that Antonio Carvajal and his associates were to fill later under Oliver Cromwell.[1] Perhaps equally prominent were the members of the Añes family, survivors also from the earlier group. These have been mentioned on an earlier page. Dr. Rodrigo (Ruy) Lopez, who had married Sarah Añes, was Queen Elizabeth's trusted physician and the most fashionable English medical practitioner of the day. Unfortunately he was involved in political intrigues by some of his distinguished patients and aroused the enmity of the Earl of Essex, the most influential Englishman of his time. Lopez was accused of conspiring to murder the Queen, and despite her unconcealed confidence in him, he was hanged. The case against him at the time was somewhat flimsy. Later researches have convinced students of English

[1] See p. 12.

history that it was baseless.[1] To what extent this group of Marranos —the disguise so far at any rate as Rodrigo Lopez was concerned seems to have been very thin—followed Jewish observances is unknown. We know, however, that in 1592 there came to England Solomon Cormano, an emissary of the Sultan who, enjoying diplomatic privilege, held Jewish religious services without concealment in his house, and these services were attended equally openly by members of the Marrano community. There was, however, no recognized Jewish community as yet, and marriages and funerals had to be conducted in accordance with the rites of the Church of England. Presumably Jewish sanctification also was given to the marriages. As to the burials it is interesting to note that it was the practice to bury all London Marranos, no matter in which parish they had lived, together side by side in one churchyard, that of Stepney, and it is not an unjustified guess to say that there had been a secret Jewish dedication of that portion of the churchyard.

Finally there is a story, which cannot be confirmed although it is not impossible, that in the year 1593 some Marrano fugitives from Portugal on a ship captured by an English vessel were landed in England. Prominent in the party were a young man, Manuel Lopez Pereira, and his sister Maria Nunez. Reports spread of the beauty of this girl and the Queen herself became interested. She was captivated by the girl's charm and offered her and her brother permission to settle in England. But the call of Judaism was stronger than personal ambition or prosperity. Settlement in England, even under royal protection, meant, they felt, the ultimate loss of their Judaism. Gratefully they refused the tempting offer and proceeded with their party to their original destination, Amsterdam, where they helped in founding a Sephardi Jewish community which in course of time became one of the parents of that which was afterwards established in Bevis Marks.[2]

The long-drawn-out trial of Rodrigo Lopez and its tragic conclusion attracted an undesired publicity to the small Jewish community of London. The prejudice to which this publicity led took an anti-Jewish form, for the Jewish past if not present of this community was, if not generally known, certainly no secret in certain English circles which the trial was effective in enlarging.

---

[1] See in particular Martin Hume, *The So-called Conspiracy of Dr. Ruy Lopez* in *Trans. Jew. Hist. Soc. of England*, vol. VI. Mr. John Gwyer read a paper on Lopez before the Jewish Historical Society of England on 19 January 1948.

[2] Although Marrano fugitives first began to settle in Amsterdam about 1550 it was not until the Day of Atonement in 1596 that there is any record of Jewish communal worship—in the house of Samuel Palache, the Moroccan envoy. In the following year a permanent synagogue was opened.

Simultaneously the political connexions of some of the more prominent members with the Portuguese Pretender, Don Antonio, and his supporters ceased to be an asset, for Don Antonio had passed out of favour. The legality of the presence of Jews in England was, to say the least, a matter of doubt and their position, as a consequence, always precarious. The time had obviously come for the Jews of England to avoid attracting any attention, and once again the small crypto-Jewish or semi-crypto-Jewish community dispersed or concealed itself. Economically also life in England was no longer as attractive as it had been for these ex-Spanish and Portuguese merchants, for Amsterdam had arisen as a competitor with London for the Spanish trade and the newly formed Jewish community of Amsterdam was as well equipped as that of London for the purpose. Yet all the members of the London community did not leave England, even though some of them were met by the traveller, Thomas Coryate, in Constantinople a few years later. Members of the Añes family in particular became absorbed in the surrounding population. In the end a bitter quarrel broke out among the remnants, in the course of which one party denounced the other to the authorities as Judaizers. The Government—James I was by now king—was forced to take notice of the charges, for the alleged offence was serious. In a number of cases it was substantiated and the offenders were expelled from the kingdom. Thus in the year 1609 another Anglo-Jewish community came to an end. It was during this period, on 6 December 1605, that Jacob Domingo, M.D., was summoned before the College of Physicians, for practising medicine in London. He produced papers testifying to his qualifications, underwent examination by a board of censors some months later, and was approved and admitted a licentiate at the *comitia majora* of the 1st of October following. Nothing beyond this is known of this physician who, judging by his name and profession, was probably one of the secret Jewish community.

CHAPTER II

THE ORIGINS OF THE PRESENT COMMUNITY

AFTER THE EXPULSION of 1609 there is another blank period in the history of the Jews in England, but only a brief one. Within less than a generation a new Marrano community had collected. The new-comers came to a large extent from the Canary Islands, previously in a sense a haven for the harassed heretics or suspected heretics of the mainland. The Holy Inquisition, however, pursued them also to this land of refuge. The new settlers were for the most part merchants of substance, probably also like their predecessors with commercial connexions with the land in which they made their new homes. The new settlement began about the year 1630. Its most prominent member was Antonio Fernandez (otherwise Abraham Israel) Carvajal, long believed to be a native of Portugal who had first settled in the Canary Islands. Carvajal was a man of considerable wealth with widespread commercial connexions. His settlement in England and the consequent transfer thither of the centre of his commercial activities were in the circumstances an obvious contribution to the English economy. Carvajal is generally thought to have been a Marrano or New Christian, born at Fundão in Portugal, but Lucien Wolf[1] suggested a more interesting alternative, that although he had lived in Portugal, he was a native of the Canaries to which islands he returned. There Wolf traced a number of highly placed Portuguese bearing the same surname and presumably relatives of Antonio. This family Wolf suggested was not of Jewish origin but was Christian for generation after generation. If this view is accepted, Antonio Fernandez Carvajal was not a New Christian, a descendant of converts from Judaism, but himself a convert from Christianity. Whether or not of Jewish origin Carvajal was certainly a Jew by religion, and as far as was possible a practising one. His wealth and influential position marked him out in commercial circles. He was accepted as the head of the small Jewish community that had collected and when this community came out into the open he was accepted also in non-Jewish circles as its representative member.

Carvajal did not, however, come to England direct from the Canaries. He lived for a time at Rouen in France, where a secret Jewish community existed in the earlier half of the seventeenth

[1] *Jews in the Canary Islands*, p. xxxix.

THE ORIGINS OF THE PRESENT COMMUNITY

century. Dissensions, however, broke out in this little community and the attention of the secular authorities was drawn to it. As a consequence the community was broken up in 1633 and its members expelled. Of these some, including Carvajal and members of the Lopes Pereira family, removed to London.

Among the other members of this new community of the fourth and fifth decades of the seventeenth century was Diego Rodrigues Arias, who came to England in 1651 by way of Amsterdam where he had lived openly as a Jew. He was Spanish by origin. Among his relatives was Lorenço Lindo, originally a Marrano of Spanish birth. Lorenço's father was João Rodrigues Lindo, a Marrano merchant, born in Badajoz in Spain and later residing at Campo Maior in Portugal. Lorenço's mother, Constança Nunez, came from the city of Guarda. A sister of his mother was the wife of Antonio Fernandez Carvajal, 'The first English Jew'. A cousin, Isabel Marquez, was burnt at the stake in 1654; a brother, Antonio Rodriguez Lindo, was condemned and punished by the Inquisition in Lisbon in 1662, and other near relatives suffered similarly. Lorenço Lindo's maternal uncle, Antonio Fernandez Nunez, was a victim of the Inquisition in Lima, Peru. Lorenço, who on his final settlement in England took the name of Isaac, and his brother, Manuel, had made several visits to London from the early 1650s, but did not then settle there. He and his wife, Perpetua Lopez, were, however, seized by the Inquisition in the Canaries in 1656 and imprisoned. They were released after two and a half years without any charge being brought against them, and finally settled in London about the year 1670. Isaac and Perpetua Lindo founded a family which is still represented in the Anglo-Jewish community. He was also related to the Fernandez Nunez and the Marques families, both well known later in Bevis Marks. Duarte Henriques Alvares (otherwise Daniel Cohen Henriques) and Antonio Rodrigues Robles had held government appointments of importance in the Canaries before they escaped to England. Alvares' first wife was an Old Christian, that is to say, not of Jewish ancestry, but after her death, having himself formally embraced Judaism, he married a Jewess, Leila Henriques, in Amsterdam. After their marriage they settled in England. This was the first appearance in England of the well-known Sephardi family of Henriques. Robles was even more prominent, for it was a consequence, shortly to be described, of the seizure of his property, as that of a Spaniard, by the English authorities on the outbreak of war with Spain in 1656 and his successful plea that as a Jew, although of Spanish birth, he was not an enemy alien, that the small Jewish community of

London came out into the open and was permitted to live and to go about its business undisturbed. Other members of the community bore the surnames Francia, da Costa Alvarenga, de Paiba, Gomez Rodriguez, Blandon (Brandon), Mendez, Rodriguez Vaes, all to become familiar in course of time in Anglo-Sephardi records.

The existence of a Jewish community in London was openly admitted and accepted only at the beginning of 1656, but there can be no doubt that this Community had then been in existence, in secret, for some years. Carvajal, a zealous Jew, had a private synagogue in his own house, although members of the community were accustomed to attend for worship in accordance with the forms of the Catholic Church in the chapel at the Portuguese Embassy. This was necessary to protect themselves against legal proceedings. For part of this period of secrecy it has been said that a Marrano held the office of Portuguese Ambassador. This was Antonio da Souza, but this claim has not been established. Carvajal in fact enjoyed remarkable favour from the Government. As early as 1655 he and his two sons were endenizened as English subjects. Among his business activities was the lucrative concession for supplying the army of the Commonwealth with corn. In another respect Carvajal, with the help of his associates, proved himself of even greater service, and here again history was repeating itself. Just as Hector Nunez had three-quarters of a century earlier supplied Elizabeth's ministers with invaluable information regarding the activities of the Spanish enemy, so now Carvajal and his associates furnished similar information to Cromwell. In fact the controls of a whole branch of the national secret service seem to have passed through the hands of Carvajal.

There was one member of the group of London Jews of the earlier half of the seventeenth century who was not a Marrano and who had not himself come from Spain or Portugal. This was Simon (otherwise Jacob) de Caceres. He was born a Jew in Amsterdam and with considerable foreign business interests had settled in London. So far from dissimulating his Judaism he seems even to have boasted of it. He lost no opportunity, when meeting his secret coreligionists, of trying to persuade them to follow his example and proclaim their Judaism. He also gave valuable service in his adopted home. The settlement of Jamaica, after its conquest from Spain, was indebted to de Caceres for advice and information obtained through his business connexions with the island. Later, as the war progressed, de Caceres put before Cromwell a plan for the conquest of Chile, where he also had interests, and he offered,

THE ORIGINS OF THE PRESENT COMMUNITY 13

if his proposal were accepted, to raise an army of Jewish soldiers to co-operate with the English forces in the campaign.

The story of the so-called Re-admission of the Jews to England —in fact the public recognition of a Jewish community in this country—its acceptance and its protection when the need arose by successive governments, has been told at length, notably by Lucien Wolf and Cecil Roth, and need not be repeated. The leading protagonist on the Jewish side was Manasseh ben Israel, the widely known Sephardi rabbi and scholar of Amsterdam. In England he was seconded by some of the prominent Sephardim, but not by all. Some of them presumably preferred to leave well alone. An opinion of the highest legal authorities in the country was secured to the effect that there was no legal objection to the presence of professing Jews in England, but Manasseh's attempt, supported by all the powers of the Protector Cromwell, to lay down the constitutional lines on which a Jewish community should be established in the country, failed. The English genius has always preferred constitutional evolution to rigid written constitutions, and the establishment of a legal Jewish Community in England was no exception to this rule. The legal recognition of the Jewish settlement came not from any decision of Cromwell's Whitehall Conference or from any other political act. It came almost incidentally from a decision of the courts. As had been already mentioned, the outbreak of war with Spain endangered the position of most if not all the Jewish merchants of England, who were at least nominally Spanish subjects. Antonio Rodrigues Robles, the first to be threatened, had not been prominent in the efforts to obtain formal recognition for the community, but in the crisis his cause was that of all the Jews of London. Within a few days of the opening of the proceedings against Robles, the Jews in a body petitioned Cromwell for permission to conduct, without molestation, religious services in accordance with the Jewish ritual, 'as they had hitherto done', and to acquire land for a cemetery. Simultaneously Robles defended himself against the threatened confiscation of his property by the public announcement that he was a Jew, reciting in a brief autobiographical note his sufferings on that account. His petition was supported by affidavits of fellow Jews. The Admiralty Commissioners found it impossible to decide whether one who was apparently by nationality Spanish could properly be relieved of his disabilities on account of his religion. The question of nationality was therefore set aside and that of religion substituted for it. On this there was unanimity. The Judaism of the petitioners was accepted as a reason for granting the petition, and the Council of

State directed that the proceedings against Robles should be stopped. Three centuries later this situation was paralleled when Jews of German birth and citizenship, refugees in England from persecution, were relieved of all disabilities on the outbreak of war with Germany, on the same ground—that they were Jewish refugees from persecution. Incidentally, the outbreak of war with Spain led to an increased immigration of Marranos. Although there is no record of any formal reply to the wider petition of the Marranos, it is clear that it was intimated to them that their prayer had been granted. Before the year 1656 had expired, on 19 December, a house had been taken in London on a twenty-one years' lease by Antonio Carvajal, and work commenced to adapt it as a synagogue.[1] In February of the following year, Carvajal and de Caceres leased land in Mile End for the purposes of a Jewish cemetery, and not long afterwards Solomon Dormido, one of the members of the small community, was admitted a licensed broker on the London Exchange, the Christological oath hitherto required on these occasions being waived.

As Mr. Wilfred Samuel has conclusively shown,[2] the first synagogue to be established in England for public worship after the Expulsion in the thirteenth century was that in London established by the small Sephardi Community, the ancestor in the direct line of the present one in Bevis Marks. It was opened at the beginning of the year 1657 in Creechurch Lane in the City of London, almost within a stone's throw of the present synagogue in Bevis Marks. Its establishment was practically contemporary with, although it slightly preceded, the acquisition of land for the Jewish cemetery in Mile End, and both were the direct consequences of the appeal ten months previously to the Lord Protector for recognition of the more or less secret community. The house—later two houses—which was to some extent reconstructed to serve the purposes of a synagogue was the property of one William Whitbey, his son and grandson, by whom the original lease was granted. The property later passed, as has been said, into the hands of the authorities of St. Katherine Creechurch, but this transfer did not interfere with the renewal of the lease when the occasion arose. The rent laid down under the original lease was £40 per annum, which amount

[1] The freehold of this building was shortly afterwards acquired by the parish authorities, payment being made in part out of a legacy bequeathed to the parish by Sir John Gayer, a former Lord Mayor. Under the terms of this legacy an annual sermon—the Lion Sermon—was endowed to mark the providential escape of the legator from the paws (and jaws) of a lion when cast away on the coast of Africa. Thus the famous Lion Sermon was for a time maintained by the rent paid under lease by the Sephardi Congregation of London.

[2] *Trans. Jew. Hist. Soc. of Eng.*, vol. x, pp. 1 et seq.

THE ORIGINS OF THE PRESENT COMMUNITY 15

was subsequently increased to £60. The site has been identified by Mr. Samuel as that of the present No. 5 Creechurch Lane. The building survived until 1857 when it was demolished.

This earliest public Jewish place of worship in England subsequent to the Expulsion was fortunate in having in effect no history. The early incidents that stand out were visits paid on two occasions by curious non-Jews, records of which have survived to be enshrined in English literature. A record has been preserved of the earlier visit in a lengthy letter from John Greenhalgh to his friend Thomas Crompton, dated 22 April 1662.[1]

'. . . lately having a desire to spend some of my time here in learning the Hebrew tongue, and inquiring of some one that professed to teach it, I lighted upon a learned Jew with a mighty bush beard, a great Rabbi as I found him afterward to be, with whom after once or twice being together, I fell into conference and acquaintance; for he could speak Latin, and some little broken English, having as he told me been two years in London. He said he was an Hebrew of the Hebrews of the Tribe of Levi, and his name (I had like to have said his Christian name) Samuel Levi. . . . He said he was brought up, and was a student eleven years, in the Jews College in Cracovia the chief City of Poland . . . and that himself had formerly been Priest to a Synagogue of his own nation in Poland . . . he told me that he had special relation as Scribe and Rabbi to a private Synagogue of his nation in London, and that if I had a desire to see their manner of worship, though they did scarce admit of any, their Synagogue being strictly kept with three doors one beyond another, yet he would give me such a ticket, as, upon sight thereof, their porter would let me in upon their next Sabbath Day in the morning being Saturday. I made show as though I were indifferent, but inwardly hugged the good hap.

'When Saturday came, I rose very early, the place being far from my lodging; and in a private corner of the City, with much ado, following my directions, I found it at the point of nine o'clock, and was let come in at the first door, but there being no Englishman but myself, and my Rabbi not being there then (for they were but just beginning service) I was at first a little abashed to venture alone amongst all them Jews; but my innate curiosity to see things strange spurring me on, made me confident even

[1] British Museum MSS. 988, folios 175 to 180. Reproduced by Sir Henry Ellis in *Original Letters illustrative of English History*, 2nd Series, vol. IV, p. 3. London, 1827.

to impudence. I rubbed my forehead, opened the inmost door, and taking off my hat (as instructed) I went in and sate me down amongst them; but Lord (Thoma frater) what a strange, uncouth, foreign, and to me barbarous sight was there, I could have wished Thoma that you had then sate next me, for I saw no living soul, but all covered, hooded, guized, veiled Jews, and my own plain bare self amongst them. The sight would have frightened a novice, and made him to have run out again.

'Every man had a large white vest, covering, or veil cast over the high crown of his hat, which from thence hung down on all sides, covering the whole hat, the shoulders, arms, sides, and back to the girdle place, nothing to be seen but a little of the face; this, my Rabbi told me, was their ancient garb, used in divine worship in their Synagogues in Jerusalem and in all the Holy Land before the destruction of their City: and though to me at first, it made altogether a strange and barbarous show, yet me thought it had in its kind, I know not how, a face and aspect of venerable antiquity. Their veils were all pure white, made of taffata or silk, though some few were of a stuff coarser than silk; the veil at each of its four corners had a broad badge; some had red badges, some green, some blue, some wrought with gold or silver, which my Rabbi told me were to distinguish the tribes of which each was common. . . .

'Their Synagogue is like a Chapel, high built; for after the first door they go up stairs into it, and the floor is boarded; the seats are not as ours, but two long running seats on either side, as in a school: at the west end of it there is a seat as high as a pulpit, but made deskwise, wherein the two members of the Synagogue did sit veiled, as were all both priest and people. The chief Ruler was a very rich merchant, a big, black, fierce, and stern man to whom I perceive they stand in as reverential an awe as boys to a master; for when any left singing upon their books and talked, or that some were out of tune, he did call aloud with a barbarous thundering voice, and knocked upon the high desk with his fist, that all sounded again. Straight before them, at some distance but upon a seat much lower, sate the Priest. Two yards before him, on midst of the floor, stood that whereon the Service and Law were read, being like to an high short table, with steps to it on one side as an altar, covered with a green carpet, and upon that another shorter one of blue silk; two brass candlesticks standing at either end of it; before that on the floor were three low seats whereon some boys sat, their sons, richly veiled, as gentle comely youths as one should see; who had each

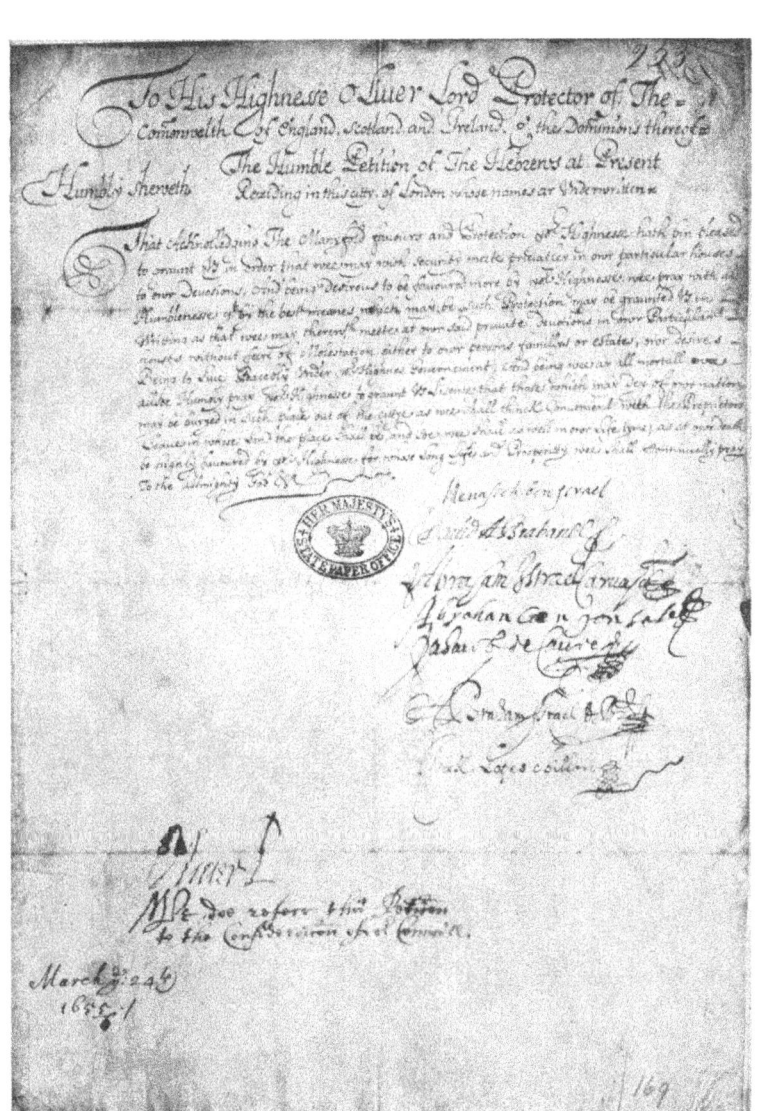

PETITION OF THE MARRANOS TO CROMWELL
24 March 1655/6

LAST PAGE OF THE FIRST CODE OF ASCAMOT, WITH SIGNATURES (1663) his Service Book in hand, in Hebrew without points, and were as ready and nimble in it, and all their postures as the men.

'There was brought in a pretty Boy at four years old, a child of some chief Jew, in rich coats, with black feathers in his hat, the priest himself arose and put a veil over the child's hat of pure white silk, fastening it under the hatband that he should not shake it off, and set him upon a seat among the boys; but he soon leaped off, and ran with his veil dangling up and down; once he came and looked at me, wondering perhaps that I had no veil; at length he got the inner door open and went to his mother; for they do not suffer the Women to come into the same room or into the sight of the men: but on the one side of the Synagogue there is a low, long and narrow latticed window, through which the women sitting in the next room, do hear; as the boy opened it, I saw some of their wives in their rich silks bedaubed with broad gold lace, with muffs in one hand and books in the other.

'At the east end of the Synagogue standeth a closet like a very high cupboard, which they call the Ark, covered below with one large hanging of blue silk; its upper half covered with several drawing curtains of blue silk; in it are the Books of the Law kept. Before it, upon the floor, stand two mighty brass candlesticks, with lighted tapers in them; from the roof, above the hangings, two great lamps of christal glass, holding each about a pottle filled up to the brim with purest oil, set within a case of four little brass pillars guilded. In the wall at either end of the Synagogue are very many draw boxes, with rings at them like those in a Grocer's Shop; and in it (as I came sooner in the morning than many or most of them) I saw that each Jew at his first entrance into the place did first bow down towards the Ark wherein the Law was kept, but with his hat on, which they never do put off in this place; but a stranger must; for after a good while two Englishmen were brought in, at which I was glad, being alone before, and they were bareheaded until they were set down amongst them, which then put on their hats. ... Each Jew after he had bowed went straight to his box, took a little key out of his pocket, unlocked it, took out his veil and books, then threw his veil over his hat and fitted it on all sides, and so went to his place and fell a tuning it upon his Hebrew Service Book as hard and loud as he could; for all is sung with a mighty noise from first to last, both of priest and people; saying some prayers; and all was done in the right true Hebrew tongue, as my Rabbi affirmed to me afterwards; which, to this end, they do industriously teach all their children from their infancy, having their schoolmistress on purpose, especially their Service books, which they have at their finger's end. There was none but had a book open in his hand, about the bigness of our hand Bibles. I looked upon several of their books as they sate by me and before me, yea I could plainly see both lines and letters in the Priest's book wherein he read, I sate so nigh him, and all were the true Hebrew letters, but in all the books without any points. The Priest's son, a comely youth standing at the Table or Altar alone, sung all the former part of the service which was a full hour long, all the rest singing with him, with a great and barbarous noise; this consisted mostly of the Psalms of David with some prayers intermixed, which they sung standing up looking East, and with a lower noise and tune not unlike to that when the reading Psalms are sung in our quires; but their reading Psalms they sung much what like as we do sing ballads; and I observed that when mention was made of the Edomites, Philistines, or any enemies of David, or Israel's, they stamped strongly with their feet, that all the Synagogue sounded again. There were two or three composed Hymns, which they, all standing up and looking toward Jerusalem, sang very melodiously. After this former part of the Service finished, the Priest's son officiating hitherto, which was about an hour, there was deep silence for a pretty while; then the Priest arose and some of the chief Jews with him, and they went with a grave, slow pace, up the Synagogue, to fetch the Law of Moses, and when they came to the Ark wherein it was kept, the priest drew the curtain, and opening the double door of it, the Law appeared, then the whole assembly stood up and bowed down just toward it, and the priest and those chief ones with him, stood singing a song to it a little while. The Law was written in two great rolls of very broad parchment (as my Rabbi told me afterwards, and he told me the meaning of each thing that I desired, to which you must impute all that I here interpret). . . . Then there arose one out of the assembly and came unto the priest, making low reverence: when the priest asked aloud whether he desired to hear the Law read, who saying "yes" the priest bade him pray then, and he looked upon his Hebrew Service Book which he had in his hand, and read over a short prayer very fast; then the priest read a few lines of the Law with a loud voice in a thundering barbarous tone, as fast as his tongue could run, for a form only; then asked the man whether he had heard the Law, who saying "Yes" he bad him give thanks then, and he read a short prayer out of his book as before: so, bowing himself to the Law and the Priest, he went to his place, and another came, and did in like manner until five or six had thus heard the Law read to them; which they count a special piece of honour to them. . . .

'I confess that looking earnestly upon them in this, and thoughts coming into my mind of the Wonders which God wrought for their fathers in Egypt, and who heard the Voice of God speak to them out of the midst of the fire on Sinai, and seed of Abraham the friend of God, I was strangely, uncouthly, unaccustomedly moved, and deeply affected; tears stood in my eyes the while, to see those banished Sons of Israel standing in their ancient garb (veiled) but in a strange land, solemnly and carefully looking East toward their own Country. . . . After this, for a conclusion of all, the Priest read certain select promises of their restoration, at which they showed great rejoicing, by strutting up, so that some of their veils flew about like morris dancers, only they wanted bells. This forenoon service continued about three hours, from nine to twelve, which being ended, they all put off their veils, and each man wrapping his veil up, went and put it and his Hebrew Service Book into his box, and locking it departed.

'My Rabbi invited me afterwards to come and see the feast of Purim, which they kept he said for the deliverance from Haman's Conspiracy, mentioned in the Book of Esther; in which they use great knocking and stamping when Haman is named. Also he desired me to come and see them at the Passover . . . afterwards I understood that several had been there to see them eat it, who brought away some of their unleavened bread with them, and showed to some who told me, one year in Oliver's time, they did build booths on the other side of Thames, and kept the Feast of Tabernacles in them, as some told me who saw them; but since the King's coming in, they are very close, nor do admit any to see them but very privately.

'When I was in the Synagogue I counted about or above a hundred right Jews, one proselite amongst them, they were all gentlemen (merchants) I saw not one mechanic person of them; most of them rich in apparel, divers with jewels glittering (for they are the richest jewellers of any) they are all generally black so as they may be distinguished from Spaniards or native Greeks, for the Jews hair hath a deeper tincture of a more perfect raven black, they have a quick piercing eye, and look as if of strong intellectuals; several of them are comely, gallant, proper gentlemen. I knew many of them when I saw them daily upon the Exchange and the Priest there too, who also is a merchant. . . .'

The Samuel Levi, Greenhalgh's 'rabbi', is presumably identical with Samuel Levy, an Ashkenazi, who was not rabbi but *Samas* to the Community. He was one of the few Ashkenazim who became members of the Congregation. He died in 1701 and is buried in the first Sephardi cemetery in Mile End. The 'priest' whom Greenhalgh mentions was Moses Israel Athias, a kinsman of Carvajal, who came to England from Hamburg in 1656. In Hamburg he was Assistant *Hazan* and teacher in the Talmud Torah. In England he was employed by Carvajal in his business, but Athias also officiated in the Synagogue, was in fact the first formal minister of the Congregation and lived in the Synagogue building.

Less than two years after Greenhalgh's visit a more distinguished visitor attended a service in the synagogue in Creechurch Lane and left a record of his impressions. This was no less a person than Samuel Pepys, the garrulous diarist. His visit was paid on *Simhhat Torah* (the Festival of the Rejoicing for the Law) when the decorum of the worshippers is never at its highest and Pepys was not very favourably impressed, as is clear from the entry in his diary of 14 October 1663.[1]

'... after dinner my wife and I, by Mr. Rawlinson's conduct, to the Jewish Synagogue: where the men and the boys in their vayles, and the women behind a lattice out of sight; and some things stand up, which I believe is their Law, in a press to which all coming in do bow; and at the putting on their vayles do say something, to which others that hear him do cry Amen, and the party do kiss his vayle. Their service all in a singing way, and in Hebrew. And anon their Laws that they take out of the press are carried by several men, four or five several brothers in all, and they do relieve one another; and whether it is that every one desires to have the carrying of it, I cannot tell, thus they carried it round about the room while such a service is singing. And in the end they had a prayer for the King, which they pronounced his name in Portuguese; but the prayer, like the rest, in Hebrew. But, Lord! to see the disorder, laughing, sporting, and no attention, but confusion in all their service, more like brutes than people know the true God, would make a man forswear ever seeing them more; and indeed I never did see so much or could have imagined there had been

[1] This was not the first visit of Pepys to the synagogue. He had previously, in 1659, attended the service in memory of Antonio Fernandez Carvajal.

THE ORIGINS OF THE PRESENT COMMUNITY 21

any religion in the whole world so absurdly performed as this. . . .'[1]

The Rawlinson to whom Pepys refers was Daniel Rawlinson, of the Mitre tavern in Fenchurch Street, the father of Sir Thomas Rawlinson who was Lord Mayor in 1706. A great-great-nephew of Daniel Rawlinson afterwards acquired the business of grocers and tea merchants, of Fenchurch Street, founded in 1650 and now occupying premises, exactly opposite the site of the synagogue in Creechurch Lane to which Daniel Rawlinson took Pepys and his wife in the autumn of 1663. Rawlinson must have been familiar with the Synagogue and probably friendly with some of its members.

The names of the principal members of this early community have survived and they are entitled to be designated the founders of the present Sephardi Community of London. Outstanding among them is Antonio Fernandez (otherwise Abraham Israel) Carvajal, who has already been mentioned. Simon, otherwise Jacob, de Caceres was the somewhat aggressive, fire-eating Jew who had never concealed his Judaism and had devoted part of his energies to persuading his more timid fellow (crypto) Jews to follow his example. As co-signatory with Carvajal in the transactions that led to the acquisition of land for a cemetery he must in the first years of the open life of the Community have been one of its most prominent members. Of less importance communally at first were David Abrabanel (otherwise Manuel Martines) Dormido, Abraham Israel de Brito, Abraham Cohen Gonzales, and Isaac Lopes Chillon. All of these had signed the petition of March 1656 in which they avowed themselves Jews and asked for freedom as such to live in the country. Others among their contemporaries were the earliest known bearers of names later familiar in London Jewry: Domingo (otherwise Israel) Rodrigues Francia, Manuel Rodrigues Nuñes, Manuel da Fonseca and Alonzo da Fonseca Meza, David da Costa, and Bento de la Costa. Wolf identifies the last-named with Alvaro da Costa, a wealthy London merchant a few years later. There is one other outstanding member of the group, but his connexion with the synagogue is problematical. This is Augustin Coronel Chacon, a supporter, perhaps an agent, of the future Charles II before the Restoration, who had been settled in England for some years. It was he who suggested the marriage of the King with Catherine of Braganza after the return of Charles to England and for this service he was knighted

[1] Henry B. Wheatley's edition of 1903, vol. III.

but first he had to accept baptism. Chacon, or Sir Augustin Coronel as he was known, was one of the leading merchants of the group and financial agent of the Portuguese Government. However, misfortune overtook him, and he became bankrupt. He must have returned to Judaism for in his last years, after having left England, he was maintained by some of his relatives, the Mendes and da Costas, and after his death his widow was supported by the London Community. This reversion, however, did not affect his title, and thus he was the first English Jew, although not the first Englishman of Jewish birth, to enjoy the honour of an English knighthood.

Two lists of names, compiled by informers, who attempted unsuccessfully to secure the destruction of the Community after the Restoration, at the end of 1660, survive. From these it would appear that the Community counted from thirty-five to forty families, including London Jews, who it is known were temporarily absent when the lists were compiled. Among the new names are Joseph and Michael d'Oliveira, two brothers named Pereira, Moses and Jacob Baruh or Barrow, better known as Baruh Lousada, Stephen Rodriguez, Franco Gomes, David and Aaron Gabay, Manuel Rodrigues Nunes, and Francisco Rodrigues Francia, brother of the Domingo or Israel already mentioned. Doctor Boyno was Doctor Joseph Mendes Bueno 'Phision to the Jewes', the first of the long list of official physicians to the Community. Solomon Frankhes was a rabbi, Solomon Franco, who had been teaching Hebrew at Oxford as early as 1652. He later settled in London as a member of the Community but accepted baptism eight years after the compilation of this list. He and afterwards his widow were for long a source of trouble to the Community.

In these lists there were also the names of four converts, two of whom, Samuel Swinock or Swynock, a West Indian merchant, with probably Jewish business connexions, and Bellamy the cooper, had been associated earlier with Carvajal in some of his non-Jewish activities. This small group of founders of the Community comprised merchants, gem importers, financiers, bullion dealers, and physicians. Judging by their banking accounts, kept by Mr. Alderman Blackwell, most of them were men of considerable means.

The marriage of Charles II with Catherine of Braganza improved the standing of the small Sephardi community. Coronel, despite his apostasy, was still an asset and the Community included also a few others who had stood by the Stewarts in the time of their

THE ORIGINS OF THE PRESENT COMMUNITY

adversity. In the retinue of Catherine came Duarte and Francisco da Silva, men of wealth, who had been entrusted by the King of Portugal with the management of his daughter's dowry. The da Silva brothers were, however, not the only Jewish recruits whose arrival in England coincided with the Portuguese marriage. There was at the same time a resurgence of the activities of the Inquisition and in consequence a new emigration from Portugal. The newcomers seem to have been some rich, some poor, but inevitably no record of members of the latter class has survived. Among the wealthier new-comers was Fernando Mendes da Costa. Fernando Mendes da Costa was much exercised by the sufferings of his kinsmen and other Marranos at the hands of the Inquisition and perhaps in conjunction with his brother, George Mendes da Costa, who had settled in Rome, and other coreligionists, had conceived a plan for settling the sufferers in Italy and England and allowing others to return to Portugal. In England King Charles and in Rome the Pope were interested. Indirectly the principal result was the suspension for a time of the activities of the Inquisition in Portugal.

CHAPTER III

THE ORGANIZATION OF THE COMMUNITY

AS HAS BEEN mentioned an immediate consequence of the official recognition in 1656 of the legal existence of a Jewish settlement in London was the acquisition of a building to be adapted as a synagogue. Two months later land was leased at Mile End, then outside the farthest eastern limit of London, to be used as a cemetery. The lease was granted to Carvajal and de Caceres, and the first to be buried in it was Judith, the widow of one of the little group of founders, Domingo Vaez de Brito, who had predeceased her by a few months. A month later Sarah, the wife of Rabbi Moses Athias, followed her. The friendly relations between the local church authorities and their Jewish parishioners cannot be better illustrated than by the mention that on the occasions of these and other Jewish funerals the church bells were tolled, and for the first of them the church authorities lent their pall.

The direction of the Community in the days in which it first came out into the open rested with those men of relative distinction to whom earlier the recognition of a Jewry as part of the larger English community was due, and in this group Carvajal was the outstanding figure. But he survived the Protector by only a few months and was in his grave when Charles returned to England. After Carvajal, de Caceres was perhaps the most prominent figure. He had avowed himself a Jew years before such a step was taken by his colleagues. He had, however, been very active in his support of Cromwell and the Protectorate, and it is probable that in the complete change of political circumstances involved in the Restoration it was considered wiser that he should retire into the background. He died in London in 1704. A third prominent member of the group, who, Mr. Wilfred Samuel suggests, was the presiding warden on the occasion of Greenhalgh's visit to the synagogue and to whose dictatorial manner Greenhalgh calls attention in his description of that visit, was David Abrabanel Dormido. Dormido had himself suffered on account of his faith at the hands of the Inquisition until he managed to escape from Spain in 1632. Although a Marrano, he had held public offices before the Holy Office had turned their attention to him and was a man of wealth. From Spain he went to Amsterdam, after a short stay at Bordeaux, one of the first stages of the journey of the Marranos to a land of

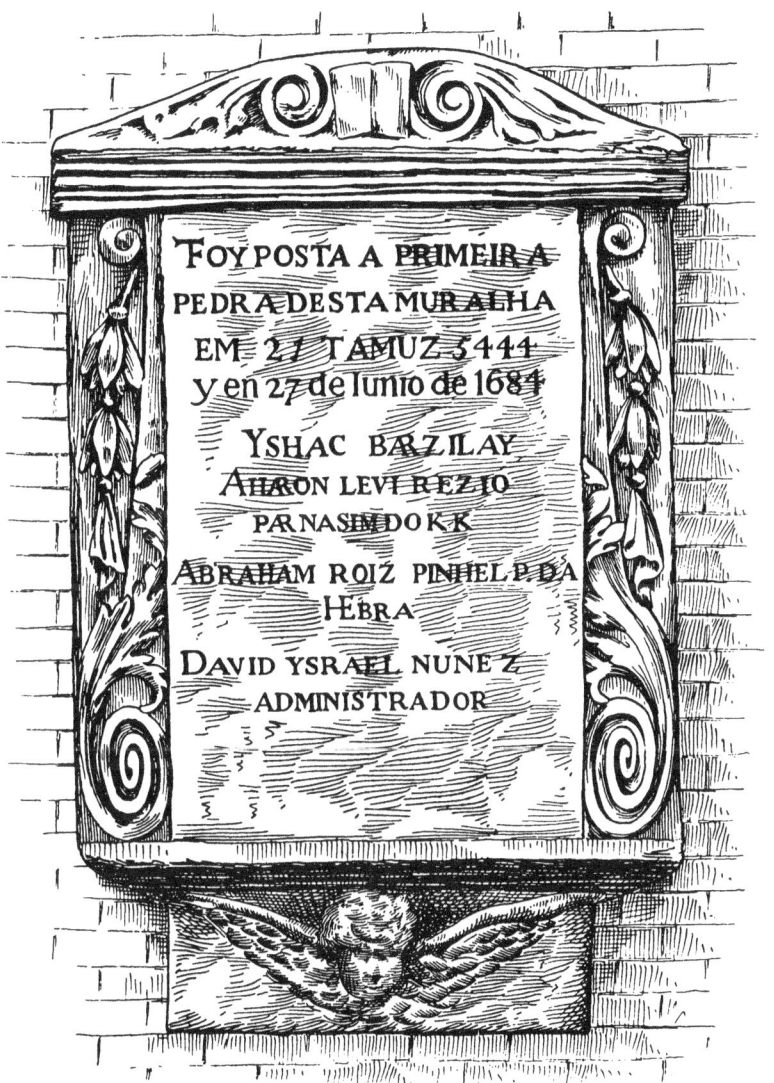

CEMETERY INSCRIPTION, 1684

freedom. In Amsterdam he occupied a prominent place in the Synagogue. The conquest of Brazil by the Portuguese involved Dormido in considerable losses and to restore his fortunes he turned to a new land, England, where he settled in 1654, shortly before the arrival of Manasseh ben Israel. In London also he avowed himself a Jew. He at once joined the little Jewish community and signed the petition asking for permission for Jews to live in the country undisturbed. At the same time he petitioned Cromwell to intercede with the King of Portugal for the restoration of his property, lost when the Portuguese seized Brazil. As has been recounted, the more general petition had no success at that time, but on the personal one Cromwell did as he was asked. Dormido was probably the first presiding warden after the Community had been formally organized. He certainly occupied that office when the first *Ascamot* or constitution was adopted in 1663. He died in 1667 and was buried in the cemetery at Mile End. His widow, who had also suffered at the hands of the Inquisition in Spain, died a year later and lies by his side. Their son, Solomon Dormido, was in 1657 the first Jew to be admitted a member of the London Exchange, the necessity for taking a Christological oath on the occasion being waived in his favour.

That Dormido was a *Parnas* before 1663 is probable, although not certain. The earliest honorary officer of the Community of whom there is a positive record is Aaron Veiga or de Veiga, who in a later minute of the *Mahamad* or governing body of the Synagogue is mentioned as having been a former *Gabay* or treasurer, probably in the previous year. Of Veiga nothing further is known, but there were other members of the family in London in his time until well into the nineteenth century, and the name also appears in the small secret community of the middle of the sixteenth century.

Within a year of the return of Charles the position of the Community had been well established. The new régime—despite the justifiable fear that in Jewish matters as in others the policy of its predecessor would be reversed—was showing itself as sympathetic as had been that of Cromwell and even that of the short-lived intervening one of the ineffectual Richard Cromwell. The period of provisional status had passed and the Community seemed now on a permanent basis. On such a basis it was possible to build. The first step was to appoint a regularly elected governing committee. In this the precedents of the ex-Marrano communities in Venice and Amsterdam were followed, and a Mahamad consisting of the already mentioned David Abrabanel Dormido and Elias de

THE ORGANIZATION OF THE COMMUNITY 27

Lima as *Parnassim* or wardens and Mosheh or Moses Baruh as *Gabay* was appointed on 18 November 1663. Of de Lima nothing is known, but Mosheh Baruh was the first member in England of a family that flourished and multiplied in this country and in the West Indies and which has given pillars to the synagogue and distinguished men to English public life. A century has passed since the name last appeared in the records of Bevis Marks, but among the members of the West London Synagogue there is today an Anthony (Baruch) Lousada, an exact namesake of the Gabay, Mosheh Baruch, known in the wider world as Antonio Lousada, which name he or his family bore in Portugal, and slightly modified to Moses Barrow for business purposes in the City. Three of his brothers and also his two sons settled in Barbados and Jamaica, and for a time both names were unknown in Anglo-Jewry. But in the West Indies some of the family were known as Barrow and some as Baruch Lousada. The Jewish community of Jamaica still includes Barrows among its members. In the middle of the eighteenth century both Barrows and Baruch Lousadas, men of wealth, left the West Indies to settle in England, and for a century they and their descendants were prominent at Bevis Marks. Today only one small Lousada branch remains within Anglo-Jewry. There are, however, many non-Jewish Barrows—including a whole dynasty of British generals and other soldiers—and of Baruch Lousadas. When Charles III, King of Naples, was crowned King of Spain in 1759, he conferred on his Grand Chamberlain, a member of the family, the title of Duke de Losada y Lousada, creating him at the same time a Grandee of Spain of the First Class. The Duke died without issue, and almost a century later the title was revived in favour of a Jewish member of the family, Isaac Lousada, who was born in Jamaica, but settled in England and died there in 1857. Francis Baruch Lousada (1813–70), a younger son of one of his successors to the title, who was British Consul-General in Boston, U.S.A., was created by the Grand Duke of Tuscany, Marquis di San Miniato. The son of Francis inherited both titles. The last of the Lousada dukes was Edward Eugene, who succeeded to the title in 1916 and then returned to Jamaica. This branch of the family had, however, a number of years previously withdrawn from the Jewish community.

Second only to the appointment of a Mahamad was the drawing up of laws and regulations, the adoption of a constitution for the young community. The Ascamot in which this constitution was formulated followed in many details those of the *Kahal Kados*[1] of

[1] Holy Congregation.

the *Talmud Torah* of Amsterdam and of the Sephardi Congregation of Venice. These two Communities, especially that of Amsterdam from which city many of the original members of the London Community came, may consequently with justification be considered the parents of the *Kahal Kados Sahar Asamaim* (The Holy Congregation of the Gate of Heaven), the name by which the London Congregation is known. These laws or Ascamot, as formulated in 1663 and adopted on the 1st of Nisan, the eve of the Festival of Passover 1664, numbered forty-two. The first of them forbade, under penalty of *Herem* or excommunication, the formation of any other Sephardi congregation in the City of London or its surroundings or even the assembly of ten persons (a religious quorum) for the purpose of worship, except on the occasion of a wedding or in the house of mourners, with a prophetic proviso, however, that some day in the future in other circumstances the establishment of a second congregation might be authorized by the Mahamad. Next came the provisions for the election of a Mahamad, consisting of two parnassim and one gabay to be elected by the members of the retiring Mahamad and two elders nominated by them. For the election of a new Mahamad a majority of four votes to one was necessary. Two kinsmen 'unto the third generation' were not eligible to serve simultaneously. New members of the congregation coming from abroad were not eligible for election until they had resided two years in London, and a Parnas could not be re-elected until after an interval of two years. The Mahamad were given absolute power. 'The Mahamad shall have authority and supremacy over everything, and no person shall rise in the Synagogue to reprobate the decisions which they may take, nor shall they draw up papers concerning it, and they who shall do so shall be subject to the penalty of Herrem.' There was, however, one safeguard against the abuse of this absolute power. 'The Mahamad that shall be elected, on entering upon their duty, in the presence of the Mahamad that shall be retiring, shall take an oath with the doors of the Ehal[1] open, promising to fulfil their duties with truth, justice, and fear of God, without respect or despite to the prejudice of parties, and this shall be observed inviolably.' In the seating arrangements in the synagogue there was to be absolute equality, with no right—apart from the members of the Mahamad for the time being—to any particular place except that preference was to be given to strangers and to brides present on the first occasion after their marriage. Refusal of honorary office or resignation 'even though he may have reasons

---

[1] The Ark containing the scrolls of the Law.

that appear very just' was prohibited 'in order not to interrupt the order of the elections; and he who shall be obstinate shall pay as penalty £10 sterling, and shall not be admitted for the period of three years to any Misva,[1] nor shall he be called to the Sefer'.[2]

Members of the Congregation who might have business disputes with one another were bound to refer them in the first instance to the Mahamad for arbitration. The decisions of the arbitrators were however, not binding and any party who was not satisfied with them was 'free to seek and defend their rights before whom they may please'. The arbitrators were in effect conciliators. The one exception was in the matter of brokerage. 'No broker shall summon to justice any one of his brethren for brokerages, except before the Mahamad.' If he did so he was liable to a monetary penalty and to exclusion from the synagogue until he had paid it. The enticement away from a fellow Jew of a serving maid seems also to have been prohibited under *Ascama* 26, the wording of which is somewhat obscure. 'No person shall speak of hiring a house, or actually do it, of another Jew without his express permission; and it shall be the same with serving women or maids, practising no collusions to that end by causing them to be spoken to by some Goy;[3] and he who should do so shall pay as penalty five pounds sterling for the Sedaca.'

There were special provisions to safeguard the Community as a whole, at the time a notoriously alien community in English environment. The printing of books in Hebrew, Ladino, or any other language, in England or elsewhere, by any member of the Congregation, was subject to the permission of the Mahamad. Anyone who transgressed this law was liable to immediate excommunication, 'because it thus conduces to our preservation'. Arguments on religious subjects with non-Jews and attempts at proselytization were forbidden, 'nor may offensive words be spoken to them against their profession (religious beliefs), because to do otherwise is to disturb the liberty which we enjoy and to make us disliked'. In a further Ascama conversion of non-Jews is expressly forbidden.

The lampooning, libelling, or slander of others is emphatically denounced and threatened with excommunication. Included with these offences, somewhat curiously, was the 'retaining of papers of others'. A similar penalty was threatened in the case of any member of the Congregation who, without authority, put himself forward as their spokesman. The Mahamad shall in no circumstances

[1] Synagogue honour.   [2] Scroll of the Law.   [3] Non-Jew.

intervene on behalf of any member who may be charged by the civil authorities with crime, 'but they shall consent that he be punished by the law according to his crimes, as an example to others, and that thereby the stumbling-block in our midst be removed and God's people be free'. In some matters the Mahamad kept a tight control even over their own rabbinical authorities. No one without the consent of the Mahamad was permitted to grant a *get* or divorce or to celebrate the marriage of a bride (no matter her age) without the consent of her parents.

The comments by Greenhalgh and Pepys on the decorum in the synagogue are supported by the laws it was found necessary to enact to modify the unruliness, at any rate on some occasions, of some of the congregants. Ascama 21 runs, 'No person in the Synagogue or its district shall lift his voice or raise his hand to harm his fellow, nor shall he come to it with weapons of offense; and him who should do the contrary we hold straightway as placed in Herrem and separated from all our brethren, and he shall not be admitted into the Synagogue, even though he do penance, without paying first ten pounds sterling for the Sedaca.'[1] This Ascama dealt with acts or threats of violence. The following one was enacted to deal with a far less serious, although annoying, offence, perhaps an echo of strictures from outside. 'To those who are reading their prayers it shall not be permitted to raise their voices in such wise as to impede (others) from hearing clearly the Hasan, in order that the Kahal may be able to follow him according to Din, besides which it is small courtesy to cause disturbance with discordant voices, impeding others who are praying and giving ground to strangers to be able to blame.' Again, 'no person may talk in the Synagogue during the time of the Tephila or of reading the Sefer, nor likewise may they go out after the raising of the Law, because the Misva is not only to see it, but it is needful to hear it read, besides that it causes much scandal and disturbance; wherewith it is recommended that there be improvement in this matter, unless it be for especial need.' A whole series of laws deals with finance. For general purposes the revenue of the congregation depended primarily on the *Imposta*, a sort of income-tax, based on the value of goods bought or sold and other business transactions. The maximum rate at first was two shillings on every hundred pounds sterling of all commodities bought or sold. The rates were, however, soon increased to keep pace with the increase of expenditure. All Jewish residents in England, Ireland, and Scotland were liable for this imposta 'so long as there be not

[1] General communal funds; properly charitable fund.

established another (congregation) in the parts where they live'. There was some reason for mentioning all three kingdoms, for at any rate in Dublin a few ex-Marranos had already settled with Manoel, otherwise Isaac, Lopez Pereira, as their principal colleague. Lopez Pereira, born in Rouen, had left that city when the Jewish community there was broken up. For a time he lived in London, where he was among the supporters of Manasseh ben Israel in his efforts to secure the position of the Jews then already settled in London. He with his brother, Francisco, as well as a third ex-Marrano, Jacomo Faro, was settled in Dublin and prospering there in business in 1660, and although Manoel afterwards returned to London, where he was Parnas of the Sephardi community in 1694, his business and members of his family continued in Dublin, where in 1718, nine years after Manoel's death, a grandson of his, Eliau Lopes Pereira, was prominent both in commerce and in the direction of the small Jewish community. Manoel and Francisco Lopez Pereira were sons of David Lopez Pereira who died in Bordeaux. Another brother, Gaspar, otherwise Gaspar de Vitoria, was caught by the Inquisition while on a business visit to Spain, tortured, confessed, and imprisoned for life. Another member of the family, Diego Lopez Pereira, escaped from Portugal, settled in Vienna, where he was ennobled as Baron d'Aguilar by the Empress Maria Theresa, and later settled in London, where he died in 1759. Descendants of his still exist in England, but not in the Jewish Community.[1]

A second regular source of income, although intended to be temporary, was a tax on meat of a farthing a pound. Another consisted of voluntary offerings (*promesas*) and *Nedabot* made on being called to the reading of the Law and on other occasions. In the disposal of these offerings the decision rested to a large extent with the donor. He could and often did indicate some poor individual or communal institution as the recipient, but this freedom operated only with second and subsequent offerings. The first offering made by any individual had to be paid into the general funds of the Congregation known as the *Sedaca*. On the occasion of *Purim* a general collection was made, mainly for the benefit of the poor. Private and other collections of money for those of the Congregation and others who were in need were strongly discouraged. 'The Mahamad will furnish with Sedaca (out of communal funds) those who may deserve it and be in want, in conformity with their need.' The one exception to this rule was in the case of an emissary from the Holy Land, who was considered to be

[1] *Trans. Jew. Hist. Soc. of Eng.*, vol. XI, pp. 162-4.

travelling on an exceptionally sacred errand. The visits to England for this purpose date from the formation of a regular community, if not earlier. In 1657 Rabbi Nathan Spira of Jerusalem was in England collecting funds for the distressed Jews of Jerusalem. His mission was primarily to non-Jewish sympathizers of whom Henry Jessey and John Dury, nonconformist divines, gave him much encouragement and support.[1] Apart from the general fund of the Congregation, there were already in those early days two special ones to which offerings could be devoted and gifts made. The one was that for *Terra Santa* or the Jews of the Holy Land. The other also, less remote in time and space, was one whose thread is visible almost throughout Jewish history, especially if the title be interpreted generously. This was the fund for the benefit of the *Cautivos* or captives, devoted to the ransom of Jewish victims of piracy or other similar violent proceedings.

The accounts for the first year balanced at £336 12s. 6d.

The Ascamot came into force on the 1st of Nisan 1664, and a copy of them is retained in the earliest surviving Minute Book of the Congregation, itself a copy of an earlier record. They were signed by the three members of the Mahamad, already mentioned, and also by the other principal members of the Congregation. Among these was Samuel da Veiga, the jeweller and banker, who died a victim of the plague in the following year, probably a relative of the first known Gabay. He had been endenizened in 1661, and in 1663 had been admitted a freeman of the City of London—the first professing Jew to be admitted—on the personal recommendation of the King. Others of these signatories were Jacob Gomez Serra, Parnas in 1675; Abraham Cohen Gonzalez, one of the signatories to the petition to Cromwell of March 1656; Jacob Netto, a member of a family that was later to give two *Hahamim* or Chief Rabbis to the Community; and Aron Veiga, already mentioned as an ex-Gabay. Yet others whose names became later familiar in the Community were Isaac Barzilay, Isaac d'Azevedo, Jacob de Chaves, Jacob Pardo, and Benjamin Nunes. Jacob Sasportas, the first Haham, also signed the record at a date necessarily later than the others. He had not yet arrived in England when the Ascamot were enacted.

The community consisted of *Yehidim* or ordinary members, who comprised the general body of members and by virtue of their membership contributed to its funds; the more prominent of the Yehidim, the *Velhos* or Elders, who became the consultative body;

[1] C. Roth, *A History of the Jews in England* (1941), p. 166 n., and *Jew. Hist. Soc. of Eng.*, Misc. II, pp. 99 et seq.

HAHAM DAVID NIETO (NETTO)
From an engraving by James McArdell, after David Estevens

HAHAM JACOB SASPORTAS
From an engraving by P. van Gunst

DR. FERNANDO MENDES
From a water-colour by Catharine da Costa

THE ORGANIZATION OF THE COMMUNITY 33

and the executive, the Mahamad, consisting of two Parnassim and a Gabay (the last named concerned specially with financial matters), elected for one year and chosen almost without exception from among the Elders. At first, until the adoption of the first set of Ascamot, the administration of the Community rested with the whole body of Yehidim, acting in general meeting, but the authority soon passed to the Elders and, after a short interval, to the Mahamad. The original ascamot were, however, approved and signed by the Elders, and later, in 1671 and 1673, new Ascamot, imposing the *imposta* (later *finta*) on temporary residents from abroad and laying taxes on brokers, were approved by the Elders. Subsequently, at times, changes in taxation required the approval of the Elders, who also, in 1681, elected Jacob Abendana Haham. The Yehidim did not, however, comprise all of the Jews of England of that day. Not only were there undoubtedly some, too poor to pay any contribution to the communal funds, who were on that account excluded from membership although not from worship in the synagogue. But among the wealthier members also there were noticeable omissions. Outstanding among these was Simon de Caceres, who from his arrival in England had almost aggressively proclaimed his Judaism, who had taken his part in securing the recognition of a Jewish community and with Carvajal acquired the lease of the first Jewish cemetery. He died in 1704 and was buried in that cemetery, but he never seems to have been a registered member of the Community. Others of his name, however, possibly relatives, appear in the early lists of members. Another member of the earliest pre-recognition group, Isaac or Lorenço Lindo, seems to have delayed many years before he joined the congregation, Whatever influence affected him did not play on his descendants, one or more of whom has been a *Yahid* from that day until this. Another prominent London Jew who never formally joined the community although all his children married Jews or Jewesses and were among the most prominent members of the Congregation, was the wealthy Alvaro da Costa who had settled in England in 1660, was endenizened seven years later, and died and was buried at Mile End in 1716. It is difficult to understand why these and others who were buried among their brethren and were, at any rate socially, active among them, neglected formally to join the Community. In the case of de Caceres, who was certainly not mild-mannered, some persisting quarrel may have been the cause. In other cases, a shrinking from circumcision—all of these abstainers were of Marrano origin—was unquestionably the reason. In a census of the community made about the year 1684 the names appear of five families to which the note 'Portuguese who are not circumcised' is attached. This list includes the names of Alvaro da Costa and Antonio Rodrigues Marques, the brother of Abraham Hezekiah Marques who was dead by then. Another name in the list is that of Dr. Fernando Mendes, court physician in the time of Charles II, who had married a niece of Abraham Hezekiah Marques, herself a professing Jewess.

One further step was taken in the earliest days of the Community to complete its organization. A few months before London Jewry came out into the open and was publicly recognized, Moses Israel Athias, a relative of Carvajal, had come from Hamburg for the dual purpose, as has already been mentioned, of assisting Carvajal in his business and of taking charge of the services in the synagogue. As soon as the new building was opened and the Community organized, it was felt that a man of higher scholarship and standing was required as its spiritual head. The choice for this purpose fell on Jacob Sasportas, a rabbi of Amsterdam and a scholar of repute. Sasportas was born in Oran, North Africa, in 1610, and claimed descent from Nachmanides, the famous Spanish Talmudist and exegete. After short periods of office as rabbi at Tlemcen and Fez in Morocco, brought to an end by serious differences with the ruling authorities, he fled to Amsterdam where he met Manasseh ben Israel, who had not yet gone on his mission to England. Sasportas, however, soon made his peace with the Sultan of Morocco, who sent him on a mission to the King of Spain. It was not exceptional in those days in Moslem lands for the services of Jews to be employed in inter-governmental diplomacy. After the conclusion of his mission Sasportas returned to Amsterdam, and it was while he was there, in 1663, that he was invited to come to London as Haham and Hazan. Sasportas came to England early in 1664 but did not remain for long. Terrified by the Great Plague of the following year, of which his predecessor Athias died, he returned to Amsterdam. For short periods he lived in Hamburg or Leghorn, but soon returned to Amsterdam to become one of the principal rabbis there. He died in Amsterdam in 1698 at a very ripe old age, after seventeen years' service, widely respected as a scholar and as a courageous and outspoken opponent of the Sabbathaian heresy which he had denounced from the beginning, despite the widespread and fanatical support it had secured in Jewish circles throughout the world. In Amsterdam he published a number of works of Talmudic lore. Although Sasportas never returned to London he remained in correspondence with some of his acquaintances there, and in particular with his several successors in the office of Haram, and when he died general mourning was displayed in London Jewry as in that of Amsterdam. Two of his sons settled in London.

CHAPTER IV

SET-BACKS AND ADVANCES

THE FIRST YEARS of the Community in its new home and under its new constitution were not without tribulations, troubles, however, for the most part not peculiar to itself but general to the larger community of which it formed a part. The year 1665 was that of the Great Plague, as a consequence of which London Jewry lost a number of its members—an appreciable loss in view of its small size—including its first rabbi, Moses Athias, and Samuel da Veiga, the jeweller. It lost also, not through death but none the less as a consequence of the scourge and the state of terror that accompanied it, its Haham, Jacob Sasportas, who returned to the Continent. The following year came, perhaps as an at the time unrealized blessing, the Great Fire of London, which, however, in its immediate effects still further reduced the amenities and prosperity of London as a whole, and in these losses London Jewry necessarily shared. This was plainly reflected in the finances of the community. Whereas, as has already been mentioned, the income of the Congregation in the first year (1663-4) for which accounts survive was £336 12s. 6d., three years later, in the year of the Great Fire, it had fallen by more than a third, to £213 13s. 5d. This was the lowest point the Congregation's income ever touched. Henceforth almost year by year it rose continuously until, after a not very long interval, the income and expenditure of the Congregation were counted not in hundreds, but in thousands of pounds. One other tendency that began, or at any rate first comes to light, in the year succeeding that of the Great Fire and was perhaps due to the depression that that scourge and its predecessor, the Plague, brought in their wake was the annoying practice of depositing waifs and foundlings at the door of the synagogue or at those of prominent members of the Community. Thus the accounts of the churchwardens of St. Katherine Creechurch for the year 1667 contain the 'item paid for nursing of ye child that was left at the Sinagogue Dore and for things when it was sick 2-6', and similar entries in respect of 'Mr. Rodrogus (Rodrigues) his dore', 'Mr. Dopostos dore', 'Mr. Mirandos (Miranda's) dore' in subsequent years.[1] There is no reason to suggest that these

[1] Mr. Wilfred Samuel has called attention to these curious entries. See his 'The First London Synagogues of the Re-Settlement", *Trans. Jew. Hist. Soc. of Eng.*, vol. x.

waifs were the children of Jewish parents. They were probably left at the doors of the Jewish Community as a result of the general belief in the wealth of the Jews or possibly also as a consequence of their reputation for human feeling and charity. The local Christian authorities seem to have shown no hesitation in accepting responsibility for the maintenance of these abandoned infants. If there had been any reason to believe that they were of Jewish birth the Jewish authorities would have been required to accept responsibility for them and would have done so.

A very much more serious threat, endangering the very existence of the Community, was that engineered by two men of position, partly, it seems, out of commercial rivalry, partly probably in view of the prospects of blackmail that it offered. The opportunity came with the enactment of the Conventicle Act of July 1664 which placed all but members of the Established Church under disabilities. Under this measure heavy penalties were prescribed against participants in any religious gathering (apart from those of a household in which not more than five persons took part) not conducted in the form laid down in the Book of Common Prayer. The Act was directed against the Puritans, but there could be no question that the holding of services in accordance with the Jewish ritual in the synagogue in Creechurch Lane transgressed the new law. Nevertheless, despite this legislation, the services in Creechurch Lane continued as heretofore. But although not interfered with by the authorities this persistent and notorious breach of the law did not pass unnoticed. Paul Rycaut, who had connexions with Turkey and was associated with the Levant Company whose members resented the Jewish threats to their commercial monopoly, and the Earl of Berkshire called the attention of the heads of the Jewish Community to the new legislation. Berkshire went further and stated that the King had placed the Jews of England in his charge and he suggested to the leading London Jews or to some of them that to avoid the consequences, so far as they were concerned, of the Conventicle Act it was probably worth their while to pay him for his protection. The threat failed entirely. The Mahamad, instead of responding to Rycaut's and Berkshire's approaches, went direct to the King and appealed to him for protection. Charles had, apart from its effect on the Jews, little liking for the legislation which he had been forced to accept—as he said in another connexion he had no desire to resume his travels—and his response was immediate. He denied having given to Berkshire or to anyone else any jurisdiction over the Jews of England or authority to interfere with them and told them in the form of a communication from the Secretary of State that 'they may promise themselves the effects of the same favour as formerly they have had, so long as they demean themselves peaceably and quietly with due obedience to his Majesty's Laws and without scandal to his Government'. This was for the time being final. Outside of the very small circle of prospective blackmailers there was no interest whatever in the proceedings of the Jews behind the walls of their synagogue. The services there continued without interruption, and although they unquestionably infringed the law and were by no means conducted in secret, for the next ten years no attempt was made to interfere with them.

The Ascamot, although drawn up with very great care and meticulousness, were never considered above amendment. In fact, like everything that enjoys life, they were accepted as subject to revision almost before the ink in which they were written was dry. The first amendment or rather addition was enacted in Elul 1664, less than a year after the Ascamot as a code of laws was accepted. The necessity for this addition showed that visits of non-Jews to the synagogue were not very exceptional and as a consequence, although the opposite has been suggested, the holding of Jewish services in these early years of Charles II was not a matter of strict secrecy. The new ascama runs:

'To avoid the scandal and hindrance that it causes in this Kahal Kados on the occasions when English ladies come to see the ceremonies of our religion, it is forbidden, and ordained that from this day henceforth no Yahid of this Kahal Kados may bring them to it, nor rise, nor move from his place to receive them, nor (persons) of any other nation that may be, in order to accompany them, or give them place; and the same applies to the gentlemen who may come to this Synagogue, reserving to the Señores of the Mahamad the power to act as they ought according as may seem good to them.'

The Community had not been long established before steps were taken to form the first of the network of subsidiary institutions that have developed into a group that surrounds the parent institution today. The earliest, as in all Jewish communities, was for the provision of Hebrew and religious instruction for the children. This developed later into the establishment of a specific institution. From the beginning arrangements were made for this instruction, for in the agreement made with the first Haham, Jacob Sasportas, it was laid down that he should arrange for his son, Samuel, to give four hours a day instruction of 'such students as may be' and that the Haham himself should give instruction in Gemara to more advanced students. That the twin call of charity was also not overlooked is evident from the provision made in the original code of laws for the relief of the poor, both those of the local community and also new-comers or wayfarers from abroad. Of these visitors some at any rate were assisted to proceed farther. This benevolence served as an attraction to London and the burden became almost heavier than the young community could support. In the end, in the year 1669, it was compelled to appeal to the City corporation for assistance in coping with the swarm of destitute new-comers by which the Congregation was beset, and as a consequence the mendicants were ordered to leave the country within five days under the penalty of exclusion from the synagogue, with the promise, however, of the Synagogue authorities to contribute towards the expenses of their journeys farther afield. Furthermore, a new ascama was adopted to the effect that no new members from abroad should be admitted into the Congregation until they could show that they had the means of unaided subsistence, which step was considered 'to tend greatly to the preservation of the Nation in this city'. The assistance of the poor—the germ of the later distinct institution of a Board of Guardians—was provided from the general funds of the Congregation. The first charitable institution to be established was the *Hebra de Bikur Holim e Guemilut Hasadim*, a society for the care of the sick and for burying the dead, which came into existence in 1664–5. Its funds were to be derived from special collections from the members of the Community to be made every Thursday, but if these were inadequate they were supplemented out of the General Fund. The administrator of the *Hebra* was given charge of the *Beth Haim*[1] or cemetery with authority to make arrangements for all burials in it. But in this matter there was one proviso. 'The Administrator shall not have authority to allow the burial of any uncircumcised man, nor any of his belongings (i.e. dependants) without holding a meeting of six of the Elders of the Hebra, so that in company with the Mahamad they may consider what seems good to them, which he shall be obliged to follow.' This regulation explains the position of those ex-Marranos who were in the Community but not of it. The earliest application of this rule seems to have been in the year 1670 when Diego de â Mesquita, a visitor coming from Holland, was taken ill and died. Of Marrano origin, he had failed to enrol himself fully in the Jewish community in the place of his settlement (Bordeaux), nor had he had his son circumcised. But it was learnt that he had

---

[1] Literally: House of Life.

before his death arranged for his son to be taken to Bayonne, where there was an ex-Marrano community, for that purpose, and it was agreed to bury his body in the Beth Haim in Mile End, but 'in a place separate from our brethren'. Another regulation provided for the appointment of a physician of the Hebra. Ultimately this post developed into that of physician of the Community.

David Abrabanel Dormido and his colleagues were succeeded on the expiration of their term of office by Isaac Barzilai and Isaac de Azevedo as parnassim and by Isaac Israel Nunez as Gabay. New names that appear in the list of the Yehidim, according to the record of those who contributed to make good the deficit in the accounts for the year 5424 (1663–4), were those of Isaac de Andrade, Isaac de Paiva, Jacob Pardo, Jacob Gomes Serra, Jacob Aboab, Isaac Vaz Nunez, Abraham Roiz da Costa, and Abraham and Isaac Soares, all of which reappear later in this narrative.

It was soon discovered that the rate of taxation imposed on the members of the Community was insufficient to meet its public needs and within a very short time it had to be increased, in some respects doubled. Almost from the first day recourse had to be had to *fintas*, which were at first payments in advance of the imposta or the regular tax, to balance the accounts. This was obviously an unsatisfactory financial system, and in order to reform it 'the heads of the houses of this Nation', that is to say, the Elders resolved 'unanimously and harmoniously' to double the rate of the imposta, always with the threat of *Herem* or excommunication (a threat in those early days frequently employed although not so frequently made effective) against those who evaded their increased liabilities or refused to accept them. The Mahamad, to strengthen their position, secured the agreement of the Yehidim to an additional ascama to that effect. The Herem was not, however, complete, for it was 'only permitted them to speak and trade with such a person in order not to disturb commerce'. And in the event of repentance and payment of all arrears of imposta and finta the offender would be received back into the Community. That disinclination to pay their dues was not limited to the less affluent members, and was also not due only to difficulty in paying, is clear from a long-standing dispute with the brothers Abraham and Isaac de Francia, two of the wealthiest members of the Community, who were at the time of the adoption of the new ascama in default. However, the breach was later healed, for each in turn became subsequently a parnas and also a generous donor to the Congregation's funds. Isaac, otherwise Domingo Rodrigues Francia, was an ex-Marrano who, with other members of his family originating in Portugal, had removed to Malaga in Spain, thence escaped later to Bordeaux, and finally in 1655 settled in London. In that city he was circumcised and was one of the original principal members of the Community. In conjunction with his brother he founded in Leadenhall Street a wealthy firm of Spanish and East Indian merchants and shipowners.[1] A grandson of Isaac, Francis Francia, was in 1716 the centre of a notorious trial for high treason.

After the immediate effects of the Plague and the Great Fire had passed the finances of the congregation began to improve. Under the care as Gabay of Abraham, otherwise Polycarp, de Oliveira, the accounts showed a surplus, despite the call of relief of the poor, including those recently arrived from abroad, which absorbed almost a quarter of the total revenue. The accounts for this year, 5428 (1667-8), included a final payment on account of an anonymous mulatto who died in that year. The relation between him and the Community and the basis of their liability in respect of him is nowhere explained, but he was probably a servant or slave of one of the members who had, after his admission to the Jewish Community, brought him from the West Indies and left him as a legacy to the London Sephardim. In later accounts there was definite record of the assistance of ex-slaves or servants admitted to the Jewish Community.

The vacancy in the office of Haham caused by the departure of Jacob Sasportas in 1665 continued for five years until the appointment of Joshua da Silva of Amsterdam, a friend of Sasportas. Like his predecessor, he was required also to act as Hazan and to teach the boys of the congregation and in the Talmud Torah. He was to receive a salary of £50 (almost £300 in present-day money) per annum with a free residence in the synagogue building, the same as had been received by Sasportas at the beginning of his term of office. Sasportas had, however, very soon found that salary inadequate and it was increased to £70. Da Silva, however, received no regular increase of salary throughout his seven years of office, but had to be satisfied with his £50 and free accommodation. Although appointed also Hazan of the Congregation he was able, however, from the beginning to share the duties of that office with Benjamin Levy. Levy, one of the small group of Ashkenazim in London, had been appointed *Shochet*[2] and *Bodek*[3] of the

---

[1] For the Francia family, see a note of Lucien Wolf in vol. XI of the *Trans. Jew. Hist. Soc. of Eng.*, and also Lucien Wolf, *Jews of the Canary Islands* (1921).

[2] Ritual slaughterer of cattle.

[3] The examiner of cattle after slaughter to ascertain whether it was free from disease.

congregation in succession to Samuel Sasportas, the son of the former Haham. The synagogue accounts of 1665 were also the last in which a payment appears to Solomon Lopez, who had been brought from Amsterdam in the previous year to act as samas. He seems to have been specially qualified for that office by his skill in 'cupping', for which under the terms of his appointment he was authorized to charge a shilling an operation.[1] Lopez held this office for less than two years. Then came the disturbance caused by the Plague and the Fire, and in the accounts for 5427 (1667) Samuel Levy (presumably also an Ashkenazi) appears as Samas and continues there for several years. In the same year Benjamin Levy was appointed Hazan at a salary of £10 per annum to cover all his duties. He seems to have been a man of business as well as a communal official, for in 1671 the meat tax of a farthing a pound was farmed to him in return for an annual payment of £20, the sharing of the reading of the prayers in the synagogue with the Haham and the performance of the duties of shochet and bodek without further payment. Benjamin Levy's tender was accepted in preference to a higher one of £35 a year by a bidder who did not propose to perform these ancillary duties.

There is a not surprising tendency to confuse this Benjamin Levy with a namesake and younger contemporary, also of Ashkenazi origin, who loomed much larger in the early records of the Spanish and Portuguese Jewish Community of London. This other Benjamin Levy came to England from Hamburg, and in the absence of an Ashkenazi community of any size or standing joined that of the Sephardim into which he was accepted as a full member. Outside of the Synagogue he also after a time took his place among the more prominent of the Jewish merchants and men of affairs, being one of the original twelve Jewish brokers who were admitted to the Exchange as Jews by special legislation in 1697. Levy, a Sephardi by adoption and a loyal and devoted son of the Community, never set aside his recollections of his Ashkenazi origins, recollections which were probably kept bright by the relatives who in the course of the years followed him to London. The number of Ashkenazi residents in London had grown appreciably by the end of the seventeenth century and they must have turned inevitably to Benjamin Levy as their outstanding representative. The growth in size of this Community led to a movement for the erection of a synagogue larger and more worthy than the modest,

---

[1] Lopez was presumably also the barber to the Congregation and the professions of cupper or bloodletter and barber were then closely connected.

half-concealed centre in which they had hitherto worshipped. The need was even more insistent for a cemetery of their own, for the Ashkenazi dead were beginning to overcrowd the cemetery of the Sephardim. In 1696 Levy purchased land in Alderney Road, not far from the Sephardi cemetery, for an Ashkenazi one. Four years earlier he had also helped towards the acquisition of a larger place of worship, and the first rabbi to serve in this new house of prayer was a relative of his who had come for the purpose from Hamburg. Benjamin Levy died in 1704, at the age of forty, the last appearance of his name in the records of the Sephardi Community having been two years earlier. He had originally made a request that he should be buried near his children in the Sephardi cemetery, but on the death of his wife, shortly before his own, he left instructions that his remains should rest in the grave next to hers in the Ashkenazi cemetery that he had purchased. He left legacies to both communities, for the poor, for dowries, for orphan girls, for the Sephardi orphanage, and also for the Christian poor of the parish and for the Klaus or Talmudical College of Hamburg, his native city. In 1699 Levy had married Hitchele, daughter of Samuel Heilbuth (otherwise Helbert), also a member of the Sephardi community of Ashkenazi origin. Levy left two sons, Menachem who died unmarried, and Elias who was a child of two when his father died. Elias inherited a considerable fortune from his father, married a relative, and was on the way to succeeding to his father's position in the City when he also died. Elias' only son, Benjamin, died as a young man unmarried: his daughter within a year of her marriage, also childless. Elias' widow, Judith or Judy Levy, known as the Queen of Richmond Green, where she had a house, still surviving in Maids of Honour Row, as well as one in Albemarle Street, died in 1803 at the age of ninety-seven. On account of her age, her position in Anglo-Jewry and her benefactions and also perhaps her eccentricities, she became a well-known figure in London—in and out of Jewry. Her father-in-law had contributed handsomely to the building of the Ashkenazi Great Synagogue, and when the time came for its rebuilding she resented the suggestion that anyone but herself should provide the means. When she died she left a great fortune but no will. Her relatives, the Franks, secured most of the fortune, but her husband's family were not satisfied, and until very recent times there were still occasional echoes of the claim by descendants of Elias Levy's sister, Abigail or Golly, to their share of the Levy millions.[1] But the story of Benjamin Levy and his

[1] In other respects some of the descendants of Golly Levy, who married Moses Adolphus, attained to distinction. One of their six sons, Dr. Joy or Simcha

descendants after the establishment of the Great Synagogue does not belong to that of the Sephardim.

In the meanwhile the narrative of the Sephardi community continued on its course. The problem of the poor took up a considerable part of the thought and attention of the Governors of the Community. The fame of the prosperity and contentment of London Jewry—no doubt with the usual exaggerations—began to spread and London increased its strength as a magnet to attract new-comers—not only Sephardim—from the Continent. These new-comers were in most cases a burden, which added itself to that of some of the immigrants who had preceded them. They led also to the appearance and growth of a nuisance against which the Mahamad found itself compelled to legislate. A class of vicarious philanthropists began to appear—men who adopted protégés among the poor and who thought fit to pester the Mahamad to give them undue favours. To deal with this development the Gentlemen of the Mahamad resolved on the 4th of Elul 1674 'that no Yahid intercede for any foreigner, under penalty of 20s., and to the same penalty shall be liable any who may go drawing alms for them', but these foreign poor were permitted to continue to appeal themselves to the Mahamad for assistance 'and the Senhores of the Mahamad will order the help to be given them that they may think fit'. Of the total expenditure of £401 4s. 3d. for the year 1671, £71 9s. 4d.—a portion being expended on returning recipients of relief to the Continent or of sending them farther afield—was spent on the poor of the community and a further £40 14s. 6d. on new-comers including the cost of their journeys to more distant destinations. One family in particular is mentioned in the records of relief or assistance in these earlier days, and this was one that had influential support. Mention has been made on an earlier page of Rabbi Solomon Franco, one of the earliest members of the London Community, who subsequently apostatized. He seems to have been a source of trouble from the beginning, and as early as 1664 the accounts show a payment to him of £12 11s. in settlement of all the claims he had against the Community. This was, however, not the end, for there is mention

Adolphus, who was for a time personal physician to Frederick the Great of Prussia, subsequently returned to London, and from him was descended John Adolphus, celebrated as an advocate and historical writer, and his son John Leycester Adolphus, the literary critic and authority on Sir Walter Scott. Sir Jacob Adolphus, the army surgeon, who held the rank of a British General, during the earlier half of the nineteenth century, was also one of the numerous descendants of Moses and Golly Adolphus. Another Jacob Adolphus was one of the few Ashkenazim who were early admitted to membership of the London Sephardi Community.

in the accounts for 1670 of a further payment in respect of an action, presumably a lawsuit, to Franco two or three years earlier. These payments probably related to the employment of Franco in some minor capacity in the first years of the history of the Congregation. The date of Franco's death is not known, but he left an unappreciated legacy to the Community. Perhaps he was not dead, but his wife and daughters declined to follow him in his apostasy and claimed the support of the Congregation. In 1671 the Lord Mayor intervened, and on his instructions the Mahamad had to pay an allowance of three pounds a quarter to the wife of Solomon Franco for the maintenance of her two daughters. These payments continued not very willingly on the part of the Mahamad, with occasional additional payments for clothing for the daughters. In the end Mrs. Franco took legal proceedings against the Mahamad, received further payments but was still not satisfied. Finally the case reached the Privy Council, who decided against her claim, and the proceedings were stayed. The Franco case was not without precedent, for some years earlier, in 1662, the then Lord Mayor had ordered the Community to make a weekly payment to Abraham Monday, an apostate, and after his death, in the Plague year, a reduced grant to his widow,[1] who had never been a Jewess. The allowance was reduced on the plea that the Community had suffered severely by death and removal as a consequence of the Plague. There is a hint, however, that changes of religion were not all in one direction at this period in a resolution of the Mahamad of the 15th of Tebet 5431 (1671) by which Ascama 32 prohibiting the acceptance of proselytes was expanded and the employment, even temporarily, of maids who had been converted to Judaism was prohibited. It seems that there were, despite the earlier prohibition, at least occasional breaches of the law.

This period was one of some anxiety for Anglo-Jewry. The country was in the grip of an intense anti-Catholic agitation, and in those who directed it there was a tendency to bracket foreigners with Catholics. The members of the Jewish Community were without exception either of foreign birth or the children of foreigners, and in consequence found themselves objects of widespread suspicion. In fact a Select Committee of the House of Commons, appointed in 1670, was instructed not only to inquire into the spread of Catholicism in England but incidentally 'to enquire touching the number of the Jews and their synagogues, and upon what terms they are permitted to have their residence

---

[1] See W. S. Samuel, *Miscellanies of the Jewish Historical Society of England*, vol. III, pp. 7 and 8.

here'. The committee, however, ignored this part of its reference, but nevertheless some not surprising alarm was aroused in the London Jewry. Next, the law was strengthened against unauthorized assemblies for prayer. This was directed against Nonconformists, but was not without the possibility of effect on the position of the Jews. The forced withdrawal, in 1673, of the Declaration of Indulgence of Charles II raised a threat against the Jews who had lived comfortably enough without the Declaration and must have deeply regretted that it had ever been made. It soon became evident that there was justification for the foreboding, for an application was almost at once made to the Quarter Sessions at the Guildhall indicting the Jews of a technical riot for having met together for religious worship. A true bill was returned by the Grand Jury, and the leading Jews, in a state of alarm, petitioned the King, who by an Order in Council instructed the Attorney General to stop all proceedings. In those days it was not always desirable to rely solely on the administration of the law or of justice. In fact, so far as the law was concerned, the position of the Jews was not altogether secure. The value of having friends at court was also widely recognized. The Jews of London had hitherto been very sympathetically treated by the King and his advisers, but less highly placed friends might also be of value. The position of the Lord Mayor of London was one of considerable power, and the synagogue authorities did not delay long in recognizing that it was worth while to secure his friendship. Gifts to holders of office were then not exceptional. Two centuries and more had to pass before it was generally accepted that it was undesirable for anyone in public office to put himself under obligation to a wealthy individual or group. The Mahamad therefore decided to follow what was then to some extent the fashion. In the accounts for 1671 there is an entry of the payment of £48 for a pipe of wine presented to the then Lord Mayor, Sir Richard Ford, who had in the same year ordered the Mahamad to make provision for the widow and daughters of Solomon Franco, and of twenty guineas to the Lord Mayor's son. Five years later there was an expenditure of £6 4s. on the banquet which 'Melormer gave to the Nation', and in the same year £4 15s. 'By wine for the sword bearer of Melor mer'. By 1679 these gifts had taken a more formal form. In that year the sum of £30 3s. 10d. was expended on a silver salver presented to the Lord Mayor and henceforth for a century the presentation of a similar gift became an annual event. In this the Jews did not stand alone, for year by year the Communities of Dutch Protestants and French Huguenots also

SET-BACKS AND ADVANCES

made gifts of pieces of silver plate in anticipation of securing the active sympathy, if the need arose, of the City authorities. The gifts of the Dutch and the Huguenots ceased in 1739 by which year they considered their position was fully secure: among the Jews they continued for another forty years. The Jewish gifts at first took the form of salvers; later they were replaced by cups which in beauty and in value by no means fall below the salvers. These receptacles were generally piled up with chocolates or other sweetmeats. On occasions towards the end of the period purses of gold were substituted for pieces of plate.

Apart from the institution of an annual gift to the Lord Mayor, there were other echoes in the annual accounts of the Community of the uneasiness from which its members suffered during this period. In 1671, lumped together with the £48 for the pipe of wine for Sir Richard Ford, twenty guineas for his son, and £10 'ordered to be given at once to the wife of Solomon Franco', there was also a further sum of £22 18s. 10d. for various expenses on solicitors and goings and coming to the Parliament and bottles of wine that were presented, and £6 7s. 6d. for a paper of a Court of the Aldremans'. Another similar echo is probably to be heard in the entry 'By outlay in the house of Ishack Alvarez with the Duchess of Bokingham—£10 17s. 6d.' No details of the expenditure are given. For the entertainment even of a duchess the amount seems excessive in those days. Isaac Alvarez was a very prominent member of the Community, a jeweller, who had been gabay of the Congregation during the Plague year and held the office again later. In the Community he was generally known as Isaac Israel Nunez, but in his business transactions he appeared as Isaac Alvarez. He was the court jeweller, or one of them, and in this capacity found at times difficulty in obtaining payment for gems supplied to King Charles. There is in the Privy Council Register for January 1675-6 an entry relating to Alvarez's urgent request for the payment of a sum of £4,000 long overdue to him and an order to the Lord High Treasurer to give Alvarez the satisfaction he required.[1] As court jeweller Alvarez doubtless met members of the nobility, and it is probable that the Duchess of Buckingham was among them. The Duke was the son and successor of Charles I's favourite and at times one of the most influential men in the kingdom. He had been brought up with Charles II and his brother, and had held high office under the former king, although at the time of the visit of his wife to Alvarez he was out

[1] See W. S. Samuel, *Miscellanies of the Jewish Historical Society of England*, vol. III.

of favour. Nevertheless the Duchess was in a sense a friend at court, and the Gentlemen of the Mahamad doubtless considered her favour worth cultivating.

But to return to the inner life of the Community. Its numbers were continually growing, and although the richer members were becoming richer and probably increasing in number, the poorer ones were increasing at a greater rate. The tradition of Jewry has always been to support its own poor, but even if that had not been the case the City authorities would have been quick to send to them any poor Jew who might ask for assistance. The item in the accounts 'outlay on foreigners to despatch them abroad' often exceeded the expenditure on the local poor. There was also a prospect of increased expenditure for other purposes in the near future. There was no suggestion that the settled members of the Community were in any respect lax in their payments, but this does not seem to have been the case with those who came to England for temporary stay. Some of these seem to have stayed in the country until they died, and although the Ascamot had laid down that these visitors were expected to pay their due contributions, a practice had grown up on their part of securing all the advantages of membership of the Community without its liabilities. Early in 1673 it was decided to call these defaulters sharply to account, and it was further decided that the penalties laid down in the original ascama would in future be strictly enforced. All Sephardim living in England, possessing any means of consequence, were required to join the Community, and steps were early taken to see that they did so. Even temporary visitors to London were expected to contribute to the Community's funds. To attain this end the Mahamad took to itself the power of electing Yehidim without even mentioning in advance the intention to the gentlemen primarily concerned. But there was another difficulty that had not been foreseen, and provision to deal with which had within a few years to be made. It was not altogether infrequent for members taking offence or being dissatisfied over some matter of more consequence to themselves than to their fellow members to resign their membership. To prevent a man resigning or to control him in any way after his resignation was beyond the power of the Mahamad, autocratic as it was. But these seceders generally resigned in a fit of pique from which they recovered after a not very long interval. This gave the Mahamad their opportunity, and to take full advantage of it they enacted in *Adar Sheni* 1674 that 'a Yahid who resigns as a consequence of a quarrel or disinclination to fulfil his obligations and wishes to return must pay a penalty of

SET-BACKS AND ADVANCES 49

two pounds for the first year of his absence and six pounds for the second'. Since a Yahid could not resign without the permission of the Mahamad he was in addition liable for the imposta and other charges that had accrued during his absence.

Another regulation made at the same time was to the effect that silver and other articles of value were not in future to be deposited in the synagogue for safe custody unless they comprised ritual or other sacred objects. Anybody who deposited his property in the synagogue did so at his own risk. This doubtless followed burglaries by which property entrusted to the synagogue for safe custody was stolen. Three years later the first ascama, that forbidding meetings for divine worship, other than that of the Congregation, 'in this City of London, its districts and environs', was revised and extended. The prohibition was more clearly defined. It was limited to within four miles of the existing synagogue. Permission to arrange a second place of prayer within these limits could be given only with the agreement of two-thirds of the Yehidim assembled in general meeting. In 1673 also a congregational physician was appointed at a salary of £10 per annum. The first incumbent was Dr. Abraham Perez Galvão. In 1660, however, in the list of the Jewish residents in London appeared the name of Doctor Boyno (Bueno) 'Phision to the Jewes'. He does not appear to have held an official appointment, or in any event not any paid one. Successors followed without interruption until with the resignation of Dr. Sydney Mellins in 1948 the office, which had become a sinecure, was abolished. In the same year (1673) the agreement with Benjamin Levy (the elder) for the farming of the meat tax expired and a new agreement was made with Isaac de Ramos at a rate of payment double that agreed to by Levy—evidence of the growth of the Community within a few years. Further evidence in support of this growth was the pressing need for an increase in synagogue accommodation. The Community had outgrown that which was ample fifteen years earlier.

The provision of this additional accommodation was taken in hand energetically, but before the whole of the attention of the Mahamad was directed to it, one small reform in the conduct of the services was adopted. The decorum observed in the synagogue, according to the evidence of Pepys and others, fell below that generally observed elsewhere in similar circumstances at the time. Simhhat Torah in particular seems to have been the season at which it was realized that the congregation was accustomed to pass beyond the limits of decorum. The need for greater restraint was evident, and in 1674 the Mahamad resolved to deal with the matter. A new ascama was adopted. This ran, 'The Senhores of the Mahamad, considering the tumult and disorder which the decorations made on Simha Torah and Sabath Beresitt cause agreed that from this day henceforth it be not permitted to the Bridegrooms of the Law to decorate the Synagogue with wreaths of myrtle nor of anything, and it is only allowed them (to do so) with landscape tapestries or gilt leather, as also flowers on the candelabra.' At the same time another small reform which it was hoped would help towards the more orderly conduct of the services was adopted. The boys of the congregation, like other boys at all times, were not as quiet and subdued during the services as was desirable, and in order to keep them under control a new office, that of Parnas of the Talmud Torah, was created. The duties of the gentlemen chosen for that office, the first of whom was Abraham Rodriguez Pinhel, consisted in the first place of taking charge of the pupils of the Talmud Torah while in the Synagogue, of 'controlling them, restraining them so that they do not raise their voices inordinately, and if they should do so they shall have power to rebuke them, and afterwards to chastise or order to be chastised those who may deserve it, for the wanton acts that they may do or scandal that they may raise in the streets'. For this purpose the Parnas of the Talmud Torah was given a seat in the Synagogue where all the students could see him. The new officer was, however, not concerned solely with discipline in the Synagogue. He had also duties closer to the primary function of the Talmud Torah, that of education. It was his duty to attend at the Medrash every day and be present at the weekly examinations on Thursday. It was his duty to punish those of the pupils whose progress was unsatisfactory, 'in order that in this manner they may be eager to study it; and to the end that the respect and decency on the part of the scholars may be more effective, their fathers shall take care to introduce them to him'.

The boys were, however, not the only culprits who showed lack of decorum in the synagogue. There were others whose behaviour at times called for far more serious notice. For instance, in 1683 Samuel de Caceres, presumably a kinsman of the aggressive fire-eating Simon de Caceres of Cromwell's time, became so unruly as to cause a scene during service. He demanded the right to recite a special prayer, *Kaddeesh de Rabanan*, on the occasion of the death of a cousin, a right which was granted under the regulations of the Congregation, only on the occasion of the death of a parent, or, very exceptionally, of a brother. De Caceres, persisting in his demand, was ordered to leave the synagogue, but refused to do so and had to be ejected. In the course of the scuffle he drew a knife and threatened anyone who approached him. For his offence in disregarding the order of the Mahamad he was summoned before a special meeting of the Mahamad and the Elders and sentenced to pay a fine of £5 and to be excluded from the synagogue for six months. He, however, quickly made his peace, for within two days the Mahamad and Elders remitted the exclusion from the synagogue and de Caceres was free to resume his devotions in his accustomed surroundings, but presumably unarmed. Some years later, in 1694, another incident is recorded in which the synagogue was not the scene of the unseemly conduct, but the place of punishment for it. The two *rubis* or teachers in the congregational school, Abraham de Leon and Joseph Abendanon, seem to have been on very unsatisfactory terms, and the culmination came when the Mahamad had to take notice of their unseemly quarrels and the abusive language they used to one another. They were not only dismissed from their offices in the school but ordered to remove to prominent seats side by side in the men's gallery in the synagogue—a sort of pillory—where all could see them and realize the punishment such persistent disturbers of the congregational peace deserved. If either refused to take the place allotted to him, the customary and generally very effective punishment was to be imposed—exclusion from the synagogue. Abendanon had been brought from Amsterdam only two years earlier to teach in the school. A member of a scholarly family, he had fled from Belgrade on the occasion of its sack and had spent some years wandering in Europe. His exclusion from office was not permanent, and in 1700 he succeeded Isaac Israel d'Avila, who had been appointed in 1676, as congregational rubi and bodek. After his dismissal in 1694 he opened a private school, and the Mahamad agreed two years later when David Pardo, who had been appointed rubi in 1679 and Hazan in addition in 1681, asked to be relieved of his duties as congregational teacher, and that his pupils in the congregational school should be transferred to Abendanon's school, so that he might be able to devote himself to private teaching and other remunerative employment. Abendanon was a scholar of some standing and always resented the inadequate consideration he felt that his learning received. He was unhappy in the subordinate position he occupied, and this dissatisfaction is probably the cause of the many quarrels in which he became involved. Among his opponents was Jacob Fidanque, and it was against him that he appealed to his friend Jacob Sasportas whom he knew when he was living in Amsterdam. Abendanon died in 1740.

These quarrels and disputes were, however, only exceptional incidents. The lack of decorum in the synagogue seems to have been a perennial matter, and even in an age in which a lower standard than that of today was accepted was not considered satisfactory. At length, in Sivan 1699, the Mahamad had to give very serious consideration to it. 'In view of the great disorder in synagogue due to some persons rising at certain passages of the prayers and others at others, and the scandal this causes to those who come from without, the Mahamad on 2 Sivan 5459 (1699) resolved to convene the Elders and the Haham who with a view to our preservation and tranquility ordained that henceforth no one should rise at *Vaibarech David* or *Istabach*.' A fine of 5*s*. was imposed for the first offence on those who in responding to the Kaddeesh did so with disturbing voices, without regard to the devotion and respect due to the synagogue.

CHAPTER V

THE ENLARGEMENT OF THE SYNAGOGUE

WITH THESE RELATIVELY minor matters out of the way, the Gentlemen of the Mahamad and to a less extent the members of the Congregation as a whole were able to direct their attention to the pressing need for larger synagogue accommodation. The conduct of the negotiations and the approval of the consequent plans fell on the former body which consisted at the time of Isaac Israel Nunez and Abraham do Porto, the Parnassim, and Jacob Gomez Serra, the Gabay. So that this work on their part could continue without interruption an innovation in the selection and appointment of the Mahamad was made. Hitherto these gentlemen were appointed for one year only, but on this occasion, for the first time, the three officers at the end of their year of office were re-elected for a further term of six months. This step was taken on a petition by a number of the *Velhos* or Elders of the Congregation. Under the constitution of the Congregation the new Mahamad was always elected by the gentlemen who were retiring, assisted by two of their predecessors of the previous year, and no member of the retiring Mahamad could be re-elected except after an interval of two years. The Mahamad in office agreed to the extension, and thus the Mahamad under whose direction the enlargement of the Synagogue was commenced saw its completion. The Senior Parnas, Isaac Israel Nunez, was the court jeweller, Isaac Alvarez. Abraham, otherwise Antonio, do Porto, an ex-Marrano, had been a member of the group since the time of Manasseh ben Israel. He had previously, in 1670, served as Gabay. Jacob, otherwise Antonio, Gomez Serra, the Gabay, had held the same office in 1667 and was one of the signatories to the original Ascamot.

The original twenty-one years' lease of the house—later two houses—in Creechurch Lane which Carvajal had taken in 1656, was approaching its end and provision had to be made for the future. The Community had outgrown the accommodation originally provided, and the two alternatives before them were the acquisition or erection of a new building or the remodelling and rearrangement of the old one so as to provide room for a larger number of worshippers. The latter course was decided on. In the first instance a new agreement was made with the parish authorities

—the ground landlords—for the extension of the lease for a further period of twenty-four years until midsummer 1698. This extension secured, the Mahamad proceeded to arrange for extensive alterations of the interior of the structure. The two houses, hitherto separate, were combined and the yard attached to one of the houses built on. The whole of the first floor of the two houses was turned into one large hall, which became the main synagogue. The floor above was to a large extent cut away, leaving galleries for the women on the north and south sides with two rows of seats. There was a third gallery on the western side, but since the seats in this were not hidden from the male worshippers below by lattice work, it was presumably intended for men. The architecture of the entrance and the internal decoration were on a generous scale and, according to a French traveller who when in London presumably visited the Synagogue, need not in those respects have feared comparison with the synagogues of Venice. It has been estimated that there was accommodation in the enlarged building for 172 men and 84 women, more than twice as many as hitherto. The estimated cost of the work on the building was £222, apart from other expenditure on the fittings and also incidental expenses, but when the accounts came to be paid it was found that £760 16s. 4d., including £100 for the extension of the lease, was required. This expenditure was of course outside the normal accounts of the congregation. The first step taken to cover this extraordinary expenditure was the making of offerings in the synagogue for the purpose. This realized £265 18s. 6d., more than the whole of the original estimate.

From the list of donors that has survived, one can estimate the relative wealth of the principal members of the Community. At the top of the list came Isaac Israel Nunez (Alvarez), one of the Parnassim, with £25. After him came Abraham Israel de Sequeira (Gomez Rodriguez), a former Parnas and generous supporter, and Jacob Baruhiel (Berahel), otherwise Francisco de Liz, also a former Parnas, with £15 each. Close behind was the second Parnas, Abraham do Porto, with £14. The future Sir Solomon de Medina gave £10, Moses Baruch Lousada, the Gabay of 1663, £5 10s., Samuel Sasportas, the son of the first Haham, who was by then a broker on the Exchange, £2, and Benjamin Levy, apparently the former Samas, 10s. Isaac bar Abraham, a proselyte, contributed 12s., Samuel Haim and Manasseh Hart, Ashkenazim, 10s. and 2s. 6d. respectively. Mayer (Michael) Levy, the 'solicitor' of the Congregation, their agent in dealing with the public authorities and his anonymous nephew gave £2, Eliezer bar Joseph, probably

THE ENLARGEMENT OF THE SYNAGOGUE

also an Ashkenazi, £1. Four residents in Hamburg or Amsterdam who were at the time in England or had connexions with the Community were also in the list. Moses Mocatta, the first of the family to appear in the records of the Community—the earliest mention of him was in the list of payments of *imposta* in 1671— was there with a member of another family later well known in Anglo-Jewry, Isaac de Andrade, whose name first appeared in the Synagogue records in 1664.

Since the cost of the work exceeded considerably the original estimate, further resources had to be obtained. The *Nedabot* or special donations were supplemented by a finta, that is a loan to be repaid by deductions from future annual payments due. This finta produced a further total of £235 10s. from eighteen members, of whom the principal contributors in addition to the two parnassim, the Gabay, Abraham Israel de Sequeira, and Solomon de Medina, were the brothers Abraham and Isaac de Francia, Jacob de Miranda, Jacob Jessurun Alvarez, and Moses Mocatta.

On the other side of the ledger was the expenditure, some of the items of which are of particular interest.[1] £100 was paid for the extension of the lease, £2 2s. 6d. 'To the painter who began to paint and did not continue his work', a surprising reminder that certain modern practices are after all not so modern. Then comes 13s. 10d. 'For what was spent in the Tavern when the Contract of the Synagogue was made'. Not the whole of the expenditure can properly be debited to the work itself. Some of the expenses were ancillary. 'To Mr. Cooll, stonemason, for passage through his house for the ladies for 16 years . . . £12.' £8 for sixteen weeks' rent of a temporary place of worship. 'To Manuel Mocata for 7 weeks besides while the Sr. H.(aham) was residing in the said house . . . £1 15s.': and also 10s. 6d. to the Haham for the expenses of his temporary removal 'and messuzot and other minor matters'. There is a detailed account of the cost of the Tablet of the Ten Commandments, probably the ones still familiar to visitors to Bevis Marks.[2] 'For the canvas on which were painted the Commandments £1 17s. 6d. to Sr. H. Avilla for the gold £1 10s. for his labour £3 to Aron de Chavez for the painting £5', £11 7s. 6d. in all.

Once the alterations were completed, the workmen departed and the synagogue once more in full use, the somewhat placid life of

[1] These amounts should be multiplied by about six to bring them into relationship with present-day values.
[2] There is, however, an entry in the accounts under the date Sivan 28, 5448 (1688): 'Paid to an Italian for remaking the panel on which are the Commandments . . . £6.'' De Chavez' work had therefore soon to be restored.

the Community was resumed, to be disturbed only in 1680 when the arrival in London from Holland of a Jewish girl, Eve Cohan and her Christian lover, and the spread of the news that she intended to embrace Christianity, caused such a scandal in London Jewry that the Sephardi authorities or at any rate their representative *vis-à-vis* the public authorities, the 'solicitor' Michael Levy, felt themselves obliged to intervene. The line taken by the London Jews to prevent her baptism was to secure her arrest on a trumped-up charge of debt. There was no legal case against her, and the Lord Mayor in dismissing the charge went out of his way to threaten the whole of the Community 'for daring to offer such an affront to the religion and nation of the land'. He went further and called for a statement of all legal disabilities under which the Jews might be suffering in England. Fortunately the matter was soon forgotten, unless an abortive proposal a little later to reorganize the constitutional position of Anglo-Jewry on a sort of ghetto basis was an echo of it.

The death of Charles II in 1685 brought a more serious threat to the Jews of England. So long as he lived it was recognized that the position of the Jews in England was secure. With his death their business rivals believed or hoped once again that their opportunity had come. The campaign began with a pamphleteer, Samuel Hayne, who drew up a list of all the statutes that affected the trading of aliens in England and then proceeded to argue that the Jews who had settled in the country had infringed the whole of the series. The Corporation of London, never hitherto very friendly, became interested, and finally two brothers, named Beaumont, applied for writs for the arrest of all the prominent members of the Community under a statute of Queen Elizabeth, directed against Roman Catholics and long a dead letter, which imposed a penalty on anyone who abstained from attendance at church. Writs were accordingly issued against forty-eight prominent Jewish merchants, thirty-seven of whom were arrested at the Exchange. The accused pleaded the precedent of 1673. The heads of the Synagogue at the same time, acting on the advice of the Attorney General, petitioned the King to permit the Jews of his kingdom to continue as heretofore. James confirmed the decision of his predecessor and ordered the Attorney General to stop all proceedings—'His Majesty's intention being that they should not be troubled on this account, but quietly enjoy the free exercise of their religion, whilst they behave themselves dutifully and obediently to his Government.' The incident, although it did not cover a lengthy period, caused the Community much anxiety and also

THE ENLARGEMENT OF THE SYNAGOGUE 57

expense, the greater part of which consisted of the fee or gift of two hundred guineas paid to the Earl of Peterborough who had actively championed the Jewish cause at court. Henry Mordaunt, the second earl, was a Cavalier who had once been a Roundhead. His services to the King had been considerable, and they had been suitably recognized. He had thus much influence at court, and although James would probably have in any case granted the prayer of the Jews, especially in view of the anti-Catholic legislation that had been invoked, the support of Peterborough was certainly of service. This was the last occasion on which the free practice and observance of Judaism in England was threatened.

Once these anxieties had passed away the Community again resumed its course of uninterrupted progress. In 1675 the first of a long series of legacies earmarked for special purposes was received. With the help of these legacies, which have come as acts of piety and appreciation from Yehidim covering a wide social range, most of the subsidiary institutions of the Community have been built up. The benefactor on this occasion was Abraham Hezekiah Marques, otherwise Diego Rodriguez, one of the leading Jewish merchants of London, who died in 1675. He left a sum of £30 to the Congregation, subject only to the condition that a lamp should burn in the Synagogue in his memory during the first year after his death, and his memory should in other manner be perpetuated. But there was also another legacy by him which is as living and fruitful today as on the day on which it first became effective. He left to his widow on trust a sum of a thousand pounds out of the interest on which she was to pay fifty pounds every year for a dowry to a poor orphan girl of the Community, preference to be given to a member of his family if one were qualified. His widow survived him by only two years, and the disposal of the fund thereupon came before the Court of Chancery. By this authority a scheme for the administration of the legacy was drawn up by which the master of the court was made responsible for the fulfilment of the conditions laid down, but the nomination of the beneficiaries was to rest with the wardens of the Synagogue. The fund is still being administered by the Court of Chancery, the Mahamad nominating the recipients of the dowries. In the following year, 1676, another generous legacy was received. The benefactor on this occasion was Jacob Berahel, otherwise Francisco de Liz, who had from early days in its history been prominent in the life of the Community, and had been a Parnas in 1666–7 and again in 1671–2. His legacy also consisted of £30 and was left subject to the same conditions as those that governed the earlier one of similar amount of Abraham Rodriguez Marques. In 1680 the Mahamad received a sum of £15 from Isaac bar Abraham of Hamburg, a Tudesco who had probably visited London. Another legacy of a still earlier date came from a more unusual source. This was a proselyte, Debora Israel, who seems to have in 1669 left the whole of her estate to the Community to apply it to whatever object they might consider suitable. After placing a memorial stone on her grave and providing for the recital of a memorial prayer (Kaddeesh) on the anniversary of her death, the Mahamad devoted the balance of her bequest to the purchase of silver ornaments for two scrolls of the Law, and to perpetuate her memory and to secure that these ornaments should be a perpetual memorial of the pious donor a special ascama was adopted. 'And thus it is made known to all this Kahal Kados that it is recorded in the Book of the Escamoth, in order that it may so remain firmly, and that this order henceforth may not be liable to be subverted; and that it has the same force as the other Escamoth and ordinances of this holy Kahal Kados, which God prosper, and may He bless all his people "Israel" with peace. Amen.'

The rebuilding of the synagogue and the payment through the generosity of members of the congregation of its cost somewhat relieved the finances of the Congregation. In the year 1676, when Solomon de Medina was Gabay, it was found possible to abolish the additional taxation that had been introduced ten years earlier. The records for the same year showed the appeal for assistance by the widow and family of Sir Augustine Coronel, the supporter of Charles II who had accepted baptism to qualify for a knighthood. This appeal was granted. Another new item that appeared in the accounts of the same year was one for a 'special watch at different times and firing weapons' and 'cost of two muskets and bandoliers, powder and bullets for the watchmen who offered themselves'. There had been earlier payments in respect of 'guards of the parish', and these more detailed accounts may have related to a similar service. On the other hand, the later expenditure may have been on account of special protection, perhaps of the cemetery in an age when such protection was sometimes necessary. The accounts for the year 1677 show that out of a total expenditure of £621 12s. 10d., £61 6s. 6d. was spent on the local poor, apart from special distributions such as gifts on the occasion of festivals, and £181 5s. 9d. on foreign poor, including the cost of sending some of them abroad, and also £53 given during the same year to the widow of Augustin Coronel. Another item of interest in the

THE ENLARGEMENT OF THE SYNAGOGUE 59

expenditure for the year 1677 was £18 1s. 'Paid for the liberation of Jewish prisoners in this (City)' and also grants to certain individuals mentioned by name, sometimes 'in distress', sometimes as a consequence of 'a suit' brought against him. The sum of thirty shillings was also paid in this year for the redemption of the lease of the Beth Haim four years earlier.

The *Hebra de Bikur Holim e Guemilat Hasadim* (Society for visiting the Sick and Charitable Deeds)[1] was active for some years and then lapsed into quietude. In the year 1678 it was realized that the effective dissolution of this society had left a gap that it was desirable to fill, and in response to a petition by thirty-five members of the Congregation the Mahamad consented to the organization of a new society with the same objects as its predecessor, 'to execute any meritorious charity in case of poverty or death'. However, the enthusiasm of the new founders or their successors in office did not continue, for by the year 1693 the new society also had become moribund. It was resuscitated in that year and a new constitution given to it. In the new regulations the members of the society were placed under obligation, in person or by deputy, to nurse the sick when the necessity arose. In the end, in 1747, the functions of the society were separated. The Hebra retained its functions relating to the dead; the care of the sick and the poor was placed in the hands of the Beth Holim, or communal hospital. By this reform the provision of medical assistance was completely revolutionized.

The Haham, Joshua da Silva, died in May 1679,[2] and after an interval of two years and four months Jacob Abendana was chosen to succeed him. Da Silva's widow was granted a pension of £1 a month. Abendana's salary like that of his predecessor was £50 a year with free accommodation, and his duties included those of Hazan, or reader in the synagogue, and teacher of the boys 'in the Prophets' and of the students in the Talmud. Born in Spain, Abendana, who was fifty-one years old at the time of his appointment, had been taken to Hamburg as a child. He was educated at the famous *Yeshiba de los Pintos* at Rotterdam. After a short stay at Antwerp, Abendana proceeded to Amsterdam as rabbi, in 1658, and remained there for some years. He was also a Jewish scholar of some standing and was one of the earliest Jewish writers

---

[1] See p. 39.
[2] The address at his funeral was given by Isaac Aboab, Haham of Amsterdam, who also wrote his epitaph. Nine years after his death, in 1688, da Silva's widow, who had made a selection of his addresses in synagogue, published them in Amsterdam, this being the first publication of any Jewish sermon delivered in England.

whose works were commended by non-Jewish authorities. He had been in England on a visit previously, and as his younger brother, Isaac Abendana, had been resident in this country for almost twenty years, he was not on his arrival for permanent settlement unacquainted with conditions in England. In 1663, eighteen years before his appointment as Haham, and even before his first visit to England, Jacob Abendana had acquired English connexions through Sir William Davidson, a Scottish merchant resident in Holland, who had been prominent in his support of the King in exile. Davidson's business interests brought him into contact with the English colony of Barbados where there was then already a flourishing community of Sephardi Jews. Thus Jews were by no means strangers to Davidson,[1] and, on the other hand, Abendana had, apart from his brother who had settled in England, also English interests. Both brothers were scholars and had published results of their researches. Jacob's translation of Jehuda Halevi's *Cuzari*, published before he left Holland, was dedicated to Sir William Davidson. Isaac also published books but was more notable as a teacher of Hebrew and Cabbalistic literature at Cambridge and later at Oxford, and a friend and correspondent of English scholars. While at Cambridge he spent twelve years translating the *Mishnah* into Latin with the encouragement of the leading English scholars of his day. This translation was never published. More fortunate was he with his series of Jewish Calendars, dedicated to Oxford scholars, which he compiled and published from 1692 onwards. These productions were much more than their title indicates. They included also essays of Jewish antiquarian interest and two on the liturgy—and were sought for long after their author's death. Some of these essays were republished in one volume as *Discourses of the ecclesiastical and civil polity of the Jews* in 1706, with a second edition three years later. These books were the first written and published in England by a Jewish resident, although on two previous occasions Jewish residents in Holland, both also Sephardim (Manasseh ben Israel and a little later Judah Leon Templo) had published English translations of their writings.

Jacob Abendana's term of office as Haham lasted for only four years, for he died in 1685. The year of his appointment was marked by a great honour paid to the London Jewish Community. In that year the Princess Anne, daughter of the King, who was herself later to be Queen of England, paid a visit to the Synagogue

[1] Mr. Wilfred Samuel has in vol. XIV of the *Trans. Jew. Hist. Soc. of Eng.* sketched the dealings of Davidson with the Sephardi merchants of Barbados.

THE ENLARGEMENT OF THE SYNAGOGUE

during Passover. No record of the visit has survived, but there is in the archives of the Congregation an account of the expenses necessitated by the entertainment, after the service, of the Princess in the house of the Gabay, Abraham, otherwise Francisco, de Liz, the son of Jacob Berahel (another Francisco de Liz), an earlier parnas. At the end of the service the royal party proceeded to de Liz's house in the neighbouring Bury Street.[1] There we learn of a total expenditure, for which the Gabay claimed refundment, of £4 11s. 6d. 'For collation that was given in the last days of Passover in my house to the Lady Anne, daughter of the Duke of York, who came to see the Synagogue:

For dry sweetmeats of all sorts—25 lbs.	£3 5s.	0d.
Wine of different sorts and olives, and to the woman who got ready the plates	19s.	0d.
Fruits and flowers	5s.	0d.
Hire of pewter in which it was served without counting chocolate and other sweetmeats that were in the house	2s.	6d.
	£4 11s.	6d.

Although the first occasion on which a member of the English royal family visited a synagogue in England, this was not the first visit of an English princess to a synagogue. Thirty-nine years earlier, before the presence of Jews in England was recognized, Henrietta Maria, the Queen of Charles I, while on a visit to Amsterdam, had in the company of the Stadtholder of the Netherlands visited the synagogue in Amsterdam where they had been received by Manasseh ben Israel.

A few months after the visit of the Princess Anne, the Congregation made its contribution to the fund that was being raised for the rebuilding of St. Paul's Cathedral, destroyed in the Great Fire. The contribution was one guinea (£1 1s. 6d.). Five years later another contribution was made for church purposes. The local Church authorities who were the landlords of the synagogue building decided to install a new organ in their own place of worship, and for this purpose set about raising the cost from their congregation and their friends. By invitation or on their own motion a number of members of the Sephardi community also came forward with their contributions. The sum of £12 1s. was

---

[1] '*Berry Street* which is very handsome and cleanly kept, with good uniform Buildings on both Sides, well inhabited, mostly by Jews, who dwell privately, without shops.'—Wm. Maitland, *The History of London* (1756), p. 777.

received from nine of the members—all being names familiar in the annals of Creechurch Lane. There were other connexions between members of the Community and the churches of the parishes in which they lived. Superficially at any rate they were not so cordial, although as has been suggested their roots may have been in the desire of public-spirited English Jews to take their share of some of the burdens of the larger community of which they were a part. The churchwardens and overseers, elected annually, were drawn from among the lay residents of the parish, and from 1686 the practice began of occasionally selecting Jewish residents for these offices. Duties were attached to them which Jews felt themselves unable to perform, and on refusal of the office they, in common with non-Jews who might also find themselves unable or unwilling to take up the office, were fined. It may be that some at any rate of the Jews were quite willing to contribute to the Church funds in this manner, but without penetrating below the surface, it would seem that the choice of Jews in these circumstances was somewhat ungenerous. Later the attitude of Jews was changed. The office was looked on as public rather than religious, and Jews chosen for it gladly accepted and performed its duties. In the end one Jewish ratepayer, who happened to be a member of the Sephardi Community, actually protested against not being selected, and it was the vicar who had to object on the ground that the choice of a Jew for the office appeared to be inappropriate.

By this time the size of the Community had grown. A list is extant which was drawn up after the arrival of Jacob Abendana in London in 1681, but before April 1684 when the author, Abraham Israel Zagache, left England, of all members of the Community then resident in London.[1] Their number, men, women, and children, was 414 of whom five men were stated not to have been circumcised. Of these last five, two—Alvaro da Costa and Dr. Fernando Mendes, cousins and brothers-in-law—were among the most distinguished Jews of England of the time. They, through a series of inter-family marriages, became the ancestors of the Mendes da Costa family whose members, generation after generation, loomed large in Anglo-Jewry and from whom most of the older Sephardi families are descended. In fact, probably all the older Sephardi families of England can trace their descent back to Alvaro da Costa and Fernando Mendes. Alvaro da Costa had been one of the agents of the King of Portugal in the payment of the dowry of Catherine of Braganza. Fernando Mendes was the court physician. He followed the Queen to England and attended

[1] The names of the seatholders in 1682 are given in Appendix III.

THE ENLARGEMENT OF THE SYNAGOGUE 63

Charles II in his last illness. The Queen was the godmother of his daughter Catharine. Alvaro da Costa was the first Jew to own real estate in England. These two outstanding men, although in their lives not fully members of the Jewish Community, were buried among their brethren in the Beth Haim in Mile End, and their children took a full part in the life of the Community.

Among those in the list who were unequivocally members of the Community, there are several who have already been mentioned in these pages and others who names subsequently became prominent. Of the Henriques there were four families and one bachelor, but not yet a Quixano Henriques. Gutterres, however, appears in the list. Moses Barrow, the early Gabay, appears as Moses Baruch Lousada, with his wife, daughter, and son, together with an Abraham Baruch Lousada and his wife, and another Moses Baruch or Barrow, a bachelor. Isaac Lindo, his wife, mother, three daughters, and two sons are there and Solomon de Medina, his wife, and daughter. Moses Mocatta, his wife, two daughters, and two sons, are accompanied by another Mocatta, Immanuel, with his wife, three daughters, and son. Among the new names are Moses Henriques de Mesquita, three de Paiva families, Madam Salvador and her children, Joseph Henriques Sequeira and his daughter, and two da Silva families and also David Mendes Silva, a bachelor. Only one proselyte is mentioned, and in this case neither the name nor sex is given.

In the year 1689, the second occasion in its short history, the Synagogue suffered from burglary, the loss on this occasion being relatively serious. The principal objects stolen, so far as has been recorded, were silver ornaments and other appurtenances for the scrolls of the Law, but the thief or thieves, whoever they may have been, were interested also in the day-to-day private performance of the ritual, for among the losses were the *talet* or praying shawl and *tephillin* or phylacteries of the Gabay, Moses Henriques de Mesquita. Not only did the Congregation lose property, but some of its members, who had deposited ritual objects with it, suffered also. The property was never recovered. An earlier similar robbery, but on a smaller scale, had taken place in 1666, but only one set of *rimonim* or silver ornaments for the scroll of the Law seems to have been stolen on that occasion. The burglary, unpleasant as it was, was, however, dwarfed in the eyes of the members of the Mahamad and their constituents by a greater anxiety. The Revolution and expulsion of James II, whom his son-in-law and daughter succeeded on the throne, left their aftermath, a feeling of unsettlement and uneasiness that it took time to dissipate. The small

Jewish community was still an alien element in the larger one and at times attracted disproportionate attention. The recent civil war had led to undue expenditure, and the necessity to replenish the Treasury was evident. One proposal to this end was the imposition of special taxation on the Jews, and a motion to this effect was introduced into Parliament. The leaders of the Community—acting in this as an embryo Board of Deputies—were quick to take up the challenge. Every legitimate means was taken—doubtless with the energetic assistance of the 'solicitor' of the Community, Michael Levy—to defeat the proposal. These efforts were successful, but they cost the Community an 'extraordinary expenditure' of £193 8s. 9d., including a present of £20 5s. 7d. to Lady Littleton, presumably the wife of Sir Thomas Littleton, the Minister and future Speaker of the House of Commons, and another lady who remains anonymous, and another of £21 13s. 6d. to the Serjeant (of the House) (? Mr. Tuffan), and £5 1s. for chocolate and vanilla. The threat, however, had its repercussions. Not only the political and financial but also the economic situation of the country was unstable. A drain of silver from the country set in and according to the report of a committee of the House of Commons which went into the matter some Jews were engaged in the traffic. The Mahamad recognized that even a suspicion might be a source of danger, and acted promptly. On the 6th of Tebet (December) 1690 it enacted an ordinance forbidding any of the members to export silver from the realm in any circumstances, and when a few years later new rumours to the effect that Jews were endeavouring to depress the value of the currency, members of the Community were forbidden, under penalty, for a period of a fortnight to deal in currency, and later it was decided to put under strict control all dealings in bullion. In other respects also business transactions were placed under careful surveillance.[1] The Mahamad was always anxious to keep high the reputation of the Community, and as subsequent events will show was not unsuccessful in doing so. The reputation of the Community in view of the character and personalities of its best known members was considerable, and

---

[1] 14 Nisan 5451 (1691). 'The Mahamad having observed the scandal caused to natives of this land by our brother Jews making bets and raising insurance policies on the chances befalling Government and successes of war in which this realm is concerned, this being very contrary to our preservation, as we enjoy the tolerance and kindness of Their Majesties, whom God preserve, to allow us to live in this Kingdom quietly and peaceably, the Mahamad with the agreement of the Haham and past Mahamad ordain that henceforth no Yahid shall make such bets or insurances nor ask for them, directly or indirectly by himself or by agent. The offender will incur Herem and be cast out from our Nation.' This ascama remained in force for almost two and a half years, being repealed in Elul 1693.

TABLETS OF THE LAW
From a painting by Aron de Chavez (1674)

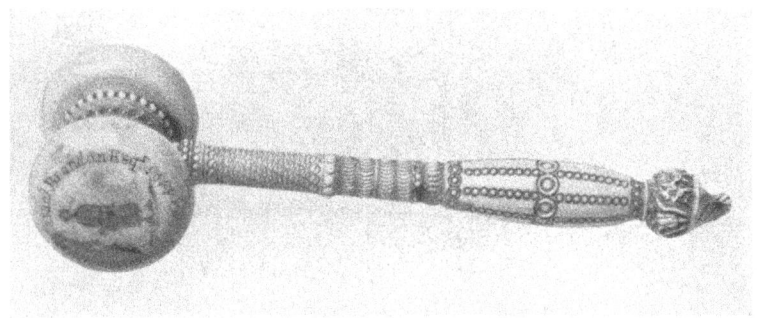

CHAIRMAN'S MALLET
used at meetings of the Gates of Hope School Governors (*c.* 1835)

DON JOSÉ CORTISSOS

THE ENLARGEMENT OF THE SYNAGOGUE 65

every Mahamad as they succeeded to office was determined to keep it undiminished. The Mahamad had considerable power over the Yehidim, and they wielded this power sometimes somewhat dictatorially, but their object was the welfare of the Community as a whole and this was recognized.

There were other matters in which the Mahamad kept a firm hand on the Yehidim, which will probably cause some surprise to the reader of the twentieth century. One was very close to the private life of the individual. On the 3rd of Nisan 1678, the minute book shows, a gentleman, whose name is still today well known in the public life of the London Community, was summoned by the Mahamad on a charge made by the Haham and Rabbi Avila, the rabbi of the Talmud Torah, that he had broken a vow not to play cards for four years. He was ordered to keep within his house for seven days, at the end of which period he would be released, provided that he undertook to comply with the terms of his vow. If he failed to do so a sentence of excommunication was passed on him. A few weeks later the prevalence of an offence of a more public character was brought to notice. 'It was reported to the Mahamad that some Jews, both congregants of ours and non-congregants, to the great profanation of God's name and of the sanctity of the Sabbath day and notable scandal for their people, with base ambition take and go to fetch on the Sabbath letters to the post with such insolence that they scandalize even strangers.' The Mahamad ordained that no Jew, whether a member of the Congregation or not, should commit such an offence, whether or not money passed in the transaction, and that anyone who did so would be excommunicated.[1] In 1698 a very curious offence was recorded. Moses Rodriguez de Leon was forbidden the synagogue for three months for having tried to induce Jacob Gomez de Herera and David de Castro to act as confessors to a dying Spaniard.

The Sephardi authorities were also frequently worried by the subject of proselytes. There was a longstanding tradition, if nothing more, that, when the conditions on which the presence of Jews in England was to be tolerated were under consideration, an undertaking had been given that the Jews would refrain from making or attempting to make converts from among the Christian population. At any rate, proselytization was always discouraged,

[1] This ban held for fifty-five years, for it was not until 26 Sebat 1733 that the Mahamad 'summoned the Haham and Beth Din and ordered them to lift the penalty of Herem "which appears in Ascama No. 5 of the 3rd of Ellul 5438", regarding the prohibition of the carrying or collecting mail on the Sabbath'. The Minute continues: 'This penalty was lifted in order to avoid further annoyance.'

5

and more than one law adopted by the Mahamad was directed against that practice. Nevertheless there were always a few proselytes in the Community. The records of voluntary offerings and also of grants to the poor occasionally show donors of non-Jewish origin. When the Community was formally constituted in 1657 there were at least four proselytes within its fold. In the records of marriages kept at Bevis Marks there are a number of proselytes mentioned, men very infrequently, more often women. Most of the latter—bearing unquestionably Sephardi names—were the daughters of members of the Community who had married, presumably in church, non-Jewish women. These girls may have been treated exceptionally, but it is certain that the synagogue authorities as a rule refused to accept proselytes, and it seems that those who were determined to enter the Jewish fold had to go to Holland where the synagogue authorities had no similar objection to accepting them. Early in the seventeenth century, years before there was any known Jewish community in England, individual Puritans occasionally adopted Jewish practices and went even further, some going to Holland for formal admission to the Jewish Community. Whatever attitude might be adopted towards proselytes who had been accepted into the Jewish community abroad, the official attitude towards any non-Jew who sought similar admission in England was consistently hostile, although from the legislation of the Mahamad on the subject it is clear that Jewish public opinion in England was not, so far as an appreciable section of it was concerned, in agreement. It was not until the middle of the nineteenth century that proselytes admitted by the Ashkenazi Community, which seems never to have had similar prejudices, were accepted by the Sephardi authorities. In Tammuz 1678 a new Ascama was adopted to deal with the subject. By that law those who harboured proselytes 'even for one night' were liable to penalties similar to those laid on those who clandestinely admitted them into the Community of Jewry. Proselytes made subsequent to the year 1660 were not to be permitted to pray in the synagogue, but the dead were more favourably treated. If they had always borne themselves as Jews they might be buried in the communal cemetery. These regulations applied to English proselytes only. Proselytes of other nationalities should be treated as the Mahamad might think fit. And then comes a passage touched with human charity. 'These ordinances are not from lack of the love which by Divine Law we owe to those of the Gentiles who have associated themselves with it, but it is wholly directed to our preservation and in order to fulfil what we are recommended by His Majesty, whom

THE ENLARGEMENT OF THE SYNAGOGUE

God guard, and peace upon Israel.' Three years later (in 1681) there was further legislation. It was laid down that anyone who took any part—even merely by his presence on the occasion—in the admission to Judaism of a proselyte should be fined £10 and excommunicated.

In Adar 1696 a new trouble developed. Under the constitution of the Community, as prescribed in the Ascamot, the Community secured to itself a monopoly in the supply of meat to its members, and from the tax of a farthing a pound it enjoyed a small but welcome revenue. Evasion of the tax necessarily reduced the cost of the meat, and there had grown up a 'black market'. To cope with this new trouble the Mahamad had recourse to the only sanctions in effect at its disposal for any purpose of punishment or prevention of offence—excommunication, as a rule in a modified form, and fine. It was accordingly ordained that anyone who should try to buy meat not killed by the communal shochet should be excluded from the Congregation, and anyone cognizant of the offence but not reporting it should be fined 20s.

The arrival of William and Mary in England in 1688 brought a new immigration of Jews in its wake. Wealthy Dutch Sephardim were said to have been among those who gave William financial support, and Francisco Lopez Suasso, later created Baron d'Avernas le Gras, two of whose sons later settled in England and held high office in the Community, has been mentioned in particular. The new-comers came for the most part from the Netherlands and included both *Ashkenazim* and *Sephardim*. Throughout the period from the Restoration there had been a flow of new-comers but not a considerable one. There was little opportunity for poorer Jews in England, and their arrival was, as has been seen, not encouraged by the City authorities or by those of the Community. Nevertheless new-comers came, and the growth of the number of Ashkenazim was so considerable that the time soon came for organizing an Ashkenazi sister community on a sound and permanent basis. In this work Benjamin Levy, the prominent member of the *Sahar Asamaim* of long standing but of Ashkenazi origin, took a leading part.[1] An increase in the number of Jews in London was not the only consequence, so far as Anglo-Jewry was concerned, of the arrival of William in England. The pacification of England was followed by the conquest of Ireland, and this led to a temporary revival of the Sephardi Community of Dublin which, first established

---

[1] See p. 42. The story of the foundation of the London Ashkenazi Community has been told by Mr. Cecil Roth in his *History of the Great Synagogue, London, 1690–1940* (London, 1950).

about 1660 and always small in size, had nevertheless survived. William had not only had the financial support of some of the Jews of the Netherlands preparatory to his crossing the North Sea. He had also the good wishes of a large part of the Community in Holland who prayed in their synagogues for his success and—those who were so gifted—wrote poems promising him success. Of greater practical value perhaps were the services of the firm of Machado and Pereira and their representative, Francisco de Cordova, to whom the provisioning of the expedition was entrusted. Similarly when Ireland was invaded, William turned to English Sephardim for their assistance. Isaac Pereira of the Dutch firm came over with the army, and in his new undertakings had the co-operation of Solomon de Medina—later to become even better known in a similar line of activity—and Affonso Rodriguez (Isaac Israel de Sequeira), a son of Abraham Israel de Sequeira or Gomez Rodrigues, the ex-Marrano, who had for long taken a prominent part in the direction of London Jewry. To look after their interests they sent to Ireland David Machado de Sequeira, a relative of Abraham Israel de Sequeira, and Jacob do Porto, a grandson of Abraham Israel de Sequeira and a son of the Abraham do Porto who had served as Gabay and as Parnas in London.[1] These two settled for a time in Dublin, and it was to them and to their fellow Sephardim who accompanied them that the resuscitation of the Dublin Jewish Community was due. David Penso, alias Alexander Felix, Jacob do Porto, and David Machado de Sequeira were three of the four Dublin Jews to whom the lease of the cemetery was assigned in 1718.

Haham Abendana died in 1685 on the first or second day of the Jewish New Year, and after an interval of four years a successor was appointed. The choice fell on Solomon Ayllon, then about twenty-nine years of age. Born in Salonica of a family of Spanish origin he had spent most of his life in Palestine, at Safad, the centre of religious mysticism. Sent on a mission to Europe to collect funds for the Jews of Palestine, he, in the course of that mission,

[1] Incidentally, Abraham do Porto had already left England with his wife and elder son in 1681 and settled in India. He died in Madras, of which city he was one of the earliest freemen, in 1690. Abraham's father had been burnt by the Inquisition in Lisbon in 1609, and he with his mother, brothers, and sisters figured in an *auto da fé*. He escaped to England in 1665. Members of the London Sephardi Community were prominent in the beginning of the development of the British possessions in India. Abraham Israel de Sequeira and his relative, Diego Rodrigues Marques, had been of considerable service to the East India Company, and it was through their intercession that Jews were first permitted to settle in Madras. De Sequeira's three sons all became freemen of the Company and the youngest, Jacob, was one of the principal founders of the municipality of Madras in 1688.

reached London, where he was persuaded to settle and accept the office of Haham. In selecting him, however, a considerable departure from precedent was made, one that proved itself a failure. Living in Safad, a centre of Cabbalism and steeped in Messianic beliefs, one of the last centres in which the Sabbathaian heresy lingered, Ayllon had been brought up and remained to some extent under the influence of that heresy. The London Community, on the other hand, was one of the few in Jewry that had retained their mental balance even at the height of the Sabbathaian madness, and its Haham at that time, Jacob Sasportas, had been and continued to be one of the most stalwart of the anti-Sabbathaian polemists. The atmosphere in London was very different from that in Safad, and Ayllon speedily discovered this fact. His situation in London was consequently by no measure a comfortable one. In addition to the suspicion of heresy under which he lay, he had the misfortune to find in London two of his most bitter enemies, Jacob and Abraham Fidanque, father and son, who throughout his residence in England pursued a vendetta against him. Abraham Fidanque made definite charges against him, but these when investigated by the Mahamad were found to be baseless, and Fidanque was ordered to be excluded from the synagogue until he had publicly asked pardon of the Haham and the Congregation. On this occasion the elder Fidanque, Jacob, was found guiltless, although the feud seems to have started with a quarrel between the two some years before Ayllon had settled in London. The decision of the Mahamad did not bring amity or even peace to the contestants. Despite the earlier absolution of Jacob Fidanque he became involved when the feud broke out again, and the charges were again examined not only by the Mahamad but by a larger committee which included a number of the other influential members of the Congregation. These decided unanimously that the Haham was innocent of the offences alleged and expressed their complete confidence in him. But even this conclusion did not bring the peace and quietude that was desired, and at length in 1700 Ayllon felt that he could no longer remain in London and resigned his office after an uneasy tenure of eleven years. The Mahamad did their utmost to dissuade him from this step, but he was resolute and returned to the Continent and was appointed Haham in Amsterdam, the Mahamad making him a grant of fifty guineas in appreciation of his services. Two years after his settlement in England the Mahamad had purchased his collection of books to form the basis of the congregational library of Hebraica. As to Jacob Fidanque, it was resolved that he should be excluded from office in the Community for all time and declared ineligible for certain synagogue honours and in particular prohibited from performing any functions in any way related to the office of Haham.[1] At the same time, and possibly in the same connexion, the shochet and bodek, Daniel Peres was dismissed. Ayllon settled in Amsterdam, but the worries caused by his unpopular views still continued, and the controversies in which he was involved led to estrangements between him and his colleagues in his new home. He lived, however, until 1728.

In the meanwhile the size of the Community still continued to grow and a new complexion was coming over it. Originally its members were without exception, or almost without exception, of foreign birth. The worshippers in Creechurch Lane formed a self-contained foreign community, as foreign and as clannish as were three centuries later the communities of Belgian and later of Central European Jewish refugees in England. Even more so, for many of the last named found a kinship among the English Jews, whereas those of the seventeenth century had no English coreligionists with whom to come into touch. This was the position in 1660. In the succeeding forty years a generation, two generations, of English-born Jews had grown up. The regular worshippers in Creechurch Lane still included a considerable foreign element—survivors of the original members and new-comers—but perhaps they were no longer even a majority. Many of those who sat at the feet of Haham Ayllon were natural-born English subjects—not dependent on an act of the King or Parliament for the enjoyment of the privileges of English subjects and English citizens but born with the right to them. An English Jew might and did differ from his non-Jewish neighbour in the extent of his rights, but as English subjects they were equal.

A census was taken of the inhabitants of London in 1695, and the Jewish names, or those that appear to be Jewish, have been extracted.[2] Of an apparent total of 716 men, women, and children, 519, judging by their names, were Sephardim; of these, 501 lived within the city limits and 18 without the walls. Most of the Jews of London lived in the parish of St. James, Dukes Place, the second, third, and fourth most popular parishes being St. Katherine Creechurch, All Hallows, London Wall, and St. Andrew Undershaft respectively. The Sephardim were by no means all men of means, and some were not even Yehidim or enrolled members of the Community. They were not on that account unwelcome in the

---

[1] Jacob Fidanque died in London in October 1701. For much of his time in London he conducted a private Talmud school. Abraham died seven years later.
[2] By Mr. Arthur P. Arnold.

Synagogue and in the records of voluntary gifts to the communal funds appear occasionally the names of men who were not formal members. There was by the date that has now been reached a small Ashkenazi synagogue in which presumably most of the Ashkenazim or *Tudescos* worshipped, but a few had for so long been incorporated in the Sephardi Community as to be accepted as Sephardim. Two Benjamin Levys, Mayer or Michael Levy, Samuel Heilbut, have already been mentioned. So has Greenhalgh's 'rabbi', Samuel Levy. As early as the year 1684 the list of offerings contained an appreciable number of Ashkenazi names, not only the familiar ones of Levy, Heilbut, and Adolphus, but others later prominent in the records of the Ashkenazi Community, such as Franks and Keyser and many others of whose careers no records have survived. Jacob Keyser obviously prospered in London, for in 1700 he was able to contribute five pounds to the fund raised for the erection of the new synagogue, whereas sixteen years earlier his offerings were of the neighbourhood of sixpence or a shilling. After 1702 the names of Benjamin and Michael Levy disappear from the congregational books, the former devoting himself to the new Ashkenazi community for the last two years of his life. At the same time there was a continual flow of new Sephardi congregants who generally appeared first as *foresteiros* or strangers, but later became incorporated as Yehidim or members. Among them in these early years was a third member of the Mocatta family, Isaac. The beneficiaries from the communal charity were also by no means all Sephardim, even after a formal Ashkenazi community had been constituted.

As has been mentioned, as early as May 1669 the Community found itself compelled to make formal application to the Lord Mayor, for protection against the swarm of foreign mendicants that was besetting the synagogue, and ten years later the Mahamad had formally to decree that honours and privileges were not to be accorded in the synagogue to *Tudescos*, except with the approval of ten elders. Michael or Mayer Levy, the younger Benjamin Levy and the samas, Samuel Levy, were, however, excluded from this disability. Samuel Heilbut would probably also have been exempted, if he had been a Yahid at the time. His membership of the Community was, however, subject to interruptions apparently due more to disputes than to inability to pay the imposta. This discriminatory legislation was repealed after three years, but a disability was imposed on Heilbut for a further year. In 1680 consideration had to be given to the subject of indigent Jews arriving in England without any prospect of self-support. Hitherto, as a rule, in these cases the cost of the journey to any destination the visitor might propose was defrayed. This practice necessarily led to much abuse, for it was found that London Jewry was paying a large part of the expenses of emigration of Continental Jews to other lands. In that year it was laid down that the cost of the journey back to their country of last departure only should be defrayed and the growing practice of paying for passages to France, Italy, the eastern Mediterranean, and North American and other colonies was brought to an end. But 'this is not to apply to those stricken by misfortune; for example, shipwreck: for them the Mahamad will use due consideration.' Not long afterwards the assistance granted to foreign Ashkenazim was limited by ordinance to five shillings a head, and then only on condition that they returned by the first available ship to the Continent. But all difficulties were not yet removed and in Elul the Mahamad had yet again to legislate on the subject. 'Having learnt that some Yehidim go about on the Exchange and outside collecting alms for mendicants' the Mahamad decided to impose a fine of 25s. on members of the Community so engaged. 'No one may collect for a Yahid of this Kaal nor try to help foreigners from abroad without authority of Mahamad.' The practice had become a public scandal. However, the evil still persisted, and thirty-four years later, in Tishri 5475 (1714), the Mahamad had to resolve,

> 'Various Yehidim having remonstrated with the Mahamad against the scandal caused to the Nation among whom we live by the help given to the Poor who beg alms at the Bourse and Exchange and such help being moreover directly contrary to an Act of Parliament and consequently a source of disgust to the Yehidim, they resolved to remedy the matter so far as lies in their power by requesting all the Yehidim to desist from giving alms to any poor person whatsoever, neither at the Bourse nor at the Exchange.'

Nevertheless, as late as 1753 there is reference in the Minutes of the Mahamad to the scandal caused by the begging by poor Jews at the Exchange and in Change Alley.

There is a contemporary account also of the service in the synagogue at the end of the seventeenth century.

> 'On Saturday (or Sabbath) January 25, 1690, I went to Creek Church-Alley (about midway between the royal exchange and Al-gate, where was the Jewish synagogue, divided in 3 parts as were the tabernacle and temple; The court for the people, the

THE ENLARGEMENT OF THE SYNAGOGUE 73

sanctum for the priests, and the *sanctum sanctorum* where was the ark and the law in it folded up in a very long parchment inclosed into several broidered mantles and a silver ornament of three tier height, all hung about with small bells on the top of the staves about which the law was written, and the like, but of less value on the top of the staves on which the prophetic books and hagiographa were written and incased about. The Jews have bad English, some Latin, but all of them Hebrew, and do not read it as their Rabbi goes before them. These broad parchments of the law are solemnly taken forth, with psalms, all the house using a motion as if betwixt reading and singing, no way harmonious. The Rabbi or scribe has a pulpit inrailed, or rather a table before him having many seats behind it within the rails for those two who hold the books by turns. The scribe in a black garb, a cloak laid aside, putting a veil of white taffeta about his hat, ranging all about him (as have all the multitude, being about 150 men, about the room, 60 boys in the middle, and 7 or 8 women in the galleries above, hardly perceived by any). Only the women had no veils. When the Rabbi (who looked not like a grave learned man; for he and many Jews would have laughed and talked when they ended a paragraph) read, all did read audibly enough in Hebrew, all said Amen. They never prayed, nor discovered their heads, nor bowed the knee. The Rabbi called 6 or 7 to come to him after another and taught them, pointing with a silver pen. They had no methodical worship. They were all very black men, and indistinct in their reasoning[1] as gipsies.[2]

This is an account by an uninformed visitor. The 'silver ornament of three tier height' is presumably the *rimmonim*. Scrolls of the Prophetic books and hagiograph are, to say the least, very unusual.

---

[1] Presumably pronunciation which was inevitably for the most part foreign.
[2] The Commonplace Book of the Rev. Robert Kirk of Aberfoyle, quoted by Donald Maclean and Norman G. Brett-James in *London in 1689-90*. *Trans. of the London and Middlesex Arch. Soc.*, New Series, vol. VII, pt. i, p. 151.

CHAPTER VI

A NEW HAHAM AND A NEW SYNAGOGUE

DESPITE THE FORMATION of a stable Ashkenazi Community and the consequent withdrawal of Ashkenazi worshippers from the Sephardi synagogue the pressure on the available accommodation still continued and even increased. This accommodation had already previously been doubled and no further increase in the existing building was possible. The only alternatives were the acquisition of a larger building elsewhere or the erection of a new one. And with every member of the Community living within a mile of Creechurch Lane a site for a new synagogue must necessarily not be far distant from the existing building. At first the possibility, despite the difficulties, of enlarging the existing building were considered, and as early as 1694 there is a hint of preliminary negotiations with the ground landlords, the churchwardens of St. Katherine Creechurch, on the subject, but it was soon realized that such a project was impracticable, and the bolder plan was decided on. In the same year already a joiner named Henry Ramsay was commissioned to prepare a model for a new building, and within a year the raising of funds to defray the relatively large expenditure that was in front of the Community was taken in hand. It is interesting to note a couple of Ashkenazi names in the list of contributors: Benjamin Levy, who gave the largest contribution in the first list, inevitably—he was still one of the leading members of the Community—and Jacob Keyser. Both contributed generously to most if not all the several collections made for the same purpose. These preparations continued over half a decade, until, on 12 February 1699, Antonio Gomes Serra,[1] Menasseh Mendes, Affonso Rodriguez,[1] Manoel Nunes Miranda, Andreas Lopes, and Pantaleão Rodriguez, on behalf of the Sephardi Community, made a contract with a builder, Joseph Avis, for the erection of a new synagogue in the neighbouring Bevis Marks at a cost of £2,650, this sum to be paid by instalments. Nine months later a document was signed by the same six representatives of the Community by which Lady Anne Pointz, otherwise Littleton, and Sir Thomas Pointz granted a lease of Plough

[1] Gomes Serra had long been prominent in the councils of the Community and had filled most of its offices. He signed the agreement for the enlargement of the synagogue in 1674. Affonso Rodriguez was one of the wealthiest of the Jewish residents in London.

Yard and some houses in Bevis Marks for the erection of a synagogue building. The site as well as that of the earlier synagogue in Creechurch Lane was on the land of the medieval Priory of Holy Trinity or Christ Church, Aldgate. In 1557 the property passed by marriage to the Duke of Norfolk, from whom are derived the names Duke Street and Duke's Place. Heneage Lane later ran along the outside wall of the neighbouring garden of Sir Thomas Heneage, successively Keeper of the Tower Records, Paymaster of the Forces, Vice-Chamberlain, Chancellor of Lancaster, and Vice-Chamberlain to Queen Elizabeth, who was a member of the Commission that tried Dr. Rodrigo Lopez in 1594. The earliest mention of Bevis Marks in the form Bewesmerkes to be traced was in 1407. In 1450 it was Bevys Marke. Later it appears as Buries Markes, Bevers Market, and Beavis Markes. Apparently the name was derived from the Abbey of Bury St. Edmunds in whose possession the land was from before 1156. On the dissolution of the Abbey by Henry VIII the land and the buildings on it were given to Thomas Heneage, the father of Sir Thomas Heneage. The lease was to run for sixty-one years from 24 June 1699 and thereafter for a further thirty-eight years if the lessees so desired. The rent was to be at the rate of £120 per annum. The lease was later transformed into a freehold. Special donations were given by members of the Community to defray the cost. The foundation stone was laid on the 6th of Elul 5460 (1700), which was a day of festivity in the Congregation when every member gave within his means and the poor who were unable to contribute received instead gifts from the congregational funds. Henceforth the work on the new synagogue continued without interruption. An extension of time had, however, to be given to the contractor, for when the contract was drawn up he had not realized that no work was to be carried out on sabbath or the Jewish festivals. The building was opened for worship on Sabbath eve, the 27th of Elul 5461 (1701). The event is recorded in the minutes of the Mahamad. 'On the 27th of Ellul 5461, Friday, on the Eve of Sabbath, was the opening ceremony of the new synagogue—may God grant that it shall be for this Holy Congregation to enjoy it many years with peace, unity and increase—the wardens and treasurer being the Senhores Isaac Israel Correa, President, Isaac Lopes Pereira, Abraham Vaes Martinez and Isaac Israel Henriques, Wardens, and Moses Francia, Treasurer.' This is the building which is still today the centre of the Sephardi community of England. In form and in appearance it has remained practically unchanged. The system of lighting is still as in its earliest days composed of innumerable candles placed in magnificent hanging candelabra, one of which, a gift of the Amsterdam Sephardi Community, was brought from Holland for the original installation. It was not until 1929 that, for the sake of convenience, this somewhat elementary system of lighting was to a small extent supplemented around the sides of the building by electricity, arranged to resemble candles. But on the Day of Atonement and other great occasions, when the interior is illuminated solely by candles, some idea can be realized of the effect the new building must have had on its first worshippers and visitors two and a half centuries ago. Some of the wooden benches also were brought from the earlier synagogue. It used to be believed that the builders utilized in the construction an oak beam presented by the Princess Anne who was to succeed to the throne as queen in the following year. But this is probably a legend, an echo perhaps of her visit to the earlier synagogue some years before. A description, published half a century later, is near enough to depict the Synagogue as it was when opened. After a reference to the 'Great House', formerly the property of the abbots of Bury in Suffolk, it continues

> 'This House and Ground is now increased into many Tenements, and amongst the rest, the *Portuguese Jews* have built themselves a large Synagogue here, wainscotted round. It stands East and West, like one of our Churches. The Great Door is on the West; near to which West End is a long Desk upon an Ascent, somewhat raised from the rest of the Floor, where the Law is read. The East Wall is in Part railed in, and before the Wall is a Door, which is to open with a Key, where their Law seems to be laid up. Aloft on this Wall are the *Ten Commandments*, or some Part of them, inscribed in golden *Hebrew* Letters without Points. There are seven great branched candlesticks on Brass hanging down from the Top, and many other Places for Candles and Lamps. The Seats are Benches, with Backs to them, that run along from West to East; and the Galleries above, for the Women to sit in, have Lattices before them.'[1]

Apart from the lighting, and the provision of additional seats, few other minor alterations have been made in the course of time. As has been said, an agreement had been made, before the work commenced, with Joseph Avis, the builder. The amount agreed upon, it later transpired, exceeded the cost to which Avis was put.

[1] *The History of London from its Foundation to the Present Time*, by William Maitland, F.R.S., and others (London, 1756), p. 782.

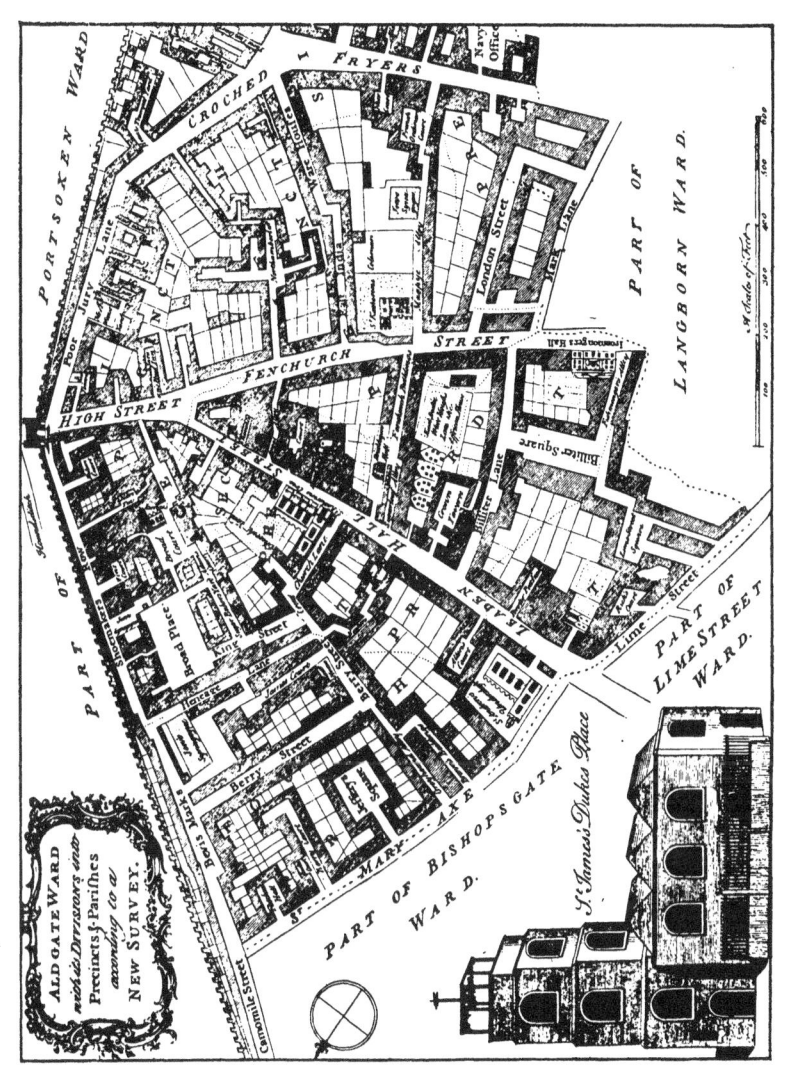

PLAN OF SYNAGOGUE DISTRICT, 1756
From Maitland's *The History of London*

Avis was a Quaker, and it would have gone against his conscience to have made a profit from a building to be devoted to the worship of God. So he refused to accept the whole sum agreed upon. There is another incident worthy of mention in connexion with the erection of the new building. During the two years in which the work was being carried on the pressure on the accommodation continued unabated and for the last year it was found necessary to exclude the women from the synagogue, their galleries being placed entirely at the disposal of male worshippers. Incidentally, the resolution of the Elders that laid this down also ordered that no worshipper should stand up during a service, except on the appointed occasions 'unless he do so from devotion on Kipur near his seat'. The new building provided accommodation for about 400 men and 160 women.

The Congregation still owned the lease of the building in Creechurch Lane. It should have expired at midsummer 1698. A fresh lease for seven years was, however, granted and this was later extended until midsummer 1723. During the extended period the building was utilized in part for congregational purposes, such as the school, and in part as residences for the Haham and other officials.

The erection of a new synagogue building was, however, not the only outstanding event in the history of the Sephardim in England at the opening of the eighteenth century. Contemporary with it, although not dependent on it, were changes among the officials of the Community of which one was of outstanding importance. There being a vacancy for a Hazan, David Pardo having died while the new synagogue was being built, it was decided to choose a qualified person to fill it. And here a precedent was created. There were two candidates. The one was Joseph Abendanon, the quarrelsome *rubi* or teacher who has already been mentioned and who intended to associate his son with him in the office if he were elected. The other was Isaac de Chaves. The election was clearly considered a matter of much importance, for the Yehidim were not only urged to record their votes but threatened with fines of 20s. if they did not do so. As a result de Chaves was elected by an overwhelming majority, 116 against 7 for Abendanon and 3 blank votes. De Chaves was in consequence appointed Hazan, and also Rubi in the school, at a salary of £40 per annum. David Pardo, who had been appointed Hazan in 1681, was the son of a predecessor in the same office, Joseph Pardo, who died in 1677. The two Pardos were the most scholarly occupants of the office until the time of David de Sola. Joseph Pardo compiled an edition of

A NEW HAHAM AND A NEW SYNAGOGUE

the *Shulhan Tahor*, a compendium of the rites and ceremonies required to be performed by observant Jews. Written in Hebrew, it was without delay translated by his son David into Spanish with which language his prospective readers had a better acquaintance than with Hebrew. The younger Pardo was a fine *sofer* or scribe and a remarkably accurate reader of the prayers, and throughout the twenty years of his tenure of office there is no record of his having been fined for errors for which members of the congregation were always on the watch. This cannot be said of his successor, who was fined five shillings on four occasions in his first year of office.

In the meanwhile Samuel Levy, the Samas, was growing old and was no longer capable of performing his duties. It was consequently decided to retire him, and his assistant, Isaac Purim, also a *Tudesco*, was appointed in his place at a salary of £12 per annum for which he was expected to perform all the duties of the office. As Assistant Samas he had received an annual salary of £8. Purim died in 1704, but in 1699 the Congregation appointed a second Samas, Abraham Nunez de Almeida, who had offered to fill the office without salary for the lifetime of Levy, provided that he received half the sum of the offerings made for the benefit of the samas, and whose offer was accepted. During the preceding years there had also been changes in the office of Rubi or teacher. At the end of the century there were two holders of this office—Joseph Abendanon, who had been appointed in 1692, and Abraham Judah Leon, six years earlier, in succession to Isaac Israel d'Avila, who, however, did not die until 1691. Abendanon was dismissed in 1705 and his place was taken by Daniel Peres. Two years later Judah Leon died. He had two joint successors, Abraham Lopes Henriques and Samuel Abenatar Mello, both appointed in 1707. Peres filled the office for eleven years until 1716, when so far as is known no successor was appointed. In 1724 Mello died, and in the following year Joshua de Mattos was appointed rubi. Abraham Lopes Henriques held the office until 1726. These men were all qualified rabbis and as such acted as a rule also as *dayanim* or members of the *Beth Din* or rabbinical court of law.

The outstanding new appointment was, however, that of Haham in place of Ayllon, who had resigned a few months before. This election was unanimous, the choice falling on David Nietto or Nieto of Leghorn. His salary was £100 a year, twice that of his predecessor, with a house and a further £10 every Purim. One condition of the appointment was that the new Haham should not practise medicine but should concentrate on the functions of his office. The new Haham had been born in Venice on 18 January 1654, but had been resident for some years in Leghorn, where, according to his own account, he was 'Dayan, and Preacher of the Congregation and Physician'. He apparently also practised medicine privately. According to Daniel Lysons in 1735, who gives Daniel de Castro, the secretary of the London Sephardi Community, as his authority,[1] Nieto had studied and graduated in 'physic' in the University of Padua. For a list of his activities one may quote his epitaph, composed of course years after his arrival in England, some of which activities may have been dormant until after his settlement in this country. As is usual with epitaphs[2] this may have suffered a touch of exaggeration, but it nevertheless helps to describe the man. 'Sublime Theologian, profound Sage, distinguished physician, famous Astronomer, sweet poet, elegant preacher, subtle logician, ingenious physicist, fluent Rhetorician, pleasant Author, expert in Languages, learned in History.' He is said to have been proficient in Hebrew and its related languages, in Spanish, Portuguese, Italian, Latin, French, Greek, and English. He was an astronomer and an expert on the calendar of some distinction. The calendar covering a period of eighty-three years, with many astronomical details, which he issued in 1717, was accepted by his Community as their guide for the dates and times of the Sabbath and Jewish festivals during that period. He produced also a number of annual calendars in more detail. He wrote also Hebrew poems, theological works, and works on the Inquisition. One work of his at least was written before his settlement in London, although not published until later. This was a book in Italian entitled *Pascalogia Overo Discorso della Pasca*, on the relationship in the calendar between the varying dates of the two Easters and Passover, occasioned by the unusual falling of the Latin Easter in the year 1693, a month less a day earlier than that of Passover. As a rule when Passover and Easter do not coincide, the former is celebrated earlier. The dedication of the book to Cardinal Francisco Maria de Medici illustrates Nieto's standing in Italy. Nieto brought the manuscript of this work with him to London, where he published it in 1702. The place of publication appears, however, on the title page not as London but Cologne,

[1] *Environs of London* (1735), vol. III, p. 478.
[2] There is a longstanding tradition in the Community that epitaphs should be strictly factual and that all elaborations should be avoided. The principle that governs this rule and also that of a degree of uniformity in tombstones, which in Sephardi cemeteries are invariably laid flat on the graves, not erected, is that in death all are equal. There have occasionally been difficulties in the application of this principle, mourning widows demanding the right to record the virtues of their lost husbands more generously than the Mahamad would permit.

THE JERUSALEM INFIRMARY
(A satire on the Beth Holim, 1749)
From an engraving

DR. JACOB DE CASTRO SARMENTO, F.R.S.
From an engraving by Andrew Miller, after H. Stevens

A NEW HAHAM AND A NEW SYNAGOGUE 81

the explanation being that, emanating from a heretic centre, as London was considered, it might be regarded with prejudice in Roman Catholic circles.[1] Nieto arrived in London in September 1701, and two months later he issued his first publication in England, 'A fervid and humble prayer addressed to the Great and Omnipotent God of Israel by the Congregation of Jews in London, in which they implore the assistance and help of Heaven at the Deliberations of His Majesty the Invincible King William III, their sovereign, of his Supreme Council, and of both the Chambers of his August Parliament.' This was the first of a long series of sermons and learned studies that issued from his pen and were published during the subsequent twenty-six years of his life. Above all, David Nieto stands out as a resolute opponent of the Sabbathaian heresy. At the beginning of the eighteenth century there was a recrudescence of this heresy of which Nehemiah Hayyun, one of Sabbathai Zevi's earlier followers, was the principal protagonist. The leading opponent in London was the new Haham who was tireless in the production of polemical writings devoted to the suppression of Sabbathaiism. Nieto's predecessor, Ayllon, was suspected, apparently not altogether without reason, of sympathy with the heretics. Although he had left the country some of his influence still remained. Thus when Nieto arrived in England, and for some years afterwards, there was a Sabbathaian undercurrent to be recognized and fought. It is by no means improbable that the difficulties with which Nieto had to contend and the opposition and hostility he encountered during his first years in England were to some extent to be attributed to the underground activities of these disciples of the Sabbathaians.

Previous to these events a slight reorganization of the administration had been effected. Originally the offices of Gabay or Treasurer of the three institutions, the *Terra Santa*, or interests of the Jews of the Holy Land, the *Cautivos*, or the ransoming of prisoners, and the *Talmud Torah*, or school, had been combined. In 1689 that of the Cautivos had been detached and in 1699 those of the Terra Santa and the Talmud Torah were formally separated. The Cautivos was by no means a sinecure, as the records show, for with the Mediterranean infested with Barbary pirates and their Christian competitors, the Knights of Malta, it was seldom that the need did not arise for the ransom of Jewish travellers or wanderers who had fallen into their hands and would be, unless released, destined to life-long slavery. This service was undertaken

[1] For a detailed biography of Nieto, see I. Solomons in the *Trans. Jew. Hist. Soc. of Eng.*, vol. XII.

by all the principal Sephardi communities equally, and London was not behind the other centres in this mission of humanity. Not all the victims were Sephardim, but this did not count with those who readily came to their aid. Incidentally, this work of charity kept the London Sephardim in continuous touch with their brethren in Venice, Leghorn, Amsterdam, Marseilles, and elsewhere.

With a new Haham who, by his reputation and acquirements, stood out above the heads of all his predecessors, and with a new synagogue which also at once took its place among the outstanding Jewish communal buildings of Europe, a new era opened for the Sephardim of England. But not all of the old worries and annoyances by which the successive guides of the fortunes of the Community in England were beset disappeared with the more obvious changes. The one continuous trouble was the poor which have throughout the history of the Community, in varying degrees, been a cause of anxiety. Thus there is an entry in the minutes under the date 20 Tishri 5456 (1695) to the effect that in view of the many foreign vagrants who come to London expressly to beg, 'to the prejudice of our own poor, it is ordained and to be announced from Teba that not more than 5s. is to be given to any of these "dishonest strangers"'. It was not only Ashkenazim who were discouraged. Later when an immigration of poor Sephardim set in, new legislation was enacted. This, in 1710, was directed specifically against 'Berberiskos' and 'Italianos'. The maximum relief to be given to them was laid down at ten shillings and food for three days, and then only on condition that they left the country at once. This affected the new-comers from abroad, but in 1703 legislation was found necessary to deal with a new class of the local poor of whom nothing had previously been heard. On the 15th of Kislev 5464 (1703) it was resolved that henceforth no relief or help from the Sedaca should be given to persons arrested for debt or to their dependants. Furthermore, any official of the Congregation who might be arrested for debt was at once to be suspended from his office, and any person in receipt of sedaca should forthwith forfeit his allowance. The Mahamad did not encourage indebtedness on the part of anyone within their control.

The care of the sick had always been one of the more urgent functions of the Community and, as has been mentioned, early in its history the communal physician appeared in the list of its functionaries. The *Hebra de Bikur Holim e Guemilut Hasadim* (society for the assistance of the sick and for good deeds, i.e. the performance of the last offices for the dead), instituted in 1665, suffered several vicissitudes before its activities ceased.[1] A revived interest was displayed in 1709 when the *Hebra de Bikur Holim* was established. This followed on a resolution by the Mahamad two years earlier, reaffirming that of 1693 to the effect that recipients of sedaca (poor relief) must be prepared, if called on, to tend the sick of the Community. Other functions of the earlier society of 1665 were revived in 1724 by the *Honen Dalim, Menahem Abelim, Hebrat Yetomot e Hebrat Moalim* (the succouring the poor, comforting the mourners, the society for female orphans and the society of circumcisers), whose duties were to assist poor women in confinement, to give allowances to mourners while away from work, and marriage portions to fatherless girls.[2] This institution is still active. Finally the provision of medical attendance was reorganized (in 1747) in the *Beth Holim*, originally a communal hospital for both the sick and confined women, to which was attached a home for the aged, now limited to the last-mentioned purpose, except for the occasional provision of accommodation for a woman in confinement.

Troubles, however, arose and quickly surrounded this institution. The foundation of the hospital was decided on at a meeting held on 18 October 1747, at which three medical members of the Community, Dr. Jacob de Castro Sarmento, Dr. Philip de la Cour (otherwise Abraham Gomes Ergas), and Dr. Joseph Vaz da Silva, of the first two of whom more will be learnt later, offered their services free. Later Jacob de Castro, a surgeon, joined these three in their offer. Apparently from the beginning there was some opposition, for obscure reasons, to the institution, and anonymous threatening letters induced the Governors to hire a guard for its protection. Regulations for the administration of the institution were drawn up by de Castro Sarmento and de la Cour, and the hospital was opened in Leman Street, Goodmans Fields, in the summer of 1748. Dr. Vaz da Silva, however, ignored these regulations, and as a consequence 'great disorder in the hospital' was caused. The clerk, Moses Pereyra de Castro, also proved unsatisfactory, and before the close of the year 1748 he was dismissed. Then came trouble with the Apothecary, Mordecai de la Penha, who was accused of immorality. A meeting of the Governors was devoted to the matter, but in the end the motion that he be dismissed was defeated by eight votes to three. The whole matter

[1] See p. 59.
[2] The constitutions of the *Honen Dalim* and the *Mehil Sedaca*, both established mainly for the provision of dowries, were approved by the Mahamad in 1735 and 1736 respectively.

is recorded in a scurrilous anonymous print[1] depicting a meeting of the Governors in which all the aforementioned and several other well-known contemporary members of the Community appear. These dissensions led soon to the resignation of de Castro Sarmento and de la Cour. However, the hospital recovered from these tribulations, and there is an account of it and its activities in William Maitland's *The History of London from its Foundation to the Present Time*, published in 1772.[2]

These disputes and scandals in the medical sphere did not, however, begin with the establishment of the *Beth Holim*. In the period of its predecessor there were others, similar although less public. Two entries in the minutes of the Mahamad throw light on these. Under the date, 24 Iyar 5484 (1724), the minutes record that

'The Mahamad and their adjuntos (co-opted elders) considered a complaint formulated by Sampson Gideon against Doctor David de Chaves, and having called and examined witnesses from both sides, and having given due and just consideration to the matter, they resolved that Dr. David de Chaves is to blame; and in order to show to the world that the Mahamad and their allied bodies are the Fathers of the Nation and are careful to respect the families thereof and detest tell-tale talk against their honour, they resolved unanimously that Dr. David de Chaves be dismissed from his office of Doctor of the Hebra for one year, and that the Sedaca shall not assist him in any form during the said term; and may Almighty God bring peace upon us.'

Eight years later the doctors of the Hebra appeared again in the minutes. They had been displaying undue extravagance in their prescriptions and were duly reprimanded and warned.

'On the 11 Tebet 5492 (1723) the Mahamad issued instructions to the Doctors of the Hebra not to order chicken for the sick except in cases of serious illness or childbirth, and they confirmed their previous orders warning them that they would be deprived of their office on the first complaint made against them, and they are not to prescribe sugar with chicken, nor mutton, except it be found necessary.'

The society, *Mahasim Tobim* (good deeds), founded in 1749, devoted itself to the constructive work of granting loans to Sephardim

[1] This print has been reproduced by Mr. Alfred Rubens in his *Anglo-Jewish Portraits*, where it is explained point by point and a brief account of the incident as a whole is given.
[2] Vol. II, book vi, p. 1325.

in need of them, to the apprenticing of boys and girls and also the training of *shochetim*. Ten years earlier a wider attempt had been made to deal with the problem of the local poor on more statesmanlike lines than the mere doling out of relief. A subscription was opened for the raising of a special fund for the establishment of a society for the employment of those who were capable of useful work. The aim was to raise a minimum sum of £150, and if that minimum were not reached it was agreed that the project could not go forward. Only about £50 was obtained, and the scheme had to be abandoned. During these years more than one charity was endowed, as a rule under wills, for the assistance of the poor of the community. Widows in particular were the object of those testamentary benefactions. Isaac da Costa Villa Real, who died in 1730, made provision in his will, not only for the education of poor girls,[1] but also for their clothing. Under a deed of gift executed by Haim and Rachel Esteves in 1740 an annual income was provided for the relief of poor widows, and in the following year Hannah de Avila bequeathed a sum of money for a similar purpose. In 1756 Moses Lamego, a very wealthy member of the community who died three years later, made a deed of gift in memory of his son of £5,000, four-fifths of which was to benefit the orphan society and the remainder the Gates of Hope School. If the attempt to form an employment and presumably also training organization for the poor and unemployed had failed, another attempt to put relief on a more satisfactory basis was more successful. This related to the friendless orphans of the Community. In 1703 the Brotherhood of the *Saare Orah Veabi Yetomim* (the Gates of Light and Father of the Orphans), the Sephardi Orphanage, originally for fatherless boys, later extended to benefit motherless boys also, was established. The occasion was taken for celebrations. The Haham, David Nieto, preached an inaugural

[1] The regulations adopted in 1739 laid down the following 'Conditions to be observed by Miss Sarah Luzeno regarding the instruction and establishment of the School, as follows: There shall be a teacher who can read write and count in Portuguese and English to instruct the twenty girls, also teach them to read and pray in Hebrew; the teacher must attend at the said school daily as follows, from the going out of Passover till Tabernacles from 7 o'clock in the morning till 8 to teach Hebrew reading, from 8 till 9 to read write and count in English, from 9 till 10 to read and write Portuguese or Spanish, and from 10 till 12 sewing, flower-designing, embroidery and anything further the said teacher can teach them, from then from 2 till 4 they shall sew, from 4 till 5 they will learn Hebrew. From the going out of Tabernacles till Passover the teacher shall attend at the school in the same way as indicated above starting at 8 till 4 in the afternoon; the inclusive salary for the said teacher shall be 30 pounds per annum payable quarterly commencing 2 March 1732/3, given under my hand in London 15 Iyar 5493. Furthermore, the Mahamad promised 24 sacks of coal per annum.'

sermon on the second day of Passover and on a Sabbath later in the month one of the beneficiaries of the newly established institution gave an address, being followed by two sons of the Haham, Moses and Isaac, the latter later to succeed his father as Haham, both still boys, who gave discourses. Other formal institutions for the relief of poverty and distress followed at intervals. A relief project of a completely different character was launched in the year 1709. One of the periodical appeals for assistance from foreign Jewries had reached London. Not Sephardim but Ashkenazim were affected on this occasion. It was the Jews of Poland who were suffering and who appealed for help. The response of the London Sephardim was immediate. A collection of money was organized and the response provided £276 9s. a by no means inconsiderable amount in those days.

Another perennial trouble was that which may be termed widely the behaviour of members of the Community within and without the synagogue. This topic has received notice more than once in the foregoing narrative. The Community was still largely self-governing, on lines followed almost without exception at that period by Jewish communities everywhere. The members preferred to settle differences among themselves and to refrain, except as a last resort, from calling in the non-Jewish authorities. This procedure was accepted in the early eighteenth century by every Jew, with hardly an exception, and it was also recognized that if the outside authorities were not to have jurisdiction, some of the powers necessary to a government must be given to a Jewish one. Thus the Mahamad enjoyed powers that must appear strange to the Yahid of today. In the administration of the synagogue and its institutions this is not surprising, but when it extended also to outside affairs, domestic as well as commercial, not to mention relations with the national and local authorities, in the modern mind there must be some difficulty in realizing the position of the Jew in the general community.

There has been mention in the foregoing pages of the steps taken to preserve law and order in the synagogue and to direct the members to follow approved lines in external matters. These lines were generally followed for the greater part of the eighteenth century. Legislation had even to be adopted to this end, for in the Ascamot of 1685 it is laid down that

> 'should any person rise in Synagogue to oppose or reprobate any of the orders of the Mahamad, or of him who may be presiding, or contradict or offend the said President in the said

Synagogue or in its court, or form parties in any place to oppose the orders of the Elders of the nation, or of the Mahamad, or distribute papers murmuring at or reprobating any of their orders, he shall pay such a fine as the Mahamad shall deem proper according to the nature of the offence, not being, however, less than £10 nor more than £20.'

There was evidently reason for such legislation. Joseph Abendanon, the rubi who had already attracted undue attention, appeared again in the record for the year 1700, but on this occasion he was the victim and not the aggressor. On the 28th of Nisan of that year it was recorded that one Moses del Cano had attacked and 'injuriously maltreated' him in the synagogue building. The offender was ordered to pay a fine of five pounds and to ask pardon for his offence publicly in the synagogue. Del Cano ignored the sentence, and he was therefore forbidden admission to the synagogue until he complied with the decision of the Mahamad. Nothing further is heard of him, and it cannot be said whether or not he ultimately submitted. Two years later there was another undesirable scene in the precincts of the synagogue. The two samasim, Abraham Nunes de Almeida and Isaac Purim, actually came to blows in the courtyard. The Mahamad ordered that they should both be excluded from the synagogue until the following Friday when they should be required between the afternoon and evening services to ascend the Tebah (reading desk) and ask pardon of God and the congregation for their offence and to suffer deductions of twenty shillings each from their salaries. In that year also Joseph Abendanon again got into trouble. It had been laid down that so far as the London Community was concerned the Haham alone was entitled to give decisions on Jewish law, and that no one else was permitted to do so. This regulation was doubtless galling to qualified rabbis, such as Abendanon, who on one occasion at least ignored the regulation. On the 3rd of Elul he was formally charged with having transgressed Ascama No. 33 by having given such a decision. The Mahamad constituted itself a judicial court. Witnesses were called and heard. Abendanon was found guilty and fined two pounds and warned that if he repeated the offence he would be dismissed from all his offices. He had, it will be remembered, been removed from office some years before, but the punishment of removal from office seems to have been more often temporary than permanent.

In 1703 another personal communal dispute came to a head. Jacob Mendes de Brito and Abraham Lopes de Brito, kinsmen, if not descendants, of the Abraham Israel, otherwise Domingo Vaes de Brito, one of the founders of the London Community who had given evidence on behalf of Antonio Robles in 1656, taking offence for one reason or another, probably at some decision or action by the Mahamad or other officer of the Congregation, had not been seen in the synagogue for more than two years. According to Ascama No. 25 the Mahamad was entitled to dispose of the seat of any Yahid who absented himself from the synagogue for a longer period than a year. After having waited twice the minimum period the Mahamad decided to act on this Ascama. So far as the two gentlemen immediately concerned there was no response, but a reaction showed itself very soon. A daughter of Abraham Lopes de Brito married, but the bridegroom, Isaac Rodrigues Nunes, could not induce his father-in-law to agree to the drawing up of a *ketuba* or marriage agreement by the Haham, as laid down in the regulations. He was, however, very uneasy about the proceeding, and informed the Mahamad and Elders of what had happened, agreeing to submit to their decision. This decision, so far as one knows the circumstances, was unduly oppressive. The bridegroom seems to have done all that could have been expected of him in the circumstances. Nevertheless a very heavy fine of £20 was imposed on him.

The following two offences among others on which the Mahamad adjudicated were of a different character. On the 12th of Ab 1734 Moses de Morais Pereira cited before the Mahamad Dr. de Castro Sarmento, the most distinguished English Jew of his day, whose name will appear in this narrative again later, for having had his daughter, the widow of Jacob da Còsta Villa Real, arrested by the civil authorities, without obtaining the permission of the Mahamad, and he was fined five shillings. Presumably Dr. de Castro Sarmento met with difficulty in obtaining payment of the fees due to him for his professional services and, losing patience, had had recourse to the civil law. Five years later, in 1739, Abraham Torres, the bloodletter,[1] complained that Abraham Duque, a tailor, had summoned him and had him arrested by the law of the land without leave of the Mahamad or coming to them in spite of three messages, and when charged with breaking Ascama No. 16 he had answered that he was not bound to obey it for he was not a Yahid and that the Mahamad helped and protected perjurers: for which the Mahamad declared him incapable of ever becoming a Yahid or making offerings or have a place in the Synagogue or be buried

---

[1] A barber who combined with his functions that of cupper or bloodletter.

in *Beth Haim*. This was also presumably a business dispute. However, this ostracism did not remain permanent, for it is further recorded that on the 13th of Elul following when the most solemn season of the year was approaching Duque made his submission and begged pardon of the Mahamad, who granted it, but only from the approaching Day of Atonement. These transgressions against law and order in the Community were almost incessant. In Tamuz 1752 the records relate that Nathan Henriques had transgressed Ascama No. 15 by shouting at Raphael Orbino in the Synagogue and that the Mahamad had condemned him to pay a fine of five pounds and publicly to ask pardon from the Tebah of the Synagogue for his offence. Exactly a year later, on the Sabbath, Jacob Moreira approached Jacob Buzaglo in the Synagogue, and in the course of a dispute cursed him and expressed the hope that Buzaglo and his family would starve. Buzaglo, his temper aroused, struck Moreira. For this outburst he was fined ten pounds and also ordered publicly to ask for pardon of the Congregation from the Tebah. Furthermore, he had to ask pardon of Moreira or in default pay him two guineas (? damages). The latter gentleman, who thus started the quarrel with his curses, seems to have not only escaped scot free, but to have made a profit out of the proceedings.

These were internal matters. Unfortunately the behaviour of members of the Congregation—in essence quite innocent—sometimes attracted undesirable attention from outside. On Rosh Hodesh Hesvan of 1701 the following announcement was made from the Tebah: 'The Magistrates of the City having complained to the Mahamad of the great scandal caused by our people gathering in the streets on Sunday, the Mahamad begs all our Yehidim not to gather on Sundays in the district of the old synagogue or in Bury Street. If they do they will be treated as disturbers of the peace.' A few months later there was another announcement from the Tebah at the conclusion of the sabbath, also a consequence, even though a less direct one, of a direction by the civil authorities. 'In view of the Queen's proclamation urging abstention from all play on Sunday, the Mahamad order that no Yahid meet in a public or private house to play on Sundays, under penalty.' A regulation of the same year, with which the civil authorities had no concern, related to the disorder that was arising in the synagogue on the occasion of wedding celebrations. To deal with the matter the Mahamad and Elders resolved that in view of 'the great scandal and annoyance caused by the company brought by brides to Esnoga (the synagogue) it was decided that from Roshodes Adar next no bride, whether of a wedding or of Hatan Torah or Hatan Beresit may bring more company than two godmothers, the mother and brothers'. Finally, in 1749, the Mahamad had to deal with the annoyance and also damage caused not only by the boys of its own congregation but also by those of the neighbouring Ashkenazi synagogue, by resorting to the courtyard of the Bevis Marks Synagogue for play. The Mahamad did not consider this a suitable playground, although they could offer no alternative. However, they were determined to send the boys elsewhere, so the samas was instructed to keep the gates of the courtyard closed from half an hour after the end of a service for prayer until half an hour before the beginning of the subsequent service and, since there seems to have been a fear that the heart of the samas might prove softer than that of the Mahamad, appended to this instruction was a rider to the effect that if the samas failed to carry out this instruction he would himself be fined half a crown for every default.

But these were after all only minor matters. Far more serious ones absorbed the attention of the Mahamad and others during these years. Above all was that of the position of the Haham. The London Sephardi Community had the privilege of having one of the most distinguished Jews of the day as its spiritual head. In Nieto they had a man who had earned respect in Jewish and non-Jewish circles, one who shone as a scholar in religious and in secular spheres, who had behind him a brilliant record, and in front of him the promise of an even more brilliant one. This was fully recognized by the leaders and directors of the London Community as well as by the members as a body. But, as always —independence of thought is so Jewish a characteristic or perhaps more properly a characteristic so widespread among Jews, and a tendency towards criticism so strong—there was a group of critics, with a capacity for respect and admiration inadequately developed, who seemed to believe that in most, if not in all, matters their opinion was as justified as that of anyone else, if not more so. In the past, self-opinionated critics of this character had helped to make the life of at least one Haham of London a misery and despite the support he received, in the end he had to resign. Nieto was a far greater man than Ayllon, but this fact did not silence detractors. They appeared almost as soon as Nieto settled in his new home, for a few months after his arrival, towards the end of the year 1701, the Mahamad resolved—doubtless with good reason —to strengthen an Ascama of 1699, that anyone who should speak unbecomingly of the Haham either at the time in office or retired should be liable to a fine of five pounds. And to strengthen this enactment it was at the same time laid down that the same penalty would be imposed on anyone who hearing such an expression of disrespect failed to report the offence to the Mahamad. What had been foreseen in 1701 was realized three years later when Moses de Medina reported that Joshua Sarfaty had referred to the Haham as a heretic and worshipper of Nature. Sarfaty was summoned before the Mahamad for having spoken 'very indecently' of the Haham. He admitted the charge but denied that he had acted wrongly and, remaining contumacious, was ordered to be excluded from the synagogue until he had made such amends as might seem proper to the Mahamad. Sarfaty's reply was to resign his membership of the Congregation. Such resignations had occurred previously, and the Mahamad was therefore not unduly perturbed. It anticipated that when the heat that the subject had caused would have died down Sarfaty would reconsider his resignation and to prepare themselves for that event it resolved that he should not be readmitted to the congregation until he had given satisfaction to the Mahamad and the Haham for his 'scandalous and indecent' attacks.

Sarfaty's attack was but an incident in a larger campaign. On 20 November 1703 Nieto had preached a sermon on the subject of 'Divine Providence' which caused considerable excitement among some of his hearers who claimed to discover in it heretical tendencies, inspired by the pantheistic teachings of Spinoza. Nieto was accused of having taught that God and Nature were one. Sarfaty was in particular disturbed and was so affected as to insult the Haham publicly by refusing to enter a house in which he was attending a wedding festivity. Sarfaty when summoned before the Mahamad reiterated his charge of heresy, challenged them to submit the case to any Jewish authority anywhere, and if the decision were given against him offered to forfeit £100 as a fine. The challenge was declined. The Mahamad themselves adjudicated in the case. Sarfaty had been told to put his case in writing before the Mahamad, but when he did so he was referred to the Haham, who, the Mahamad undertook, would explain and satisfy him. Sarfaty, however, refused to meet the Haham, and he was thereupon ordered, as stated above, to be excluded from the Synagogue. A minor protest against this, made by Sarfaty, was that the Mahamad had no right to exclude him from a building to the cost of the erection of which he had contributed. Sarfaty later published his case in detail. Simultaneously Nieto had put his case in writing and had published it under the title *De la Divina Providencia*, one of the best known of his writings.

But Sarfaty did not stand alone. A group of sympathizers with his view gathered around him. They showed themselves as determined as their spokesman and were excommunicated in a body. The Mahamad did not, however, appear to be altogether certain of their position, and they therefore referred a case to the Attorney General, Sir Edward Northey, for his opinion.[1] The questions, put in the somewhat quaint language of the day, were:

(1) 'If any member of the sinagogue doth Transgress any ordre, and the church Wardens either for Peace sake avoiding of scandall or any other reason against a Crime Commited shall declare him in Excumanication, and the party so declared shall complain to any Court of Judicature thereof wether they will or Cann take any notice thereof, and if there is any statute against Excumonication or any particular Court (and wich) where this matter proprely shall bee Litigated,

(2) 'If any member shall transgers the second above ordre and should Come to Dye without ffullfilling said ordre having paid his Five pounds mencioned in the third ordre[2] whether the Church Wardens may not hinder this body to be interred in our burring place, hee having Forfeted his said Five pounds in not obeying the ordre hee subscribed to, or whether they Cann bee Compelled by having received the said Five pounds to burry the same.'

The opinion of the Attorney General gave support to the Mahamad.

'I am doubtful that the pronouncing excommunicating being an act of ecclesiasticall Jurisdiction, the Synagogue of the Jewes are not allowable by the Lawes of England to exercise the pronouncing of same, and for assuming the exercise of ye power in England, may be prosecuted by indictment or Information, and may be prohibited from pronouncing ye like by writ of prohibition to be granted by the Queen's courts of Law—

'As to ye 2nd Qu. I am of opinion the inheritance of the burying place being in the Churches trustees they may lawfully exclude such from burying there who have transgressed the said second they having only a permission to bury there on ye termes mentioned in ye order.

'Edw. Northey. June 12, 1705.'

[1] In those days and for two centuries afterwards the Law Officers of the Crown were accustomed to undertake private work while in office.
[2] This was the fee for future provision of a grave required of every Yahid on admittance to the Congregation.

A NEW HAHAM AND A NEW SYNAGOGUE

Among others Joseph Abendanon entered into the fray—there were few disputes of the first rank in the community from which he could keep away—and, as a consequence, he was again dismissed from his office of Rubi of the Congregation's school. While the members of this group were still excommunicate, one of them, Joseph Cohen d'Azevedo, died. His body was not allowed to be interred in the Sephardi cemetery, and his tomb is still to be seen in the neighbouring Ashkenazi one, as close as is possible to the wall that separates the two cemeteries. There are other Sephardi graves in this cemetery, of men probably buried in similar circumstances or of others who had voluntarily withdrawn from the Sephardi Community. Excommunication, however, could not settle the controversy. In the end, after some months, the Mahamad took the step for which Sarfaty had asked in the first instance and referred the question of the orthodoxy of Nieto's views, as expressed in the offending discourse, to the Sephardi Beth Din of Amsterdam, constituted of the Haham, Solomon Ayllon, formerly of London, and Rabbi Salomon de David Israel d'Oliveyra. Simultaneously, but independently, a group of London Sephardim —supporters of Sarfaty—wrote to the Mahamad of Amsterdam, asking them to obtain the opinion of their Beth Din on the phrase to which they took particular exception, 'They say that I have said in the *Yesiba*, that God and Nature and Nature and God are the same. I did say so. I affirm it, and I will prove it.' The Beth Din of Amsterdam, however, could not agree on a decision. The intervention of this group and the ear the Amsterdam Mahamad had given to it in the meanwhile aroused the resentment of the London Mahamad. Considering themselves offended, they consequently resolved that in no future circumstances should any request be made to the Beth Din or Mahamad of Amsterdam on any subject on which the London Community desired enlightenment. The dissidents, who included some of the best-known names in the Community, thereupon again approached the London Mahamad, reiterating their desire for an authoritative decision. The London Mahamad was still willing to seek one, but was in a quandary. Recourse to Amsterdam had failed. The next obvious court was that of Hamburg, but the office of Haham there was at the time vacant. The *Parnas* of the London Ashkenazi Synagogue, Reb Aberle or Abraham Nathan of Hamburg, at this juncture intervened with a suggestion. This was that the case should be submitted to the Ashkenazi rabbi of Altona, Rabbi Zevi Ashkenazi, better known perhaps as Haham Zevi, revered and respected on account of his character and learning equally by Sephardi and

Ashkenazi. The decision of Haham Zevi and his two coadjutors was in favour of Nieto.

The dissidents, however, still lay under the ban of excommunication. Still further to assuage the passions that had been aroused, Nieto himself stepped in. A petition had been sent to the Mahamad by four of the principal members of the Community who had kept outside the controversy, to annul the sentence of excommunication. This petition was very strongly supported by Nieto himself, who pleaded that in the Days of Penitence 'in which God sits to judge His people' it was the Mahamad's duty to bring about peace and unity in 'the Nation'. The prayer was promptly granted and peace once again reigned in London Jewry. Haham Zevi subsequently visited London and was received with enthusiasm by Sephardim as well as Ashkenazim. It is even said that he was offered the appointment of Haham of London, but this is apocryphal. When he died, in May 1718, the mourning among the Sephardim of London was as sincere and general as it was in the several cities on the Continent in which he had held office.

Education with charity, from the beginning the principal care of the Congregation, after the Synagogue itself, continued throughout these years to hold its position of prominence. The *Shaare Tikva* or Gates of Hope School for boys dated back to 1664, and the Villa Real or similar one for girls to 1730. The former institution was supported out of congregational funds, including special donations for the purpose: the latter was endowed by Isaac da Costa Villa Real, who died in 1737. It was opened in 1731 with sixteen girls nominated as pupils. Over a century later it was amalgamated with a National and Infant School that had been founded in 1839. Originally close to the synagogue in Heneage Lane, the school was in 1897 removed to Thrawl Street. But it had before that year, in 1885, been transferred to the control of the London School Board, and in 1923 it ceased all activity as an ordinary school. These boys' and girls' schools survive as Hebrew and Religion classes for the children of the Congregation. The boys' school, the *Shaare Tikva*, has developed into the *Medrash* of *Heshaim*. Originally intended solely for instruction in Hebrew and Judaism, it is often referred to as the Talmud Torah, and the several Rubis mentioned in the course of this narrative were members of its staff. Originally it was administered jointly with the funds for the *Cautivos* and *Terra Santa*. The institution was reorganized in 1690 and again in 1733. In 1736 the teaching of English subjects and of arithmetic was added to the school curriculum, and in 1758 the institution was again reorganized. The teaching at that time covered a wide range, from the elementary classes in which the teaching opened with the Hebrew alphabet to the study of Rashi, the *Shulchan Aruch* and the *Gemara* in the highest class. The elementary classes were closed long ago, but the highest still survives, for adults not boys.[1] Finally, in 1734, Benjamin Mendes da Costa, prominent both in his share in the administration of the Community and for his benefactions to the poor and needy of all creeds, established and endowed in memory of his only son, Raphael, the *Yeshiba Mahané Raphael*, a preparatory school for admission to the highest class of the Medrash and mainly for the support of the students. Benjamin Mendes da Costa, in cooperation with another benefactor, Isaac de David Levy, established and endowed another *Yeshibah*, the *Assifat Haberim*, whose functions included, as was usual in those days, the payment of allowances to the students. Both these institutions were later absorbed in the Medrash.

Before the present chapter is brought to an end, there is one other subject relating to the internal history of the Anglo-Sephardi community that calls for mention. From the very beginning of the record of the Sephardi Community there was always an element that displayed a degree of reserve when participation in congregational activities was required. This disinclination for communal service was not at first serious, for the available supply of men qualified to fill in rotation the several honorary offices in the Community was quite adequate. Yet almost from the beginning provision was made in the governing regulations for dealing with any member who refused, without good reason, to accept any office to which his fellow members wished to elect him. And it was not long before occasion came for putting these regulations into force. As early as the year 1679 the normal punishment for refusal of office was increased from a fine of £10 as laid down in the original Ascamot to one of £25, and to exclusion from all other office for a period of two years, but after the lapse of three years the fine was reduced again to £10. The reduction did not, however, improve matters: it rather worsened them. Even the enthusiasm aroused by the erection and opening of the new synagogue in Bevis Marks did not effect an improvement. At the end of the

---

[1] Another benefactor of the *Heshaim* was Moses Lamego, who in 1757 gave £1,000, the interest from which was earmarked for the salary of a teacher of English.

The *Medrash Heshaim* still meets weekly for the study of the Talmud. The publication of successive editions of the prayer books is in its charge.

year 1700, while the new building was being erected, Isaac Lopes Pereira and Isaac Israel Correa were fined £20 each for refusing to serve as Parnassim. It was realized that the stability of the Community was threatened if this disinclination to accept office on the part of those best qualified persisted. An immediate reaction was an undertaking given by nineteen of the Elders to accept the office of Parnas or Gabay in the event of their being chosen. Nevertheless in the following year four prominent members of the Community were fined in similar circumstances. Three of them were Abraham de Brito, Daniel Penso, and Jacob Mendes de Brito, who had signed the undertaking. The fourth was Solomon de Medina, presumably the future knight who had previously taken his full share in the work of the Community. The dispute with the de Britos that came to a head three years later was probably already brewing. It is possible that Medina's extra-communal activities left him at that time no leisure to devote to the work of Anglo-Jewry. In other respects this undertaking, however, did not entirely relieve the situation, for three years later there is a record of the laying down of a penalty of a fine[1] of one pound on any elder who neglected without a satisfactory explanation to attend any meeting to which he might be summoned, and before the end of the first quarter of the century it had become a rule for hardly an election to pass in which one or more of the successful candidates, or more properly nominees, did not refuse to serve. It had become almost the exception for the Mahamad to have its full complement. These instances of disinclination to take a proper share in the work of the Community may have some relation to the general lack of interest in communal affairs that began to show itself among members of the wealthier circles who, feeling themselves a part of the English nation and in particular of the more privileged section of that nation, discovered other interests and attractions that led not towards but away from their smaller community. In a later chapter a number of instances will be given.

By the end of the seventeenth century the flow of Marranos and ex-Marranos from Portugal began to slacken, but new sources of immigration took their place. The immigration from Holland has already been mentioned. A little later, one, not very considerable, began from Italy, stimulated no doubt by the settlement in England of David Nieto. From early in the eighteenth century dates the arrival of later well-known Sephardi families of Italian origin such

---

[1] This practice of imposing fines for refusal of office or absence from meetings was in force in the Ashkenazi Community also.

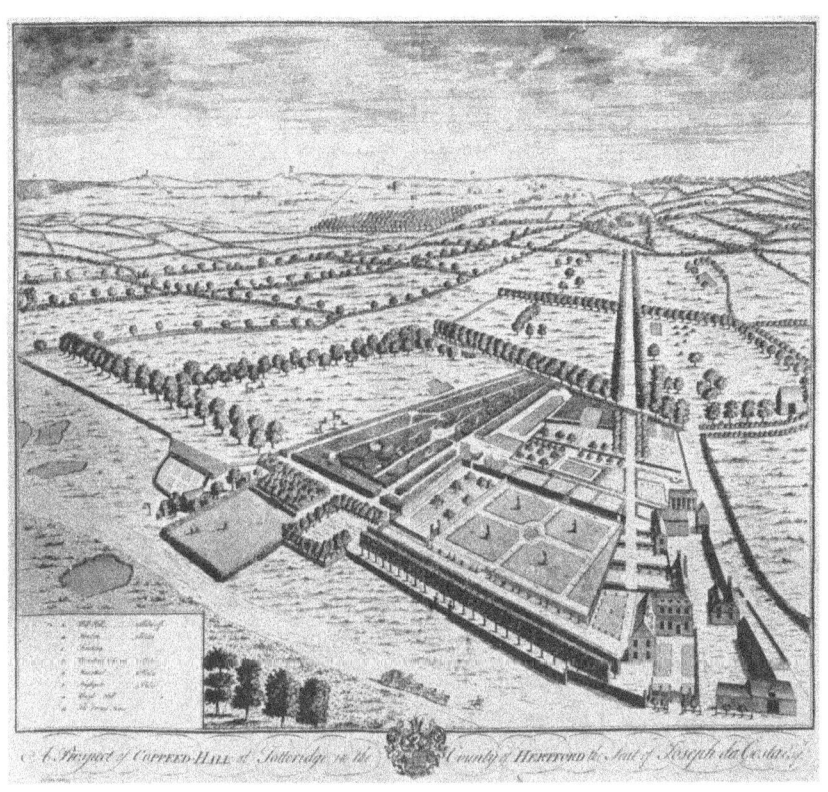

COPPEED HALL, TOTTERIDGE, HERTS.
(Home of Joseph da Costa, c. 1730)
From an engraving

SILVER SALVER PRESENTED TO THE LORD MAYOR
(Made by John Ruslen, 1708/9)

A NEW HAHAM AND A NEW SYNAGOGUE

as Soncino, Uzzielli, Pacifico, Tedeschi, Rieti, Disraeli, and Treves from Venice, where Nieto was born, and Franco, Ergas, Treves, Supino, Ottolenghi, Montefiore from Leghorn, where he lived. These men for the most part engaged in commerce, building up a trade between their former and their new homes. Some of these Italian families came originally from Spain or Portugal. Others had, however, no Iberian origins, but were gradually assimilated by the more virile new-comers. Coral, for the most part worked by Jews in Leghorn, was exported to India by Anglo-Jewish merchants, who brought back diamonds in exchange. At the same time, in the middle of the eighteenth century, the greatest part of the Spanish West Indian trade was still in the hands of Jews. Another course of immigration that began in the eighteenth century, smaller and less noticeable, but which gained greater strength towards the end of that century, was that from North Africa, direct or by way of Gibraltar which became a British possession in 1704. Among the families, who have secured mention in the records of the Community who came at one time or another from Gibraltar, where those of Almosnino, Bensusan, Benoliel, Benaim, Benzimra, Abecasis, Seruya, Sarfaty, Nahon, Benzecry, Beriro. The new-comers were at first accepted somewhat grudgingly, hardly welcomed. Many of them were looked down upon as inferiors not only materially but also culturally, being known generally as *Berberiscos*, and were grouped with the poorer Tudescos, who formed the great majority of the Ashkenazim, and *Polaccos*.

INSCRIPTIONS ON THE CHAIRMAN'S MALLET USED AT MEETINGS OF GOVERNORS OF THE GATES OF HOPE SCHOOL.

CHAPTER VII

SOME EIGHTEENTH-CENTURY PERSONALITIES

WHILE THE COURSE of the story of the Sephardim in England was developing, the position of individual members of that Community was also undergoing a change. When Sephardim first appeared in England, and for generations afterwards, they lived and deliberately kept themselves closely shut up in a self-imposed ghetto, physical and intellectual, out of which they never came except for the solitary purpose of commerce. In commercial dealings, but in no other matters except for a very few individuals, did they come into contact with other inhabitants of the country. Alien in origin with few exceptions, who themselves were living in an entirely foreign environment, their manners, their ways of life, their beliefs, their hopes, even the language of their homes, were entirely strange to the Englishman. Contact was limited solely to the very narrow field of commerce. As time passed, however, the at first almost insurmountable barrier between the two peoples gradually began to crumble away. Commercial intercourse was soon followed by the entry of Jewish physicians into English homes. Commerce led to prosperity, and prosperity opened many doors at which English Jews had previously often looked somewhat wistfully. All the time the early settlers who had come from abroad were being replaced by their sons and daughters, born in the country. To these the English language was familiar almost from birth, and English customs no longer strange. In exceptional cases these English-born Jews began to move outside the Jewish quarter in the city and to settle farther afield. Here they found new interests and new friends, far distant from those of their fathers in Bevis Marks and Creechurch Lane. Thus, from the beginning of the eighteenth century and earlier, Anglo-Jewry was undergoing a noticeable change and a new generation, very different from the old, was arising. This change, this 'emancipation from the ghetto', was also one of the prime causes of the drift from Jewry which also began to become evident among some of the sons of the *esnoga* who had attained wordly affluence or were influenced by the respect shown them for their intellectual successes in the new circles into which they entered.

The founders of the Community in 1657 and in the following

SOME EIGHTEENTH-CENTURY PERSONALITIES 99

years were to a large extent men of substance, merchants and dealers, many of whose names have already been mentioned, and men of the same class were necessarily the first to gain prominence. This is not the occasion for compiling a list of these merchants nor of publishing an embryonic dictionary of Anglo-Jewish biography. A few brief details regarding some of these men may not, however, be considered out of place. There was Alvaro da Costa, who died in 1716. He may be said to have been the founder of the great Anglo-Jewish family of Mendes da Costa whose story, Lucien Wolf once said, composed the greater part of modern Anglo-Jewish history. Alvaro da Costa came to England in 1655 and was naturalized in 1667. A man of wealth he had a country house at Highgate as well as a town house in Budge Row in the City and lived in grand style, generous in his hospitality. He was one of the first of the members of the new Community to live outside the quarter of the city that most of them had made their own. Although he, himself, a former Marrano, was never circumcised, his family was fully within the Community. In the Thurloe Papers under date November 1656 he is described as 'a Jew named Da Costa, a great Merchant in London, who hath and is presently to receive the sum of £4,000 for the use of Charles Stuart'. Of the next generation of the da Costa family there was Moses (Philip) Mendes da Costa, whose death was recorded in the *Gentleman's Magazine* as that of 'a very rich Jew merchant' who died on 14 October 1739. Another Moses, otherwise Anthony, da Costa, Alvaro's grandson, who died in 1747, was one of the Jewish merchants who took a leading part in the activities against the attempt, at the opening of the reign of William III, to impose Alien Import Duties on endenizened merchants, many of whom were Jews. So high was his reputation and standing that the story gained currency that he was one of the directors of the Bank of England, but there is no basis for this claim. In 1727 he had taken legal proceedings with success against the Russia Company which had refused to accept him as a member on account of his religion, and the Company, persistent in their aim, had to go to Parliament for an amendment of their charter so as to have the right to refuse membership to a Jew. Anthony da Costa was one of the three prominent London Sephardim who were appointed subcommissioners for the colonization of Georgia in North America. Yet another member of the same family who shone in commerce and finance was John (otherwise Abraham), a son of Moses (otherwise Philip) da Costa and a son-in-law of Alvaro da Costa. John Mendes da Costa was one of the three London merchants who in 1710 provided £300,000 for the supply of necessities for the army in Flanders. Joseph Cohen d'Azevedo was one of the directors of the Scottish East India Company formed, and suppressed, in the previous reign to compete with the monopoly-holding East India Company. These Jewish merchants were from the beginning especially prominent in foreign trade. They brought with them their connexions with Spain and Portugal to which they very soon added others with Holland, whence many of them had come, and with the West Indies and North America where relatives of theirs had settled. Later came an interest in India, and they and their relatives in other Sephardi centres were in continuous correspondence with Italy and the eastern Mediterranean countries generally.

There is a curious claim made during the period with which we are dealing on account of the alleged services in founding the Bank of England, of one Henriques, of whom nothing is known except that he was a hunchback vendor of lottery tickets. The claimant was his son, Jacob Henriques, a lottery promoter and also a dealer in lottery tickets, who himself suggested the restoration of the national finances by means of a lottery.[1] Despite all these efforts the younger Henriques did not prosper financially, and in the end felt himself compelled to petition the King, George III, on the occasion of his coronation, on the strength of the alleged services of his father. The petition which so far as is known led to no result was in part in the following terms:

> 'The race not being always to the swift, nor the battle to the strong, but time and chance happening to all, by various dispensations of Divine Providence, after using every honest and laudable endeavour, grudging no talent or expence for the public service, find myself so circumstanced, that with the greatest humility I most earnestly entreat your Majesty's royal favour, so as to enable me to pass through the few remaining days of my pilgrimage with less solicitude, affording me some relief from the cares and anxieties of this life, that I may be fitter to prepare for my last great change, which at the fartherest cannot be far off. I have seven daughters to maintain. Hitherto my sorrows and disappointments have been many and frequent; but if what I now offer, with the most profound reverence, shall incline your Majesty on mature deliberation to consider me, my grey hairs will not go down sorrowing to the grave, and my eyes will be closed in peace. . . .'

Jacob Henriques later returned to Holland whence his father had

---

[1] Lottery transactions in those days were quite respectable.

come and died there on 1 January 1768, seven years after the date of his petition, in his eighty-fifth year.

From commerce and finance the step to contracting for supplies to the armies was not wide. And at the end of the seventeenth and the opening of the eighteenth centuries opportunities for such activities were not lacking. The story of the part taken in this sphere by English Sephardim begins on the Continent, in the Netherlands and in the Iberian Peninsula. Mention has already been made of the contribution made by Dutch Sephardim to the provisioning and supplying of William III's armies, including those for the invasion of England and the reconquest of Ireland. Outstanding among the earlier group of Sephardi army contractors was Joseph Cortissos who claimed descent from Emanuel José Cortissos, Marquis de Villa, a grandee of Spain of Jewish origin, of the late fifteenth century. For a time Cortissos was in the Spanish diplomatic service. In those days in Spain and elsewhere men of outstanding activity did not devote the whole of their energies to one sphere. Known by the English military commanders in the peninsula he was pressed by them to supply the needs of the Portuguese authorities—on credit. He hesitated to do so, but urged by Lord Galway, the Commander of the English Army, and Lord Stanhope, then English Ambassador at Madrid, who virtually pledged the English Government to see that all sums due to Cortissos by the Portuguese Government would be paid, he agreed. His supplies and services kept the English and Portuguese armies in the field, but at the conclusion of the war his pessimistic anticipations were realized. His claim against the English Government was for £25,000 and that against the Portuguese one for £70,000. Of the latter he received nothing: of the former less than half. In 1712 he came to England to press his claims and for the succeeding thirty years England was his home. To his descendants, the last of whom was still living in London until well into the nineteenth century, he left little beyond his claims and his strikingly handsome portrait in oil, now the property of the London Sephardi Community. It is said that while on active service in Spain a son was born to him, and secure under the protection of the English forces he had the child formally accepted into the Jewish Community by a mohel,[1] whom he brought, presumably from Gibraltar or Morocco, the first occasion of a ritual circumcision in the Iberian Peninsula for more than two centuries.

Another great Sephardi who settled in England—great not only

[1] A circumciser.

on account of his international standing but also on account of his wealth and the size of his family—was Diego, otherwise Moses, Lopes Pereira, Baron d'Aguilar. Coming of a wealthy Marrano family of Portugal, around whom many romantic legends cluster, he was invited to Vienna in 1725 to advise the Government on the creation of a tobacco monopoly. In Portugal his family had farmed very successfully a similar monopoly. Safe in Vienna, Lopes Pereira threw off his Christian disguise and founded the Sephardi community in that capital where his name is still recited at the head of the list of benefactors every Day of Atonement. Gaining the favour of the Empress Maria Theresa, he was appointed her Treasurer and created a Baron of the Empire, the first professing Jew to be ennobled. Among other of his transactions was the provision of the money for the erection of the royal palace of Schönbrunn. In 1756 Lopes Pereira settled in England, where he had been on a visit thirty-four years earlier, with a great fortune and a family of fourteen children. In England he was endenizened without delay, but died three years later, in 1759. His children married into the leading families of Anglo-Sephardi Jewry, and for the next century and longer many of the most prominent members of the Sephardi community derived from him. He was the ancestor also of two well-known English military families—those of d'Aguilar and of Lopes Pereira. His eldest son, Ephraim, succeeded him in the title. Ephraim was also a man of great wealth, for, apart from the fortune he inherited from his father, his first wife, Sarah, daughter of Moses Mendes da Costa, brought him a dowry which was stated to amount to £150,000. She died in 1763, after a few years of wedded life, leaving several children. Four years later the widower married the widow of Benjamin Mendes da Costa, who was born a Pereira and also brought with her a fortune. Ephraim d'Aguilar at first took a full part in the work of the Community, holding in succession a number of offices, including those of Parnas and Gabay. But later he developed eccentricities which gained such control over him that life with him became intolerable. At first he lived with his wife in considerable style in a mansion in Broad Street Buildings, but financial losses which still left him a wealthy man affected him so as to drive him into seclusion, and he withdrew from society, from the Community and from his family. After having deserted his wife for twenty years, he suddenly returned to her, but only to persecute her. Her life became unbearable and she was forced to have recourse to the civil authorities for release. Among d'Aguilar's other eccentricities was his essay in farming. He bought land in Islington on which he kept cattle. But he was too miserly either to feed his cattle properly or to sell them. As a consequence the victims of his treatment became a public scandal, and his farm was popularly known as Starvation Farm. Yet there was another side to his character, for while he was perpetrating these cruelties, he was at the same time devoting large sums to charity, including the upkeep of institutions which he had himself founded for the assistance of those in need. He died on 16 March 1802 in his house in Shaftesbury Place, Aldersgate Street, his death being hastened, it was said, by his refusal of any comfort that cost money. Although he had long before detached himself from the Community he was buried in the Beth Haim at Mile End, leaving a considerable fortune.

Among Jewish army contractors a well-known figure was Sir Solomon de Medina, who over a series of years supplied the armies of Marlborough during the war in Flanders, and was the first professing Jew to receive the honour of an English knighthood. He had the further honour of being visited in his home by the King, William III. He was, however, ultimately involved in the disgrace of Marlborough, after appearing before the Commission that inquired into Marlborough's financial transactions, but he passed through the ordeal without any reflection on his character. Medina was born in Italy and left this country to die in Holland, although his will was proved in London and members of his family remained here. Medina, during the greater part of his life in England, took an active part in the work of the Sephardi Community, and his name appears frequently in its records, over nearly half a century.[1] Later, during the Seven Years' War, Abraham Prado, who lived the life of a country gentleman at Twickenham, was in charge of the army commissariat. His office was a civil not a military one. He enjoyed a wide measure of independence and was far more a contractor than an official. To assist him in his work he gathered a group of men around him, of whom most if not all were family connexions. These included his son Samuel, Elias Buzaglo, a member of a London family of which mention will be made later, and above all David and Jacob Mendes da Costa, brothers of the both famous and notorious Emanuel Mendes da Costa and a member of the distinguished Anglo-Jewish family.[2]

[1] A detailed account of Medina and his activities was contributed by Dr. Oscar Rabinowicz to the Jewish Historical Society of England, but has not yet been published.

[2] Three of the letters of David Mendes da Costa, written from the Army headquarters while on active service, have been published. Two of them are addressed to Abraham Prado, and deal with business matters, except for a passing mention of a Prussian victory. The third letter is addressed to his brother, Jacob, and is entirely personal. Cecil Roth, *Anglo-Jewish Letters*, pp. 136–40.

Two other Sephardim who were for a time prominent in the public eye, but who do not fit into any of the regular categories may be mentioned here. Franz van Schoonenberg otherwise Francisco de or Jacob Belmonte (of which name Schoonenberg is a translation) was a member of one of the ex-Marrano families of Holland. A relative, Don Manuel de Belmonte, was Spanish resident at the Hague until he died in 1704. Francisco was also a member of the diplomatic service—but of the Netherlands—and was Minister and Envoy Extraordinary of the Prince of Orange —William III of England—to the Court of Spain from 1678 to 1702. For his services he was created a marquis by the Emperor Charles VI. After his retirement he settled in England, where he was naturalized as Jacob de Abraham de Belmonte and was probably an occasional worshipper in Bevis Marks. He died in 1717 in Lisbon, where he was at the time the envoy of the Government of the Netherlands. Regarding Francis Francia, there has been considerable mystery, which still to some extent persists. He was a grandson of Domingo or Isaac Francia, one of the Jewish residents in London in the time of Cromwell, who died in 1687 after a third of a century of prominent activity in the Jewish Community. Francis was, however, born in Bordeaux, about the year 1675, when the practice of Judaism in that city was still prohibited and the Jews there were brought up as Marranos. In the course of his trial he was described as having become a Christian, although of Jewish origin, but as he refused to take the oath on the New Testament and produced a Hebrew prayer book for the purpose, one can assume that his Christianity was nominal. Francia was charged in the year 1717 with high treason and put on trial. His offence, it was stated, took the form of assistance to the Old Pretender in his attempt to seize the throne two years earlier. Francia was acquitted, although the evidence against him was strong and he is fully implicated in the Jacobite plot in correspondence that came to light in Italy many years later. The explanation of the acquittal seems to be that the Government had some hope of making him one of their agents and to this end influenced the court, and from the extracts from the papers published by Mr. Marcus Lipton[1] one is justified in believing that Francis, while still (after his acquittal) ostensibly devoted to the cause of the Pretender, was in effect an agent of the English Government.

After commerce and finance, as has been said, medicine was the principal road from Jewry into the larger world. In England, as elsewhere, the physician has always been favoured and treated as

[1] *Trans. Jew. Hist. Soc. of Eng.*, vol. XI, pp. 190 et seq.

the exception among Jews and in the earliest period of Anglo-Jewish history and also in the intervening period during which the presence in the country of acknowledged Jews was not tolerated, exceptions were always made in favour of Jewish physicians, as a rule for the treatment of royal and other distinguished personages. Mention has already been made of Dr. Fernando (Moses) Mendes who attended Catherine of Braganza and Charles II. No Jewish successor until the present century[1] attained to so fashionable a position as this, but for almost a third of the eighteenth century Meyer Löw Schomberg, of the Ashkenazi section of Anglo-Jewry, reigned first in London, later at Bath, as the most fashionable medical attendant in the country. Yet, when he first arrived in England and became the physician of the Great Synagogue, he was so poor that when admitted a licentiate of the Royal College in 1721-2 he was unable to pay the fees due, whereupon the College accepted a bond for payment on some future date. Of his five sons, Ralph (or Raphael) and Isaac, a twin, were also physicians, Ralph also a minor poet, but in neither capacity did either attain to the distinction of their father. Henry, another son, received a commission in the army, and Alexander, later Sir Alexander Schomberg, took part as naval captain, in command of a man-of-war, in the capture of Quebec. But this was after the family had left Jewry. The naval and military traditions persisted in the family, and among the descendants of the former physician of the Great Synagogue there appear the names of four admirals, three generals, and other officers of lower rank. The *Dictionary of National Biography* contains biographies of Dr. Meyer Löw Schomberg and of seven of his descendants.

Dr. Philip de la Cour, one of the founders of the Beth Holim, was also a fashionable physician in London and Bath. He married a niece of the famous Sampson Gideon. The later part of his life was unfortunate and he ultimately returned to Holland, where he died in 1786. Somewhat earlier Isaac de Sequeira Samuda, who died in 1730, appears in the list of the Yehidim. Sequeira Samuda was a fellow of the Royal Society. This learned institution was founded in 1662 when Charles II granted it a charter and the first Jewish fellow, Isaac de Sequeira Samuda, was elected in 1723, three years after he had graduated in medicine at the University of Coimbra in Portugal, in which year also he began to contribute papers to the Royal Society. He was admitted to the Royal College of Physicians in 1721. Sequeira Samuda was a physician of some

[1] Sir Felix Semon, the throat specialist, was one of the medical advisers of Edward VII.

repute and was elected on his professional attainments, although wealth or station were often accepted as an alternative in those days. He was also a poet and he delivered one of the funeral orations on the occasion of the death of Haham David Nieto in 1728. At first, like other Sephardi physicians of the eighteenth century, he was the physician to the Community. He was at the same time the medical attendant at the Portuguese Embassy and Honorary Physician Extraordinary to the Prince Regent of Portugal.[1] His close friend was another physician and F.R.S., Jacob de Castro Sarmento, who stood out among the practitioners of medicine in England in his day. Himself a Marrano who had escaped from Portugal and settled in England, at first also as physician to the Sephardi Community—he had received the degree of Doctor of Medicine from the University of Coimbra in 1717—de Castro Sarmento was one of the first, perhaps the first Jew to graduate at a British university. He was a doctor of medicine of the University of Aberdeen and Marischal College, the degree being granted in July 1739, one of his sponsors being Sir Hans Sloane, the President of the Royal Society. Ralph Schomberg received a similar degree about the same time, but it is not certain that he was still a professing Jew. Although a refugee from Portugal and a Jew, de Castro Sarmento was appointed physician to the Portuguese Ambassador. He gained a great reputation as being particularly skilled in curing fevers and has been credited with having introduced vaccination against smallpox into England fifty years before Jenner. He was elected a fellow of the Royal Society in 1729, one may perhaps say on philo-Semitic grounds. One Daniel Flores had accused him of having assisted the Inquisition in Portugal, before he left that country, by denouncing to them fellow crypto-Jews, and his election was endangered by the prejudice this aroused. To support his application he therefore applied to the authorities of the London Sephardi Community of which he was a member, to hold an inquiry. This they did and exonerated him completely. He was thereupon elected a fellow of the Society. The record of the conclusion of this affair appears in a contemporary leaflet, the only known copy of which was discovered in the Bodleian Library by the diligence of the late Israel Solomons:

'Dr. Jacob de Castro Sarmento, having been proposed to be admitted a Fellow of the Royal Society, and a certain Gentleman

[1] For biographical details of Sequeira Samuda, see *Bulletin of the Institute of Medicine*, vol. IV (1936).

having industriously propagated a most scandalous Report, highly reflecting on the Doctor's character; it is thought proper to publish the following Extract, which is a true copy of the Entry in the Registry Book of the Synagogue.

'Conclusion of the false and malicious Testimony, that was rais'd against Dr. Jacob de Castro Sarmento, and the Result of the second Meeting of the Elders of the Synagogue, after a very exact and true examination of the same, in which meeting were present the following gentlemen, viz.:

Mosseh de Medina, President
Ishac Cohen Peixoto, Parnas ⎫
Joseph de Crasto, Parnas ⎬ or Wardens of the Synagogue
Ishac Vas Martines, Parnas ⎭
Ishac Nunes Fernandes, Adjunto ⎫
Joseph Telles da Costa, Adjunto ⎪
Ishac da Costa Alvarenga, Adjunto ⎬ or Elders' Assistants[1]
Abraham Dias Fernandes, Adjunto ⎪
Mosseh Lopes Dias, Adjunto ⎭

It having been divulg'd among our holy Congregation, that Dr. Jacob de Castro Sarmento had been the cause of many of our Brethren's imprisonment of the City of Beja, in the Kingdom of Portugal (a very Inhumane and Cruel Crime of itself), he the said Doctor petition'd the Elders of the Synagogue, that they would be pleas'd to examine the case, either to punish him with all the Rigour and Severity (if he should deserve it) or (if innocent) to acquit and free him from such a Scandalous Imputation, and the Consequences thereof, which still he unjustly suffers, without Examination or Conviction: The Elders of the Synagogue, being touch'd with Zeal and Justice, summon'd an extraordinary Meeting, and after mature Consideration of the Case, found there was not sufficient proof to decide it, and adjourn'd to another meeting, that better Evidences might appear. Several Gentlemen of very great Credit and Reputation, having since come over from Lisbon, do declare the said Report to be false and malicious: besides several Letters, which have come from faithful Persons, who were themselves in the said Prisons, and then suffer'd very rigorously, do likewise confirm and attest the said Report as false and groundless; and all the above-said appearing very manifestly and evidently before the

---

[1] An *Adjunto* is an Elder who has previously held office as Parnas or Gabay. The Mahamad was accustomed to call in adjuntos when a decision of considerable importance had to be taken.

Elders of the Synagogue, and their Assistants, at a second meeting, which they had only upon this Account, unanimously resolved to make a publick Declaration in this Holy Place (the Synagogue), to the end that the Truth might appear, and that the same Dr. Jacob de Castro Sarmento might be re-established to his entire Credit.

'And we pray God to keep his people from raising false Witness against their fellow-creatures, and to give Peace upon Israel.

'David Lopes Pereyra, Gabay or
'Treasurer'

De Castro Sarmento, although for long a zealous and active member of London Jewry, did not die within its fold. Born at Braganza in Portugal about the year 1691, he was settled in England before he was thirty. His wife Sarah died in Sebat 1756 and was buried in the Sephardi cemetery in Mile End. Shortly afterwards he married a Christian woman and withdrew from the Synagogue. The letter that he sent to the authorities of Bevis Marks on this occasion was published in *The Annual Register* for 1758.

'Dr. de Castro, a member of the Royal College of Physicians, and Fellow of the Royal Society of London, separated himself from the community of the Jews, by a letter which he wrote to the elders of the Synagogue in the following words: "Gentlemen, The different opinion and sentiments I have entertained long ago, entirely dissenting from those of the Synagogue, do not permit me any longer to keep the appearance of a member of your body; I now therefore take my leave of you, hereby renouncing expressly that communion in which I have been considered with yourselves. I do not however renounce the intercourse I may have with you in the general society of men of honour and probity, of which character I know many among you, and whom, as such, I shall always esteem. I have sent the key of my drawer, that you may dispose of my place. J. de Castro Sarmento."'

De Castro Sarmento died in 1762 at his house in King's Road, Holborn, and was buried in the churchyard of St. Andrew's, Holborn. He left two sons by his second wife, of whom the elder, Henry, became a British general. Dr. de Castro Sarmento was a voluminous author not only on medical subjects. A close friend of David Nieto, he on at least one occasion—Kippur 1724—preached in his stead in the synagogue. He also delivered one of the orations on the occasion of the Haham's funeral. Both of these sermons were published. In 1724 he also published in Spanish verse a paraphrase of the Book of Esther.[1] He contributed to the *Transactions* of the Royal Society papers on astronomical observations and Brazilian diamonds.

There was yet another medical man who stood out in the circle of worshippers in Bevis Marks during the earlier half of the eighteenth century. This was the surgeon Jacob de Castro, who has sometimes been confused with his contemporary de Castro Sarmento. Both were among the honorary medical officers of the *Beth Holim* when it was first instituted. He was born in 1704 and lived until 1789. Jacob de Castro was the first member of the Corporation of Surgeons after its separation from the Barbers. Three or four pamphlets on medical subjects, one of them on the smallpox, have been attributed to the surgeon, but they cannot have been written by him, for they were published when he was only seventeen or eighteen years of age. They must have been written by the F.R.S. who was accustomed occasionally to omit the latter part of his name, Sarmento. A younger contemporary, Ephraim Luzzatto, shone more as a poet than as a physician. A member of a very distinguished Italian Jewish family, he was born in Gorizia in 1729 and took his doctorate in medicine at the University of Padua in 1751. Twelve years later he settled in London, where he was at first medical officer to the Beth Holim, an office filled by more than one Sephardi physician who otherwise attained distinction. In 1792 he left for Italy to consult a specialist, and died on the way, at Lausanne. Luzzatto's duties at the Beth Holim involved long attendances there, and as those duties were not very onerous he used to while away the time by writing poems on odd pieces of paper that came his way. A very large number of these poems left by him at the hospital were unfortunately destroyed by some careless or ignorant attendant. Luzzatto was a master of the Hebrew language and in this tongue most of his poems were written.[2]

But there were other Sephardi fellows of the Royal Society in this early period. Scientific distinction was at first not the only qualification for election. Wealth had an almost equally strong claim,

[1] There is much about Jacob de Castro Sarmento in *Trans. Jew. Hist. Soc. of Eng.*, vol. XII (Monograph on David Nieto by Israel Solomons), and in the *Miscellanies* of the same society (Dr. R. N. Salaman, 'Jewish Fellows of the Royal Society'). There is also a biography in the *Dictionary of National Biography*.

[2] For Ephraim Luzzatto, see *Trans. Jew. Hist. Soc. of Eng.*, vol. IX (Ephraim Luzzatto, 1729–92, by Mrs. R. N. Salaman).

and it was on this ground, coupled with a general interest in the objects of the Society and their personal high stan ding,that gained admission for Alvaro (Jacob Israel) Suasso in 1735, Anthony (Moses) da Costa in the following year, and Joseph Salvador in 1759, all leading men in the city and generous supporters of the Community. Among all the earlier Jewish fellows, however, stands out Emanuel (a son of Abraham otherwise John) Mendes da Costa (1717-91), eminent as conchologist, mineralogist, antiquary, and naturalist in general, who was actually elected secretary of the Society. Unfortunately his moral character was weak. He abused his office, robbed the Society and was inevitably dismissed from office and expelled from the Society. On the scientific side, however, Emanuel Mendes da Costa was the most distinguished Jewish fellow, at any rate until well into the nineteenth century.

Mention has already been made incidentally of a few Jewish writers and men of letters of this period—David Nieto, Jacob de Castro Sarmento, Ephraim Luzzatto, Isaac de Sequeira Samuda —but these names by no means exhaust the list. *Cacoethes scribendi* seems to be a Jewish characteristic everywhere and at all times, and London Jewry of the eighteenth century was no exception to the rule. Not surprisingly the first literary efforts of English Jews were made in one of the languages with which they were best acquainted—Spanish, Portuguese, or Hebrew. Such a one, Daniel Israel Lopez Laguna, introduced with his first publication in England, in 1720, a veritable galaxy of Anglo-Jewish writers. Laguna had been born in the south of France about 1653, of Marrano parents. Going to Spain for his studies, he was arrested by the officials of the Holy Inquisition. After some years of imprisonment he escaped and went to Jamaica, where the prosperity of the local Jewish Community at that time almost rivalled that of London. There he openly avowed his Judaism. From Jamaica, Laguna after some years went to London. He brought with him a metrical version of the Psalms in Spanish on which he had been engaged for twenty-three years. In London he found a Maecenas in Mordecai Nunez de Almeida, a cultured member of a cultured family. The book appeared in 1720 with a glowing approbation by the Haham, David Nieto, and with engraved illustrations from the hand of Abraham Lopes de Oliveira, who was also a member of the London community. Most noteworthy, however, was the number of laudatory sonnets and other introductions by which the work was prefaced. These numbered twenty-two, of which most were in Spanish. Three of the sonnets in Spanish were by women—Manuela Nunez de Almeida—the mother of the generous patron who also contributed a sonnet, and Sara de Fonseca Pina y Pimentel and Bienvenida Cohen Belmonte, his sisters. Other poetical contributors were David and Jacob, respectively son and grandson of the author. Joseph Abendanon, the scholarly and quarrelsome rubi of the congregation, wrote in Aramaic verse; Jacob de Sequeira Samuda and David Chaves in Latin; and Sampson Gideon, later prominent as financial statesman, Abraham Bravo and an anonymous contributor in English—the first appearance of Jews in English *belles-lettres*. Laguna seems to have stayed but a short time in England, for he died in Jamaica, where his wife and family had remained, about three years after the publication of his book. A contemporary man of letters was David Machado who lived for a time in Dublin. After retiring from business he settled in Bordeaux, where he preached in the Synagogue and wrote poetry. Far better known in English letters is, however, the banker-poet, Moses Mendes, stockbroker, dramatist, *bon vivant* and wit, a grandson of Fernando Mendes, Queen Catherine's physician. Moses Mendes, who died in 1758, had left the community and married a non-Jewess. Their sons took their mother's maiden name, Head, in place of Mendes, and their grandsons became prominent, the elder as Sir George Head, Assistant Commissary General, and Deputy Marshal at the Coronations of King William IV and Queen Victoria, the younger as the Rt. Hon. Sir Francis Bond Head, Bart., one of Wellington's officers at Waterloo and later Lieutenant-Governor of Upper Canada. Both followed the example set by their father, and contributed to English literature. A cousin of theirs, Jael Henrietta Mendes, who married a brother of the Poet Laureate, Henry James Pye, wrote minor verse, but like the Heads she can hardly be counted as a member of the Jewish Community.

Mention of the Mendes family directs attention to another member of it, Solomon Mendes. In a story such as this the distance between the man of letters and his patron is not long, although Moses Mendes needed no patron, and his niece, Jael Henrietta, needed none in the ordinary sense. Solomon Mendes, who died four years after his kinsman, the banker-poet, was, although not himself a writer, the centre of a literary coterie. A number of letters to and from him have been published.[1] These introduce some of his friends and correspondents—Richard Savage, poet and playwright, James Thomson, author of *The Seasons*, Robert Dodsley, the publisher, bookseller, poet, and dramatist, the Rev. Thomas Brock, secretary to the Royal Society,

[1] By Mr. Cecil Roth in *Anglo-Jewish Letters* (1938), pp. 105–14.

and John Armstrong, the Scottish poet, physician, and essayist. Thomson wrote an epitaph for him in a somewhat jocular vein.

Solomon da Costa Athias, merchant, notary, scribe, and philanthropist, immortalized himself in a different way. By his gift to the newly established British Museum of a valuable collection of Hebraica, 179 Hebrew printed books, one Spanish and three manuscripts, (all once the property of Charles II who had lost his right to them by neglecting to pay the bookbinder), he laid the foundation of the great collection of Hebraica which the Museum now houses. The 180 volumes comprised more than 220 works, in some cases more than one being bound together in a volume. Athias in making his valuable gift accompanied it by a somewhat florid Hebrew epistle to which an English translation was thoughtfully attached. Da Costa Athias was a master of literary Hebrew and also an excellent Hebrew and English calligraphist, so that the manner of presentation was worthy of the gift. The letter and gift seem to have aroused considerable interest, and the former was printed more than once in the public press as well as as a broadsheet. The social relations between Jew and non-Jew in the higher classes that were developing are well illustrated in the easy friendly tone of a letter from da Costa Athias to a friend and neighbour, Sir Nicholas Carew, in which he asked a favour for a friend and co-religionist, James Mendez, who incidentally is mentioned as having lived in the rural district of Mitcham since about the year 1730. The character and personality of da Costa Athias are summed up in a passage by the antiquary Thomas Hollis.

'This Solomon da Costa is no other than a broker; but a man of knowledge and virtue; and of such rare ability in his own profession, that he hath acquired by it, during the course of his life, one hundred thousand pounds: and this without public scandal or private fraud or meanness. Much of this has been nobly scattered, from time to time, in deeds of piety and beneficance, as well to his own straggled beggar nation as to ours. For many years he has spent annually among the latter, to my own knowledge, in the counties of Surry [sic] and Kent alone, above one thousand pounds. This has been done in a district of about thirty contiguous parishes, to which he rode and rides by divisions weekly: and where he relieves the aged and disabled worthy poor with clothes, and food, and money: and causes the industrious but necessitous young to be clothed, instructed, and placed out with farmers, and such like laborious

THE OLD MAHAMAD CHAMBER

THE OLD BETH HAIM
SHOWING THE TOMBS OF HAHAM DAVID NIETO AND HIS WIFE

HAZAN DAVID ISAAC DE CRASTO (CASTRO)
From an engraving by W. Hincks

HAHAM MOSES COHEN D'AZEVEDO
From a painting

honest men. To which ought not to be forgotten, that the whole is conducted without bustle or affectation. . . . To this same gentleman several of our leaders in the House of Commons have been in no small degree indebted for their fame there in funds and money matters, which no one understands more clearly, deeply, than himself, nor probably so well; and by his credit with them he has been enabled to effect, at times, even national good offices. . . .'[1]

Joseph d'Almeida, a wine merchant of Cowpers Row, Crutched Friars, and later of Watford where he died in 1788, was a patron of literature and the drama. It was he who was the principal Jewish supporter of Mozart when he was in London in 1764. He also encouraged the Sephardi Jewish comedian, Jacob de Castro, and gave him a useful introduction to the manager of Covent Garden Theatre. Outside of the Community he showed also his interest in public affairs. His name appears in the list of original members of the Cumberland Society which was founded at Inverness in 1746. But d'Almeida had his financial vicissitudes. His wine business was apparently not always successful. For eleven years, from 1754 to 1765, he was one of the twelve Jewish registered brokers of the City of London. Four years after his retirement from the Exchange he became bankrupt, but in 1773 he was admitted a member of the Scriveners Company, having by then recovered his prosperity. Apart from his handsome engraved portrait in the possession of Bevis Marks, there is another living memorial of him there. In 1779 he presented a short set of steps to raise to the required level boys too small to reach the reading desk when reading the *Haphtarah*. It is still in use.[2]

David Alves Rebello has been described as merchant and numismatist. This is correct so far as it goes, but it does not go far enough. One of the group of prominent Sephardi merchants, he was also one of those who took his full share of the work of the Community. Of ample means, he devoted a part of them to works of charity and also to the encouragement of young writers of promise. Equally well known was he for his hobby—numismatics. He made a considerable collection of coins as well as of objects of scientific interest and was the first person to issue private token

---

[1] For Solomon da Costa Athias, see Roth, *Anglo-Jewish Letters*, pp. 123–5 and 144–7; *Occident and Orient* (Gaster Anniversary Volume) (1936), p. 264; and *Trans. Jew. Hist. Soc. of Eng.*, vol. XII, pp. 96–9.

[2] A brief biography of d'Almeida as well as of other Anglo-Jewish worthies of the eighteenth century is to be found in 'Anglo-Jewish Notaries and Scriveners', a paper read by Mr. Edgar Samuel before the Jewish Historical Society of England in December 1949.

coins, intended presumably for collectors. By his will he bequeathed to the Congregation a legacy of £500, the interest on which was to be spent on the purchase of underclothing for those in need.

From literature to the arts the passage is not difficult. First comes music. Anglo-Jewry produced no great musical creator in the early half of the eighteenth century or at any time, but the support and patronage of wealthy, cultured Jews certainly made easy the course of one great composer, George Frederick Handel, who made England his home and composed his masterpieces there, and of the youthful Mozart when on a visit to England later. Handel would doubtless have been Handel without his Jewish friends. But they smoothed his path and made it easier for him to give full play to his genius. It was, however, a Sephardi Jew from Italy who lived until he had passed his century, Giacobbe Cervetto[1] or Basevi—familiarly known as Nosey for an obvious reason—an uncle of Naphtali Basevi, a president of the Jewish Board of Deputies and the maternal grandfather of Lord Beaconsfield, who introduced the violoncello into England, where he reigned as its master for two generations. After him his illegitimate son, James Cervetto, succeeded as the master of his instrument. The lives of father and son covered more than a century and a half. But the younger Cervetto was never a member of a Jewish community, and it is doubtful whether the elder one ever passed through the doors of Bevis Marks. Thomas Pinto, who was born in England of Italian parents about the year 1710, was a violinist of renown, living successively in London, Edinburgh, and Dublin, where he died in 1773. It is not certain that his parents were Jewish. If they were, they would have been of the Sephardi branch of the Community. Other musical members of the family were Charles Pinto, who died in 1791, and G. F. Pinto described in the *Gentleman's Magazine* as 'well known in the musical world', who died in 1806. Even better known was Charlotte Brent, the vocalist, who married Thomas Pinto, but she was certainly not a Jewess.

Abraham Lopes de Oliveira has already been mentioned as an engraver. He was also a goldsmith and designer. Products of his art are among the treasures of Bevis Marks and also of the Hambro and New Synagogues. Eighty years later John Foligno was recorded among the London goldsmiths. In the more authentic sphere of art the first English Sephardi name is that of Catharine or Rachel da Costa, the daughter of Fernando Mendes, the physician

---

[1] Cervetto, a name taken from the arms of the family, a hart Bar. Tsebi).

of Queen Catherine after whom she was named. She married her cousin Moses, otherwise Anthony, da Costa, the merchant and F.R.S. of whom more will be heard. The portrait of her father, now in the possession of the Spanish and Portuguese Congregation, is from her brush. She painted also other portraits. Contemporary with her was another Anglo-Sephardi engraver, Aaron Mendoza, of whom only the engravings of his *Laws of Shechita and Bedika* (1733) are known. Other contemporary artists of whom hardly anything is known were David Estevens, who painted a portrait of David Nieto, and Samuel da Silva, who similarly portrayed the features of Nieto's successor, Moses Gomes de Mesquita. At the end of the century there was a Mrs. de Castro who exhibited her work at the Royal Academy in 1777 and 1778.

Related to the arts is the stage. There Hannah Norsa, who died in 1783, reigned. The daughter of a publican in Drury Lane, she was one of the famous creators of the part of Polly Peachum in Gay's *Beggar's Opera*. She appeared in that part at the revival with which Covent Garden Theatre was opened in 1732. Her sister, Laura, married Sir Edward Walpole, brother of the Earl of Orford and son of Sir Robert Walpole. Their daughter married the Duke of Gloucester, brother of George III, who was so annoyed that he had enacted the Royal Marriages Act which prohibits the marriage of a member of the Royal Family without the permission of the King. Jacob de Castro (1758–1824), whose memoirs were published during his lifetime, was the principal of the group of actors 'Astley's Jews', as well known in Dublin and in Edinburgh as in London. Born in Bishopsgate Street, he described himself as the son of a rabbi. His father cannot be identified, but he was certainly a member of the family that in addition to other servants of the Congregation gave two successive secretaries, and another, David Isaac de Castro or Crasto who died in 1785, Hazan from 1749 to 1783. Solomon Rieti, a relative of the d'Israeli family, by creating Ranelagh Gardens in 1742 increased appreciably the opportunities for pleasure and enjoyment in the Metropolis during the second half of the eighteenth century.

Next comes a miscellaneous group of frequenters of the Sephardi synagogue or their near kinsmen whose activities help to illustrate the extent to which by this period the Sephardim of England had begun to enter into the complete life of the English people. Abraham Mendes, who died in 1756, was a professional thief-catcher. Born in Spain as a Marrano, he came to London from Holland as a child about the year 1690. He was officially attached first to Southwark, later to Newgate Prison. His best known success was the capture of Jack Sheppard. Mendes and Jonathan Wild, the latter little better than the arch-criminal Jack Sheppard, were colleagues and associates in the profession of thief-catcher. Abraham Buzaglo, a member of a family of Moroccan Jews, a member of which became prominent in quite another capacity, flourished as a quack and an inventor. In the latter capacity he produced and put on the market a new form of heating stove. He found, however, the promise to cure diseases more profitable. From an advertisement in the first issue of *The Times* in 1784 we learn that he was prepared to cure gout by muscular exercise alone. He promised that sufferers who placed themselves in his care would be out of pain and danger within a few hours, completely and permanently cured within ten days and in better health of body and mind after his treatment than they had ever been. He offered further, by similar means, to cure corpulency, lack of appetite, and indigestion, completely or partially, as the patient wished. His absurd boasting advertisements encouraged the satirist even to surpass him, and as a consequence there appeared in 1783 an engraving published by P. Sandby at 'St. Georges Row, Oxford Turnpike', entitled 'Les Caprices de la Goute, Ballet Arthritique' in which is depicted a corpulent Buzaglo in a ridiculous posture, with two of his patients watching him intently. As is not exceptional on these occasions, a small orchestra in the background gives a musical accompaniment, presumably to drown the groans. A contemporary 'Dr.' Bossy, whose original name was Garcia, was selling quack medicines in Covent Garden in 1790.

The English Sephardim of this period who carried a knowledge of the Community into external circles were, however, not all of the character and characteristics to which reference has been made. There were the philanthropists, in the full sense of the term, who knew no limits of community, class, even of race, to whom all sufferers were equally human beings, to relieve whom they felt and proved to be their mission. They and their successors (for Anglo-Jewry fortunately has never been without such men and women) did not neglect those in need in their own small community in the interests of those of the larger one. Two or three of these men whose hearts were always attuned to suffering in others have already been mentioned. Others have been passed by—Benjamin Mendes da Costa, for instance, for long the recognized head of Anglo-Sephardi Jewry, a grandson of Alvaro da Costa, has been described as 'a man endowed with a large heart, and whose unbounded charity on its most extended form had endeared him to Jew and Gentile'. He was honoured and respected by all, for he looked on

SOME EIGHTEENTH-CENTURY PERSONALITIES 117

everyone in trouble as a fit subject for his unbounding generosity. In his will he made provision for the continuation throughout the lives of the beneficiaries of the allowances he had made to them. All debtors were released of their obligations to his estate, on the ground that everyone who had recourse to borrowing must undoubtedly be in need. The beneficiaries under his will included both Ashkenazi and Sephardi institutions. Another family that stood out in devoted service to the Community in the middle years of the eighteenth century was that of Salvador, better known in the Synagogue as Jessurun Rodrigues. Joseph Salvador, who cooperated closely with Benjamin Mendes da Costa, took an even more prominent part in the public affairs of the Community and was chosen as the sole representative of the Sephardi Community when a united deputation was sent to court to present the congratulations of Anglo-Jewry to the Princess of Wales on the accession to the throne of her son, George III. Joseph Salvador, the head of a very wealthy firm of city merchants, Francis and Joseph Salvador, which took Sampson Gideon's place, after his death, as financial agents to the Government, had a large house in White Hart Court, Bishopsgate Street, which bore until three-quarters of a century ago his name and the inscription on the foundation stone which his daughter Judith had laid. He had also a country house and wide estate at Tooting. He devoted his life, apart from his commercial activities, to work for the benefit of Anglo-Jewry. An heir to considerable wealth, he was able still further to increase it. He was the first Jewish director of the East India Company. Misfortune, however, ultimately overtook him. The earthquake in Lisbon where he had much property led to the loss of most of it. This was followed by the failure of the Dutch East India Company in which many English Sephardim as well as Dutch co-religionists had invested part of their fortunes. One blow following another dissipated practically all his property in the Old World, and when he died in 1786 he was in effect a poor man. Salvador owned also large tracts of land in North America to which in the days of his prosperity little attention was given. After his losses in Europe, his nephew and son-in-law, Francis Salvador, went there, apparently to settle, and purchased a part of these lands. Francis, however, became involved in the American rebellion, and taking part with the rebels among whom he quickly reached a position of influence was wounded and scalped in battle with the Red Indians at the early age of twenty-nine. In 1784, eight years after the death of his nephew, Joseph Salvador himself settled in Carolina, where by then he had sold almost the whole of his vast estate, presumably living on the proceeds. He died two years later at the age of seventy in circumstances very different from those to which he had long been accustomed. Quoting *The Charleston Morning Post and Daily Advertiser* of 30 December 1786, 'Yesterday died Joseph Salvador Esq., aged 86 years.[1] He was formerly a most eminent merchant in England, being one of those who furnished that Government with a million of money in two hours' notice, during the rebellion in the year 1745: and likewise was one of the greatest landholders in this country.'[2] As late as 1845 the Community received a legacy bequeathed by Jacob Salvador, a nephew of the Francis Salvador who was killed in North America. Of Sampson Gideon, another outstanding English Sephardi of the eighteenth century, mention will be made later.

This present series of brief biographical notes may be brought to a close with a reference to a *cause célèbre* which at the time attracted widespread attention—the breach of promise case of da Costa *v.* Villa Real. The defendant in this case, Mrs. Catharine (or Kitty) Villa Real was a daughter of Joseph da Costa, a son of Alvaro, who married Leonora, daughter of Dr. Fernando Mendes. While they were both children it was arranged that Kitty should marry her cousin Philip (or Jacob) Mendes da Costa, a brother of Emanuel Mendes da Costa, F.R.S. Philip, however, as he grew up, showed himself to be an undesirable character. In the meanwhile a very wealthy Marrano family named da Costa Villa Real escaped from Portugal and settled in London, and Kitty da Costa, at the age of seventeen, was married to a member, Joseph or John (also known as Isaac), a man much older than herself. He died after three years of married life, leaving his widow with an infant daughter and son and a very large fortune. Within three weeks the young widow engaged herself to Philip Mendes da Costa. Her father and other members of the family objected very strongly to the marriage, and Kitty was taken away to her father's country house at Totteridge where she was kept under restraint. Philip, being unable to see her or to get her to carry out her promise, after waiting a year, took proceedings against his fiancée for breach of promise in the Arches Court of Canterbury—the first instance of the recourse of Jews to the English high courts. The case was dismissed, but the disappointed suitor thereupon took further proceedings, claiming £100,000 damages. This claim was also rejected without troubling the defence. Mrs. Villa Real, perhaps

[1] This should of course be 70.
[2] For Francis and Joseph Salvador, see B. A. Elzas, *The Jews of South Carolina* (Philadelphia, 1905).

estranged from her kin by these events, later married William Mellish, later M.P. for Retford, and she and her two Villa Real children were baptized. Her daughter Sarah (Elizabeth) married the second Viscount Galway, and from her was descended among others the late Marquess of Crewe whose second wife was a descendant of Nathan Meyer Rothschild. If their son had survived he would in himself have united the families of Villa Real, Mendes da Costa, Cohen, and Rothschild.[1]

[1] The best account of the Villa Real romance is given in the *Trans. Jew. Hist. Soc. of Eng.*, vol. XIII, by M. J. Landa. Some of the letters that passed between the parties have been published in Mr. Cecil Roth's *Anglo-Jewish Letters*.

Some confusion was caused for a short time by the discovery by Mr. Richard Barnett in the archives of the Community of a letter in Portuguese addressed to the Mahamad, of which the following is a translation.

'My dear Sirs,
I beg to convey to you my most sincere thanks for the favour which you have shown for an unhappy and unfortunate man. It is my desire to ask of you that my turbulent and mad sister should be interred at the foot of her ancestors, husband, son, aunt and grandfather, she having requested her nephews that they should grant her the burial, which they did grant and I for my part will fulfil in every respect whatever you decide.

'ISAAC MORAIS PEREIRA.'
December 2nd 1756.

Preserved with this letter were two others in English. They run as follows.

'Blyth, *6 December 1756.*
'Dear Sir:
'You acted very right in regard to the Burying Ground and I am ready at any time to sign any Thing you think proper.
'I am,
Your affectionate Br.
'W. MELLISH.'
'To Benjamin da Costa Esq.
at the General Post Office, London.

'Gentlemen, By order of Mr. William Mellish, Lord and Lady Gallway and Mr. Villa Real I was to have acquainted Mrs. Villa Real that she might have that ground which was my sisters as she desired it so much. Being acquainted this day with her death, Mr. Mellish and Mr. Villa Real being out of town it is impossible for them to sign the order soon enough for her burial. If this will not do I will get Lord and Lady Gallway to sign any order as they are in town and Mr. Mellish as soon as he returns, and send it to Mr. Villa Real to sign. I am, Gentlemen, Your most obedient humble servant,
'Benjamin da Costa.'
2nd December 1756.

'To the Gentlemen of the Mamad.'

Further, the arrangement is confirmed by an entry in the Minutes of the Mahamad, dated 5 Kislev 5517 (December 1756) to the following effect: 'Rachel da Costa Villa Real having died the Gentlemen of the Mahamad have received a letter from her relative Isaac Morais Pereira asking for her to be interred in a grave reserved in the old Bet Haim by Isaac da Costa Villa Real to which they had agreed. This document was deposited with others in the safe.' Finally, in the cemetery there is a row of Villa Real graves, the last two of these being those

120   THE SEPHARDIM OF ENGLAND

The disjointed story told in this chapter indicates the road taken by the wealthier and more cultured of the English Jews as soon as they felt themselves securely settled in this country, out of the social and intellectual ghetto to which they had hitherto been accustomed, and in some cases there have been hints of the destination to which that road sometimes leads. The first Jewish settlers, however, lived also in a physical ghetto, self-imposed but none the less a ghetto on that account. This ghetto had no walls, but it had limits. It was not long before these limits were exceeded. The synagogue in Creechurch Lane and later in Bevis Marks remained for more than a century the physical centre of Sephardi Jewry, and most of its members lived very close to it. For many years they continued to live within easy reach, even though in a number of cases they moved to other and more fashionable parts of the City. But the practice also grew for the wealthier members to have country houses in addition to their town residences: country

of Isaac, buried in 5491 (1731) and Rachel, buried in Kislev 5517 (December 1756). This last grave was the one reserved by Isaac da Costa Villa Real for his wife, the future Mrs. Mellish.

Mrs. William Mellish had been Rachel or Catharine da Costa Villa Real before her marriage to William Mellish. The W. Mellish of Blyth of the second letter was her second husband and the Benjamin da Costa to whom it was addressed, her brother, who on marrying a non-Jewish wife had left the Jewish Community. He died less than three years later at the age of forty-seven. As Deputy Receiver-General of the Post Office, he was the first post-Resettlement civil servant of Jewish birth. The Lady Galway and Mr. Villa Real in the letter of Benjamin da Costa were the daughter and son of Mrs. William Mellish by her first husband. In view of these identifications it seemed at first sight that the Rachel da Costa Villa Real who was buried in the Bet Haim in December 1756 was identical with the Catharine Mellish, previously Rachel da Costa Villa Real (the only name recognized by the Jewish Community) who was buried in Blyth churchyard in 1747. The suggested explanation was that after nine years the body had been exhumed and reburied in Jewish consecrated ground. However, further investigation did not support this surmise. Abraham da Costa Villa Real, the refugee from Portugal who had settled in England with his family and died in 1737, had two sons, Isaac, otherwise Joseph, who married Catharine or Rachel da Costa and by her had two children of whom one, the daughter, was the future Viscountess Galway. The other of Abraham's two sons was Jacob, who died in 1733, two years after his brother. Abraham had also two daughters, of whom one, Mariana otherwise Sarah, married Moses de Morais Pereira. They had a son, Isaac, the writer of the letter to the Mahamad, and a daughter, Rachel. The last mentioned, Rachel de Morais Pereira, married her mother's brother, Jacob da Costa Villa Real, who died in 1733, leaving her a widow with a son Abraham, who died in August 1756. Rachel da Costa Villa Real (née Morais Pereira) died four months later, leaving a request that she should be buried at the feet of her grandfather (Abraham), her husband (Jacob), and her son (Abraham). The promise that this should be done, so far as it was in their power to do so, given by her nephews, Lord Galway and William Villa Real, was fulfilled. The only unanswered question that remains is, why did Isaac Morais Pereira refer to his sister as 'turbulent and mad', epithets that might not in all the circumstances have been inappropriate if applied to his aunt, the earlier Rachel da Costa (or Kitty) Villa Real?

SOME EIGHTEENTH-CENTURY PERSONALITIES 121

houses that is to say in districts that have long since been incorporated in Greater London. The extent of this dispersion of London Jewry can be learnt from the addresses of English Sephardim given in connexion with marriage, birth, and death announcements in the fashionable periodicals. Some of these, taken from the *London Magazine* for 1732 to 1785, give in chronological order:

'Highgate (1736: Fernando da Costa), Mincing Lane (1747: Mr. Lopez), Fenchurch Street (1750: Mr. Franco), Lime Street (1750: Miss Sally Salvador), Lincolns Inn Fields (1752: Miss Paiba), Lime Street (1753: Mr. Montefiore—a great uncle of Sir Moses), Wimbledon (1757: Joshua Levi), Stanmore (1760: Jacob Pereira), Red Lion Street, Holborn (1762: Solomon Mendes—the patron of literature), Islington (1769: Aaron Nunes Pereira), Devonshire Square (1772: Isaac Ximenes), Devonshire Square (1779: Jacob Mendes da Costa), Wimbledon (1782: Moses Isaac Levy—a president of the Jewish Board of Deputies).'

A similar story is told by the obituaries in the *Gentleman's Magazine* between 1731 and the end of the century. Taking the Sephardi names, most of the bearers of which are known, but a few of whom may have left the Community before the years stated, we get the following list:

'1736, Fernando da Costa at Highgate: 1737, Daniel Delvalle in Bunhill Fields; 1753, Joseph da Costa at Totteridge; 1750, Naphtali Levi Sunsino in Hackney; 1757, Joshua Levi in Wimbledon; 1759, Moses Lamego in Hackney and Jacob Fernandez Nunez in Stoke Newington; 1760, Joseph Treves in Mincing Lane; 1762, Samson Gideon at Belvedere, Kent; Solomon Mendes in Red Lion Street, Holborn and Siprut in Chelsea; 1764, Levi Pardo at Clapham Common; 1766, Salerno at Fulham and the Hon. Mrs. Salvador, Baroness Suasso, at Tooting; 1767, Francis Lindo at Isleworth; 1769, Daniel Baruch Lousada at Hackney; 1771, Mendes da Costa, in Bow Street, Covent Garden and Mr. Sylva in Moor Lane; 1774, Joseph de Aguilar at Margate; 1776 Abraham da Costa at Hampstead and Samuel da Costa in Broad Street Buildings; 1777, Samuel da Costa at Hackney; 1781, Mrs. d'Almeida at North End, Hampstead; 1782, Aaron Capadoce at Stanmore and Abraham Prado at Twickenham; 1784, Solomon de Medina at Stoke Newington; 1785, Elias Lindo in Devonshire Street; 1788, Joseph d'Almeida at Watford, Jacob Ancona in New Street, Bishopsgate, and Isaac Mendes da Costa in Heydon Square; 1789, Hananias Modigliani at Blackfriars; 1791, Mrs. Siprut (mother of Mrs. Benjamin d'Israeli), in New Broad Street; 1795, Mrs. Esther Franco in Charlotte Street, Bedford Square; 1796 Mordecai Rodriguez Lopez at Clapham Common, and David Alves Rebello in Hackney; 1798, Nathan Basevi at Billiter Square, and da Costa at Enfield Highway; and 1799, Jacob Mendes Furtado at Godstone, Surrey, and David Ximenes in Devonshire Street, Portland Place.'

As to their financial positions a few of the dowries and estates mentioned in the public press may be quoted:

'Miss Mendes da Costa to Mr. Aguilar, £30,000 (1756); Miss d'Aguilar to Mr. Azulay, £10,000 (1762); Fernando da Costa, "said to have died worth £300,000" (1736); Abraham Franco, "said to have died worth £900,000" (1777); Moses Lamego, £100,000 (1759); Benjamin Lara and Miss Jessurun, £10,000 (1758); Mr. Nunes and Miss da Costa, £11,000 (1756); Aaron Nunes Pereira, £100,000 (1769);'

and money had a very much higher value in those days than in these.

CHAPTER VIII
EXTERNAL AFFAIRS

WE HAVE SEEN how the individual members of the organized Jewish Community in this country, or many of them, in the course of the first century of its life, gradually began to pass out of a state of isolation into the fuller life, that of the people among whom they had made their home. So, in the same way, the organized community itself also began to develop interests outside of the narrower ones of London Jewry. In some respects they had always done so. No matter how much the fathers of Creechurch Lane desired to limit their own interests and those of their members to their own affairs, they were occasionally forced by circumstances to take cognizance of outside events and of their demands. This was particularly the case when the status, not yet finally established, of the Jewish Community seemed to be threatened. As time passed, relations between the Community and the Government and other constituted authorities of the land developed and instances occurred of legislative proposals and other acts of the administration in which Anglo-Jewry was deeply interested. In other directions also English Sephardi interests spread. Political affairs continued to take their place in the agenda. So also did the interests and doings of foreign Jewries, primarily but never exclusively Sephardi Jewries. In some cases the approaches of London Jewry to the authorities related solely to the welfare of foreign Jewries. In yet another respect the thoughts and efforts of those who guided the fortunes of the London Sephardim passed outside their own immediate circle. This took the form of co-operation with the Ashkenazi branch of Anglo-Jewry which had by the middle of the eighteenth century grown to a position approaching in influence that of the Sephardim, apart from outstripping them in numbers.

To turn to the first group of above-mentioned activities. The opening of a new synagogue in Bevis Marks practically coincided with the first step in the development of another institution which, wider than the synagogue and the Sephardi community, for long occupied the recognized position of the most influential in Anglo-Jewry. It is usual to date the establishment of the London Committee of Deputies of British Jews, more familiarly known as the Jewish Board of Deputies, to 1760, and in the narrower sense this is correct, for the history of that institution is continuous only from that year. The establishment of this committee was, however, the crystallization of an idea that had been floating in the minds of the directors of the London Sephardim for half a century and more, sometimes taking form, but only an ephemeral form, never until the middle of the eighteenth century striking permanent root. The seed first began to sprout on the 28th of Adar (March) 1702 when the Mahamad and Elders had under consideration a bill then before Parliament for compelling Jews to maintain those of their children who might accept the Protestant form of Christianity. The legislative proposal arose out of the refusal of Jacob Mendes de Brito to maintain his daughter who had been baptized.[1] To meet the threat the Mahamad appointed a committee, consisting of Jacob Gonzales, John Mendes da Costa, Jacob Salvador, and Moses Francia 'to attend to the business of the Nation which is before Parliament' and to take such measures as they might consider suitable, subject to the approval of the Mahamad. The measures that were taken, however, proved unsuccessful and the legislation to which the Jews took exception became law in May of that year. This legislation arose out of an appeal to the House of Commons by the clergy and lay authorities of those parishes in the City of London in which most of the Jews then lived. Parliament went into the matter thoroughly and heard a number of witnesses, including Jacob Mendes de Brito who said that the girl was not his daughter but a foundling who had been left on his doorstep in Portugal when he was still living in that country. The London Jewish Community petitioned against the bill, but this was of no avail. The churchwardens, before they appealed to Parliament, had taken proceedings at Quarter Sessions to compel de Brito to maintain the girl and had received the order for which they asked, but this decision was upset on appeal. The Committee, having been appointed for the one purpose only, was dissolved on its final failure, but the affair cost the Community over £255 in expenses. Twelve years later the Mahamad took another step which led also towards the establishment ultimately a permanent Board. George I, the first monarch of a new dynasty, ascended the throne in August 1714, and within a few weeks the Mahamad and Elders resolved to take steps to offer him their respectful assurances of loyalty. A generation later a still more positive step was taken in the same direction. A bill had been introduced into the Irish Parliament for enabling Jews to be naturalized but had been defeated in the Irish House of Lords by one vote.

[1] The records of the Community refer to the girl bluntly as de Britos' bastard.

It was felt in Bevis Marks that the failure was probably a consequence of the lack of interest shown on the part of the London Sephardi community. The Mahamad thereupon bestirred themselves, and it was on their motion that the Elders resolved

> 'that a Committee be appointed to make use of any opportunity that there may be for the benefit of our Nation, and recommend them to take, in case of necessity, in time the advice of the best legal authorities of the realm, and power is given them to call to their assistance any person of our Nation and to treat with the persons whom they may think fit; and this meeting promises to pay all the expenses that may be incurred and to seek, if possible, by any means to do so without the funds of the Nation being diminished; and moreover it is recommended to the said Senhores Deputados that they should keep a Minute-book, and this meeting promises that neither the Senhores of the Mahamad nor they will ever call upon them to produce it, and that they shall not be able to do anything without permission of the majority of the said Senhores Deputados in the affirmative.'

This resolution gave the Committee a certain measure of permanence by the introduction of a minute book, and also a certain amount of independence. The members appointed to the Committee were Benjamin Mendes da Costa, Daniel Jessurun Rodrigues (otherwise Francis Salvador), Jacob Fernandes Nunes, Jacob de Moses Franco, and Benjamin Mendes Pacheco. The first two of these shared between themselves the lay headship of the Community, and Jacob Fernandes Nunes was also prominent both in the City and in the affairs of the Community. When the Board of Deputies was finally established in 1760 two of these, Benjamin Mendes da Costa and Jacob de Moses Franco, were among the representatives of the Sephardi Community then chosen. Whether or not as a consequence of the appointment of this committee, the Naturalization Bill was again introduced into the Irish Parliament and on this occasion passed through both Houses (1747), but the royal assent was never given.

More serious in its possibilities was a charge, circulated by means of leaflets in 1732 by one Osborne, a person of no standing, to the effect that Portuguese Jews in London had cruelly murdered a Jewish woman with her newly born child, whose father, it was alleged, was a Christian. Osborne went further and said that such crimes in similar circumstances were usual on the Continent. These charges had their intended effect on the populace, and some recent Jewish arrivals from Portugal were attacked and assaulted in the London streets. The reaction of the Mahamad was immediate. Proceedings were instituted in the Court of Kings Bench and, after a little hesitation on the ground that the libel was general and no individuals directly affected by it could be indicated, the Court decided against Osborne on the ground that the libel was 'necessarily tending to raise tumults and disorders among the people and inflame them with an universal spirit of barbarity against a whole body of men, as if guilty of crimes scarce practicable and totally incredible'. The mob excitement aroused by Osborne's libels, however, did not subside immediately but gradually, and for the next few years the Congregation's accounts show payments to the City Marshal and the constables in acknowledgement of their services in keeping the rabble under control.

Another lawsuit—this time a civil one—in which the Community was involved some eleven years later had a less satisfactory conclusion. Elias de Paz, a member of the Community, bequeathed in 1743 a sum of £1,200 for the establishment of a *Yeshiba* for religious study and for the advancement of Judaism. Doubt arose whether this was a valid bequest inasmuch as the legacy was intended for the propagation of a religion other than Christianity. The case came before the Court of Chancery. Lord Hardwicke, the Lord Chancellor, in giving judgement, decided that the legacy must be disallowed. 'This is a bequest for the propagation of the Jewish religion, and though it is said that this is a part of our religion, yet the intent of this bequest must be taken to be in contradiction of the Christian religion, which is a part of the law of the land.' As to the disposal of the bequest the court decided, after further consideration, that it should be devoted to some other charitable object. In the end £1,000 went to the Foundling Hospital and the balance went in costs. This judgement concerned the propagation of the Jewish religion only, and was followed later in 1783 in a case in which money was bequeathed for the support of an (Ashkenazi) synagogue. Legacies for the benefit of Jewish charities were, however, unaffected. The earlier cases of the endowment of Jewish schools and houses of learning were gifts during life and not legacies and were undisputed. The several instances of legacies to the Congregation both before and after the year 1783 were presumably tacitly accepted as for the furtherance not of its religious but of one or more of its other functions.

Although the minute book or other records of the Committee appointed in 1746 to watch over the external interests of the Community—the forerunner of the Board of Deputies—have not survived, it is not to be taken that this committee was inactive, even if opportunities for action were infrequent. For instance, in the year 1753 there were two measures before Parliament in which Jewish interests were concerned. The one was a Marriage Bill, commonly known as Lord Hardwicke's Act, after the Lord Chancellor who was in charge of it, to regularize marriages and to prevent clandestine ones, in which provision was made to safeguard Jewish, and also Quaker, interests by waiving in the case of their marriages the requirement of banns or licences. The other still stands in Anglo-Jewish and in English history as the Jew Bill, a measure intended to facilitate the acquisition of English citizenship by foreign Jews resident in England. The importance of these two proposed measures was at once realized, and they were both at once referred to the standing committee of Deputies for their views. Both legislative proposals were favourable to Jewish interests, and both became law against little opposition. The Marriage Act was accepted without objection by the people generally and remained law until superseded by further legislation more than eighty years later.

The Jewish Naturalization Act of 1753 had, however, a different history. Until the year 1609 there was no bar to the naturalization as an English citizen of any foreign Jew settled in England. In that year, however, the acceptance of the Sacrament and the taking of the Oaths of Allegiance and Supremacy were made conditions of naturalization. This act was deliberately directed against Catholics: incidentally, it affected Jewish candidates, if there had been any, similarly. There was a slight modification of the law, which did not affect Jews, in 1663. Otherwise the legislation of 1609 continued in force until 1740 when the disability, so far as Jews resident in the American Colonies were concerned, was removed. After the legislation of that year a Jew living in North America had advantages over his kinsman in England. Naturalization was no longer barred to him, and in the subsequent thirteen years some two hundred Jews—men of substance, for the privilege was not for the poor—became English citizens, some of whom settled in England, where they retained their English citizenship. Those foreign Jews, however, who had been resident in England all the time remained under disability. Mention has already been made of the abortive attempt to secure facilities for the naturalization of foreign Jews in Ireland in 1745 and 1747. In 1753 the Whig Government of Henry Pelham decided to go forward and provide similar facilities in England. Their measure was accepted unanimously by the House of Lords. In the Lower House there was some opposition, but the measure was finally passed against a continually growing opposition by 96 votes to 55. This, however, was not the end of the story. A general election was almost due, and the Tory opposition took full advantage of the prejudices and ignorant fears that the controversy had aroused. Scurrilous attacks on the Jews and their supporters had appeared already in the debates in Parliament. When the scene was shifted to the press —the realm of the pamphlet and the broadside—the extravagance of the campaign grew still further. The caricaturists also entered the campaign, and many of their products that have survived well illustrate how political controversies were conducted in those days. In the end the Government was forced by public opinion to give way, and the pro-Jewish legislation was repealed. It was only after many years, and in a different age of political controversy, that this further step was retraced. The Jewish Community kept on the whole in the background throughout the controversy, but was by no means uninterested. The committee of Deputies watched the proceedings as they developed and their agent, Philip Carteret Webb, an attorney who was also an antiquary and politician, took, as the opportunity offered, whatever steps he considered desirable to secure the success of the Jewish cause. He certainly participated —anonymously—in the pamphlet war that broke out.[1] Pressure was also brought to bear in another direction. Joseph Salvador was in the ordinary course of his affairs in contact with public men. Among these were members of the Government and there has come down a memorandum submitted by him in January 1753 to the Duke of Newcastle, the brother of the Prime Minister, who was himself a secretary of state and in 1754 succeeded as First Lord of the Treasury. This memorandum put under seven headings the case for the legislation that was then under consideration. There can be no doubt that Salvador acted with the encouragement if not the approval of the Mahamad. In fact the Mahamad seems to have gone further than was justified in its quiet support of the legislation.

Sampson Gideon (in the Synagogue Abudiente) was the most

---

[1] An account of the development of the controversy together with a list of the publications to which it gave rise is given in vol. VI of the *Trans. Jew. Hist. Soc. of Eng.* which contains also an illustrated article, 'Satirical and Political Prints on the Jews' Naturalization Bill 1753', by Israel Solomons.

The accounts show total payments to Webb of £542 12s. 10d. 'in relation to the applications to Parliament concerning Naturalization' covering the years 1742 to 1753. Of this sum £290 12s. 10d. was on account of Webb's fees. Webb's expenses include payments to House of Commons clerks and others in official positions. Such payments were not then unusual. The details of the accounts show that the Mahamad was, through Webb, in close touch with members of the Government during the period of the preparation of the measure. Webb did other legal work for the Congregation during the same period for which he received additional payment.

THE TOWN HOUSE OF JOSEPH SALVADOR
From a water-colour by T. Hosmer Shepherd (1835)

CARICATURE OF SAMPSON GIDEON
From an engraving (1753)

prominent English Jew of his day. He came of a Sephardi family that, having escaped from Portugal, lived for a time on the Continent and then settled in the West Indies. Later Rehuel Abudiente (Rowland Gideon) and his brother, the elder Sampson, together with Rehuel's son, the younger Sampson, settled in London. There Rehuel took a prominent part in the direction of the Community, holding most of its honorary offices in turn. His brother Sampson also took his share in the work of the Community. Rehuel, a prosperous West Indian merchant, was the second Jew to become a freeman of the City of London (1722) at a time at which there were considerable difficulties in the way of the attainment of the desire of Jews for that privilege. The younger Sampson also at first showed some interest in Jewish affairs and was one of the literary contributors to Daniel Lopez Laguna's poetical translations of the Psalms. Sampson Gideon was twenty-one when his father died. His earliest interests were in finance, of a sort. He began his business life as a lottery ticket dealer. From that occupation he rose, at the age of thirty, to become one of the twelve Jewish members on the Exchange. Thence he developed into one of the leading financiers in England—for a time the leading one—the financial adviser and trusted councillor of successive governments, the supporter of the Government of the day in every crisis that arose, a man under whose advice and with whose support the fortunes of his country rose continually while his own private fortune expanded at the same time. At the time of the Forty-five panic when the Young Pretender and his army were already in Derbyshire and the Hanoverian King was preparing to retire to the Continent, Gideon placed both his valuable advice and his outstanding credit at the disposal of the Government and in this support he was seconded by the other Jewish brokers and merchants to a man. The Government, in the emergency, needed money. Gideon placed himself at once at the head of a small group that provided the Government with £1,700,000 for its immediate needs. Together with others he formed an association, when the credit of the Bank of England seemed to be becoming unstable, to purchase its notes at par, and the whole body of the Jewish merchants, encouraged by the Synagogue authorities, came forward in their support. Others devoted their efforts to importing bullion from abroad and lodging it ostentatiously with the Bank of England. Those who owned sea vessels placed them unreservedly at the disposal of the Government. The Jews of England both native and foreign born, in that time of crisis came out wholeheartedly in the defence of their country, and at their head was

Sampson Gideon. This outstanding loyalty of the Jews of England was fully appreciated in Government and other political circles. When after the crisis had passed a delegation was sent by the City to congratulate the King, a Jewish citizen was chosen as a representative of his community to be a member of it, and the Congregation was invited to send representatives to a meeting held in the Guildhall to express the loyalty of the City of London to the Crown. The Jewish Naturalization Bill of 1753 was undoubtedly to some extent intended to be a recognition of the services of the Jews during the crisis. Sampson Gideon, as a part acknowledgement of his services, had one of his ambitions gratified. Whether or not a Jew could own land was a matter of doubt. Gideon had a great desire to be a landowner, and a private Act of Parliament was therefore passed to enable him to own land. Another of his ambitions was to receive a title. But the time was too early for a Jew in England to be ennobled. However, a compromise was arranged. Gideon, although remaining a member of the Community, had married a non-Jewess and their children were not Jewish. His son was at Eton, and while still a boy was made a baronet and, later in life after his father's death, a peer, under the title of Lord Eardley. The peerage died with him, but from his daughters were descended Hugh Culling Eardley Childers, the Liberal statesman of the nineteenth century, Robert Erskine Childers, the novelist and rebel or patriot, according to where one's Irish sympathies lie, Sir Culling Eardley, the religious philanthropist, the present Lord Auckland, and a former Duchess of Norfolk. There is one other living survival of the family. Occasionally the name Rowlanda is found in some old-established English family as far from Jewry as it is possible to be. Yet this name is an echo of Rehuel Abudiente, otherwise Rowland Gideon, Sampson's father, and denotes descent from him. In the same way the curious female name Tryphena, also occasionally to be met with in families far removed from Jewry, indicates descent from Jacob Barrow (otherwise Baruch Lousada) and his wife Tryphena, daughter of Baron Lyon de Symons, and the equally distinctive Phila from Abraham, otherwise Naphtali Herz Franks, one of the earliest prominent Ashkenazim in England. That the Jewish services to the State were widely realized became clear in the course of the debates on the Naturalization Bill. One speaker in support of the measure mentioned a Jewish merchant of foreign birth, who, hearing in 1745

> 'that the Government was in distress for want of a sufficient number of small ships of war to guard our coasts, in order to

prevent the rebels receiving any succour from France, came to the Lords Commissioners of the Admiralty, and told them, that he had then no less than five stout privateers in the rivers, all ready to put to sea every one of which should be at the Government's disposal, and, further, that he was so far from expecting any recompense or reward for this testimony of his loyalty, or for the service they might be of, that as long as the Government had occasion for them, he would maintain them all at his own expense.'[1]

Sampson Gideon himself showed no interest in the campaign for naturalization facilities. As a natural-born English subject it could be of no benefit to him. Nevertheless he was too prominent an English Jew not to be brought into the discussions, an introduction that could have given him no pleasure. In one hostile pamphlet[2] in which it was foretold that if the measure was made law all the rich Jews of the world would flock to England and set up the Messiah, Sampson was offered as a candidate for the office, with the remark that he was certainly as well qualified as Cromwell, an allusion to the rumour current a century earlier that a deputation of Jews had come to England to satisfy themselves whether or not the Protector Cromwell was the Messiah. In the political prints of the time Gideon appeared more than once, as often as not mixed up with the alleged bribing of the supporters of the Naturalization Bill. In one the statue of Queen Anne, in front of St. Paul's Cathedral, has been pulled down and one of Gideon substituted for it. In fact so intense was Gideon's annoyance at the manner in which his name was brought into the agitation and at an unauthorized indiscretion whereby the Jewish authorities gave the impression that he shared their ardour in the cause, that the controversy led direct to his final severance from the Community. In their advocacy of the measure the Mahamad and Elders spoke in the name of the entire community as they were fully entitled to do. They, however, mentioned Gideon, the most prominent English Jew of the time, by name, without his authority or even informing him. This increased his annoyance, and on 5 September 1753 he wrote formally to the Mahamad.

'The receipt of this will not be more displeasing to you than the writing is to me. All the satisfaction I have is, that your Selves have given the occasion, and made is necessary.

[1] *Parliamentary History*, vol. XIV (1395–1402).
[2] *An Answer to a Pamphlet*, p. 33.

'Your assuming a power of representing me in point of political or Civil Interest, as I understand you have done in a late Instance, is certainly as little consistent with prudence, as with the Law of Nature, or of the Land, and the more so, as you knew the matter solicited for, to be directly contrary to my declared Sentiments, and my dislike to all Innovations. But to prevent all future, as well as to rectify all past mistakes, Take notice, that I for my Self do in the most solemn manner disavow all power that you may at any time have assumed, in civil or secular Affairs, and more especially that, which you, without any Colour, have taken upon your Selves, to represent the Jews in general, and to request things in their names, or undertake for them, in any manner whatever, and whatever you may have done in this respect, of what kind or nature soever, I hereby, as to me in particular, declare null and void, without force and of no Effect. I do further declare and desire you will take notice, that I am thoroughly satisfyed you never had, nor have, nor can have, any such power or Authority from me, and if you should at any time pretend to it, I absolutely protest against it, in all Instances, as against reason, Custom, Law and Justice, and that I neither am, nor ever will be, concluded or bound by it, and the more effectually to prevent my being any ways affected by any such unwarrantable and unjustifiable Steps or Attempts for the future, I hereby declare that I am not, nor will be from henceforth, any Member of your Society or Congregation by whatever name you may have entered or distinguished me therein; and if my name is any where entered, and stands as one of the Members of such Society or Congregation, I desire it may be forthwith erased or struck out, and that I may not be any longer considered as a member thereof in any respect.'

The letter was signed 'Samson Gideon', not 'Abudiente' as he was known in the Congregation, and was sent by hand by means of a notary, by whom the signature was witnessed. The receipt of this letter was duly recorded in the minutes of the Mahamad under the date 3 Heshvan 5514 (1753), and it was resolved by the Elders by twenty votes to six, 'that the resignation as a Yahid by Simpson de Rehuel Abudiente be accepted, he having resigned in the name of Sampson Giddion'.

But this was not quite the end. Gideon died nine years later, in 1762, and when his will was opened it was found that he had bequeathed a legacy of a thousand pounds to the Congregation, as well as other legacies to the Congregational Orphanage and the

Beth Holim, asking that he be buried with his people in the Jewish cemetery and that annually, on the Day of Atonement, his name be commemorated with those of other benefactors of the Congregation. Furthermore, it transpired that, although he had formally withdrawn from the Community, his contribution to the Synagogue funds had been regularly paid anonymously through a member with whom he had continued his friendship. His wishes were complied with and his legacy accepted. To this day an attentive listener in the Synagogue in Bevis Marks as the evening service on *Kippur* comes to a close will catch, in the lengthy list of benefactors of the Congregation, the name of Simpson de Rehuel Abudiente.[1] Eighty years later, in 1842, the family of Sampson Gideon asked for permission to restore his tombstone, and this permission was at once given.

The Forty-five or the Young Pretender's invasion of England and the support given to the Government by Sampson Gideon and other prominent members of the Community have already been mentioned. These individuals did not, however, stand alone in Anglo-Jewry. One method of showing the loyalty of the nation as a whole to the House of Hanover was the inscription of the names of citizens in the Association Oath Rolls. This movement was widely and eagerly taken and the Jewish citizens of London were not behind their Christian fellow citizens in this respect. Among the Sephardim the matter was taken up officially, for the Mahamad under the presidency of Joseph Dias Fernandez ordered a proclamation in the Synagogue in the following terms:

> 'Inasmuch as in this time of peril to these realms all good and loyal subjects of His Majesty have demonstrated their good zeal by joining associations and making other efforts for the public welfare, and as an association of all the residents in this City has been opened in the Guildhall, it is recommended to all gentlemen of this Nation that they join it, because it will do honour to our Nation, and will be well received; and the Gentlemen of the Mahamad do not doubt, from the good disposition which they have always seen in the said gentlemen, that they will shew themselves ready to give their aid in all the exigencies that there

[1] There is no adequate biography of Sampson Gideon, who is well worthy of one. Scattered in a number of publications much information regarding him is to be found, especially in the *Dictionary of National Biography*, in Part I of the *Bevis Marks Records*, and in vols. VI and XIII of the *Trans. Jew. Hist. Soc. of Eng.* Miss Lucy Stewart Sutherland, C.B.E., read a paper before the Jewish Historical Society on 'Sampson Gideon' on 25 April 1949, in which much further material was produced for the first time. This paper has not yet been published.

may be in this critical time, as is the duty of all who live under this Government.'

As a practical step in the same direction the Mahamad in advance and at once paid their contribution to the extraordinary levy or tax that was imposed for the maintenance of the Militia. At the time of another crisis, in 1779, when the country was surrounded by jealous enemies and threatened with invasion, the Elders were called together to consult with and advise their Deputies for public affairs as to what measures the Community should take in the emergency. After a discussion two resolutions were adopted, the English as well as the Portuguese text being recorded in the minutes. In the one the Yehidim were advised to respond generously to the appeal that was about to be made for contributions to the fund that was being raised for the defence of the kingdom. The other resolution was in these terms: 'That in Case of an Actual Invasion in any part of Great Brittain it is recommended that Our Yehidim and Others of our Community should enter Chearfully Personally or otherwise into such Loyal Associations which may be formed.' And the resolutions of the Elders were in due course reported to the sister Ashkenazi congregations.

The Jewish Board of Deputies, as at present constituted, came into existence in 1760. The immediate occasion was the accession to the throne of a new king, George III, and the desire of his loyal subjects who worshipped in Bevis Marks, dutifully to offer to him their congratulations. The Committee of Deputies which had been constituted in 1746 was not used for this purpose. It seems to have lapsed, killed perhaps by the unfortunate end of the Naturalization agitation. The function of the new committee was not to be merely that of courtiers—but also to revive the functions of the earlier committee. On the 24th of Heshvan 1760 the Elders of 'the Portuguese Nation' resolved

> 'That 7 Gentlemen of this body be appointed. That it be left to three of them to consider what should be done on the present occasion to testify to His Majesty our homage; and thereafter to deal with the most urgent matters which present themselves in connection with our Nation. And that the said Gentlemen should not seek for new privileges for such Nation without first communicating the matter to the Elders. And that the said Gentlemen have power to confer with any persons whom they should think necessary. But that no business be transacted unless one of the three said Gentlemen be present.'

The seven original members of this committee were Jacob de Moses Franco and Benjamin Mendes da Costa, survivors from the earlier committee, Jacob Nunes Gonzales, Moses de Joseph da Costa, Joseph Jessurun Rodrigues (otherwise Salvador), Isaac Jessurun Alvares, and Isaac Fernandes Nunes, all prominent Sephardi merchants. The first business of this committee was to take steps to present an address of congratulation to the King, and to this end Salvador, who had already connexions with the Government and the court, was deputed to wait on the Lord Chamberlain, the Duke of Devonshire, a former prime minister, to seek his advice and guidance. Salvador reported that he had been very sympathetically received and advised that the Congregation should send a deputation with an address to the Prime Minister and that the latter would see that it was presented to His Majesty. This they did and in return received a message from His Majesty to the effect that he had received the congratulations of the Congregation with extreme pleasure and desired to assure them of the esteem in which he held them, and that he would always keep them in his favour. At the same time the Committee sent a similar address to the Princess of Wales, congratulating her on the accession of her son to the throne. The Princess of Wales in reply ordered that the Deputies be summoned to pay in person their respects to her, and they were consequently received by her and her son and daughter.[1]

[1] A related matter was the offering of prayers in the Synagogue on the 7th of Kislev 1737 for the recovery of Queen Caroline who was seriously ill. Offerings amounting to £37 were made on the occasion, and this sum was devoted to the relief of the non-Jewish poor of the city. The prayer for the King was a normal part of the service in England as elsewhere. Pepys mentions it on the occasion of his visit to the Synagogue in 1663. The form of prayer which differs but little from that still in use has survived. It was given in English in Leon da Modena's *The History of the Rites, Customs and Manner of Life of the Present Jews throughout the World*, published in London in 1650, and is worthy of being quoted in full.

'He that giveth salvation unto Kings, and dominion unto Lords, He that delivered his servant David from the sword of the enemy, He that made a way in the sea, and a path in the strange waters, blesse and keep, preserve and rescue, exalt and magnify, and lift up higher and higher, our Lord—The King of Kings defend him in his mercy, making him joyfull, and free him from all dangers and distresse. The King of Kings, for his goodnesse sake, raise up and exalt his planetary star, and multiply his dayes over his Kingdome. The King of Kings for his mercies sake, put into his heart, and into the heart of his Counsellors, and those that attend and administer to him, that he may shew mercy unto us, and unto all the people of Israel. In his dayes and in our dayes, let Judah be safe, and Israel dwell securely, and let the Redeemer come to Israel, and so may it please God. Amen.'

In 1741 a special service was held in the Synagogue in support of an appeal by the King but the object of the appeal has not been recorded.

In 1756 and 1759 fasts were ordered by the King, George II, when the French, in the course of the Seven Years' War, were mustering a fleet as if to invade England. Sermons in Spanish, which were printed, were preached on these

A week later the Board of Deputies held its first business meeting on 26 November. The business to be considered was a communication from the Jewish Community in Jamaica, a body for the most part Sephardi which had been established almost as long as had been the Sephardim in England. The communication received from the Jamaica Community cannot be found, and as only the decision of the committee survives, its subject is a matter of conjecture. The middle of the eighteenth century, however, was a period of considerable excitement among the Jews of Jamaica. Hitherto, like their co-religionists in England, they had been excluded from the political franchise. The Act of Parliament of 1740 which had, in other respects, eased their position, was taken as a peg on which to hang demands for further concessions. In particular the Jews of the island, or more properly the majority of them, demanded political emancipation; on the other hand, there was a proposal for the imposition of a special tax on the Jews. In these circumstances a state of unsettlement and excitement was inevitable. There were, furthermore, other events and movements

occasions by Isaac Nieto and Moses Cohen de Azevedo. On the death of George II in 1760, a sermon in Spanish was preached in the Synagogue by Isaac Mendes Belisario, the rubi or teacher in the Congregational school, and this was later published in English. Later in the same year Moses Cohen de Azevedo preached a sermon of congratulation on the accession of George III, and sixteen years later, in December 1776, in the course of the war with the rebel American colonists, a special service was held on the occasion of a fast day appointed by the King 'to humble ourselves before the Supreme Being, imploring pardon for our sins'. The order of service and sermon preached on the occasion by de Azevedo, who had by then become Haham, were printed both in English and Spanish, as was also his Accession Sermon. In the midst of the war with the French Republic, during the Feast of Hanucah in 1792, Hasdai Almosnino, the Dayan of the Community, at the request of the Mahamad preached a sermon impressing on his congregation the virtues of loyalty to their King and Country, and in the following year a special service was held for 'the repentance of our sins and the success of the British arms, by command of His Majesty', also on an officially appointed fast day. There were other special services and prayers in the course of the same long-drawn-out war—on 19 December 1797, in thanksgiving for the naval victories of Jervis and Duncan; 'for pardon of our sins . . . dearness and scarcity of provisions, the success of His Majesty's arms and the spreading . . . peace over us' on 13 February 1801; for the recovery of the King's health, on 2 May 1801; on the signing of the Treaty of Amiens in 1802. When war broke out again in the following year, there was another service at which prayers were offered for the success of the army. The victory of Trafalgar was celebrated in all the synagogues in 1805, and the King's Jubilee on 25 October 1809, when the Haham gave an address. Finally the end of the war was again prematurely celebrated in the Synagogue in Bevis Marks in 1814 and yet again, after the Battle of Waterloo in the following year. In the year 1814 also, in the Sabbath service of 23 October, 'a form of praises and thanksgiving to the Almighty God for the abundant Harvest lately granted' was incorporated. Later, in the midst of the Crimean War, on 26 April 1854, there was a service for 'Repentance and Success of our Arms', and in 1878 one 'To celebrate the restoration of peace and the Proclamation of religious liberty in Bulgaria, Servia and Rumania'. This which concerned the Jews only as part of the general population. The immediate difficulty arose out of one of these latter, the proclamation of martial law, a consequence of a negro rebellion in the course of which many whites were massacred. The Committee of Deputies, after taking the letter from the Jamaica Community into consideration, resolved that sympathy should be expressed with them in their trouble and that all possible assistance would be given to them, but, in view of the recent death of the King and its possible effect on the status of the Jews of England, the English Jews themselves were a little apprehensive. However, the newly appointed Governor of the Colony, William Henry Lyttelton, who had not yet taken up his office and was still in England, would be approached. The Jews of Jamaica must, however, remember that, so long as martial law was in force, it was their duty to obey without question all orders that were published, even though they might involve the desecration of the Sabbath. Nunes Gonzales and Salvador had interviews with Lyttelton and Thomas Pownall, the Secretary to the Board of Trade, an office which in that day

latter marked the end of the Russo-Turkish War. In 1883, on the first day of the Feast of Tabernacles, the service was devoted to prayers for 'the success of our Arms' in the first Sudan War, and there was a second special service for the same object in 1885. The South African War, at the end of the nineteenth century, was marked in the Synagogue by a weekly prayer during its duration and special services in aid of the National War Fund, and on 11 June 1902 on its cessation. In this war period also fell the special service, on 2 February 1901, in memory of Queen Victoria. On the occasion of her Diamond Jubilee there had also been special services at Bevis Marks, Manchester, and Ramsgate. There were special services also, the ark and reading desk being draped in black, on the occasions of the funerals of George III, George IV, and William IV. On the last occasion, as the funeral was appointed for a Saturday, the service in Bevis Marks was held on the following day, a choir taking part in it and the sermon being preached by a lay member of the Congregation, Abraham Alexander Lindo, and when in 1843 the Duke of Sussex, a son of George III, who had shown much interest in Jewish affairs and was on friendly terms with several prominent members of the Community, died, a similar service was held in Bevis Marks in his memory. On this occasion the preacher was Louis Loewe, an Ashkenazi scholar, who had assisted the Duke of Sussex in his Semitic studies and was also 'Oriental Secretary' to and the companion of Sir Moses Montefiore on some of his missions on behalf of foreign Jewries. Many years later Loewe's grandsons became Yehidim. Special prayers were also recited on the frequent occasions of the birth of a child to Queen Victoria and on the infrequent ones of attempts on her life. On the occasion of the birth of the future King Edward, David Meldola was asked to consult with the Ashkenazi authorities so that as far as possible the prayers recited in all the synagogues on the occasion should be uniform, and in 1864, on that of King Edward's elder son, the future Duke of Clarence, a special prayer was recited. There was a special service in his memory when he died in 1892.

Earlier, in 1694 and 1702 respectively, elegies in Hebrew on the occasion of the deaths of Queen Mary and King William were written by Joseph Abendanon, but not published, and in 1700 a similar one on that of the Heir Presumptive, the Duke of Gloucester.

included also the functions of the Colonial Office of today. The interview was in all respects satisfactory. The deputation was reminded that instructions had been repeatedly sent to Jamaica that the special taxation of the Jews was contrary to Government policy and would not be tolerated even though the local legislature should adopt such a proposal. On the subject of the militia and the consequent necessity for Sabbath duty, the Governor would endeavour to ease the situation so that the Jews, while serving by the side of their fellow citizens, might be relieved of the need for performing tasks on the Sabbath that were contrary to their conscience. Shortly afterwards news was received to the effect that the proposed special taxation of the Jews had been rejected by the island legislature by fifteen votes to thirteen, and a new First Lord of Trade and Plantations having been appointed in the person of Samuel, Lord Sandys, Salvador and Isaac Jessurun Alvarez waited on him to congratulate him on his appointment and to take the opportunity to discuss the Jamaica troubles. From him they received further assurances and were told they need have no fear. But it was not desirable that publicity should be given to the matter nor was it good policy that Jews should be given a privilege over their non-Jewish fellow citizens and exempted from service in the militia.

Since the previous occasion in 1746 on which the Mahamad and Elders had appointed a Committee of Deputies to watch over the interests of the Jews of England and to represent them *vis-à-vis* the Government and other public authorities, the numbers and importance of the Ashkenazi branch of Anglo-Jewry had considerably increased. With this growth had come a new sense of pride and a feeling of responsibility. With a preponderance of the poorer classes and very few members who could meet the leading Sephardim as equals, socially or in substance, they had previously been satisfied to leave the defence and representation of Jewish interests to the senior branch of the Community, which they recognized was far better fitted for the task. But by the middle of the eighteenth century there had been a change. The members of the large family of Franks had no need on any occasion to withdraw into retirement in the presence of Sephardi magnates. Other Ashkenazi families, mostly of Dutch origin, the several Salomons, Levy, Adolphus, had settled in England and were prospering there. They were no longer satisfied to leave everything to the Sephardim and, although with no desire to act independently, wished to share in the external public activities of Anglo-Jewry. When therefore the Ashkenazim learnt of the approach to the King that had been made by the

Sephardi Deputies, the heads of the two Ashkenazi Congregations —the Great and the Hambro—Aaron Franks and Levy Salomons, the great-grandfather of the future Sir David Salomons, very temperately inquired why they had not been asked to join their Sephardi colleagues. It was explained that in approaching the King, the Sephardim had only been following a long-standing precedent, but if the Ashkenazim wished to follow their example they saw no objection. On the other hand, the Ashkenazim might prefer to join in the delegation to the Princess of Wales that was being arranged. To this the Ashkenazim agreed, and the deputation that was received consisted of Salvador for the Sephardim and Franks for the Ashkenazim. This agreement led to a firmer one, one not only for representation at court and elsewhere on somewhat similar occasions of the Jews of England. At first there were two parallel committees, and it was resolved 'that each Nation should communicate to the other what they were doing in public affairs'. But it was not many years before the two independent committees became a joint one, and although the Sephardi Community, as the numbers of the Ashkenazim and of their synagogues increased, not only lost their predominance but obtained in numbers but an insignificant membership of the Board this agreement and co-operation continued for almost two centuries. Henceforward the foreign and external affairs of the Community were taken over by the Committee of Deputies, the Mahamad and Elders being kept informed of whatever steps were taken.[1]

There was, however, another group of dealings with public authorities other than the Government—a section of the external relations of the Community during the eighteenth century—that calls for mention. The relations between the Community and the City Corporation were necessarily close, and although the plane on which they met was lower the occasions of contact were far more frequent. The relations between the City and the Jews, at the beginning not very friendly, gradually but slowly improved. Perhaps the annual gifts to the Lord Mayor and to some of his entourage, of which mention has been made, contributed to this *rapprochement*. At any rate they continued, uninterrupted and subject to only minor changes, until 1780, a silver cup being substituted for a salver or a purse, well filled, at times, or chocolates taking the place of sweetmeats. It was not only the Lord Mayor who benefited from these gifts. The expansiveness of the donors

---

[1] A chronological record of the principal activities of the Committee of Deputies from its constitution in 1760 is given in *A Century and a Half of Jewish History* by C. H. L. Emanuel.

spread, more or less willingly, further. For instance, at the end of the year 1685 there is not only an entry in the accounts of the payment of £25 7s. for the salver, weighing 86 oz. 18 dwts., and of £5 10s. for the sweetmeats, but of the payment of a further ten shillings to the servants of the Lord Mayor, and four weeks later of £2 0s. 5d., the cost of twenty pounds of chocolate for which it would seem a request had been made. In 1689 the salver, although a little lighter in weight, cost twelve shillings more, and the sweetmeats, '40 lb. of various qualities', £4 13s. 8d. But this year 14s. 6d. had to be paid in addition to the Lord Mayor's men for fetching and delivering the present. By 1707 the price of silver had fallen tenpence an ounce, but the total expenditure on the gift was little changed. Thirty pounds of sweetmeats were sent with it, and again the Synagogue had to pay 14s. 6d. to the Lord Mayor's officers for delivering it. The earliest entry in the series was in 1678 when £55 4s. was expended on presents to the two 'Maiores' (? the Lord Mayor and a colleague). The following year the cost of the gift fell to £27 11s. for a piece of silver weighing $85\frac{3}{4}$ oz. (£18 5s. 10d.) with sweetmeats. In 1692 the Congregation more or less willingly provided sweetmeats at a cost of 25s. for a party to the friends of the Lord Mayor. By the year 1738 the cost had increased appreciably. The plate, weighing $111\frac{1}{2}$ oz. in that year, cost £40 10s. and fifty pounds of chocolate £10 12s. 6d. The accounts say at 4s. a pound, but this is an understatement. That year the officers of the Lord Mayor received £1 6s. for delivering the gift. Finally, as has been said, the practice was brought to an end in 1780. The minute recording this decision runs as follows: 'Resolved (1) that it will be convenient and proper for the future to cease giving the present which hitherto has been given to the Lord Mayor after this year. (2) That the best manner of doing it becomingly will be that the Senhores Parnassim who should bring the present this year should insinuate that henceforth we shall be obliged to discontinue it for various reasons which the said Senhores will be able to give.' The Senhores Parnassim do not, however, seem to have been sufficiently explicit on this occasion, or perhaps their message was not passed on by the Lord Mayor to his successor, for the following year the new Lord Mayor, not having received the usual gift, inquired through a member of the Congregation the reason for the omission. The Mahamad were therefore forced to give a formal explanation and write as follows:

'Sir, The Wardens of the Portuguese Jews' Synagogue having received by you a Message from the Right Honourable Lord

Mayor concerning the usual present made to the Lord Mayor direct me to request you to acquaint his Lordship most respectfully that the great increase of the Portuguese Jewish poor and the Decrease of the Finances given for their Support, had lain the Elders of their Nation under the Necessity amongst other Savings to Adopt the Discontinuance of the Present usually made to the Lord Mayor, which they very reluctantly acquainted his Lordship's Predecessor, with the Motives which induced them to take that Measure; As that Present was made out of the Monies contributed for the Relief of the Poor for which that Fund is greatly insufficient. They hope his Lordship will not consider the Resolution taken in this Matter as any ways tending to a particular Mark of Disrespect to his Lordship, but that it solely arises from the Necessity of their Situation, and that sentiments towards his Lordship are those of the most unfeigned and respectful esteem. J. Moron, Gabay.'

This letter brought the story to an end, at any rate, so far as the Congregation was concerned. The Lord Mayor and his staff were, however, not the only recipients of the Congregation's generosity. Under the date 17 Sebat 5489 (1729) appears the entry 'To the servants of Sir Robert Walpole 18/–'. Walpole was then at the height of his political career.

That these courtesies were not always on the one side only appears from an entry in the minutes for the year 1703. The Mahamad had learnt that invitations to the Lord Mayor's Banquet of that year would probably be received, and the Elders, or some of them, were in consequence much perturbed. They would have preferred to have remained in the obscurity in which they felt themselves more comfortable. The problem as to what steps should be taken in the event of such an invitation being received could, however, not be evaded, and it was therefore decided, after a ballot, that if such an invitation were received the Mahamad should nominate sixty persons, twenty of whom should attend each of the banquets. And if a member nominated refused the invitation he should be fined two guineas, and if he failed to pay he should not be given any *mitzva* in the Synagogue. Both the hospitality of the Lord Mayor and the social modesty of the ordinary member of the Community were more patent in those days than in these.

There were, however, more important matters in which the City and the Congregational authorities came in contact in those days. The one was the eligibility of Jews for the Freedom of the

City. In the past Rowland Gideon (Rehuel Abudiente) had been a liveryman of the Painter Stainers Company and a Freeman of the City, and on his death his son, Sampson Gideon, had succeeded him. Some years later Isaac Rathom had been a liveryman of the Loriners Company and a Freeman of the City, and when he died his son, Abraham Rathom, one of the *samasim* of the Congregation, applied to succeed him, not without the encouragement of the Mahamad, for exclusion from the Freedom deprived those who so suffered of some highly prized economic advantages. Rathom's petition was dismissed. The decision rested with the aldermen. In the course of the hearing, it transpired that in the past Jews had occasionally been granted the Freedom. This discovery scandalized the aldermen, for implicitly if not explicitly Jews should have been refused the privilege. An inquiry was ordered and it was found that no less than six members of the Jewish Community—all Sephardim—had been admitted since the admission of Joseph Robles in 1687. The rejection of Rathom's application, in the eyes of the Elders of the Congregation, seriously affected the interests of their members, and early in 1738 they appointed a Committee of Deputies to watch developments and to take whatever steps they might consider desirable. This committee instituted proceedings in the Court of King's Bench to require the City Chamberlain to show cause why Rathom should not be admitted to the Freedom. The reply was that an oath taken on the New Testament was required before anyone could be admitted and that Rathom had refused to take one. The Chief Justice upheld the City Chamberlain, and almost a century had to pass before a Jew was again admitted to the Freedom of the City.

The subject of admission as sworn brokers was to some extent related to that of the freedom of the City, since, so far as non-Jews were concerned, this freedom was an essential qualification. At first admission to this profession was accorded to Jews, and even before 1660 one Jew, Solomon Dormido, had been accepted. In the subsequent thirty-seven years twenty-one other Jewish brokers —two or three of whom had been previously baptized—all Sephardim, were admitted. By that year the number of Jewish brokers had so increased that the corner of the Royal Exchange in which they were accustomed to gather became known as Jewes Walk. The entire subject of the admission of brokers, however, got into a state of disorder and in 1697 the Corporation of the City obtained Parliamentary authority for making regulations. The number of brokers was in consequence limited to 124, of whom twelve were to be Jews and twelve non-Jewish aliens. These figures gave to the latter two classes brokers far in excess of their proportion in the population. The Jewish brokers were at the same time formally relieved of the necessity of being freemen, and the oath of admission was modified in their favour. Of the twelve Jewish brokers appointed in that year ten were Sephardim and an eleventh, Benjamin Levy, also a member of Bevis Marks.[1] But the Jewish prospective brokers were not satisfied with the number allotted. The members of the French and Dutch communities were equally dissatisfied, but had had their petition for an increase in the number allotted to them rejected in 1708. Thirty-one years later, in 1739, a step was taken by Jewish would-be brokers. The minutes of the Mahamad record that on the 5th of Shebat of that year Isaac Levy and Gabriel Lopes de Brito on behalf of themselves and other members of the Congregation, represented that the number of Sephardi sworn brokers was inadequate and asked the Mahamad to consider the advisability of approaching the Lord Mayor and Court of Aldermen with a view to an increase in their number. The Mahamad referred the matter to the usual Committee of Deputies, consisting on this occasion of Moses da Costa, Daniel Jessurun Rodrigues (Francis Salvador), Benjamin Mendes Pacheco, Benjamin Mendes da Costa, and Jacob Israel Suasso, to take whatever steps they might consider suitable to attain the desired end. The Deputies prepared a petition which they proposed to present to the Lord Mayor and Court of Aldermen and, the Mahamad assenting, the petition was presented. This action, however, obtained no noticeable success, for it was not until 1745, six years later, that another Jew was admitted. This was Isaac Levy, the principal petitioner to the Mahamad in 1739. But his appointment was not a new creation. He merely succeeded Jacob Alvares who had been admitted in 1714. In the same year, 1745, a second Jew, David Salomons, an Ashkenazi, was admitted.

In the year 1777 an attempt was made to impose Church rates on the authorities of the Synagogue. The wardens were called on by the vestry clerk of Cree Church to pay these rates. They, however, objected, producing legal opinions from leading authorities in support of their objections. These opinions were accepted and no further claim was made against the Synagogue authorities.

In one other matter at the beginning of the eighteenth century the Mahamad came into relation with the authorities of the City and at the same time showed one of the then very rare occasions of co-operation with the Ashkenazi authorities. The approach to

[1] For the names of the Jewish brokers, see *Miscellanies of the Jewish Historical Society of England*, vol. III.

the Corporation was at the instance of the Ashkenazim. There had been a serious quarrel within the Ashkenazi Community and aggrieved members threatened to establish a new congregation, independent of the original and until then the only one. One of the laws of the Sephardi Community prohibited, with very heavy penalties for transgression, the opening of any other Sephardi place of worship or even the holding of private worship, without the permission of the Mahamad, within six miles of Bevis Marks. The Ashkenazi authorities, although they had no similar law, were anxious to enforce a similar practice. Both communities considered themselves too small for the luxury of more than one place of worship. Furthermore they were disinclined to tolerate a second and probably, ultimately at any rate, rival community. In this matter of the establishment of a second community the views of the Ashkenazim and of the Sephardim were identical. Aaron Franks, the Parnas of the Great Synagogue, thereupon approached Abraham Mendes, who held a similar office among the Sephardim, and together they petitioned the Court of Aldermen to prohibit the erection of a second Ashkenazi synagogue. Their prayer was granted. Marcus Moses, the leader of the rebels, had to admit himself defeated. After a time he went abroad but returned to England in 1721 with a considerable fortune. He then commenced to build a synagogue in his garden. The heads of the Duke's Place (Great) and Bevis Marks communities again appealed to the City authorities, who once more ordered the work to stop. This time, however, Marcus Moses ignored the prohibition. The work proceeded and the new synagogue, afterwards called the Hambro, was completed and opened in 1726. The other parties to the dispute silently acquiesced in the *fait accompli*.

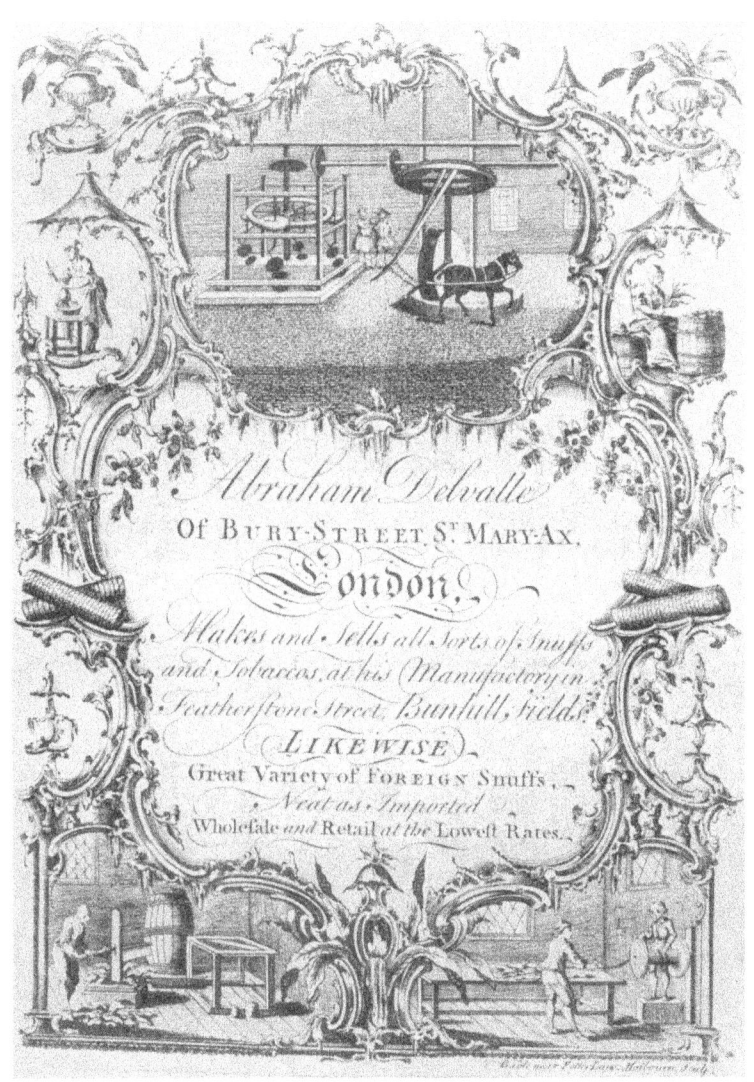

TRADE CARD OF ABRAHAM DELVALLE
(Grandfather of David Ricardo and of Mrs. Rebecca Lowry)

NAPHTALI BASEVI
Grandfather of Lord Beaconsfield: Warden of
the Congregation (1791-2)

DAVID ALVES REBELLO
From an engraving

CHAPTER IX

THE SEPHARDIM BEYOND THE SEAS

AS HAS BEEN mentioned incidentally on an earlier page, the first founders of the Amsterdam Sephardi and Jewish community, refugees from Portugal, tarried for a short time in England before they made their way to their final destination in the Netherlands. In greater but by no means full detail the story has been told of the return some two generations later of some of the first Jewish settlers in Amsterdam to join with fellow Sephardim—some direct from Spain or Portugal, others after a temporary residence in France—to establish a community in London. Thus the London Sephardi community may be considered a child of that of Amsterdam. The parent of the Bevis Marks Community is known and so are her children—those communities in the western hemisphere that owe their existence in greater or less measure to the support given them by the mother community in London. The eldest of these is that of Dublin, except that the present Jewish community in that city passed generations ago out of the Sephardi orbit and has now for almost two centuries been counted among the centres of Ashkenazi Judaism. Yet, as has already been mentioned, the establishment of an organized Jewish community in Dublin is almost contemporary with that of one in London, and for nearly a century the relationship between the two was very close. As time passed, the Sephardim of Dublin gradually gave place to Ashkenazim, but so late as 1718 when the lease of land for a cemetery at Drumcondra was acquired, of the four signatories on behalf of the Jewish Community three were Sephardim. Twenty years later, in 1738, the London Community made a contribution towards the defraying of some expenses in connexion with this cemetery and in 1747 Bevis Marks when appealed to by the small Dublin Community relieved its anxieties by settling the claims of creditors who were pressing the trustees. At the same time Bevis Marks sought further information about the condition and capacity of the cemetery. In the end the lease was extended at the expense of the London Community for a thousand years at a peppercorn rental, and the title deeds were sent to Bevis Marks where they still remain. This cemetery was closed in 1908, a few years after the burial there of perhaps a distant kinsman of the original trustees. The Portuguese Consul at Holyhead having died, it was found that he had left a request that he should be buried among Jews. A member of the Roman Catholic Church, he presumably alone kept the closely guarded secret that he was of remote Jewish origin. He was in fact a Marrano, perhaps even a crypto-Jew, and it was according to his wish that his body was taken to Dublin and buried among his long estranged kinsmen. The sense of gratitude on the part of the Jews of Dublin remained vivid for very many years. As late as 1836 when the Mary's Abbey synagogue was consecrated the Mahamad was asked, in view of the assistance they had given to the Dublin community many years before in the repair of their cemetery, to honour them by accepting the trusteeship, and one of the earliest visitors from without and worshippers in the new house of prayer was Sir Moses Montefiore, who was in Dublin on business. There was also a Sephardi community or at any rate a group of Sephardim living in Cork in the middle of the eighteenth century as may be deduced from a minute of the London Mahamad dated 3 Tamuz 1753 which deals with the supply of *Kasher* meat to Yehidim living 'in Cork and other parts of Ireland'.

The Sephardi Community of New York, *Shearit Israel* (Remnant of Israel), although not a child of that of London was to some extent a foster-child. The original Jewish settlers in New York, then New Amsterdam, were Sephardim from Brazil and the West Indies, many of whom had previously come from Holland. The earliest surviving grave in the communal cemetery is that of Benjamin Bueno de Mesquita, a London Jew who had lived for a time in Jamaica before 1660 and subsequently settled in New York, where he died in 1683. After the English had taken the city in 1664 these were reinforced and a stream of Jews from England, which, very small at first, later grew in volume and, despite occasional slackening, never ceased from that day to this, set in. In the first decades most of these new-comers were Sephardim. The present *Shearit Israel* synagogue of New York was not opened until 1730, although the formation of a Sephardi community antedates this by a number of years. In fact one was organized in 1706. From the beginning the membership of this community was largely Ashkenazi, and very soon there were more Yehidim of Ashkenazi origin than of Sephardi. In little over a generation, by 1766, of the four principal honorary officers, three had Ashkenazi names (Adolphus, Jones, and Jacobs), and of the five *adjuntos* four were similarly named (Jacob Franks, Myers, Simson, and Levy). Jacob Franks, one of the principal founders, who was as much at home in London as in New York, a member of the leading London

Ashkenazi family, members of which had settled in North America, was Treasurer of the Building Fund and Parnas of the Congregation in the second year of its home in its new building and he filled that latter office on six subsequent occasions. Other Jews of Ashkenazi origin succeeded him, and by the year 1742 Sephardi names in the lists of honorary officers had become rare. The connexion between the Sephardi communities of New York and London was close from the beginning. Among the contributors whose names appear in the preliminary list drawn up when the new building was only in contemplation there were three London Sephardi donors, Aaron Israel Pereira, Jacob Mendes da Costa, and his kinsman, the outstanding philanthropist Benjamin Mendes da Costa, in addition to five Ashkenazim. In a further list of donors for the same purpose, two years after the opening of the Synagogue, appears the name of Isaac de Fonseca. In all £52 14s. was contributed by residents in London. Abraham Mocatta, the founder of the present London family, came forward with an offer to contribute £150, in the conditions of those days a princely sum, more than the total contributions of any community outside of New York, the total cost of the land for a synagogue and a cemetery, provided he were given the honour of the land being registered in his name. 'Considering the few Days a man hath to live and that every man hath an obligation to assist an other and more particular in such good works. The day after the finishing of the Fabrick and your Publick Enterence be made I will give Both (plots of land) Kodes (dedicated) to God.' The trustees had, however, with deep regret to refuse this very generous offer, since the land had been registered in their names and they no longer had any power to transfer it to anyone else. They suggested, however, that Mocatta should devote his proposed gift towards the cost of the erection of the building and offered him, if he agreed, the honour of laying the first stone. This offer was kept open for some time, but was not accepted. There is no record of any reply from Mocatta.[1] Jacob Mendes da Costa, in addition to his contribution to the Building Fund in 1728, defrayed the cost of a subsidiary building for the Yeshiba and *Beth Hamedrash* or school. Jacob Franks and three English brothers, Abraham, Isaac, and Aaron, all contributed. The Ascamot of the newly organized Community, their method of keeping accounts and minutes, all followed closely those of London and their ritual and conduct of the services were

---

[1] The correspondence is given on pp. 28–31 of *The Mill Street Synagogue (1730–1817) of the Congregation Shearith Israel* by the Rev. D. de Sola Pool (New York, 1930).

on the same lines. The new synagogue also followed generally the architectural pattern of Bevis Marks. In one respect they differed. There was no Haham in New York. When the opinion of an ecclesiastical authority was necessary, resort had to be had to those in London or Amsterdam. On one occasion in 1791, when the extension and development of the City of New York threatened the stability of the old Sephardi cemetery which that extension had surrounded, the Beth Din in London, consisting of Aaron de Saa Silveira, David Henriques Julian, and Hasdai Almosnino, was consulted whether the bodies might be removed and transferred to another cemetery. Authority was given for this transfer, subject to the fulfilment of certain conditions. As late as 1855 when similar circumstances arose the Mahamad of Shearit Israel applied again to the Beth Din in London for a ruling.

As in the case of all the other English colonies, England was the source from which officers of the Congregation were generally drawn. In 1757 Bevis Marks was asked to send a Hazan from London. A salary of £50 a year in addition to voluntary offerings and fees was offered. The duties laid down were 'to serve as Hazan and teach the poor children Hebrew, English and Spanish'. 'A young man, of good morals and strictly religious, with the advantage of an agreable voice and capacity for teaching of Hebrew and translating it into English as well as Spanish,' was the specification. Joseph Jessurun Pinto was the paragon selected.[1] When he resigned in 1765, after six years' service, he returned to London, and a successor was advertised for at the increased salary of £80, with an annual grant of not more than £20 for rent and wood and matzo[2] 'as customary to other Hazans'. The emissary who conducted the negotiations between New York and London that led to the appointment of Pinto was Moses Franks, a member of the well-known Ashkenazi family who was also at home in both capitals. The New York Community has never forgotten its indebtedness to Bevis Marks and twice a year, on the Day of Atonement and during Passover, a *Misheberach*, or prayer in honour of the London Community, is still offered in the synagogue of Shearit Israel.

In the minutes for 1775 there appears an entry that is reminiscent to some extent of experiences elsewhere, especially in English provincial congregations of the same period. It is worthy of quotation in full. Moses Levy, Parnas of Newport (Rhode Island), wrote suggesting that the two congregations should join in

[1] The first English Jewish publication in North America was a thanksgiving prayer by Pinto in 1760. In the following year and in 1766 he published there English translations from the Prayer Book.
[2] Unleavened bread.

defraying the cost of sending to London Haham Cohen, a *shaliach* or messenger who had arrived from the Holy Land on a mission to collect funds for the poor of Hebron.

'The Parnas presented a letter he had received from Mr. Moses Levy, Parnas of the K.K. of Newport (R.I.) together with a letter from the Rev. H. H. Samuel Cohen, requesting the assistance of this Congregation to relieve our distressed brethren of Hebron, and Mr. Moses Levy requesting our assistance in despatching the said H.H. Samuel Cohen to London as it would prevent their sending the said Haham to this place, and the same being taken into consideration, Resolved that we will bear the expenses towards maintaining and despatching the said H.H. to London and the Parnas is hereby empowered to pay the same.'

An appeal from London in the same year for contributions to a fund that was being raised for the poor of Smyrna was declined.

The Sephardi Community at Newport, Rhode Island, *Jeshuat Israel* (Salvation of Israel) was founded in 1658, and in 1763 it constructed the present synagogue building, the oldest on the continent. When this building was still only in prospect the governing body of the Congregation wrote to sister communities for assistance, and that of Bevis Marks was one of those that responded. As in the case of so many other of the early Sephardi synagogues in English-speaking lands, the architectural design of the London synagogue was followed. Furthermore, there is a copy at Newport of the Tablets of the Law painted by Aaron de Chavez in 1675 for the London building that was then being remodelled.

The Sephardi Community of Philadelphia, *Mikveh Israel* (Hope of Israel), was formed later, in 1782, by refugees from New York and the British forces, who were threatening that city, under the lead of its Hazan, Gershom Mendes Seixas, whose family had connexions with Bevis Marks. Although by then the North American colonies had severed their connexions with Britain, relations between the new community and Bevis Marks continued. In November 1823 there was a grant of fifty pounds by the London Community to that of Philadelphia, and as late as the year 1828 the Philadelphia Community wrote to the authorities of Bevis Marks asking them to recommend a successor to their recently deceased Hazan. The London Mahamad readily responded. They asked for further particulars, and in the meanwhile invited candidates to apply for the appointment. Over a year passed and then the London Mahamad learnt that the Philadelphia Congregation, despite their application, had appointed their own candidate to the vacant position. The London Mahamad was most indignant at this lack of courtesy, and wrote to Philadelphia asking that at least some compensation should be made to the three London candidates who had been kept so long in suspense.

The organized Sephardi Community of Canada dates from 1768 when Jewish settlers in Montreal, originating in England and the West Indies, met and decided to found a congregation to be known also as Shearith Israel. A synagogue building was, however, not erected until 1777. From the first the relations with the mother congregation in London were close. The ritual was the same, and all questions that called for a rabbinical decision were referred to the Haham in London. The two *sepharim*[1] used from the beginning for the conduct of the services were gifts from the Community in Bevis Marks. For eighty years this was the only synagogue in Canada. The laws of the Community, the internal arrangements of the synagogue, all followed the models of Bevis Marks, and already in the second year of its existence four of its members were fined for refusing office. As in New York, the Community was from the first mixed in origin—Ashkenazi as well as Sephardi—and like New York also, the former element in the end predominated. Early in 1778 the London Community was asked to select a Hazan for the Montreal Community, and in response Jacob Raphael Cohen was sent to Canada as Hazan, Shochet, and teacher. His appointment was not altogether successful, for, claiming arrears of salary which were contested, he took legal proceedings which passed through several courts, splitting the community into hostile parties in the process. In the end, in 1784, judgement on appeal was given against Cohen, who thereupon left Montreal. His intention was to return to England, but the ship on which he sailed was diverted to New York, where it was requisitioned for the repatriation of British troops on the close of the American War of Independence. Gershom Mendes Seixas, also a member of a London Sephardi family, the Hazan of the New York Community, had withdrawn to Philadelphia with those members of his Community whose sympathies were with the rebels, and Cohen took his place. When Mendes Seixas returned to New York, Cohen went to Philadelphia as Hazan of the Community there, remaining until his death in 1811. No permanent Hazan was appointed in Montreal for several years, and then came David Piza, selected by the London authorities at the request of those of Montreal, who remained in office until he was invited to

[1] Scrolls of the Law.

London in 1847 to take up the office of Hazan at Bevis Marks. In his place Abraham de Sola was sent from London. In the history of the Jews of Canada de Sola's name stands out as the most distinguished occupant of a Jewish pulpit there. He was born in London in 1825, a son of the learned Hazan David Aaron de Sola and a grandson of the Haham, Raphael Meldola. In Montreal the young Hazan carried on the traditions of his ancestors. He founded a dynasty of ministers and also of lay leaders of the Community. Some of his descendants later settled in England and became prominent in the Community there. Abraham de Sola died in 1882. To this day a *Misheberach* or prayer for the welfare of the Community is offered in the Synagogue in Bevis Marks on the Eve of the Day of Atonement on behalf of the Sephardi Community of Montreal as well as of that of New York.

Barbados is the oldest of the British colonies, having been settled in 1627, and almost from that year Sephardi Jews began to make their homes there. They were among the pioneers of sugar planting. So relatively numerous were they and so prosperous did many of them become that at one time there were two independent Sephardi communities in this small island of the size of the Isle of Wight. The lands of origin of the Sephardim of Barbados were the same as those of the Sephardim of England, and there was for long a close relationship between them, wealthy Barbados Jews often retiring to the larger community and opportunities of London, and in the later period younger members of the London community settling in the island to seek their fortunes there. Thus some of the best known names in Bevis Marks—Baruch Lousada, Henriques, Massiah, Barrow, Abudiente (Gideon), Navarro (Nabarro), Bueno de Mesquita, and others—were equally familiar in the island. The smaller community was established independently of London, but it was to London that its eyes were turned whenever help or advice was needed and especially when disputes in the local community had to be composed. And when finally, early in the twentieth century, the Barbados community was extinguished through lack of members, it was to the Sephardi Community of London that was entrusted the synagogue building and cemetery and such other property as remained. But the benefits of the relations between the two communities did not all run in one direction. The minute books of the former Hebrew Congregation in Bridgetown show many entries similar to the following:

6 March 1774. Letter received from Haham Moses Cohen D'Azevedo of the Portuguese Congregation in London asking

for help for co-religionists in Jerusalem. A vote for £20 granted.'

'November 1791. £20 sent to Mr. Jacobs, agent for K.K.N.I.[1] in London, for the distressed Jews in Tetuan.'

'1798. £1,152 subscribed by the congregation to be sent to London to assist His Majesty's Government in carrying on the War.'

'21 August 1801. £25 sent to the Parnassim of London to assist our distressed brethren in Tiberias.'

'2 October 1815. Remittance. £25 sent to London for the relief of our brethren in the Holy Land.'

'26 November 1824. Mr. Simon Barrow of London presented to the Kahal a Sepher Torah formerly the property of his uncle Joseph Barrow.'

'3 August 5600—1840. At a meeting held this day it was determined to remit to Mr. Sampson Samuel, Secretary to the Board of Deputies of the British Jews in London, £50 towards the relief of our suffering brethren in Damascus and Rhodes.'[2]

'6 August 1840. £50 was directed to be handed to Baron Lionel de Rothschild, Treasurer of Deputies of British Jews, to be appropriated in aid of "our foreign brethren now suffering from a despotic government".'

'Bridge Town Committee Room, 3 Tebet 5601—25 January 1841. It having been suggested by the Committee appointed to co-operate with the London Committee for the relief of the suffering Jews in the East that most probably a valuable testimonial would be voted by the latter to be presented to Sir Moses Montefiore expressive of the gratitude of the Congregation for the alacrity evinced by him in undertaking, and the ability exhibited in executing his most arduous commission, it is deemed advisable that this ancient and respectable Kaal should be prepared to meet them in the execution of such a desirable object. They therefore propose that the sum of £10 sterling be placed at the disposal of the London Committee for the purpose, and hope that the contributing members will by their unanimous vote empower them to carry the same into effect.'

The seatholders of the congregation at that time numbered barely forty. As late as 1883 assistance was given to the Jewish

[1] *Kaal Kadosh Nidhe Israel* (the Holy Congregation of the Remnant of Israel), the name of the Congregation in Barbados.
[2] This relates to the historic blood accusations at Damascus and Rhodes that aroused the conscience of the Christian and the Jewish worlds.

Community of Jamaica for the rebuilding of their synagogue destroyed in a fire.

Not all of the Congregation's contributions for the welfare of other Jewish communities, however, passed through London. The minutes for the period covered by the above-quoted entries contain also the following:

'3 November 1772. Letter from St. Eustacius[1] asking assistance towards rebuilding their Synagogue. Aid granted.'

'June 1792. Assistance asked for and £25 granted towards the building of a Synagogue in Charleston, U.S.A.'

'7 March 1819. Aid asked and 500 dollars granted to Jews of Philadelphia towards building a Synagogue.'

'17 Ab 5598—8 August 1838. The Secretary here read a letter from Mr. J. W. Lyon, Edinburgh, dated 30 May 1838 and a circular from Joshua Sararus dated Charleston, 8 May 1838, applying for assistance to rebuild their several Snogos:[2] the former was replied to 16 July regretting the incapability of this Snogo to assist and the latter will be replied to by an early opportunity.'[3]

In those days appeals came to the West Indies even from British congregations—not to mention those of the United States.

If the small community was accustomed to reply generously to Jewish appeals from England and elsewhere over this long period, for a part of the time it was also indebted to the Community in London for assistance in another form. In particular it relied on *Saar Asamaim* for keeping its pulpit, or more properly reading-desk, occupied, for London was then the only suitable source on which it could rely for ministerial recruits. And also, if a newcomer might accept such an appointment, it did not necessarily follow that he would retain it for long. There were often greater attractions elsewhere. In some cases the nominees were unsuitable. The minutes to which access has been had cover only the period 1752 to 1840, during the latter part of which the Barbados Community was in decline. In March 1799 it is recorded that Hazan Emanuel Nunes Carvalho had been sent by the Mahamad in London. After six years he was discharged, the reason not being stated, but he was, however, at once reinstated and again discharged in 1808 when he received an appointment in North America. Three years later he was appointed Hazan to the

[1] A Dutch West Indian island.
[2] Synagogues.
[3] These extracts are taken from a contribution by Edward S. Daniels to vol. 26 of the *Publications of the American Jewish Historical Society*.

Community in Charleston, S.C. In the meanwhile Moses Belasco had been sent, in April 1801, by the London Mahamad to take up the offices of Shochet and Bodek in the island. After the retirement of Hazan Carvalho one Abendana was sent from London to take his place, but he also did not remain long, for in less than four years, in September 1812, he was dismissed, no reason for the dismissal being recorded. In October 1819 another Hazan was sent from London, Moses Henriques Julian. It is mentioned that other applicants for the post—Moses Judah Mudahy, Isaac N. Martinez, and Abraham Jessurun—were considered by the London Mahamad at the time, but Julian had been selected. Julian, however, unfortunately died after little more than a year. The Barbados Mahamad acted very generously. They made a grant to the widow of £200 in addition to £50 to cover the cost of her return to England and a suitable tombstone was placed on the grave of the late Hazan at the expense of the Congregation. The finances of the Congregation were at this time deteriorating as a consequence of the reduction in its numbers, and the customary expenditure could no longer be continued. Occasionally a local Jew would be appointed Hazan: more often some member or members of the Community performed the duties honorarily. The Barbados Community never forgot its relationship to that of Bevis Marks. As late as 1845 when the Ashkenazi Chief Rabbi, Nathan Adler, was attempting a sort of census of Jews in the British Empire, a request reached Bridgetown for statistical information. This was collected, but sent to the London Mahamad. 'As you are aware that this Kaal has ever acknowledged yours as the parent synagogue we leave the matter entirely at your disposal and shall be guided accordingly.' In the end the congregation shrank to less than a *minyan*, for the most part members of the Daniels and the Baeza families, not all of them Sephardim, who between them performed all the necessary duties without payment. The Community died out as recently as 1927 appointing the Bevis Marks Community its executor and heir. There were Sephardi communities also in other of the West Indian colonies, in Nevis, where there was a synagogue in 1688, and for the care of whose cemetery Bevis Marks accepted responsibility as recently as 1924, in Tobago, and in Trinidad in the eighteenth century, but these have long since died. That in the then Danish island of St. Thomas, which has always had close English Sephardi affinities, received in 1832 a grant of twenty pounds towards the cost of rebuilding their synagogue which had been destroyed by fire.

The largest and the most important of the West Indian

Communities was that of Jamaica, which has survived—as a joint Sephardi and Ashkenazi community—until the present day. There were Sephardim—crypto-Jews—in Jamaica before its conquest by Cromwell in 1655—a conquest in which, as has been mentioned, Sephardim had some part. These Jews had been brought to the island by Columbus to whom it had been allotted after its discovery, and had been protected and encouraged by him. They remained there, but it was not for another twenty years that their numbers were appreciably increased, by immigration from Holland and England and also from Brazil and Surinam, when these colonies passed out of Dutch or British rule mostly, and by men and women kin of the Jewish worshippers in Creechurch Lane and later in Bevis Marks. The approaches by the London Sephardi Community through its Committee of Deputies to the British Government on behalf of the Jews of Jamaica, have been narrated on an earlier page. The Jews of Jamaica early acquired denization and the unquestioned right to own landed property. But for long the Community had to pay special taxes in addition to the ordinary ones for which all residents in the island were liable. On the other hand, the greater part of the trade, especially that with the Spanish Main, was in their hands. This matter of special taxation was one over which the local legislative assembly had control. Successive governors, appointed from England, and the English Governments that appointed them were opposed to it, but it was only after many disputes, covering a period of years, that the latter had their way. Until about 1780 the Jews of Jamaica were almost exclusively Sephardim. The change in their complexion did not, however, sever the relationship between Kingston and Bevis Marks. When in 1839 the Kingston Community needed the services of an assistant Hazan, teacher and preacher, it was to Bevis Marks that they turned. Moses Abendana was selected, but unfortunately he died shortly after his arrival in Jamaica. In the same year the London Community voted £50 towards the cost of repairing the Kingston synagogue. Four years later the tables were turned. The Jamaica community had a suitable young man among themselves, but he needed training. He was sent to London to study and all facilities were placed at his disposal by the London Community. The Rev. Abraham Pereira Mendes, as he afterwards became, married a daughter of Hazan de Sola.

The connexion between the Sephardim of London and the settlements that have been mentioned arose after they were already established. In no case did the new communities owe their establishment to the Community in London or to any of its members, apart from those who might have themselves been among the original settlers. In the Sephardi communities of what was then British North America the connexion was closer. The settlement of Georgia grew out of the efforts of a group of English philanthropists at whose head was John, Viscount Perceval, later the first Earl of Egmont. As a member of a parliamentary committee appointed to inquire into the condition of debtors' prisons he had been profoundly moved by what he had learnt. He was determined to do whatever was possible to alleviate the condition of the unhappiest classes in the country. He and others who shared his sympathies and his hopes, obtained from the Government the grant of a wide extent of virgin territory carved out of the colony of Carolina in North America. Perceval and his associates were appointed trustees of the new colony, with wide powers of administration. Fortified by a parliamentary grant, they appealed to the public for financial support which was generously forthcoming. The collection of funds was entrusted to commissioners, and among these commissioners were three of the leading members of Bevis Marks, Anthony or Moses da Costa, the wealthy merchant, Francis Salvador, the financier and founder of the family in England, and Alvaro Lopez (otherwise Jacob Israel) Suasso, Baron Suasso, a son of the second Baron d'Avernas le Gras. Baron Suasso was a son-in-law of Anthony da Costa. Still more important in the present connexion was that he was at the time of his appointment Presiding Warden of the London Sephardi Community. Both the other commissioners had held or were to hold the same office. The three in fact were among the leading members of the London Community. It has hitherto been believed that these three commissioners were appointed in their private capacities and that for what later transpired they alone were responsible. An entry in the minutes of the Mahamad, however, puts a different complexion on the development of events. Under the date 9 Nisan 1732 it is recorded that 'The Mahamad and Ajuntos met and resolved that Messrs. Moses da Costa, Joseph Rodrigues Sequeira and Jacob Israel Suasso should interest themselves with those who have permission to arrange settlements in the English colony north of Carolina provided that there is no charge on congregational funds without informing the Mahamad.' Of these three when the commissioners were appointed by the trustees, Sequeira was substituted by Francis Salvador. The three Jewish commissioners succeeded in raising a relatively considerable amount, but instead of handing it over to the trustees they spent it in sending about forty poor Ashkenazi families, whom they themselves selected, to the settlement of Savannah which was being prepared for the new-comers. These Jewish immigrants arrived in Georgia almost simultaneously with some thirty-five families of authorized non-Jewish immigrants whom the trustees had sent. This was in July 1733.

The trustees had six months earlier learnt of the irregularities the Jewish commissioners had committed, and proposed to commit, and had called on them to surrender their commissions. Suasso and his colleagues, however, delayed, and when at length they did so, after more than a year of procrastination, the new immigrants had arrived.[1]

James Edward Oglethorpe, formerly a soldier of fortune and Jacobite, but who had by then settled down and become a respectable Member of Parliament and had in fact been the chairman of the Parliamentary Committee on which Lord Perceval had sat, was the trustee who represented his colleagues in Georgia, in effect the administrator of the new settlement. Confronted with the boatload of indigent Jews he was at a loss to know what to do. He referred to his colleagues in London for their advice. They on their part were smarting under the treatment they had received at the hands of the Jewish commissioners, and replied in effect that no consideration should be given to these Jewish interlopers. The interval between his inquiry and the reply had given Oglethorpe the opportunity to consider the problem at his leisure. His decision was to treat the Jewish new-comers similarly to the authorized immigrants. This he could do the more easily in view of the generous terms of the charter of the embryo colony which laid down full liberty and freedom of worship for men of all faiths except Catholics. Simultaneously there was another Jewish immigration into Georgia. This consisted of Sephardim of some means, hitherto resident in most instances in London. These people paid for their own passages, and on their arrival sought for no assistance from Oglethorpe, devoting themselves largely to wine and silk cultivation. Some of them had already followed these pursuits in Portugal, and their contribution to the welfare and development of the new settlement was readily acknowledged. Among these new-comers were such familiar London Sephardi names as Nunes Henriques, Bornal (? Bernal), Lopez de Oliveira, de Paiva, Gideon, Lopez de Crasto (Castro), Lopez de Vaz, Villa Real, Miranda, and Cohen Delmonte.

---

[1] Relative extracts from the Minutes of the Trustees are given in *Historical Collections of Georgia* by the Rev. George White, 3rd edition (New York, 1855), pp. 328 and 329.

The first business of the Sephardi new-comers was to open a synagogue in Savannah. In this they placed a *sepher torah*, the gift of one of the London Lindos, which they had brought with them. A few years later Benjamin Mendes of London sent them a second sepher torah, a *menorah*,[1] and a number of prayer books, by the hands of Isaac de Cunica who was travelling to Georgia. In 1740 many of these Sephardim, together with a number of their Christian fellow settlers, indignant at the prohibition of rum and slaves on which the administration was determined, left the colony and settled in the neighbouring South Carolina. So large was the exodus that the congregation was temporarily dissolved and the synagogue closed, but most of the Jews ultimately returned to Georgia.

Suasso and his colleagues, having at length surrendered their commissions, the authorities at Bevis Marks determined to go ahead independently. They were still anxious to find a land of settlement for members of the poorer class for whom there appeared no prospect of employment in England. They therefore, in 1734, appointed a committee of their own to pursue the matter. This committee approached the trustees of the Georgia Settlement, but their requirements of land for an exclusive Jewish settlement— on the lines apparently of the proposals of Mr. Zangwill and his fellow-members of the Jewish Territorial Organization almost two centuries later—were not met. Although the Georgia project had failed, the requests of the Sephardi authorities did not, however, lack sympathy, and, as an alternative, land for settlement in the neighbouring South Carolina was suggested by the trustees. Here also mutually satisfactory conditions could not be agreed upon, and no settlement was organized. The Bevis Marks Committee, however, remained in being and was still in existence in 1745. In fact it must have had a hand in 1748 in the petition of John Hamilton, a London financier, to the Committee of Council for Plantation Affairs for the grant of 200,000 acres in that colony for the settlement of Jews. The London Mahamad took this proposal very seriously for a committee consisting of Francis Salvador, Benjamin Mendes de Costa and Solomon da Costa—presumably the aforementioned committee—was instituted to treat with Hamilton and any other parties that were concerned. The Committee of the Council also took Hamilton seriously, but as he was unable to fulfil the conditions laid down his project came to nothing. The possibility of the settlement of Jews in this part of the world during this period was, however, by no means original. The

[1] Candelabrum used on the Feast of Dedication.

somewhat mentally unstable Sir Alexander Cuming or Cumming, a Scottish lawyer, went to South Carolina in 1729, inspired, so it was said, by a dream of his wife. He got himself appointed chief and lawgiver of the Cherokee Nation[1] of Indians and in the following year presented seven of the Cherokee chiefs whom he had taken to England to the King and also drew up a sort of treaty between them and the British Government, further proposing a Jewish settlement on a large scale on their lands. His proposals included the settlement of three million Jewish families in the Cherokee mountains, as a consequence of which eighty million pounds of the National Debt could be paid off. This project also proved abortive. Apart from those who had come from Georgia it was not until 1750 that Jews began to settle in South Carolina, but then as independent not assisted immigrants.

The new-comers, together with those from Georgia who had remained, set about without delay in forming in Charleston (then Charles Town) an organized community. Seven years later, in 1757, they acquired a cemetery, the authorities of Bevis Marks as well as those of the Jewish Communities of Kingston (Jamaica), Barbados, New York, Newport (R.I.), and Savannah (Georgia), all joining that of Charleston as parties to the lease. Although there were a number of Ashkenazim among their members the Charles Town Community followed the lines laid down in the Sephardi Communities of London and Amsterdam, and it may properly be considered an offshoot of Bevis Marks. The Community gradually became overwhelmingly Ashkenazi in membership, but the ritual remained that of Bevis Marks until as late as 1850. All the officials were honorary. One, Moses Cohen, of whom nothing is known except that he had come from London and that he had opened a shop in Charleston, was somewhat grandiloquently described as Haham and Ab Beth Din. This was presumably but an honorary title, for there is no reason to believe that Cohen had any qualification for either office. More important, communally, was the Hazan, Isaac da Costa, who had been trained in London under Haham Nieto and had arrived in Charleston and taken up office there shortly after the establishment of the Community. Da Costa was also in business and combined the reading of the prayers on the sabbath with the selling of merchandise on other days. He remained Hazan until 1764. During the rebellion he was driven out of Charleston by the British and went to Philadelphia, where he was in 1782 one of the founders of the Sephardi congregation

---

[1] 'by the unanimous consent of the people he was made lawgiver, commander, leader, and chief of the Cherokee Nation, and witness of the power of God'.

there. Jacob de Oliveira, one of the Jews who had left Georgia in 1740, died not long afterwards. In his will he did not forget his old Community in London, for he left a legacy of £10 to that synagogue with the customary request that his memory should be kept alive there once a year. Another of the original or very early members was Moses Lindo. He came from London, where he was active in the work of the Jewish Community, a merchant of standing and an authority on dyes. It was on account of his standing among experts in indigo and other dyes that he came to Charleston, a centre of the indigo export trade, and settled there. In Carolina he soon opened in a relatively large way of business, and after his reputation had grown sufficiently he was appointed to the specially created Government office of Surveyor and Inspector-General of Indigo. He died in Charleston in 1774 at the age of about sixty-two. Almost exactly a year before his death, in testimony of his loyalty, he had sent a jewel which had been found in the colony, 'a water sapphire or topaz', by the hands of Lord Charles Greville Montagu, for presentation to the Queen. As late as 1805, a generation after the secession of the North American colonies, application was made to the authorities of Bevis Marks to select a Hazan to fill a vacancy. In the stilted language then in use the Mahamad were informed that the vacancy had occurred as a consequence of 'the feat of the omnipotent Being who thought proper to consign him (the former Hazan) to the Cold Tomb'. Benjamin Cohen d'Azevedo, a son of an earlier Haham, was selected by the London Mahamad and arrived at Charleston in due course. He, however, did not prove satisfactory and was returned to London after eighteen months of service in North America. The London authorities very strongly resented the incident, which was the last in the story of the mutual relations of the two communities.[1] The younger Cohen d'Azevedo was appointed a teacher in the London Community.[2]

From 1811 to 1814 Emanuel Nunes Carvalho was the Hazan of the Congregation which did not in consequence have an easy time. He was the son of a London worker in coral, jet, and similar material, and in his spare time he studied languages. Getting into trouble on account of his political views, Emanuel Carvalho left England in 1799 and first went to Barbados, where he was

---

[1] In 1939, however, the Charleston Congregation appealed to the London Mahamad for assistance towards the rebuilding of their synagogue, and was given £25.

[2] For the history of the Jews of South Carolina, see B. A. Elzas, *The Jews of South Carolina* (Philadelphia, 1905), and Charles Reznikoff, *The Jews of Charleston* (Philadelphia, 1950).

appointed Hazan. After a short time as Hazan at Charleston, he removed to New York, where he taught in a Talmud Torah, but not being comfortable there he returned to Charleston, whose climate he preferred, and where he had a brother in business and a nephew who was an artist. There is a detailed reference to Carvalho in one of the letters of that eccentric, Mordecai Manuel Noah, among whose frustrated ambitions was the creation of a Jewish state—a new Jerusalem—in New York State. Writing as an onlooker, from Charleston on 10 May 1812, to his uncle, Naphtali Phillips, he said:

'In my last I enclosed to you a bill of fare relative to a singing match established by Mr. Carvalho. Within this last week the Congregation has been in a state of warfare sanctioned and approved by that gentleman, unheard of in the annals of religion. It appears he had taught the children to sing the concluding psalms of the Sabbath Morning Service in a very handsome manner which in a measure did away (with) the discordance which attends every Synagogue. For a whim or capour he discontinued this ceremony and forbid the children to sing. The private adjunta conceiving it to be his duty to continue a system which was generally approved of, respectfully requested him to allow the children to continue, which he refused to do and on application for some other branch of his duty he treated the adjunta with disrespect and they suspended him for five days which suspension terminated on Saturday at 10 o'clock when he performed the prayers—Saturday evening being a meeting of the adjunta in general body he collected a rabble composed of all the vagrant Jews and had a petition signed by them to give him redress. This petition was handed the Parnass who could not act upon it, being in express violation to the constitution. Mr. Carvalho in person aided and abetted the confusion and riot which took place. In a short time the whole meeting, parnass and all, were battling with clubs and bruising, boxing, etc., during which his reverence and brother[1] and friend Lipman came off with a few thumps. This outrageous and disgraceful (?) produced by the interference and co-operation of Mr. Carvalho terminated without any serious injury. The result has completely destroyed the small remnant of respectability and character yet left for Mr. C. His duty was not to take the law in his own hands but to submit with respect to the conduct and resolve of the private adjunta who are composed of the most

[1] Presumably David Nunes Carvalho (1784–1860).

respected and indeed the most enlightened part of the Congregation. Mr. C. should have taken a lesson from Mr. Seixas[1] book and studied the character and views of a man who after forty-five years public service retains the respect, the esteem and regard of his Congregation and holds a place in the general estimation and opinion of the public.'[2]

Litigation followed, for there is a record of a case, some years later, in the South Carolina courts—State *v.* Carvalho—where the decision given was that 'disturbing a congregation of Hebrews was an indictable offence at common law, although the offender was a member of the same'.

Despite this incident, so picturesquely described, Mr. Carvalho was tolerated by the Congregation for another two years, until he resigned to become Hazan of *Mikveh Israel* in Philadelphia. After his death there in 1817 an *ascaba* in his memory was regularly offered on the evening of the Day of Atonement in the Synagogue of Charleston.

---

[1] Gershom Mendes Seixas (1745–1816), Hazan of the *Shearit Israel* Congregation, New York, and, during the rebellion against Britain, of the *Mikveh Israel* Congregation in Philadelphia. Carvalho preached a sermon on the occasion of his funeral.

[2] Isaac Goldberg, *Major Noah: American Jewish Pioneer*, pp. 51 and 52. Charles Reznikoff, *The Jews of Charleston*, pp. 114 and 115.

CHAPTER X
THE GREAT PERIOD IN SEPHARDI HISTORY

THE RELATIONSHIP BETWEEN the Community in Bevis Marks and those in the colonies was, when not that of father and son, one of father and adopted son, and favours or benefits conferred upon these latter from time to time may be considered in no way extraordinary but in the normal course. The relations, however, between Bevis Marks and the communities of western Europe were different. So far as Amsterdam was concerned, that Community could, to a certain extent, claim to be the parent or foster-parent of Bevis Marks. There were Sephardi communities also in Hamburg and in the neighbouring Glückstadt and in Italy, but with those there was the connexion only of common membership in a larger community, except that Amsterdam, whence London drew its inspiration, on its part drew a similar inspiration from Venice. There were relations, not often noticeable and seldom of any consequence, with these communities—except that of Amsterdam which was in a class by itself—but as a rule it was London that was the benefactor and the Continental community the beneficiary. For instance, when in 1682 the small community of Glückstadt, then in Denmark but close enough to be almost a suburb of Hamburg, appealed to its fellow communities for assistance in the restoration of its synagogue building the Mahamad of Bevis Marks voted a hundred marks for the purpose. Ex-Marrano Sephardim had settled in Glückstadt in 1616, within two or three years of the toleration of the presence in Hamburg of similar settlers. It was, however, not until 1627 that the Jews of Hamburg were permitted to build a synagogue, and yet another three years before those of Glückstadt were officially recognized. Even the *Beth Israel* Congregation of Hamburg appealed, in 1832, for assistance in rebuilding their synagogue and £30 was voted for the purpose. A similar appeal from Ragusa three years earlier was, however, refused.

The grant to the Glückstadt Community was a small matter. A more important one was that of Venice. The history of the Jews in Venice goes back to the thirteenth century and that of the Sephardi community there to the end of the fifteenth. For many years Venice stood out as the foremost Sephardi centre of the world and although Amsterdam and London grew in opulence and in influence, Venice retained this position for centuries. But in the nature of things this could not be for ever. The position of the whole Mediterranean was changing, if only gradually, and that of Venice with it. And as the wealth and influence of the Queen of the Adriatic declined, so did those of its Jewish Community. Thus the once proud premier Jewish Community in Europe had by 1737 been compelled by circumstances to appeal for assistance to its sister communities. Foremost among these was that of London, whither in the wake of Haham David Nieto, a migration of Sephardim from Venice had turned. At the end of that year Jacob Saraval, the most eminent rabbi of the city-state, and a colleague, Jacob Belilios, were sent to London and also to Amsterdam to raise loans. In London they were fully successful and a total sum of £4,825 was subscribed, not by the Community as a body but by individual members, in response to an appeal made to them by the Mahamad. The Mahamad took charge of the management of the loan, and it was agreed that it should be repaid in half-yearly instalments over a period of ten years, two per cent interest being paid on the amount outstanding. For a short time this undertaking was observed, but the borrowers soon fell into arrear. In the end the Venice Community, having ceased all payments, pleading inability to continue, applied for a second loan which was, however, refused. Later small payments were resumed on account of interest, but the capital amount was never refunded nor the whole of the interest due paid. The last payment was in Sivan 1802, and then the loan passed into oblivion.

In 1689 a fund was raised for the relief of the Jewish fugitives who were fleeing from the war that was raging around Belgrade, and twenty years later a similar fund was raised for the benefit of 'our brothers in Poland'. As late as the twentieth century, appeals for assistance still came from foreign communities. In 1911, the Antwerp Jewish Community asked that of Bevis Marks to help them to defray the cost of rebuilding their synagogue. The request was refused. In 1920, after the conclusion of the first World War, the Sephardi Community of Hamburg, perhaps remembering the help they had received almost a century before, appealed once more to Bevis Marks to come to their assistance. Oran and Mogador in North Africa, Madeira (where in 1852 a community had only recently been established), Corfu, Smyrna, Larissa, all appealed for help and in most cases small grants were made. In 1921, after the Jewish quarter of Salonica had been devastated by fire, four Sepharim were presented to that Community. Two years later came an application from Amsterdam. In 1928 Surinam, whose community is contemporary with that of London, many of the founders in both cases being related, received a grant for repairs to its cemetery. In 1931 came an appeal from Porta Delgada in the Azores for a contribution towards the salary of its Hazan, and to encourage a favourable response the request was accompanied by a deed of trust making Bevis Marks the heir of this small community. Next came an appeal from the small island of Cos in the Aegean Sea for assistance in the erection of a synagogue. Very few members of the community could previously have known even of the island, still less of its Jewish community. And throughout the decades appeals from Palestine became ever more frequent. With the outbreak of the National Socialist persecution of the Jews of Germany in 1933, the London Sephardi Community was the first Anglo-Jewish institution to make its formal protest. Its members joined at once in the efforts to succour these sufferers, and within a short time subscribed over ten thousand pounds for this purpose. This was, however, only the first step in a series of similar efforts towards the same end.

The case of Bohemia as of Poland was different. There was no Sephardi Community in Bohemia; the Jews of that kingdom all followed the Ashkenazi rite. Jews had been long established there, when in 1745 the Empress Maria Theresa, annoyed by certain shortcomings or fancied shortcomings of another section of her Jewish subjects, those in Alsace, determined to impose a vicarious punishment and to expel the Jews of Bohemia from their homes. In their terror the Jews appealed to Jewish communities in all parts for assistance. A copy of the appeal came to Bevis Marks, and announcement was made from the Teba one Friday night to the effect that a subscription was being opened for 'our afflicted brothers in Germany', to which all *Yehidim* were urged to contribute. A sum of almost £900 was collected, and the Parnas Presidente, Moses de Jacob da Costa, was requested to consult with the heads of the two Ashkenazi communities or either of them within his discretion, regarding the disposal of the money. A touching prayer was at this time composed by the Haham, Moses Gomez de Mesquita, for the relief of the anxieties and sufferings of the Jews of Bohemia. The appeal from Bohemia was, however, primarily to the Ashkenazi communities, and political intervention even more than financial assistance was hoped for. The heads of the Great Synagogue, Aaron Franks and Moses Hart, responded to it. They secured an audience with the King, George II, who listened attentively to their recital, and at its conclusion expressed his deep sympathy with the sufferers. This sympathy was not merely verbal. Instructions were sent without delay to the British Ambassador in Vienna to make representations in the name of his Government to that of the Empire on behalf of its Jewish subjects. As an ally of the Empress, King George was in a strong position. He was supported by other diplomatists, the representatives of the Netherlands, Denmark, Venice, and even the Holy See. Their representations were successful. The edict of expulsion was revoked, and the Jews of Bohemia were allowed to remain in their homes undisturbed.

Within a few months of this successful intervention on behalf of the Jews of Bohemia came an invitation from another continental government to Jews to settle within its jurisdiction. The number of Jews in Sweden has never been large. Until as late as 1782 they lived there only as individuals, with their Judaism more or less concealed, the profession of Judaism then being forbidden. Today the Jewish population of Sweden is estimated to number less than twenty thousand. But if two centuries ago the residence of Jews in Sweden was prohibited, the possibility of a Jewish settlement was not absent from the minds of its rulers. On 3 January of the year 1746 an invitation was addressed on behalf of the King of Sweden to a number of Sephardi communities, of which London was one, to Jews to settle 'in Sweden and in all the countries dependent on the Swedish crown'. The invitation was extended specifically to the 'Portuguese Nation' spread throughout the world. Gothenburg was mentioned in particular as the centre in which such Jews would be free to establish synagogues and schools, with their own rabbis and teachers, to pursue from there worldwide commerce and finance and to establish fishing and other industries. The offer was, however, limited to 'rich Jews of the Portuguese Nation'. The reply of the London Community, dated 20 May, was polite but not encouraging. After an expression of thanks for the generous offer that had been made, the reply continued: 'You cannot be unaware of the great kindness that our very illustrious monarch and his illustrious parliament have always shown towards us. Our establishment here, which is already of long duration does not permit us to think of leaving our country where we are so well treated. Furthermore our duty to our country does not even allow us to consider the suggestion.' The reply continued to say that it was most unlikely that any of the Jews of England or of Holland had any desire to leave their homes. It was 'respectfully suggested however that our brethren in France and Italy might not share our views'. There could, however, be no hope of succeeding even there unless the invitation of the King of

THE GREAT PERIOD IN SEPHARDI HISTORY 167

Sweden were made in general terms, without discrimination between rich and poor and the conditions of settlement in Sweden were made clear and definite. 'If those conditions are accepted the Mahamad of London would be ready to assist with all the means at their disposal in meeting the wishes of the Swedish Government.' However, both the Swedish Government and the Jews of Europe had to wait yet another generation before the portals of Sweden were opened to the latter.

David Nieto died on 10 January 1728, terminating a period of office during which the position and reputation of the Community was raised to a level commensurate with that of its Haham. His death was received with widespread mourning throughout Anglo-Jewry and beyond. Several addresses were delivered, on the occasion of his funeral, by men of eminence who shone outside the synagogue. Isaac de Sequeira Samuda, who also composed the epitaph on the tombstone, spoke at the graveside as did also Jacob de Castro Sarmento and the dead Haham's son and successor, Isaac. Among the addresses that were published was also one by Abraham Mendes Chumaceiro. Isaac Nieto was, however, not appointed Haham for another four years, until 1732. His salary was £85, less than that of his father, but it was laid down in the minutes of the Mahamad that he was to receive in addition £20 every Purim.[1] David Nieto's widow was granted a pension of £35 a year. Isaac Nieto, as was to be expected of a son of a man and scholar of the eminence of his father, was also a scholar, but he did not attain to the distinction of his father. Both father and son suffered from attacks from critical, dissatisfied, or jealous congregants. David Nieto, as has been shown, overcame them: Isaac Nieto was not so successful, and after eight years he resigned the office which he presumably felt to be beyond his powers. As successor, Moses Gomez de Mesquita, who came from Amsterdam, was appointed Haham. He, however, held office for only seven years, dying in Iyar or May 1751 at the age of sixty-three. Very little has survived of his activities. In fact more is known of his death than of his life, for his funeral was noteworthy for two graveside addresses, the one by Rabbi Aaron Hart of the Ashkenazi

[1] The relative value of money in those days can be gauged from an account that has survived of the payment by the Mahamad in 1741 for fittings in one of the houses that belonged to the Congregation. The total payment was £2 16s., for which sum were supplied 'a blowing stove with Dutch tyles', two tables and shelves, a cupboard and shelves with lock, 'another blowing stove with Dutch tyles', dresser and shelves, a buffet with glass doors, 'a pair of grates', a leaden cistern sink, and another dresser and shelves.

Great Synagogue—somewhat surprising in view of the growing jealousy between the two communities—and the other by Gomez de Mesquita's predecessor, Isaac Nieto, who was also to be in a sense his successor.

In the administration of the Community also there were changes and developments. In particular the finances adequate for an earlier period began to prove less so as time passed. Later, in the year 1732, a special committee that had been appointed to investigate the financial position reported that the Community was in debt to the extent of £1,300, that the expenditure which was in the neighbourhood of £4,000 per annum exceeded the income, and that although it might be possible to reduce the former without undue hardship, on the existing basis it was impossible to balance ordinary income and expenditure. On the other hand, the invested funds derived from legacies amounted to £4,750, and it was essential that in future all legacies should also be invested, the interest on them only being treated as income. Members were appealed to for special donations so as to relieve the situation. This report was accepted and a financial reorganization was effected. Eight years later the maximum sum of £750 was fixed for the Finta. Judging by the amounts paid, the wealthiest members of the Community at that time were Isaac Israel Suasso, Jacob Jessurun Alvarez, Jacob de Abraham Mendes da Costa, Jacob de Moses Mendes da Costa, Jacob Pereira de Paiva, Moses Lamego, Moses de Abraham Pereira, Benjamin Mendes da Costa, and Daniel Jessurun Rodrigues or Francis Salvador.

The threat of fire was then relatively frequent, and although the synagogue edifice providentially has always escaped destruction or even serious damage, the threat has sometimes come very near to it. In the winter of 1737–8 there was a very serious fire in the course of which neighbouring buildings, the property of the Community, were destroyed, the roof of the synagogue damaged, a number of the poorer members rendered homeless, and three lives lost. In addition to the direct losses the Community was put to expense in fighting the fire and protecting their property. The property was insured for £1,000, but this sum was not sufficient to make good the losses. The Congregation was consequently called together and addressed by the Parnas Presidente, whose pious and moving peroration ran as follows: 'May God who delivered our Holy Habitation be magnified and praised and may he grant us his help to serve Him, and may He remove His righteous anger from His people and incline our hearts to perform what is desirable in His Divine eyes.' The response of the

THE GREAT PERIOD IN SEPHARDI HISTORY 169

Congregation was immediate, and within a short time £2,478 was subscribed and devoted mainly to the relief of the sufferers. Less than four years later, in Tishri 1741, there was another devastating fire from which, however, the synagogue building again fortunately escaped. Special offerings were made in the synagogue as an expression of the gratitude of the members and the proceeds devoted to the relief of the sufferers. The danger of fire, although ever present over a long period, was not as pressing as that of burglary, the possible consequences of which were, however, not so serious. Mention has already been made of two burglaries from which the Congregation suffered. There were also others in later years. In 1715 the burglary or theft was relatively unimportant. During the night of Purim, three silver plates were stolen. A reward of five pounds was offered for their recovery, but whether or not the object was attained was not recorded or the record has not survived. A burglary in 1744 was more serious. In Iyar of that year the Chamber of the Mahamad was broken into and a large quantity of congregational silver stolen. A much larger reward was advertised on this occasion and other steps taken, but again there is no record whether or not they were effective.

The Congregation had to spend £1,700—a large amount in those days—in making good the damage to the synagogue building caused by the fire of 1741, and the work was not completed for eight years. In the meanwhile the lease of the property had been purchased by Benjamin Mendes da Costa, in 1747, and presented by him to the Congregation. The property was, however, still only leasehold, and it was many years later when it was transformed into a freehold.

Originally the Community, although overwhelmingly of a Sephardi character, included among its number a few Ashkenazim who happened also be resident in England, and those whom it did include were accepted wholeheartedly as Yehidim or congregants equally with their fellow worshippers of Sephardi origin. The number of these Ashkenazim was few, but they included one, Benjamin Levy, who acquired an influential position in the congregation, and a group of others who obtained minor offices. When on the establishment of a stable Ashkenazi community Levy and two or three others transferred their interest to that community, no resentment on the part of the older one was apparent. In the early days the charity of the Community was distributed indiscriminately among Ashkenazim and Sephardim alike, and in no case, except in the few instances in which conditions were attached to charitable bequests, does anything but need seem to have been taken into consideration when relief was distributed. In fact as the

Jewish population of London increased, it is probable that the sum of the relief granted to Ashkenazi poor represented an almost undue proportion of the total. When appeals came from abroad from Ashkenazi communities, Bevis Marks, as has already been shown, was not deterred from responding by the fact that members of another branch of Jewry than themselves were concerned, and when the interests of Anglo-Jewry as a whole were involved they did not hesitate to co-operate with the other section of the Jewish community. But the authorities of Bevis Marks were always jealous to preserve the Sephardi complexion of their own smaller community and although they were as a rule willing to accept and absorb individuals they were continuously watchful lest the numbers of these individuals should become too large so as perhaps to threaten the preservation of their Community as a Sephardi one, without qualification. This determination governed their attitude towards marriages between their members and Ashkenazi women. Marriages between Ashkenazi men and Sephardi women were out of their control, while those with non-Jews or non-Jewesses, even more deeply reprobated, could not be influenced at all. The Synagogue declined altogether to recognize them. The records of the marriages in the Community show a continuous and consistent development along these lines. The very few marriages of Ashkenazim at first were cases in which neither party was Sephardi in origin. The first obvious marriage between an Ashkenazi man and Sephardi woman was in August 1706. This example began to be imitated and as the number of imitations grew the strength of the discouragement increased. The outstanding case occurred in 1745 when Jacob Israel Bernal, the Gabay of the Community, resigned his office preparatory to marrying a Tudesca, Jochabed Baruch, daughter of one Gershon Levy. Bernal wished to be married in his own community. The Mahamad felt they could not decide in so momentous a case. They summoned the Elders for joint consideration. In the end they gave their consent to the marriage, but most grudgingly. None of the rabbis or *Hazanim* of the Congregation was to be present at the marriage. The bridegroom was not to be called in that capacity to the Law. No offerings were to be made in his honour. No celebration of any kind in connexion with the marriage was to be held in the Synagogue. In 1772 the Mahamad went even further, and without any explanation Asser del Banco was peremptorily refused permission to marry a Tudesca. In later similar cases the marriage is duly recorded, but the bride is often contemptuously described as a Tudesca, not by name. In one instance even this term is omitted, the space for the name of the bride being left blank. It was not until after the end of the eighteenth century that this extreme expression of disapproval was modified, and the prejudice began to be broken down. The marriage of a member of the Montefiore family, Moses, to a daughter of Levi Barent Cohen in 1812, and of his brother Abraham to a sister of Nathan Mayer Rothschild, by then already in a position of supremacy in the City and in society, three years later, gave it its *coup de grâce*. Marriages between Mocattas and Goldsmids quickly followed. The Gabay, Jacob Israel Bernal, was a member of a family that had come from the West Indies and whose members took their full part in the administration of the London Community. After his marriage he naturally withdrew from communal activities, although remaining a loyal member of the congregation.[1]

After a time the control over marriages seems to have become lax, and any Jew or Jewess, provided the consent of the Mahamad had been obtained, could be married under the auspices of Bevis Marks. The regulations were, however, later again made more stringent, but it was as recently as the year 1944 that it was laid down that marriages were not normally to be celebrated unless the bridegroom was a Yahid or at least a congregante.

Related to this attitude towards marriages between Sephardim and Ashkenazim was the reconsideration in 1751 of the regulations for eligibility for office and the introduction of others more stringent. In Nisan of that year the Elders resolved that, without affecting the position of existing Yehidim and their descendants, any who were not of Sephardi origin who might be admitted to the Congregation in future should not be eligible for election as Parnas or Gabay. On at least one occasion early in the eighteenth century a meeting of the Yehidim was convened to instruct the Mahâmad to punish one of their number who had repeatedly committed the offence of taking part in the worship in an Ashkenazi synagogue. Towards the end of the eighteenth century, however, there began to appear the glimmerings of a more tolerant attitude. In the revised Ascamot of 1784 it was laid down in No. 7 that

> 'at any time when Sura[2] is to be made in synagogue, either for the celebration of nuptials, or Berit,[3] or other particular cause, the Parnas Presidente, or he who presides in his stead, may call up to Sepher and give Misvot to persons belonging to the Congregations of German Jews, who may be relatives or friends

[1] See p. 197. [2] A list of prospective recipients of honours.
[3] Circumcision.

of those who are interested in such Sura, provided always that the giving of such Misvot and calling up to Sepher are not considered as entitling such persons to be admitted Yehidim of the Kaal.'

A generation and a half later, when a new atmosphere had arisen in Sephardi-Ashkenazi relations, the Elders went further.

> 'It appears to the Mahamad that connected as the two nations at present are by intermarriage between them and it would be advisable to make some alterations in the existing custom so to authorize the calling to Sepher and giving Misvot to such individuals on particular occasions and with this feeling they shall submit to your consideration an alteration in the 7th section of the Ascama No. 7 in order to provide for this purpose under limitations.'

The Mahamad at once acquiesced and on the same day (23 October 1825) resolved, a little guardedly,

> 'on special family occasions Ashkenazim may be called to the Law or given Mizvot but such Mizva or calling to the Law must not be considered as entitling such persons to be admitted Yehidim of the Kaal'.

The frequent differences that arose in the Congregation from individual members resenting rulings by the Mahamad led many such persons to withdraw, as a rule temporarily, from the Community. These seceders were able to find shelter within the portals of the neighbouring Ashkenazi synagogue and also, if they died while still out of communion with their original community, a last resting-place in the Ashkenazi cemetery which was separated only by a wall from that of the Sephardim. Apart from the solitary case in 1730 that has already been mentioned when penalties were inflicted on a member of the Community who persistently attended service in an Ashkenazi synagogue, the authorities seem to have turned a blind eye to the seceders. Presumably as they were for the time being excluded from Bevis Marks and were suffering from a form of temporary excommunication the Sephardi authorities considered that their movements and attendances were no longer a matter of concern to them. There were, however, other and more important secessions, the causes of which went deeper than the often trivial differences that led to these temporary exclusions.

THE GREAT PERIOD IN SEPHARDI HISTORY 173

Those who established the Sephardi Community of London were almost without exception men who had for generation after generation nursed their religious faith in secret and clung to it sometimes at the cost of torture and the risk of death. To them their Judaism was the greater part of their life. They had paid almost the heaviest of prices for it, and once they had found an opportunity of practising their religion openly and without restraint, they practised it with a rigidity unknown to those who had lived as Jews in easier conditions. And this rigidity brought with it a trace of intolerance. To the sons the sufferings of the fathers, the price they had paid for their Judaism, were becoming but a tradition. The Jewish characteristic of intellectual speculation and scepticism was also displaying itself and the second generation in England, still more the third, was consciously or unconsciously beginning to examine the bases of the faith of the ex-Marranos which to the first generation were as unassailable as rocks. Even among this first generation a few sceptics raised their heads. Among the later generations also the attraction of the outside community began to display itself. Mention has already been made of prominent Jews or members of well-known families in the Community who succumbed to this attraction from outside. As the eighteenth century lengthened, this outside attraction grew in strength and by its end an appreciable number of families that stood out in communal service at its beginning were no longer to be found within the portals of Bevis Marks. There were means of recruitment, but the Sephardi authorities were never fully desirous of taking advantage of them.

One of these sources was that of proselytization. To this allusion has been made on an earlier page. Although when the Community was organized in 1657 there were four proselytes among its members, and from time to time others were accepted, proselytes in general were never wholeheartedly welcomed. A strongly rooted tradition in London Jewry—one for which no basis can be found —that one of the conditions on which Jews were permitted to establish themselves in this country was that they should make no proselytes among Christians, and the legislation of the Mahamad and Elders for long went in the direction of fulfilling this assumed condition. In the earliest code of laws the making of proselytes was emphatically prohibited. This, for instance, was the reason for prohibiting the employment of Christian serving women in Jewish households. Women were assumed to be more susceptible than men in these matters. Those proselytes who subsequently appeared in the congregational records were received into the

Jewish Community—even though they were English-born—not in this country, but on the Continent.

About the middle of the eighteenth century (December 1751) the Sephardi authorities became exceptionally nervous on the subject. As a consequence a formal resolution was taken. This was to the effect that

> 'It having been represented to us that some foreign Jews not inhabitants of England make it their practice to convert Christians to the Jewish faith, in order to put a stop to so pernicious and unlawful practices, we the aforesaid Presidents and Gentlemen of the Vestry come to the following resolution, that in case any person or persons shall attempt making of proselytes, he or they so offending shall be immediately expelled the synagogues and also be deprived of the benefit of being buried in the Jewish burial grounds and to be denied all other privileges appertaining to the Jewish religion. These penalties are not to be understood as merely personal but even to extend to their wives and children.'

This resolution was communicated to the governing bodies of the two Ashkenazi Congregations.

> 'The President and Gentlemen belonging to the German and Hamburg Jews' Vestrys.' 'Being persuaded that you will join with us in all things that tend to preserve the present happy toleration, we take this opportunity to acquaint you, as worthy representatives of your congregation of a growing evil among us, viz: that of permitting proselytes, for which end we have heard that two or three Christians have come hither from Norway with that intention, and lest these practices should extend to create English proselytes also which is contrary to the express conditions annexed to our first establishment here, we have thought proper to forbid in our Synagogue any from aiding and assisting them therein in any manner whatsoever, under the penalties as we send you enclosed.[1] Do not doubt but you will

[1] 'No Jew shall dispute or argue concerning religion with any person of another religion whatsoever, for to persuade them to follow to our laws, neither shall they speak anything indecent against their professions.

'No Jew shall circumcise any person whatsoever that is not born a Jew.

'It is also ordered that no proselite shall be bathed, neither shall any person give them employment, and whosoever incurs therein shall be proceeded against with the utmost rigour as disturbers of our Libertys.

'And as it is of the utmost importance to our tranquility we do order that whoever should hear that any person intends to be circumcized or bathed (to

THE GREAT PERIOD IN SEPHARDI HISTORY 175

also concur with us to endeavour to prevent the same from taking effect amongst you in the manner that may be judged most expedient. We pray God to preserve you for many years.'

The response of the Ashkenazi authorities was immediate (2 January 1752). They 'concur with you in opinion that we ought to do everything in our power to prevent the ill consequences that may arise from making of proselites, contrary to the known laws of this Kingdom.' On their part they 'The Presidents and Gentlemen belonging to the Vestrys of Dukes Place and Magpye Alley synagogues' issued the following pronouncement:

'That in case any person or persons shall attempt making Proselites, he or they so offending shall be immediately expelled the Synagogues, and also be deprived the benefit of being buried in the Jewish burying grounds, and to be denied all other privileges appertaining to the Jewish religion. These penalties are not to be understood as merely personal, but even to extend to their wives and children.'

Only members of two classes were treated as exceptions. The one consisted of Marrano fugitives from Portugal, the stream of which continued until well into the eighteenth century. Marranos or secret Jews, although nominal Christians, could not be considered real ones. The practice was for the men on reaching England to be formally admitted into the Community. In most cases married and accompanied by their wives they were then remarried in the synagogue according to Jewish rites. Not the least touching of the entries in the long roll of marriages under Sephardi auspices in London are the entries in which the Spanish or Portuguese surname is the same for both husband and wife to which the note 'Vindos de Portugal', refugees from Portugal, is attached. Some of these, of course, may have been cousins, for the practice of marriage of cousins and also of uncles with nieces was very prevalent in Jewry in those days. Many of the families subsequently prominent in Anglo-Jewry can be traced back to the marriage of one of these *Vindos de Portugal*. There were cases even of men escaping from Portugal, being accepted into the Community and then returning to their original home. The Mahamad most definitely disapproved of such proceedings. For instance, in Nisan 1733 it was learnt that two refugees from

become a Jew) he shall immediately give notice thereof to the Gentlemen of the Vestry in order that they may prevent it, in failure whereof they shall be proceeded against with the utmost rigour. And this order is directed particularly to the Circumcizers and Bath Keepers.'

Portugal, Moses de Jacob Rodriguez da Costa and David Orobio Furtado, who had earlier been circumcised and admitted members of the Community, had subsequently returned to Portugal. They were promptly expelled from the Community. One of the two subsequently returned to England and was re-admitted a member. Three years later, in Adar 1736, Isaac de Lara was ordered on the occasion of a similar offence, to ascend the Teba in the synagogue and beg pardon of God and the congregation. The incentive for men, women, and even children, even of remote Jewish origin, as late as the end of the seventeenth century to flee from Portugal is clear from the following extract from a contemporary publication. The author was Chaplain to the English factory at Lisbon from 1678 to 1688 and was later Chancellor of Salisbury.

> 'Great numbers upon their having any of their Relations taken up by the Inquisition, do flee from Portugal, notwithstanding that it is so difficult for them to make their escape, by reason of their not daring to go into Spain; which is the only way they have to escape by land. The way by which they commonly make their escape, is, by getting aboard an English or Dutch man-of-war; and tho when they are aboard these ships they are as safe from the Inquisition as they are in England and Holland, no officers, Civil or Ecclesiastical, being ever suffered to come a-board those Ships to make any Search, yet these poor Wretches, tho they do know this, and upon the Knowledge of it put themselves on board, yet, if they happen to hear Portuguese spoken upon the Deck, or in any of the Cabins, they tremble Hand and Foot, as if the Familiars of the Inquisition were come to carry them away.'[1]

The second class of proselyte, though not Jewish, was not in the full sense Christian. So far as is known the admission of the members of this class into the Community was principally for the purposes of marriage, but the 'conversions' were none the less sincere on that account. As the eighteenth century advanced, the number of marriages between Jewish men and non-Jewish women increased. The progressive removal of the social barriers between Jew and non-Jew made this inevitable. And since the admission of proselytes into Jewry was severely frowned on, to the young man in love there was no alternative but to marry the object of his affections in church. But the Church ceremony did not

[1] Michael Geddes, *Miscellaneous Tracts*, vol. 1, 'A View of the Court of Inquisition in Portugal' (1714), p. 518. I owe this reference to the kindness of Mr. Wilfred Samuel.

eradicate all Jewish sentiments and although the synagogue authorities expelled these offenders from the Jewish community, Jewish friends and relatives seem to have been often more tolerant. This is evident from the number of instances in which the children of these mixed marriages, for the most part daughters, after admission to the Community as proselytes were married to sons of its members. There are a number of instances in the record of marriages of such unions, from two in 1699 onwards, although as in these early cases the surnames of the brides are not given, they may have been ordinary proselytes. But by no means all the children of these marriages entered the Jewish community. One finds traces of others with unquestionable Sephardi names among highly placed civil servants and holders of other offices for which Jews were at the time ineligible. By this means are explained, for instance, Moses Sierra (1709–92), who was Secretary to the Russia Company and his wealthy sister, Zipporah, who left a fortune of £60,000; Benjamin da Costa (1712–59), a son of the wealthy Moses or Anthony da Costa, who on his marriage to a non-Jewess left the Community. He was Deputy-Receiver General of the Post Office; his son, also Benjamin (1739–82), was Accountant General in the Excise Office; and yet a third Benjamin da Costa (1779–1854) fought as a naval officer under Nelson at Trafalgar.

The other source of recruitment was by immigration. Refugees from Portugal were always welcome and newcomers from other parts of Sephardi Europe—such as Italy or Amsterdam—were equally well received. Those coming from North Africa or the Levant, even though they were of Sephardi origin, were not so welcome. The movement from the West Indies could hardly be considered an immigration. The new-comers were kinsmen of members of Bevis Marks and they as a rule came to England as a land of retirement after successful careers in the colonies. In fact there were movements in both directions between London and the West Indies and so long as the prosperity of Jamaica and Barbados continued, there was always a movement westwards of young Ashkenazim as well as Sephardim going to the West Indies to seek their fortunes. Thus the settlement in England of Gideons, Henriques, Lopezes, Baruch Lousadas, Barrows, and others was balanced by the emigration from England of Montefiores, Lindos among the Sephardim, Lucases, Leviens, Elkins, and others among the Ashkenazim, many of whom later returned to the land of their birth.

Another matter in which circumstances compelled the two

communities, despite the inclinations at any rate of one of them, to co-operate, was that of *Shechita* or the ritual preparation of meat for consumption by Jews. On this matter the laws of both communities were identical. Nevertheless until well into the nineteenth century they refused to set up a joint administration and each community went its own way with its own set of officials and administrative rules and regulations. In one respect, however, they had to support one another. In the absence of such co-operation both parties would have suffered and neither would have gained, for under the existing system both the Sephardi and the Ashkenazi communities derived revenues from the sale of meat, and it was to the interest of both of them ruthlessly to suppress any interlopers in the field. It will be remembered that, in the first instance, the Sephardi Community, while licensing and paying their own *shochetim* or slaughterers, so that the orthodoxy of their method of slaughter should be above question, farmed out the monopoly of supplying meat to members of the Community. This system was, however, abandoned after a time. In 1732 a system of free trade in *Kasher* or ritually approved meat was introduced, subject, however, to the employment by the butchers of shochetim licensed by the Congregation. A further condition was that the butchers should pay a tax to the congregational funds—2/6 per head for cattle, 1/3 for calves, sixpence for sheep and fourpence for lambs. The new system, however, did not remain unchanged for long. In less than six months it was brought to an end or rather radically altered. Not less than four congregational shops, with licensed shochetim and other officials, were to be set up, at which Kasher meat could be sold. Licences to open these shops were to be given by the Mahamad, within their discretion, to any Jew or Christian, who applied for one. Butchery may not have been a popular trade in London Jewry at that time, but it must also be realized that the restrictions against the carrying on of retail trade by Jews within the limits of the City of London militated against the opening of butchers' shops by Jews. This arrangement continued for a time, but Shechita troubles were perennial, and early in 1745 there was a conference between the Sephardi and Ashkenazi authorities on the subject. By the middle of the next decade the difficulties had grown considerably. The principal trouble was the doubt that had arisen about the ritual correctness of some of the meat that was placed on sale. In 1756 a committee—by no means the first for a similar purpose—was set up to inquire into the abuses that were said to be rife. The investigations were widespread and it was found that at least some of the charges were justified. The steps taken were drastic. They included the dismissal of the shochet at fault. For a time everyone was satisfied, but not for long. As has been said, Shechita disputes and irregularities in Sephardi Jewry and also elsewhere were perennial. The old troubles and complaints again appeared and again disturbed the Community. On one occasion, later in the eighteenth century, one of these disputes almost started a quarrel between the two London Jewish Communities. Jacob Kimhi, a Jew from Constantinople, who spent his time in London writing learned Hebrew books, selling Turkish slippers at the Royal Exchange, and criticizing the communal authorities, began to express doubts of the reliability of the Sephardi shechita. In his own Community he obtained little support, so he turned to the Ashkenazim, and appealed to the recently appointed Rabbi of the Great Synagogue, Hart Lyon, who promised to inquire into the charge and formulate an opinion. When this intention came to the ears of the Wardens of the Great Synagogue, they quickly intervened, ordering Lyon to refrain from interfering in the affairs of the sister community. Lyon, of course, acted on their instructions, but the episode gave Kimhi fuel for the fires that he was always stoking.

There was another movement into England at which the Mahamad and also most of the Yehidim looked askance. For the immigration of Ashkenazim from eastern Europe—coming as they thought to an *El Dorado*—no one in Bevis Marks had anything good to say. Opportunities for the immigrants to find employment with members of the Community were small—the principal one seems to have been that of domestic servant in a wealthy Sephardi household—and non-Jewish employers—in view of the requirements of sabbath observance—were particularly barred.

New-comers who had not the means of setting up independent businesses—and Jews were at that time debarred from opening retail shops within the City of London where most of them lived to be near their co-religionists—had therefore little prospect of supporting themselves. They became a burden on the existing community and frequent is the mention in the records of the giving of alms and of projects for the permanent relief of the donors from their moral liabilities. One such was certainly the project for the Jewish settlement in Georgia. The poorer element in the Jewish population, however, consisted not only of Ashkenazim. There was a Sephardi one also, coming from the north of Africa, but with an occasional individual from farther afield. Although of the Sephardi rite, in some cases descended from exiles from Spain or Portugal, their culture and way of life were very different from those of the well-established Sephardi families of England. Materially they were as a rule on a far lower level and culturally also there was a wide gulf between them. This difficulty had been evident from the beginning, but with the growth of the London Community it had increased, despite discouraging legislation of the Mahamad and occasional intervention by the City authorities. On one occasion the City Corporation intervened but in a manner that the Mahamad did not welcome. One, Uzily or Uzzielli—a Jew of Italian origin—of whom the Mahamad had had considerable experience, none to his credit, finding that he could get nothing more from the Community, appealed to the Lord Mayor for relief. The Lord Mayor ordered the Mahamad to provide for the man, but this they refused to do, arguing that Jews who paid the same poor rates as Christians were equally entitled to assistance from those rates when the necessity arose. To secure themselves they, however, sought counsel's opinion, applying to no less an authority than the future Lord Chancellor Thurlow. He was at the time, in 1772, Attorney General. 'I am of opinion', he said, 'that the poor of whatever nation or religion, must be maintained by the officers of the parish, where they are found, and that no other person is compellable to relieve them, except under especial circumstances, which make no part of this case.' This opinion was supported by John Dunning, a former Solicitor General, and accepted by the Lord Mayor. However, Uzielli was not satisfied and summoned the Wardens of the Congregation before the Lord Mayor, who, in deciding in their favour, added a rider to the effect that they should assist Uzzielli if they could conscientiously do so. In the end Uzzielli made a complete submission to the Mahamad, who accepted his repentance and put him again on the roll of the congregational *sedaca* or charitable relief.

The accounts show a curious collection of objects of relief and other miscellaneous payments. There are many entries, back to ten or fifteen years after the organization of the Community, relating to the return to the Continent of poor Tudescos. In the year 1681 appears the entry of the payment of fifteen shillings to Jacob Abensur 'to remove an Indian from a slave-boat bound for Carolina, whom the Jews were reported to have sold' and a further payment of five shillings to Notary Hayward 'for obtaining from the mouth of the said Indian a statement to the contrary', apparently a less irksome or dangerous undertaking. In 1686 appears the surprising entry under 'Sums paid to the Poor of this

Town' of: 'On the 4th Nisan given to Abraham and Adam Rison to go to be touched by his Majesty whom God preserve—11/–', obviously an instance of being touched for the King's Evil by King James, and the expenditure of eleven shillings to make the two sufferers respectable in appearance so as not to bring discredit on the Community. Then follow a grant of 7/6 to Manasseh Hart, a Tudesco, for his son and after two successive payments for the sabbath to Isaac Carballo, a final one of a pound to Jacob, probably an error for Isaac, to get him out of the country. For the year 1698, out of a long list of miscellaneous payments one can extract one for the shipment to Leghorn of Isaac Meshiach and Isaac bar Abraham, the latter presumably a proselyte. Isaac bar Abraham returned later. Later in the same year come a payment of the considerable sum of £4 14s. 3d. to Abraham da Silva for help in getting him out of prison, and one of £2 7s. 'for taking out of pawn a watch pawned by David Alvarengha and belonging to Isaac Tegger'. In 1707, £6 1s. 7d. was spent on Jonathan, a proselyte, and a further £2 to defray the 'amount owing by him to the Ale House'. Five shillings are given to Sara Lopez, a mulatto, apparently a slave or ex-slave brought by some member of the Congregation from the West Indies. Then comes the payment of £1 5s. 6d. to 'the Printers of the papers declaring Antunes to be a Catholic', and thus presumably relieving the Community of the responsibility, moral if not legal, for his maintenance. Payments in respect of soldiers or watchmen were frequent. Some of these were for night guards at the cemetery: some for protection of the synagogue or the Jewish quarter at times of threatened civil commotion. Some of these payments were obligatory. On the occasion of the Coronation of William and Mary the Congregation had to supply a soldier for a double guard. When they failed to provide the soldiers for which they were responsible a penalty was imposed. 'For eight times that we failed to send a soldier. There should have been three, but there were only two. Agreed with the Captain 3/– each time—£1.4.0d.' There were also records of sundry douceurs or fees scattered about the accounts. 1682: 'Paid to an officer of My Lord Mayor and to other officials in respect of a libel against the Nation published in the Gazette and its denial in the following publication 10/6'. 1691: 'For a dozen bottles of wine presented to the Sergeant at Arms in Parliament—£1.3.6d.'. 1693: 'Paid to David Penso for wine for the Sergeant of Parliament—£2.8.6d.' But it must be remembered that in those days it was the general practice to make gifts to holders of office.

CHAPTER XI

THE INTERNAL LIFE OF THE SEPHARDIM

MOSES GOMES DE MESQUITA died in 1751, leaving the office of Haham again vacant, and for some years it was unfilled. During the interregnum Isaac Nieto, who had gone abroad after his resignation, but had later returned to England, carried out most of its duties. Nieto, during this second term, took the title of *Ab Beth Din* or President of the *Beth Din*. The reason for this may be that after his previous resignation he had been admitted a notary and was unwilling to retire from the practice of that profession. It will be remembered that his father had practised medicine before he came to England and on his appointment as Haham in London had to give an undertaking that he would not continue to do so. Isaac Nieto's second term was also not untroubled. Dissensions were almost continuous, and after five years he again resigned. The principal cause of difference was Moses Cohen d'Azevedo. This young man had also come from Holland and had married a daughter of the Haham, Gomes de Mesquita. D'Azevedo secured friends in the London Community and when a vacancy in the Beth Din occurred he was appointed to it, Isaac Nieto himself having earlier conferred on him his qualification, the rabbinical diploma. Nieto's hostility to him, perhaps a consequence of jealousy, however, had grown with time. He objected as strongly as he could, to the appointment, and within twenty-four hours of it Nieto himself resigned. The resignation was promptly accepted, and shortly afterwards, so that there should be no room for doubt, Nieto was specifically forbidden to give rulings on Jewish law so far as the London Community was concerned. This was in accordance with the Ascamot, since Nieto was no longer a member of the Beth Din. The resignation of Nieto did not lead to peace in the Community. From his retirement he poured out a stream of criticisms of the decisions of his successors and he went so far as to declare that the meat provided under their control was improper to be eaten by Jews. At one time he and a group of his supporters—for he obtained a measure of support among the Yehidim—went so far as to threaten to appoint their own Shochet and provide meat in the Kashrut,[1] of which they had full confidence, for themselves. This raised not

[1] Ritual correctness.

THE INTERNAL LIFE OF THE SEPHARDIM   183

only an ecclesiastical but also a financial question, for the Community was to some extent dependent on a revenue derived from the meat eaten by its members. The threat which for a short time was obviously to be taken seriously was, however, withdrawn and the unity of the Community, despite these bitter dissensions, remained unimpaired. For four years the *status quo* continued, and then in 1761, after d'Azevedo had completed his fortieth year, the step that Nieto seems always to have anticipated and against which he had struggled so strenuously, was taken, and d'Azevedo was appointed Haham. Nieto fought this appointment to the last, and it was not made until his objections had been referred by the London Mahamad to the Beth Din of Amsterdam. This last body overruled them all and d'Azevedo's appointment was confirmed. Nieto survived this defeat for twelve years, dying in 1773. During his last years he continued his scholarly work, leaving as a memorial his translation of the prayer book into Spanish, the first volume of which had been published in 1740 and on which he had been engaged for a third of a century.

This was Nieto's *magnum opus*. It was the basis of all subsequent translations into English. In the words of a successor in his high office who also enriched the Community with an edition of the prayer book for English worshippers

'His translation has become the household translation of the Community, and for close upon a century has enabled people unacquainted with the Hebrew idiom to commune with their God in a form as near approaching the beauty of the original as a translation can ever be. It has uplifted and comforted them through its contents and through the form in which it was conveyed to them.'[1]

This was not Nieto's only literary work that survives. Sermons by him were printed: some of his Hebrew poems remain in manuscript. His sermon preached in February 1756 on the occasion of a Government-proclaimed fast was also published in English. The occasion was 'to implore God's blessing upon our fleets and armies, and for humbling, in view of His late visitation by earthquake, more particularly in neighbouring countries in alliance and friendship with us.'[2] This was the earliest Jewish sermon to be published in English. Nieto also, in 1763, published a calendar covering a period of fourteen years. In 1761 there appeared anonymously, in Salonica, a small volume in Spanish recording the whole of the

[1] M. Gaster, *History of the Ancient Synagogue* (1901), p. 138.
[2] The devastating Lisbon earthquake had occurred a few months earlier.

dispute that was then still raging in London over the subject of *Shechitah*. From internal evidence this brochure appears to have been printed in London and to have come from the pen of Nieto.

All of these works that were published in London appeared under the authority of the Mahamad as required by the Ascamot. The authority of the Mahamad was exercised over the entire field of literature so far as the members of the Community were concerned. For instance, in 1734 Jacob de Castro Sarmento, having written a Portuguese-English dictionary and wishing to publish it, had first to obtain the permission of the Mahamad, which was granted. But similar permission was by no means always forthcoming. In 1721, one Joseph Messias published or attempted to publish a Spanish translation of the Daily Prayer Book without the permission of the Mahamad, which apparently he had been unable to obtain. Only one copy of this book, which bears the name of Rachel de Castro, a cousin of Isaac d'Israeli, as owner, is known and it looks as if the book was published and later suppressed. In 1766 an English translation of the Prayer Book by Isaac de Pinto appeared in New York in consequence, it is believed, of the refusal of the London Mahamad to license it, and in 1772 a Spanish translation, also without the sanction of the Mahamad, appeared in London under the *nom de plume* of Aaron Nodnarb, which hardly troubles to conceal the name of Brandon, one of the Yehidim. In 1734 the struggle between the author and the Mahamad became more intense. In that year Moses Nieto, a son of David Nieto and a brother of his newly appointed successor, applied for permission to publish an English edition of the prayer book. This permission was peremptorily refused. The author, however, ignored the refusal and proceeded with his preparations for publication. Whereupon the Mahamad, acting on the authority of the Ascamot, fined Moses Nieto £10 for printing the book and a further £15 for disobeying the Mahamad, with the further threat that unless he surrendered the manuscript of his work and gave an undertaking not to proceed with the publication he would be expelled from the Community.[1] Furthermore, all Yehidim were warned from the Teba to avoid the book as if it were poisonous and that if anyone read, bought or sold it he would be punished by a fine of five pounds. Moses Lopez Diaz, however, who in the same year asked for permission to print some papers (presumably advertisements), required to further his business of

---

[1] The manuscript passed later into the possession of David Aaron de Sola and is now the property of his descendant, Mrs. G. H. Mosely.

THE INTERNAL LIFE OF THE SEPHARDIM 185

selling Imperial bonds, received the required permission. The mere request illustrates how far the arm of the Synagogue authorities stretched. Moses Nieto also, after he had made his peace with the authorities, was given permission to print an extract from his calendar in Spanish. Successive generations of this family, until half a century ago or so, have published Jewish calendars. Eight years later there was further trouble. The attention of the Mahamad was called to the publication, without any reference to them, by Moses Barzilai of a book with the challenging title of *Bigotry, Superstition and Hypocricy worse than Atheism*. He was fined ten pounds. Barzilai was not powerful enough to fight the authorities, and submitted. He undertook not to print or sell any further book without the required permission, and was forgiven.

The rule of the Mahamad was very strict and dictatorial. Resort was frequently had to the penalty of excommunication, but as the ban seems to have been easily and speedily raised this penalty was by no means as severe as its title suggests. Offences covered a very wide range and went far outside the province with which the Synagogue today is concerned. The penalties also are often surprising to the modern mind. For instance, on one occasion an offender was forbidden to shave for six weeks, and if he failed to repent during that period he was to have been excluded from the synagogue and in the event of death he was not to have been buried in the communal cemetery, but 'beyond the board', that is to say, in a part reserved for undesirables of Jewish origin. The jurisdiction of the Mahamad was in fact very wide, but it is not to be understood that it was by any means in all cases oppressive. In most cases this jurisdiction was readily accepted. In disputes between members the Mahamad acted as an arbitration court and as such it had to adjudicate in a variety of matters, as it has been said, from the price of a warming-pan to the settlement of a breach of promise. In a breach of promise case which was adjudicated in 1808, judgment was given in favour of the plaintiff, the lady, to whom damages of £80 were awarded against—not the gentleman, but his father. But the jurisdiction of the Mahamad was not always readily accepted. For instance, in August 1734, the distinguished physician, Jacob de Castro Sarmento, who has already been mentioned in these pages, was summoned before the Mahamad by Moses de Morais Pereira for having taken proceedings in the Civil Courts against the latter's recently deceased brother-in-law and also son-in-law, Jacob da Costa Villa Real, and was fined five shillings. As will be remembered, this was not the first occasion on which de Castro Sarmento had committed a similar transgression. He was, it seems, accustomed to have recourse to the courts of the land to secure payment for his professional services. For a time the Mahamad actually went into business on behalf of the members of the Community. This activity arose out of the difficulties, in particular of the widows and other dependants of Yehidim who were left by the death of their supporters in straitened circumstances, or of officials of the congregation who were no longer fit for work. To deal with their needs the Congregation sold life annuities, but as the prices of these annuities were not based on actuarial calculations but more often on the means of the purchaser, the undertaking could not remain solvent without outside assistance. The Great (Ashkenazi) Synagogue also adopted this practice, which was prevalent in continental communities.

Difficulty in getting qualified members to accept the burden of honorary office was also a recurring trouble. The fine imposed on any Yahid who refused the office of Warden or Parnas varied from time to time and rose at times as high as £40. The office carried with it a certain financial liability or possible liability, for every Parnas on entering office had to take an oath before the opened Ark in the Synagogue that he would administer his office justly and without favour and would respect all the laws of the Congregation, and also to deposit the sum of £100 which might be drawn on if the funds were in deficit, but which was to be repaid at the end of the term of office. In the case of the Gabay or Treasurer, the deposit amounted to £600. These regulations did not, however, mend matters, which were rendered worse by the continued drift away from the Community during the second half of the eighteenth century of men who by their parentage and their position were marked out as members of the reserve from which the leaders should have been drawn. In the end, in the year 1791, once again a group of members including many of the best known names in Bevis Marks gave an undertaking that 'in consideration of the dilemma in which this Congregation now finds itself, no person being willing to accept the post of Parnas, we hold ourselves ready to discharge this duty whenever our turn would come'. The signatories to this undertaking were Isaac M. Pereira, Raphael Brandon, Jacob Israel Brandon, Gabriel Israel Brandon, M. Lopes (presumably Mordecai Rodrigues Lopez, the father of Sir Manasseh Lopes), E(manuel) Baruch Lousada, Jacob Samuda, Benjamin Mendes Pereira, David Alves Rebello, Benjamin Lara, David de Leon, Isaac Aguilar, and Abraham Lopes Pereira, all members of prominent Sephardi families, many of them themselves prominent in the Community. A hundred and fifty years later but one of these names appears in the list of Yehidim. Even when men well qualified did accept the office the working did not always run smoothly. This is evident from a remarkable dispute with Moses, otherwise Anthony, da Costa, records of which have survived. Moses da Costa was one of the outstanding members of the Community, a grandson of Alvaro da Costa and Dr. Fernando Mendes. He was elected Parnas in 1769, but neglected to intimate his acceptance or refusal of the office. After some delay he did accept, but then he neglected to pay the deposit of £100 required of every parnas on acceptance. Then followed a series of meetings and resolutions by the Mahamad and the Elders, culminating in a not very edifying correspondence. There was, however, some grievance on the part of others which has a connexion with the election of da Costa but does not fully come to light. Da Costa was elected Parnas on the 6th of Nisan, and on the 17th of that month—the first of the intermediate days of Passover, a semi-holiday on which all but the most urgent business was avoided—an emergency meeting of the Elders, called on the requisition of a number of them, was held at which voice was given to the 'widespread annoyance caused by the great affront' given to two of the oldest and most respected Yehidim, apparently by not electing them as Parnassim. These two 'victims' were Gabriel Lopes de Brito and Pinhas Gomes Serra. Three days later Gabriel Lopes de Brito was elected to fill a vacancy, that does not appear to have yet existed—presumably in anticipation of one occurring, and it was also decided that the first further available vacancy should be filled by the election of Pinhas Gomez Serra. After waiting nearly three months it was decided to give da Costa a further month in which to make the deposit and if he still neglected to do so to conclude that he refused election and to fine him forty pounds in accordance with the usual procedure. Still da Costa made no move, and on the 14th of Ab, more than four months after the original election, the office was declared vacant. A few weeks before the final date, however, the Mahamad still anxious not to estrange da Costa, sent their secretary to him with a verbal message. His report sums up the not very pleasant reception he obtained. The secretary: 'The President and the rest of the Gentlemen of Mahamad desired me to call upon you with their compliments and to acquaint you that this is the last day for you paying the hundred pounds and if you do not your place of Parnas will be vacant and that they must proceed in a regular course.' M. da Costa's reply: 'Being contrary to the Law of God for to condemn a man unheard the sentence of itself is reversed that declaring that they will deem it a refusal they cannot as I now am and will continue a parnass unless they have an Ascama or Power to turn me out for the vote of itself is making black white.' The following day da Costa followed this verbal reply with a lengthy letter, also in English, protesting in extravagant terms against the action of those whom he considered his colleagues in the Mahamad. The further proceedings were not recorded, and possibly there was a vacancy in the office until the next regular date for an election, when da Costa was not re-elected. There were several symptoms of financial weakness at this period, due possibly to the gradual withdrawal, by death or otherwise, of many of the wealthier members of the Community. Yehidim got noticeably in arrear in the payment of their fintas, and recourse had to be had to the very unsatisfactory step of treating as ordinary revenue money received as legacies. But this step did not bridge the gap. Others were necessary. The subventions to the congregational charities had to be drastically reduced, and in the process perhaps some reorganization was effected. By these means the difficulties were overcome, but it seems that the most prosperous period in the history of the Community had passed.

The Ascamot or body of laws governing the Congregation, drawn up and adopted in 1664, had never been considered the acme of perfection but had been under a continuous course of revision. As the necessity showed itself amendments and additions had been made, and by the period that has now been reached in this narrative it was generally realized that the amended and re-amended versions then in force needed a thorough recasting. This was accordingly taken in hand and a new version of the Ascamot was adopted and printed at the opening of the year 5545 (1784). The fundamental laws of the Community adopted more than a century earlier remained untouched, and the absolute control remained in the hands of the small group of Elders—consisting of ex-members of the Mahamad—by whom the Mahamad, an executive committee, was appointed. The powers of the Elders were even increased, and every member of that body, on election, had to take an oath before the open doors of the Ark that he would administer the laws of the Community, following the established usage, without fear or favour. The prohibition on the opening of a second place of worship was continued, subject, however, to the agreement of two-thirds of the Yehidim. The prohibition applied, however, only within four miles of Bevis Marks. Previously the distance had been indefinite—in the City of London and its surroundings. The minimum finta, by now no longer a loan but one of the principal sources of revenue for the

Community, payable by a Yahid, was fixed at two shillings and the maximum at fifteen pounds, the total expected to be derived from this source being placed at £600. This figure, however, did not remain for long. It was soon raised to £750 and then again to £900. The minimum and maximum were also altered, the former to two shillings and sixpence and the latter to seventeen pounds ten shillings. Any Yahid proposing to leave the Community was required to pay an additional year's finta as a sort of fine, but no provision was or could be made for enforcing the payment.

It was laid down that the Mahamad should be elected by the members of the retiring Mahamad in conjunction with eight other recent holders of the office. If anyone of these neglected to take part in the election he was to be fined one pound unless he had a satisfactory excuse for his absence. And since, as it seems, there was a general disposition to excuse absence, if those who did attend neglected to fine their erring colleague they were as a body themselves liable to a fine of five pounds. An election could take place if seven of these electors were present. Otherwise all the other Elders should be invited to participate in the election. The voting was by means of a complicated system of lots. The minimum age of the Gabay who was in effect the executive officer of the Mahamad and on whom in that capacity most of the administrative work of the Community fell, was twenty-five years. For a Parnas the minimum age was fifty, unless he had already served as Gabay, subsequently reduced to forty-five and later to forty. The heavy deposits hitherto required of holders of these offices were no longer required.

The precedence and privileges of the honorary officers of the Community were defined almost meticulously. It was enacted that

'Should anyone rise in Synagogue to oppose or reprobate any of the orders of the Mahamad, or of him who may be presiding, or contradict or offend the said President in the said synagogue or in its court, or form parties in any place to oppose the orders of the Elders of the Nation, or of the Mahamad, or distribute papers murmuring at or reprobating any of their orders, he shall pay such a fine as the Mahamad shall deem proper according to the nature of the offence, not being, however, less than ten pounds nor more than twenty.'

In the event of the offender being without means he should be required publicly from the Teba in the course of service, 'in an audible voice' to ask pardon of God and the Congregation for his offence.

In the interests of the preservation of the Community and the proper religious behaviour of the Yehidim special care was to be taken in granting membership. No one was to be accepted who was not of Portuguese or Spanish Jewish birth, of twenty-one years of age or upwards. Widows and single women could be admitted as *Yehidot*, but no provision was made for the admission of married women. Admission to the Community was to be made by a two-thirds majority of the Elders. Any Yahid or Yahida who was three years in arrear in the payments due was to be removed from the list of members and anyone who removed from London, without the permission of the Elders, was also to cease to be a member unless subsequently he could satisfy the Elders that his membership should be retained. Any Yahid found to be profaning the Sabbath was to be summarily expelled. Anyone who married a non-Jewess or who was intimate with one should also be expelled. For more than half a century it had been the practice to refuse to bury a member of the Community who had married a non-Jewess.

Anyone who caused damage to the synagogue buildings or to its surroundings, including Heneage Lane specially mentioned, was to be fined, as was also anyone who assaulted or insulted another member of the Community. The prohibition of proselytization was again enacted. The selling of goods, apart from prayer books and religious appurtenances, in the courtyard of the synagogue was prohibited. Another prohibition that was re-enacted with emphasis was that of publishing or printing without the permission of the Mahamad, who should consult the Haham, anything in any language relating to religion or politics or the Government of the country. The legislation against participation in political matters had been in force for at least sixty years. In the case of a vacancy for a Haham the Elders must be convened within three months to take steps to elect a successor.

Yehidim were not permitted to marry below their social rank without the permission of the Mahamad, but this prohibition does not appear to have applied to Yehidot. Marriage with Tudescos was not prohibited, but it was still sternly frowned on. The Haham was not to officiate at such a marriage, and any member who married a Tudesca or the widow of one was disqualified from benefit from the Sedaca.

The *imposta* or tax on trade or mercantile activities, once the principal source of revenue of the Congregation, still lingered on but was gradually diminishing until in the end it faded away.

Occasionally the story of the Sephardim in England is illuminated by a romance, as a rule in accordance with the pattern of other such romances in eighteenth-century England. One such which aroused widespread interest within and also without the Community was that of the elopement or runaway match in 1772 of Sarah Ximenes or Ximenes Cardoso and Joshua Lara, both members of prominent families. The story is told at length in a pamphlet that was published at the time. The young lady, it seems, was on a visit in the house of her brother-in-law and sister, Joseph Capadose and Abigail Ximenes. (Something unusual happened with regard to the Capadose marriage also, for after having been married in Paris, in Tebet 1772, although they were members of the London Community, they were married again in London two months later.) One evening the young lady did not appear for dinner, and after some inquiry and hours of suspense it was learnt that she had taken a post-chaise to meet Joshua Lara, had accepted a ring from him in the presence of two witnesses—the minimum form of marriage service—and had accompanied him to St. Albans. The young couple then went to Paris, where they were remarried in accordance with full Jewish rites. Before leaving England they asked the bridegroom's brother-in-law, Jacob Mendes Furtado, to accompany them to act as a witness to this marriage. This he declined to do but he agreed to his wife, Joshua Lara's sister, going to Paris. When the angry father heard what had happened he turned to the Haham to intervene. He presumably considered that one elopement per family—that of the Capadoses—was sufficient. The young couple were promptly excommunicated and the marriage declared null and void. This was bad enough, but the irate father was not yet satisfied. He followed the couple to Paris, arriving a few hours after the second marriage had taken place, and turned for assistance to the police, whom he is alleged in the pamphlet to have bribed. The police authorities duly responded. They proceeded to the house in which the young couple were staying, and at two o'clock in the morning arrested and separated them. For fifteen days the young couple were under arrest. In the meanwhile Mr. Ximenes returned to London to collect the decree of excommunication and returned with it to Paris, intent on having the marriage annulled on the ground that Lara had forced his daughter to marry him. In this, however, he was not successful. In the meanwhile members of the bridegroom's family, also not without influence, joined in the dispute. They also brought pressure to bear on the Haham, who had had the support of the Mahamad, and he began to realize that his action had perhaps been precipitate. Gradually and grudgingly he began to retrace his steps, and ultimately all the decisions he had given were withdrawn and cancelled. The Mahamad, however, did not capitulate without a struggle, and after the couple had returned to England set up a sort of court of inquiry. The first court of inquiry having failed to inculpate Lara of having forced the girl to marry him, a second one was set up, but Lara and his wife declined to recognize this court or to appear before it. The young couple, supported by the Mendes Furtados, were completely successful. The irate father, the Haham, and the Mahamad all capitulated, and the young couple were not even required to remarry within the shadow of Bevis Marks as had the Capadoses.

It has been mentioned previously that to marry a girl of the Community without her father's or guardian's consent had been made an offence subject to severe penalties. This edict was by no means a dead letter, for it is recorded in 1737 that a young man, having committed such a serious offence, was promptly excommunicated for 'young men should not entice the daughters of Israel to act contrary to divine and human laws or against the wishes of their parents and the fear of God should prevail and the family honour and reputation'. And so as to discourage imitators this pronouncement and decision was read publicly in the synagogue on three successive sabbaths.

At the close of the eighteenth century, in 1793, there was another of these Sephardi romances—one that arouses perhaps less sympathy even among the tender-hearted—which also attracted undue attention. Two well-known families were again involved—the Lindos and the Mendes Belisarios. Esther Lindo, a young orphan, was induced by one of the Mendes Belisario family, a man much older than herself, to enter into a secret or irregular marriage with him. The ceremony was on this occasion also reduced to the lowest limits—the acceptance of a ring and the recital of the marriage formula. After the ceremony the couple separated and never met again as husband and wife. This time the Haham and the Beth Din—perhaps cautious after their earlier experience—refused to commit themselves to a decision whether or not the marriage was binding in Jewish law. The girl's guardian, Abraham de Mattos Mocatta, thereupon appealed to the Court of Chancery to protect his ward. The Lord Chancellor accepted the responsibility and ordered that a suit of jactitation of marriage should be entered in the Court of Consistory. The case was argued before Lord Stowell, who felt he could not adjudicate without expert opinion. He knew that consentual marriages among Jews were recognized and that the ecclesiastical courts had held that the validity of Jewish marriages was to be decided in accordance with

Jewish law. To help him to a decision Lord Stowell had recourse to a number of authorities, early and contemporary. Among others the three members of the Sephardi Beth Din, Juliano, Almosnino, and Delgado; Isaac Ximenes, former Haham of Hamburg; and Solomon Lyon, the Hebraist of Cambridge, were consulted. The opinions given by these authorities differed and the court remained in a state of uncertainty. After further consideration it gave judgment against a marriage. The parties, the court decided, were only betrothed and the contract was determinable by either party at will. As the lady did not wish to continue further in the marriage there was no obligation on her to do so. This decision was in accordance with the opinion given by the Beth Din. Mendes Belisario appealed against this decision to the Court of Arches, which rejected the appeal.

The last quarter of the eighteenth century was a period of incipient social upheaval in England. The Jewish as well as the general community was affected, and at a time when the number of criminals was increasing and their activities becoming continually bolder it is not to be expected that some of the less disciplined and less responsible members of the Jewish community should remain immune. That the Mahamad must have been disturbed by the wave of crime that was attracting undesired public attention is clear, for in December 1775 it inserted advertisements in the following terms in a number of London newspapers:

'The Parnassim or Directors of the Portuguese Jews residing in the City of London, ever willing to bring offenders to justice but more immediately so, those of their particular Community, do hereby promise a reward of thirty guineas to be paid by their Secretary to any person or persons who shall within the term of three years from the date hereof seize and bring to justice any individual belonging to the aforesaid Community so that such culprit may be convicted capitally in any court of assize in Great Britain.'

Occasionally, at intervals throughout the eighteenth century, a Jew —sometimes a Sephardi—had been hanged at Tyburn but these advertisements do not seem to have brought any response, at any rate followed by a conviction, unless the John Franque who was hanged in the year 1780 was both a Jew and Sephardi. This execution was in any case probably too late to be a consequence of the advertisements.

A more pleasing incident was the interest shown in the Congregational manuscripts by Benjamin Kennicott, the biblical scholar, who in the course of the preparation of his great work on the text of the Hebrew Bible asked for permission to examine them. This permission was readily granted.

The officers of the Congregation at that time, apart from the honorary ones, mention of whom in the foregoing pages is frequent, consisted of the Haham, Rubis or teachers who also with the Haham constituted the Beth Din, one or more Hazanim, Samasim, the doctor and also a secretary sometimes designated chancellor. At first it seems that the Gabay acted as secretary and the minutes are as a rule written by him by whom they were almost invariably signed. The Gabay probably became tired of the routine work of the office, and at the same time the financial position of the Congregation improved sufficiently for the expenditure on salaries to be increased. In these circumstances the office of secretary or chancellor came into being. Of these secretaries the earliest known is Aaron Nunes, who resigned in 1732. He was succeeded in that year by Solomon de Castro, the first of several members of that family to hold the office. He resigned in 1740 when another de Castro, Abraham, was appointed in his place. Abraham de Castro was also the first secretary of the Jewish Board of Deputies in its present form, being appointed to that office in 1760. Abraham de Castro died in 1779 and was succeeded by Elias Lopes Pereira, of the family of the wealthy Barons d'Aguilar. He resigned in 1786 on inheriting a fortune. He did not, however, cease his service to the Community. In the subsequent years he filled several honorary offices, including those of Gabay and Parnas and, when he died, he bequeathed a considerable legacy to the Congregation. Lopes Pereira was succeeded by yet another de Castro, Daniel Jacob, who on his death in 1821 was followed by Solomon Almosnino, who had acted as clerk or assistant secretary, a grandson of the Haham Isaac Almosnino who had come to England as a refugee during the siege of Gibraltar in 1781. Almosnino's emoluments on appointment were a salary of £75 a year and a house free of rent, but he was required to enter into a bond for £500 that he would perform his duties to the satisfaction of the Mahamad and Elders. Shortly before the publication of the revised code of Ascamot in 1784 Haham d'Azevedo died. A month later Isaac Almosnino, the former Haham of Gibraltar, followed d'Azevedo to the grave. Although he held no office in the London Community he was accepted as second only to the Haham, and his opinion was often sought. More than one of his descendants held office in the

Congregation. The community suffered other losses at this time. One of the Hazanim, who was also a communal rabbi, David Isaac de Castro or Crastro, died on 3 January 1785 after thirty-five years' service, and three weeks later his fellow rabbi and a teacher in the communal school, Benjamin Dias Lorenço. After the death of Haham d'Azevedo there was again an interregnum, one of twenty-two years.

During this period developments which will be dealt with later were considerable. Although the records of the Congregation continued to be kept in Portuguese, after Hebrew still the language of the Synagogue, the advance of English was continuous. Even before the middle of the eighteenth century, English words and phrases began to find their way into the minutes of the meetings, and probably also into the discussions these reported, to an ever-increasing extent. English had some years earlier been admitted to the congregational schools, and the need for an English version of the prayer book had been manifest and had been met by more than one writer.

Before this chapter is closed and the story of the new century is opened, there are one or two matters that call for mention. Jewish cemeteries were not exceptional at the end of the eighteenth century in suffering at the hands of a body of men who set out to supply the hospitals with corpses for anatomical research, and the Jewish authorities, in common with their Christian colleagues, had to take steps for the protection of their dead. On the enlargement of the communal cemetery, in 1786, precautions had to be taken at once to prevent desecration of the graves. Many suggestions and experiments were made, but none proved satisfactory. In the end it was agreed that there was no alternative to the hiring of watchmen, and items of expenditure under this heading henceforth appeared in the accounts for a number of years. There were every night two watchmen on duty. As time passed, the private employment of watchman was also introduced. The watchmen were provided with a sort of small movable fortress on wheels, in which they were expected to spend the hours of darkness. By this means the bodies of the dead were given protection. That this occupation of cemetery watchman was a not unhealthy one is evident from the grant of a gratuity in January 1821, in accordance with precedent, of five pounds to James Mason, watchman at the burial ground, aged eighty-five, who had resigned after thirty-five years' service. Five years later, in May 1826, 'In consequence of Abraham Silva, one of the Watchmen at Beth Haim being advanced to 82 years of age, and quite enfeebled and having been in the Service of the Synagogue for upwards of 45 years, it was resolved that he should relinquish his situation, and be allowed 5s. per week during his life.' Jews and non-Jews were both employed in this office, but it seems that as a rule the couples in which these men were on duty consisted of one Jew and one non-Jew.

A few years earlier there was an incident of an entirely different character that led to quite unexpected consequences. As has previously been remarked, the decorum in the Synagogue did not always conform to the standards laid down today. The Mahamad from time to time realized this and made attempts by legislation to keep the conduct of the services within more orderly bounds. There were occasions, however, when this proved almost outside the limits of practicability. One of these was the celebration of the Feast of Purim. To express their execration of Haman and his exploits and intentions it was the custom on the part of the more religiously exuberant section of the Congregation to create such a din at every mention of Haman's name as to shock and annoy the more moderate members. The Mahamad decided in 1783 to keep these manifestations of exuberant Judaism within some limits. Expressions of reprobation were to be permitted, but not the noise and din that had hitherto been prevalent. The new Ascama on the subject ran in part as follows:

'1. In future no person of our nation of either sex or of any age, shall on Purim or at any other time of the year, appear in the streets in masquerade, or disguised in the dress of the other sex, though only to pass from one house to another, this being as well a violation of decency, as of the laws of God and of this kingdom: and whoever shall do so in defiance of this prohibition shall be fined by the Mahamad a sum not exceeding five pounds for Sedaca. 2. Also in future, on the evening and morning of Purim while the *Megillah* is read, or at any other time, no person of whatever condition, age or sex, shall beat, or make a noise in Synagogue with a hammer, or any other instrument, since apart from the scandal to which such a bad custom would give rise, it may prevent many devout persons of our congregation from going to Synagogue on these occasions.'

The penalty in such a case was a fine not exceeding twenty pounds. The noisy section on the evening of the subsequent Purim ignored the new regulations, and on the following morning they found two constables within the synagogue, put there to preserve order. The rioters ignored their presence until they found themselves promptly ejected from the building. The offenders were summoned before the Mahamad, and all, with one exception, submitted and in some cases had to pay trifling fines. The exception was Isaac Mendes Furtado. Furtado belonged to a Marrano family that had escaped from the clutches of the Inquisition. Members of the family came to England where they settled and prospered. One, Abraham Mendes Furtado, later went to France, where he held a prominent place in Napoleon's Sanhedrin. Another married into the d'Israeli family. In England members of a later generation were well-known musicians. Isaac Mendes Furtado was scandalized by the proceedings in the Synagogue on this Purim. He objected to the interference by the constables in the service. He objected to the prohibition on celebrating the Feast in the manner that most appealed to him. He rejected the jurisdiction of the Mahamad and withdrew from the Congregation which he considered unworthy of his membership. To mark the incident he named a row of houses that he was erecting in east London, Purim Place. In the end the family withdrew from Judaism altogether, and most of its members are buried in the churchyard of St. Mary's, Stoke Newington.

This describes the loss to Bevis Marks of one family. Another, about this time, was that of a more distinguished one, the Bernals. The trouble caused on the occasion of the marriage of Jacob Israel Bernal to a Tudesca has already been mentioned,[1] but this did not lead to the withdrawal of the bridegroom from the Community. He was only barred from office. His sons, Isaac and Jacob, both withdrew from the Community, but for other reasons. Isaac was deeply offended by his failure to secure election to the honorary office he desired. Jacob withdrew on more general grounds. In doing so he denounced the Mahamad as being dictatorial and of competing with the Inquisition in the torture of those more delicate minds which they were unable to penetrate. The lines followed by the two Bernals led in different directions. Isaac had married a non-Jewish wife, who, however, followed Jewish practices, and their children were brought up as Jews. For thirty-four years Isaac had kept away from the synagogue, but had nevertheless and despite his non-Jewish wife lived as a Jew. After his death his daughters were admitted as Yehidot. He was buried in the Beth Haim in Mile End in 1820.[2] His brother who had denounced the

[1] See p. 170.
[2] The Synagogue authorities had not considered that there was sufficient reason for his withdrawal from the Congregation and had not agreed to it. He was therefore theoretically heavily in debt to the Congregation for payments due over a period of thirty-three years, but it was intimated that on payment of only £17, burial in the Community's cemetery would be permitted. 'The sum is rated with great moderation in consequence of his pecuniary circumstances for several years past.'

synagogue authorities as a body, withdrew from Jewry completely. He had married a Sephardi Jewess, and his son Ralph married a wife of Sephardi origin even though not in synagogue. This son, however, in whatever religious community he was born, did not die a Jew. He was the Ralph Bernal who was Chairman of Committees of the House of Commons for twenty years and a famous art collector. Ralph Bernal's son, also Ralph, obtained a commission in the Army and later also entered the House of Commons, being appointed in course of time Parliamentary Secretary to the Admiralty. On his marriage to a daughter of Sir Thomas Osborne he added Osborne to his surname, and in the social history of England he stands out as Ralph Bernal-Osborne, distinguished as a wit. His grandson is the Duke of St. Albans.

CHAPTER XII
MORE PERSONALITIES

AS THE YEARS passed, the interests of the Jews of England continued to widen until in a growing number of cases—although the total was still small—non-Jewish interests took the place of Jewish ones to an extent that was foreboding. From political activities English citizens of the Jewish faith were still excluded. Yet it seems that the attraction of general political life and discussion was not lacking, for provision had to be made in the Ascamot for the avoidance of the risk which it was still feared, in view of a feeling of uncertainty which although diminishing still survived, incursions into the sphere of politics might bring. However, not only was the still existent feeling of nervousness gradually passing away: even the definite disabilities under which professing Jews in England laboured were, though very slowly, hardly perceptibly, passing into desuetude. For instance, Jews might be debarred from voting at parliamentary elections, but by the end of the eighteenth century very few could remember a returning officer refusing any Jew the right to do so.

However, this was the limit of the political rights or privileges at the end of the eighteenth century. It was into other fields, in which there were no legislative hindrances, that Jews were penetrating. In the year 1758 there occurred the death of Moses Lumbrozo de Mattos, described as 'broker in bullion to the Bank of England'. This was a son-in-law of Abraham Mocatta, a merchant of wealth and standing, who had died seven years earlier. The Mocatta family goes back in Anglo-Jewish records without a break from father to child to one of the two Moses Mocattas who were living in England while Cromwell was still Protector. These two and also a contemporary Immanuel Mocatta had come to England from Amsterdam, where members of the family had been living almost from the beginning of the Jewish settlement there. Earlier Mocattas had been living in Italy, having come there from Spain a few years before the expulsion from that kingdom. The name, which is of Arabic origin, denotes a very early residence in Spain, possibly as long ago as the eighth century, after the defeat and death of Roderick, 'the last of the Goths'. One branch of the family, however, remained in Spain as crypto-Jews. This branch, as was the custom among other Marranos, took a non-Jewish name, that of the town or Christian family with which they were connected. In the case of the Mocattas this name was Marchina or Marchena. Moses, the ancestor of the present family in England, was known first as Antonio de Marchena, and only later as Moses Mocatta. He was presumably of the Marrano, not of the Italian, branch of the family. There was, as has been said in an earlier chapter, another Anthony de Marchina living in England over a century before the arrival of Moses Mocatta, one of a group of crypto-Jews living in London towards the end of the reign of Henry VIII. The members of this group admittedly 'came for religion to England'.

To return to Moses Lumbrozo de Mattos, 'the broker in bullion to the Bank of England'. The Bank of England was founded in 1694, and if not from the beginning, very shortly afterwards, a Lumbrozo de Mattos became one of its agents for the purchase of bullion. The Abraham Mocatta who died in 1751 had a brother Isaac, who had died twenty-two years before him. Of his descendants, if any, nothing is known. Abraham's daughter, by her second husband, Moses Lumbrozo de Mattos, left two sons of whom the elder, Abraham, on the death of his grandfather, took the name Abraham Lumbrozo de Mattos Mocatta, succeeding in due course to the businesses of his father and grandfather. After a time Abraham Mocatta was authorized to drop the names Lumbrozo de Mattos. It is said that in his petition he explained that to write out his name in full every time he signed a business or official document imposed too great a strain on him. Henceforth he passed as Abraham Mocatta, and in that name held high office in the Sephardi Community. Later the firm of Abraham Mocatta joined forces with that of Asher Goldsmid, and under the name of Mocatta and Goldsmid it is still flourishing in the City of London as bullion brokers to the Bank of England, having acted in a similar capacity also to the East India Company as long as that institution existed. Among the partners today are Mocattas and a Goldsmid, the former are direct descendants of Abraham Mocatta, but of a branch that withdrew from Bevis Marks over a century ago and helped to found the West London Synagogue of British Jews. One of this branch of the family, Mr. Owen Mocatta, is today the President of the West London Synagogue.

Another family well known in the Sephardi Community to which it has given leaders and guides for generation after generation is that of Montefiore. This family, as its name denotes, is of Italian origin and its first English members came from Leghorn early in the eighteenth century. The first of the family to come to England were the brothers Joseph, who married in London Rachel Chamis Vaz at the beginning of the year 1753, and Moses Vita (Haim), who had married Esther Hannah Racah in Leghorn some months earlier. Later came two other brothers, David and Eliezer. Of these four, Moses Vita was the eldest, and it was from him that is descended the branch of the family that later became so prominent in Anglo-Jewry. Nothing is now known of the present-day descendants of any of the other brothers. The four brothers engaged in commerce, and in due course prospered. Moses Vita had a large family—eight sons and nine daughters, most of whom married and in their turn had large families. Two married Tudescos and two, daughters of Abraham Mocatta. Three of the sons lived for a time in the West Indies—whither the sons of Anglo-Jewry at that period often went to seek their fortunes— Eliezer, the father of, among a number of other children, Jacob, one of the Commissioners for the Colonization of South Australia, and Joseph Barrow, who ultimately settled in that colony; another Jacob, a London merchant, apparently a victim of a press gang, who died in Barbados at the early age of twenty-eight shortly after his arrival there; and Joshua, whose career exceeded in adventure the combined ones of all of his sixteen brothers and sisters. Born in 1762, Joshua married Esther Lupino, who left him a childless widower at the age of twenty-five. Unable to settle down, we find him three years later engaged in a sort of Bevis Marks expedition to the west coast of Africa bent on the conquest and colonization of the island of Bulama there. 'A Bevis Marks expedition', for the undertaking seems to have been financed disproportionately by members of the Sephardi Community, several members of which took part in it. In command was Moses Levi Ximenes or Ximenes Cardoso, later Sir Morris Ximenes. Among the contributors who stayed at home were Emanuel Baruch Lousada, Jacob Mocatta, Samuel Vita Montefiore, a brother of Joshua, Abraham Levi Ximenes, Abraham Texeira, and Manasseh Lopes, later the famous baronet. Among the participants, in addition to Ximenes and Joshua Montefiore, were Benjamin and Mordecai Pereira and another Levi Ximenes, Isaac. The expedition was, however, not a success, and Joshua Montefiore returned to England. In England he had a variegated career, if his recollections are to be trusted, although his imagination seems to have been the more intense. At one time or another he claimed to have graduated at the University of Oxford, although his name can be found nowhere in the university records, to have held a commission in the Army— employment by the military authorities in a civil capacity for a short time at York seems to have been the basis of this claim—and to have been a member of the Bar. As a professing Jew, Montefiore could not at that time have fulfilled any of these claims. He, however, was admitted as a notary and was the author of some books on commercial law, and he was also admitted at the age of twenty-two a member of a lodge of freemasons. Montefiore also said that he had been offered a knighthood by King George III in 1803, possibly in appreciation of his exploits in the Bulama expedition four years earlier, and to have refused it. Unable to settle down in England, Montefiore went to Jamaica, where he endeavoured, on the strength of his record, to be admitted to the Bar, but was refused on account of his Judaism. He then returned to England. In the end he settled in the United States, where he practised law. At the age of seventy-one he married a second time, a non-Jewess, and before he died ten years later he had had seven children. His Jewish consciousness continued until the end, for he was accustomed as each boy was born to send the child to Boston, a week's journey, to be circumcised. Montefiore was buried more or less with Jewish rites in his garden at St. Albans, Vermont, a translation of the Jewish burial service having been written by him from memory, in anticipation, while on his death-bed.

The two brothers, Sir Morris and Sir David Ximenes, were members of a family whose names appear repeatedly in the records of the Sephardi Community during the seventeenth and eighteenth centuries. Their mother was a Mendes da Costa. In the end the Levi Ximenes family died out, but not before its last members had withdrawn from the Community, offended, it is said, at their election, without their consent, to office. Both the brothers were at first in the city, but, being men of wealth, they soon retired from it. Moses or Morris Ximenes was an amateur soldier. David made the Army his profession, and it was as Lieutenant-General Sir David Ximenes that he died in 1848. Sir Morris Ximenes when he applied for a grant of arms in 1807 represented 'that he and his family have always used as arms . . . which appear to be similar to those used by Cardinal Ximenes, Archbishop of Toledo, Primate and Prime Regent of all Spain and Castile, from a branch of whose family he is traditionally descended'. This claim must, however, not be accepted without question. Similarity of name between Marrano and Spaniard did not always denote relationship. Mention has been made also of Sir Manasseh Masseh Lopes. He was a member of one of those wealthy West Indian families, all of which seem sooner or later to have settled in England. In this case it was the father of the baronet, Mordecai Rodrigues Lopez, who came to England about the middle of the eighteenth century and lived at Clapham, then a part of the pleasant countryside in the neighbourhood of London. Manasseh Lopes had political ambitions, and like his forerunner, Sampson Gideon, was covetous of a title. The attainment of neither was possible to a Jew, and Lopes, on whom his Judaism sat lightly, had no qualms about accepting Christianity so that he might qualify for both. Having accepted baptism, Lopes was successful in the attainment of both of his ambitions. Not only did baptism open to him the path into Parliament, but in 1805 he was created a baronet, with the exceptional remainder, since he had no son, to a nephew, Ralph or Raphael Franco, who was the son of his sister Esther, and of Abraham Franco, a member of another prominent English Sephardi family, of Italian origin. From Sir Ralph Franco who took the name of Lopes were descended Lord Justice Lopes (Henry Charles Lopes), later created Lord Ludlow, Lord Roborough (Sir Massey Henry Lopes), and the future Viscount Bledisloe. There was much heartburning over this succession, for Esther was not the eldest sister. Another had married a Pereira in Jamaica, and their son, Benjamin, always felt that he had been deprived of his birthright and his feelings were not concealed. As a further reward for his baptism Manasseh Lopes was elected to Parliament in 1802 for New Romney, and in 1812 for Barnstaple. His next constituency was Grampound, but here he got into trouble. As was subsequently proved, he had, through an agent, distributed before the election £2,000 among its sixty electors. When this became known the politicians, of the other party, were scandalized. Lopes was indicted for bribery and corruption and convicted. In the meanwhile, however, he had stood again, this time for Barnstaple, and had been elected, at a cost of £3,000 distributed among the three hundred electors. Lopes was convicted of this offence also, and in punishment for both fined £10,000 and sent to prison for two years. The corrupt borough of Grampound was disfranchised. These incidents did not, however, interrupt Lopes's political career, except for an interval of two years, during which he found himself not at liberty to attend to his parliamentary duties. On his release from prison he was elected for his own pocket borough of Westbury, of which he was also recorder, and remained in Parliament as its representative, with one interval, until 1829, when he resigned to provide a seat for Sir Robert Peel, the future Prime Minister, who, on account of his change from hostility to support of Catholic Emancipation, had been defeated in the University of Oxford. Despite these adventures Lopes remained undisturbed in his membership of the magistracy in the county of Devonshire, where he had been tried and convicted, and in Wiltshire or in his recordership of Westbury. It is said that when, on his death-bed in 1831, his mind went back to his early days, before the road was clear to the attainment of his ambitions, he asked for Jewish ministration. A message was sent hastily to the nearest Jewish community, in Plymouth, for someone to be sent to him, but the request went unheeded. Sir Manasseh Lopes left the immense fortune of £800,000.

The story of Isaac d'Israeli is more familiar by virtue of his illustrious son. Like the Francos and the Montefiores, the d'Israelis were also of Italian origin, Benjamin d'Israeli, senior, Isaac's father, having come to England about the same time as the earlier Montefiore brothers. The first Benjamin d'Israeli entered commerce. His son felt no call in that direction and devoted himself to letters. He, like the Ximenes, although little more than a nominal member of the Community, was elected a parnas against his will, and as a consequence withdrew altogether from it,[1] but although he was buried in non-Jewish surroundings, he never formally abandoned Judaism or adopted Christianity. In 1842, six years before his death, he attended the opening of the West London Synagogue of British Jews, whose teachings and development he had to some extent anticipated in a little book *The Genius of Judaism*, which he had published anonymously in 1833.

A contemporary of a different character and whose path led for other reasons away from the synagogue was David Ricardo, one of the creators of the science of political economy. A member of one of the families that had come from Holland, his father had acquired wealth and given sterling service to the Community. David, on marrying a Christian lady and leaving the Jewish Community, was discarded by his father, but found influential friends elsewhere. In 1814, at the age of forty-two, he retired from the Stock Exchange with a considerable fortune. He then turned to the building up of a system of political economy as his life's work. He entered Parliament in 1819 and very soon attained there a position of such influence that in economic matters successive governments, not to mention future generations, found themselves in his debt. David Ricardo's intellectual interests were wide. For instance, he was one of the original members of the Geological Society. In the House of Commons he had probably the unique distinction of on one occasion being 'loudly called upon from all sides of the House' to speak on Peel's measure for the resumption

[1] See p. 242-6.

of cash payments. He had on an earlier occasion and in different circumstances said that he was so frightened by the sound of his own voice that in Parliament he should probably think it wisest to give silent votes. Ricardo died in 1823 at the early age of fifty-one, leaving a great name and a great fortune. Most of his near relatives followed his lead out of Jewry, but the family is still represented in the Sephardi Community. Outside of that community the Ricardo family has secured for itself a position of honour and respect. A nephew, John Lewis Ricardo, whose father, Jacob, married a Jewess and remained in the Jewish community after David had left it, died also at an early age. He followed his uncle into Parliament, where he devoted himself to the application of the teachings of his illustrious relative. Outside of Parliament he was a pioneer in the development of the railways and of the electric telegraph system. John Lewis Ricardo married Catherine Duff, a sister of the fifth Earl of Fife, whose son, created Duke of Fife, married the Princess Royal, the daughter of King Edward VII. John Lewis Ricardo was thus by marriage an uncle of the late Princess Royal.

Another occasional worshipper in Bevis Marks during this period, whose Judaism, however, seems to have been only an interlude between two periods of non-Judaism or crypto-Judaism, was John Charles Lucena, described in the *Gentleman's Magazine* on the occasion of his death in 1813 as 'Thirty years agent of affairs and consul-general from the Court of Portugal'. Lucena was a Marrano, born in Lisbon about the year 1750. His family, like that of other Lisbon families of Jewish origin, was much disturbed by the great earthquake of 1755, and a few years later the Lucena family left their home and settled in Newport, in North America. There they lived as Jews. Later the family removed to Savannah in Georgia, where there was at the time a more virile Jewish community. Involved in the rebellion of the colonists, as loyalists to the English cause, the Lucenas had to leave Georgia. James, the father of the family, returned to Portugal, where, since their departure from that country, the activities of the Inquisition had been much reduced. The son, John Charles, however, went to England, where, possibly with the assistance of his father, he was appointed Consul-General for Portugal in London. In England, however, there is no evidence that he connected himself in any manner with the Jewish Community. If he wished to retain his official position it was hardly possible for him to do so.[1]

---

[1] For an account of the Lucenas, see *Publications of the American Jewish Historical Society*, vol. XXXVIII.

The da Costa Alvarenga family, although not prominent, is long-standing in the annals of Anglo-Jewry, reference to members of it going back to the seventeenth century. One member only seems to have attained notice out of the ordinary rut in which most of the Sephardim of London were then and later confined. This was one of a branch that had transferred its home to Jamaica. Isaac da Costa Alvarenga, a member of this branch, chose medicine as his calling and the State as his employer. For forty years he served in the medical branch of the British Navy and retired with the rank of rear-admiral. A sister of da Costa Alvarenga married Jacob Orobio Furtado, a member of one of the most illustrious of the Marrano families, and among their grandchildren was Sir John Simon, who settled in England where he attained great distinction at the Bar, in Parliament, and in the service of the Jewish community. In 1730 David and Rachel Orobio Furtado escaped from Portugal to England, where they were at once remarried according to Jewish rites.

One group of settlers in England in the latter half of the eighteenth century consisted of diplomatic emissaries of North African rulers. The first of these had come a century earlier in the person of Jacob Sasportas, the first Haham of London, who had previously been sent by the Ruler of Morocco on diplomatic missions. Not long after him, in the year 1675, Chayim ben Daniel de Toledo or Toledano was in London as an envoy of the ruler of the same empire. Jewish residents in Moslem lands were especially fitted for this service, being qualified, by the dispersion of their families and the close and continued connexion between the members, to act as the links between Islam and Christendom. Jacob Benider, although an accredited emissary from the Sultan of Morocco, was a British subject by birth, having been born in Gibraltar, after the annexation of that fortress. In fact he began his official career as vice-consul in several British consulates in Morocco. From these minor offices his activities extended. On one occasion he was seconded for service with the Venetian Ambassador. In 1772 Benider came to London as the Ambassador of the Sultan of Morocco, having the full confidence, it seems, of both governments. Quoting from the *Gentleman's Magazine*,[1]

> 'The bearer of this Imperial letter is Jacob, the son of Abraham Benider, a person equally beloved of his sovereign and country, and who has your Majesty's interest to heart. I have entrusted him with full powers to treat, and from his knowledge

[1] Vol. XLII, p. 433.

of public affairs and his attention to our mutual affairs, I doubt not that he will conduct to a successful issue the negociations I have empowered him to carry on with your Majesty's Government.'

Benider, although in the service of the Emperor of Morocco, kept his family and home in Gibraltar, until the latter was destroyed and his son killed in the bombardment. His wife and daughter then joined him in London.[1] In 1794 another Jewish envoy of the Moroccan Government arrived in England. This was Joseph Sumbel. More is known of his matrimonial adventures than of his diplomatic activities. His family, while still in Morocco, seems to have been of service to the British Government, and their services were acknowledged. In London, Sumbel became involved in litigation with his brothers over some family property in consequence of which he was committed to the Fleet prison. There he met a Mrs. Mary Wells, a not very reputable actress, whom he married after she had accepted Judaism. The marriage was, however, not successful. There were many quarrels, and in the end Sumbel left his wife and settled in Altona.[2]

Somewhat later, in 1813, Masahod Macnin arrived in England on a mission from the Sultan of Morocco, and fourteen years later came a kinsman and namesake, Meir Cohen Macnin, in a similar capacity. The latter was accompanied by a relative, Solomon Sebag, who is described in his application for denization as 'Clerk to the Moorish Minister Meir Cohen Macnin'. Macnin and his entourage seem to have combined commerce with diplomacy, and they were soon absorbed into the commercial life of London. Solomon Sebag married a daughter of Joseph Elias Montefiore and was the father of the heir of Sir Moses, his brother-in-law. A Macnin, Abraham Cohen, was a member of the London Stock Exchange until his death in 1840. In September 1826 he protested against the claims made against him by the Congregation, and his finta was reduced by the Mahamad. Still later he attained to undesirable prominence in the Synagogue records on account of his matrimonial relations and their connexion with his status as Cohen.

Still later, in 1851, another member of the same family, David Cohen Macnin, finding himself in difficulties, applied to the

[1] For an account of Benider, see C. Roth, in *Miscellanies of the Jewish Historical Society of England*, vol. II.
[2] *Memories of the Life of Mrs. Sumbel, late Wells, of the Theatres Royal Drury Lane, Covent Garden and Haymarket* (1811) contains much about the joint career of Sumbel and his wife. My attention was directed to this work by Mr. Cecil Roth.

Mahamad for assistance. He was given five pounds on condition that he left the country—a condition not infrequently made in similar cases. At the end of the period he repaid the grant—apparently with interest—and the Mahamad seems to have been so surprised as to pass a special vote of appreciation of his action. David Cohen Macnin's career consisted of a series of vicissitudes. In 1830 we find him holding office as the first Treasurer and shortly afterwards President of the recently opened Shaare Tikva Preparatory School. But his end was unenviable. In the year 1866 he was admitted as a pauper inmate to the Beth Holim, the office of Parnas of which his namesake and probable kinsman, a Cohen Macnin, had refused in September 1830.

Another contemporary arrival was Abraham Belais. He was said to have been born in 1773[1] in Tunis, where he had been Treasurer to the Bey, but, on account of financial troubles, had been obliged to leave the country and settle in Jerusalem. Travelling on the Continent, he obtained support and assistance from men of influence everywhere—King Victor Emanuel of Sardinia, French statesmen, and others. From the Duke of Sussex, a son of George III, he received a letter of recommendation written in Hebrew. For a time he was rabbi of Nice, but in 1840, fortified by letters of introduction to the Duke of Sussex and the Dowager Queen Adelaide, he came to London, where he was appointed Rubi or teacher in the Sephardi school, and was occasionally called on to sit in the Beth Din to complete the quorum of dayanim. But his salary in this office proved inadequate for his support, and there are frequent references to him in the sedaca accounts of the Congregation. He soon got into other trouble, however, for in February 1841 he was called to account for publishing a volume of poems without the permission of the Mahamad and was admonished. He pleaded that in publishing without permission he was unaware that he was transgressing any law. Two years later he asked the Elders to pay for the publication of a work he had written, but they refused. He was by then again in financial difficulties, for a few months later the Elders found themselves compelled to make him an urgent grant, and these exceptional grants were frequently repeated. In January 1844 Belais was elected a student of the *Yeshiba*, which office carried with it a small stipend, and the hope was at the same time expressed that the need for assistance from the sedaca would thereupon cease. He wrote many books in Hebrew, mostly biblical or Talmudical. He was also a poet. As such he specialized in the writing of odes in honour of potentates

---

[1] At the time of his death in 1853 he was reputed to be ninety-five years of age.

JOHN KING (JACOB REY)
From 'Town and Country Magazine' (1787)

DAVID ABARBANEL LINDO
Drawn by J. H. Lynch, from a daguerrotype

PELLEGRINE TREVES
From an engraving (1801)

EPHRAIM LOPES PEREIRA,
SECOND BARON D'AGUILAR

and other men of distinction—George IV, Louis XVIII, Louis Philippe and other French princes, King Victor Emanuel, Ferdinand of Naples, and others. Belais died in London in 1853, leaving a widow to the Community. The Elders felt a moral, if not a legal, obligation to support her. They, however, attempted a compromise. They offered her a sum of money provided she left the country for good. She accepted the gift, but seven years later she was still in England, a pensioner of the Community. She died two years later and was buried at the expense of the Congregation.

Another scholar who settled in England about the same time was Isaac Leonini (otherwise Joseph) Azulay, a member of a family renowned in the annals of Jewish learning. His ancestry can be traced back to Rabbi Abraham Azulay, who left Castile for Italy in 1492. The settler in England was a son of Haham Raphael Azulay of Ancona, and descendants are still to be found in the London Jewish Community. When in Berlin in 1794, before he came to England, Azulay published a Spanish comedy on the title page of which he described himself as 'Teacher of Princess Augusta and in the Gymnasium of Berlin'. In London he married Bella Friedlaender, a cousin of the Ashkenazi Chief Rabbi, Solomon Hirschel. The inscription on Isaac Azulay's tombstone in the cemetery at Mile End sums up his career after the reservations often necessary in reading epitaphs:

'In memory of Signor Yitzhak Leonini Azulay M.A., twenty two years Professor Regius to the Institute of Noble Cadets in Berlin, Tutor to H.R.H. the Princess Royal of Prussia, member of several learned societes, etc., etc. Born at Leghorn. Died 16th Tammuz—17th July 1840.'

A man of quite different type was John King. This worthy first appeared as Jacob Rey, an inmate of the Sephardi Orphanage. He left this institution after seven years, in 1771, being apprenticed as a clerk in a city house, the premium of £5 being paid by the Community. Jacob advanced rapidly in the City. Gratitude and loyalty to his Community were among his characteristics. Four years after leaving the orphanage he sent its governing body a gift of a hundred pounds as an expression of gratitude for all he owed to it. Throughout his further career he displayed an active interest in synagogue affairs, and when he died he left the Congregation a legacy of £20, one half in part payment of a debt due to the sedaca and the other half as a legacy. He even wrote at least three theological works, putting forward the Jewish point of view in the controversies with which he dealt. Outside of the Jewish community Rey had a different career. There he was known as John King or sometimes Jew King or The King of the Jews. His clerkship in a Jewish business house did not last long. He soon blossomed forth as a 'financier' on his own account. In this calling, although he suffered some vicissitudes, he on the whole prospered. At one time he was partner with a well-known Irish baronet in a banking house in Piccadilly; at another he was a partner in a bank in Portland Place. With a strong streak of independence in his character he did not as a rule agree for long with his partners. Much litigation ensued, and he was at times confined in the Fleet or the King's Bench Prison. As the writer of his obituary in the *Gentleman's Magazine*[1] said

> 'His transactions being carried on in a peculiar way, he was constantly before some of the courts of law or equity, as plaintiff, defendant, or witness, in which latter capacity he was often roughly treated by the Gentlemen of the Bar, which induced him, in 1804, to publish a pamphlet entitled "Oppression deemed no injustice towards some Individuals".'

As a hobby King turned to political writing. In 1783 he addressed to Charles James Fox *Thoughts on the Difficulties and Distresses in which the Peace of 1783 has involved the people of England*. There are other interesting publications of his, including *Letters from France* and *An Essay, intended to shew a Universal System of Arithmetic*. King married Sarah de Benjamin Nunes Lara, a sister of the wealthy benefactor of the Synagogue, Moses Lara, whom he afterwards took to Italy and divorced in order to contract a second marriage. Their son published several scurrilous volumes in which he showed his detestation of his father for this injustice. On a visit to Paris, King had met and later married the widowed Countess of Lanesborough, the only daughter of the Earl of Belvedere, who towards the end of her life inherited a considerable fortune from her brother, the second earl. King's first wife, after his death, gave two sums of £50 each to the Congregation, one in her own name, the other in that of their daughter, Rachel Charlotte Rey, earmarked for communal institutions and to be treated as legacies paid in advance.

Early in life King came under the notice of Tom Paine, the author of *The Rights of Man*, from whom a letter has survived, dated Paris, 3 January 1793:

> 'When I first knew you in Philippe Street, an obscure part of the City, a child without fortune or friends, I noticed you

[1] 1824, p. 184.

because I thought I saw in you, young as you were, a bluntness of temper, a boldness of opinion, and an originality of thought that portend some future good. I was pleased to discuss with you under our friend Oliver's lime tree, those political notions, which I have since given the world in my "Rights of Man".'

King died in Florence in August 1823, Lady Lanesborough in the same city almost five years later, at the age of ninety.

The Treves family was one of great renown in Italy and Turkey, not only as merchants of the foremost rank but also as rabbinical scholars for many generations. It even claims descent from Rashi, and if this claim cannot be substantiated it is certain that Rabbi Simeon of Treves who married a cousin of Rashi was one of its ancestors. About the year 1740 two brothers, Joseph and Pellegrin Treves, were sent to London by their father to take over a business that he had established there. Under their guidance this business speedily rose to the first rank in commerce. In London they not only prospered commercially: by their marriages they entered the highest rank of Sephardi society. Joseph Treves married a daughter of Solomon da Costa Athias, and after her death, Rebecca da Costa, a daughter of Joseph da Costa of Totteridge. His brother Pellegrin or Gershom married Rebecca, daughter of Jacob Pereira de Paiba, and on her death after eleven months of married life, Bathsheba, daughter of Moses de Paiba and a niece of Sampson Gideon. After his second marriage he moved from the rooms over his warehouse in Mincing Lane to a house in the fashionable district of West London. Later he took a house in St. James's Place near the Green Park. He also had a house in Newmarket in which he spent the last seven years of his life. In the words of the *Gentleman's Magazine* of 1817 'in the meridian of life he was the companion of royalty and the wit of society'. This reference is to Treves' close friendship with the Prince Regent, afterwards George IV, of whom he was one of the boon companions. In the will of Rebecca Pereira de Paiba there is a moving passage relating to him.

'Lastly I do hereby return my said husband my most grateful thanks for the love and kindness he hath shown to me upon all occasions, and his most tender treatment of me, and through his goodness has laid me under an obligation too great for me to repay, yet I do assure him my utmost study has been to render him all the happiness in my power. And if I have been in any way deficient in my duty towards my dear husband, I hope he will attribute it not to the least want of affection, but unknowingly, as was really the case; and I do desire all my faults may be buried in oblivion, and intreat him not entirely to wipe off from his memory one whose only happiness centred in him.'

Nevertheless Pellegrin Treves solaced himself with a new wife within five weeks of the death of his first one. He, however, reserved for himself a grave next to that of his first wife, whom he survived fifty-five years, but when he died at Newmarket he was buried in the local churchyard. He remained, however, a Yahid until the end of his life. He was survived by his second wife, who died in her house in Charles Street, Cavendish Square, on 3 January 1832, aged ninety-three, and in accordance with the wishes expressed in her will was buried 'in the Portuguese Jewish cemetery with the full rites of the synagogue'. The empty grave next to that of the first Mrs. Pellegrin Treves has never been occupied and is still recorded in the books of the Community 'Reservado por Guerson Treves'.

Pellegrin Treves had one son, also Pellegrin, by his second wife. His career was in the service of the East India Company in which he rose to the rank of Postmaster-General, spending over forty years of his life in India. There he was of course completely outside the Jewish community, marrying a non-Jewess, and his children being brought up as Christians. From them are descended an appreciable section of the Roman Catholic aristocracy of England—a former Lord Thurlow, a Lord Donington, the Countess of Loudoun, the Viscountess St. Davids, a former Duchess of Norfolk, Lord Grey of Ruthin, and the Earl of Dumfries, son and heir of the Marquess of Bute—all of whom, if not descendants, are collateral descendants of Rashi, the famous Talmudist and rabbi. In Italy the Treves family still survives in the Jewish Community.

An earlier Anglo-Sephardi gallant was Francisco Lopes de Liz, in the synagogue Jacob Berahel. His grandfather and namesake was one of the prominent members of the synagogue and appears in the London Directory for 1677 as living in Bury Street. His father, Abraham Berahel, also known as Francisco de Liz, was the Gabay who entertained the Princess Anne when she visited the Synagogue. The second Jacob, Francisco Lopes de Liz (III) in 1700 married Esther, a daughter of Isaac, otherwise Pedro, Israel Henriques, junior, a prominent London merchant. By him she had two daughters, the elder of whom died young and the younger, one of the greatest heiresses of the day, married a posthumous son of Suasso, the second Baron d'Avernas le Gras. After his marriage, however, the third Francisco de Liz left England and settled in Holland. There he lived the life of a cultured man of wealth, devoting himself to music, the drama, and gallantry. It is recorded that among his investments or speculations was one in South Sea Stock. Reckoning that this stock had reached its maximum price, he instructed his agent to sell it. The latter, however, neglected to do so, and the stock began to fall. It was then sold and the owner realized a profit of only 1,800,000 florins. The adventures of this gentleman are somewhat spitefully recorded in more than one book. In Holland de Liz moved in royal circles. When the Prince of Orange returned from England after his marriage to Anne, the Princess Royal, eldest daughter of George II, de Liz gave a magnificent entertainment at which the Prince and Princess were present.

A member of another well-known Sephardi family who attained about the same time a degree of fame, although in an altogether different capacity, was Abigail Baruch Lousada, a collateral ancestor of whom was a member of the Mahamad in the first year of the Community's corporate existence. She can best be described as 'a blue stocking', at a period when that category among English ladies was familiar. A sister of hers in the Community, although on her marriage she left it, was Rebecca del Valle, after her marriage, Mrs. Lowry. A mineralogist whose distinction was sufficient to admit her to the pages of the *Dictionary of National Biography*, she with her husband, Wilson Lowry, an engraver of repute, founded a family of mineralogists. Her sister, Abigail, married Abraham Israel Ricardo and was the mother of David Ricardo and the grandmother of John Lewis Ricardo. Isaac Henriques Sequeira, another bearer of an honoured name in Jewry, was born in Lisbon in 1738 of a family of physicians. He adopted medicine as his profession and came to England after he had qualified by graduation at the Universities of Bordeaux and Leyden. In London he was at first with his uncle, Dr. Philip de la Cour. When the latter removed shortly afterwards, in 1772, to Bath, Sequeira succeeded to his practice in London. Like other ex-Marrano physicians he was attached to the Portuguese Embassy and was also Honorary Physician Extraordinary to the Prince Regent of Portugal. Later he became a popular medical practitioner among 'the nobility and gentry'. Joseph Barrow Montefiore, who died in 1893 at the age of ninety, whom several members of the London Community must remember, was thirteen years of age when Sequeira died and well remembered him as 'a tall thin man with white hair and a very pompous manner. He always dressed in a snuff-coloured cutaway coat and white stockings and carried a fine gold-headed cane'—the badge of the medical profession in eighteenth-century England.

In the tradition of Solomon Mendes, the friend of Richard Savage, was Isaac Mocatta, a son of Abraham Lumbrozo de Mattos Mocatta. Letters that have been preserved show the close friendship, personal and literary, between him and Walter Savage Landor, the man of letters, famous for his authorship of *Imaginary Conversations*. Landor's opinion of Mocatta has been committed to writing. 'In the number of my acquaintance there is none more valuable, there is not one more lively, more enquiring, more regular; there is not one more virtuous, more beneficent, more liberal, more tender in heart or more true in friendship than my friend Mocatta—a Jew.' This, it is said, was written to show that in Landor's quarrels with Isaac d'Israeli, there was no trace of anti-Jewish prejudice. His brother Moses Mocatta wrote Jewish polemical works. Isaac Mocatta took an active part in Jewish communal life.

Sephardi Jewry also produced at the end of this century a small group of artists just as it had in an earlier generation. Samuel da Silva is known only by his portrait of the Haham, Moses Gomes de Mesquita, which he painted in 1752. Abraham Osorio, who died in 1827, was elected a member of the Society of Arts in 1800 and its Chairman of Accounts seven years later. As he had left the Community before he died, he may not have been a member of it then. In music there was Michael Bolaffi or Abulafia, musical director to the Royal Duke of Cambridge, who seems to have been alone in his generation. His greatest effort was a sonnet for voice and pianoforte, published in 1809 in memory of Haydn. A namesake and contemporary, Haim Vita or Hananiah Bolaffy, was a teacher in the congregational school and was also active with his pen. He wrote a *Grammar of the Hebrew Language*, an anthem 'to be sung by the boys belonging to the Congregation of Spanish and Portuguese Hebrews, cloathed and educated at the charitable institution denominated Shaare Tikvah' in Hebrew and English, and 'The Order of Service to be performed on the day of the Anniversary in the Synagogue of Jews' Hospital', an Ashkenazi charity. Bolaffy also translated into English the Haham Raphael Meldola's 'Form of devotional service, thanksgiving and singing for the renewal of the dedication of the Synagogue of the Portuguese Jews' Congregation in Bevis Marks, London, to be performed on Friday evening, 27 Elul A.M. 5585'. Among his claims was that of teaching Hebrew at Eton College. A curious controversy in which he got himself involved was with Rachel Fanny Antonina Lee, who called herself the Baroness Despenser. She was born about the year 1774, a natural daughter of the Lord Despenser. Mrs. Lee was a woman of striking beauty and outstanding intellectual gifts. However, she also suffered from mental derangement, as is shown by the pamphlet on her relations with Bolaffy which she published in 1824. Bolaffy who described himself as 'Professor of Languages, Author of the Hebrew Grammar, etc.', had translated into English a somewhat incoherent *A Hebrew Epistle or a Circular Epistle to the Hebrews* which she had written in Hebrew. Mrs. Lee in her later charges against him accused him of tricking her out of a twenty-pound note and also of claiming against her through his solicitors two years' salary which were not due to him.

There were other worthies who catered successfully to the amusement of the public in those days. Carlo Antonio Delpini, described as clown and theatrical manager, first appeared at Drury Lane in 1774, but later turned to the more regular drama. George Romondo or Raymondo, a dwarf three and a half feet tall and mimic, was born in Lisbon about 1765 and brought to London by an Italian who abandoned him. He started his career in England by entering a public-house unobserved and by his loud roaring as a lion aroused first the alarm and then the amusement of the company, who by their combined contributions set him on his feet. According to a contemporary 'His placid disposition is displayed in his countenance, for he is seldom to be seen without a smile upon his face, particularly when he meets females; and he declares that he is sure the ladies must see something in him that pleases them, otherwise he should not be blessed with their looks.' In London he gained his living as an entertainer at small inns. But his reputation as a mimic spread beyond that limited circle. Two portraits of him were etched and published. Maria Theresa Bland was born in Italy of Italian Jewish parents named Romanzini. The family came to England when she was a young child. In course of time she acquired both popularity and a lasting reputation in her profession of actress and vocalist, especially as a singer of English ballads. Her first appearance in public was at the age of four. Less reputable was a noted London beggar, Israel Aga, an oriental Jew, who posed as a pedlar and frequented the streets, wearing a turban, about 1780. He did not stand alone at that time. There were others like him: for instance, Jacob Kimhi or Kimchi, who has already been mentioned.[1] They and their fellows were sufficiently well known to have their portraits etched or engraved by artists of repute and reproduced and sold.

The end of the eighteenth century saw the development of boxing into an art or science. Jewish pugilists took a prominent part in this development, and outstanding among them was a group of young Sephardim—Daniel Mendoza, Aby (Abraham), Samuel and Israel or John Belasco, Isaac Bitton. The earliest of these was Abraham da Costa of Moorfields, who flourished in 1769. Mousha of Stepney was a contemporary, but it is not known whether or not he was Sephardi. Paramount among these and all the other English boxers of his time was Daniel Mendoza, the father of the modern science. The family had been living in England for at least the best part of a century, and one Aaron Mendoza, the communal shochet who published a book on his science with illustrations from his own brush in 1733, may be assumed to have been a member of it. According to his memoirs, Daniel was always ready from boyhood with his fists. He was still a youth when he took up prize-fighting professionally, and it was not long before he rose to the foremost place in his new profession, the hero of half the English nation, patronized by gentlemen of fashion at the head of whom was the Prince Regent, the future George IV. Mendoza's historic fights were the three with Richard Humphries, until then the champion of England, whose jealousy of him as time passed became insatiable. These epic fights were described at length in the press and recorded in popular ballads. *Bell's Life* in recording his death on 3 September 1836, wrote:

> 'It has long been admitted that no pugilist that ever existed so completely elucidated or promulgated the principles of boxing as Mendoza. Dan . . . may be said to have been the first "great master" of pugilistic science in this country; and to have introduced a system of attack and defence at once new and imposing.'

Abraham, better known as Aby, Belasco was a younger contemporary of Mendoza but never attained to his distinction. The two, however, were at one time in partnership in an exhibition tour. He survived his boxing days, but hardly to his credit. His brothers, Samuel and Israel, are still lower in the hierarchy of pugilists. Isaac Bitton or Bittoon was born in 1778. He is worthy of mention not only as a pugilist and teacher of boxing, but also as a fencing-master. The pugilistic period of his life was short, although he lived until he was seventy. The later and longer

[1] See p. 179.

period was devoted to teaching in Whitechapel the sciences of boxing and fencing. Other non-Sephardi Jewish contemporaries also gained distinction in the early annals of boxing.

The foregoing are a few individuals, sons and daughters of Bevis Marks, who, climbing out of the ordinary rut, claimed and secured attention for shorter or longer periods. In their many and widespread activities they help to show the extent to which the English-born Sephardim were, towards the end of the eighteenth century, spreading into almost every sphere of English life. Many, probably most, of the Jews of England still found themselves at home and at ease only in a Jewish environment. Others were equally so in Jewish and non-Jewish surroundings. Yet others were beginning to feel themselves members of the general community to an ever increasing extent and of the Jewish community to a decreasing one. Geographically also the Sephardim of London, though strongly bound to the Synagogue, were scattering. At first Bevis Marks was the centre and few lived more a short distance from it. Then they housed their extensive families in stately city mansions a little farther away, in Budge Row, in Devonshire Square, in Finsbury Square. Next the wealthier ones even left the City and settled in Kennington, in Islington, in Westminster, in Bloomsbury, in many cases with country houses in what are now parts of London but were then well outside—Stoke Newington, Shacklewell, Tottenham, Hampstead, Highgate, Merton, Morden, Tooting, Twickenham, Richmond, even as far as Totteridge in Herts. Finally the wealthier members of the Community were found living in Mayfair and Kensington, even in Belgravia.

The founders of the Community and their successors who followed them from the Continent brought with them the names they bore in Latin Europe, and, furthermore, on throwing off the cloak of Marranoism, assumed others patently Jewish. Thus Antonio Lousada was known also as Moses Baruch and Antonio or Lorenzo Lindo as Isaac. The first generations of English birth, while retaining their Spanish and Portuguese surnames, assumed or received Jewish personal names. In course of time, however, outside influences and fashions had their inevitable effect. Names prevalent among the English were adopted to a continually increasing extent. In the synagogue a Jewish name was retained, but outside of it, in very many cases, one more familiar to their English neighbours was adopted. Thus Jacob became James, sometimes John; Hyam or Haim, Henry; Elias, Edward. Hebrew names were sometimes translated; Mazaltov, a not infrequent name for girls becoming Goodluck or Lucky, and by a further metamorphosis, Lucy. The practice of naming children after near relatives was very frequently followed, as a rule a grandchild after a grandparent, although not infrequently after a parent. Thus in genealogical researches there is often difficulty in identifying an individual unless the name at any rate of the father is also given. In the Lindo family, from the arrival of the first members in England, Isaac and Elias have always alternated from father to son. Among the Mocattas, Moses and Abraham frequently recur. Those of the Baruch Lousadas were for a long period to a large extent either Emanuel or Isaac. Sir Moses Montefiore was one of five contemporary members of the family who bore the same first name. There is evidence of the Napoleon cult in England at the end of the eighteenth century when Isaac and Esther Lindo gave their son, born on 7 October 1798, the name Helectob, an exact translation into Hebrew of Buonaparte. One can speculate about the consequences to the child a few years later when Napoleon had lost his popularity in England, and was widely believed, among other enormities, to breakfast off an infant every morning.

The men and women to whom the foregoing brief notes relate were among the more picturesque members of the Community. They should not be taken as typical of the Sephardim of England in the eighteenth century. That group in English Jewry—for by now it formed only a minority of the Jews of London—consisted for the most part of ordinary people—men and women not very different in essentials from those who form the greater part of the Sephardim of England today. They may be classified as the rabbis and scholars, the principal of whom have received or will receive mention; the second class was that of the lay leaders, heads of families—as a rule very numerous[1]—prosperous merchants, looking upon office, and by no means sinecure office, in the Community as a pleasure and also a pious duty which they owed to their fathers and ancestors who had preceded them in the same

[1] Raphael Franco (1708–81), the grandfather of Sir Ralph Lopes, had twelve children. Moses Vita Montefiore (1712–89), the grandfather of Sir Moses, had seventeen; his son, Samuel Vita Montefiore, who died in 1802, ten, and another son, Joseph Elias (1759–1804), the father of Sir Moses, also ten. Dr. Judah Israel Montefiore (1778–1827), for a few years the physician of the Community, had eleven children. Abraham Lumbroso de Mattos Mocatta (1730–1800), the grandson of Abraham Mocatta, who took his grandfather's name, had twelve children, and his son Jacob (1770–1825), eleven. Abraham Israel Ricardo (1733–1812), the father of the political economist, had had twenty-two. Elias Lindo, who died in 1785, had ten children; his son, David Abarbanel Lindo (1772–1852), had eighteen; Abraham Quixano Henriques (1775–1840), ten; Simon Barrow (1787–1863), thirteen. These figures are not overstatements: in some cases they are less than the truth. David Sassoon of Bombay (1793–1864), who although he himself never visited England sent all of his sons with one exception to settle there, had eight sons and an appropriate number of daughters.

offices as well as to their contemporaries. In the course of this narrative there has been occasion to mention by name some of these devoted servants of Creechurch Lane and of Bevis Marks. But far more have necessarily been passed over in silence. It fell to them to carry on their duties quietly, modestly, almost secretly, satisfied to hand over to their successors undiminished the trust they had accepted from those who served before them. To give a list of these devoted men would be to provide a bare catalogue. The names of most of them are to be found in the record of the members of the Mahamad from the year 1663 until today. A few families whose members served for generation after generation may, however, be mentioned. Of the founders of the Community there were those of Mocatta, Baruch Lousada, Mendes da Costa, Brandon, and, above all, Lindo, the most historic of them all. The Salvador, Suasso, and other families that came later have already been mentioned. Less prominent in the work of the Community, although also making their contribution to it, were the families of Ricardo, de Pinna, Samuda, Lopes, Gomes Serra, Henriques, Capadose, de Pass, Franco, Levy Ximenes, Faro, and de Paiva. There are of course still others, for the full record, stretching over three centuries, is a very lengthy one. Many of these families have unfortunately passed out of the records of the Community, but some survive. The eldest of all with a practically unbroken period of service covering three centuries is that of Lindo, whose first member in England was Isaac or Lorenço Rodrigues Lindo.

The families were not only large. They were also closely inter-related. It was the rule for cousins to marry one another, and when the parties were not cousins they were generally uncle and niece or brother and sister-in-law. So frequent were these inter-marriages that cases are known in which instead of thirty-two great-great-great-grandparents (the number if every marriage is outside the previous circle) a man had less than ten. The girls married young, seldom after twenty, and the mortality among young wives was heavy. To provide for their large families the houses of these opulent merchants had to be similarly spacious. The houses of those days that still survive are now occupied by half a dozen families apiece.

From the foregoing may be deduced to some extent the manner of life of the worshippers, regular and occasional, within the portals of Bevis Marks at the close of the eighteenth century.

CHAPTER XIII

THE TURN OF THE CENTURY

THE END OF the eighteenth century saw the Sephardi Community with its ecclesiastical personnel much depleted. Haham Cohen d'Azevedo's place had not yet been filled. Aaron de Saa Silveira, Rubi and Dayan, had died in 1792, and his colleague, Hasdai Almosnino, was to follow him in the earlier half of the first year of the new century. Solomon Cohen, another of the Rubis, was to die in 1804. There remained only one Dayan, David Henriques Julian, and two Hazanim, Mordecai Salom and Daniel Cohen d'Azevedo, the latter of whom resigned in January 1802 and went to North America. Daniel Jacob de Castro was the secretary; Joseph Hart Myers, a son of Naphtali Hart Myers, one of the leading members of the Great Synagogue, and later himself prominent in the life of the sister community, was the Congregational physician; and Benjamin Gomez da Costa, the surgeon. Dr. Myers' successor was also an Ashkenazi, a member of the later well-known Leo family. These officials of the Community were not overpaid according to modern standards. Rubi Julian for his two offices of teacher and Dayan received the combined salary of £56 5s. per annum. The Hazanim received £60 a year each, and the secretary £84. The physician and surgeon who were not fully employed received £42 and £21 respectively. When Raphael Meldola was appointed Haham a few years later his salary was £250. This paucity of experienced spiritual guides was unfortunate, for the Community was about to enter, in fact had already entered, the most critical period of its existence. The spirit of progress and of reform was abroad in political and social spheres, and it could not be confined to them. Everywhere the shackles of the age of faith and obedience were being broken and discarded. The French Revolution and the movements, feelings, and hopes to which it gave rise had led western civilization out of the eighteenth-century world for ever. England had passed out of the era of the Stewarts and of the early Hanoverians and was looking eagerly towards the nineteenth century and to the mirage that stretched beyond it. The Sephardim of England were by now a part of the English people. In most cases English-born and the children of English-born parents, who class by class were finding their interests coincide to an ever-increasing degree with those of

THE TURN OF THE CENTURY

their non-Jewish fellow Englishmen, they now realized, almost without exception, that there was a world of which they were citizens outside of Bevis Marks, that the new liberalism of which they were hearing so much belonged to them as well as to others. But the Community lay still, according to its laws and regulations, under close control, almost the dictatorship of a small group of individuals, the hereditary aristocracy of Sephardi England. The Ascamot or Constitution of the Community had been revised a few years earlier, but this revision brought no loosening of the reins. The control of the governing families was as absolute as it had been a century and a half earlier when the Community consisted of but a small group of aliens, justifiably nervous of its status, and anxious above all to attract as little attention to itself as was possible. Conditions had changed, but, as generally happens, those in whose hands rested power had not realized the change.

It is difficult to appreciate that in the first years of the nineteenth century when the revolution, political and social, had made great strides throughout western Europe and even in other lands, for trivial offences members of the Community could be and were arbitrarily expelled and deprived of all recognition in the synagogue. If they entered to pray, they were treated as untouchables, and if they died were refused burial in the communal cemetery. Such penalties were inflicted for the offence, for instance, of occasionally meeting together for prayer in a private house. In those days the Haham was formally forbidden to take any part in the election of other salaried officials or to intercede in favour of any Jew who applied for charitable assistance, for fear lest the lay authorities 'out of respect to him, should deviate from that impartiality which it is their duty to observe'. Any unauthorized person giving legal decisions on points of Jewish law, even though fully qualified, was at once punished. So was anyone who 'either by words, writing or printing' offended the Haham or any other member of the Beth Din. So harmless a work as an English-Portuguese dictionary had to obtain the approval of the Mahamad before its author, if a member of the Community, was permitted to publish it. The publication of religious or political works—even a translation of the Prayer Book into English—or the taking of an action at law against a fellow Jew by a Yahid without such permission, which was by no means invariably given, was unthinkable. To enter into religious or political controversy with a non-Jew, to masquerade out of doors in the Jewish quarter on Purim, to make or attempt to make proselytes or to pay a visit to Spain or Portugal, was immediately visited with heavy punishment, as a rule exclusion from the Community or the imposition of a heavy fine. A member of the Community who took a wife from outside was promptly expelled and considered as having become an apostate. Anyone who bought or sold a vote in the course of an election for a Hazan was fined ten pounds. Fines were imposed for the refusal of honorary office, for declining the mitsva of being called to the Law, or for neglecting to attend congregational or committee meetings or even for being late at such meetings. An hour after the opening of such a meeting a roll-call was made and anyone who failed to respond was fined. A fine of twenty shillings was imposed on the Hazan if he omitted any name from the constantly lengthening list of benefactors of the Community it was his duty to recite in the synagogue on the appointed occasions. The mislaying of the *Ascaba* Book, or list of these names, was visited by a fine of two pounds.

The number of Sephardim living in London in the year 1800 was estimated at 4,000, about a fifth of the total number of Jews in London, probably the highest figure it has ever reached. When the Community was organized in 1657 there were about thirty-five families and this figure comprised the total Jewish population of England. There were at the end of the century many poor in the Sephardi Community, but there were absolutely and proportionately still more among the Ashkenazim, and the average standard of prosperity in the smaller community was much higher than in the larger. This disparity between the two communities was one of the causes of the failure of the scheme not only for the relief of poverty but also for its prevention, sponsored in 1795 by Joshua van Oven, a London surgeon and prominent Ashkenazi, and Patrick Colquhoun, a Metropolitan Police magistrate, whose experiences on the bench had convinced him that the problem of the Jewish poor of London needed urgent attention and that, before all else, training for useful employment was necessary. The scheme, on which van Oven and Colquhoun agreed, was one that included relief for the helpless, schools for the children, and training in trades for the adolescents. To provide for their needs an organization, representative of the Jewish community, was to be established by Act of Parliament. Its funds were to be derived in part from a proportion of the poor rates paid by Jewish ratepayers and in part from contributions by the synagogue authorities and a special poor rate levied on Jews only. The proposals appealed to the leading members of the Ashkenazi Community, and a Bill to put the scheme into effect was introduced into Parliament. The opposition to it was, however, too great. The local authorities objected on the ground that the measure would take from them part of their revenues. The Sephardi Community also objected on the ground that they were already providing on the lines indicated for their own poor and also that an undue proportion of the funds raised would come from them. The only supporters left were the Ashkenazi authorities, and since, as a consequence of the objections that had been made, no revenue for the project could be expected except from Ashkenazi sources, and this would probably be forthcoming on a voluntary basis, an Act of Parliament was unnecessary. The larger scheme was therefore abandoned. Abraham Goldsmid and other prominent Ashkenazim had, however, already commenced to collect funds for the task they had set before them. Some twenty thousand pounds, half of the sum subscribed by non-Jewish friends, had already been received, and this was devoted in 1797 to the establishment of an institution of which the present Jewish Orphanage is the descendant. Its original purpose was not only the care and training of orphans, but also the maintenance of the aged and infirm.

The period was a critical one in the history of the Community, and the absence of a spiritual leader increased the gravity of the crisis. The number of Yehidim and still more of the Congregantes was larger than it had ever been, but the complexion of the Community was undergoing a change. The Congregation in Bevis Marks was increasingly one of new-comers and at the same time the number of representatives of the older families, those which had created and built up the Community, was diminishing. The names that had been so familiar in the story of Sephardi Jewry were gradually disappearing and new ones, hitherto unknown or little known, were taking their places. There were a number of consequences of this change. Sephardi Jewry was ceasing to be the outstanding section of the Community, the only one which demanded any serious consideration in the wider history of Jewry and in the picture of the English people as a whole. Furthermore, the financial basis of the Sephardi Community was being affected. Its expenditure increased, but its revenue did not increase at a similar rate. At one time, early in the nineteenth century, a special fund had to be raised from among the Yehidim to restore the financial equilibrium. There was also a growing feeling, at any rate among the group with which the direction of the Community had hitherto rested, that all was not well in the spiritual sphere and that an improvement there was urgently necessary. At a meeting of Elders in the year 1803 Jacob Mocatta gave expression to this feeling. In particular he pointed to the unsatisfactory state into which religious and Hebrew education had fallen. Portuguese, which was after Hebrew the language of the Synagogue, was no longer familiar to most of its members and attendants, and he urged that the language that they all understood from childhood, English, should be substituted for it. Jacob Mocatta's intervention had an effect. A committee was appointed by the Mahamad to take the condition of the Community into consideration and to make recommendations. They recognized the state of affairs, for in their reference to this committee they remarked that 'in this Kahal, which had shone brilliantly for more than a century as one of the principal of Europe, the study of the Law will be entirely lost, and the Kahal will become an object of contempt and ridicule'. Among the recommendations of this committee were that a Haham should be appointed, that the communal schools should be reorganized, that the *Medrash* should be so overhauled that members might be induced to send their sons to it or alternatively to another school of religion or *Yeshiba*, the establishment of which was recommended.

One almost immediate consequence of this report was the appointment as Haham of Raphael Meldola of Leghorn. The new Haham came from a long line of Jewish rabbis and scholars, many of whom had also been physicians, going back to Isaiah Meldola (1282–1340), who was born in Spain, where he was Haham in Toledo and later settled in Italy, where he was Rabbi of Mantua. The new Haham's father, Moses Meldola, had taught oriental languages in the University of Paris, and his son, before coming to England, had been Dayan in Leghorn where he was born. One of Raphael Meldola's books, *Faith Strengthened*, was published after his death, translated into English by Moses Mocatta. Although Meldola held the office of Haham in England for more than twenty years, he was never at ease in English, in which language he was unable to write. He preferred Spanish of which language his knowledge was not extensive, or his native Italian. The new Haham on his appointment showed himself energetic. He had not been long in the country before he urged on the Mahamad the necessity to take the strongest measures to prevent the attendance of Jewish children at the schools that were being opened in the neighbourhood of their homes by the Protestant missionary societies that were being formed. The Congregation co-operated with the Great Synagogue in the matter, but the burden of the action that was taken fell on the latter. The trouble with the missionary societies continued for years. Later in 1865 the Mahamad summoned a number of parents to explain the attendance of their children at

JACOB DE CASTRO
From a drawing by Stanfield

DANIEL MENDOZA
From an engraving by Gillray

HAHAM RAPHAEL MELDOLA
From an engraving by Joshua Lopez, after F. B. Barlin

HAZAN DAVID AARON DE SOLA
From a painting

the Evening Ragged School in Wentworth Street, which was suspected of being a missionary institution. The parents explained, with one voice, that 'on its coming under their cognizance the children had been reprimanded in a suitable manner, and cautioned against a repetition of the offence. And they further stated that from their investigation it appeared that the children, chiefly amongst themselves, had been induced to repair to those schools for an evening frolic; and they disclaimed all knowledge of any bribes having been received by the children.' Meldola co-operated also with Hirschel, the Ashkenazi rabbi, in a campaign for upholding the sanctity of the Sabbath. Still earlier, within a few months of Meldola's arrival, the often mooted but never attained co-operation with the Ashkenazi synagogue authorities in matters of Shechita was at length secured. This subject had throughout the post-Resettlement history been one of worry and annoyance to the Synagogue authorities—Ashkenazi as well as Sephardi. Some of the difficulties that arose have previously been mentioned. Their culmination was perhaps the lawsuit of 1788 in which one Rodriguez, the offended and offending butcher, took proceedings for libel aimed directly against their informant, indirectly against the authorities of Bevis Marks, for having announced from the Teba in synagogue that he had been deprived of his licence to sell meat for consumption by Jews, and that it was forbidden to members of the Community to purchase meat from him. Rodriguez claimed heavy damages but lost his action, as well as a further application for a retrial. The courts decided that the synagogue authorities had acted well within their rights. Four years later proposals for co-operation were taken up seriously by the authorities of the three Ashkenazi synagogues whom those of Bevis Marks were invited to join. Linked with the proposal for a joint Board of Shechita, however, was one for the erection of a market for the sale of Kasher meat. To this the Sephardim were not willing to agree, although so far as the joint board was concerned they were in full sympathy. The Ashkenazim, however, considered the two proposals as parts of one inseparable whole, and proceeded on their course alone. They were not successful in raising the money required, and had consequently to abandon their project. A joint Board was ultimately established, but not until 1805, one of the first fruits of the activities of the new Haham. The profits of the undertaking were shared equally between the four participating synagogues, the share of each in the first year being slightly under £100. When it was necessary to denounce a butcher for irregularities of Shechita and to warn members of the Community against him, proclamation was made in all four synagogues. This agreement has remained in force, to the satisfaction of the two communities, until the present day, although the representation of the Ashkenazim has been altered; a member of the Sephardi Community being invariably included among the Honorary Officers of the Board, in addition to adequate representation on its governing committee. Eleven years earlier, in 1794, an agreement was made for the provision of *matzot* or unleavened bread at Passover. There was no opportunity on this occasion for the difficulties that had arisen in the course of the Shechita negotiations. In other respects also the Sephardim and the Ashkenazim approached one another in the course of the first years of the nineteenth century. Disputes occasionally arose between the Ashkenazi synagogues, especially on the subject of the relief of their poor or the burial of paupers, and when these were otherwise incapable of settlement the Mahamad was asked to arbitrate. These invitations were accepted and the decisions given loyally carried out. In 1790 it was even agreed to admit Ashkenazi patients, on payment, to the Beth Holim, which was, with one exception, the London Infirmary, now known as the London Hospital, for very many years still the only hospital in England in which the Jewish dietary laws could be observed. Another consequence, somewhat belated, of the Report of the 'Committee on the Ecclesiastical State' of the Congregation of 1803 was the translation into English of the Sephardi Liturgy. The officially sponsored work, in five volumes, did not begin to appear until 1836 from the hand of David Aaron de Sola who at the time of the report of the committee had not yet been appointed Hazan. This was an official publication, but earlier there had been several English versions of the Sephardi prayers, in whole or in part, produced by other English Jewish scholars but not Sephardim.[1] For these the licence of the Mahamad was not required. The earliest of these was a translation of the Liturgy in Hebrew and English by Alexander Alexander, published in 1773, of which two later editions appeared at intervals of fifteen and twenty-six years respectively. The editions of 1814 and 1815, produced by his son, Levy Alexander, contained scurrilous attacks on the Haham and also on his Ashkenazi colleague, Hirschel. In one of the periodical parts in which form the Prayer Book appeared was even a more vindictive attack on Meldola—printed on the wrapper. Alexander turned on the prayer composed by the Haham to mark the restoration of peace in 1814. The title is sufficient to indicate its contents

[1] A translation of the Prayer Book by one Messias, presumably a Sephardi, appeared in 1720, but this has not been seen, only one copy being known to exist.

—'Critique on the Hebrew Thanksgiving Prayers . . . Portuguese Synagogue . . . Thursday the 7th of July . . . General thanksgiving for the happy restoration of peace. In which the stupidity of the Rev. Raphael Meldola . . . will be clearly shown.'

The mutual approach of Sephardim and Ashkenazim had been noticeable, although it had moved very slowly, since a couple of decades before the end of the eighteenth century. In 1785 the office of Physician to the Community, hitherto a preserve of Sephardi medical men, was given to an Ashkenazi, Joseph Hart Myers. Six years later the Sephardi Community was officially and fully represented by its five wardens and four dayanim at the funeral of the principal Ashkenazi rabbi, David Tewele Schiff. In 1834 and also in later years the Shaare Tikva School was placed at the disposal of the New Synagogue for services on the holidays whenever their own building was under repair, and from time to time other Ashkenazi institutions were similarly accommodated. In 1836 the Hazanim of the Congregation were invited to take part in the consecration of the new Westminster (the predecessor of the Western) Synagogue and were given leave to do so. In 1825, however, there was an instance of co-operation of a more questionable character. Chief Rabbi Hirschel called the attention of the Sephardi authorities to the irregular proceedings of Solomon Bennett, known both as a controversialist and biblical writer and also as an engraver. Disagreements between Bennett and the Ashkenazi ecclesiastical authorities were frequent and in that year Hirschel thought that he had found his opportunity. Bennett, it seems, together with one 'so called rabbi', Jacob Michalki, had 'presumed to take upon himself the authority of officiating as priest at a ceremony of marriage, of which he determined the ordinances, and signed as witness in conjunction with the said Rabbi Jacob'. Hirschel had consulted Meldola who had agreed with him that the marriage was altogether irregular and contrary to a proper interpretation of the Law. In the name of Meldola as well as himself he approached the Mahamad with the request that a suitable proclamation should be made in the Synagogue. Such a proclamation was accordingly made. The principal occasion for the trouble seems to have been that the bridegroom was of the priestly family of Cohen and that the lady, it was claimed, was the daughter of a convert to Judaism, between whom and a Cohèn, according to Jewish law, marriage was prohibited. For this offence Bennett and his coadjutor were to be excluded from the Community of Israel.

Private or unofficial marriages were by no means infrequent.

Sometimes the parties went to the authorities for confirmation, which was by no means given as a matter of course. In the meanwhile the number of marriages between Sephardim and Ashkenazim, which were still looked on askance, was increasing at a remarkable rate. The records of Bevis Marks give only those instances in which the bridegroom was a member of the Sephardi Community. In other cases, presumably at least as numerous, the marriages were under Ashkenazi auspices. To such an extent did they increase that at one meeting of the Mahamad, in July 1835, of the five marriages authorized—all marriages celebrated by the officers of the Congregation had to be authorized by the Mahamad, who seem to have divided the candidates into three classes, the first and highest who were to be married by the Haham or Ab Beth Din; the second by one of the Hazanim; and the third by the Samas; and to have designated the officers to perform the ceremony—in four instances the brides were Tudescas. These intermarriages were not confined to any one social class. For instance, in 1786 Joseph Azulay married Rachel Lazarus and a few months later another Azulay married Simcha Gompertz—a well-known name in the Ashkenazi Community, later to be connected with the Montefiore family. In the next month another intermarriage was celebrated in the Sephardi Community and others followed at not infrequent intervals.

The secondary part played by Meldola in the matter of Bennett and the Cohen marriage may well be explained by the facts that the offenders were members of the Ashkenazi Community and that it was the Ashkenazi rabbi and lay authorities that had been affronted. There was possibly also another reason. Meldola had held the office of Haham some twenty years, during which period his relations with the lay authorities of his Community were not always of a most cordial character. These authorities invariably treated him with all the respect due to his office, but Meldola does not always seem to have been a master of tact or to have possessed the flexibility that public office requires. Furthermore, the Haham's two sons, David and Abraham, as young men at any rate, were of a somewhat hasty temper or of an unruly character, and the paternal feelings of the Haham naturally urged him to look upon their actions or remarks sometimes more generously than would have been expected from a stranger. The culmination of the differences of which Meldola was the centre came in June 1819. Moses Nunes Lara, one of the more prominent of the Elders and a very generous benefactor of the Community, who had served in its highest offices, was presiding in the synagogue one sabbath when, he complained, he was grossly and publicly attacked by the Haham and his two sons. The Meldola family, it seems, desired that one of their friends should be given a mitzva, but the presiding warden did not share this desire. Lara made a formal complaint to the Mahamad, and a special meeting of that body, reinforced by some of the former wardens, was held to consider it. The Haham and his sons were also summoned to the meeting. The Haham declined to attend on the ground that the Mahamad had no jurisdiction over him, that he was above them in all such matters. In fact the old struggle of Pope and Emperor was revived in a new setting. The Haham was required to justify this claim, and after some delay did so by means of a joint opinion given by himself and Luria, the other member of the Sephardi Beth Din, and two of their Ashkenazi colleagues. The Mahamad accepted this ruling without concealing their lack of enthusiasm in doing so. Lara was, however, not satisfied and threatened that if justice were not given him and the offenders forced to apologize and undertake not to repeat the offence, he would take legal proceedings against the Meldolas. The Haham was also not satisfied. Having gained the first round in the contest, he proceeded to the second. For three years, he said, he had suffered continuous insults, false accusations, and contemptuous treatment from Lara. 'Consider how much, how long and with what patience have I suffered under various unpleasant circumstances with Mr. Lara and in particular in the public synagogue as the whole congregation knows.' Where, however, the Mahamad unaided, although reinforced, had failed, Lara's threat of legal proceedings succeeded. The Haham was induced, but with considerable difficulty, to agree to the Mahamad acting as arbitrator, and when that body decided that through a third party, who would wait on him at his residence, he should make 'an apology for the warmth and the expressions he used on that occasion to the Parnas Presidente' he consented to do so. The two gentlemen who called on Meldola to collect the 'apology' thereupon delivered it to Lara, and everyone was satisfied, excepting the Haham's two sons.

If the Haham was outside the jurisdiction of the Mahamad and the Elders this exemption did not extend also to his sons. The part they had played in this not very seemly affair was investigated. In vain did they plead that all they had done was to endeavour to calm their father who, they had been warned, was not in any circumstances to allow himself to get excited. Without judging the case of the Haham, David and Abraham Meldola were found to be at fault, despite a counter-attack by them to the effect that

Moses Lara was accustomed to pour insults upon them in the synagogue. The punishment imposed consisted of the infliction of fines and, in the meanwhile, exclusion from all synagogue honours. This state of affairs continued for three years, neither party making a move to meet the other. The Hazanim were of course warned in no circumstances to call either of the offenders to the Law, whether or not they were instructed by the presiding officer to do so. On one occasion the Hazan inadvertently did so, intending to call up another worshipper with a similar name, and the haste and abjectness with which, as soon as the service had terminated, he went to the residence of the Parnas Presidente to explain and apologize reads after the lapse of a century and a quarter as pathetic. At the end of three years, in February 1822, the prohibition was withdrawn. The fines were remitted, but the young Meldolas were cautioned to be 'more circumspect in the style of his language than he has hitherto been in case of his having occasion to address their room in future'.

The quarrel between the Meldola family and Moses Nunes Lara had hardly been brought publicly to an end when a new feud broke out between the Meldolas and the Almosnino family, represented by the Hazan Isaac Almosnino and his brother Solomon, the secretary of the Congregation, always referred to in the Meldola correspondence as 'Your secretary'. Meldola's relations with Hazan Almosnino seem to have been especially bad, and the Mahamad had to deal with charges by the Hazan to the effect that the Haham was circulating libellous and abusive circulars regarding him. One of these documents was in Hebrew, a language with which the members of the Mahamad were not fully conversant. Without suggesting that Meldola was in any way responsible for the document, they sent it to him, with a request for a translation into Spanish—Meldola's knowledge of English was still slight. They received more than one letter in reply but neither the original document nor a translation. They had in the end to write, over the signature of Moses Montefiore, then Gabay, very peremptorily demanding forthwith the return of the document with a translation. Finally they recorded their disapproval of the publication of the document and continued 'that the Rev. Haham be requested hereafter not to print or publish for circulation, or cause any written document to be distributed amongst the Congregation, in any manner or way whatever, without such publication or document being previously submitted to the Mahamad and its approbation first obtained in writing'. However, the offending document continued to be circulated by Meldola's son, David, and Isaac

Almosnino complained that it was offensive to him and appealed to the Mahamad for 'protection against the most persevering persecution which malignity can devise and if it is not in your power to afford me that protection, then I beg that I may be at liberty to take such steps as I may consider necessary for my own redress'. The retort of the Haham was to charge Almosnino with various trivial offences—in effect with not having carried out his orders. The Mahamad proceeded to investigate these charges and counter-charges and, in order to do so, co-opted additional members, to show its realization of the seriousness of the matter. The conclusion reached by this reinforced Mahamad was that 'The Mahamad highly disapprove of Mr. David Meldola's having publicly returned a paper to an English clergyman in synagogue particularly knowing that such paper was a production that had been prohibited from circulation by the Velhos. . . .' They were very careful not to mention the Haham in the matter. But the secretary, Solomon Almosnino, also got into trouble. 'The Mahamad are very much dissatisfied with Mr. Solomon Almosnino for having expressed himself in intemperate language in synagogue. . . . The Mahamad from their experience of Mr. S. Almosnino's general conduct are satisfied that nothing but a state of great irritation could have induced him so far to have forgotten himself. . . .' Abraham Meldola's troubles, however, were not even then concluded. Less than two months before his father's death in June 1828, there is a letter from the latter to the Mahamad written 'to vindicate the character of a dutiful son, and to relieve my own wounded feelings from an attack made on him in Snoga, and to ask you particularly, why after his several applications, an impartial investigation of the affair has not taken place, and your judgment thereon transmitted to him in writing. . . . I therefore entreat you to come to a fair, cool and dispassionate decision on the late outrageous conduct of the Hazan, and your Secretary in Snoga, towards my son, without driving him to any other Tribunal, which can only disturb the whole of the Congregation, and set our national laws at defiance.'

There is further about this period long-drawn-out correspondence regarding the manner in which Hazan Almosnino pronounced one word in the course of his recital of the prayers, a pronunciation to which the Haham with the support of another of the Hazanim, who happened to be his son-in-law, took the strongest exception.[1] The several relative documents referred to in the course of these disputes are not quoted. It is therefore

[1] The dispute was over the pronunciation of the *Sheva* point.

impossible to be certain of their import, but there is reason to believe that these trifling questions of pronunciation on which more than one opinion was held had much to do with them. At any rate after the death of Meldola, when the office of Haham was vacant, Hazan Almosnino relapsed into his manner of pronouncing the *sheva* point. The matter came again before the Elders and Almosnino had to give an undertaking to abide strictly by their orders, although they could not 'but express disapprobation of a great part of his lengthy communication'. The Hazan was verbose as well as irascible.

The Meldola-Almosnino feud did not die with the Haham. Two years later—in July 1830—there was another altercation in the synagogue precincts in which Hazan Almosnino and David Meldola, by this time a rubi and dayan, were involved. Almosnino was in a state of excitement and as soon as he recovered wrote to the Mahamad a long letter of apology. Meldola, however, was not mollified. He charged Almosnino with 'the disrespectful mention of his name in synagogue'. This charge the Mahamad considered non-proven. Thereupon Isaac Costa, a colleague of Meldola, preferred a new charge, 'with using irritating language and conducting himself in a violent manner towards him' on the occasion. Almosnino, uncertain of his capacity to keep control of himself, asked to be excused from answering the summons.

> 'Gentlemen—I have received two notices from your Secretary summoning my attendance to answer complaints of Mr. D. Meldola and Mr. I. Costa. Whether may be the real motives of those Gentlemen for causing the issue of such summonses, or the objects which they are intended to further, I am desirous from respect to you, not to allow the possibility of being goaded into any expression of feeling, which the well-known bias of my mind might unguardedly lead me into, on an occasion of this kind; and I therefore entreat that you will excuse my attendance and condescend to accept of this apology, as being truly dictated by the sentiments of respect.'

The charge was considered proved, and Almosnino was fined five pounds. He was further charged with disorderly conduct in the synagogue and using disrespectful language to the Parnas Presidente. This was a more serious matter, 'but in consideration of the contrition he has expressed both by his letter and personally at the Meeting, they (the Mahamad) consider the censure conveyed in this resolution as sufficient notice of the offence'.

Almost simultaneously there was another outbreak in the synagogue with which the presiding warden—whose perplexities still arouse sympathy after the lapse of almost a century and a half—found himself quite incapable of coping. It was over another trivial matter of pronunciation on which there were two opinions, both with support behind them. One of the boys in the Communal Preparatory School was deputed—as was the rule—to read the *Haphtarah*. The presiding warden had been warned that unpleasantness would arise and when the moment for the disputed pronunciation arrived, loud and unseemly protests were made by what appears to have been the North African party led by Solomon Aloof and Solomon Abecasis, the principal parties in the unauthorized service of eight years earlier which is about to be mentioned. David Meldola, who was by now Ab Beth Din and in the absence of a Haham the acting spiritual head of the Community, took a prominent part on the other side. In between these two violently contesting parties were the little boy who was reading the Haphtarah as he had been taught and the presiding warden, Isaac Foligno—almost as worthy an object of compassion. The boy had to transfer his mizva of concluding his recital to one of the Hazanim and the service had to be brought to a premature end. A veiled description of the proceedings is given in a letter of shocked indignation sent as a consequence by one of the Elders, Jacob Mendes Belisario, who was, by temperament, given to disputation, to the Mahamad.

'Gentlemen—"Can such things be and overcome us like a summer cloud without our special wonder?" Having been at Synagogue this morning I feel it a duty I owe to the Nation as a Velho to make some allusion to what took place on the reading of the portion of the Prophets.

'I shall not enter into the merits of the cause of the disturbance, knowing myself to be wholly incompetent to entertain even an opinion upon it, but I unhesitatingly declare that conduct more extraordinary, more disgraceful and more painful to a religious bosom has not occurred within my recollection. I cannot be an accuser and shall therefore designate no one, though it may be proper to point out the mischief likely to result from such intemperate proceedings. We are few in number, and very few of that few I regret to say, attend our place of worship. I declare my feelings are so greatly outraged, as others must be by what has occurred, that it will not surprise me if many of the Congregation should absent themselves until the Nation is secured against a repetition of the insult offered to our Maker in his Holy Dwelling. The conduct evinced by the few Velhos who were present is deserving of the highest commendation and could only have proceeded from a calm and discriminating judgement. They saw, they heard and said nothing, they knew their duty to their maker, and the respect they owed to themselves. I pitied the President who was so baited as to be under the necessity of expostulating, but his power soon ceased. He was not only insulted but despised—in short after the experience of this morning it would be ridiculous to talk of a President in *Synagogue*. I will never preside without guarantees and who is to furnish them? Let me entreat you Gentlemen to take this matter instantly into your serious consideration. Either shut the doors of the Synagogue or cause yourselves to be respected. The Velhos should be convened without loss of time, as your own power is clearly insufficient to appease the difference or to obtain redress for the gross outrage committed.'

Aloof and Abecasis and a third member, Solomon Sequerra, at first refused to attend the investigation. Later they did so and to some extent admitted their offence, but urged certain circumstances in palliation. They were fined £5 each. Abecasis protested against this decision and refused to pay the fine. But this is not the end of the feud. A year later (17 July 1831) Aloof, then a member of the Mahamad, wrote to the secretary, 'Having understood that Mr. Meldola receives some emolument for making a *Daras* (a sermon or address in the synagogue), I request that you will not pay him any sum whatsoever until the Gentlemen of the Mahamad meet to decide on the subject.'

On another occasion Meldola got into trouble for performing a marriage ceremony at Cambridge between parties of whom the Mahamad did not approve—and later in the same year, 1822, for giving a certificate to the Bolaffy, to whose not altogether regular activities attention has previously been called, exculpating him from a charge of having transgressed Ascama No. 9, that relating to Shechita. The Mahamad considered 'such interference injurious to the peace of the Congregation which such Ascama is intended to promote, they consider that fit measures should be taken to prevent a recurrence of such practices'. At the end of 1827 Meldola had again to be reminded that he must not publish or distribute any document among the Congregation, without permission of the Mahamad in writing. The office of Parnas was obviously not a sinecure during the Meldola period.

These were, however, for the most part but personal disputes, illustrative of the life in the Community at that time but with no permanent effect on its future. There were others of greater consequence with which the Elders and the Haham were troubled during the later years of Meldola's tenure of office. Outstanding among these was the unpleasant episode that arose at *Shebuot* 1822 when a group of Yehidim and others, for the most part passing visitors to London, meeting in the house of one of the former for the customary study during the first night of the festival, concluded their meeting, which cannot be considered inexcusable, by joining together in the holding of divine service. By doing so they had transgressed the first Ascama which prohibited the holding of such a service within six miles of Bevis Marks. The transgression was promptly reported to the Mahamad, who, without delay, called on the offenders to answer the charge brought against them. After considering the matter the Elders gave their decision which was published to the Community.

'In the name of God, Amen. The Elders of this Nation having had under their consideration the conduct of certain individuals who have openly and many wilfully, violated the fundamental ascama of this Kaal No. 1 by holding Minyan within the limits of the said Ascama, they cannot refrain from proclaiming to the Nation their abhorrence of such practises, and warning every individual of our Community from joining such disturbers of the Peace, Union and Harmony of our Congregation. And they deem it proper to announce to the Kaal the resolutions which have been adopted by them against the principal offenders that the Congregation may know that they will not suffer laws which have been instituted for ages and sanctioned by the most eminent Rabanim jointly with the Velhos and Yehidim to be infringed upon with impunity.'

This was a general proclamation. To deal adequately with the offenders the ringleaders, Judah Aloof, in whose house the service was held, his father, Solomon Aloof, and a relative Solomon Abecasis, were each fined forty pounds and the other offenders smaller amounts. Until they made their peace they were to be excluded from the Community, and although permitted to enter the synagogue, confined to the space at the back just within the doorway. A record of the offences and of the consequent punishments was in ordinary course affixed to the door of the synagogue for the information of the Congregation generally and of any others who might have been interested.

Of the offenders those who happened to be in London temporarily had in the meanwhile returned to their homes abroad and were beyond reach. Of the others some submitted to their punishments without protest, but the remainder, including the three principal offenders, were by no means silenced, and, as was later reported, they not only ignored the punishment, neglecting to pay the fines imposed, but 'continue in their contumacy and the Mahamad have every reason to believe continue regularly to congregate for the purpose of prayer'. One of the offenders, Samuel Benrimoh, was even more militant. Being naturally offended at seeing the proclamation on the door of the synagogue in which he, among others, was denounced, he proceeded to tear it down, but before he had succeeded in doing so the Samas 'with much spirit drove him from the spot and prevented him effecting his object'. On the Sabbath following, the same offender entered the Synagogue and proceeded to his usual seat. He was told that he was not permitted to occupy it and that he must withdraw to the back of the Synagogue. This he refused to do and he was thereupon, with a token display of force, in accordance with the Parliamentary precedent, removed from his seat; in the words of the record, the Samas and the Ward Beadle, whose presence in the Synagogue yard had been secured in anticipation of the need for him, 'lifted him up from his seat and conducted him as far as the bench T where they told him he might sit: he refused to do that and went out of the Synagogue'. This was not the end of the series of events on this memorable Sabbath. 'On the Saturday during the Afternoon Prayers writs were served on Plaistowe (the Ward Beadle) and Rodriguez (the *samas*) at the suit of Benrimoh for an assault and trespass.'

At this point the Haham, Meldola, intervened by making a proclamation in the Synagogue. The Mahamad, anxious to conform to the proprieties, politely asked him for a copy of this proclamation 'without offering an opinion at present upon the propriety of making a proclamation without their approbation'. Meldola returned a very sharp reply, stating that the proclamation and its terms were his concern and not theirs, and turned the argument against the Mahamad by expressing his surprise that they had written to him on the subject 'in the Holy Day of Hol Almohed without first enquiring of the Rabbi if it was permitted to write it'. Meldola refused to move from the position he had taken, despite further correspondence with the Mahamad, whom the Elders declined to support in the matter, and the dispute between the Mahamad and the Haham ended in the success of the latter, the terms of whose proclamation are unknown. Benrimoh,

THE TURN OF THE CENTURY 237

however, was induced to cease his action for assault and trespass, and later he made his peace with the Mahamad, and asking for a reconciliation was readmitted to the Congregation on payment of the fine imposed on him, arrears of finta and the costs of the legal action into which he had entered.

The final reconciliation, with the principal offenders, however, still lingered. Solomon Aloof's wife died at the end of November 1825, and application was made for her burial in the communal cemetery. The presiding warden at once expressed his readiness to pay the fine and all other sums due from the husband. This offer was accepted and permission given for the burial. The younger Aloof and Abecasis thereupon announced that as soon as their week of mourning had expired they also would make all the payments due from them, and seats in the Synagogue were thereupon again allotted to them. The prohibition of the award to them of any synagogue honour was at the same time withdrawn. However, the Haham again intervened and the Mahamad were compelled to withdraw their instructions to the Hazanim on the subject of the award of synagogue honours. Meldola demanded and persisted in his demand that before the offenders could be restored to their previous status they must admit their errors in the Synagogue and ask for pardon. This they were naturally very loth to do. The sympathies of the Mahamad and the Elders were evidently with the Aloofs: on the other hand, they were not prepared to overrule or attempt to overrule the Haham on what he emphasized was a matter of doctrine. In the end a sort of compromise was arranged. Late in the year 1826 the three gentlemen appeared in the synagogue, and in the presence of three rabbis chosen by themselves they made formal admission that they had been in the wrong in transgressing the Ascamot, more than four years earlier. They were then fully and without qualification restored to all the rights of Yehidim. This was the *cause célèbre*. While it was still running its course a minor but similar offence came to light in which the offenders had even more justification than the Aloofs and their friends. The inmates of the communal hospital were obviously not capable of proceeding to synagogue on the Day of Atonement, and the kind-hearted steward of the institution made arrangements for the holding of service within its walls. This also was a contravention of the first ascama, which provided for no exceptions and the sympathetic official was severely reprimanded. The pressure on the steward of the Beth Holim was, however, too great to be withstood. After an interval the offence was repeated. On Kippur 1829 prayers were again read with minyan for the patients in the hospital. Again very severe notice was taken of this very serious offence. A special meeting of the *Mahamad Completo* was summoned and the steward and all the inmates who were capable of leaving their beds were called before it. It transpired that the violation of the Ascamot had been instigated or encouraged by a collector of funds who had arrived from Jerusalem—a by no means strange phenomenon—and who had accepted the hospitality of the hospital over the Holy Days. In these circumstances the steward was absolved. The *Shaliach* from Jerusalem was above the law, for although he accepted full responsibility for the transgression no punishment or reprimand was meted out to him. His apology was accepted as sufficient. The hand of the Mahamad, however, fell upon the poor inmates who were severely reprimanded. Furthermore, the Treasurer and Parnassim of the Beth Holim waited on the Mahamad and 'expressed their regret and high displeasure at the circumstances related to them and assured the Mahamad that the subject should receive every possible attention on their part so as to mark their displeasure at all the proceedings'.

In the affair of the Aloofs and in other matters Meldola was very strict in the observance of the letter of the Law and in the infliction of the penalties laid down. In others in which he considered the dignity of his office to be more closely affected he was somewhat more lax. The procedure in matters of divorce and related ones was also governed by the laws of the Community, according to which the Haham and the Mahamad had to act in co-operation. Of this procedure Meldola showed himself somewhat impatient, and on more than one occasion the Mahamad had to call the Haham to account and to require him in future to observe the regulations that had been laid down to govern these matters. Finally, in January 1822, Meldola suddenly refused to administer the oath hitherto taken before the open ark in the synagogue, required of members of the Mahamad on their entry into office, to administer their duties justly and without favour or prejudice.

Meldola died on 1 June 1828 at the age of seventy-four. *The Annual Register* devoted three-quarters of a page to his obituary notice. 'The learned rabbi, Dr. Raphael Meldola, high priest of the southern (Oriental, Spanish, etc.) Jews, in the twenty-third year of his priesthood.' This reads as having been contributed by his son. A lengthy account of his funeral was given in the general press. All the leading members of the London Jewish community, Ashkenazim as well as Sephardim, attended, at their head Solomon Hirschel, the Rabbi of the Great Synagogue, and the Hazanim

THE TURN OF THE CENTURY 239

and wardens of all the London synagogues. The funeral ceremonies lasted from ten in the morning until seven in the evening when the dead Haham was laid to rest close to the grave of the predecessor, David Nieto, whom he so deeply revered, in the old and then already disused cemetery in Mile End. 'As the procession passed Aldgate Church the bell tolled and so great was the respect shown to this gentleman, that the tradesmen's shops adjacent to the Synagogue were all closed during the ceremony.'[1] There were many addresses delivered at the graveside. Rabbi Solomon Hirschel spoke in English instead of his native Yiddish with which he was far more familiar. His 'appeal to the feelings of his congregation drew tears from all'.[1]

[1] The *Sunday Herald*, 3 June 1828.

CHAPTER XIV

THE FIRST DECADES OF THE NINETEENTH CENTURY

THE EARLY YEARS of the century were the occasion of some financial worries. The revenues as a whole did not diminish: they even increased, but the expenditure increased to a still greater extent. As the life of the Community developed new necessities arose and older ones grew in volume. The country as a whole was developing and the Jewish section of it had to develop and expand with it. In January 1809 when the situation seemed critical, the system of taxation of members was completely reorganized. To effect these reforms a new procedure was introduced. The whole body of Yehidim was called together by the Elders and the situation explained to them. The responsibility was thus thrown on the members as a body for the alterations in the administration of the Community that were then introduced. Once before, in 1746, there had been a general meeting of Yehidim. The procedure, very strange in these days of far less leisure, is described in the minutes in detail, although there is no record of the business transacted on the occasion. At the meeting of 1809 the procedure laid down on the earlier occasion was generally followed. All Yehidim who were not in default with their payments were summoned to the synagogue. At eleven o'clock the doors were locked and no one was permitted to enter or leave before the business was concluded. Quoting from the minutes of the meeting

> 'The President sat on the Teba in the Presidential Chair which had been removed from the Room of the Mahamad, and the other Members of the Mahamad sat at his side in accordance with their seniority of Office, i.e. the Vice-President was on his right and the third Parnas on his left, and the Gabay was on the right side of the Teba and the Secretary on the left at a table, with paper and ink before him. The Haham sat in his pew with Ribi Isaac Luria, the second Dayan on his left; Ribi David Henriques Juliao, the first Dayan, was at home ill. The doors were closed in conformity with the notices sent out, and the President ordered the Hazan to begin; he sang Psalm 67 in which the Kaal joined.'

Then and only then was a chairman of the meeting chosen and

JOSEPH D'ALMEIDA
From an engraving by John Jones, after William Lawranson

HANANEL DE CASTRO
From a painting

ISAAC D'ISRAELI
From an engraving by Ridley, after Drummond

attention given to mundane affairs. The Elders put three proposals before the Yehidim. They pointed out that the then income was quite inadequate, and they asked that (1) they should be given power to raise the finta from £900 to £2,500 per annum, the maximum payable by any Yahid being not more than 2½ per cent of the total finta and the minimum 10s. per annum—these amounts to include offerings by Yehidim and their dependants; (2) Ascama No. 1 should be amended so as to prohibit the holding of divine service within six miles of Bevis Marks instead of the existing less definite prohibition of four miles from the City of London and its suburbs; and (3) the tax on business transactions, the imposta, should be reduced from a shilling to sixpence per hundred pounds. This concession was intended to appear to mitigate the proposed very steep increase in the finta. Originally the finta was merely a loan or advance payment and the imposta a tax, varying year by year, on certain business transactions of members during the year. In course of time as a means of attaining a stable revenue this system had become unworkable. For many years the amount of the finta, both as a whole and as it affected individuals, had been fixed from time to time, and it had long been recognized that it was no longer a loan but a tax.

The great increase in the finta was not accepted. A more modest total of £1,400 was substituted for it, with four per cent as a maximum and ten shillings as a minimum. The two other proposals were accepted. Another proposal, that in future the minutes of meetings should be kept in English, was rejected. Still a decade had to pass before that reform was adopted. A detailed procedure for the convening on requisition of future meetings of the Yehidim was also rejected. It was still some years before regular meetings of the Yehidim became a part of the administration of the Community. The finta and the imposta, however, were by no means the only sources of revenue of the Congregation. During the century and a half of its existence there had been a continual stream of legacies from its members. Some of these were bequeathed for the general purposes of the congregation: others for specific objects. Their total was relatively considerable, and the revenue derived from their investment comprised an appreciable proportion of the congregational income. It happens that in the very year 1809 the death of Joseph Barrow brought a legacy of £2,000 to be devoted to the erection of almshouses for indigent members of the Congregation. Four years later Abraham Lopes Pereira, after leaving a number of generous legacies for specific purposes, bequeathed the residue of his estate to the congregation for the benefit of its poor. Most of Lopes Pereira's bequests were to Jewish institutions, but he did not limit his benefactions to them.

Another great benefactor of the Community was Moses Lara, of whose differences with the Haham, Raphael Meldola, mention has previously been made. Moses Nunes Lara died in 1831, leaving the residue of his estate to the Community. Five years before his death, however, he had made a very generous gift, bringing in some £650 a year, laying down the purposes to which the income was to be devoted—scholarships, marriage portions, gifts on confinement, clothing for girls, shrouds for the dead, and medical attendance for the living. The whole range of needs was thus almost provided for. There was also a loan fund financed out of the Trust. But the beneficiaries in all cases were to be limited to those of Sephardi parentage on both sides. Lara thus showed himself almost the last survivor of the opponents of mixed Sephardi and Ashkenazi marriages. A few years earlier, in 1823, Moses Montefiore, of whom much will appear later in this narrative, presented the Congregation with thirteen houses in Cock Court, Jewry Street, to be used as almshouses for occupation by the poor of the Community. This does not by any means exhaust the list of benefactions even during the first years of the nineteenth century.

The Community had another source of revenue, less admirable than those that have hitherto been mentioned. The Ascamot from the beginning laid down that every Yahid was bound to accept any honorary office in the Community that was bestowed on him, and in the event of a refusal a substantial fine was to be imposed. Fines were also imposed for other offences, but those for refusal of office were the heaviest. It soon became evident that this power of imposing office could be made a source of revenue, and advantage was taken of it. Whether prominent and wealthy members of the Community made use of it as a means of contributing, in a sense anonymously, to the congregational funds is not clear, for from the time of Sir Solomon de Medina at the end of the seventeenth century to that of Sir Moses Montefiore in the nineteenth, men prominent in communal affairs, who had served the Community previously and repeated the service later, were fined for refusal of office. One very glaring instance of this practice which completely overreached itself, but nevertheless had a direct influence on English history, was that of Isaac d'Israeli. Isaac d'Israeli, the son of an Italian Jewish settler in England, of the earlier half of the eighteenth century, was the despair of his father as a consequence of his rooted disinclination to commercial pursuits to which members of his family had always devoted themselves. From his

THE FIRST DECADES OF THE CENTURY

mother he received no encouragement to interest himself in Jewish teachings or in the affairs of the Jewish community. On the other hand, he was deeply absorbed in literature and today, more than a century after his death, it is as an Englishman of letters that he is remembered, apart from being the father of a very illustrious son. Isaac d'Israeli, however, had no antipathy to Judaism. It merely did not interest him. When he grew up he became a Yahid in ordinary course and if the quiet tenor of his Jewish life had not been disturbed he would probably have remained one until his last day. His attendance in synagogue was very occasional, and as time passed probably ceased altogether. He had other and more absorbing interests. But he paid his accounts regularly and allowed the life of the Community to flow without criticism or even comment on his part. No Yahid could be less qualified for office in the Community than he. Nevertheless it was upon him that the choice of the Mahamad fell when new Parnassim had to be elected in the autumn of 1813. D'Israeli naturally declined the honour, expressing great surprise that he should have been elected. In doing so, he added that he would be pleased to continue his usual contributions to the Synagogue's funds and to those of its charities, but that he could not take any more active part in its affairs than hitherto. The refusal was ignored, and d'Israeli was summoned to a meeting of the Mahamad. This summons he returned, remarking that it had probably been sent to him in error. The Mahamad, however, replied that he had been elected in accordance with the Ascamot, and that if he did not accept the office he would under the same regulations be fined forty pounds. Isaac d'Israeli's reply was a temperate and well-argued letter in which he pointed out that if the procedure was in accordance with the laws of the Congregation, and therefore legal, the spirit of the laws must depend on their wise administration. In announcing his withdrawal from the Community he wrote:

> 'I lament the occasion which drives me, with so many others, out of the pale of your jurisdiction.... Even the government of of a small sect can only be safely conducted by enlightened principles, and must accommodate itself with practical wisdom to existing circumstances, but above all with a tender regard to the injured feelings of its scattered members.... Many of your members are already lost; many you are losing! Even those whose tempers and feelings would still cling to you, are gradually seceding. But against all this you are perpetually pleading your existing laws, which you would enforce on all the brethren alike!

It is of these obsolete laws so many complain. They were adapted by fugitives to their peculiar situation, quite distinct from our own, and as foreign to us as the language in which they are written. Some of you boast that your laws are much as they were a century ago! You have laws to regulate what has ceased to exist, you have laws which through the change of human events, prove to be new impediments to the very purposes of the institution, and for the new circumstances which have arisen, you are without laws. . . . If you will not retain a zealous friend, and one who had long had you in his thoughts, my last resource is to desire my name to be withdrawn from your society. It remains for you, Gentlemen, to set a noble example of dignity and political wisdom. Let the award of the Mahamad be revised because they have erred in the choice of a fitting person to become a Parnass. At all events you have my warm wishes for happier days. Do not shut out the general improvement of the age. Make your schools flourish, and remember that you have had universities ere now; a society has only to make itself respectable in these times to draw to itself the public esteem.'[1]

This was, however, not the final break. A few months later d'Israeli received the usual intimation that his regular payment to the synagogue funds was due, but was asked to pay not only his finta but also the fine that he had repudiated. By this request he was naturally irritated, but replied that he was prepared to pay the sum claimed less the amount of the fine. For the time being the matter lapsed, but early in 1817 he was again called upon to pay the finta that had accumulated and also the fine and was summoned to a meeting. He replied regretting that the Mahamad was not satisfied to allow him to remain a passive member of the Community, paying his dues but going his own way.

'I have patiently sought for protection against the absurd choice of two or three injudicious individuals, but I find that you as a body sanction what your own laws will not allow. I am not a fit member of your society, and I certainly am an aggrieved one. I must now close all future correspondence, and I am under the painful necessity of insisting that my name be erased from the list of your members.'

It is obvious that it was with reluctance that d'Israeli withdrew from the Jewish community, but he felt that he had no alternative.

[1] This letter was printed in full by James Picciotto in his *Sketches of Anglo-Jewish History* (1875) and by Cecil Roth in his *Anglo-Jewish Letters* (1938).

THE FIRST DECADES OF THE CENTURY 245

That his interest in the philosophy of Judaism and also in the practical application of it survived the estrangement is evident from the publication, anonymously, in 1833 of his *Genius of Judaism* and in the fact that years later, in 1842, when a blind old man almost at the end of his days, he left his house in the country to attend the inauguration of the West London Synagogue of British Jews. D'Israeli, although no longer a member of the Jewish community, joined no other. For a time he and his family remained outside all religious communities. For the parents this course was not impracticable. The case of the children, one daughter and three sons, was different. They were all very young, the eldest, Sarah, eleven at the time of the withdrawal. Although Isaac d'Israeli could not be called an active Jew, he was quite prepared to have his children brought up as Jews and provision was made for instruction in Hebrew or Judaism of the eldest boy Benjamin, while he was at a non-Jewish boarding-school in Blackheath. With the withdrawal this presumably came to an end. The father could be outside of all religious communities, but with the children some definite step had sooner or later to be taken. Isaac d'Israeli seems to have realized this, but yet was reluctant to take any definite step. A close friend of the family, Sharon Turner, the historian of Anglo-Saxon England, was continually pressing to have the children baptized into the Church of England. Isaac d'Israeli at length half consented. Sharon Turner hastened to make the necessary arrangements, and the children were thereupon baptized in the Church of St. Andrew's, Holborn. But even then reluctance continued to be shown. The children were not baptized all at one time, but singly, the youngest first and the eldest of the family, Sarah, last. Benjamin was then in his thirteenth year. If he had not been baptized as a child, as a Jew he could not have been admitted to Parliament until 1858 instead of in 1837, and in consequence could never have risen to be Prime Minister of England. With the d'Israelis the related family of Basevi also withdrew from the Jewish community. They were also of Italian origin; Nathan or Naphtali Basevi had been one of the early presidents of the Board of Deputies, and in a later generation George or Elias Basevi was a distinguished architect.

Four years after Isaac d'Israeli's formal withdrawal, application was made to the Mahamad on his behalf by Ephraim Lindo, a family connexion, for certificates of birth of the d'Israeli children. The Mahamad refused to deal with any intermediary in the matter, and d'Israeli was consequently compelled to apply to them direct. The Mahamad refused the certificates unless the sum of '£100 2s. being owing by you to the Synagogue and incurred during the period you acknowledged yourself a member thereof' be paid. This of course included the fine that d'Israeli had repudiated. The matter was, however, referred to the Elders and by them satisfactorily settled. 'The Mahamad be desired to grant Mr. d'Israeli such certificates of his family's birth as are in their possession. The Mahamad be empowered to receive from Mr. d'Israeli what he may offer as the amount of his debt to the Congregation.' This was the resolution adopted by the Elders, but it was not confirmed. In substitution it was resolved 'that the Mahamad be desired to request Mr. Isaac d'Israeli will inform them what sum of money he is willing to pay towards the balance due by him to the Sedaca agreeably to the account rendered, and in part acknowledged by him, prior to granting the certificates he required of his family's birth'. The Mahamad was further authorized to accept from him 'what he may offer as the amount of his debt to the Congregation'. With the payment by Isaac d'Israeli and the issue of the certificates of birth, the d'Israeli family passed out of the story of Jewish history.

Ephraim Lindo had married Sarah Basevi, a sister of Miriam or Mary Basevi who had married Isaac d'Israeli. These ladies and their brother Joshua (later George), who married Bathsheba, sister of Ephraim Lindo, were children of Naphtali or Nathan Basevi, the first of the family to come to England, apart from Jacob Cervetto, otherwise Basevi, the 'cellist who has been mentioned on an earlier page. Ephraim Lindo was the eldest of the many children of Elias Lindo and Grace Lumbroso de Mattos, and a brother of David Abarbanel Lindo, a veritable pillar of Anglo-Sephardi Jewry in the first years of the nineteenth century, and a man of rigid orthodoxy. Ephraim's daughter, Olivia, married Charles Trevor, a non-Jew, and their daughter, Katherine, married Ralph or Raphael Disraeli, a younger brother of Lord Beaconsfield. Coningsby Disraeli, M.P., the last male bearer of the name, was the son of Ralph and Katherine Disraeli. Ephraim Lindo, however, did not withdraw from the Community with the d'Israelis and the Basevis. In September 1825 he was elected a parnas, which office he refused, presumably paying the usual fine, but less than four years later, in March 1829, he also took the final step and severed his connexion with Jewry.

In the meanwhile the practice of electing Yehidim to office, without their consent or even knowledge, continued and the imposition of fines followed as a matter of course, but in November 1829 one modification was made in the procedure. It was decreed that in future when a Yahid was elected to office he should at the same time be told the amount of the fine for which he was liable if he refused it. Occasionally acceptance of office was preferred as an alternative to the payment of a fine. Thus when in October 1819 Samuel Levy Bensusan was fined for refusing the office of Gabay and, despite his efforts, could not get the fine remitted, he changed his mind and accepted the office. Office, in particular that of Gabay, was by no means a sinecure. Apart from an almost uninterrupted succession of annoyances, causes of anxiety, and of worry to which the records of the Community over long periods testify, there was the financial responsibility of the Gabay who was required to make a deposit on taking office of £600, from which temporary deficits were to be financed, and if this sum proved insufficient the Gabay was expected to supplement it. The revenue derived from fines formed at one time an appreciable proportion of the income of the Community. For instance, in 1817–18 £360 was derived from this source and in the following year £460. Not only were Yehidim elected to office without their knowledge. It was the practice also to seek out Sephardim of some means who were resident in England, permanently or temporarily, and forcibly to enrol them as Yehidim and of course assess them for finta. There was the case of Solomon Abecasis, one of the prominent transgressors against the first ascama in 1822, who considered that he had not then settled in England but was only living there for the time being. After the great offence had been purged and he had been fully pardoned, he had to contest very persistently the attempt to enrol him as a permanent member, despite his willingness to pay his quota of the finta and other charges. Later he did become a Yahid and served the Congregation in the highest offices. Two years earlier, in November 1820, Isaac de Oliveira and Isaac Dias Carvalho, who were living in Brighton, found themselves elected Yehidim without their knowledge or desire. They declined the election of which they learnt 'with surprise'. Nevertheless the Elders similarly declined to accept the refusal. However, this attempted practice of compulsory membership was abandoned shortly afterwards. There was of course no means of making it effective, and although fines could be imposed, how could they be collected? Incidentally, a two-thirds majority of electors was necessary for election to membership of the Community. There was another method of raising revenue by means of fines to which full recourse was had. This was the fining of any member of the Mahamad or other body, including those non-members summoned for instance to complete a quorum, who failed to attend, except for very good cause, within a short time of the opening of the meeting.

Excuses were frequent, and as time passed, more and more were accepted. But in some years a not insignificant sum was derived from this source. Abraham Montefiore, a younger brother of Sir Moses, was an especial offender in this respect, and the number of pound fines that he was called on to pay during the periods in which he held office was noticeable. One somewhat surprising entry on the other side of the ledger was the trouble into which Jacob Netto became involved in March 1834 by refusing a grant that was offered to him by the Mahamad for the relief of his children. He was called on to make a formal apology for having rejected the generous offer.

In the meanwhile the financial state of the Congregation continued, if only sporadically, to give cause for anxiety. In December 1819 a report of the Elders called attention to the increasing expenditure on the maintenance of orphans and also the considerable increase in the expenditure on passage money for the flood of refugees from the States of Barbary and other places infected with the plague 'as well as from the distresses which many of our nation are suffering in several parts of Europe and it has always been thought most prudent to encourage the emigration of strangers from this place which must be attended with expenses'. Six years later the Community found itself involved in a financial crisis and the conclusion was that in the circumstances then existing, unless some very drastic steps were taken, the ordinary expenditure must always exceed the income. The income from impostas, once the main source of revenue, had fallen to £411 in 1809–10 and as low as £11 in 1824–5. The income under all heads except that from the investment of legacies was continually diminishing, although that of the imposta was of course an extreme case. Lack of interest was showing itself in other directions which led also directly or indirectly into the realm of finance. A report by a special committee on finance, dated 19 October 1825, of which Moses Montefiore was chairman, and his brother-in-law, Solomon Sebag, Gabay, said:

> 'From the great pains your Committee have taken to embrace the entire subject of your finances they feel emboldened to solicit the sympathy and co-operation of the Elders to devote every possible means of exerting a common zeal in the Nation; at the same time feeling how forcibly example operates they cannot omit expressing their opinion that a general determination of giving a more constant and regular attendance at Synagogue, on Sabbath days and festivals would effect a greater harmony and inspire a livelier interest among the Congregation than is now

THE FIRST DECADES OF THE CENTURY 249

felt, it is also fair to presume that by fathers of families leading the way, that the younger branches would follow in which cases much future good might be looked for from our youth becoming zealous advocates in our cause.'

The estimated income for that year was £3,525 and the minimum expenditure £4,140. Nevertheless no general improvement showed itself. Receipts continued to fall, partly in consequence of deaths and withdrawals, the voids created by which there were not sufficient new-comers to fill. By the beginning of the thirties the total estimated finta had been reduced to £1,100, but it was impossible to reach this figure. It was soon after again reduced to £1,000. In the year 1835 the total expenditure was £3,475 14s. 1d., of which £2,598 19s. 8d. comprised ordinary expenditure, and the total revenue £3,378 12s. 7d., of which £1,723 18s. 10d., more than a half, was derived from investments, representing legacies and bequests of earlier generations. In that year the total of outstanding accounts on the books was £656 4s. 7d. A new misfortune and drain on the finances was the cholera epidemic of 1831 and 1832 to deal with which, so far as the poorer members of the Community were affected, still greater expenditure was necessitated. There was no possibility of balancing the two sides of the accounts, and recourse had to be had to the realization of legacies that had been invested. In addition a special fund was raised for the relief of the sufferers from the scourge. In that year the expenditure was £3,732, of which £2,604 was classified as ordinary, and the ordinary revenue £3,474, of which £1,709 was derived from income from invested funds. Outstanding accounts for finta and offerings amounted to the relatively large sum of £679.

For its own poor, that is to say the poorer Sephardim of London, the Mahamad felt itself entirely responsible. The richer members of the Community, as individuals, also took their part in the assistance of the poor of the wider London Jewish community. There were also appeals from a wider Jewish circle from without the metropolis. Mention has already been made of request for assistance that came from time to time from Sephardi communities in other lands. These appeals seldom passed without response. The Sephardim of the world were, after all, one community, with one tradition covering two millennia, and in many cases knitted close together by family kinship. Similar appeals for financial assistance, however, came also from other sources, from Ashkenazi communities in all parts of the kingdom, to which in some cases a satisfactory response was given, in others not. Bevis Marks was still looked on as the wealthiest Jewish centre in England, and its generosity was known to rival its wealth. Thus in January 1835 the Dover Community asked for assistance; in the following June a grant was made towards the purchase of a cemetery for the Jewish Community of Jersey and fifteen months later a request from Penzance for a contribution to the rebuilding of the synagogue in that town. In June 1838 came a similar request form the Jewish Community of Sheerness. In 1842 the Bath Community asked for assistance and those of Dover and Sheerness a second time. In 1843 came one from Nottingham, which was also refused. In 1845 the Dublin Community whose relations in the past with Bevis Marks had been close, received £25 towards the rebuilding of their synagogue, and in reply sent a profuse letter of thanks. They intended, they said, as an expression of their gratitude to consider themselves in future a branch synagogue of Bevis Marks 'that we may under every vicissitude of our affairs, claim the privilege of being under your fostering and beneficent protection'. They then proceeded to mention that their *siphre torah* were either worn out or too small to read or otherwise unsatisfactory and to inquire whether the Bevis Marks authorities could not spare for them some more satisfactory ones. During the next decade or so appeals came from Great Yarmouth, Nottingham (for the purchase of a cemetery), Norwich (for help in rebuilding their synagogue), Jersey, Portsea, Edinburgh, Sheffield, Merthyr Tydfil, Leeds, Sunderland, Dover, Liverpool, and Newport (Mon.), and it was very exceptional for any appeal to be rejected in full.

These came all from the United Kingdom. The story of the generosity of Bevis Marks had, however, spread far beyond the limits of the British Isles. In 1839 £50 was given to the Jewish Community of Kingston, Jamaica, towards the establishment of a school and the repair of their synagogue and in the same year sepharim were presented to the Congregation in Montreal. The Hamburg Synagogue needed rebuilding after a fire in 1842, and its governing body at once turned to London for help. In 1846 Sydney in Australia was preparing to erect a synagogue and its eyes and its hands at once turned to London. In the same year applications for help came from Salonica, Adrianople, and Tangiers. Two years later it was the turn of the North American Continent. The Jewish Community of Louisville, Kentucky, considered that their synagogue needed repair, and at once turned to the Sephardim of London for a contribution for the purpose. In the same year a *sepher torah* was given to the Jewish Community of Terceira in the Azores; Cape Town was building a synagogue in 1850, and

Bevis Marks was asked to assist and did so. In the same year £75 was sent to Morocco for a similar purpose; in the following year £20 to Madeira, and in 1852 a grant to Corfu. In 1852 the Community in Smyrna was given assistance and in 1855 it was the turn of that of Brusa. The following year an application was received from a group of Sephardim in Melbourne, Australia— Daniel and John de Pass, Solomon Belinfante, E. S. Henriques, and others—all names well known in London Jewry—for help in the establishment of a Sephardi Community there, and the call was heard. The London Community was at that time encouraging emigration to Australia as a means of some relief from the burden of their own poor. Other appeals came from Larissa in Greece in 1856, and two years later from the Baghdad Community, who wanted to repair the traditional tombs of the Prophets, and this list is by no means exhaustive. At the same time, but less frequently, there were appeals on behalf of suffering Jewish communities abroad, in Mogador in 1844 when capital had to be realized to give an adequate response; Tiberias in 1848, the gift 'to be distributed between all Jews without distinction of congregation'; in 1858 to the North African refugees in Gibraltar. And this was a time when the congregational finances were at a low ebb, the finta at one time being reduced to £700. There were also the wider appeals for Jewish relief that knew neither Sephardi nor Ashkenazi, only Jew. Such were those that came in the wake of the Blood Accusations at Damascus and Rhodes in 1840, and another, a little more than a year later, on behalf of the sufferers from a great conflagration in Smyrna. The Congregation had voted £500 towards the cost of the mission of Sir Moses Montefiore in the earlier year, undertaken on behalf of the Damascus Jewish Community.

Furthermore, there were the general appeals to the people of England to which the London Sephardim never hesitated to respond—for instance, the fund for the relief of the victims of the earthquake in Syria in 1823, and in 1831 that for the benefit of the distressed Irish. During the cholera epidemic money was voted not only for the Jewish victims but also to the national fund raised for the relief of the consequent distress.

There was, however, one quarter, the Holy Land itself, requests from which were found increasingly burdensome. The Mahamad and the Yehidim in course of time tired not merely of the continuous requests for assistance but also of the persistence with which they were pressed. Almost two centuries earlier, when the Community was first established, the provision of help to the Jews of that country had been placed very high on the list of *Mitzvot*, and it was not long before a department of the Community's administration was created for the direction of relief to the Jews of the four Holy Cities of Palestine. *Shiluchim* or rabbinical messengers, from one or other of these cities, received a respectful welcome and were never sent away empty-handed. In the true Jewish tradition assistance to a worthy cause, in this instance a sacred cause, was felt to confer as much if not more benefit on the donor as on the recipient. But in course of time it was found desirable to examine the credentials of the shiluchim. As long ago as the year 1735 when a *shaliach* appeared in England from Safad, three of the most prominent members of the Community—Benjamin Mendes da Costa, Jacob de Moses Franco, and Abraham da Fonseca, at the time Gabay of the Community, were deputed to accompany him on his visits to members of the Community, perhaps to support his efforts, perhaps also to keep an eye on him, for his permission to make collections was subsequently cancelled on the ground that he was not authorized by those who were said to have commissioned him. It was made clear at the same time that the Mahamad was ready to support anyone who was properly authorized.

But it was not only the Sephardim who suffered. In the end, in April 1831, Rabbi Hirschel of the Great Synagogue approached the Mahamad to seek their co-operation in the establishment of a society in England to raise and distribute contributions for the Holy Land and to 'prevent the arrival of siliachem to this country for that purpose'. The Mahamad quickly responded. They considered the suggestion as one that would further 'a most desirable object' that of 'avoiding the necessity of missionaries from the Holy Land coming to this country'. The Mahamad suggested that in future an annual grant from the fund earmarked for the ransom of captives—an object that no longer existed—should be made to the Jewish Communities of the Holy Cities, and the Elders agreed to the proposal. It had been resolved ten years earlier that the proceeds of this fund should be devoted in future to the assistance of distressed Jewish communities anywhere. The authorities in Palestine who were directly concerned were informed of this decision. It was even decided to refuse in future to pay the cost of the further journey of any shaliach who might nevertheless come to England. This had hitherto been the general practice of Jewish communities. This decision, however, did not bring the nuisance to an end. In April 1835 two rival shiluchim from Tiberias appeared on the scene, each claiming to be the only legitimate one. The claims of both were rejected, and they were told that if assistance to the Jews of Tiberias was decided on, the money would be sent direct to that city. Two years later the Mahamad was warned that a shaliach was on the way from Safad and in order to dissuade him from completing his journey a sum of five pounds was sent to him post haste for 'Seda la Dareh',[1] 'as a mark of such their approval it being a grant which would not be made to any other Seliah'. The shaliach accepted the money but did not interrupt his journey. When he reached Amsterdam he wrote asking for permission to continue his journey to London 'in his individual character to procure assistance for his heavy expenses'. In reply he was warned not to come, as his proposed visit 'would be attended by expense to him and no advantage as the Congregation would not be troubled with Siluhim'. His reaction to this warning is not recorded. Palestine, although the most prolific, was not the only source of shiluchim, who were accustomed to wander about the world visiting more fortunately circumstanced Jewish communities than their own. From the east of Europe and from the Moslem lands they came in contingents and their bona fides were not always above suspicion. Occasionally their journeys were extended to inordinate length in time, if not in distance, and the communities that had originally started them on their journeys, having lost contact with them, became anxious or at any rate inquiring. Thus in April 1825 a meeting of the Mahamad was convened 'in consequence of a letter received from the K.K. of Mequinez (Meknes) complaining of the conduct of R. David Attias, an individual now in this country, who had been appointed by that Kahilla Saliah to the several congregations of Jews throughout Barbary and Europe, in order to solicit assistance in their behalf in account of their great sufferings from famine and civil war—that nearly six years had elapsed since his departure and they had not received any account nor tidings from him, tho' they were credibly informed he had collected large sums of money. Learning that the said Seliach was proceeding to London, they solicited the interference of the Mahamad to obtain from him account of the collections he had made and monies might be in his possession and transmit the same to the said Kehila.' Attias was summoned by the Mahamad and asked for an explanation. He promised a statement of accounts within a few days, and when he furnished one it showed not only that he owed nothing to his principals but that the balance of the account, for expenses, was in his favour.

Another cause of worry during these years, but in a different sphere, was that of the increasing number of wives and children

[1] A viaticum or provision for a journey.

who were deserted by those responsible for their maintenance and left to the charity of the Community. In some cases the husbands and fathers went abroad and nothing further was heard of them. In many, however, they did not trouble to conceal themselves, but merely changed their places of residence, leaving their families behind them. For these families the Community took responsibility, but as time passed with less and less enthusiasm. In the earlier years when the normal standard of living of the poor was very low and the value of money high, the cost in pounds, shillings, and pence was small, at most five shillings per child per week, and although these standards changed the payments were never large. But it was the principle more than the cost that concerned the Mahamad and the Elders. The Community had the support of the law, for by the early years of the nineteenth century fathers were under legal obligation to maintain their wives and children. In these circumstances, in May 1822, the Mahamad decided to prosecute deserting husbands in all cases in which the families were left destitute. A number of prosecutions was instituted, convictions obtained, and sentences of hard labour passed on the offenders. The governing body of the Community took the proceedings, but they were fully supported by the parish authorities. The magistrates were similarly helpful. According to a letter from the Congregation's solicitors 'the Magistrates stated, and they particularly requested that this might be communicated to you by us, that they would cordially co-operate with you in coercing the members of your body to maintain their families. . . . It is but justice to the officers of Spitalfields Parish to say that in prosecuting the cases . . . we have received the most prompt and handsome assistance from them.' There was, however, one contretemps. It was discovered that one of the husbands whom the Mahamad had prosecuted had married a Christian woman. Morally and religiously the Community had no *locus standi*, but the discovery came too late.

Mention has previously been made of the cholera epidemic that ravaged London in the winter of 1831-2. It first appeared in one of the northern ports, and the news of it there at once aroused alarm and foreboding. The authorities of the capital promptly took steps to combat the disease, to limit its spread, and to relieve its surviving victims. In all these measures the Sephardi Community took its share, spending not only a portion of its income in this work, but realizing investments also to the same end. In advance of the appearance of the scourge in London, a Board of Health was appointed in November 1831 to watch over the health of the poorer members of the Community, and other precautions were taken. In the same month special prayers were recited in the Synagogue, by the King's command, for protection against cholera and were continued weekly until the epidemic had passed. When the scourge did appear in London, the Sephardim joined with their fellow citizens in the fast that was ordered by the Government, and a special service was held in the synagogue. David Meldola, who had some months after the death of his father been appointed Ab Beth Din and Acting Haham, was invited to preach a sermon in English, but in accordance with the established practice and in view of some experiences that had been undergone he was required to submit it in advance to the Mahamad. Meldola declined the invitation as did his brother-in-law, the Hazan, David Aaron de Sola. In the end a sermon in English was preached, but by a lay member of the Community, David Rodrigues Brandon, who first submitted it to the Mahamad. This body not only approved it, but thought so highly of it that they asked Brandon's permission to print it. This he gave. At another special service of thanksgiving when the epidemic had died out, on 14 April 1833, Brandon was again invited to preach. The offerings made on the occasion of the earlier service were remitted to the Government Board of Health for disposal as they might think fit.

Haham Meldola died at the beginning of June 1828. No successor was appointed for thirty-eight years. The ecclesiastical administration had, however, to be carried on, and for this purpose in November of the same year David Meldola, a son of the late Haham who has previously come under notice, and Isaac Sebag were appointed Dayanim. Isaac Sebag died a few months later. On 21 February 1830, Joseph Benguegui, who had been appointed in August 1823 as a member of the Beth Din and who had in ordinary course succeeded as its president on the death of Raphael Meldola, also died. There had been trouble over Benguegui's original appointment against which Raphael Meldola had protested not on personal grounds, but because he had not been consulted by the Mahamad before it was made. On the death of Benguegui, David Mendola succeeded in ordinary course as Ab Beth Din and Acting Haham. To complete the bench Elimelech Mudahy and Ephraim Abraham Arditti were appointed. Arditti died at the end of 1832. Over the appointment of a successor another of the very unseemly disputes in which Meldola was so frequently involved broke out. Meldola apparently had his own candidate and in support of his candidature induced his colleague Mudahy to write to a number of the prominent members of the Community to the effect that the other candidate, Abraham Haliva, was unfit for the office. Mudahy when called on for an explanation said that he had signed the letters at the request of Meldola, without knowing their gist. They were written in English. Meldola also said that he had no time to read the letters before they were sent to Mudahy for signature. They had been written by a Mr. Walker, who understood Hebrew, after they had discussed Haliva's disqualifications. When Meldola and Mudahy were confronted 'much discrimination took place between the parties'. It transpired that the two dayanim had approached Solomon Hirschel for his opinion, stating, however, an hypothetical case without mentioning any name. Hirschel on being invited to state what he knew of the matter did so. He stated that the alleged quotations of his opinion in the letter that had been circulated were not authentic. When approached by the two dayanim he had declined to enter into the matter unless he was approached in due form by the Mahamad. The Elders proceeded severely to censure both Meldola and Mudahy and warned them that 'if there were any repetition they will visit them with the severest penalty', and immediately afterwards elected Heliva dayan at a salary of twenty pounds per annum.

The differences between Meldola and the authorities and members of the Congregation were unceasing, and complaints about his proceedings took up an undue proportion of the time of the Gentlemen of the Mahamad and the Elders. Occasional threats of actions for libel or slander interspersed these investigations. In May 1837 the Mahamad had to lay down that no discourse should in any circumstances be delivered in the synagogue until it had been submitted to an inspector to be appointed by the Mahamad and approved. This resolution arose out of an address which Meldola had delivered in which, according to complaints that were made, there were undesirable mention of personalities and unwarranted allusions. This sermon seems to have led to a retaliatory complaint that David Abarbanel Lindo, one of the lay pillars of the Community, had printed and distributed a libellous pamphlet regarding Meldola, addressed to the governors and subscribers of the Orphan Society of which he was at the time patron. The Mahamad, prudently avoiding any decision whether or not the pamphlet was justified, fined Lindo five pounds for having printed and circulated it without their permission. In order to limit the bounds of the controversy they at the same time warned Meldola not to publish another pamphlet in reply. Lindo contested this decision on the ground that the ascama under which he had been fined did not apply and appealed to the Elders against the

JACOB KIMHI
From an engraving by Joseph Singleton, after Osias Humphrey, R.A.

MOSES EDREHI
From an engraving by J. C. Hunter

KETUBA OR MARRIAGE CONTRACT
WITH HEADING AND DECORATIONS (1843)

decision of the Mahamad. The latter upheld the Mahamad, but they proceeded to censure Meldola severely for the terms of a letter reflecting on Lindo that he had addressed to the Mahamad. Within the Beth Din, as was to be expected, relations between Meldola and his colleagues were not cordial.

David Abarbanel Lindo was certainly a gentleman of a very hot temper which often involved him in disputes and altercations in the course of which he often said and did things which he regretted in his cooler moments. A noticeable occasion was early in 1832. It was the practice for the boys of the two older communal schools, those of the Orphan Society and of the Etz Haim (later Shaare Tikva), to read the Haphtara every week in synagogue in order to train them to be able in due course to take their full and expected part in the service. For this purpose the boys form the two schools were entrusted alternately with the honourable task. The two older schools were later supplemented by a third, a preparatory school for the Shaare Tikva, and not unreasonably the Gentlemen of the Mahamad agreed to let the boys of that school also have a share in the weekly reading of the Haphtara. The share of the new-comers was a minor one, six occasions as compared with more than twenty in each of the senior schools. David Abarbanel Lindo held an honorary office in the Orphan School, and at once demanded that whatever changes were made the share in the *mitzvot* of the pupils of his school should not be diminished. His demand was not met, and he thereupon sat down and wrote a letter to the Mahamad resigning his membership of the Community.

> 'Your most irreligious decision of yesterday respecting the Aphtarots, obliges me to demand that my name be erased from List of Yehidim. Now that I am no longer a member of your Congregation, I fearlessly give a *din* that it is according to *Din Torah* and the laws of this and every civilized country. Men cannot act as judges on any case that they have any direct or indirect interest in and so much for your *complete Mahamad*.'

An endeavour was made to get the Elders to intervene, but this they declined to do. They presumably recognized that the whole dispute was even less than a storm in a teacup. Lindo very soon recovered from his outburst, and on the intervention of twelve of his fellow Elders, acting in a personal capacity, in whose hands he had placed himself, he withdrew his letter of resignation and the bone of contention was buried. The incident illustrates the mixture of pettiness and rigid devotion to principle with which the Community was governed early in the nineteenth century on the eve of events of major importance to the interest of Anglo-Jewry.

In the year 1818 one of the Hazanim, Mordecai Salom, who had been first appointed in 1770, died. In his place David Aaron de Sola was appointed Assistant Hazan. He was of a Dutch Jewish family and had been born in Amsterdam in 1796. He was therefore not yet twenty-two when he was appointed to office in London, and a year after his arrival he married Rebecca, the eldest daughter of the Haham, Raphael Meldola. He was not the first of his name to hold office in the London Sephardi Community. From 1690 to 1700 Isaac de Sola was Hazan in London, and in 1722 Abraham Solas or de Sola was appointed Assistant Hazan at an annual salary of £40, and full Hazan, when Isaac de Chaves died in 1740. Abraham de Sola retired in 1749 and died four years later, being succeeded by a kinsman or namesake, Joseph Mendes de Sola, who held office until 1770. The de Sola family goes back to Don Bartolome (Baruch ben Isaac ibn Daud), who lived in Spain in the ninth century, and in subsequent generations produced eminent men in several spheres as well as martyrs of the Inquisition. Carlos de Sola (b. *c.* 1595) settled in Holland and from him are descended the English members of the family. David Aaron de Sola had a large family, and there are many descendants of him in the London Community today. His eldest son, Abraham, settled in Canada, as has already been mentioned, and was for many years the spiritual head of the Sephardi Community in Montreal. Another son, Samuel, succeeded his father as Hazan in London. David Aaron de Sola stood out in the line of Hazanim of Bevis Marks. The nearest who approached to him was David Pardo who filled the same office at the end of the seventeenth century. De Sola earned the soubriquet 'the learned Hazan', on account of his scholarship and his writings. Although a stranger to the English language, he soon became a master of it, and it was not long before he was preaching in English with a facility that might well make his hearers believe that it was his native tongue. Many of these sermons were published. To him was entrusted the translation into English of the Sephardi ritual, a translation that has been taken as the basis of all its successors. This work included a Hebrew Calendar for fifty years. De Sola also translated the ritual of the Ashkenazi Community. In co-operation with Morris J. Raphall, an Ashkenazi scholar, he began the translation into English of the *Mishna*. In this work they were encouraged by Moses Mocatta and Horatio Joseph Montefiore in order to meet 'the necessity of being supplied with an English translation of the Mishnah, from persons of their own faith'. Their work was published, with an anonymous preface without the knowledge of the translators, by Benjamin Elkin, an overzealous member of the group of those who actively advocated reforming the services of the synagogue. It led to a repudiation by de Sola and Raphall in *The Times*, in whose columns the book had been advertised. A lengthy controversy followed. These two scholars also projected a new edition of the Bible in English and Hebrew, with notes, but only the Book of Genesis appeared. The writers were in advance of their time. They co-operated with Charlotte, the wife and niece of Horatio Montefiore, and her sister Louisa, wife of her kinsman, Sir Anthony de Rothschild, in the production of a popular Jewish library, in effect a series of cheap religious tracts, then a popular form of literature. De Sola co-operated in other ways with Ashkenazi scholars in furthering Jewish adult education and also in the general activities of the Jewish community. In 1842 the Association for the Promotion of Jewish Literature was founded by a group of these scholars and patrons of learning and de Sola also took his share in this work. The Association later developed into The Jews' and General Literary and Scientific Institution, the first institution of its kind in Anglo-Jewry, popularly known as Sussex Hall, so named in honour of the Duke of Sussex. Hananel de Castro, another prominent English Sephardi, was its first president. De Sola edited, with Emanuel Aguilar, the traditional melodies of his own Community and was selected to be, with Raphall, joint editor of the first Anglo-Jewish newspaper, *The Voice of Jacob*. This last arrangement was not completed on account of the removal of Raphall to Birmingham.[1] A year or so later David Meldola became, with the permission of the Mahamad, joint editor of *The Jewish Chronicle*, then newly established, but he was soon instructed to resign this office in consequence of the publication in that periodical of an article 'containing severe strictures on the Synagogues in this City'. The Mahamad still had the will but no longer the power of exercising a censorship over the Anglo-Jewish press. This period in Anglo-Jewish history saw a burgeoning of scholarship and letters in the community, and in this movement de Sola took a prominent part.

It was in this period that the sermon began to take its regular place in the London Sephardi synagogue service. Previously discourses had been delivered, but they had been very occasional and

[1] A biography of de Sola, by his son, the Rev. Abraham de Sola of Montreal, was published in Philadelphia in 1864.

confined to some special service. They were invariably in Portuguese or in another language with which the members of the Congregation were from generation to generation getting more and more out of touch. The promotion of English at first to equal status with Portuguese as the official and, after Hebrew, the ritual language of the Community, was marked in 1819 by the decision henceforth to keep all the records in that language. It was in December 1830 that the Elders having resolved that sermons should from time to time be delivered in English in the Synagogue, invited anybody who considered himself able to deliver one to communicate with the secretary. There was only one response, and that was from the Hazan, de Sola. Three months later, at the end of March 1831, the first sermon in English to be delivered in the synagogue of the Community was given by him. The experiment was a success, and de Sola was invited to preach at regular intervals in future. So far as London was concerned this was an innovation, but these English sermons were not the first in England. Almost a generation earlier an occasional sermon in English had been preached in the Ashkenazi synagogue in Liverpool, of all the provincial communities, the one in which the English tradition was strongest. In London the earliest sermon to be preached in English was by Tobias Goodman, on the occasion of the death of the Princess Charlotte, delivered in the Denmark Court (later Western) Synagogue on 19 November 1817. For the next seven years, until his death in 1824, Goodman preached occasionally in English in other London synagogues. Two years later, in February 1833, de Sola was formally engaged to preach in English in the Bevis Marks Synagogue, at first at intervals of a month, later of a fortnight, at a fee of two pounds per sermon. At the same time Solomon Aloof, a lay member of the Community, was also authorized occasionally to preach. David Meldola was required to preach on certain stated occasions, but not necessarily in English. Later, at Passover 1839, Abraham Alexander Lindo, who had previously given an address at the service held on the occasion of the funeral of King William IV, preached again and was permitted to repeat his address on the last day of the festival in the Western Synagogue, where by this time sermons in English had also become an established although still occasional practice. These English sermons had, however, all to be seen and approved by the Mahamad before they were permitted to be delivered. The Elders were still very nervous of what might be said or done in their name. Within a week of Lindo's address on Passover 1839 he was reprimanded for publishing a small book, *A Word in Season*,

THE FIRST DECADES OF THE CENTURY 261

without previously seeking permission from the Mahamad. He apologized and promised to submit all similar works in future and as evidence that his offence had been forgiven copies of his sermon, which he had had printed, were accepted in settlement of his account with the Congregation, the copies being distributed to members and to other approved persons. Permission was given later for other occasional lay preachers, for instance, D. E. Cohen de Lara at Passover 1840, not to mention those Yehidim who preached on special occasions, and also Louis Loewe. One other sermon was given at this early period, in 1849, by Sabbathai Moraes, the unsuccessful candidate for the office of Hazan in 1845.

David Aaron de Sola stood out among the men and women of letters that the Sephardi Community produced early in the nineteenth century, but he was not by any means solitary. This is evident, if only from the mention that has been made of occasional lay preachers. There were Isaac Lindo Mocatta, a theological writer and author of books of general interest, who devoted himself also to the development and welfare of the community, and his father, Moses Mocatta, who translated David Nieto's *The Inquisition and Judaism* and other works, and published also a selection in Hebrew from *Proverbs* and *Ecclesiastes*, 'The Wisdom of Solomon'. A staunch Jew, always ready to cross swords with missionary enthusiasts, he was also a patron of Jewish scholars in general and of Grace Aguilar in particular. Moses Mocatta was prominent over a long period in the administration of the Community. Abigail, a daughter of David Abarbanel Lindo, was a Hebrew scholar. She compiled a Hebrew dictionary. Her cousin, Elias Haim Lindo, was one of the pioneer English-Jewish historians. His *History of the Jews of Spain and Portugal* can still be read with interest and instruction. Earlier he had published a translation of Manasseh ben Israel's *El Conciliador*. His Jewish Calendar, covering sixty-four years, was in constant use in the Community over two generations. It was much more than a series of astronomical tables: it was also the embryo out of which the present *Jewish Year Book* developed half a century later. Emanuel Aguilar, the musician who collaborated with David Aaron de Sola in his edition of the Synagogue melodies, has already been mentioned. He survived until 1904, dying at the age of seventy-nine. Aguilar, apart from being a minor composer, was, as *The Times* described him, 'a highly successful teacher of the pianoforte on principles more scientific and artistic than those of the average music master'. His far more widely known sister, Grace Aguilar, who died at the early age of thirty-one, fifty-seven years before him, is perhaps the most distinguished, certainly the most widely read, woman writer that Anglo-Jewry has as yet produced. She wrote for both Jew and Gentile, and in both sections of the English people she had a wide circle of readers, loyal to her in successive generations for a century. Her best known works of Jewish interest are *The Spirit of Judaism*, *The Vale of Cedars*, and *The Jewish Faith*. When she died *The Art Union Monthly Journal*[1] published a long and enthusiastically appreciative obituary notice, by a surprising coincidence signed A.M.H., most of which was reproduced in the *Gentleman's Magazine*.

'Miss Aguilar's last work *Home Influences* deserves a place in every house—whether Jew or Christian dwell therein. Her *Women of Israel* is so chivalrous in spirit, and so eloquent in style, that the Hebrew ladies did honour to themselves when they presented this noble-hearted daughter of their race with a testimony of esteem. She was one of whom they might well be proud: it will be long before we shall forget the kindly generous nature, the tender sympathy, and perfect truthfulness of the dark-eyed, full-hearted "Jewess", foremost in all good and righteous deeds. Her name may appear forced into this journal; for, although the friend of many artists, and a true lover of Art, she was not, in the ordinary sense, an artist; but it is a high privilege to be enabled to write even a brief record of a truly good woman, and to aid in preserving a virtuous example from passing unnoted down the stream of Time.'[2]

Another woman writer of this period was Miriam Mendes Belisario, a member of a family which although never in the first rank frequently obtained notice in the story of the Sephardi Community. With her sisters she kept a girls' school at Hackney, where most of the daughters of the wealthier families of Anglo-Jewry attended. Her writings were a little 'highbrow' and didactic, a Hebrew and English vocabulary and *Sabbath Evenings at Home*, treating of the inspiration and teachings of Judaism, being among them. Her kinsman, Isaac Mendes Belisario, was an artist. He is best known for the etching of the interior of the Bevis Marks Synagogue which he made in 1817. He also painted and engraved a portrait of the actress Ellen Kean, and exhibited at the Royal Academy from 1815 to 1831 and at the Old Water Colour Society.

[1] Vol. IX, p. 378.
[2] A paper on Grace Aguilar and her writings was read before the Jewish Historical Society of England on 17 July 1947 by Mrs. Beth Zion Abrahams, but has not yet been published.

Moses Edrehi was of an entirely different character. He was born at Agadir in Morocco, in 1771, and at about the age of thirty settled in Holland. Some twenty years later he came to this country. At any rate, and probably for the greater part of his career in England, he lived at the expense of the Community. In the year 1825 he received assistance from the communal charity fund on the condition that he should either return to his home or proceed farther on his travels. He took the money but does not seem to have fulfilled the condition. If he did so it was not long before he appeared again in this country. He showed himself in his writings more a charlatan than a scholar. However, he did for a short time attract an undue amount of attention in Anglo-Jewry and outside of it. In 1836 he published in English a fanciful story entitled *Historical Account of the Ten Tribes settled beyond the River Sambatyon in the East*, which when he was in Holland had appeared in Hebrew and German. He also published a volume of sermons. Edrehi died in London about 1840. In 1829 or thereabouts he seems to have been in Edinburgh, for 'Christopher North' (John Wilson) brings him into one of his series of 'Noctes Ambrosianae' in *Blackwoods' Magazine* of June of that year. In this appearance he shows or is made to show a speaking acquaintance with half a dozen languages, including Hebrew.

Haim Guedalla belonged to a different class. Born in 1815, a cousin and nephew by marriage of Sir Moses Montefiore, to whom he attached himself until the latter's death and under whose will he was provided for, Guedalla lived until he was almost ninety, until his end attracting attention wherever he went by his conservative devotion to the costume of his youth. Guedalla cannot be described as a man of letters, still less a scholar or even deep thinker. But he was always on the edge of the intellectual and sometimes also the political activities of the Community. He wrote pamphlets and other ephemera, mostly in furtherance of some cause or other. Today they would be called propaganda. Guedalla was connected with the birth of the Anglo-Jewish Press, but never took a prominent part in its support or production. In the great secession that culminated in the establishment of the West London Synagogue of British Jews and especially in its aftermath he acted as mediator, not entirely without success. He always fancied himself a diplomatist, and engaged in negotiation with Spanish statesmen for the resettlement of Jews in Spain and seems to have been quite satisfied with their result, though his success was not very evident to others. He was more successful in the campaign against the proposed demolition of the Bevis Marks Synagogue in 1886. Guedalla took an active part in the administration of the Community. For sixty-one years he was an Elder. He accompanied Sir Moses Montefiore on one of his visits to Palestine and on his mission to Morocco, whence his ancestors had come, in 1863. In these countries he derived a reflected glory from the generous benefactions of his distinguished kinsman and as a crystallization of that glory he had the dignity of Nasi or Prince conferred on him by the rabbis of the Holy Land.

Other Yehidim who acquired some distinction outside the Community in the earlier half of the nineteenth century were David Mocatta, one of the earliest architects that Anglo-Jewry has produced. He also was one of the numerous children of Moses Mocatta, in his time the 'Grand Old Man' of Anglo-Jewry. Among his work was the New Synagogue building in Great St. Helens of 1837, the earliest specially built place of worship of the West London Synagogue and the Montefiore Synagogue at Ramsgate. His secular buildings included a number of stations and other buildings on the London, Brighton, and South Coast Railway. He exhibited at the Royal Academy and was a vice-president of the Royal Institute of British Architects and a trustee of the Soane Museum. David Mocatta was also a F.R.S. After his early retirement from the active pursuit of his profession on inheriting a fortune, he devoted his time and energies principally to Jewish and general philanthropic work, in particular that of hospitals.

Samuel de Castro was a founder in 1841 and original member of the Council of the Pharmaceutical Society, and Jonathan Pereira, who was born in the same year, 1804, was a pharmacologist of distinction. He was the recognized authority of his day in England on pharmacy and gave the first complete course to be delivered in England on *Materia Medica* in 1843. Previously, in 1839–40, he had published his *The Elements of Materia Medica*. He was also a pioneer in the sphere of dietetics. In quite a different sphere of science two slightly younger contemporaries, the brothers Jacob and Joseph d'Aguilar Samuda, distinguished themselves. They came from a family that had for three generations taken its part in the administration of the Sephardi Community and in this form of public service Joseph d'Aguilar Samuda also took his share, rising to the highest office. His elder brother, Jacob, would, we may assume, also have done so if his life had not been brought to an end prematurely, at the age of thirty-two, by an accident sustained in the course of his professional work. Jacob Samuda was a railway engineer and was responsible for striking developments in the early years of railway engineering. Joseph was a shipbuilder, and built the earliest armoured vessels used in the British Navy. He was one of the founders and the first treasurer of the Institution of Naval Architects. At one time a warden of the Spanish and Portuguese Community, he later withdrew from it entirely. He was elected a Member of Parliament in 1865 and remained in the House of Commons, for the latter period for the Tower Hamlets division, greatly to the indignation of his Jewish constituents, for fifteen years. Isaac Gomes Serra was the last member of a family whose record covers the story of modern Anglo-Jewish history throughout its course; he also took his full share in the work of Sephardi Jewry. But he did more than that. To the public and social service of Bevis Marks he gave a full portion of his wealth and of his thought. He shared them also among non-Jews and non-Jewish institutions. The City of London Lying-in Hospital, the Small-pox Hospital, and also the public and private benevolent institutions of his own parish, St. Andrews, Holborn, all had a generous and wise friend in him. When he died in 1818 his epitaph was written by a non-Jewish friend and fellow worker. 'In temper placid and serene but just, in character respectable, in age venerable; as a Jew he was conscientiously strict; as a member of society, upright, benevolent and honourable.'

There was a time, many centuries ago, in which Jews took their place on the battlefield: in recent days the Jew has emerged again as a soldier. But there was a period of centuries in which no Jewish name was to be found in the rolls of the national armies of Christendom. Willingly or unwillingly they were excluded from them, for by the laws of the several Christian nations no Jew could hold a commission, or, theoretically at any rate, serve. In the year 1829, however, professing Jews were at length enabled to hold the King's commission. Jews had of course previously occasionally held commissions or served in the ranks, but these were ex-Jews or crypto-Jews. Mention has already been made of military members of the d'Aguilar and Lopes Pereira families. There was also an occasional de Castro or Capadose in the army lists. Among the officers of Jewish origin who fought in the Napoleonic war was Diaz da Fonseca, born Suasso, but who had taken his mother's name. As Jews in the ordinary course they would not have been accepted. After the army had been opened wide to members of the Jewish community several of the sons of Simon Barrow obtained commissions, and three of them rose to the rank of general, with two other generals in the next generation. These, however, without exception, all left the Community of Bevis Marks. At times of a national levy everyone was accepted, but these could not be considered soldiers in the ordinary sense. The same may be said of the Honourable Artillery Company, whose history goes back to the time of the Tudors and in whose ranks one or two men with Jewish names were frequently to be found from the time of Charles II. The press gangs also made no inquiry regarding religious belief and Jew as well as non-Jew who came within their clutches was taken. Thus even an uncle of Sir Moses Montefiore, a merchant in the city, seems to have been seized by a press gang, forcibly enrolled in His Majesty's Navy, to die shortly afterwards in Barbados. In the lower ranks, however, it was not so difficult to preserve one's Jewishness, and in the earlier half of the century there was a sprinkling of men, more or less active in Jewish affairs, who had served in their time in the army or navy. One, Sergeant Isaac da Costa, on his discharge in 1824, settled in South Africa and when he died left a legacy to the newly founded Cape Town Synagogue. That there were others is manifest from an unexpected application made in September 1836 by the sister of David Uzzielli, 'who lies dead at Greenwich where he has been pensioner for many years, and she having solemnly assured the Mahamad that he always used to observe Passover and fast on Kipur, it was resolved not to refuse sepulture to him behind the Boards'. The Mahamad in those days most certainly gave no encouragement to Jews dead or living who did not fully observe the laws of their faith.

Finally, mention must be made of a somewhat picaresque individual who for the greater part of his life lived outside of British jurisdiction, yet was a natural-born British subject, even if almost by accident. His mother, as was not unusual in those days when British citizenship was still universally prized at its full value, had come across the Straits to Gibraltar for the birth of her child. David, more generally known as Don Pacifico—he was accustomed to describe himself as Le Chevalier Pacifico—was a merchant who had for a time been in the Portuguese consular service, which he had left somewhat precipitately and unwillingly. In 1847 he was living in Athens, where it was the practice to celebrate Easter every year by the public burning in effigy of Judas Iscariot. In the Easter of that year one of the Rothschilds happened to be on a visit to the Greek capital and out of presumed consideration for his feelings, or in hopes of a loan, the Greek authorities banned the celebration. The mob, however, was determined not to be deprived of its bonfire. Don Pacifico's house was ready to hand, and it was set on fire. No personal harm was done to the owner or to the members of his family, but his property was destroyed. He promptly appealed to his Government to secure redress for him and put in a claim which no one can describe as outstanding for modesty or moderation. For instance, his original claim for £30,000 included £150 for a bedstead, £30 for a pair of sheets, and £10 for a pillow-case. In the final settlement £1,000 was awarded in all. This exuberance in estimation did not, however, deprive him of the support for which he asked. There were a few other trifling British claims against the Hellenic Government, and Palmerston, the Foreign Minister, lumping them together, demanded their prompt settlement. The Greek Government prevaricated, and at length, after negotiations extending over nearly three years, Palmerston lost patience and in support of his demand sent the British fleet to the Piraeus with instructions to seize the Greek Navy and any other Greek vessels they could find if the claims were not immediately settled. These high-handed proceedings were, however, too much for more sober public opinion. The matter was raised in Parliament and Palmerston found himself at first almost without support. The Queen, then a power under the Constitution, did not conceal her disapproval, and Palmerston's own Cabinet was hardly more sympathetic. Foreign powers also protested, and as a consequence relations with France became very strained and the French Ambassador was withdrawn from London. The House of Lords, after a very critical debate, passed a vote of want of confidence in the Government. In the Commons, where the Government's normal majority was small, the position became very difficult. The Government realized that it had to rehabilitate itself and put up a private member, John Arthur Roebuck, to propose a vote of confidence. One of the most outstanding and famous debates that Westminster has ever heard followed. The debate occupied four days, throughout remaining at a very high level. Palmerston himself spoke from 9.45 p.m. on the second night and continued for four and a half hours, concluding with the famous peroration, 'Whether as the Roman in the days of old, held himself free from indignity, when he could say *Civis Romanus sum*; so also a British subject, in whatever land he may be, shall feel confident that the watchful eye and the strong arm of England will protect him against injustice and wrong.' Palmerston secured a majority of 46 in an almost complete house. Palmerston's own comment was, 'I scarcely ever remember a debate which, as a display of intellect, oratory, and high and dignified feeling, was more honourable to the House of Commons.' This was the last debate in which Sir Robert Peel spoke. A week later he met with his fatal accident.

Don Pacifico ultimately settled in London, being admitted a Yahid in 1851 and dying three years later. A relative of his, Emanuel Pacifico, endowed the almshouses that were known by his name. A daughter of David married Abraham Hassan and there was litigation in the London Courts, instituted by Abraham's sons, as recently as 1903, on the subject of Don Pacifico's estate.

CHAPTER XV

THE GREAT SECESSION

ALL THIS TIME the new outlook in the Community was gathering force and gradually coming to the front. This movement did not begin with the nineteenth century. It had been taking shape for almost a century previously, but, with the nineteenth century, it rapidly gained momentum and what had previously been little more than the thoughts and expressions of opinion of individuals began to take the form of the considered policy of a party or a group. Originally the Sephardim of England had been one united body. At the end of the eighteenth century it was still one body, but comprised two parties. The one, consisting mainly of the original settlers, formed the progressive party; the other, largely of new-comers from Gibraltar, North Africa, and the shores of the Mediterranean, the conservative. The latter party was satisfied with conditions as they found them, holding every custom observed within and without the Synagogue, no matter what its origin, almost divinely inspired. The Progressives, in touch with outside thought and subject to the developing western influences, sought, while retaining untouched the kernel of their faith and most of its age-long sanctified customs and observances, to divest themselves of some of the accretions of the centuries, during which Jewry had lived self-centred, apart from its surroundings, and to bring the practice of their faith more into line with the new world that was opening. An illustration of this was the substitution of English, for Portuguese. Portuguese had long been a dead language to most of the Sephardim of England. Yet the records of the Community and the announcements in the synagogue were still made in Portuguese. More than one attempt had been made to substitute English for this language, but it was not until February 1819 that the Elders decided that in future their minutes and those of the Mahamad should be kept in English. The change was made at once, but the old tradition still lingered, and for some time, although the minutes were in English, there were occasional lapses into Portuguese. Three months later, it was decided to translate the Ascamot into English. But it was not until the year 1848 that all announcements in the synagogue, hitherto made in Portuguese, were made in English.

The demand for development and progress was first made

audible by Jacob Mocatta in an address to a meeting of the Elders in 1803. This address was related to a report by a committee appointed to consider the spiritual state of the Congregation. Mocatta was severe on the shortcomings to which he called attention. He mentioned the spiritual deterioration from which the Community was suffering, and in particular the neglect of religious education. Among his demands was that the use of Spanish and Portuguese in the schools should be abandoned and that English should be substituted. Mocatta's criticisms bore fruit, but only after much effort and the lapse of time. The forces of conservatism were still powerful. Nine years later, in 1812, criticisms came from a different quarter. John King, otherwise Jacob Rey, of whose adventures mention has already been made, was, despite his eccentricities, on the whole a loyal son of the Community. He also was very dissatisfied with the state of affairs. In the course of a number of letters to the Mahamad he explained his infrequent attendance at the synagogue as due to his feeling that it was no longer a place of devotion. He pointed out that he was not alone in that opinion, as the many other empty seats proved. On the behaviour of those who did attend he was most severe and censured in particular the conduct in synagogue of the boys of the congregational schools of one of which he himself had once been an inmate, foreseeing that, unless a drastic change were made, the behaviour of the next generation would be even worse than that of the present. King offered, if the Mahamad would accept his suggestions, to contribute to the cost of putting them into effect. He was also prepared to give his services to the same end. There were others who shared King's views. But the Mahamad showed itself uninterested and King had again to withdraw from the Synagogue, defeated. Yet these representations were not without effect: some of the seed dropped by them began after a time to take root.

The frequent criticisms of the quality and style of the education given in the congregational schools also began to bear fruit. First came the decision to give the English language an appropriate place in the curriculum. Early in 1821 a committee was appointed to examine and report on the state of the schools and to make recommendations. These recommendations were somewhat drastic, but were nevertheless adopted. The schools of the *Heshaim* were closed and a new one, the *Shaare Tikva* or Gates of Hope established in place of them, preference being given in admittance to orphan boys. The opportunity was taken for the complete reorganization of the education. At the same time the new school was made independent in its administration of the Mahamad or Elders and given its own budget, to which the Congregation made an annual grant, and for which offerings were made in the Synagogue. In 1830 a preparatory school leading up to the Shaare Tikva School was opened, and in 1839, the National and Infant School, founded at the expense of Mrs. Moses Lara, as generous to the Community as her late husband had been. The new school premises were opened by her in April 1844. A Women's Committee had for many years shared—in a more or less unofficial capacity—in the management of the Villa Real School for Girls. On the establishment of the National and Infant School, however, provision was made in its regulations for such a committee and henceforth this committee dealt direct with the Mahamad, if not on a level of equality, yet receiving full acceptance of its position.

The Synagogue was closed for redecoration and repair in 1824, and for its reopening, marked by a special service, the Haham, Raphael Meldola, composed a hymn, *Kol Rinnah* (The Voice of Song), which, with other parts of the service, was sung by a choir, the introduction of which was another innovation in response to the movement of opinion in the Community. This choir became in 1839 a permanent institution. Two years earlier, in 1837, the provision of relief to the poor, hitherto a function of the Mahamad and Elders, was transferred to a newly founded institution, the Board of Guardians, at first only a Committee of the Elders with a separate budget, later an independent institution. The Mahamad, however, retained for some years its own list of pensioners, and also granted occasional relief to persistent applicants. It will be remembered that an attempt was made to establish such an institution as early as 1739, but the time was then not yet ripe.

These were improvements, and they showed, even though not in a very startling manner, that those in whose hands the guidance of the fortunes of the Community rested, were not unmindful of the need for change. This need became still more evident after the death of Haham Meldola in 1828. At the end of that year a Committee of Elders was appointed to inquire—in conjunction with the Mahamad—into the means of improving the state of the Congregation generally. Daniel Mocatta, the *Parnas Presidente*, in closing the meeting at which this Committee was appointed, took the opportunity of referring to the widespread feeling of dissatisfaction among the Yehidim and to the consequent damage to the welfare of the Community and to the mutual relationship of its members. In particular, finances were suffering severely.

The party spirit that was arising must, he said, be eradicated. He appealed for 'a more conciliatory spirit amongst us and by forgetting supposed injuries and disappointed results restore that brotherly love and good understanding which until recently were ever implanted in our hearts'. The reference to the Committee was 'to consider the most effective means of obtaining this most desirable object (a proper degree of devotion and attention during the time of prayers at Synagogue) and that they be requested to bring under their consideration the propriety of some plan for having worthy sermons delivered in the English language'. The committee was appointed, however, only by the casting vote of the chairman. At the same time a revision of the *Ascamot* was authorized, prior to their being printed in both Portuguese and English. When printed, however, they were distributed only to the male members.

The Committee reported without delay. One of the conclusions reached was that it was 'most essential for the preservation of order and decorum at synagogue that the Gentlemen of the Mahamad should attend there as much as possible and not quit their places until the service is completed'. Since one-half of the Committee consisted of active members of the Mahamad and the other half of former members this conclusion seems remarkable. Parents were recommended 'to promote the cultivation of the Hebrew language by every means in their power'. Among the recommendations adopted were that the services should, as far as possible without contravening any of the laws by which the Community was governed, be shortened, for instance, by the reduction of the extent of the singing; that the boys of the Communal schools should be trained to chant those parts of the service that were usually chanted and to make the responses; that an appeal should be made to the Congregation generally to attend synagogue, to abstain from conversation while there, to make the responses in due time and order; and to remain until the conclusion of the service. All of which throw light on synagogue practice in those days. The Elders decided by fifteen votes to twelve that in future all proclamations in the Synagogue should be made in English. They also resolved that a sermon or 'moral and religious discourse' of three-quarters of an hour should be delivered in English every Sabbath afternoon, such sermons being submitted in advance to an elder selected for the purpose to see 'that it may not contain anything inimical to our religious doctrines or any matter hostile to the established institutions of the country'. When this resolution came up for confirmation, however, it was

ABRAHAM MOCATTA (1797–1880)

DANIEL MOCATTA (1774–1865)

THE BETH HOLIM (1851)
From a water-colour by T. Hosmer Shepherd

rejected by sixteen votes to thirteen. It was still considered too early for a regular sermon in English.

'In the meanwhile the life of the Congregation continued to drift. The attempt in 1822 to secure the right to hold service elsewhere than in Bevis Marks was ruthlessly suppressed, but this action did not increase the attendance. The Yehidim had by now spread over a wide area and their homes were to be found in all parts of London, many beyond walking distance of Bevis Marks. Those who were beginning to feel the ties of Judaism but lightly were probably undisturbed by this. But there was a larger number who wished to continue to worship in company with their fellow Sephardim. For them to drive or ride to Synagogue was unthinkable. If they had done so, one of the consequences would probably have been expulsion from the Community, and this was the last step these men and their families desired. Forbidden to worship together in their own neighbourhoods, too far from Bevis Marks to attend service there on Sabbath or a festival, these Yehidim had no alternative but to stay away altogether from public worship and as a consequence attendance in the synagogue continued to grow smaller. Inevitably, some of those who stayed away in course of time became estranged from the Community, but this was not so with all. The majority, probably, were anxious to join their friends and relatives in prayer, but had no opportunity of doing so, short of giving up their homes and returning to the cramped and residentially unattractive districts in central London which they had left. Some of course, steadfast in their loyalty to their religion and their community, did walk on Saturday mornings the considerable distance from their homes to Bevis Marks. Among these was Moses Montefiore, who had removed from the City to Park Lane. Even then, only a few men could walk and the men were not the only ones to be considered. Women also were progressing towards their full emancipation in the synagogue as well as outside —and their wishes also demanded consideration. Among some of those who did attend there were also other sources of dissatisfaction. Among the dissatisfied a 'Committee for promoting Order and Solemnity in the Synagogue', of which Abraham Mocatta was chairman, was formed. The title denotes sufficiently the purpose of the Committee. In particular, it was dissatisfied with the choir which had been introduced in the hope of increasing the attraction of the services. It asked permission of the Mahamad for a proclamation to be made in synagogue calling for improvements in the behaviour of the worshippers, and this request was granted.

The new committee and its objects, however, aroused suspicions in certain quarters and the reaction came within a few months, on 12 November 1838, in the formation of another society, under the chairmanship of the stalwart of orthodoxy, David Abarbanel Lindo, 'The Society for Supporting and Upholding the Jewish Religion as handed down to us by our Revered Ancestors and for preventing Innovations or Alterations in any of its Recognized Forms and Customs unless sanctioned by properly constituted religious Authorities', known more briefly as 'Shomere Mishmeret Hakodesh' (Preservers of Sacred Institutions). A circular was issued to the members of the Community by this society. The Mahamad, as soon as this circular came to their notice, strongly deprecated it. They objected to it as 'calculated to create dissension in the Congregation', and recommended the Elders to urge the founders of the Society, in the interests of the unity of the Community, not to proceed with their undertaking. In short, the Elders were recommended to call on the new society to dissolve. Meeting without delay (30 December 1838), these resolved 'That in the opinion of the Elders it is both uncalled for and dangerous for any society to exist purporting to take charge of the recognized forms and customs of our religion independent of the Elders of the Nation and not sanctioned by them. That it is also the opinion of the Elders that no attempts have been made to make innovations or alterations in any of the religious forms and customs of our Holy Religion, without being sanctioned by properly constituted religious authorities. That reluctant as the Elders must ever feel to visit with their reprobation the acts of members of the Community, still they deem it their duty to declare that a society styled "Shomere Mishmeret Hakodesh" is calculated to produce disunion in the Congregation, and in their confirmed and deliberate judgment should have dissolved itself on their recommendation and that in refusing to do so it is deserving of the censure of this body.'

Nevertheless the Society did not dissolve, and the Elders thereupon threatened to disqualify all its members from office in the Congregation if it continued to defy them. Lengthy and heated were the discussions at the meetings of the Elders. At one time their President, Daniel Mocatta, resigned his office. He later withdrew his resignation, but as the offending society still continued in existence, after an interval he withdrew his withdrawal. In the end, however, he remained in office and at the end of the year 1839 the *Shomere* Society dissolved itself.

In the meanwhile the earlier committee, of which Abraham Mocatta was the chairman, remained in existence, although quiescent. Partly to meet its wishes, the criticisms of the embryonic choir were taken to heart and a permanent choir, on a more professional basis, established. These controversies and the sharp differences of opinion in the Congregation which they disclosed led to changes in its constitution which carried it a long distance on the road to a system more in accordance with the spirit of the time. When the Congregation was first organized in the middle of the seventeenth century, following foreign precedents, an oligarchy was given control. The first Mahamad was chosen presumably by the members, who certainly acquiesced in the choice. This first Mahamad appointed their successors in office and these latter in their turn appointed their successors, and so on continuously over almost two centuries. As time passed a group of ex-members of the Mahamad grew up—elders in more sense than one—and on occasions of exceptional difficulty it became the practice of the Mahamad to call in these ex-members of the Mahamad for consultation and advice. In certain circumstances they were bound by the Ascamot to do so. In this manner grew up the body of Elders whose influence and power increased. In the end the government of the Congregation rested in effect in the hands of the Elders, using the Mahamad as a sort of executive committee authorized by custom to deal on their own responsibility only with routine matters that arose from day to day. The Mahamad, however, retained the right of electing their successors, but, as time passed, it became almost imperceptibly the practice for these successors first to be approved by the Elders. This system continued for a long period, but it was not the final form of the constitution. Under this system the ordinary Yehidim had nothing to say. Oligarchy remained, with the centre shifted somewhat from the position that it originally occupied. Mention has been made of the calling of a general meeting of the Yehidim in the middle of the eighteenth century, in 1746. The occasion of the meeting has not come down to us, the surviving minutes describing only the elaborate ritual prescribed. After the lapse of half a century another meeting of the Yehidim was convened. The elaborate formalities of the earlier meeting were repeated, but on this occasion some business was transacted. These two meetings were isolated ones, as no provision existed for treating such gatherings as a regular part of the constitution of the Congregation. That step, however, in course of time became inevitable, and the stirrings in the Community during the fourth decade of the nineteenth century were the occasion for it. Even then the Annual Accounts were not submitted to the Yehidim to be discussed by them. This did not happen until 1884, when for the first time, on the 16th of March, the Accounts were discussed. This meeting lasted five and a half hours, but not only financial business was transacted. For example, the proposal to open a branch synagogue in Mildmay Park was also taken into consideration.

As on the previous occasions, it was the Elders who at the beginning of September 1838 convened another meeting of the Yehidim which was to become the first of a regular series. The subject that led to a great reform, the participation of all the members in the government of the Congregation was that of the choir. The reference of the Elders to this first regular meeting of the Yehidim (4 November 1838) was in the words of their president, Daniel Mocatta, who provisionally took the chair, to consider and express an opinion on 'the system of a choir at Synagogue, and further to devise any other means, which in your opinion may be calculated to promote order and solemnity in the synagogue'. Mocatta then vacated the chair, and the meeting elected its own chairman. Its first business was to draw up a code of regulations for the government of its own meetings. It also decided that, in conformity with the established practice of the Elders, all its decisions would require confirmation at a subsequent meeting. After a discussion it was resolved by fifty-two votes to thirteen

> 'that it is the opinion of this Meeting that the introduction of a choir in the performance of Divine Worship in Synagogue has tended materially to the promotion of order and solemnity, and it is therefore expedient that steps be taken to establish it upon a permanent and solid foundation.'

Further the meeting recommended the Elders to devote adequate funds, which they designated £150 a year, for the maintenance of a choir. The appointment of a committee for the supervision of the choir was left to the Elders.

The next resolution placed before the meeting was

> 'That a committee of enquiry, consisting of the three (members of the) Bet Din, two Hazanim, three elders and five Yehidim, be appointed to consider and report upon the best mode to be adopted as to combine the order of our Divine Services and the times of their duration as may conduce to proper solemnity and devotion therein, such report to be submitted to a general meeting of Yehidim, to be specially convened for that purpose. . . .'

Consideration of this proposal was deferred to an adjourned meeting held a fortnight later. This resolution was then taken into consideration, but its proposals were in advance of opinion. The resolution was rejected—by fifty-seven votes to thirty. The opposition suspected an attempt at reform, to any glimmer of which they were resolutely opposed. Yet notice was given of several interesting motions for the next meeting, which, however, did not take place for more than a year—on 15 December 1839.

This second meeting was convened by the Elders again to take into consideration the state of the choir. The critics were more active or effective on this occasion than on the previous one, and it was only by a majority of twenty-seven votes to twenty-two that a resolution was adopted agreeing to the continuance of the choir, but at the same time urging the Mahamad to secure an improvement in its quality. But the great bone of contention was the proposal that the first ascama of the congregation, prohibiting divine service elsewhere than in Bevis Marks, should be amended. The meeting did, however, go so far as to appoint a committee, while voicing their deep apprehension of the consequences of any proposal for the total repeal of the Ascama in question 'thereby dissolving the union of the Congregation, which has now existed for a period of 176 years' and realizing the conviction

> 'that the complaints of a large and influential portion of the Yehidim are entitled at all times to the most patient and calm investigation, with a view if possible to devise means for redressing any grievance or inconvenience suffered by them, and more especially of one of as important a nature as the want of a place of religious worship within a reasonable distance of their domiciles'.

This committee was directed to consider and report what modification time has rendered necessary 'and may safely be made'. The committee included representatives of both points of view.

The body of Yehidim then passed to other business. They confirmed a decision of the Elders regarding the expulsion of Yehidim in debt to the congregational funds over a number of years, brushing aside a suggestion that such confirmation was unnecessary, but at the same time appointed a committee to investigate the circumstances of the debtors and to consider whether in some cases more lenient treatment was not desirable. It decided that the Yehidim should meet regularly at least once a year and that to the annual meetings statements of income and expenditure should be submitted. The Yehidim then turned to the method of assessment for finta. The practice followed hitherto was that fifteen fintadores or assessors were appointed in three classes. The one consisted of the Mahamad, the second of five elders, and the third of five ordinary Yehidim. Each class made its assessment separately, and the average of the three assessments was taken in every case. The fintadores on appointment were required to take on oath before the open Ark in the synagogue that they would act justly, and anyone who refused the service was fined ten pounds. There was obviously ground for strong objection to one or two of these conditions and this was generally realized. The oath was abolished without opposition, and a mere pledge substituted that the fintador would not 'suffer favour or affection or antipathy' to influence him. The amount of the fine was reduced to five pounds, 'and may peace prevail in Israel'. The perennial subject of the choir, however, came up again at this meeting. The Mahamad, to whom the matter had been referred, confessed themselves powerless to effect an improvement without the co-operation of the Congregation, and a committee of seven was appointed to assist them. This committee was given power to take any action they deemed fit to attain the desired end. The question of decorum, in which that of the choir was involved, was recognized as urgent, for those members who had in the past taken exception to the conduct of a section of the worshippers in the Synagogue were becoming ever more restive.

The next business that was taken at the momentous meeting of the Yehidim of 16 February 1840 was consideration of a resolution moved by Abraham Alexander Lindo for the appointment of a committee

> 'to ascertain as far as it may be in their power to acquire accurate information upon it, the actual condition, both spiritual and temporal of our Nation generally, but more especially of that portion of it residing in this country and its dependencies. That the Committee being appointed for practical purposes, be enjoined likewise to take into their consideration and suggest such measures as they may deem calculated for improving our spiritual and temporal condition, and especially for preserving that harmony and union, so indispensably necessary for promoting the well-being of our Nation in every respect. That they be empowered to communicate to the authorities of the Congregations of German Jews both in London and the Provinces the objects for which the Committee is appointed, and to invite them to co-operate in the same. That they be empowered to confer

with, and consult, such persons as may be willing to assist them in their enquiries. That so soon as materials shall have been collected for the purpose, the Committee do prepare and send to a meeting of the Yehidim a report of their labours.'

This was a very wide and almost revolutionary programme, beyond the capacity of the Yehidim, who rejected it by a majority of two to one.

The meeting then turned its attention to the report of the committee that had been appointed to consider what, if any, modifications were desirable in the first Ascama, that which prohibited the holding of divine service within six miles of Bevis Marks. The recommendation of the committee was that, although the existing ascama should remain unchanged, quoting the original preamble, 'Duly considering how important is our union, to keep us from giving offence to the inhabitants of this City, against which we have been cautioned by His Majesty King Charles the 2nd. of Glorious Memory', yet it should be supplemented by a further paragraph authorizing the establishment of another supplementary place of worship, 'in case it shall be acknowledged at anytime that a new establishment is absolutely necessary', but only with the sanction of a meeting of the Yehidim. The report proceeded to explain that the demand for the opening of a Branch Synagogue in the western district of London could then be granted, provided that the members of the new synagogue remain members of the parent congregation and that any alterations in its ritual must be subject to the approval of the ecclesiastical authorities of the whole community. As regards civil and temporal arrangements the Branch Congregation would have complete autonomy. The meeting of Yehidim accepted this recommendation after inserting the proviso that at the required meeting of the Yehidim two-thirds of those present approve the opening of a new synagogue. But the opposition was still strong. The amended resolution was carried by only twenty-nine votes to twenty-six, and when it came up for confirmation at the following meeting of the Yehidim (23 February 1840) it was rejected by twenty-eight votes to twenty-two. And so that there should be no further risk of the opening of a branch synagogue, David Abarbanel Lindo proposed a motion to the effect that no alteration of Ascama No. 1 should be made without the approval of two-thirds of the Yehidim present at a meeting convened for the purpose. This was, however, rejected. However, the Mahamad obtained the opinion of the Dayanim on the point that these resolutions had raised. It was that Ascama No. 1 could be repealed or amended only at a meeting of the Yehidim and by a two-thirds majority, and then only after satisfying themselves that 'no injury or detriment whatsoever result at any future period to the established synagogue Sahar Asamaim, or operate against the order or the rules of prayers or against our Holy Law . . . and that the said synagogue will still continue to enjoy notwithstanding all its usual privileges and advantages'.

The advocates of a branch synagogue nearer their homes, with a service conducted more in accordance with their wishes than that in Bevis Marks, had been very patient, but there was a limit to their patience. The decision of the Yehidim on 23 February marked that limit. There was a smaller group of Ashkenazim who shared their views and their needs. Members of the two groups had doubtless previously discussed the matter, and a joint meeting was held on 15 April at the Bedford Hotel in Southampton Row. This meeting was convened on the requisition of twenty-four signatories of whom nineteen were Yehidim, including several who had held the highest offices in the Sephardi Community. Of the nineteen, nine were members of the Mocatta family. There were three Montefiores and three Henriques. One of the Yehidim was of Ashkenazi origin, Solomon Lazarus, who had been received into the Sephardi community only a few years before, and another was Joseph d'Aguilar Samuda, also at that time one of the most prominent members of the Community within and without Jewry. Samuda, however, later withdrew as did also Jacob Montefiore. Of the Ashkenazi signatories three were members of the Goldsmid family. A tenth Mocatta, Aaron, attended the meeting at which Daniel Mocatta, a former warden and president of the Elders, was voted to the chair. Among the early adherents were two other Mocattas and Joseph Barrow Montefiore. The requisition or 'Declaration' on which the meeting was convened ran as follows:

'We, the Undersigned, regarding Public Worship as highly conducive to the interests of religion, consider it a matter of deep regret that it is not more frequently attended by the members of our Religious Persuasion. We are perfectly sure that this circumstance is not owing to any want of a general conviction of the fundamental Truths of our Religion, but we ascribe it to the distance of the existing Synagogues from the places of our Residence; to the length and imperfections of the order of service; to the inconvenient hours at which it is appointed; to the unimpressive manner in which it is performed and to the absence of religious instruction in our Synagogues. To these evils, we think that a remedy may be applied by the establishment of a Synagogue in the Western part of the Metropolis, where a Revised Service may be performed at hours more suited to our habits, and in a manner more calculated to inspire feelings of Devotion, where Religious Instruction may be afforded by competent persons, and where to effect these purposes, Jews generally may form an United Congregation under the denomination of British Jews.'

The resolutions adopted at this meeting were: (1) That it is expedient to establish a synagogue in the western part of the metropolis and that it be established under the denomination of Synagogue of British Jews (later altered to West London Synagogue of British Jews). (2) That a revised service be there performed in the Hebrew language in conformity with the principles of the Jewish religion and in the manner which may appear best calculated to excite feelings of devotion. (3) That religious discourses be periodically delivered in that Synagogue in the English language. (4) That a subscription be forthwith entered into in order to carry these objects into effect. £3,000 were immediately subscribed by those who were present. A congregation was, however, not formed for another two years, although a minister—David Woolf Marks, an official of the Liverpool Ashkenazi Community —was appointed, one of his principal duties being the drawing up of an order of service which was published in time for the opening of the Synagogue in January 1842. This prayer book was based very largely on that of the Sephardim, the main differences being those of omission rather than of addition. The Sephardi pronunciation was adopted. Further, the committee, anxious not in any way to withdraw from the body of Jewry, resolved that after provision had been made for their proposed synagogue and cemetery the first call on their funds should be for the relief of the Jewish poor.

The movement for the establishment of the West London Synagogue was not brought formally to the notice of the Sephardi authorities until May 1841, and this coincided with a similar step in the Ashkenazi Community. The Mahamad, in its communication to the Elders, admitted that the provision of a second place of worship for those resident too far away to attend at Bevis Marks might be satisfactorily dealt with, although it

'would be an infraction of the fundamental law of the Congregation which has been our bond of Union since our admission into this country now near two centuries, though it is a step pregnant with consequences seriously affecting the best interests and welfare of our ancient establishment . . . but when there is great reason to apprehend that their contemplated establishment is to be on principles opposed to the received religious institutions and ordinances of our Nation, that it is not to be subject to ecclesiastical discipline in religious matters and that its promoters are engaged in alterations and abridgments of our established ritual to form a new order of prayers and service unsanctioned by any competent or regularly constituted authority their proceedings then assume a character of so serious a nature as to call for the united interposition of the Jewish Nation, so by every means in its power to deprecate and check such attempts. The Mahamad, therefore, impressed with a due sense of its importance, brings this matter under your serious consideration. They do not do so without feelings of the deepest regret, yet they entertain at the same time an earnest and anxious hope, that either here or in a meeting of the Yehidim, or in concert with the Authorities of the other Congregations, some course may be marked out, some measures determined upon likely to conciliate discordant feelings and prevailing opinions, and that by a temperate and full consideration of any just cause of complaint or dissatisfaction and of every well digested plan of improvement, and above all by a cordial and sincere approximation of all parties in so good a cause, the peace and union of the Congregation may yet be restored and permanently re-established. Such are the warmest aspirations of the Mahamad and they fervently implore the God of Israel to guide your deliberations and to prosper your resolves to this great and important end.'

The Elders, after a long discussion, resolved by seventeen votes to sixteen not to proceed with the matter. The extreme orthodox party among the Yehidim were, however, by no means satisfied. They asked for a meeting of the Yehidim, and on the requisition of thirty-one of them, for the most part of North African origin, such a meeting was held on 30 May. It proceeded to pass a series of resolutions. In the first it expressed its deep concern at the step taken by the dissentient Yehidim towards the establishment of a synagogue, 'on principles unsanctioned by any regularly constituted religious authority', and declared that it would view 'as an infraction of the religious compact, binding on the whole Jewish Nation, any resolution or act of such parties, which may have for its object to alter, modify or change any of the laws, ordinances or institutions which have been handed down to us, and which it is our duty to support and maintain, and that the members of this congregation will cordially unite with those of the other Communities in this City to oppose and denounce such proceedings as subversive of the principles of our Holy religion, and destruction of that peace, union and concord, so strongly enjoined on us by the principles of our Faith'. After adopting that resolution, with only one dissentient, the meeting then proceeded to hold out a small olive branch. In this it emphasized its 'earnest, anxious and sincere desire to extend the hand of peace and conciliation'. It then exhorted and entreated the seceders to turn away from the path on which they had entered. 'It is in no feeling of anger, it is with no view of intimidation, that it urges them to weigh well the fatal consequences which have ever followed dissensions and schisms in our Nation.' The resolution ended in an appeal to the seceders to remain within their old religious community. Thanks were then accorded to the Ashkenazi rabbi, Solomon Hirschel, and to the Sephardi Ab Beth Din, David Meldola, for a communication which had been received but was not then made public, and the meeting decided by fifty-one votes to five to appoint a committee to consider the best means of carrying into effect a proposal for the opening of a branch synagogue in the western district of London. These resolutions were printed and circulated to all the members of the Community. One step taken by this committee was to invite the Sephardi seceders to confer on the practicability of the establishment of such a branch synagogue, but they unanimously declined to take part in any conference.

From this point onwards events hastened towards a crisis. On 24 August the Sephardi seceders wrote a temperate letter to the Elders in which, after pointing out that their proposals for improvements in the services had hitherto been consistently ignored or rejected, they explained the principles on which they were acting in deciding to open a place of worship for themselves and members of other Jewish synagogues who shared their views. 'In order to preserve proper decorum during the performance of Divine Worship it is essential that the whole congregation should assemble before the commencement of Prayer and remain until its conclusion.' As a means to attain this end and to gain other advantages it had been decided that service should commence at 9.30 a.m. in the summer and 10 a.m. in the winter, and except on the Day of Atonement should not exceed two and a half hours in length. To attain this end the existing service would have to some extent to be curtailed. The revised prayer book would, however, be based on that in use in Bevis Marks. Regular religious discourses in English and a choir would be introduced. The practice of calling members of the Congregation to the Law should, it was thought, be discontinued since its original purpose had long passed into disuse. Voluntary offerings were to be limited as a rule to the three Great Festivals of the year. They should not be accompanied by personal compliments and should be devoted only to two purposes, the relief of the poor and the maintenance of the Synagogue. 'It is not the intention of the Body of which we form part to recognize as sacred days which are evidently not ordained as such in Scripture.' The Sephardi pronunciation of Hebrew would be employed. Discarding the appellations of both Portuguese and German Jews, the reformers decided to call their place of worship the West London Synagogue of British Jews. Their object was not to create a schism 'but through a sincere conviction that substantial improvements in the Public Worship are essential to the weal of our sacred religion, and that they will be the means of handing down to our children and to our children's children, our holy faith in all its purity and integrity'.

'In thus establishing a new Synagogue on principles not hitherto recognized or approved by your body, we may possibly encounter considerable differences of opinion, and a strong prejudice against our proceedings, but having been actuated solely by a conscientious sense of duty, we venture to hope that on further consideration our intentions and our motives will be duly appreciated, and that those kindly feelings which ought to exist between every community of Jews, will be maintained in all their force between the respective congregation which you represent and the small body whose views we have herein endeavoured to explain. Before concluding, we are anxious to impress upon your minds that we are most desirous of continuing to make through you a contribution towards the Relief of the Poor, and to devote some of our time and attention to the superintendence of those excellent institutions connected with the Parent Synagogue. Influenced as we are by a sense of duty to offer our assistance in these works of charity towards our poorer brethren we should derive no small gratification, if in thus co-operating with you to satisfy the claim of humanity, we should find that we are thereby establishing a bond and symbol of connection with the old Congregation and assuring you that its welfare will never be a subject of indifference with us, we shall but express the words which we utter so frequently in our daily orisons "May He who maketh peace in his high heavens, in His mercy, grant peace unto us, and unto all Israel, Amen".'

This letter was considered by the Elders on 29 August, the day also on which the new prayer book was brought to their notice by the Mahamad. The result was that the signatories were warned that if they persisted in their course they would render themselves liable to exclusion from the Community.

'Painful indeed will be such proceedings on the part of this room, for it cannot lose sight of the fact, that the members who have addressed them have always been zealous supporters of our Ancient Congregation and its valued institutions, and that their rank and station in the Community entitled them to every consideration; a severance therefore from such valued and respected friends, numbering amongst them some who may trace their descent from the original founders of our Establishment, must be considered a deep sacrifice of personal feeling to a sense of religious duty. This meeting therefore most earnestly exhorts them as brethren, well intentioned but mistaken in their views, to yield their individual opinions to the united voice of their congregation, to abstain from all objectionable measures, and to recollect that the Yehidim of this Congregation have given proof of a desire to grant them their great desideratum, a synagogue westward, and let them above all, consulting their own interests and welfare, not lightly discard the protection of their ancient and parent congregation, and if they will but seriously reflect on all this, this meeting may yet entertain the hope that the severance so much to be deplored may still be avoided.'

There being no response to this appeal the declaration of Hirschel and Meldola which had hitherto been withheld was ordered to be published. It was proclaimed in the Synagogue and distributed to all Yehidim and to Sephardi communities everywhere—to all parts of the Empire, on the Continent, North America, Turkey, Palestine, and Lisbon. After a certain amount of hyperbole the declaration proceeded to denounce the 'Forms of Prayer, used in the West London Synagogue of British Jews, edited by D. W. Marks' as contrary to Jewish ecclesiastical law and warned all Jews against using or in any manner recognizing the book 'and whoever shall use it for the purpose of prayer will be as counted sinful'. The declaration was signed by the spiritual heads of the two Communities, and the members of the respective *Botai Din*, Abraham Haliva signing with Meldola on behalf of the Sephardim.

The seceders, however, went on their way. The new synagogue in Burton Street was opened on 27 February 1842, the first wardens being Abraham Mocatta and Joseph Barrow Montefiore of the Sephardi Community, and Francis Goldsmid, later Sir Francis H. Goldsmid, Bart., V.C., M.P., of the Ashkenazi. Daniel Mocatta was the chairman of the Founders. The seceders had expected that their letter of 24 August couched in conciliatory terms would have called forth an equally conciliatory response. To their surprise it had not done so. To the last they had hoped that the reforms that they had introduced could have been carried out under the aegis of the parent Synagogue. In the circumstances they saw no alternative to resignation from the parent congregation. This they offered on 13 January 1842, concluding with a blessing on the members of the Congregation they were leaving. The seceders were told in reply that they had no power to withdraw from the Community as an earlier Haham and Beth Din had ruled that all Jews of the Spanish and Portuguese Community on residing in London became automatically members of the Sephardi Community and could not divest themselves of that status or its responsibilities. The resignations of the seceders were, however, accepted after a few weeks and, lest they wished to retain any connexion with their old Community, they were disqualified from all offices in the Synagogue, and if they attended at it they would be relegated to Bench T near the entrance door. No gifts or contributions were to be accepted from them and, if they died, they were not to be buried in the communal cemetery. But if they withdrew from their contumacy they might be readmitted on payment of the fines to be imposed on them. This was a decision of the Elders and was adopted by eighteen votes to six. The seceders had, however, no desire to avoid their responsibilities in the charitable work of the Community, and proposed to continue their share in it. The members of the Beth Din thereupon called the attention of the Elders to the continued presence of seceders at meetings of the charitable institutions and requested them to take steps for the exclusion of the seceders in future. This the Elders did on the ruling of Meldola and Haliva that 'members of the Burton Street Place of Worship [so it was henceforth invariably designated] during their contumacy' cannot be considered members of any of the communal institutions. Instructions were also given that no members of the new congregation were in future to be invited to congregational meetings of any character. However, these instructions do not seem to have been meticulously observed, and it was not everyone in the Community who wished them to be. Three months later David Abarbanel Lindo had to protest against the use of the Mahamad Chamber for meetings of the governors and subscribers to the Shaare Tikva School on the ground that members of the secessionist congregation had been invited, but he was promptly overruled by the presiding warden.

A few days before the consecration of the new synagogue a joint meeting was held of the wardens of all the London synagogues, with Sir Moses Montefiore in the chair. It was then decided to distribute as widely as possible in Jewry another denunciation by Hirschel and Meldola and their supporting rabbis.

'Information having reached me, from which it appears that certain persons calling themselves British Jews publicly and in their published Book of Prayer reject the Oral Law, I deem it my duty to declare that according to the Laws and Statutes held sacred by the whole House of Israel any person or persons publicly declaring that he or they reject and do not believe in the authority of the Oral Law cannot be permitted to have any communion with us Israelites in any religious rite or sacred act. I therefore earnestly entreat and exhort all God-fearing Jews (especially parents) to caution and instruct all persons belonging to our faith that they be careful to attend to this declaration and that they be not induced to depart from our Holy Laws.'

So far as the Sephardi Community was concerned this needed confirmation. The Mahamad decided by three votes to two that this declaration should be read in the synagogue on the following Sabbath. Abraham Lindo Mocatta, the presiding warden, who as a close relative of many of the objects of this denunciation was in a delicate position, protested against the decision and recorded in the minutes: 'That he protests against the public notification of the above document emanating from the Rev. Dr. Hirschel and other gentlemen of the Beth Din, he deeming the same to be a highly imprudent act to be carried into effect, decided by the majority of the Mahamad.' The other members of the Mahamad present on the occasion were Sir Moses Montefiore, Judah Guedalla, Hananel de Castro, and Isaac Jalfon. De Castro was presumably the other member who opposed the resolution. The Mahamad at the same time published the following proclamation:

'The Gentlemen of the Mahamad with deep regret publish to the Congregation a Declaration signed by the Ecclesiastical Authorities of our Nation in this Country which has been forwarded to them for publication. The Mahamad at the same time having received information that a place of worship is about to be opened by persons calling themselves British Jews, wherein a ritual is to be observed, which has been proscribed by Authority; the Mahamad caution every true Israelite from attending any such place of worship, or sanctioning, or countenancing by their presence such an establishment.'

Meanwhile even among those Yehidim who were the strongest opponents of the new movement there were some who were not fully satisfied with the existing state of affairs. In April 1840, probably too late for any influence to be had on the new movement, another serious effort was made to improve the decorum in the synagogue which, apparently, had again fallen behind. To this end the Mahamad appealed to Yehidim to co-operate with them *inter alia* by each individual

'reciting his prayers, and making the usual responses, in a tone of voice *considerably lower* than is at present practised; so that the service generally may be conducted with greater order, and the chanting of the choir be more prominent and free from interruption.

'The members of the Congregation must be aware, that the establishment of a Choir *alone*, will not affect all that is required to secure order and decorum in Synagogue; much more is necessary to be done, or rather to be avoided: and the Committee most earnestly call the attention of the Congregation to the following Regulations, which they strongly urge on their observance: 1st. That all persons on entering or quitting the Synagogue should do so in the most quiet and orderly manner. 2nd. That all conversation be strictly avoided, and that on no account should any person quit his seat during the service, or take any other place than the one assigned him. 3rd. That no one should quit the Synagogue, nor make preparation for so doing, until *the entire conclusion of the Service.*'

At the same time renewed consideration was given to the desirability of opening a branch synagogue in West London. A committee that had been appointed by the Yehidim in June 1841 to consider this proposal reported in the following December. The result of this committee was little more than an appeal to the seceders to hesitate even at the brink of a withdrawal and to desist from putting their intentions into effect. 'With the greatest satisfaction will this meeting hail a return of the individuals in question to a right feeling and understanding of their present position, and in thus expressing the hopes and wishes of the Nation, the Meeting trusts, as regarding this lamentable difference, that it will be the last duty it will have to perform.' This committee, however, at

THE GREAT SECESSION 289

once approached all members of the Congregation who were resident west of Temple Bar, numbering thirty-six in all, and invited them to co-operate with them. Among those who accepted the invitation were four who were connected with the new movement, but six of their colleagues said in reply that matters had proceeded too far and that after the denunciation to which they had been subjected, co-operation on the lines suggested was no longer practicable. The attempt at co-operation proved abortive, and the committee saw no alternative but to surrender its mandate. It was accordingly discharged.

But this was not the end of the matter, even for the time being. A further resolution, adopted at the same meeting, ran: 'The present state of our Congregation is such as imperiously calls for the serious consideration of the collective body of the Nation so that an investigation be made into the causes which have produced it and some remedy suggested for the evils which now assail it.' Another committee was thereupon appointed. One move in a new direction which, although at the time ineffective, and perhaps never expected to influence the flow of events, yet showed that the consciences of some of the Yehidim were disturbing them, was the notice of a motion given at this meeting by David Brandon 'That in the opinion of this meeting the penalty of *Herem*, as denounced by the Ascamot Nos. 1 and 3, is at once inoperative and repugnant to the spirit of legislation of the present time. The said penalty is therefore declared to be abolished.' Objection was at once raised on the ground that the proposal was contrary to the fundamentals of the faith. The point was referred to a Beth Din, specially constituted for the purpose, and a decision, obviously a compromise, and an indefinite one, was given. The Yehidim were competent to consider the resolution, but 'the meeting of Yehidim should be attended by as many congregants as possible'. The Beth Din, in another ruling given at the same time, laid down that all Portuguese Jews in London, 'whether they are subscribing members or not' were liable to the penalties of Herem for infringement of any ascama in which Herem was specified as one of the penalties. The decision of the Beth Din was recorded, but the meeting proceeded. Brandon moved his resolution and thereupon one to the same effect but in stronger terms was moved in the form of an amendment. Both the amendment and the original resolution were, however, defeated.

The committee appointed at the meeting on 9 January 1842 had still to report. It realized that, in some respects, the laws and regulations of the Community were out of date.

'They could not dismiss from their minds the conviction that laws enacted in remote periods of time, under a state of things totally different as regarded our civil and religious condition, might reasonably require change, to render them more efficient and salutary and more consonant with those enlarged views of policy which regulate legislation in the present day.'

The committee unanimously came to the conclusion that some modifications were called for. They recommended therefore, as a first and immediate step, that the much disputed Ascama No. 1 should be repealed and substituted by an alternative. This alternative retained the prohibition of the holding of divine service within six miles of Bevis Marks so that the union 'as recommended to us by His Majesty Charles the 2nd. of glorious memory' should be preserved, but suggested certain exceptions, for instance, on the occasion of a wedding, a funeral, at the Beth Holim (provided that only patients and officials participated) and, subject to the permission of the Mahamad and their adjuntos, and the payment of a capitation fee, occasionally, in a private house more than three miles from Bevis Marks. Members of the Community, Yehidim and Congregantes, residing at this distance might also, with the permission of the Mahamad, attend service in other established synagogues. (This permission did not include the West London Synagogue in Burton Street which in the eyes of the Sephardi ecclesiastical authorities was not a synagogue.) It was specifically laid down that this Ascama or law applied to all Spanish and Portuguese Jews residing in London or in future residing there, whether Yehidim or not, and anyone aware of an infringement of this Ascama who did not report it to the Mahamad was equally liable to punishment. The possibility at some future date of the establishment of a branch synagogue elsewhere in London was, however, envisaged, but this could be authorized only by the Yehidim in meeting, with the approval of two-thirds of those present. The penalties to be imposed for violation of this ascama were exclusion from membership of the Community and forfeiture of all rights, honours, and immunities as a member of the Congregation, fines of varying gravity and, for those dying in contumacy, refusal of burial in the grave next vacant in the cemetery, but instead interment in the section reserved for those who were more or less in disgrace at the time of their death. This amended Ascama was accepted by thirty-seven votes to twelve and confirmed by thirty-five votes to nine.

In the meanwhile the campaign, in which the leading part was

THE GREAT SECESSION

taken by Hananel de Castro and Haim Guedalla, for the removal of the Herem on the Sephardi members of the West London Synagogue continued. In January 1845 the Elders formally resolved that 'this room taking into consideration the alteration that has taken place in the Ascama of Kaal No. 1 is of opinion that the Ascama should in the present form be submitted to the Gentlemen Dayanim, for their opinion whether the alteration therein made could not admit of any relaxation of the penalties enacted against the members of the Burton Street Place of Worship so to admit them as members of all or any of our charitable institutions'. But the Dayanim were, on the general question, as adamant. The seceders were in Herem, and no measures could be taken to relieve them from the Herem 'so long as the individuals that have estranged themselves from the Congregation neglect or refuse to abide by the principles of our Holy Religion'. This decision was signed by David Meldola, Abraham Haliva, and Abraham Belais, the last named having been called in to complete the quorum. They asked for ten days' leave from their ordinary duties to consider this question, but were given only ten afternoons. The Dayanim, however, made one concession. Later in the same year they gave a decision that 'We cannot find the least objection for the marriage of any individual taking place with the daughter of a member of the Burton Street Community'. Still the Elders felt very uneasy, and in November of the same year they resolved that

'As it is deemed doubtful whether the members who seceded from the Congregation in 5603 are or are not in *Herem* and as this body has never sanctioned nor does it desire to sanction the enforcement of this penalty, a committee be appointed to consult with our rabbinical authorities and others, if deemed by them advisable, to ascertain beyond question the state of the case and should it appear that the said parties are actually in *Herem*, then to adopt such measures in the name and on the part of the Congregation as may be necessary, to absolve them from the said Herem, leaving in force all the other penalties which by order of this body have been declared against them.'

This was carried by ten votes to six.

The year 1847 opened with a requisition from fifty-seven Yehidim calling on the authorities to remove the Herem imposed on the seceders as being 'repugnant to justice', and pointing out that their congregation was the only one that had imposed the ban. The signatories included both Yehidot and Yehidim. A resolution in accordance with the terms of the requisition was carried, and the Elders were asked 'to endeavour to devise some means' to put the wishes so widely expressed into effect. The Elders fully sympathized with the majority of the Yehidim in the matter and decided to make further efforts to persuade the Beth Din to relieve the situation. However, they did not hesitate to expel from the Congregation Jacob Cohen de Solla and his family because three of his sons were members of the choir at Burton Street. Incidentally, one of these, Henri, was some years later appointed choirmaster at Bevis Marks. The Beth Din still remained immovable. An ever-growing number of Yehidim continued to press for the lifting of the ban on the seceders, supporting their arguments on the important new fact that since the imposition of that ban the laws of the Congregation had been so amended that Herem could no longer be imposed in similar circumstances. On every occasion a resolution to that purpose was moved and carried. But no civil resolution could overcome the impediment of the ecclesiastical authorities. An attempt in April 1847 to override the local Beth Din by referring the matter for decision to the Sephardi ecclesiastical authorities at Amsterdam was rejected by the Elders. Another attempt, nine months later, to the same end by appealing to the Ashkenazi Chief Rabbi, Nathan Adler, for a decision, was defeated by the Yehidim by a small majority. The English Sephardim were very jealous of their independence. The next step was to carry, by a still narrower majority, a resolution declaring that there was grave doubt whether the original herem was intended for a religious offence, and since such a penalty in respect of a civil offence had since been abolished, this point should be put to the Ashkenazi Chief Rabbi for his advice and decision. The opponents, however, did not abandon the fight, and when a fortnight later this resolution came up for confirmation it was rejected by a majority of four to one. But the advocates also did not abandon the struggle, and Hananel de Castro at once gave notice of a new resolution 'That every person who may have incurred the penalty of Herem by an infraction of the old Ascama of Kaal No. 1 (new repealed) shall no longer be considered under that penalty'. The Beth Din intervened and secured the addition to the resolution of the words 'but subject only to the same pains and disqualifications as are in force against the members of the Burton Street place of worship, under the declaration of the Ecclesiastical Authorities of the United Congregations'. This was carried on a majority of one vote, but failed to secure confirmation.

The end of the long-drawn-out controversy was by now near at

THE GREAT SECESSION

hand. Although not unanimous, the opinion of members of the Community was strongly in favour of relieving those who had withdrawn from the Community, now nearly ten years before, of the interdict that had been imposed upon them. The first step was for the Elders to adopt de Castro's resolution as amended. This they did on 21 January 1849. Hananel de Castro, at the time president of the Elders, and Haim Guedalla then approached David Meldola, the acting ecclesiastical head of the Community. They made it clear that the ostracism of the seceders, which by now was to a large extent nominal, must be ended. Meldola, there is reason to believe, was made to understand that a way had to be found to this end. In any event a way was quickly found. The resolution of the Elders was formally communicated to Moses Mocatta and others affected, and it was intimated to them that if they would authorize de Castro and Guedalla to inform the ecclesiastical authorities that they admitted having transgressed Ascama No. 1 by having established and attended service in an unauthorized place of worship and asked to be relieved of the penalties imposed on them, the Herem would be raised. This Mocatta and his colleagues did. De Castro and Guedalla thereupon delivered the message to the Dayanim, and the Herem was withdrawn. For seven years de Castro and Guedalla had striven actively towards this end. At length they were rewarded.

The battle had been lost but the ecclesiastical authorities would admit it, even to themselves, only grudgingly. Several relatively small points still remained over for settlement and on the decision of these the Dayanim could give rulings. One was whether or not contributions to the communal charitable institutions could be accepted from members of the West London Synagogue. The Dayanim were asked this question. Their reply was so involved that the committee appointed by the Elders to go into the matter had to report 'Your Committee regret to observe that the answers given are not of that direct and straightforward character which they would have desired to present to you'. The Elders found that in the circumstances the position was unchanged. So far as the educational institutions were concerned it seemed that the money of the Reformers might be accepted, but the donors must be excluded from all meetings of the societies and committees and not allowed to influence them in any way. In 1863 it was at last ruled that offerings and legacies might be accepted from the seceders. A resolution to this effect with the addition that the customary announcements and records of these gifts should be made was adopted by the Elders. At first it was rejected when it came forward for confirmation. The conciliators, however, despite all disappointments persisted, and at length, later in the year, the Elders carried again their resolution with the addendum and on this occasion it was confirmed. In the intervening years, however, the volcano showed occasional signs or threats of activity. The refusal to recognize the 'Burton Street Place of Worship' as a synagogue, entitled to representation at the Jewish Board of Deputies, was final and accepted for a generation, but at the end of 1853 there was an attempt to get round the disqualification if not in regard to the synagogue, at any rate so far as its members were concerned. At the elections of September of that year four Orthodox Ashkenazi provincial communities chose members of the West London Synagogue as their representatives at the Board. The Board refused to accept them, but only after long and not very orderly discussions and then by the casting vote of the chairman, Sir Moses Montefiore, who had, despite the participation of some of his near relatives in the new movement, been inflexible in his opposition. Montefiore was unwilling to concede a fraction of an inch. Other members of the Board, although their orthodoxy could not be questioned, were not so rigid. At their head was the future Sir David Salomons, a connexion by marriage of the president, and supporting him were Baron Lionel and Baron Anthony de Rothschild. Among the representatives of Bevis Marks, Nathaneel Lindo was his only supporter, but Haim Guedalla (Canterbury) and Aaron de Pass (Great Yarmouth) voted on the sam side. Montefiore, one of the representatives of Bevis Marks, conducted the meeting somewhat imperiously, and after two sessions gained his way by nineteen votes to eighteen. Among his supporters were the other representatives of Bevis Marks—Judah Aloof, Isaac Foligno, Moses H. Picciotto, Joseph Sebag, and Solomon Sequerra.[1] Salomons and his followers were defeated. A heated controversy ensued in the Jewish press, in the course of which Salomons and one of his colleagues in the representation of the New Synagogue on the Board, Laurence Myers, resigned. But the authorities of the New Synagogue were as proud of their distinguished member, Salomons, as were the Sephardim of Montefiore, and Salomons and Myers after having been asked in vain to withdraw their resignations were at once unanimously re-elected. The Sephardi Community also was not slow to record its support of Montefiore. A meeting of the Yehidim was held on 9 January 1854, at which a letter from Montefiore was read. The Yehidim,

[1] These meetings of the Jewish Board of Deputies were reported at length in *The Jewish Chronicle* of 2 and 9 September 1853.

after discussion, approved of the course Montefiore and the other representatives of the Sephardi Community had taken. 'They desire to offer to Sir Moses Montefiore and to the other deputies, with whom his casting vote was given, their best thanks for the firm determination evinced by them to maintain in its full integrity the constitution of the Board of Deputies as recognized by the United Congregations of this Country.' An attempt was further made to start a controversy on the subject with the New Synagogue and in particular with Mr. Alderman Salomons, but, after reflection, this attempt was abandoned. The main controversy thereupon died away.

The act of reconciliation of December 1863 was the last public action of Hananel de Castro. Three weeks after the receipt of the final letter from Mocatta he was dead, stricken down without warning at the age of fifty-five. He was rightly described in the obituary notice in *The Jewish Chronicle* as one of those Jews 'who are the glory and the pride of British Judaism'. 'Though he belonged to the Sephardim [sic] Congregation, his charitable heart was too large to admit of narrow-minded distinctions between that Congregation and the German one.' He was very active in charitable and cultural institutions in both communities and at one time or another president of several of them. 'His heart was warmed with charity and it felt for everything charitable.' In his last years his most absorbing interest was probably the Jews' and General Literary and Scientific Institution, or Sussex Hall. This institution was the forerunner of the many successors, important and unimportant, that provide and have provided for *die Wissenschaft des Judenthums*, or a specific modern Jewish culture, among the Jews of England. Around de Castro's bier there gathered Jew and Christian, Orthodox and Reform, Sephardi and Ashkenazi, united in one common mourning.

In 1892 a happier epilogue was written to the story of the great secession. In that year the West London Synagogue celebrated the jubilee of its establishment. A special service was held at which all the principal Orthodox congregations were represented. Those who came on behalf of the Sephardi Community were two of the parnassim, the Gabay and the secretary. The Board of Deputies was also represented by its president, Joseph Sebag-Montefiore, the nephew and heir of Sir Moses Montefiore, the lay leader in the struggle against the Synagogue whose anniversay was being celebrated. Haim Guedalla, one of the heroes of the reconciliation, was also present.

CHAPTER XVI

THE SEPHARDIM AND THE ASHKENAZIM

THROUGHOUT MORE THAN a decade during which the controversies raged around the modification, and to some extent the modernization, of the synagogue services the Community was stirred by another movement, one concerned more with its external relations. Among the active partisans of reform in this sphere the Sephardi section of Anglo-Jewry played only a small part. The movement for the political emancipation of British Jews began in 1830, immediately after the grant of a similar political emancipation to Roman Catholics, and continued for a generation. Both Jews and Christians were active in securing the reforms—Christians far more than Jews. A few Jews devoted their time, their thought, their energies, their wealth to the attainment of the end to which they looked forward, but only a few, and among these few no Sephardi names appear except Disraeli and Ricardo, those of men who had left the Jewish Community. Of those still grouped around Bevis Marks, the only Sephardi name mentioned, and that only as an illustration and on a side issue, was that of Emanuel Baruch Lousada, one of the first Jews in England to be made a Justice of the Peace. The Sephardim as a whole, even those who helped to establish the West London Synagogue, showed very little interest in the movement. The Jewish Board of Deputies, at the instance of Isaac Lyon Goldsmid, had at first taken the matter up energetically and prepared petitions to both Houses of Parliament. And two of the deputies of the Sephardi Community, Moses Mocatta and Moses Montefiore, were among the members of the small committee, which had the matter in hand. But the Jews' Emancipation Bill of 1830 was rejected by the House of Commons, and the advocates of the reform were left with little more than a heavy bill to pay. Of this expense the Sephardi Congregation paid £328 14s. 7d., a little under a third, of which £120 was subscribed privately by individual Yehidim. The active advocates of emancipation were not prepared to accept this defeat as final, and proposals for further action were put before the Board of Deputies. On this question the Sephardi representatives at the Board asked for direction. 'As there appears a considerable diversity of opinion in your Body on this important subject we are most anxious to be relieved from the apprehension of not acting in unison with the sentiments of the

Majority of our Constituents.' The Elders gave due consideration to this request for guidance and resolved by nine votes to five that no application should be made to Parliament at any rate in the coming session. In later years the Sephardi Community, as a Community, was occasionally asked to join with other Anglo-Jewish organizations in the campaign, but was always loth to do so. It seems that Sephardim with political ambitions made it a habit to leave the Community and those who remained within the fold were not interested. Early in the campaign, in February 1834, Bernard van Oven, writing as honorary secretary of the Committee of the Jewish Association for obtaining Civil Rights and Privileges, invited the co-operation of the Mahamad, in their exertions 'in any way you may deem best. The Committee are particularly desirous of circulating as extensively as possible copies of the enclosed circular, and they will feel obliged if you will assist them as far as the members of your congregation are concerned.' The request was a very modest one, but the Mahamad was very nervous about getting involved. They were probably, consciously or unconsciously, still obsessed by the supposed pledge given at the time of the first official recognition of a Jewish community in England, to refrain from interference in political matters. There were no Ashkenazim in England in those early days, and the members of the Ashkenazi community that subsequently grew up not only did not suffer from the obsession, but were quite uncônscious that there could be any basis for one. The reply of the Mahamad was: 'The nature of their (The Wardens') office does not allow them to co-operate with the Jewish Association for obtaining Civil Rights and Privileges but they will readily forward to the members of their Congregation copies of the Circular you have handed them free of any expense.'

The Jewish Board of Deputies, at first not very enthusiastic in the movement, perhaps on the account of the considerable Sephardi influence in its councils, did at length take some part in it. Early in the year 1840 it circulated to congregations resolutions that it had adopted to the effect that Parliament should be petitioned to grant the desired measure and that in support of the petition a public meeting should be held. The communication of the Board of Deputies was referred to a meeting of the Yehidim, who gave their approval to the proposals. When at length, in 1847, a Jew, in the person of Baron Lionel de Rothschild, secured election to the House of Commons, the Elders passed him a formal vote of congratulation, but only by the casting vote of the chairman. In April 1853 the authorities of the Great Synagogue wrote to those of Bevis Marks that their wardens intended to petition the House of Lords in favour of the Jews' Relief Bill and expressed the hope that the Mahamad would follow their example. The Mahamad, however, declined their invitation, as the subject was considered to be one that concerned the Board of Deputies, to whom it was referred. The Elders actually declined, in October 1855, to congratulate Alderman Salomons on his election as Lord Mayor of London, but they were overruled by the Yehidim.[1] In the last stage of the campaign, in 1857, the Mahamad agreed to the circulation among the Yehidim for signature of a petition to the House of Commons, prepared by the Board of Deputies, but it was made clear that the petition, so far as the Sephardi Community was concerned, was from individuals, not from the Congregation as a corporate body. The attainment of political emancipation in the following year passed, so far as the Congregation was concerned, unnoticed. In 1870 the Elders authorized the presiding Parnas to sign a petition to the House of Lords in favour of the abolition of religious tests.

The Community was always conscious of the obligations into which it entered, or believed it entered, when its formation in England was first authorized. Formal record of this was to be found in its frequent references, when legislating, to King Charles II, the first monarch whose favour and sympathy it had enjoyed. Another was the vigorous objection that it showed over two centuries against admitting converts from the general population. Other instances appeared in the anxiety always to conform closely to all legal requirements. When in 1840 Dr. Zachariah Lindo, who had been elected Parnas of Terra Santa, claimed exemption from serving in that or any other honorary office in the Community on the ground that he was a Fellow of the Royal College of Surgeons and thereby exempt by law from all parochial offices, the Mahamad, with the agreement of the Elders, accepted his contention and excused him. Four years later Nathaneel Lindo claimed exemption on similar grounds, that he was an attorney and solicitor, and as such exempt by law from serving in any office in which personal service was required. He accepted the office of Gabay to which he had been elected, but called the attention of the Mahamad to his right of exemption if he claimed it in future. This question was also referred to the Elders, who not only accepted the contention, but went further and decided that Parnasim and

[1] This may, however, have been a reflection of the resentment felt over Salomons' opposition to the course taken by the representatives of the Congregation in the Board of Deputies regarding the acceptance as Deputies of members of the West London Synagogue. See p. 294.

Gabayim who practised medicine or the law should be exempt from fines in case of failure to attend meetings in consequence of their professional engagements. In the year 1841 a question of marriage law arose. Until 1837 Jewish marriages in England were to a large extent governed by Jewish law, a marriage between Jews, certified as such by an authorized Jewish authority, being accepted as a legal marriage. By an Act of Parliament of 1836, however, changes were made, marriages in England between Jews, for instance, being brought into line with other English marriages so far as prohibited relationships between the parties were concerned. All marriages solemnized under the auspices of Bevis Marks had always had to have the prior approval of the Mahamad, which laid down the conditions under which the ceremony could be conducted and also nominated which of its officials, ranging from the Haham to the Samas, should solemnize it. Occasionally permission was altogether refused, even though one, or even both, of the parties were Sephardi. The question that arose in September 1841 was whether the marriage of a man, who had divorced his previous wife in Smyrna in accordance with Jewish law, was permissible in accordance with English law. The question was referred to Joseph Phillimore, the outstanding ecclesiastical lawyer of the day, who ruled that such a marriage would not be contrary to English law. Finally, in 1844, a general decision was given by the Elders on the subject of marriages.

> 'Until a judicial decision or a legislative enactment shall determine the state of the law as to Jewish marriages within the prohibited degrees of affinity and consanguinity established by the law of this country, the Mahamad be requested to withhold their license for such marriages in our Congregation.'

In 1849 when changes in the marriage laws were under contemplation and it was feared that the Jewish Community would be unfavourably affected, the Yehidim at a meeting decided that an endeavour should be made to secure that all possible doubt regarding the validity of Jewish marriages should be removed.[1]

Other marriage questions, apart from those relating to the requirements of the law of the land, arose from time to time. Marriages between Sephardim and Ashkenazim, once most exceptional and when contracted looked on by the authorities of the Congregation and probably by most of the members with intense

[1] Incidentally, it was not until 1849 that the Board of Deputies made a rule that no marriage secretary of a Jewish congregation would be approved until a certificate had been furnished by the Jewish ecclesiastical authorities to the effect that the Congregation was a properly qualified Jewish Synagogue.

and unconcealed disapproval, had by the middle of the nineteenth century become so frequent as no longer to attract any attention. According to the records of the Community, by the middle of the nineteenth century marriages in which the bride was a *Tudesca* far outnumbered those in which she was a Sephardi. On one occasion, in 1860, all five marriages authorized were with Ashkenazi brides, and on another, in 1864, six of the nine brides were Ashkenazi. The highest percentage was probably reached in September 1934, when of seventeen marriages authorized on one occasion, fifteen were with Tudescas and a sixteenth with a *Geura*. There was a general agreement between the London synagogues that such marriages should be contracted under the auspices of the synagogue of which the bridegroom or his father was a member. Thus the Mahamad authorized marriages only in those cases in which the bridegroom was a member of the Sephardi Community, apart from an exceptional one in which he was a member of no English Jewish congregation. However, when the marriage was at a distance from London, permission was as a rule given for it to be celebrated by the officers of the local Jewish congregation which was necessarily Ashkenazi.

Early in June 1847 a young man named Heilbut, a namesake of one of the earliest members of Ashkenazi origin of the London Sephardi Community, who had become a Yahid only a few years before, wrote to the Mahamad that he proposed shortly to marry. His letter is touching in its obvious sincerity and perplexity.

> 'You are aware that my father-in-law is very anxious that the Rev. Dr. Adler should officiate at my marriage and that he exerted himself in this behalf to obtain permission of your Congregation, but unfortunately without success. He cannot persuade himself to act differently to what he expressed to you. I am therefore compelled, I confess with the utmost reluctance, to comply with his wishes, for what can I do? I hope, dear sir, that you will take this in consideration and be persuaded that I have, not intentionally, transgressed on the law, and that I may be allowed, without any penalty to remain a member of your most respectable congregation to which I belonged nearly seven years. If I can persuade you again, most faithfully, that no efforts on my part have been left untried, but that my Father-in-law contends that he claims but to what considers himself entitled. I hope, Dear Sir, you will no longer hesitate to allow me the above prayer for favour and that I may be soon pleased to receive an answer of you to that effect.'

THE SEPHARDIM AND THE ASHKENAZIM 301

The Mahamad's heart was, however, hardened. It refused. 'The Ascamot leave no power to the Mahamad to authorize marriages but by the officers appointed for that purpose and persons contravening are liable to heavy penalties.' The bridegroom naturally persisted in his course and the Mahamad thereupon referred the matter to the Elders.

'The Mahamad has felt itself called upon to convene you thus hastily[1] in consequence of the unprecedented case of a Yahid of our Congregation being about to have his marriage solemnized by the Chief Rabbi of the German Congregations under a right claimed by his intended father-in-law, a member of the Great Synagogue and which right the President and Officers of that Synagogue has admitted. As it is a subject involving grave considerations and affects the good understanding which ought to exist between the congregations in this City, the Mahamad have thought it their duty to put you in possession of the steps they have taken in the matter that you may determine on what further measures it may be deemed proper to adopt under the circumstances.'

The Elders protested to the authorities of the Great Synagogue in moderate terms 'against this unprecedented proceeding deeming it calculated most seriously to disturb that union which has hitherto existed between the United Congregations in this City and which it is still the urgent wish of the Elders to preserve and maintain'.

The reply of the Great Synagogue was that E. I. Symons, the father of the bride, as a free member of that synagogue, had the right to require the marriage to be performed by the Chief Rabbi under their auspices, and they had not the power to withold their consent. The Mahamad continued to protest, but the marriage was celebrated under the auspices of the Great Synagogue on 16 June. The Elders thereupon protested to the Chief Rabbi, who replied that he had no alternative under the laws of the uniting synagogues, whose officer he was, but to consecrate the marriage. This caused still great perturbation among the Mahamad, and another evening meeting of the Elders was held. It was there resolved to expel Heilbut from the Congregation 'considering such act as a grave offence to the Congregation of which he is a member and calculated to disturb its peace and union'.[2] It was further

[1] To an evening meeting, being an urgent case.
[2] Heilbut was never readmitted a Yahid, but he was permitted to rent a seat in the Bryanston Street Synagogue, and when he died in 1886 he left a legacy to the Congregation, and his name was duly inscribed on the legacy board.

resolved that 'This meeting considering the right claimed and exercised by the Great German Synagogue in the case of Mr. Heilbut as a most unjust interference with the authority of this Congregation in regard to its own members and one which it will behove the Elders seriously to deliberate upon at their annual session, and adopt the measures rendered necessary by the unprecedented proceedings of that Congregation.'

Two years later another worrying and exciting question arose over a marriage in the Community. It was learnt that a young member of the Congregation, under age, had marriage a German Jewess 'in contravention of the Ascama of Elders No. 25 for preventing clandestine marriages'. The bridegroom was summoned to appear before the Mahamad, expressed his deep regret and explained that he had taken the step 'apprehending his father would not have granted his consent, never intending to offend the Congregation and that it was his intention to solicit that the marriage rites might be allowed him in our Synagogue'. The Mahamad were of the opinion that the young man had committed a very serious offence, and they felt that they needed time to consider what steps they should take in the matter. The parties were subsequently married by Bevis Marks.

The Heilbut marriage led to somewhat of an estrangement between the Bevis Marks and the Great Synagogues, but this did not prove serious nor did it last. And soon the relations which from the beginning of the century had been growing more cordial, and opportunities for co-operation increasing, resumed their course. For instance, as early in the century as the year 1832, when the accommodation for Sephardi orphans was temporarily inadequate, arrangements were made with the Ashkenazi authorities for the acceptance of them in the orphanage of the sister community, and as a mark of appreciation of the friendliness thus shown the Elders made a grant to the Ashkenazi orphanage which was renewed year by year over a long period. A reciprocal move—the acceptance of Ashkenazi women in the maternity section of the Beth Holim—was proposed some years later when that section was not fully occupied, but the proposal was not as readily accepted. This was in 1851 when the new building was in Mile End, whither it had been removed from Leman Street, Goodman's Fields, in 1792. The recommendation came from the governing body of the Beth Holim and the arguments in favour of its adoption included the absence of a similar institution among the Ashkenazim and the support given to the Sephardi institution by a number of members of the Ashkenazi Community. The Elders referred the proposal to a committee which was more cautious and expressed the opinion that it would be unwise to extend the benefits of the institution beyond the Sephardi Community. The proposal was revived five years later and again rejected. Of greater moment was the decision of the Elders in 1842 that Ashkenazim who married Sephardi girls might be accepted as Yehidim, provided they applied for admission not later than six months after the marriage. This proposal, when first made, was considered so revolutionary that its consideration had to be deferred, but its principle was in course of time accepted. By this and other means there was throughout the nineteenth century, through marriage with Sephardim, a continuous influx of men and also of women of Ashkenazi origin into the Sephardi community. These when admitted were accepted without reservation. Some of them took an active part in the work of the Community, the first of them to be elected Parnas being Naphtali Hart Lyon in 1848.

As the decades of the nineteenth century followed on another, greater recourse had to be had to the services of non-Sephardim. In the early days of the Community there were two or three instances, which have been mentioned, of the appointment of an Ashkenazi as samas, but the thought of filling a higher office from outside the Sephardi ranks had never been contemplated. Sometimes there was difficulty in finding a suitable incumbent within the Community, but the difficulty, sooner or later, was always overcome. Even the office of communal physician was reserved for members of their own Community until, in 1849, not only no Sephardi candidate was forthcoming, but of the four applications received only one was from a Jew, an Ashkenazi. In the spiritual sphere the first break with tradition came in 1854. In 1833, however, Sir Moses Montefiore had established a private synagogue close to his country house near Ramsgate. To this, although primarily intended for Sir Moses and Lady Montefiore and their guests, all Jews were welcome, and around it, in course of time, grew up a small local community, consisting of Ashkenazim as well as Sephardim, in which the ritual was that followed in Bevis Marks, although Ashkenazim predominated. But if the ritual was Sephardi the personnel was not. The first two Hazanim of this little congregation were the brothers Isaac Henry Myers and Emanuel Myers. Isaac Myers held the office for forty-four years, until his death in 1877. In 1844 he was admitted a Yahid of the London Community and, although he died at Ramsgate, he was buried in the Sephardi cemetery in Mile End. Emanuel Myers was more a shochet than a Hazan. He also became a Yahid. He held his office until 1860, when he resigned to devote himself entirely to the private school he had established. Emanuel Myers' two immediate successors were, like him, Ashkenazim. The senior office after the death of Isaac Myers went to a Sephardi. The Myers were more personal chaplains of Montefiore than ministers of a congregation. To an even greater extent was this true of Louis Loewe, Montefiore's secretary and travelling companion whom he first met in Rome in 1839 while on the way to the Holy Land. Loewe was born in Prussian Silesia in 1809 and came to England as a young man. He had already then acquired a reputation as an oriental scholar and a traveller. Between 1839 and 1874 Loewe accompanied Montefiore on thirteen of his missions abroad on behalf of different sections of Jewry. In England, throughout the greater part of his life, he was always in close contact with Montefiore. When in Ramsgate or at Broadstairs, where he established a private school, he worshipped in the Montefiore Synagogue, but he seems never to have become a member of the Sephardi Community. He was, however, in contact with them also and occasionally preached in the Synagogue. In 1844 he was appointed, on his own suggestion, honorary teacher of Abraham de Sola and Solomon Sebag,[1] two of the most promising students in the communal school 'to qualify them for religious office'. Both of these students progressed under his guidance and qualified for the service of the Community. Neither, however, received the appointments to which they might justly have aspired. Sebag taught in the communal school and occasionally when the necessity arose took the services in London or Ramsgate. Abraham de Sola, as has already been mentioned, settled in Canada, where he was for many years the spiritual guide of the Sephardi Community of Montreal. A closer Ashkenazi connexion, one that created a precedent and led to a far more important appointment, was the acceptance in 1849 of Barnett Abrahams as a student of the Medrash with a bursary of 7s. 6d. a month. He was then only eighteen. Later, doubtless with a thought for the future, the Elders sent him to University College, London. At the same time the managers of the Sephardi Orphanage sent one of their promising boys, Abraham Nieto, a descendant of the two Hahamim of that name, to the City of London School for his secular education, studying at the Medrash in the evenings, with the eventual intention of entering the Jewish ministry. He eventually did so, but in North America. So remarkable was the intellectual development of Abrahams that two years after his

---

[1] Not to be confused with his namesake, the brother-in-law of Sir Moses Montefiore and father of Sir Joseph Sebag-Montefiore.

admission to the Medrash, when he was still a boy of twenty, he was invited to preach in Bevis Marks on *Shemini Hatzeret*, and obviously made a very favourable impression. In 1854 not only was the Community without a Haham—the vacancy created by the death of Raphael Meldola having never been filled—but the only surviving member of the bench of dayanim, Abraham Haliva, having died a few months after his colleague David Meldola, the Community was devoid of all advisers in ecclesiastical matters. Barnett Abrahams, who had been at University College only a few months, was nevertheless chosen for the office, at first under the title of Assistant Dayan, despite the fact that there was no full dayan to assist. After two years Abrahams was given the full title. This appointment absorbed him completely into the Sephardi Community. He married a Sephardi girl, Jane, daughter of Abraham Rodriguez Brandon, and for the few remaining years of his life Abrahams was, except for the accident of his birth, in the full sense a Sephardi. On one occasion only he got into trouble with the Elders. While still Assistant Dayan he was asked to preach in the newly opened branch synagogue in Wigmore Street and did so without having first asked permission of the Mahamad. For this oversight he was censured and thought it proper to resign his office. But no one wanted to lose his services. His resignation was promptly refused and his apology and acknowledgement of error accepted in full settlement. Two years later he received permission to accept the appointment of headmaster of Jews' College, vacated by the resignation of Louis Loewe, holding both offices jointly until his death.

The foregoing matters, although they affected the Sephardim as a community, touched only individual members of the sister Community. There were others in which the two groups approached one another as communities. In this *rapprochement*, on the Sephardi side, the Hazan, David Aaron de Sola, was one of the principal instruments. He was in close and friendly relations with his Ashkenazi colleagues, and as time passed took an ever-increasing part in the general work of the community, especially on its cultural and intellectual sides. He had also contacts that many others of the leading members of the Community still denied themselves. More tolerant than some of his contemporaries, de Sola looked on the seceders of 1842 more as erring brothers than as heretics and was not afraid to be seen in their company or to have friendly relations with some of them. Of course it was out of the question for him to enter the portals of the Reform Synagogue or to be invited to do so. But those of Ashkenazi synagogues, in the provinces as well as in London, were not similarly closed. Thus when in 1855 the Birmingham Jewish Community laid the foundation stone of a new synagogue building, de Sola was asked to take part in the ceremony, and when the time came for its consecration he was again welcomed to Birmingham. Six years earlier there had been an even greater act of *rapprochement* when the Chief Rabbi, Nathan Adler, had preached in Bevis Marks and had after the service been entertained by the Mahamad, the leading members of the principal Ashkenazi congregations being also present. The Mahamad was so impressed by the address that it asked to be permitted to print and distribute it among the Yehidim, but the Chief Rabbi was too modest to accede to the request. In his opinion a sermon must be heard rather than read, 'for on paper the spirit is apt to evaporate'. The leading officers, lay and clerical, of the Sephardi Community were of course always invited to what may be termed the state funerals of Anglo-Jewry; for instance, to that of Chief Rabbi Solomon Hirschel in 1842, and in return for the compliment an *ascaba* (memorial prayer) in his memory was offered in the synagogue in Bevis Marks. Three years later the Dayanim attended by invitation the installation of the new Chief Rabbi. In return the Ashkenazi ecclesiastical and lay authorities used to attend on the occasion of the periodical reopenings of the Sephardi synagogue after redecoration or repair, and when a special service was held on the occasion, in 1864, of the return of Sir Moses Montefiore from his mission of succour to the suffering Jews of Morocco not only were the ecclesiastical and lay heads of the Ashkenazim invited, but Barnett Abrahams having died and there being still a vacancy in the office of Haham, the Chief Rabbi preached the sermon. An earlier Ashkenazi preacher in 1844 was Moses Nathan, the Hazan of the Ashkenazi Community of Jamaica, who was in England on a visit.

There were more than one proposal, all emanating from the Ashkenazim, for a much closer co-operation, but these were invariably rejected, very politely, lest such co-operation would lead in the end to the disappearance of the Sephardi Community as a distinct entity. In 1840 a suggestion for a joint Beth Din was made by Hirschel, but was not entertained. The proposal for a Chief Rabbi jointly for both communities was first made in November 1842, after the death of Solomon Hirschel and during the interregnum between the death of Raphael Meldola and the long-deferred appointment of his successor. The proposal came from the Great Synagogue, and it was that a Chief Rabbi should be appointed 'as the spiritual guide and Director of the Jews in this Empire'. The Elders agreed to take the proposal into consideration, but that no commitments should be entered into without the approval of the Yehidim as well as of the Elders. A committee was appointed for the purpose, but it failed to come to any conclusion on which to draw up a report. Its reference was consequently returned to the Elders. The Elders resolved that 'foreseeing that great difficulties would arise from important points of long established usage with us and desirous ever of maintaining the courteous and friendly intercourse with all German congregations as heretofore, we deem it proper to decline taking part, or interfering in any shape with the proposed appointment'. This decision was taken by eleven votes against ten, after an amendment had been rejected by thirteen votes to ten to the effect that 'this meeting, having given its best consideration to the resolutions adopted by the representatives of the various synagogues, as forwarded to this Board do coincide in the general tenor of those resolutions, but with the clear understanding on the part of this Congregation, that its usages, forms and customs, as Spanish and Portuguese Jews, are above all interference, on the part of any ecclesiastical authority which may be elected'. A similar proposal was made after a long interval, in 1858, when an Ashkenazi Chief Rabbi had for some years been in office and the office of Haham was still vacant after the death of Raphael Meldola thirty years before. This invitation came from a body styled 'The Committee relating to the Office of Chief Rabbi', and was dealt with somewhat more curtly than was its predecessor. 'The Elders of this Congregation having some years since (in 5603) given their serious consideration to the subject of a union under one ecclesiastical head, the present meeting sees no reason to alter the determination then arrived at.' Some years earlier (in 1850) when both communities were contemplating the opening of branch synagogues in the West End of London, the authorities of the Great Synagogue approached the Elders with a suggestion that the two communities might co-operate. The Sephardi Congregation was invited to discuss the proposals, and it was suggested that Sir Moses Montefiore, Joseph Israel Brandon, and Joseph Mayer Montefiore, all of whom lived in West London, should be appointed delegates for the purpose. The plans for a Sephardi branch synagogue were, however, already far advanced and for this reason as well as others the Elders were disinclined to join the Ashkenazim in the matter. They unanimously resolved that although they looked with favour on the proposal to establish a synagogue in West London, in view of 'differences in ritual and the usages, Customs and practices of the two synagogues to which the members of both communions must be equally as anxious respectively to preserve' the suggested co-operation was not considered practicable. Two years later the long projected Sephardi branch synagogue was opened, and from its opening Ashkenazi residents in its neighbourhood were almost as prominent among its worshippers as Sephardim.

In one other communal institution the two communities were able to co-operate from its establishment. Jews' College, the Jewish Theological Seminary, was opened in 1855. It was essentially a child of the Ashkenazi Chief Rabbi, Nathan Adler, and to that extent it was an Ashkenazi institution. The Chief Rabbi was its first president, but the first vice-president was Sir Moses Montefiore, as prominent in Sephardi circles as was Adler in those of the Ashkenazim. And it was Montefiore who presided at the meeting that put the project before the Jewish public. As has been mentioned, the second principal was at the same time Dayan and Acting Ecclesiastical Head of the Sephardi Community. Later the Chief Rabbi became *ex-officio* president, and the Haham *ex-officio* deputy president. Prominent lay Sephardim were always on the council, and several of them held high executive office. Later, after the Sephardi theological college at Ramsgate had been closed, the connexion between Jews' College and Bevis Marks became closer. The Montefiore Trust which was under the control of the Sephardi authorities voted £1,000 a year to the College for a number of years, and although this sum was later reduced for financial reasons, an annual grant continued with little interruption. In return the Sephardi Community was given ten representatives on the council of the College and an undertaking was given that, if Sephardi students were sent to the College for training, provision would be made for their instruction in the Sephardi liturgy. It was at this time that the Haham became *ex-officio* deputy president.

This close co-operation was envisaged when the project was first communicated to the Elders in 1852, and in return for the representation on the governing body, provision for the special instruction of Sephardi students and the acceptance of at least one of them without charge, a grant of £500 to the initial fund was voted. The Elders, however, after a little reflexion rescinded its resolution and in place of it resolved that 'experimentally' £35 should be voted annually for a free scholarship at the College, such scholarship to be awarded by the Elders to a boy, preferably from one of the educational institutions of the Congregation, and that a member of the council of the College be nominated by the Elders. Samuel de Sola, a son of the Hazan who was later to succeed his father in that office, was the first holder of this scholarship.

The suggestions for co-operation with the Ashkenazi community by the appointment of an ecclesiastical head of all the principal orthodox London synagogues were encouraged by the long period that had passed since the death of Haham Meldola. There was more than one reason for the length of this interval. Meldola's term of office had not been an easy one for the lay leaders of the Community, and it can well be understood that an interval of rest was welcome to them. Furthermore, there was, in the earlier years at any rate, no obvious candidate for the office, except perhaps the late Haham's son, Dayan David Meldola, and he was too closely involved in the differences and disputes between the Mahamad and his father for any enthusiasm to be generated in his favour. Thus he became *de facto* the ecclesiastical head of the Community. This created a new difficulty when the question of appointing a Haham was considered. As time passed, it became more and more difficult to contemplate the deposition of David Meldola by the appointment of a Haham above him. At the same time the relations between Meldola and the lay authorities continued to discourage them from entrusting him with the power and authority of Haham. Another factor that militated against the appointment of a Haham was financial. A considerable loss in the financial sphere as otherwise was sustained by the withdrawal of the founders of the West London Synagogue, who included a number of the wealthiest of the Yehidim. There was little money to spare in these circumstances for the salary of a Haham.

In 1844 we find Dayan Meldola's bench of dayanim in trouble. As the minute of the Mahamad records:

'The Mahamad having been informed that the Gentlemen of the Bet Din had given a certificate to one of the Readers of the Burton Street place of worship (the West London Synagogue) as to his competency as a Hebrew Scholar they requested the attendance of those gentlemen to ascertain the fact, when they stated that it was not true. They had given a certificate of that description to Mr. Breslau, simply that he was a competent Hebrew scholar. The Mahamad asked to see a copy of the certificate but they could not supply one as the original was in the hands of the party. The Mahamad expressed to them their extreme regret that they should have given any document of the kind.'

A few years earlier, in February 1838, Meldola received an

unwelcome prominence in the minutes of the Mahamad in his individual capacity.

'I am directed to acquaint you that the President has called the attention of the Mahamad to an excuse given by you at a late meeting of the Heshaim for your absence from the Medrash and Synagogue in the afternoon of Tuesday the 11th Sebat (6th February). The excuse you made was that with regard to your non-attendance at the Medrash, you had been engaged with the Lord Mayor on business concerning the Nation, and for your absence from synagogue that you had been detained by the Lord Mayor or at the Lord Mayor's which was the cause that prevented you—and the declaration was made under a solemn assurance to Mr. Abecasis, with whose report the meeting was satisfied. As the President entertained doubts of the correctness of your statement, he made enquiries and ascertained that there was no one officiating at the Mansion House between the hours of 3 and 6 on that day and therefore commissioned Mr. Abecasis and Mr. Montefiore to ascertain from you whether your original statement was correct, and these gentlemen have since reported that you were at the Mansion House on the day and time stated, that you were not certain whether the Lord Mayor was there in the afternoon, but you are sure it was the Lord Mayor you saw in the morning. As the President still conceives that your excuse is not founded on facts, for he has information that the Lord Mayor did not sit at all on that day, the Mahamad make this communication to you to afford you the opportunity of verifying the statement you have made, and you are therefore requested to furnish the Mahamad as early as possible with such proof as may remove any doubt on the subject.'

Before these incidents it began to be felt that the vacancy in the office of Haham had lasted sufficiently long and that it was time that steps were taken to fill it, and in March 1843 the Elders at length decided to take such steps. The difficulties in the way were, however, found to be still insuperable, and by the end of the year it was agreed to appoint not a Haham but a *Rosh Yeshiba*, in effect a Haham without a title, candidates to be 'men of general information', not exceeding forty-five years of age and conversant with the English language. Meldola had by then just passed his forty-fifth birthday and was disqualified, as were also, by the language requirement, probably every other possible candidate. In the circumstances it is not altogether surprising that the resolution of the Elders was not confirmed. The later meeting, however, decided to declare vacant the office of Haham at a salary of £300 a year. The resolution was carried by a majority, but not of the required two-thirds. As a consequence David Meldola continued in his seat as Ab Beth Din. For six years there was no further move, but in April 1849 the forces that were anxious for a reform of what was termed 'the ecclesiastical department' were again mobilized. On the 29th of that month a very drastic proposal was put before the Elders:

'Considering that in a congregation of our standing it is imperative that our Dayanim should be persons not only of learning, but men that can command respect, and whereas the gentlemen now in office are incapacitated from so doing, the Reverend David Meldola owing to his infirmities, and the Reverend Abraham Haliva, not understanding the English language,'

it is hereby resolved 'that notice be given to terminate the services of these two dayanim at the end of the Calendar year and that steps be taken to appoint successors', understanding or engaging to know the English language within two years, so as to be able to give a discourse at least once a month. This resolution was carried by the casting vote of the chairman, but confirmation was refused at the subsequent meeting by thirteen votes to two. The victory of the opposition was complete, for a counter-resolution was adopted to the effect

'That it is essential to our peace and welfare and to the high standing and respect of our Community that the Body of Elders should at all times extend to the religious authorities of the Congregation its support and protection in the discharge of the onerous and important duties of their office, and that whilst the Elders will be ever ready to investigate and redress any just cause of complaint connected with the Ecclesiastical Department, and be equally disposed to strengthen and increase its efficiency, so that it should be more in unison with the feelings and wishes of the Congregation at large, they feel called upon at the present juncture to declare that they see no reason to withdraw from the present Dayanim the countenance and support of this room, and the Elders cannot but deprecate any proposal for the dismissal of any officer of the Kaal, without previous notice having been given and some specific charge proved to justify such course of proceeding.'

This resolution was carried by fourteen votes to one.

The next attempt to secure a change was directed at Haliva, who was offered, in December 1851, a pension of £30 a year and one of £15 to his widow if she survived him, provided not only that he retired but that he also left the country. The offer was not accepted, and Haliva retained his office until he died in August 1853, a few months after the death of his colleague, David Meldola. Haliva's widow was at once voted a pension of £25 per annum, and shortly afterwards granted £30 to pay for her emigration to the Holy Land. But that was not the end of the widow of Dayan Haliva. As late as July 1861 the Mahamad voted £10 towards a fund that was being raised for her assistance. She was then apparently living abroad, presumably in Palestine. It was the practically simultaneous death of Meldola and Haliva, the only surviving dayanim, that led to the hurried and perhaps speculative appointment of Barnett Abrahams.

Although the seceders of 1842 had left the Community, they left behind them the beginnings of a movement that in course of time had a decisive influence on its fortunes and its developments. The Reform movement at its beginning rested to a large extent on a desire for a place of worship within reasonable reach of the homes of those who ultimately withdrew from Bevis Marks. This request was rejected almost without any consideration until consideration was too late. The establishment of another synagogue within six miles of Bevis Marks was contrary to the basic law of the Community. Those who demanded the repeal of this law consequently withdrew, but they left behind them a party whose members also had transferred or were shortly to transfer their homes from the City and desired opportunities for public worship in the neighbourhood of their new homes. This movement gathered strength and could not be ignored. No question of doctrine arose: only one, of administration.

The subject which had for long been canvassed was first brought formally before one of the governing organs of the Congregation by the Mahamad in their annual speech to the Elders on 31 October 1852. The Mahamad called the attention of the Elders to a matter involving 'the future welfare and the highest interests of this our Ancient Congregation'.

> 'Looking to the prosperous state of our Holy Synagogue both as regards its annual revenues and its permanent capital, bearing in mind the prospective advantages which are secured to it, and above all reflecting on how greatly the blessing of Divine Providence has always attended that time honored Establishment;

it does appear to the Mahamad that, under these gratifying circumstances, a duty, an imperative duty, devolved on that sacred establishment, and on you as its representatives, to afford to its members residing at a distance the facility of religious worship in a locality more easily accessible to them, than our present synagogue. The Mahamad advocates no hasty or rash measure. They will merely suggest that, under a limited expense, an experimental trial for two or three years should be made, and that for maturing a plan and carrying it out, a Committee be appointed, whose arrangement when completed shall be submitted to your approval, and subsequently to the sanction of the Yehidim, in conformity with the Ascama. Should the attempt succeed you will be amply rewarded in having achieved so great an object; should it fail, you will have given proofs to the Congregation of an anxious desire on your part to consult their feelings and wishes and to promote the union, concord and contentment of every member of our respected Community.'

The Elders, after giving the suggestion due consideration, resolved to refer it for decision to a special meeting of the Yehidim. The Yehidim met on 21 November and also gave long and anxious consideration to the revolutionary proposal. They finally agreed that the establishment of a Branch Synagogue 'in all respects subject to the same rules and regulations as those which govern this Congregation' was desirable and appointed a committee consisting of Sir Moses Montefiore, Edward Foligno, Joshua Benoliel, Moses Picciotto, David Brandon, Moses Guedalla, and David de Pass to go further into the matter. This committee's report was considered on 14 March following. It stated that the committee had found a suitable building, within reasonable distance of the residences of most of the Yehidim who were specially interested, in Wigmore Street, Cavendish Square, which could be adapted to the purposes of a synagogue. They recommended that a short lease of this building should be secured, the Congregation contributing £250 towards the cost of adapting and fitting it and that the Congregation further guarantee a payment of £400 a year for three years towards the cost of maintenance. The remainder of the money required, it was expected, would be contributed by individual members. This recommendation was adopted and the committee was re-appointed with two changes, in conjunction with the Mahamad, to see the resolution put into effect and the building made suitable for a synagogue. The next step was to secure a lease of No. 4 Wigmore Street at an annual rental of £200, and of a part of No. 5 at a rental of £30 per annum. A premium of £50 had to be paid for the portion of No. 5. These two buildings, transformed into a synagogue, provided accommodation for 200 men and 80 women worshippers. The shop and basement were sublet for £50 per annum, to a neighbour who threatened otherwise to make himself a nuisance to the new-comers. Steps were taken to enlist staff. For the office of Hazan two applications were received, neither of them satisfactory; for that of Samas there were six candidates, all equally professionally qualified. The choice fell on Israel Mendoza, 'who having a large number of sons and bearing an excellent character, was considered the most suitable for the office'. It was this Israel Mendoza whose family six years later brought trouble upon him. A letter from the secretary of the Congregation of 9 November 1858 enlightens the reader after almost a century.

> 'Mr. Israel Mendoza—Complaints having been made to the Gentlemen of the Mahamad and the Committee of the Branch Synagogue, of the very noisy and disorderly conduct of your family, which causes much annoyance and disquiet to your neighbours. The Mahamad also learn that the business you follow and carry on at the house is from its dirty character more fit for a stable or mews than for a private dwelling... All these circumstances are extremely displeasing to the Mahamad and Committee....'

Failure to secure a Hazan in England was followed by inquiries abroad, but in the meanwhile the temporary services of Solomon Sebag having been secured, the new synagogue was consecrated in time for the New Year of 1853. In the following year Joseph Piperno, who had come from Leghorn, was appointed Hazan. Financially the expectations of the sponsors of the new synagogue had been exceeded. The contributions from Yehidim and Ashkenazi friends had been unexpectedly generous. Including the grant of £250 by the Yehidim they exceeded £1,150, a sum considered more than sufficient to pay for the alterations in the building and its fitting up as a synagogue. The management of the Branch Synagogue was vested in the Mahamad with four local Yehidim who were to act in rotation as presiding wardens. The first of these wardens to be appointed were Naphtali Hart Lyon, Abraham de Pass, Abraham Cohen, and Abraham Mocatta.

This synagogue remained in use until June 1860 when the lease was surrendered. The experiment had proved successful, for steps were at once taken for the erection of another building planned from the beginning as a synagogue. Its foundation was laid in Bryanston Street, somewhat farther to the west, on 25 March 1860. And the new building was consecrated in the following year. The architect was Hyman H. Collins, a member of the Ashkenazi Community. From the first, Ashkenazi residents in West London as well as Sephardi had been accustomed to worship in the Branch Synagogue. When the erection of the new building was contemplated one of these Ashkenazim, Louis Cohen, a nephew by marriage of Sir Moses Montefiore and one of the leading members of the Ashkenazi Community, made the generous offer of a gift of £1,000 towards the building fund, provided that he was allotted a seat in the new synagogue. The Mahamad was, however, compelled to decline the gift as it was unable to comply with the condition. Although all Jews were welcome at the services, under the regulations in force only Yehidim could be allotted seats. Some years later, in 1873, Samuel Montagu, the future Lord Swaythling, a member of one of the city Ashkenazi synagogues who was resident in western London, applied for a seat in the Branch Synagogue. The City Ashkenazi synagogues had some thirteen years earlier established their own branch synagogue in Great Portland Street, and in 1863 the Bayswater Synagogue, also in the first instance an affiliate of the City synagogues, had been opened, but Montagu preferred the Sephardi place of worship, even though he was also a seatholder in Bayswater. He was informed that the governing body of the Bryanston Street Synagogue was not authorized to let seats to others than members of the Sephardi Community, but that without a formal letting a seat would be placed at his disposal. In the following year the Mahamad raised the prohibition on the letting of seats, and the first of the Ashkenazim to become seatholders at Bryanston Street were Samuel Montagu and Reuben Heilbut, who had been expelled from the Sephardi Community on the occasion of his marriage some years before. On the opening of the New West End Synagogue, of which Samuel Montagu was one of the founders, in 1879, he surrendered his seat at Bryanston Street. In February 1865 the management of the Branch Synagogue was entrusted to a committee elected by the regular attendants, with instructions in particular for 'promoting a better attendance'. At the same time it was decided to complete the building of the fabric.

The first branch synagogue was only a provisional undertaking: that in Bryanston Street was a permanent one. There was no question now that there was a real need for a place of worship in West London. But it must not be thought that the opening of a larger synagogue meant that there was or had been overcrowding in the earlier building. The number of members of the Congregation was adequate to fill it comfortably, but regularity and frequency of attendance in synagogue no longer reached the standard of the eighteenth century. Many were the complaints of sparse attendance. As time passed, the difficulty in getting a quorum for public worship, except on sabbaths and festivals, grew greater, and the records of the Community in the middle of the nineteenth century and later are filled with laments on that account. In the end the hope of an adequate spontaneous attendance at synagogue on weekdays had to be abandoned and recourse had to be had to a procedure that would doubtless have severely shocked the founders of the Community in the seventeenth century and even their grandchildren, the payment of men to attend synagogue. Even before the withdrawal of the seceders and the decision to open a branch synagogue—as early as the year 1830—the small attendances at Bevis Marks were attracting attention. And this declining interest was not limited to synagogue attendance. Similar difficulties arose in the administration. It was by no means exceptional for meetings of the Elders or of the Yehidim to be adjourned on account of lack of a quorum. On one occasion—in 1857—it is recorded that only eight Elders attended their annual meeting, the most important of the year. Even the regular business meetings of the Yehidim, for which they had long struggled and which marked the transition from an oligarchic to a democratic system of government, once obtained, soon failed to secure an adequate attendance and, as the Mahamad remarked somewhat plaintively in one of their reports to the Yehidim, 'it too often happens that a quorum is with difficulty obtained for election of parnassim'. There was also the recurring trouble of disinclination to accept office.

By now the Community was in the fortunate position of not being entirely or even mainly dependent on the yearly contributions of its members. A series of pious donors had, generation after generation, bequeathed to it legacies, large or small, the total of which by now was large enough to assure a revenue from investments equal to half the expenditure of the Congregation. The other half was made up of yearly contributions by the living, in the form of finta and voluntary offerings. By 1847 the Yehidim had gained control of the appointment of the Fintadores or assessors of finta, apart from the members of the Mahamad, who held also that office *ex officio*. In that year the Ascama governing the distribution of the finta was completely remodelled. The maximum payable by any Yahid was fixed at £40 and the minimum at 20s.

The total amount of the finta was to be laid down by the Elders, and Fintadores appointed every second year to distribute this total among the Yehidim. An oath was no longer required of the Fintador, but a pledge 'not to suffer favour and affection, or antipathy to influence him or his votes', was accepted as sufficient. Those who refused election as Fintadores were fined five pounds. The finta was first established as an organized system of assessment at a meeting of heads of families in the year 1707 when the amount to be raised was fixed at £600. This amount was increased to £900 thirty-one years later at a meeting of the Yehidim. In 1809 it reached its highest point at £1,400. These sources were always maxima, which the Elders in fixing a definite figure year by year were not free to pass. After 1809 this maximum began to fall until it reached the low point of £700. On the opening of the Branch Synagogue seats in it were allotted in return for payment in addition to the finta. It was only in 1844 that special seats in the women's gallery of the Bevis Marks Synagogue were first allotted to the wives and daughters of members. Hitherto any woman could sit where she could find room, but no personal seat was allotted to her, except that brides on their first appearance in synagogue after marriage were given seats in the front of the gallery. In the year 1823 the annual income amounted to about £4,000. In 1840 revenue amounted to £3,483 and the expenditure to £3,908. In 1841, on the eve of the secession, the total revenue was £3,638 and the expenditure £4,222 of which £393 was on account of 'Extraordinary Works and Repairs'. Of this revenue £1,767 was derived from 'Dividends on Funded Property'. In the succeeding year both the income and expenditure had fallen considerably, the two sides practically balancing at £3,270. The income from 'offerings, Finta, Imposta and Rents', all of which were grouped together had fallen by £230. The year 1843 showed a small improvement in income but a larger one in expenditure. The year 1844 showed a further improvement, due to reductions on both sides, the larger one under expenditure. Attention was, however, called that year at the annual meeting of Yehidim to the appreciable reduction since 1838 in the number of members. Revenue and expenditure continued to fluctuate for some years. In 1848 the deficit amounted almost to £600. In 1852 there was a surplus of £375, although the revenue had fallen to the low figure of £3,702. The following year it was still lower and the surplus a bare £20. The Gabay certainly held no sinecure in those days. These figures all relate to the general income and expenditure of the Congregation, apart from receipts for specific purposes. In 1842, the year of, but after the Secession, the total finta was assessed at £800. Then it was reduced to £700. In the meanwhile the revenue from Impostas, originally the main source of income, had entirely disappeared; that from fines, also at times an appreciable source of income, had fallen to five pounds in 1848. There were sudden variations in revenue and expenditure, most annoying to the Mahamad and in particular to the Gabay, who had the responsibility for preparing the estimates, and at this period of the history of the Community unexpected deficits not infrequently disclosed themselves at the end of the year. Quoting, however, the address of the chairman of the Elders at the end of 1856 'and although by the blessings of Providence, our Holy Synagogue has on various occasions found itself unexpectedly extricated from difficulties, still it is incumbent on us not to rely solely on that Benevolent Source, but timely to consider this all important subject', that is to say the balancing of the two sides of the Congregation's accounts. In short, 'God helps those who help themselves.' One consequence was the raising of the finta to £800 a year later. But the Congregation was not yet out of the financial wood, for in 1861 the assessment of the finta had again to be reduced—to £750.

During these earlier decades of the nineteenth century there were other events and occurrences in the history of the Congregation which, although for the most part not of great consequence, yet call for mention. A certain extent of disorder or freedom of behaviour in the synagogue which in the past at times attracted the attention of visitors and led to steps by the governing authorities is no longer evident from the records. But in May 1846 it was resolved to prosecute Isaac Garcia for 'most riotous and insulting conduct' towards Judah Aloof, one of the parnassim, in the Mahamad Chamber, 'this not being his first offence in so misconducting himself'. A probably connected incident is mentioned in the Mahamad minutes eight years later in 1854 when Daniel Hamis da Fonseca wrote to the Mahamad offering to apologize to Solomon Abecasis for having insulted him in synagogue, also in the year 1846. The offer was accepted and the Mahamad decided to reduce the fine of ten pounds, that had been imposed on da Fonseca at the time of the offence, to one of two pounds, provided that he wrote an approved letter to Abecasis. But da Fonseca changed his mind. No letter of apology was written, and the unpaid fine of ten pounds remained on the books of the Congregation. The probable connexion between Aloof and Abecasis on this occasion is interesting to note. It will be remembered[1] that they

[1] See p. 233.

appeared together on previous occasions of a different character. Unseemly conduct in the synagogue may have by now passed out of fashion, but human nature does not change quickly and disputes and quarrels, accompanied by occasional outbursts and displays of temper on the part of Elders, Yehidim, and Congregantes equally, still persisted in the Congregation. Even as recently as 1909 the Mahamad had to order a notice to be affixed to the door of the Bevis Marks Synagogue appealing for better decorum. Honorary office was certainly no sinecure. Now and then some aggrieved individual refused to accept a decision of the Mahamad and threatened legal proceedings.

If the behaviour of the Congregation in the Synagogue was more seemly, there does not appear to have been a similar improvement outside its precincts. One of the Community's pensioners in 1852 considered that the Community was in her debt by her acceptance of their relief. 'In consequence of the unruly conduct of the widow of David Paz Cardozo and her daughters notwithstanding the repeated warnings given to them, notice was personally given to them by the Mahamad that they were to quit the buildings (placed at their disposal free of rent) on or before the 4th of June next.' The Widow Cardozo treated this notice with the contempt that she considered it deserved, and application was thereupon made for an order of ejectment. But the magistrates decided that they had no jurisdiction and the widow remained triumphantly in possession. Three months' consideration was given by the Mahamad to the deadlock. They then made an attempt to break it.

> 'It appearing to the Mahamad that the only effectual method of restoring proper order and decorum in the Synagogue Buildings would be by discharging the whole of the inmates and readmitting under new regulations only such as have had no complaints made against them, and are the most orderly, it was ordered that notice be served on the whole of them to quit within one month from this date.' (8 September 1852.)

This drastic action proved successful. The inmates of the almshouses promptly came to heel and the resolution of the Mahamad was suspended. Even the widow Cardozo presumably remained undisturbed.

Further cemetery accommodation soon became a matter of pressing urgency. The original cemetery, commonly called the 'Velho' or Old Cemetery, was acquired in 1656 and opened in 1657 on a small plot of land called 'The Soldier's Tenement' behind the present Beth Holim, or Old People's Home.[1] The inscription on a tablet affixed in 1684 reads:

'The first stone of this Wall was placed on the 21st Tamuz 5444 & the 27th June 1684

Isaac Barzilay
Aaron Levi Rezio
Parnasim of the Congregation
Abraham Roiz Pinhel, Parnas of Hebra
David Israel Nunez, Administrator'

This burial ground or 'House of Life', as it is called poetically in Hebrew, was soon filled and an adjoining plot was secured. This again was not available for long, and in 1724 a second plot was bought at a few hundred yards' distance farther along the Mile End Road. This was an area of 2½ acres, known as the 'Cherry Tree', and was bought for the Congregation by Joseph da Costa and Gabriel Lopes for £450. It was the property of two brothers, Joseph and Jonathan Hardy, and is generally described on eighteenth-century maps as 'Hardy's Gardens'. But it was not opened as a cemetery until March 1733 when articles of agreement were drawn up for enclosing the burial ground with a brick wall. A tablet was then affixed to the north wall, as had been done in the old ground, bearing in Spanish an inscription which, translated, reads 'On the 17th of Nisan 5493 (1733) the building of this wall was begun. Parnassim being Abraham Alvares Corcho, Moses Lopes Dias, Jacob de David Mendes da Costa, David Lopes Pereira; Benjamin Mendes Pacheco, Gabay. Parnas of Hebra being David Abarbanell.' Then follows in English the verse from the twelfth chapter of Ecclesiastes, 'Then shall the Dust return to Earth as it was, and the spirit shall Return to God who gave it.' Later in the same year the fine mortuary chapel, needlessly pulled down in 1922, was built. An expenditure of £2,000 on the ground, fencing, and buildings was authorized. The cost was largely defrayed by the purchase of reserved graves by practically all the Yehidim who were in a position to do so. This was in 1734 when Jacob Mendes da Costa, the elder, and Benjamin Mendes da Costa were added to assist the Mahamad of the day as trustees. This additional space, called the 'Novo' or new ground was sufficient for about a century after which period the acquisition of new land again became urgent. The new acquisition was close to the 'Velho' and belonged to one Collins. The transaction was not completed till 1849. This extension was, however, taken into use in 1853, and a second tablet was added (page 325). After the main portion

[1] See L. D. Barnett, *Bevis Marks Records*, vol. I, p. 5.

CEMETERY INSCRIPTION, 1733

of the 'Novo' had passed out of use, only that 'behind the boards' reserved for persons in disgrace for one reason or other at the time of their death remained partly free. In 1862 this too was fully occupied, and a part of the extension was reserved for a similar purpose.

Meanwhile the cemetery guard which had been instituted many years before was still in existence. It had been reduced in 1842, and its continuance was by now hardly necessary. The guard was finally abolished in 1876. The watch in the Synagogue yard had been discontinued in 1840.

Throughout this period the needs of the poor continued to impose themselves on the attention of the Mahamad and the Elders. A subsidiary institution, the Board of Guardians with a separate budget, had been established in 1837 to deal with these needs and their related problems. Previously the relief of the needy of the Community had been the concern of the Mahamad. The foundation of the Board of Guardians did not, however, relieve the Mahamad of the whole of the burden, for the two organizations for many years continued side by side to dispense relief, independently of one another but presumably more or less in consultation. As a rule the Mahamad were concerned with the pensioners, inmates of the almshouses and other recipients of regular relief, while the Board of Guardians gave their attention to occasional, irregular, clients. These latter fell into two classes, the 'stragglers', those who received assistance 'for once', but remained in the country, and 'despachos' who applied for assistance to leave England. The latter also fell into two classes: those who wished to return to the country from which they had come, and emigrants to North America, Australia, or the Levant. The Board of Guardians assisted members of all these classes, in the case of the 'despacho' in the hope and understanding that they would not be seen again. Emigration to Australia was much encouraged. In the colonization of this continent two of the members of the Montefiore family took part: Jacob and Joseph Barrow, both of whom for a time settled there, Jacob Montefiore being one of the commissioners appointed by William IV to organize the government of South Australia. On the other hand, there was a continuous immigration from North Africa and Holland. In the words of the Annual Report of the Mahamad of December 1862:

'For some years past they (indigent Sephardim) have been emigrating to this country in considerable numbers, and are still constantly arriving with large families, encouraged to come over

PLAN OF CEMETERIES, 1786
From Bowles' *The Cities of London and Westminster* (1786)

by their relatives, who hold out to them the advantages of immediate admission for their children into our schools and to sharing equally with our native poor in all the charities of our Congregation. The facilities of marrying is another inducement of which they fail not to avail themselves and thereby pauperism is augmented.'

In fact in 1856 the Mahamad had to write to the congregational authorities in Amsterdam to call their attention to the increasing number of poor Sephardim who were coming from Holland and to announce their intention in future to withhold assistance from such new-comers. Four years later the last of the refugees from Portugal arrived in England. In October 1860 the widow of Abraham Sabah, who had been born in North Africa but had accompanied her husband to Lisbon where he had died, arrived in London with her three little children and applied to the Mahamad for relief. She had had to leave Portugal, she said, as otherwise, being destitute, she would have had to place her children in a Roman Catholic institution. Her story was confirmed. The assistance that she required was given her and steps taken for her return to Mogador. When the size of the Sephardi population of London was estimated in 1829, almost a half was receiving some relief, and there was a further number on the edge of poverty.

The subject of the Sephardi poor began to attract attention outside its own Community and, although the Sephardim had their own hospital and medical service, nearly twenty years later, in 1847, the Ashkenazi authorities felt themselves compelled to draw the attention of their Sephardi colleagues to the number of Sephardim who were filling the Jewish wards of the London Hospital. This institution was a special favourite of Ashkenazi philanthropists. Moses Hart, who died in 1756, had left it the then very considerable legacy of a thousand pounds: his son-in-law, Elias Levy, was one of its early governors. The hospital on its part, from its foundation shortly before Hart's death, has always made provision for special food for its Jewish patients. In fact as early as 1745, one of the five houses of 'The London Infirmary', its predecessor, was known as 'The Jews' House'. The Mahamad in their reply to the three Ashkenazi Congregations expressed their regret at the cause of their remonstrance, especially as the Sephardim had a hospital of their own in which their sick could find accommodation. They went on to say that the existence of this hospital was the reason why individual Sephardim did not take as large a part in the support of the London Hospital as did their

CEMETERY INSCRIPTION, 1855

Ashkenazi co-religionists. But there were Sephardim among its governors, and other members of their Congregation contributed to its funds. In these circumstances the Mahamad did not feel that their Congregation was called on to vote a grant to the hospital. The services rendered by other non-Sephardi institutions to the Sephardi poor were recognized by grants, for instance, to the Fever Hospital at Islington in the winter of 1852–3 and to the Jewish Soup Kitchen annually over a series of years. The threat of a cholera epidemic in the late autumn of 1853 led the authorities of the Great Synagogue to approach those of Bevis Marks with a suggestion for co-operation, so far as the poor of the two communities were concerned, but the Sephardim, always jealous of their independence, preferred to act alone. They considered that their Board of Guardians was able to deal with the situation. In the ordinary day-to-day work of relief in the Community the Sephardim continued on their road unaided. One of the communal societies formed in that winter was 'an Association formed by ladies of our Congregation for rendering assistance to the industrious working classes of our Community, by supplying them during the winter with bread and potatoes at reduced prices'. A Mr. B. Lindo, honorary secretary of this society, wrote to the Mahamad, submitting the plan organized and (somewhat mysteriously) requesting on the part of the ladies 'the protection and assistance of the Mahamad should they be exposed to imposition or insult whilst carrying out the arduous task they have undertaken'. The Mahamad replied at once. 'The Ladies might rely on all the assistance and protection it was in their power to extend to them.'

Other changes made new resources available for the assistance of the poor. The Beth Holim was originally a hospital for the sick, but had for long almost entirely abandoned that function and become a home for the aged and infirm. The Moses Lara Trust Fund of 1827 came to its assistance in the pursuit of this object and enabled it to carry on this work free from all financial worry. The office of Parnas of the Cautivos or Warden of the Captives had by now become a sinecure. In fact the funds reserved for the ransom of Jewish prisoners of the Barbary pirates or the Knights of Malta had been formally made available in 1821 for the assistance of congregations in distress and in particular for those of Safad and Jerusalem, which were permanently in need. As late as 1835, however, a grant was made towards the ransom of a prisoner then in Constantine in North Africa. It was not until 1872 that the offices of Parnassim of Terra Santa and Cautivos were formally

THE SEPHARDIM AND THE ASHKENAZIM 327

combined. In 1856 another trust was created by a gift from Judah Guedalla, the interest on which was to be devoted to grants to the students of a Yeshiba or College in Jerusalem which had been founded by the donor, and secondly for the provision of clothing for the children attending the Community's National and Infant School in London. Legacies and gifts occasionally came from unexpected quarters. Thus as long ago as 1746 Daniel Jessurun Rodrigues, otherwise Francis Salvador,

> 'petitioned the Mahamad to ordain the distribution of the proceeds of the fifty pounds which they had received from the Executors of Timothy Motteux which by will he left to be distributed among poor Jews, together with another fifty pounds which was received by Moses Hart and Aaron Franks,[1] and that this distribution be made among the poor of the Nation as from the roll and be entered on Mahamad's books for permanent record.'

The legacy was accepted and the proceeds distributed in accordance with the wishes of the testator. Timothy Motteux was a brother of the French translator and dramatist, Peter Anthony Motteux. They both came to England, probably on the Revocation of the Edict of Nantes in 1685. Peter ultimately became an East India merchant. Timothy, who was a director of the French Hospital in London, left money also to the Walloon and Dutch churches there. He must have had Jewish contacts, probably in the course of his business dealings. A hundred and two years later there was perhaps an even more surprising gift. This was one of ten pounds by Louis Cohen, one of the leading members of the Ashkenazi Community, in memory of Joseph Hambro. The gift was accepted and the name of the deceased was ordered to be inscribed on 'the Legacy Table'. Baron Joseph Hambro was the Danish Jewish banker who settled in England where he founded both the bank that bears his name and the family that has been prominent in business and society throughout the past century. He had one son, Baron Charles Joachim Hambro, whom he had had baptized, it is said, on *Kippur*. Joseph Hambro throughout the thirty-four years of his residence in London never showed any interest in Jewish affairs, until two years before his death, when, attacked by a serious illness, he became a member of the Great Synagogue in whose cemetery he was buried. He left a legacy of £500 out of a very considerable fortune to that institution. Yet another unexpected 'in memoriam' gift was one from a group of

[1] The heads of the Great Synagogue.

Christian friends of Isaac Foligno, who in his lifetime had taken his share of the work of the Sephardi Community and had been president of the Jewish Board of Deputies. The entry on the Legacy Board reads 'A tribute of respect to the memory of the late Isaac Foligno by Protestant friends and presented by his widow —£50.' The previous year the Mahamad had been informed of a legacy of ten pounds by Moses Emanuel of Portsea, who expressed a desire that a lamp in his memory should be kept burning in the synagogue for a year after his decease. A reply had to be given that the fulfilment of his wish would have been contrary to the usages and customs of the Community but that 'due honour would be paid to his memory by the recital of the usual ascaba or memorial prayer'. The roll of legacies from members of the Congregation continued unabated, with occasionally one from a member of the Ashkenazi Community. In August 1836 came a donation from Mrs. Nathan Mayer Rothschild of £25 'to be distributed amongst the poor of the Synagogue' on the occasion of the death of her husband. The legacy by Chaim Samuel Jacob Falk otherwise 'Haham Falcon', 'The Baalshem of London', was more picturesque in its origin. Although of Sephardi origin, in England, whither he came about the year 1742, his connexions were only with Ashkenazim and non-Jews—as a rule members of the aristocracy, sometimes of royal lineage. In Germany he is said to have been condemned to be burnt as a sorcerer, and during his forty years in England many miracles were attributed to him. On his death in 1782 he left legacies to the Great Synagogue, its rabbi for the time being, and the Ashkenazi Beth Hamedrash. He remembered also the Sephardi Congregation, leaving annuities of £15 to the Synagogue and £10 to the Beth Hamedrash, which are still received. Later there were legacies by Benjamin Cohen, a brother-in-law of Sir Moses Montefiore, Lawrence Levy, and Sir David Salomons. These legacies by Ashkenazim were to some extent paralleled by similar occasional bequests by Sephardim— Benjamin Mendes da Costa, Moses Gomes Serra, and others—to the Great Synagogue.

Marriages and proposed marriages also sometimes created difficulties, as has been mentioned. The Mahamad reserved to itself the right to refuse permission for a marriage when the bridegroom was a member of the Sephardi Community. In particular it set its face against youthful bridegrooms, but after the Marriage Act of 1836 these generally faced the Mahamad with a *fait accompli* by arranging a civil marriage without the consent of the Mahamad and very often also of the parents. The Mahamad, like the parents, had then no alternative to capitulation. Occasionally there was something of the nature of a *cause célèbre* in more prominent circles. Intermarriage with Tudescos had by now become so frequent as no longer to arouse general interest. Marriages with proselytes were also growing in number—despite the continued prohibition of the admission of proselytes into the London Sephardi Community. These ladies no longer had to go abroad to secure admission to the Jewish Community. The Ashkenazi ecclesiastical authorities were more complaisant than those of the Sephardim, and it was not unusual for the brides to become Jewesses by way of one of the Ashkenazi synagogues. A sensation must, however, have been caused in the year 1837 when Gabriel, son of Jacob Israel Brandon, at the time presiding warden, married Miriam bat Abraham Abinu, otherwise Miss Ellen Griffin. Shortly afterwards Gabriel Brandon was elected to one of the minor offices in the Community, but declined to serve. Abraham Meldola, after the death of the Haham, his father, his brother, however, being Ab Beth Din, applied for permission to marry a proselyte. Technical difficulties were at first raised, but these were overcome and the marriage was celebrated, but not with enthusiasm on the part of either the lay or the ecclesiastical authorities. Another marriage in 1859 for which permission was given was that of Joseph Mayer Montefiore, at the time president of the Mahamad, to Henrietta Francisca, daughter of Solomon Bernhard Sichel of The Hague, a Tudesca. They were married in the Ashkenazi synagogue of Frankfort on Maine, from which city the Sichel family had come.[1] This marriage, however, created no precedent in the Montefiore family. The bridegroom's father, Abraham Montefiore, a brother of Sir Moses, had himself married as his second wife—his first wife was not a Jewess—a Frankfurt Tudesca, Henrietta, daughter of Mayer Amschel Rothschild, and other members of the family who had already taken a similar course were Sir Moses himself, four of his aunts, Nathaniel and Louisa, brother and sister of Joseph Mayer, and others. It was about this period that another sensation was caused in the Community by the resignation and later baptism of Joseph d'Aguilar Samuda, who had served in almost every honorary secular office and had been prominent in the counsels of the Community for a generation. Samuda had at the beginning of the Secession Movement ranged himself with the founders of the West London Synagogue, but after a short interval he returned to Bevis Marks and resumed his activities there until his resignation at the

---

[1] A child of this marriage was the future Sir Francis Montefiore, Bart., president of the Elders for many years.

end of 1858. It is curious that of the three members of the Mahamad who were elected in the autumn of 1848 Joseph d'Aguilar Samuda left the Jewish Community; Judah Varicas transferred his allegiance to the Ashkenazim and left a very generous bequest to the Western Synagogue; Naphtali Hart Lyon, the only one of the three to remain staunch to Bevis Marks, was of Ashkenazi origin. Another secession of one whose family was well known at Bevis Marks was that of Simon Barrow, the father and grandfather of the British military family. He had long been residing in Bath. Although he resigned from the Congregation shortly after the death of his wife Tryphena, daughter of Baron Lyon de Symons, a prominent member of the Ashkenazi Community, he does not seem to have been baptized. His wife was buried in the Sephardi cemetery at Mile End: Simon Barrow lies in non-Jewish surroundings at Bath. In 1861 the name of Sassoon first appears in the roll of Yehidim, Sassoon David Sassoon, the first of the family to settle in England (in 1858), being elected a Yahid in that year. He at once threw himself into the work of the Community, filling several of the highest offices before his premature death, six years later, while serving in the office of Parnas. He was followed in England and in Bevis Marks by several of his brothers, Sir Albert Sassoon, Arthur, Reuben, and Aaron.

At the end of March 1851 a census of the population of the country was undertaken, and included in this census was a count of the attendances at the several places of worship. So far as the synagogues of the country were concerned the days appointed were Friday evening, 28 March, and the following Saturday. The return given shows that the accommodation in Bevis Marks then amounted to 850 seats, of which 300 were reserved for assessed members and the remainder available to all worshippers. The synagogue was open for public worship every day, on weekdays morning and evening, on sabbaths and festivals in the afternoon also. The census on the Friday evening showed an attendance of 168 with 45 scholars in addition. On the Saturday morning the attendance was 260 with 84 scholars, and in the afternoon 216 with 88 scholars. The attendance on festivals and days of Holy Convocation was given as ranging from 500 to 800. There is no estimate of the number of Sephardim in London at that time, but in 1829, twenty-two years earlier, one of about 2,500 was given. The number, however, was not increasing, probably diminishing, and it is improbable that such a number could have been mustered in 1851. Estimates of the size of population are necessarily, as a rule, little better than guesses, and the Sephardi population of London was and is no exception to that rule. The rise and fall in the number of births (the number of female births is certainly an understatement), marriages, and deaths during this period are, however, not without interest. But it must be remembered that all births in the Community were not recorded, that marriages of Sephardim were sometimes outside of the jurisdiction of Bevis Marks, and not every London Sephardi was on his death interred in the communal cemetery.

The following figures are taken from the official records. The fluctuations must be to some extent accidental.

	Births		Marriages	Deaths		
Year	M.	F.		M.	F.	CHILDREN
1838	21	19	6	20	22	15
1839	36	16	16	16	17	16
1840	21	15	16	14	13	14
1841	17	17	12	13	7	10
1842	25	19	11	14	21	7
1843	26	15	12	15	11	8
1844	21	24	18	10	11	11
1845	26	20	14	8	10	8
1846	34	20	13	14	13	8
1847	28	14	15	16	17	5
1848	24	16	9	12	18	13
1849	—	—	—	12	8	12
1850	40	17	18	16	16	9
1851	24	23	17	7	13	20
1852	—	—	—	10	12	17
1868	81		11	29		33
1870	70		17	33		43

In the year 1872 there were 76 Sephardi interments, of which 43 were 'charity funerals'. In the last years of the nineteenth century the number of burials ranged between 55 and 60 per annum.

Another return, for 1853, showed that on the occasion of the Holy Days the offerings made in the Bevis Marks Synagogue amounted to the not inappreciable amount of £520—this figure being surpassed by the Great Synagogue (£830) and the New Synagogue (£620).

CHAPTER XVII

SIR MOSES MONTEFIORE

THE ASCAMOT, THE constitution by which the affairs of the Community were administered, although strictly and sometimes rigidly observed, were never considered immutable and, like all living creations, underwent development and adaptation as time and the generations passed. Attention has already been called to some of these changes which commenced not in the nineteenth century but almost from the day on which the first code of ascamot was drawn up. On two or three occasions these ascamot had been entirely revised, although in essence the changes were not considerable. Until the year 1841 not only were Yehidim compelled to accept office, willingly or unwillingly, and heavily fined if they declined to do so or neglected their duties, but in the case of the wardens they were required to make large deposits as a guarantee that they would carry out their duties and also as a means of financing the congregation at times of scarcity of ready money. This system was not completely abolished in that year, but it was considerably lightened. The deposits required of the Parnassim were abolished altogether, that of the Gabay was reduced from £300 to £100. One consequence of this reform, which was not altogether unexpected, was that the reserve on which the Gabay had previously been able to draw when the accounts were in deficit was much diminished and consequent difficulties arose. Three years later another concession was made in favour of members of the Mahamad by the abolition of fines for absence from meetings, if the offender were forty miles or more from the place of meeting, either as a permanent resident or temporarily. But these were matters of detail, not touching the Yehidim as a body. The demand for a far more drastic revision was in the meanwhile gaining strength.

In one respect, almost unnoticed, a very great change was developing. Originally the government of the Community was of the nature of an oligarchy, the members of the Mahamad originally appointed choosing their successors and they in turn selecting those who followed after them. As time passed, the Mahamad became accustomed to refer to the Elders, first for advice, later sometimes for decision, matters of difficulty that arose, and in the end the Elders acquired by custom such a place in the constitution that the Mahamad in many matters became merely their executive.

This resulted in a broadening of the basis of government, but it was still an oligarchy, and, as the nineteenth century advanced, more and more opposed to the spirit of the age. A great advance was registered shortly after the securing of the great extension of the parliamentary franchise and the reform of government in a democratic direction by the English people in 1832. Almost as a consequence the Yehidim similarly acquired an assured position in the counsels of the Congregation. Its administration no longer rested only with the Mahamad and the Elders: the Yehidim also had gained a share in it. The powers of the Yehidim, once established, quickly grew. At first entitled only to meet annually to receive reports from the Mahamad, they soon met more frequently and were given or assumed definite powers. Even the Mahamad came under the influences that were stirring public opinion. Among their functions was that of electing periodically the representatives of the Congregation at the Board of Deputies. For almost a century these elections had been quite perfunctory. There had never been a contested election and the thought of going outside the small select circle for candidates had never arisen or at any rate been expressed. In 1844, however, a new departure was recorded. Not only was there a competition for election to the Board, but for the seven seats available twenty-one candidates were nominated and went to election. Five years later when two vacancies occurred, there were nine candidates. In these circumstances the existing ascamot were clearly out of date. Furthermore, the great secession had stirred everyone and stimulated their communal consciousness. Whatever the individual sympathies might be it was felt generally that changes were desirable.

The first movement came from the Yehidim at their meeting on 12 January 1845. It was there resolved, with a very small attendance, by sixteen votes against six,

'that this meeting impressed with the conviction that the progress of time, the altered position of our Congregation, and moreover the principles which govern legislation in the present day, had rendered necessary a revision of the constitution of our Community it most earnestly recommends to the consideration of the Elders the propriety of their appointing a committee to consist of five members of their own body and five of the Yehidim, to consider and report on the changes deemed necessary so to render our ascamot more in unison with the feelings and wishes of the Yehidim at large, more cheerfully obeyed and followed and, if need be, more readily and effectually put into force.'

This resolution was confirmed at a second meeting, at which there were seventeen votes in its favour and ten against. The Elders, however, rejected the proposal, by nine votes to eight. The response of the Yehidim was to resolve to appoint a committee of their own for the purpose, but this resolution did not secure the necessary confirmation. In its place the Elders were asked to revive a committee which had been appointed three years earlier and had apparently become moribund and to give it power to co-opt some representatives of the Yehidim and for that committee to be instructed to pursue the question of the reform of the constitution.

In the following year this committee reported. Its recommendations were drastic. The aims of their proposed reforms, they said, were

'a limited, periodical and responsible board of legislation. By this new system every Yahid will have a vote in the return of the members of the Board of Government and consequently a degree of control over the proceedings of their representatives, while the Representative himself will be invested with that power and authority that the great body of Yehidim at large can alone confer. By limiting the number of legislators you will ensure to the Board that dignity and respectability that an unlimited number cannot secure. In electing the Board of Legislators for a definite period, the advantages to the Congregation are obvious, both in regard to the proceedings of the Board, and also to the view of affairs that the whole body of Yehidim may happen to take from time to time, and to the representative himself it gives an opportunity of release in case of ill-health or other causes that may arise.'

The committee proposed that in future the Mahamad, the executive body, should be recruited from the Elders, and that the Elders should be elected by the Yehidim periodically by ballot, that they should be limited in number to twenty-one, one-third of whom were to retire every year, but that those at the time in office who were seventy years of age or upwards should be declared honorary elders and be additional to the twenty-one to be elected. Anyone refusing the office of elder or parnas was to be fined £40, but no elder should be fined more than once in three years for refusing the office of parnas. Any Yahid, twenty-five years of age and not more than one year in arrear with his finta should be qualified for election as an elder. This meat was, however, too strong even for the Yehidim, and, after an abortive attempt to adopt the preamble to the effect that 'the Board of Elders as at present constituted is not in accordance with the spirit of the age, nor in unison with the principles that govern the appointment of all legislative and public bodies in the present day', and then to leave to the Elders the task of effecting the desired reforms, the matter dropped and nothing further was heard of it until the beginning of January 1848. The Yehidim at their meeting on the second of that month appointed without opposition another committee consisting of five of their members, with power to add to their number, to revise the ascamot, and shortly afterwards, without awaiting the report of this committee, they resolved in favour of the elective principle being adopted for the appointment of elders, the age of thirty years or upwards and membership of the body of Yehidim for a minimum period of three years being the qualifications for election, a fine of ten pounds to be imposed in the event of refusal or resignation of office. This further resolution was, however, rejected when it came up for confirmation.

The committee appointed at the beginning of 1848 reported a year later, but did not deal with the fundamental matters that had hitherto been under consideration. In the end the revised ascamot were accepted, first by the Elders and then by the Mahamad. In these the existing system was retained, providing for the election of a new Mahamad by those retiring from office, with the assistance of adjuntos drawn from among the Elders, and for the automatic attainment of the office of Elder for life by all who served or were elected to the office of parnas, gabay, or deputy. Three years later there was another attempt by the Yehidim to set up a committee in conjunction with the Elders, to consider the advisability of altering the methods of election of the governing organizations of the Congregation, but this was defeated when it came up for confirmation. In 1858, however, drastic changes were made by the Elders in the regulations governing the election of the members of the Mahamad. These elections were to be made by the Yehidim in general meeting. The minimum age for candidates for the office of parnas was reduced from thirty-five to thirty, unless the candidate had already served as Gabay, and for that of Gabay to twenty-five years. The further qualifications for election were membership as a Yahid for at least two years and the payment of finta and offerings combined of a minimum of six pounds per annum for the same period. No Yahid who was in arrear with his payments for two successive half-years could vote. The voting was to be by ballot and no canvassing for votes was permitted. The penalty for the refusal of office was a fine of £20 except in the case of Yehidim of seventy years and upwards. The members of the Mahamad were entitled to nominate their successors as was also any Yahid who was qualified to vote. The first occasion on which the Yehidim elected members of the Mahamad was on the 30 August 1858. The candidates nominated by the Mahamad for election on this occasion were as Gabay, Abraham Mocatta, and as parnassim, Abraham Levy Bensusan and Edward Foligno. A further nomination for the office of parnas, made by two of the Yehidim, Solomon Aloof and Edward Foligno, was that of Abraham de Pass, who as a consequence was elected instead of Foligno, his seconder. In the following year there was again a contest in the election of parnassim. Three candidates were put forward in opposition to the two nominees of the retiring Mahamad, both of whom, Edward Foligno and Joseph Mayer Montefiore, were elected. In 1860 there was a further step in the transfer of power to the Yehidim when the election of all stipendiary officers of the Congregation was entrusted to them.

The new edition of the Ascamot was printed and circulated to members in the year 1850. Differing from its predecessors it was composed in English, although that of 1819 was printed also in English as a translation from the Portuguese. A comparison of the new version with that of 1663 will show how considerable were the changes that had taken place during the two centuries. The new version consisted of 37 ascamot, 2 ascamot of the Yehidim, and the others ascamot of the Elders. In the version of 1663 there were 42 ascamot, all of one class—not divided between Yehidim and Elders. Of the 35 ascamot of the Elders, eight related to subsidiary institutions and trusts that had been created during the intervening period. The comparison is therefore between 42 ascamot in 1663 and 29 in 1850. The first of the ascamot of the Yehidim was the original Ascama No. 1, with, however, important changes. The prohibition on the establishment of another Sephardi congregation was limited to within six miles of Bevis Marks, and a congregation could be formed even within this limit if a meeting of the Yehidim approved by a majority of two-thirds. Furthermore, the penalties for transgressing this ascama were membership of the Congregation and refusal of burial in the normal reduced to a fine of varying amount, deprivation of rights of place in the Communal cemetery. The second of the ascamot of the Yehidim dealt with the institution of the finta and its distribution. In this matter great changes had also been effected in the course of the two centuries. Then came the ascamot of the Elders. The election of the Mahamad still rested with the retiring

SIR MOSES MONTEFIORE, BART., F.R.S.

HAHAM BENJAMIN ARTOM

SOLOMON ALMOSNINO

members, assisted by seven adjuntos or ex-members of the Mahamad. For the office of Gabay a candidate must be at least twenty-five years of age and for that of Parnas, thirty-five unless he had already served as Gabay. Candidates had to be Yehidim of at least two years' standing. No gabay or parnas could be re-elected to that office except after the expiration of an interval of four years. The penalty for refusal of acceptance of office was a fine of £30 and of absence of an elector, without good cause, 20s. Candidates of seventy years and upwards who declined candidature were exempt from fine. The Elders, apart from the adjuntos, were not to interfere in the election of the Mahamad except that they had the discretion to remit fines on those who refused election. 'Every person who has served or been fined for the office of Parnas or Gabay' shall from the time of his election become an Elder.

The admission of Yehidim rested with the Elders, who were enjoined to exercise great care and consideration in the office. 'Spanish and Portuguese Jews, or the descendants of such, who shall have congregated with our Community for at least twelve months ... those who, coming from abroad, have always followed our ritual, and those who shall have married, or be about to marry the daughter of a Yahid' were eligible for election as Yehidim, as were also widows and single women, but not married women. Nominations for election as Yehidim were to be made to the Elders by the Mahamad, but men whose qualification was marriage to a daughter of a Yahid should not be nominated without their consent. All others who could qualify could be nominated and elected without their agreement or knowledge. Any Yahid in receipt of relief or indebted to the Congregation for three years lost his privilege of being a Yahid. 'Should any Yahid of this Congregation depart from our Religion (which God avert), either by being baptized, publicly professing some other religion, or publicly profaning the Sabbath, such person shall be immediately excluded from the list of Yehidim.' Any Yahid convicted of a criminal offence was also summarily expelled. The disinclination against disputes between members of the Community coming before the public courts of justice still persisted. Any member of the Congregation submitting a dispute to such a court before placing the matter before the Mahamad was liable to a fine of £5.

The election of Hazanim rested with the Yehidim, but candidates, who were required to conduct the service in the synagogue for one week in turn, were invited by the Mahamad. 'All persons buying or selling any vote at any election shall be excluded from voting on that occasion.' In the event of a vacancy occurring in the office of Haham the Elders were bound to decide within three months whether the office should be filled. The election when held should be by a two-thirds majority of the Elders. Among the Haham's duties were the marrying of all members of the Congregation, but only with the written permission of two members of the Mahamad. 'He shall not intercede in favor of any candidate for an office in the Kaal, or applicant for assistance from the Sedaca, lest the respect due to him should induce a deviation from impartial justice.' The minor offices in the Community were also similarly filled by the Elders except that a two-thirds majority of the votes was not required.

The Sedaca fund was the main support of the Congregation out of which all of its payments, except those made under bequests or trusts, were made. Into it passed similarly all the free revenue of the Congregation, including offerings. Every person called to the Sepher had to offer a minimum of a shilling to this fund. He could also make further offerings for other specific purposes. In certain circumstances the Mahamad were bound to make equivalent offerings up to a maximum of 2s. 6d. each. On Purim three members of the Mahamad had to make collections among the congregation, and on the five minor feasts the secretary had similarly to take the collecting plate round among the worshippers in synagogue.

The distribution of seats in the synagogue rested with a complete Mahamad and were to 'be made with equity and to avoid the confusion or displeasure which the failure thereof might cause to any of the Yehidim'. 'As death makes no distinction of persons, it has been a very laudable custom in our Congregation and one which we ought to preserve, not to make any distinctions among the deceased, whether in respect to the graves, or the honours conferred in Synagogue.' As a consequence all Yehidim or Congregantes who died were to be buried in the *carrieras* or rows in the cemetery in the order of their burial, except for those buried in graves previously reserved for them (children to be in separate rows). The further exceptions from this rule were those who were considered by the Mahamad unworthy to lie next to their fellows. These were buried 'behind the boards'. All tombstones were to be equal in size and uniform in style, except in those cases in which the stones covered two graves. To this rule no exception was permitted. Similarly the size of the graves was limited. The prohibition on the making of proselytes was still strictly enforced. Other prohibitions were against contracting of marriage with a person of another faith or the consent 'to any such person passing by his name, this being at once a high religious offence, and tending to the injury and disquiet of the congregation'. Persons under the guardianship of parents or guardians were not allowed to marry without the consent of their guardians, nor were any members of the Congregation permitted to marry except with the permission of the Mahamad. Offenders against these regulations could be punished by a fine up to £20 or to expulsion from the ranks of the Yehidim. Despite the registration of births, marriages, and deaths that had a few years earlier been imposed by Parliament, similar registers were to continue to be kept for members of the Congregation, both the relative Hebrew and civil dates being entered in the registers. Ascama No. 22 recited the regulations governing the representation of the Congregation on the Board of Deputies of British Jews, the Deputies to be elected by the Yehidim. These Deputies were required to report to the Elders twice a year, and these reports could be discussed and instructions on them given to the representatives of the Congregation at the Board.

Among the regulations governing the grant of relief there was one for which presumably there was adequate need.

'Should any person summon the Gentlemen of the Mahamad, or the Elders of the Congregation, or anyone of them as an Elder before any Magistrate or Court of Justice, to complain of their not having answered his petition, or granted the charity he required, or any other complaint against our government, he shall be excluded from all benefits which he received or might receive from the Sedaca or Synagogue, until he have given satisfaction to the said Elders or Mahamad whom he have summoned.'

Finally (Ascama No. 27):

'The better to secure obedience to the penalties imposed by the different Ascamot. In all cases and at all times when any person shall be condemned by the Mahamad, in complete Mahamad, in any penalty, and shall not conform to the same within thirty days from the imposition thereof, no Misva shall be given him, nor shall an offering of more than a shilling be accepted from him, and that only for the Sedaca, nor shall any benefit from the Sedaca be granted to him except Matsot, but if at any time afterwards he shall profess himself ready to submit to the said penalty, and to what further the Mahamad and their Adjuntos shall impose on him, in consideration of the time he persisted in his contumacy, he shall be relieved from the above named penalties.'

In many respects these ascamot followed those of 1784.

In the meanwhile the office of Haham vacated by the death of Raphael Meldola in 1828 remained unfilled. As has been said, during this long interval the duties of this office were performed, as well as they could be, by a succession of dayanim who when necessary called in rubiim attached to the Medrash to form a quorum. The arrangement was not entirely satisfactory, but for one reason or another there was no alternative to it. Barnett Abrahams died at the early age of thirty-two after a few days' illness, in December 1863. His death was a great loss. Not only was he himself a tower of strength but also a beacon of promise. His youth and his brief term of office, both weaknesses that time would have removed, were the only hindrances to his appointment later as the spiritual head of the Community. His Ashkenazi origin might have been a hindrance, but that he had already neutralized by his complete absorption into his adopted community. And, furthermore, the appointment of a rabbi of Ashkenazi origin as a Haham would not have been without precedent. A generation later such a step was taken, even by the London Community. If Abrahams had lived a normal span and, as is very probable, had been appointed Haham he would probably have taken his place among the most distinguished holders of the office in the roll of Bevis Marks. He died at the beginning of his career, leaving a widow and six little children and a vacant office that there was no one to fill. As a temporary measure the three Hazanim—David Piza, Samuel de Sola, and Joseph Piperno—were appointed a provisional Beth Din, and urgent consideration was given to the question of appointing a Haham. Abrahams' eldest son, Joseph, as he grew up was carefully educated at the expense of the Community with a view to his entering its service. He did become a Jewish minister, but not at Bevis Marks. His brother, Moses, also entered the Jewish ministry, at Leeds. The most widely known of the four sons was the third, Israel, man of letters and for very many years a leader in England in Jewish life and thought. A brother of Barnett Abrahams, Mordecai, joined the Community shortly after his brother's death. He remained connected with it in a subordinate capacity, generally in reserve for temporary employment whenever the necessity arose, throughout his active life. He had two children of whom the brilliant son, Sir Lionel Abrahams, K.C.B., rose to the high office of Assistant Under-Secretary of State in the India Office in London—dying at the early age of fifty.

Turning back, of the Hazanim, Isaac Almosnino, who had been appointed in 1819 and died in 1843, was a member of the family that had come from Gibraltar and gave several trusted servants to the London Community. Steps were taken to appoint a successor, but before doing so an attempt was made to change the method of remuneration to bring it into accordance with the new attitude towards ministers of religion. Hitherto the remuneration of the Hazanim had been partly in the form of salary, partly by voluntary offerings made in the Synagogue by worshippers week by week, which of course varied in total. The proposed alteration took the form of fixing an inclusive salary, the whole of which would have been paid out of the congregational funds, leaving to those funds any voluntary offerings. For the time being this proposal was defeated, and when in August 1845 David Piza of the Spanish and Portuguese Jewish Congregation of Montreal was appointed to fill the vacancy caused by the death of Almosnino it was at a salary of £100 a year and a residence free of rent, and in addition one-half of the offerings made for the benefit of the Hazanim. But this was not for long. Before the end of the same year consolidated salaries were substituted for the varying payments to the Hazanim and also to the Samas, who was paid under a similar system. The salary of the Samas was fixed at this time as £12 a year with a frock coat with gold lace every two years and a hat with a gold band every year. Piza was, however, not elected unanimously. Other candidates were put forward, but there was only one other serious competitor, Abraham de Sola, a son of the Senior Hazan. At the election Piza received forty-seven votes from the Yehidim and de Sola thirty-one. Of the other candidates Sabbathai Moraes, who later attained distinction in North America, secured only three, and David Bolaffy and Judah Mudahy, both with London Sephardi connexions, none. Abraham de Sola, failing to secure an appointment in London, succeeded Piza in Montreal.

At the same time Abraham Mendes who had some years before been sent from Jamaica to England to study returned to Kingston as Hazan in the Sephardi Community there. He did not, however, remain there for long, but returned to England.

David Aaron de Sola died in 1860 in his sixty-fourth year and in the forty-third of his ministry, and his son, Samuel de Sola, was appointed to succeed him, but at first as assistant to the Hazan, Piza becoming Senior Hazan. Samuel de Sola had been the first nominee of the Sephardi Community to be educated at Jews' College, and was, in fact, designated from his childhood for the office to which he was elected after the death of his father. Two years later steps were taken to define the duties of all Hazanim who might be appointed in future. They were to be required, in addition to the normal duties of the office, to preach in English at regular intervals and to attend occasionally 'at the educational establishments of the Congregation'. An attempt was made to lay down also that they should be bound to visit the sick and the poor, but this condition, adopted in the first instance, failed to secure confirmation. The duty was apparently left to the option of the officials concerned. Samuel de Sola died in September 1866, aged only twenty-seven, a few days after the long-delayed appointment of a Haham. Two years earlier Abraham Pereira Mendes had been appointed, as a private arrangement, preacher by the worshippers in the Branch Synagogue.

But the conduct of the services, important as they were, was of less importance than the spiritual guidance of the Community, and for this there was no provision. At first steps were taken to find a haham and a candidate was interviewed. Whether or not he was considered suitable for the office cannot be said, for that point in the procedure was never reached. The Elders could not agree among themselves on the salary to be appropriated to the office. £500, £400, £300 a year were all successively proposed at a meeting of Elders and defeated. £250 secured a majority, but not one of two-thirds as was required by the Ascamot. The proposal to appoint a Haham was thereupon abandoned for the time being, and applications for the office of 'Head Dayan' at a salary of £200 a year with a residence invited. But there was no response. The terms offered were obviously not sufficiently attractive. The advocates of the appointment of a spiritual head were, however, not dismayed. The campaign was transferred from the Elders to the Yehidim as a body and within a few days of a year from the day on which the proposal had been wrecked on the rock of finance, the Yehidim decided that an ecclesiastical head of the Community should be appointed, if possible within six months, at a salary of £400 a year and a residence. There was still some disinclination to act on this instruction, but when a candidate was proposed who seemed fitted in all respects for the office, and who might be expected to bring lustre to it, an appointment no longer lagged. Benjamin Artom, a young man of thirty, a scholar in secular subjects as well as in the Hebrew and Jewish theological sphere, was invited to come to London to be interviewed. A man of strikingly handsome presence, outstanding and inspiring as a preacher, he was in addition a musician. Born at Asti, near Genoa, he was at the time of his appointment in London Haham of Naples whose Jewish community he may be said to have created. He came to London and found favour with everyone whom he met. His first sermon delivered in London on 29 April 1866 was in French, for he knew no English. But so speedily did he acquire the language that he was able to preach in it when he next addressed his congregation. The Yehidim recommended his election to the Elders. This recommendation the latter at once accepted, appointing a salary of £350 a year and a suitable residence in the City Road. The Mahamad overruled the Elders by increasing the figure which was, however, a matter of minor consequence, for on Artom's marrage seven years later to a sister of Mrs. Reuben Sassoon, a member of the leading family in the Community, his salary was increased to £700 a year. The couple were married in the house of Reuben Sassoon in Lancaster Gate, and another precedent was created in Anglo-Jewish history when the marriage ceremony was conducted by the Ashkenazi Chief Rabbi, Nathan Adler.

In the meanwhile the congregation was showing signs of continued development and growth in other respects. An attempt to reconsider the method of admitting Yehidim, made in 1840, failed, and the high-handed procedure of imposing compulsory membership of the Community on any Sephardi Jew who happened to be resident within reach, even though far more than a sabbath day's journey, of Bevis Marks continued to be followed. The imposition of fines for refusal of office or failure to attend meetings also remained in force, despite attempts, supported by the Mahamad of the day, to introduce a more liberal practice, and they continued to be imposed until 1882. The Gentlemen of the Mahamad were, however, in 1854 relieved of the compulsory offerings to which they were subjected on certain occasions. The Ascamot underwent another revision early in 1871 with a view to the issue of a new edition of them in the following year. The question of the holding of regular services outside the walls of Bevis Marks also arose again, but that battle had been finally fought and won with the opening of the Branch Synagogue in Wigmore Street in 1853. Even earlier, in 1833, a Sephardi synagogue had been opened at Ramsgate, but this was of course for worshippers to whom attendance at Bevis Marks was out of the question. In the meanwhile the rigidity of Ascama No. 1 had been removed and permission to open a synagogue elsewhere, even within six miles of Bevis Marks, had been left to the discretion of the Yehidim. Thus when, in 1865, Solomon Haim Andrade asked for permission to open a synagogue which he had had built in his garden in the Lower Road (now Essex Road), Islington, the Mahamad told him that under the Ascama his request could not be granted, but that if his health prevented his attendance at synagogue, permission would be given for prayers to be read in his house on the New Year and the Day of Atonement. The application was, however, pressed and referred to a meeting of the Yehidim, who at once gave the required permission, provisionally for one year, and sepharim were lent to Andrade for use on the approaching festivals. Unfortunately Andrade died before the year expired. At its end the request was renewed by his widow and at once granted unanimously. These services continued until 1884 by which time the congregation had become too large for the small synagogue that had been erected. Solomon Pool, a son-in-law of David Aaron de Sola, an Ashkenazi who had on his marriage been admitted to the Sephardi Community and had attained to an influential position in it, received permission in 1883 to open in place of it another synagogue in Canonbury, later removed to a neighbouring site and for long known as the Mildmay Park Synagogue. This was given a permanent status in 1886, with financial, if not ecclesiastical, independence. The normal attendance on the sabbath was at that time 24 men, 21 women, 73 children, and 3 Ashkenazim. These represented 63 seatholders. The full accommodation was, however, 200. This small congregation grew and flourished. But fashions in place of residence change. Middle-class Jewry left Canonbury and Highbury for other suburbs, and by 1928 the congregation was virtually extinct. It lingered on with services only at New Year and *Kippur* until 1936, when the Synagogue was finally closed. Some of its fittings were ten years later transferred to the 'Little Synagogue' that was opened as an adjunct to that of Lauderdale Road. Reuben Sassoon had also almost twenty years earlier received permission to hold divine service occasionally in his private house in London which was certainly within six miles of Bevis Marks and still closer to Bryanston Street.

Nevertheless there was continued difficulty in securing a quorum in the Western Branch Synagogue on weekdays. Artom had not long been inducted into office—on which occasion it may be mentioned recourse had to be had to the services of the Ashkenazi choirmaster of the Great Synagogue, Julius (Israel) Mombach, far more than a choirmaster, also a composer of renown of synagogue music—when after a visit to the Branch Synagogue in Bryanston Street he reported that that synagogue was 'nearly always in a deplorable solitude'. Since the members could not be induced to attend in sufficient numbers Artom pressed for the engaging of a paid minyan. The strength of his case was admitted but the number of Sephardim living within easy distance of the synagogue, and willing to attend regularly even on payment, was too small to complete the required quorum. In the circumstances there was no alternative to the engagement of Ashkenazim for the purpose, but this step was taken only after much hesitation and some delay. There was at this period also much dissatisfaction with the state of the choirs in both synagogues. This dissatisfaction covered a long period. In the end, early in 1871, the choirs in both synagogues were drastically reorganized and a choirmaster, a trained musician, was appointed, in the person of Henri de Solla, who as a boy had been expelled together with his parents from the Community for taking part in the choir of the West London Synagogue. An alternative candidate on this occasion was Michel or Michael Bergson, the father of the philosopher Henri Bergson. If he had been elected, the worshippers at Bryanston Street, perhaps the choristers, would have included, at any rate for a time, one of the most famous of the sons of Jewry. The arrangement with de Solla did not, however, last long, for, objecting to the conditions it was proposed to impose on him, he resigned and the choirs soon relapsed into their previous unsatisfactory state. De Solla was reappointed to his old office in 1877.

Artom held his office in London for too short a period to leave a permanent influence in the Community. His principal contribution that survived is the prayer of the Barmitzvah which he composed and introduced. This also was one of the first steps he took after his appointment. Previously the practice had grown up, for which formal permission was given in 1852, for the Barmitzvah to give an address in synagogue. Artom was not only a musician but also a composer, and some of his compositions are still sung in the synagogue. He was a regular preacher, and many members of other communities used to attend to hear him. In these circumstances it is not surprising that he received and accepted many invitations to preach in Ashkenazi synagogues. In the West London Synagogue he of course could not preach, but there was no prohibition on his making friends among its members. In this he was merely following the example set by an earlier Hazan, also a scholar and a man of general culture, David Aaron de Sola. Artom's influence spread far beyond his immediate community and the fruits of that influence outside returned in an enhancement of the prestige of the Sephardim of England, a prestige that had declined during the long interregnum. In the sphere of communal education also the personality of the new Haham showed itself. Early in 1869 the Villa Real School for Girls and the National and Infant School were combined in one institution, the description of

Villa Real pupils to keep alive the memory of Isaac Villa Real, the founder of the senior institution, being retained for the girls of the highest class. The other principal educational or cultural institution of the Community, the Heshaim, underwent a thorough investigation by the Elders in 1842 in the course of which disagreements rose to so high a pitch that the President of the Elders, David Abarbanel Lindo, produced a written resignation, which he had presumably prepared before coming to the meeting. Lindo was apparently a very difficult person with whom to work in committee, and his colleagues had experienced many previous troubles and unpleasantnesses. Lindo resigned and left the room in the middle of the meeting. His place was taken by Edward Foligno, the President of the Mahamad, and under his direction the business proceeded. A fortnight later Foligno was formally elected President of the Elders in Lindo's place. At the meeting at which Lindo resigned, the Elders approved of the proposals of the governors and subscribers to the Heshaim. These were revolutionary. In future 'a classical education' was to be provided for 'a limited number of youths so as to qualify them in time to be received as students in the Medrash, or to fill clerical or civil offices with the Congregation'. This was in effect a forerunner of Jews' College, but limited to the Sephardi Community. The programme was too ambitious, for no scholar in secular as well as religious subjects is known to have come out of the Medrash. Twenty-three years later reform took another direction. The Medrash, which founded in 1664 was, apart from the synagogue, the oldest of the institutions of the Community, was combined with the Yeshiba Mahané Rephael, an institution with kindred objects, founded in 1734. They continued their activities under the title of Heshaim and Mahané Rephael.

All this time, slowly but increasingly, the Community was taking its share in the larger life of the country. In common with other religious communities the English Sephardim joined in the national joys and the national sorrows. When Queen Victoria was married in 1840 the Congregation, in co-operation with the other principal Jewish congregations of the country, offered its humble duty and congratulations to the Queen, the Prince Consort, and the Queen's mother, the Duchess of Kent, and on the occasions of the successive births of princesses and princes that followed, the Congregation similarly gave expression to the loyalty and pleasure of its members. In 1849 when the cholera scourge reappeared special prayers were offered in the synagogue every Monday and Thursday, and on its end a special sermon was preached by David Aaron de Sola. Five years later, in the midst of the Crimean War, when funds were being raised for the relief of the dependants of the members of the armed forces engaged, Bevis Marks also came forward and took its part. And when in 1862 the American Civil War brought unemployment and starvation to the cotton workers of the north of England and their families, the members of and worshippers in Bevis Marks held a special meeting at which to give expression to their sympathy.

'That this meeting recognizes it as a sacred duty to assist to the utmost, the efforts now making for the relief of the suffering operatives in the North of England, and that for this purpose a committee of five members be appointed, jointly with the Gentlemen of the Mahamad, to collect and receive contributions from the Congregation in such a manner as they may deem advisable, with authority to transfer the sums so collected to the Central Committee at the Mansion House,'

was the resolution unanimously adopted. A total of almost £250 was collected for the purpose. In the year 1873 the Metropolitan Hospitals Sunday Fund was instituted. The Sephardi Community appears to have been overlooked by the Lord Mayor when he took his first steps for the constitution of the fund, but, as soon as his attention had been directed to the omission, it was made good with an expression of regret. The Haham, Benjamin Artom, was appointed the representative of the Community on the council of the fund and took his seat at its table. He preached a sermon at the first hospital Sunday service held on Sunday, 15 June 1873, and almost £200 was subscribed by members and transmitted to the Mansion House. Henceforward the Hospital Sunday Service was until 1950 a regular feature in the Synagogue year. Coincidentally, there were the usual appeals for assistance from Jewries in all the four corners of the world, and to most of them a response was given. But the story of these is to a great extent a part of the larger one of the world-renowned philanthropist of the nineteenth century, Moses Montefiore, in many respects the greatest and most distinguished son whom Bevis Marks has produced.

Although much of importance in Anglo-Sephardi history happened in the course of the nineteenth century and has already been recorded, that century in Anglo-Sephardi and also in world Jewish history was essentially the era of Sir Moses Montefiore. Occasionally reference has been made to him in the preceding pages, for it would have been impossible to write any part of the story of the Sephardim in England after the second decade of the nineteenth century without mention of Montefiore, if only in passing. Moses Montefiore was of the third English generation of his family, being a grandson of another Moses Vita (or Haim) Montefiore, one of four brothers who came to London from Leghorn in the middle of the eighteenth century and settled there. This was a continuation, almost the end, of the Jewish immigration that followed in the wake of the appointment of David Nieto, also from Leghorn, as Haham. In England the family engaged in business in which some of them attained success, but until the time of Sir Moses none of the family could be considered wealthy. He, however, entered finance as one of the licensed brokers, to which he was introduced by his wealthy connexions, above all, his father-in-law, Levi Barent Cohen, his brother-in-law, Nathan Mayer Rothschild, and his maternal uncle, Moses Mocatta, and was so successful that he was able to retire on his fortune at the age of forty-two to devote the greater part of the long life that was before him to public service. In the course of his business career, among other activities, he was concerned with Rothschild in raising in 1835 the loan by which the British Government was able to emancipate all slaves still remaining on British territory. He was one of the founders of the Alliance Assurance Company and of the Imperial Continental Gas Association, the pioneer in gas lighting on the Continent, of which organization he remained president until his death. He was also a director of the South Eastern Railway Company and of the Provincial Bank of Ireland, and had the opportunity, which he declined, of being an original director of the Suez Canal Company.

Montefiore early showed his interest in Jewish public life and administration. At the age of thirty he served as gabay and five years later he was elected a parnas, being elected again to that office for five separate terms. These were only his principal offices in Bevis Marks. His influence in the counsels of the Community grew from year to year, and it was not long before, whether or not he happened to hold office at the time, his influence in Anglo-Jewry surpassed that of any other Yahid. In Anglo-Jewry as a whole, for among the Ashkenazim as among the Sephardim he reigned supreme, he was recognized by all as the leading Jew of England. He was first elected a representative of the Sephardi Community on the Jewish Board of Deputies in 1825 and became its president in succession to Moses Mocatta in 1835. He remained a member representing his congregation, during the last years no longer an active one in consequence of his increasing years, until 1874 when, despite the pressure of the Yehidim to remain, he refused re-election. Until that year he remained president, although only nominally so during the last few years. Occasionally, when absent on one of his missions abroad, he would be replaced for a few months, as a rule by a kinsman or family connexion, but always on his return to England Montefiore resumed the office. When he finally retired he was succeeded by his nephew, Joseph Mayer Montefiore. More or less a part of his duties as president of the Board was the series of missions he undertook to foreign governments in the interests of the suffering Jews of their dominions. On these missions he went nominally as the emissary of Anglo-Jewry, but more properly, if not officially, as the ambassador of Jewry as a whole. The first of these missions was in 1840 to Alexandria, the capital city of Mehemet Ali, at the time ruler of Syria as well as of Egypt, and later to Constantinople to whose rule Syria returned while he was still absent from England. The occasion of this mission was the accusation of ritual murder brought against a number of the leading Jews of Damascus, and the risk not only of their conviction, under pressure by the French representative, but also of their execution. Montefiore had the open support of the British Government in his mission, and with the aid of the British Consul-General in Alexandria secured not the pardon which was at first offered so as not to annoy the French, at the time Mehemet Ali's only friends, but the quashing of all proceedings that had been taken, on the ground that they were not based on justice. On his return to Europe, Montefiore, who was accompanied on this mission by Louis Loewe, passed through Istanbul (then Constantinople), where he obtained from the all-powerful Sultan a promise of humane and equal treatment for all his Jewish subjects as well as for those in the other *millets* or minority religious groups. In the *Hatti Sherif* which the Sultan Abdul Medjid issued on this occasion, he denounced the ritual murder charge, wherever made against Jews, as baseless, and ordered the Chief Justice of his Empire to note this ruling and to put it into effect whenever the occasion arose. Montefiore had gone to the East with the encouragement of Queen Victoria and her Government. On his return he was received by the Queen, who 'in commemoration of these his unceasing exertions on behalf of his injured and persecuted brethren in the East and the Jewish Nation at large' granted him the exceptional distinction of supporters to his arms. Four years earlier he had been made a knight at the end of his term of office as Sheriff of London in the year of the Queen's accession. Montefiore was the second English Jew to hold the office as sheriff. The first was his wife's nephew, David

Salomons, later Sir David Salomons, Bart., M.P., who was elected to the office two years earlier. Montefiore also was the second professing English Jew to be knighted, his predecessor in the reign of William and Mary having been Sir Solomon de Medina, a kinsman of his great-grandmother, Sarah Medina. Later, after his first mission to Russia in 1846, the Queen conferred on him the dignity of a baronet. In the words of the letter from the Prime Minister, Sir Robert Peel,

> 'This mark of royal favour is bestowed upon you in consideration of your high character and eminent position in the ranks of a loyal and estimable class of Her Majesty's subjects agreeing with you in religious profession and in the hope that it may aid your truly benevolent efforts to improve the social condition of the Jews in other countries by temperate appeals to the justice and humanity of their rulers.'

The mission on behalf of the Damascus victims was the first of those undertaken by Montefiore. There followed that of 1846 to Russia for the purpose of dissuading the Czar Nicholas from the course on which he had set himself, of deporting a large number of his Jewish subjects inland from their homes in the frontier provinces. Simultaneously the Czar had intimated that he would be pleased if Montefiore would come to Russia to consult with the Russian Government on the subject of proposed educational reforms for the Jews of the Empire, to which the Jews had shown themselves resolutely opposed. The following year a new charge of ritual murder, again supported by the local consular representative of France, was made in Damascus—in which the alleged victim was found after an interval unharmed in the not far distant town of Baalbec—and Montefiore went to Paris as a consequence and was granted audience by the King, Louis Philippe, and his Prime Minister, Pierre Guizot, on the subject. In 1858 Montefiore went to Rome in an unsuccessful attempt, despite the support of the British, French, and Austrian governments, to secure the restoration to his parents of a Jewish child, Edgar Mortara, who had been secretly baptized by his nurse. On this occasion Montefiore failed even to obtain an interview with the Pope, despite the support of the British and French representatives. In 1863, although almost eighty years of age, he did not hesitate to proceed to Morocco to intercede on behalf of the Jews of that empire in response to an appeal by them, being received by Queen Isabella of Spain and her Prime Minister in order to secure their support when passing through Madrid. By then Montefiore had become the generally acknowledged representative of the Jews of the world. In his address to the Sultan of Morocco he was able to say, 'I come supported by the sanction and approval of the Government of Her Majesty, the Queen of Great Britain, and on behalf of my co-religionists in England, my native country, as well as on the part of those in every part of the world.' On his return journey he was received again by the Queen of Spain and also by the Emperor of the French, and in England by the Queen. Three years later, when trouble arose in Persia, he determined to undertake an even more arduous journey for a man of his age, eighty-one, and was dissuaded only with great difficulty from doing so by the Foreign Office. The address that he desired to present to the Shah was taken charge of by the British Minister in Tehran, who obtained a reply as gratifying as any that could have been given to Montefiore himself. This was, however, not the end of Montefiore's journeys on behalf of Jewry. In 1867 he went to Rumania. On this mission he received not only British support, but also that of the Russian Government, and the encouragement of those of Prussia, France, Austria, and Italy. The Ruling Prince was friendly, but the people hostile almost to a man, and as a consequence, despite the influential support he received, his efforts to secure an improvement in the political and social position of the Jews of the newly constituted state were not successful. His second visit to Russia was of a different character. The bi-centenary of the birth of Peter the Great fell in 1872. The Jewish Board of Deputies adopted a resolution of congratulation for the occasion and Montefiore, its president, then eighty-eight years of age, undertook to present it in person. He received a cordial welcome from the Czar, Alexander II, who actually left the military manœuvres that were proceeding to return to his capital to receive his visitor, sparing him a further journey. On his return through the Jewish districts of western Russia and Poland, Montefiore was received by the Jewish population who came out in their thousands and their tens of thousands, as a returning conqueror, or perhaps more appropriately as the forerunner of the Messiah. He even contemplated another journey to Russia in the following year to present in person an address of congratulation adopted by the Board of Deputies on the occasion of the betrothal of the Duke of Edinburgh, second son of Queen Victoria, and a Russian princess, but he was dissuaded from this course by the Russian Ambassador. Included in the reply of the Czar was a personal message to Montefiore.

A philanthropist in the full sense of the term, Montefiore did not limit his sympathy to his fellow Jews. His benefactions, public and private, which were widespread, included Christians, Jews, and Moslems among their recipients. When in Morocco his attention was drawn to the case of some Moslems who, he was of opinion, had been improperly convicted and sentenced to death. His appeal on their behalf saved their lives. Earlier in 1860, when the Christian population of the Lebanon suffered severely at the hands of their neighbours, the Druses, his heart was touched. It was on his initiative that the British Syrian Relief Committee was founded. He was elected chairman of its executive committee, and until a year of his death he was a frequent attendant at its meetings. Recognition of his services and of his labours was universal. Of the Jewish response both in England and on the Continent mention has already been made. So has the support given him by Queen Victoria and her successive governments and the honours conferred on him by the Queen. On his return from Morocco in 1863 Austen Henry (later Sir Henry) Layard, the Under-Secretary of State for Foreign Affairs, in the House of Commons bore testimony to 'the noble and generous spirit of humanity and philanthropy which actuates him, without reference to any sect or creed, which extends to the people of every nation who are suffering wrong and injustice'. At a public meeting held to welcome him back the resolution of thanks was moved by Sir Anthony de Rothschild and seconded by William Ewart Gladstone, the Chancellor of the Exchequer and future Prime Minister, and at a distinguished gathering in the Guildhall the Freedom of the City of London was conferred on him. In Montefiore's own Community special services were held in his honour on the occasion of the return from every one of his missions abroad and sometimes to speed him on his journey. The first of these was that of 1840 after his return from Constantinople, and a copy of the firman issued by the Sultan in response to his intercession was transcribed on vellum and ordered to be exhibited in a conspicuous position in the Mahamad Chamber. In 1846, on the return from Russia, Lady Montefiore was specially included in the celebrations. The address presented to the couple on that occasion was so effusive as almost to overshoot its mark. 'The Elders gladly avail themselves of this opportunity to convey to Lady Montefiore in the name of the Congregation their grateful acknowledgements for the heroism she has displayed in sharing the trials and dangers of her honoured partner in his philanthropic missions.' Lady Montefiore as a rule accompanied her husband on these missions. At the special service held in Bevis Marks on the occasion of Montefiore's

JACOB QUIXANO HENRIQUES
From a photograph

SIR JOSEPH SEBAG-MONTEFIORE
From a painting by Solomon J. Solomon, R.A.

HAHAM MOSES GASTER
From a painting by Moses Maimon

return from Morocco in 1864 prayers, prepared for the occasion by Moses Picciotto, the President of the Elders, were recited. This Moses Picciotto was the father of James Picciotto, the first of the Jewish historians of Anglo-Jewry. He was called on by the Mahamad on other special occasions to compose prayers. The last two birthdays of Montefiore were not limited in celebration to his own Community. The whole of Anglo-Jewry, the whole of World Jewry, joined in them. He was not of the Sephardim of England alone. The Jews of all the five continents claimed their share in him.

Montefiore's passion for the welfare of Jewry in all the lands of its habitation was rivalled only by one other passion, that for the welfare of Palestine, Jewry's ancient home. Seven times did he visit the country and not as a tourist, but as a student and a pilgrim, making not merely a week-end excursion, but on every occasion remaining for a lengthy stay. So long as she lived Lady Montefiore always accompanied him on these visits. The first of the series, the visit of 1827, a year after his retirement from the Exchange, was made partly as a devout pilgrim to the Holy Land of his religious beliefs, the land in which his ancestors first became a people, partly as a student to learn the state of the country and of its people and the means of improving them if improvement were called for. The lands of the Levant—and the seas also—were then in a state of disturbance, a state to which that part of the world had long been accustomed, and visitors from the West ran some risk in travelling there. Furthermore, a visit to the lands of the Levant was in those days a costly and uncomfortable undertaking. Visitors were consequently few and far between. Jewish visitors from the West were even more exceptional than Christian ones and if one designated the Montefiores as the first Western Jews of modern times to visit Palestine the statement would not need much, if any, correction. The pilgrims were away from England for ten months. The battle of Navarino, which sealed the independence of Greece, was fought on the day preceding that on which they started on their return journey. At Malta they met the victorious commander, Admiral Sir Edward Codrington, and it was to Montefiore that he entrusted his dispatch in which he described the battle. On his arrival in London, Montefiore's first business was to deliver the dispatch at the Admiralty where he was received by the future King William IV. After the conclusion of his year as Sheriff of London, in 1837, the Montefiores set out on their second visit. During the intervening twelve years he had given much thought to Palestine. This time he went out not as a curious visitor, but as one intent on studying a problem and finding means of solving it. This problem was the overwhelming poverty of the Jews of the Holy Land, the consequent desire of the younger and more ambitious ones to leave the country and the hopelessness of those who remained. To the solution of this problem Montefiore devoted much of the remaining years of his life. He speedily reached certain conclusions. Unless something were done to inspire and unify the Jewish population of Palestine there could be no more hope for their future than for their present. Alms and more alms were insistently necessary, but these were not the end. Jewish religious observance and study were very close to his heart and deserved every encouragement, but they also were not the only end. His aim was a healthy body as well as a healthy mind for the Jews of Palestine—study and religious observance supported by the work of one's hands. To secure these was the aim Montefiore put before himself. The need for alms was in the meanwhile great, and Montefiore did not stint himself in supplying this. But as a philanthropist and perhaps also as a statesman he did not close his eyes to the needs of the other inhabitants of the land. Among the Arabs also there was dire poverty and to relieve this also he assisted. Whether or not he ever looked forward to the political future of the Jews of Palestine there is no evidence. If he did it must have been to ensuring a land in which Jew and Arab would live together in peace as fellow citizens.

In the course of his subsequent visits to Palestine and in the intervals between them Montefiore gave much attention to the possibility of agricultural revival. He spent money on two projects aimed towards this end. The one was Jewish agricultural settlement in Upper Galilee, in the neighbourhood of Safad and Tiberias, where another prince in Israel, Don Joseph Nasi, had three centuries earlier endeavoured to found agricultural settlements of Jews. Montefiore's scheme, like Nasi's, was a failure. But both failures helped to fertilize the ground in which others who came after them were able successfully to plant. Another effort of Montefiore in the same sphere was the purchase of land near Jaffa and the settlement of a Jewish family on it in the hope that from this small plot as a nucleus a Jewish agricultural settlement would spring. But this also was a failure, and it is doubtful whether the farmer or gardener—the plot was later known as the Montefiore Garden—made sufficient profit by his exertions to maintain himself and his family. This project has in a sense survived. Whereas even the site of the project in Galilee is forgotten and cannot be identified, that near Jaffa has retained the name Montefiore. On it is built the Montefiore Quarter of Tel Aviv. The other reminders—apart from tradition—of Montefiore in Palestine today are the Montefiore mill in Jerusalem, built by him to enable the local Jews to grind their corn, but never used, the neighbouring Montefiore colony or suburb, originally a group of almshouses built out of a legacy of £10,000 bequeathed by a North American Jewish philanthropist, Judah Touro, with Montefiore as trustee. Montefiore himself largely increased the sum at his disposal and, with the almshouses as a nucleus, other houses, privately built, grew up around them. The only worthy concrete object in Palestine with which Montefiore's name is connected is, however, the groups of houses built and disposed of on a building society plan which were financed by the Sir Moses Montefiore Testimonial Fund raised in London in 1875 to commemorate his services to the Jewish Community and devoted to the erection of Jewish suburbs of Jerusalem. One of these suburbs or districts consisting of comfortable middle-class houses is known by his name, and another older group of houses now well within the city bears the name Zichron Moshe, the Memorial of Moses.

Montefiore's ninety-ninth birthday was celebrated with worldwide rejoicing, led by a personal message from the Queen herself and a vote of congratulation by the Common Council of the City of London, presented by a delegation that went to Ramsgate for the purpose. The following year his hundredth birthday was celebrated with even greater enthusiasm—throughout the British Empire and the Jewish world—in the midst of which the Queen again sent a personal message and a service of thanksgiving was held in the Bevis Marks Synagogue at which the Ashkenazi Delegate Chief Rabbi, Hermann Adler, preached. The Synagogue was decorated with red and yellow flowers, the Spanish national colours. A banquet was given by the President of the Elders: dinners were arranged for five hundred of the poor of all communities, the women being presented with half a pound of tea, and the men with two ounces of tobacco each. There were also festivities for the children of the communal schools and the adult inmates of the congregational institutions. Montefiore died before another year had passed, at Ramsgate on 28 July 1885. The whole of Jewry mourned, and the English people joined respectfully in the mourning. In his death Montefiore thought above all of the needs of his fellow Jews. Of the fortune that he left, a large portion was bequeathed in trust to the Spanish and Portuguese Congregation, of the income of which added to that of his existing endowment of 1866[1] some £4,000 a year was earmarked for the endowment and maintenance of the Judith Lady Montefiore College at Ramsgate which he had built and supported in memory of his wife who had predeceased him in 1862, and the synagogue there. Stocks and shares of the nominal value of £32,000 bringing in £1,240 a year were to be devoted to the assistance of the Jewish poor in the four Holy Cities of Palestine, and a further £13,000 of investments, bringing in £650 a year, to the provision of coals and blankets for the Jewish poor of London, one-half to be administered by the Ashkenazi Community and double portions to go to those who had followed his example and married members of the sister community. There were also legacies to the Repairs Fund of the Congregation and to the *Yeshiba Assifat Haberim* which had been amalgamated with the Heshaim or Beth Hamedrash. In Jewries abroad, in those of the East, in Europe and in Asia, it was long before it was realized that his life was ended. Like other great men in history—Alexander, Napoleon—by those to whom in life he was a name and a tradition he was thought to be immortal. Men like him could never die. Many years had to pass before appeals for assistance from the farthest limits of the world of Jewry finally ceased to arrive in many languages addressed to Sir Moses Montefiore, at East Cliff Lodge, Ramsgate.

[1] This endowment consisted of the college premises, ten dwelling-houses with their contents, including a valuable library. The funds, the income from which was to be devoted to the upkeep of these buildings, consisted of £9,000 Bank of England Stock and 500 shares in the Alliance Assurance Company.

CHAPTER XVIII

A THREAT TO BEVIS MARKS

BENJAMIN ARTOM DIED quite unexpectedly on 6 January 1879 after a few hours' illness while on a visit to Brighton. He was only in his forty-fourth year and had held the office of Haham for but twelve years. At the time of his appointment a new era had opened in which the qualifications required for the office of Haham were not only Jewish scholarship and a character and influence in line with those of the outstanding spiritual leaders of Jewry, but also that he should be a man of culture, in the English sense of the term, of a wider education than that of the Jewish theological college, and with the *savoir-faire* of the new world that had by now opened. Artom was fortunate in being able to meet these requirements. Men with his gifts were not yet numerous in the world of Jewry. His premature and sincerely lamented death meant consequently an overwhelming loss. Artom lived too short a life to make a deep impress on English Jewish life, but his memory and influence lasted long and the lengthy interval that ensued before a successor in his office was appointed was a tribute to the high standard that he had set. Around Artom's bier the whole of Anglo-Jewry stood in mourning. Hermann Adler, the son of the Ashkenazi Chief Rabbi and later to be his successor, gave the memorial address, in place of his father who was unwell, and a second address was given by Aaron Levy Green, after the Adlers the outstanding preacher and minister in the Ashkenazi Community. The United Synagogue into which the principal Ashkenazi synagogues of the capital had by now been federated, the West London Synagogue, the rebel daughter of Bevis Marks, the principal provincial congregations and also the leading lay institutions, with the Board of Deputies and the Anglo-Jewish Association at their head, were all represented. At the end of the week of mourning a memorial service was held at which the address was given by Joseph, a son of the Dayan, Barnett Abrahams, who was being trained at the expense of the Community. A second memorial service was held at the end of the month of mourning at which Abraham Pereira Mendes preached, and at the end of eleven months there was yet another memorial service in the Bryanston Street Synagogue—at which Hermann Adler was invited to give the address.

Two actions of Artom during his term of office stand out and had their clear permanent effects. The one already mentioned was the introduction of the prayer for the *Barmitzvah*; the other was the precedent created by the admission of a proselyte to the Community, the first in its history. This step was taken in July 1877—revolutionary inasmuch as it went directly contrary to the traditional condition on which a Jewish Community in England had first been tolerated, a tradition that had become as sacred almost as any of the historic practices of world-wide Judaism. The condition, if at first probably for only a short time, observed by the Ashkenazim also, had long been ignored by them, and the Sephardi authorities never hesitated to accept proselytes who had been admitted by the Ashkenazi authorities in England or by either Ashkenazi or Sephardi authorities abroad; but Esther, daughter of Angelo Paris, who on her acceptance was given the name Miriam, was the first *Guera* to be admitted by the Sephardi authorities in England.

There was one other outstanding event during Artom's tenure of office. Hitherto the only Sephardi congregations in England had been in London. There was a synagogue in Ramsgate, but this was as yet hardly the centre of a community, more a private synagogue of Sir Moses Montefiore in which local Jewish residents were welcome. Small groups of Jews had from time to time come together in other cities of the kingdom and had occasionally arranged for the holding of services in accordance with the Sephardi ritual. One in Dublin has previously been mentioned. There are traces of Sephardi services having been held in Liverpool about 1750 for the benefit apparently of prospective emigrants or travellers to Ireland or North America, and there was at one time in the eighteenth century a group of Sephardim in Cork, but these were all transitory. The one exception was Manchester, hitherto not much more than a large village which the industrial expansion of the end of the eighteenth and the beginning of the nineteenth centuries transformed into the second largest city of the kingdom. There were Jewish residents in Manchester earlier, but it was not until 1780 that the first synagogue was opened there. This was for Ashkenazi Jews. Almost a century later, in 1872, the small Sephardi group that had in the meanwhile settled in the northern city, decided to establish a community of their own. The founders of this community and those on whose behalf they acted were Jews of the Orient, who had come from North Africa, Turkey, and the Levant, attracted by the growing commerce between England, especially Lancashire, and the lands of their birth. For ten years these strangers in a new land had met together for divine worship in one rented room after another, never remaining for long at any address. In February 1872, however, a number of them met and resolved to form a permanent congregation and to erect a synagogue of their own. The fourth day of that month was in fact the birthday of the Manchester Sephardi Community, which now, after the lapse of almost eighty years, is well established with its three handsome houses of prayer. The names of those who took the lead in the movement should be mentioned. Elia Negrin convened the meeting. Isaac D. Belisha, the grandfather of the Rt. Hon. Leslie Hore-Belisha and the great-grandfather of Mr. Manuel Cansino, was the first president of the Community, and one of his sons, Barrow I. Belisha, its assistant honorary secretary. The vice-president was Moses B. Messulam, the treasurer, Victor Levi, and the honorary secretary, Levy A. Cohen.

The first step taken was to approach the authorities in Bevis Marks, to whom the new congregation wished to look as to their parent. The desire was mutual and the approach of the Manchester group was met with equal cordiality in London. The new synagogue was intended to be formally quite independent of that of London, but both felt their kinship and the Manchester group instinctively accepted the spiritual guidance of that of London. The Elders of Bevis Marks were the first to be informed of the new project, and it was to them that the plans were communicated before the end of the month. The Mahamad and the Elders at once gave their encouragement and without hesitation promised their support to the appeal for funds that was about to be made to the Yehidim of London. The Elders headed this list of subscribers by voting three hundred guineas from congregational funds originally earmarked for captives, to which Sir Moses Montefiore at once added a gift of fifty pounds. Eight hundred pounds had been subscribed at the initial meeting in Manchester. A plot of land was purchased in the Cheetham Hill Road. The foundation stone was laid on 11 June 1873 by Sir Albert Sassoon in the presence of Sir Moses Montefiore, the Haham, and others from London, and the synagogue was consecrated by the Haham eleven months later, all the local Jewish ministers, orthodox and reform, participating. Hazan Piza, three sepharim and six boy choristers were lent by the London Community for the occasion. The Ascamot of the new synagogue were based on those of Bevis Marks. The first Hazan or minister, who acted honorarily, was Henry Pereira Mendes, a son of Abraham Pereira Mendes of London, and a grandson of the former Hazan of Bevis Marks,

David Aaron de Sola. Pereira Mendes, however, was appointed Hazan of the *Shearit Israel* Congregation of New York after three years, and was succeeded, in 1878, by Judah Henriques Valentine, who had held minor offices in the Sephardi Community in London. Subsequent hazanim were also drawn from the London Community. The increase in number of the Sephardim of Manchester and the movement away from the neighbourhood of the synagogue led, in 1904, to the erection of a second synagogue, with the full agreement of the members of the older one, in the suburb of Withington. It was consecrated by the Haham, Moses Gaster, on 4 September of that year. A few years later the two congregations united in one governing body. But even these two synagogues in course of time proved inadequate, and in 1924, a third, the *Shaare Sedek* Synagogue in West Didsbury, was consecrated.

Eighteen months were allowed to elapse after the death of Artom before steps were taken to find a successor. The first of these steps were, in accordance with the practice, taken by the Mahamad. There was one protégé of the Community who had been indicated almost from his birth for its service and, as the years passed, his suitability one day for even the highest office became ever more patent. This was Joseph, the eldest child of the Dayan Barnett Abrahams whose life and service had been so tragically cut short. Joseph Abrahams was in a sense a ward of the Community. He had been educated by them at Jews' College and University College, London, where he had graduated with distinction. From London he had proceeded to Berlin, where he was at this time studying at the University and at the Rabbinical Seminary under the distinguished guidance of Esriel Hildesheimer. When the question of appointing a new Haham arose the thoughts of many in the Congregation must have turned towards Joseph Abrahams. In fact, either at the suggestion of friends in England or of his own accord, he did write to the Mahamad to the effect that he hoped shortly to receive the Rabbinical Diploma and then proposed 'to place his services at the disposal of our Congregation'. About the same time advertisements were inserted in newspapers published in the Jewish centres on the Continent, but they produced no applications, and Abrahams was invited to make formal application for the appointment of Haham. In reply he made the suggested application, but at the same time asked to be permitted to continue his studies for a few months longer. Hildesheimer, while enthusiastically recommending Abrahams for the appointment, supported this request. No objection was raised by the Mahamad, but the opinion began to gain expression that perhaps Abrahams was not yet old enough for the office. He was at the time only twenty-six. These feelings grew stronger and the Mahamad suggested to Abrahams that he should withdraw his application and accept temporarily the post of Dayan and lecturer carrying with it the acting spiritual headship of the Community with a view to his appointment as Haham at a later date. Abrahams, however, declined. He was not prepared to accept any office inferior to that of Haham. This was the end of the negotiations with Abrahams and also, for the time being, of the project for the appointment of a Haham. Further unsuccessful efforts were made to find a suitable candidate on the Continent. When advertisements were published a few months later, Abrahams, who had in the meanwhile received the Rabbinical Diploma, again applied for the higher office. Time passed and no decision was taken. In the meanwhile an invitation came from the Melbourne (Australia) Hebrew Congregation to accept the office of Principal Minister of that Community. This Abrahams accepted and Melbourne's gain was London's loss. That this was realized at the time by some in London is evident from the efforts made by Joseph Sebag, later Sir Joseph Sebag-Montefiore, the successor of his uncle, Sir Moses, as the virtual head of the Community, to induce Abrahams to change his mind and remain in London as Haham.

Thus the situation remained. The Congregation had no spiritual head and in fact no spiritual direction. In cases in which decisions were required recourse had to be had to the Ashkenazi ecclesiastical authorities. After a short interval, Joseph Sebag, who had failed to secure the election of Abrahams, came forward with far more drastic a proposal. The Mahamad, at a meeting held on 24 April 1884, recorded its opinion that in consequence of the apparent impossibility of securing a suitable Haham, the Congregation's 'Ecclesiastical Department has been in a very sorry condition'. Sebag, who was then president of the Elders, consequently proposed that the Portuguese and German Congregations should establish a 'joint Ecclesiastical Board and Beth Hamedrash . . . under the presidency of the Chief Rabbi for the time being for a tentative period of three or five years'. The Board would consist of the Chief Rabbi and three dayanim, two to be elected by the Joint (Ashkenazi) Congregations and one by the Spanish and Portuguese Community. In the event of a vacancy in the Chief Rabbinate occurring during the existence of the Joint Board both Sephardi and Ashkenazi scholars should be eligible for appointment. This proposal was referred for consideration to a specially convened meeting of the Elders. In the meanwhile, a new applicant for the post of Haham appeared in the person of Alessandro da Fano, a rabbi of Florence. His qualifications were examined, but a new doubt arose, whether the finances of the Congregation could support the expense of a haham. It was decided, by the casting vote of the president of Elders, not to proceed with an election at that time. In the midst of these considerations and inquiries Sebag's revolutionary proposal, which had never aroused much enthusiasm, was forgotten. Six years later a somewhat similar proposal came from the Ashkenazi authorities. On 22 June 1890, when the office of Ashkenazi Chief Rabbi was vacant, an invitation came from the United Synagogue to consult on the subject of the appointment of a joint Chief Rabbi. The suggestion of the United Synagogue was that even the West London Synagogue should be brought under the direction of the one Chief Rabbi. The invitation was considered at a meeting of the Yehidim and refused on the grounds (*a*) that the Sephardi Community already had a Chief Rabbi (Moses Gaster had been appointed Haham three years before), (*b*) the Congregation already possessed the necessary machinery for carrying into effect any desired modification of the ritual and service. Finally, the Spanish and Portuguese Congregation considered that it would be in any event impracticable for one Chief Rabbi to preside over communities with such differences in custom and practice as those of the Spanish and Portuguese, German and Polish, and West London Jewish Communities.

The unanimous election of Moses Gaster by the Yehidim on 23 March 1887 had at length filled the office of Haham and a generation had to pass before it became vacant again. Gaster was an Ashkenazi by birth, the first, and so far the only one, to be chosen in England for that high office. Every effort had been made on this occasion to find a suitable candidate in the Sephardi communities of the Old World and the New, but they were without avail. The new Haham was in his thirty-first year. Born in Bucharest, he had been educated at the University there and at that of Leipzig. For his rabbinical studies he attended the Rabbinical Seminary at Breslau. Returning to Rumania, he lectured for a time at his old university on Rumanian literature and comparative mythology. He also held a junior appointment in the Ministry of Education. Realizing that, as a Jew, there was little scope for his abilities in his native land and, furthermore, getting into trouble on account of his political opinions, he left

Rumania and came to England. In Rumania, Gaster had already laid the foundations of his reputation as a scholar in a very wide field: in Jewry, on account of his participation in the work of the *Chovevé Zion* or Society for the resettlement of the Jews in Palestine, his reputation had overstepped the frontiers of the land of his birth. Thus when he arrived in England in 1885 he was known there, both in academic circles, at Oxford, where he was almost at once appointed Ilchester Lecturer in Graeco-Slavonic Literature, and in Jewry, especially in those sections in which the interest in Palestine was growing. Not long after his settlement in this country Gaster was approached to ascertain whether he would accept the vacant office of Haham. Gaster was a man of strong character, accustomed to express his opinions on a variety of subjects, with vehemence, and not always submissive to criticism, no matter from what direction it came. He was, above all, a personality, whom no one could overlook, no matter in what milieu he found himself. A master of half a dozen languages, he was equally at home in half a dozen and more fields of scholarship. In the Jewish community he quickly found himself in the front rank: outside of it he was accepted everywhere as one of England's leading, or at any rate most versatile, scholars. The appointment of Gaster at once raised the status of the Spanish and Portuguese Community, which during the long leaderless interregnum had in many respects fallen since the days of Meldola's prime.

Since the death of Barnett Abrahams there had been no regular dayanim. When the necessity arose, recourse was had to any member of the Community who happened to possess the rabbinical diploma. Once, in 1879, there was an attempt to appoint a dayan, but the rubi chosen—Joseph Elmaleh—declined the office. After a time none even of these occasional, honorary dayanim seemed to be available and recourse had to be had to the Ashkenazi Beth Din for a ruling. With the appointment of a Haham it was perhaps possible to dispense with the services of a dayan. Those of a Hazan or Hazanim were, however, essential. With two synagogues the number of these officials had to be increased and, looking to the future also, the practice grew up of appointing assistants to the Hazanim, who later in some cases became Assistant Hazanim and even Hazanim. In June 1869 Simson Jechiel Roco of Amsterdam was elected Hazan, in a contested election. There were five other candidates, but four of them received no votes at all. Roco had 59 votes and Abraham Haim Nieto, a descendant of David Nieto, the Haham, 32. Nieto had been and remained for some years more or less unofficially attached to the synagogue, his services being drawn on as occasion required. His relations with his fellow hazanim, especially Piperno, were not of the best, and on at least one occasion an altercation took place in the synagogue when Piperno refused to permit him to share in the conduct of the service. However, the fault was not altogether on one side. Nieto became over-persistent in pressing his services on the Congregation and in the end the Mahamad found it necessary to restrain him. Finally Nieto followed the example of several of his predecessors and settled in the United States of America.

Some ten years earlier the scale of salaries of the officials was revised, in recognition of the fall in the value of money. Offerings in the Synagogue for the Hazanim had by then been abolished. Under the new scale the salary appointed for the Haham was £720 per annum, for the Secretary £280, for the Hazanim £230 to £250, for the Assistant Secretary £175, and for the Samasim £115 to £135.[1] The monthly payments were also equalized by the substitution of the secular for the Hebrew month. In the cases of the Hazanim and the Samasim and also at first the secretary, residential accommodation was provided, and it soon became the practice to provide the Haham, when there was one, with a house. In 1888 David Piza retired, to die two years later, after having served as Hazan for more than forty years. On the retirement of Piza, Solomon Conquy, a young man who had come from Gibraltar, was appointed Assistant to the Hazanim, to become successively Assistant Hazan and Hazan (in 1895) and to die in 1914 at the age of forty-three. Piperno remained in office for fifty-six years, throughout his career attached to the Branch Synagogue in West London, until 1904, being succeeded by Mr. David Bueno de Mesquita, whose duties differed from those of all the Hazanim who had preceded him in that not only was he a Hazan but also a preacher. He had been trained under the auspices of the Congregation for the office he was to hold and had been assistant to the Hazanim from early in 1901. Piperno died six years after his retirement. After the death of Conquy, Mr. Joseph Gomes de Mesquita, choirmaster in Amsterdam who had been appointed

---

[1] The Congregation was, however, not so parsimonious as would appear at first sight to the reader of today, if comparative standards are taken into consideration. The emoluments of clergymen in this country have, with a few exceptions, always been small, and many priests of the Church of England had in 1860 no larger emoluments than had a Hazan. In *The Times* of 17 October 1850 there was an advertisement for a Superintending (presumably the equivalent of Chief) Constable of Watlington in which the salary offered was £60 per annum with a house or lodgings 'but not with a horse or clothes, excepting a great coat and cape', and in the same issue one for a House Surgeon to the Royal Pimlico Dispensary at a salary of £100 per annum 'with apartments, coal and candles'.

Assistant to the Hazanim a few months earlier, succeeded him as Hazan, retiring in 1948. Roco retired in 1921 after fifty-two years' service, and was succeeded by Aaron Nunes Vaz, who died in 1945. Roco died in 1926.

Until the appointment of Mr. Bueno de Mesquita it was invariably the duty of the Haham, and not of the Hazan, to give addresses in the synagogue, the only exceptions to this rule having been David de Sola, who was on occasion invited or given permission to address the congregation, and Piza, who was permitted to do so on one or two occasions.[1] In the late eighteenth and the early years of the nineteenth centuries, as has already been mentioned, laymen were occasionally permitted to address the Congregation. In those days the Haham was seldom moved to do so, and when he did, it was generally in a language foreign to them. Consequently, if an address in English was desired, one had to go outside the official circle. Artom was, of course, an exception to this rule, but when he died he left no successor. However, there was one man in London who was able to fill the void. Abraham Pereira Mendes, a Sephardi by birth and upbringing, had been trained under the auspices of the London Sephardi Community, had ministered for a short time in Jamaica, the country of his birth, and also in the Ashkenazi Community of Birmingham. He had married a daughter of David Aaron de Sola, and had finally settled in London where, after a period as Headmaster of the Ashkenazi Jews' Hospital and Orphanage, he was directing a school in Northwick Terrace at which many of the sons of the more comfortably circumstanced Jewish families attended. In July 1879 he was appointed Lecturer at both synagogues. The appointment was a temporary one, an experiment, but it was renewed a year later. In 1882 Pereira Mendes asked that the appointment should be made permanent and regular. But this the Mahamad would not do. Efforts were at that time being made to find a suitable haham and if one had been found, the office of Lecturer would have been redundant. Finding that there was no alternative, Pereira Mendes accepted a renewal of the appointment on the former terms. He did not, however, hold it for long, for in January 1883 he left England finally, following his two sons, Henry Pereira Mendes and Frederick de Sola (previously Pereira) Mendes, who had obtained ministerial appointments in New York. On the resuscitation of the Sephardi

---

[1] When the duties of the Hazanim were defined in 1862, preaching in English at regular intervals was included among them. The younger de Sola, the only one at the time capable of preaching, however, died within four years.

Community of Newport, Rhode Island, Abraham Pereira Mendes became its Minister. He was killed in a street accident in New York City on 4 April, 1893.

After the resignation of Pereira Mendes recourse was had to the services of ministers of the Ashkenazi Community who were from time to time invited to preach at Bevis Marks or Bryanston Street. Even earlier, in 1880, Dr. Berendt Salomon, later Ashkenazi Minister in Manchester, preached on one occasion in place of Pereira Mendes, who was ill. At the head of these guest preachers was Hermann Adler, the Delegate Chief Rabbi, who was also Minister of the Bayswater Synagogue. After him came Aaron Levy Green of the Central Synagogue, Morris Joseph, at the time Minister of the North London Synagogue, later to become the Chief Minister of the West London (Reformed) Synagogue, and Simeon Singer, of the New West End Synagogue. Still later came some of the senior students of Jews' College who had not yet received appointments. The delivery of sermons might have been made a regular feature of the service at this time, when the prospect of the appointment of a Haham had receded far into the background, for the Congregation advertised for a regular minister. The response was, however, not satisfactory, and the practice of inviting visiting preachers continued. At Ramsgate, however, the case was different. On the death of Sir Moses Montefiore the synagogue came completely under the control of the Elders of Bevis Marks. In 1886 Edgar Séches of Paris and Hermann Shandel, an Ashkenazi, were appointed Hazanim. Neither, however, was capable of giving an address to the Congregation, nor was preaching included in the duties laid down for their offices. Séches' health soon broke down and he had to retire. His place was taken by George Belasco, who had been trained under the auspices of the Congregation, was well capable of preaching, and, under the terms of his appointment, was required to do so.[1] A few years later the delivery in the synagogue at Ramsgate of at least four addresses in the course of the year was one of the duties of Gaster on his appointment as Haham. He was, of course, also expected to preach in the synagogues at Bevis Marks and Bryanston Street.

The choir or choirs were always a source of trouble, and in the minutes of the Congregation over a long period there are frequent records of complaints about them. Henri de Solla's second appointment was terminated at the end of 1879 when it was decided that the choirs of the two synagogues would have to be

---

[1] Belasco held the office until his death in 1929.

thoroughly reorganized. De Solla was later appointed Choirmaster of the Great Synagogue, London and it was while he was in that office that he offered to take charge of the choral part of the service on the occasion of the marriage of the Haham, Moses Gaster. The offer was not accepted. On the retirement of de Solla, Elias Robert Jessurun was appointed with instructions to carry out the required reorganization. He set to work on his task, but when he had completed it, the complaints of the musical members of the Congregation, or those who considered themselves musical, did not cease. But Jessurun left his name in the records of Bevis Marks by his edition of *The Ancient Melodies of the Liturgy of the Spanish and Portuguese Jews*, originally produced by the David Aaron de Sola in conjunction with Emanuel Aguilar. Jessurun died in 1933, after fifty-three years' service, and was succeeded by Mr. Jacob Hadida.

The other principal office in the Community was that of the secretary. Elias Haim Lindo,[1] a family connexion of Almosnino and a member of one of the historic families in Anglo-Jewry, was appointed Assistant Secretary at the beginning of 1863 and Secretary in 1875 on the retirement of Almosnino. Almosnino, if only on account of the length of his service—fifty-six years— had become one of the communal institutions. There were few in Anglo-Jewry at the time of his retirement who could remember a Bevis Marks without Almosnino as secretary. On him had fallen the task of guiding the Community, also often its directors, in fair weather and foul, in times of storm as well as in calm waters. His services were fully appreciated. Not only was his pension of the same amount as his salary and his occupation of the residence attached to the office left undisturbed. When he died two years later, the Mahamad in addressing the Yehidim referred to 'the important and valued services he had rendered to our Synagogue, during a period of nearly sixty years and his invariable urbanity were recognized by the Members of our Congregation in the affectionate regard which they entertained for him and the remembrance of his irreproachable conduct through life will always be retained by this room'. Lindo's assistant secretary, originally clerk, was Samuel Isaac Cohen, a son of Isaac Cohen, Hazan of the New Synagogue. He in due course succeeded Lindo as Secretary on his retirement in 1893, ten years before his death. Cohen died unexpectedly in 1910, to be succeeded by Paul Goodman, who had been appointed first as Assistant to the

[1] This Lindo should not be confused with his uncle and namesake, the historian of the Jews in Spain, who died in 1865.

Secretary fifteen years earlier. Goodman, like Cohen, was Ashkenazi in origin, as is also Goodman's successor, Mr. Michael Marchant. In Goodman, however, a new precedent was set, inasmuch as he was not only the secretary of the Community, but also its historian. He had not the leisure to undertake a full-length history of his adopted Community, but he wrote several brochures on different aspects of its history. His pen was, however, not confined to the story of the Community that grouped itself around Bevis Marks. He wrote on other branches of Jewish history and even of polemics. In the past the Community had many men of letters in its service: Goodman was the first to serve as its secretary.

Even at the end of the nineteenth century the salaries paid by the Congregation to its officials could not be described as in any respect lavish. They had increased inevitably from the figures of the seventeenth and eighteenth centuries, but nevertheless seem barely to have kept pace with the rise, if slow, in the cost of living. As late as 1823, when the annual income of the Community was about £4,000, the newly appointed dayan received a salary of only £20. It is true that the appointment did not absorb the whole of the time and thought of its incumbent, and he was free to devote himself to other occupations, but there must have been very few remunerative ones which he could combine with the very responsible one of dayan. Salaries did not, however, in all cases represent the whole of the emoluments of the stipendiary officers of the Congregation. For many years, until 1845, they were supplemented in the case of the Hazanim and the Samas by offerings of worshippers on being called to the Law. The amount of these supplementary receipts in the case of individuals cannot be stated, but the total in no instance can have been considerable. At the end of the nineteenth century, after these offerings had been abolished and the salaries of the Hazanim increased in compensation, the range of those salaries ran from £200 to £300 a year, with in some instances a house in addition. In 1824 Judah Israel Montefiore, a first cousin of Sir Moses, was appointed physician to the Community at a salary of £30 a year, to be increased nine months later to £40 on his election as a Yahid. At the same time the Hazan, David Aaron de Sola, received a vote outside of his salary of £25 'in consideration of his large family'. Grants, supplementary to salaries, were frequent; on the occasion of a holiday, of illness, of marriage of the official or his daughter, on the birth of a child; and in the end were recognized as regular emoluments. Judah Montefiore was not the only member of a prominent family to serve as communal physician. One of his successors was Emanuel Meldola, a son of the Haham. When Meldola retired at the beginning of 1874, the two offices of communal physician and surgeon were combined. James S. Sequeira, a member of one of the old Sephardi families, was appointed to the joint offices and after him, in 1920, Henry J. Sequeira, his son.

One reason for parsimony was undoubtedly the difficult financial position in which the Community found itself, sometimes over long periods. The time when the Congregation was able to defray its expenses by means of the contributions of members alone had long since passed. Yehidim, however, fortunately for their successors, were generous in death as well as in life, and although the contributions from the living varied from year to year, sometimes rising, sometimes falling, there was seldom a year in which there was no windfall disclosed in the will of some recently deceased Yahid. The finta, once an emergency fund, had long become the principal source of revenue, apart from income from investments. This should have been an elastic fund, always ready to hand to be increased. But in practice this was not so. It was found too often that there was a close relationship between the finta and the offerings made in synagogue. As one rose the other fell and the total in the end was much the same. Not only was the number or amount of the offerings reduced, but the finta fell into arrears. In 1707, when the finta was first introduced as a regular source of revenue, the total was assessed at £600 a year. In 1738 it was raised to £900, and in 1809 to £1,400. This figure was, however, beyond the capacity of the Community. It proved to be an ideal that could not be attained and the more practicable figure of £1,000 was soon substituted for it. The withdrawal of a number of the wealthier members in 1842, was followed by a fall in the maximum assessment, but after a time this loss was recovered, and henceforth at varying but shorter intervals it continued to grow. In the year 1864 it was still only £850. Three years later it was raised to £950, in 1873 to £1,100, and in 1876 to £1,250. In the following year there was a small increase, of only £50. In 1894 the maximum was raised to £1,600 and by 1902 to £1,850. Three years later there was a relatively large increase, to £2,500, the maximum to be paid by any Yahid being raised to £40 and the minimum to £2. A proposal to increase the maximum to £50 was rejected by the Elders. In 1901 the letting of seats in Bevis Marks permanently or temporarily for the New Year and Day of Atonement, to non-Yehidim, was introduced. Later the maximum finta was reduced to £2,000, again to reach £2,500 in 1923. In the subsequent half-century there were further increases, with an occasional reduction, until in 1950 the maximum was raised from £3,900 to £5,900, with a maximum for any one Yahid of £65 10s., consolidating and including, however, the different subsidiary taxes, such as those for the Board of Guardians, the Beth Haim, and others. In 1910 contributions by the Yehidim to the Beth Haim and Repairs funds had been made compulsory.

Nevertheless, over a long period of years the financial situation was not satisfactory. In 1863 the Elders appointed a committee to examine the state of the congregational finances with a view to balancing the income and expenditure, although in the previous year there had been a precarious surplus of £104. The following year the two sides were equal, the surplus being three pounds. These years showed a turning-point in the financial fortunes of the Community, the year 1866–7 showing a surplus of over five hundred pounds, the largest the Congregation had enjoyed for more than seventy years. It seemed that the efforts of this committee had proved successful. The increase of the finta in 1867 brought both the income and expenditure for the first time above £5,000, the expenditure being the greater by £95, but this was only a momentary flash, for this total fell again within a year. In the year 1867 both sides fell, but the financial position remained stable for the time being. In 1869 the surplus was £474, in 1870 £395, and in 1871 £320. Then the wheel became erratic. In 1872 there was a deficit of £330. In 1873 this was replaced by a surplus of £131, in 1874 by one of £39, and in 1875 by a relatively very large deficit of £436. By the year 1878 the situation had again become serious. The income had persistently fallen below expectations and the expenditure had at the time continued to increase. In the year 1876–7 there was a deficit of £577, due very largely to the persistent neglect of Yehidim in the payment of their dues. The position was that there was an accumulated deficit amounting to £1,800 with no immediate prospect of liquidating it. For the future the income would have to be increased or the expenditure reduced, or recourse had to both means of relief. Some step had, however, to be taken immediately. This was taken, but with great reluctance. Apart from the financial unsoundness of the step, there was a feeling that it was impious. A capital fund had been carefully built up out of the bequests of pious members of the Community. The total of these pious bequests was by now considerable and the upkeep of the Congregation was to a large extent dependent on the income derived from them. In the position in which the Congregation found itself, however, there seemed to the Elders and the Yehidim to be no alternative to realizing part of this capital for the payment of debts. £2,000 of capital was thereupon realized in the hope that it would prove possible to replace the amount out of future surpluses. This hope was to some extent realized, for in the following year there was again a surplus—of £596—the total income being raised to the unprecedented height of £6,854.

The improved state of affairs did not, however, last for long. A cause of the trouble was again laxity among too many of the Yehidim in meeting their obligations. By the beginning of the year 1885 there was an accumulated total of arrears in finta and offerings of £2,283, in some instances going back as far as twenty-five years. The Elders had in the past adopted legislation intended to deal with cases of this kind, and in accordance with that legislation Yehidim in arrear for three years should have been deprived of their rights, but there was a natural disinclination to enforce such legislation, especially when acquaintances, sometimes friends, were concerned, and the legislation in consequence had become a dead letter, to be reanimated spasmodically from time to time. The efforts made, following the disclosure of 1885, led to an improvement, and by the year 1886 there was a surplus of almost £200. Early in 1892, there was, however, another investigation by a special committee into the financial state of the Congregation. This committee made very far-reaching recommendations. It recommended that all the property in Bevis Marks and Heneage Lane, apart from the synagogue and courtyard and land to be appropriated for the building of houses for two officials, should be let on building leases and that the school in Heneage Lane should be rebuilt farther east, the surplus land in Mile End, reserved for an extension of the cemetery, should be sold, since it was doubtful whether the Congregation would be permitted to extend its cemetery there, and land for a new cemetery should be acquired elsewhere. The several almshouses of the Community, some of which were a financial burden, should be concentrated and rebuilt farther east and the land thereby set free, let on building lease. Provision should be made for the holding of services in the new almshouse building. The result of these transactions would, it was foreseen, be a normal small surplus instead of an average deficit of almost £500 a year. The committee foresaw, however, that in the not distant future the erection of a larger synagogue farther west in place of that at Bryanston Street would be necessary. This report was signed by Gabriel Lindo,

A. D. de Pass, Elim H. d'Avigdor, Sir Francis Montefiore, and James Castello, members of Mahamad, Solomon Sebag, Eleazar S. Pool, and Percy M. Castello, Yehidim. The report was referred by the Yehidim to another committee for further consideration. It was ultimately adopted and proved to be the basis of the financial regeneration of the Congregation.

But the Congregation was not yet out of the financial wood. These recommendations took some years to translate into facts, and in the meanwhile the position was again sometimes difficult. By 1899 there was again a debt to the Bank of £2,300—which had been accumulating for some years, and capital had again to be realized to liquidate it. The persistent financial difficulties led to consideration whether the finta should not be abolished and seat rentals, as in the other London synagogues, substituted, but the conclusion was reached that the change would lead not to an increase but to a reduction in revenue. Similar suggestions were occasionally made later, but the conclusion was always the same. The only change was that a few years earlier, in 1894, the practice was introduced of charging seat rentals, at a minimum of 21s. a year to regular attendants in the Synagogue at Bevis Marks, but care was taken to impose these charges only on those who could afford to pay them. The sale of securities in 1899 made the Congregation free from debt, but only for a short time. By 1901 it was again in debt to the Bank, to the extent of £1,200, and again recourse had to be had to capital. It was only in 1903 that the accounts were made to balance—the first occasion in a decade —and then the surplus was only £4 8s. 7d. A surplus of any consequence—£449—was not attained until 1912. When the first World War came the Congregation's finances again fell into deficit.

The recommendations of the committee of 1892 for a wide and statesmanlike approach to the financial problem did not appear suddenly out of a vacuum. The principle that underlay them had been under consideration for at least a decade. Already in the early eighteen-eighties the centre of the Community had finally and unquestionably shifted away from the City to the West End of London. All the better circumstanced, not only the wealthy, members of the Community had by now removed their homes to new localities, more than a sabbath day's journey from Bevis Marks. These, of course, comprised a majority of the Yehidim, none of whom were therefore able to attend service in the synagogue there, except on an occasional week-day. To ride to synagogue on the Sabbath was still unthinkable for a Yahid. The result was that so far as the greater number of the Yehidim was concerned the synagogue in Bevis Marks served no practical purpose. Furthermore, in the course of the centuries the Congregation, by purchase and by gift, had acquired in the vicinity property, land and buildings, originally residences, which by now, with the withdrawal of private residence from within the confines of the City, had lost their original purpose. Land of increasing value was being occupied by small houses, not in very good repair, let, sometimes not let, at rents far below its then market value. It was clear that the time was ripe for a development, and one that would enhance the whole of the Congregation's property in the region of Bevis Marks was obviously preferable to one that would deal with only a part of it. The earliest reference to a project such as this to be found in the records of the Congregation was at the beginning of the year 1883. Quoting from the Annual Report of the Mahamad of 14 January of that year:

> 'The time had in their (The Mahamad's) opinion arrived for admitting that our Ancient Synagogue no longer serves its purpose nor is it resorted to for prayer by a large number of the Congregation. The entire body of its supporters has left the neighbourhood and the Synagogue is practically deserted. On some sabbaths not one Yahid except our own officials is to be seen there.'

A special committee, consisting of all the Elders, was constituted and by this committee detailed consideration of the proposals was given. Only then were the recommendations unanimously approved.

The Freehold Lands Scheme, as it came to be known, covered a wide range. It not only comprised the letting on building leases of the whole of the Congregation's property in Bevis Marks and Heneage Lane and the consequent demolition of all the congregational buildings, including the Synagogue itself, but also the closing of the synagogue in Bryanston Street and the erection in place of it a larger one farther west in a more convenient situation —for Bryanston Street was no longer the centre of the new Jewish settlement in West London—with accommodation for 350 men and 250 women, with offices for the Congregation and residences for the Haham, two Hazanim, the secretary, and other officers The needs of those congregants who were left in East London were, however, not to be ignored, for it was further proposed that another synagogue should be erected in the neighbourhood of Commercial Road, in the heart of the Jewish Quarter. This should provide accommodation for at least four hundred worshippers, men and women, and subsidiary buildings should be erected for the communal schools, almshouses, offices, and a house for a Hazan. These proposals secured practically unanimous acceptance—in any event no serious objection to them was voiced—by the Yehidim, and the Elders took steps for the sale on building leases of the sites of their properties. Tenders were invited, but none was received. This gave the synagogue—the building around which the subsequent struggle centred—a respite, and in the subsequent fifteen months a considerable opposition arose. The controversy was perhaps more active without the Sephardi Community than within it. A group came into existence, partly Ashkenazi, partly Sephardi, that began to educate opinion into the realization that the old synagogue fabric was the property not only of the Sephardim but of the entire Anglo-Jewish Community, perhaps of England or London as a whole. That this last view was shared and accepted outside was shown some years later when, in 1929, the Bevis Marks Synagogue was scheduled as an Ancient Monument by the Royal Commission on Historical Monuments, and thereby permanently preserved, except for an accident or an act of war. Some enthusiasts, prominent among whom were Haim Guedalla and Abraham Anidjar Romain among the Sephardim, and Lucien Wolf, Leopold J. Greenberg, many years later to become Editor of *The Jewish Chronicle*, and Alfred Alvarez Newman, who in his short life—he died in 1887 at the age of thirty-six—rose to an outstanding position within the Community and without as an art worker and antiquary, formed 'The Bevis Marks Anti-Demolition League'. This body presented a petition to the Mahamad in February 1886, asking that the decision to demolish the synagogue building be reconsidered as

> 'your petitioners harbour the keenest love and reverence for the Bevis Marks Synagogue, a building forming as it does the monument of Anglo-Judaic liberation, associated as it is so intimately with the return of Jews to this happy land, where from the day that your renowned ancestor, Manasseh ben Israel, set foot, our liberties have deepened and broadened with the progress of our country. They feel that the demolition of such a building would be an irreparable loss to the Jewish Community at large and they believe that notwithstanding the fact that under present circumstances the synagogue is attended mainly by the poorer portion of your Congregation you will see fit so to amend your original scheme as to leave to your petitioners the ancient building in its entirety.'

The Mahamad were not very sympathetic. They pointed out in reply that the principle for the demolition had been almost unanimously approved at a largely attended meeting of the Yehidim.

The final decision, however, did not rest with the Mahamad. The objectors found a powerful supporter in the person of Joseph de Castro, originally one of the sponsors of the scheme, who later realized the force of the objections to it and at a meeting of the Yehidim a month later urged that that portion of the scheme that related to the synagogue building should be rescinded. He was opposed by an equally influential Yahid, Gabriel Lindo, who, however, in the course of the discussion, modified his amendment to the extent that no final steps should be taken without the further approval of the Yehidim. In the end Lindo's amendment was adopted, by 37 votes to 32, the minority presumably consisting of a coalition of supporters of de Castro and of advocates of demolition in all circumstances. In fact this vote meant the reprieve of the Bevis Marks building. Apart from the demolition of the Synagogue, the remainder of the scheme in so far as it related to the development of the Congregation's City property aroused no opposition. Nevertheless it lagged. Tenders for the leasing of the property were again invited, but still no response that deserved serious consideration came. The time was not propitious. All the land was, however, let in course of time and warehouses erected on it, with consequent permanent improvement in the Congregation's financial position. The National Infant and Villa Real School, which had been placed under Government supervision in 1891 and in return given an annual grant, was transferred farther east to Thrawl Street at the end of 1894 and the new building opened by the Duchess of Albany, a daughter of the Queen, early in 1897. Another rebuilding scheme, accompanied by the consolidation of resources, was the transfer of the Congregational Almshouses, all by now in unsuitable neighbourhoods and in a state more or less of disrepair, to Devonshire Street, Mile End, in 1894. The new building was consecrated by the Haham and opened by Sir Samuel Montagu, later Lord Swaythling, all the principal Jewish institutions, Reform as well as Ashkenazi, being represented.[1]

The remaining part of the scheme was the closing of the Synagogue in Bryanston Street and the erection of another farther west. This also was put into effect, except that the only ancillary buildings were houses for the Hazan and Samas and another to

[1] These almshouses were destroyed in an air raid during second World War.

serve as the Congregational orphanage, which had already been removed from the City to a temporary home. That there was a case for the erection of a larger synagogue farther west than Bryanston Street was clear. It was evident from almost the beginning of the eighteen-nineties, when in 1892 it was ascertained that there were only 34 Yehidim residing within a mile of Bryanston Street, whereas 93 lived within the same distance of Clifton Road, Maida Vale. 62 per cent of the Yehidim, who between themselves contributed 78 per cent of the total finta and offerings, were living in West and North-west London. However, still half of the Yehidim were not directly interested in synagogue accommodation in West London. The other half, however, were less inclined to acquiesce in the postponement of a decision. They, or many of them, in a group approached the Elders with a request that their needs should be met. As a consequence another committee was appointed by the Yehidim, and this committee, in April 1895, recommended the erection of a new synagogue and minister's house at the junction of Lauderdale and Ashworth Roads in Maida Vale. From this point the approved programme was carried out without hitch. The new Synagogue was opened on 4 October, 1896. It was a success from the beginning. The attendance, even on week-days, so surpassed that which had become the normal at Bryanston Street, that the engagement of Minyanistas (men required to form a quorum) was found unnecessary. In the last days in Bryanston Street a qualified Cohen had actually to be engaged and paid to attend synagogue at all times at which the Law was read or the presence of Cohanim was necessary, or at any rate desirable. Religion classes were opened at once and were attended in adequate numbers by the Sephardi children of the neighbourhood. The building cost £9,800 with a further £918 for the seating. Half of this total was voted from Congregational funds and the remainder was contributed in individual donations. In addition, there was a long list of gifts, each according to the donor's means, for the embellishment of the new House of Prayer and its ritual objects. The *Ehal* or Ark placed in the building under the contract with the builders was not considered worthy of it, and a more handsome one was substituted without delay, at a cost of £233 16s., that originally placed in the synagogue being presented to the Home and Hospital for Jewish Incurables. At the same time, in accordance with the plans that had been approved, a building to house the communal orphans was erected next to the Synagogue at a cost of £2,692. This building is now adapted as a Communal Centre, the orphanage having been closed in 1940. It was not very long before it was found that a larger synagogue was desirable to satisfy the demand for accommodation and the possibility of enlarging the building was given consideration. Much encouragement was given by a generous offer, in 1922, by Aubrey J. David, at the time one of the parnassim, to defray a quarter of the cost of enlargement, up to a maximum of £3,000, but some of the conditions that accompanied the offer were impracticable. On this disappointment the project of enlargement was not pursued.

CHAPTER XIX

THE PENULTIMATE HALF-CENTURY

ANOTHER BURNING QUESTION that throughout the latter half of the nineteenth century aroused controversies, was whether or not offerings made by members during service should be announced in the synagogue. Such a practice was from the beginning an accepted custom, and as a consequence not only was the service to some extent lengthened—a not very serious matter in the seventeenth and eighteenth centuries—and the Reading of the Law interrupted—also a matter to which not great exception would then be taken—but it led to a sort of auction which, as time passed, became less and less to the taste of a section of the Congregation whose opinion was becoming increasingly entitled to respect. The earliest date on which a decision was taken in this matter was 1885, when the Yehidim recommended to the Elders that such offerings be abolished for a tentative period of two years. The recommendation was accepted after a not great delay, for within a few years its working was causing some anxiety by the *post hoc* if not *propter hoc* serious diminution in the revenue derived from offerings. In the hope of making good these losses, protracted endeavours were made to reverse the decision. For a time a compromise was accepted under which the service was not interrupted, but the announcement of all offerings was made at its conclusion. Restoration of the original procedure was achieved at the beginning of the year 1904, but after the lapse of exactly a year this decision was again reversed and the public announcement of offerings prohibited. After another five years the practice was, however, again introduced, and continued unchanged until 1948, when mention of the amount offered was suppressed.

The second half of the nineteenth century saw a noticeable advance in what may be termed the constitutional development of the Sephardi Community. The laws and regulations by which this Community was governed were, as has previously been mentioned, embodied in the Ascamot. In the very first years, as the occasion arose, amendments were made and this process of development continued without cessation. Whenever the text became complicated and perhaps obscure, as a consequence of the accretion of amendments, a new code would be drawn up. This step was, however, considered a matter that demanded grave consideration, and much time and thought were given to it. A joint committee of the Elders and Yehidim that reported on the subject in June 1884 recommended *inter alia* that permission might be given to any Yahid to hold service in his home, provided that all offerings made were paid into the Congregational funds, that instead of electing four parnassim and one gabay, twice a year, for a period of office of one year, there should be five parnassim, without distinction of title or function, and that they should be elected for a term of two years. Apart from life elders (those already holding office), the number of elders should be limited to twenty-five, including the wardens at the time in office: the others being elected for a limited period. 'All persons of the Jewish faith (should) be eligible for admission as. Yehidim.' Candidates for the office of Haham should in future be selected by the Elders, but the election should rest with the Yehidim. For a tentative period of two years the announcement of offerings in the synagogue should be abolished. Most of these recommendations were accepted by the Elders. The most important that failed to secure acceptance were those relating to the election of Parnassim and the appointment of elders. One of those that was accepted opened the portals of Bevis Marks to all Jews, whether of Sephardi or other origin, but the decision in every individual case remained with the Elders. During the decade that preceded these radical changes there had from time to time been occasional ones tending to liberalize, even though cautiously, the constitution. In February 1874 the Elders were authorized to let seats in their synagogues to members of other Jewish congregations, without, as it was specifically laid down, giving them any claim to membership of the Sephardi Community. It was at this time that a seat was allotted in the Bryanston Street Synagogue to Samuel Montagu.

The subject of the imposition of fines for refusal of office, absence from meetings, or even attending late or leaving meetings before their conclusion was, however, not ready for settlement. But it was brought into prominence at the end of the year 1878 when Reuben and Arthur Sassoon, two of the most prominent of the Elders, were automatically fined ten shillings each for failure to attend a meeting of the Elders. The fines were at once remitted by formal resolution, probably before the offenders had been made aware of them, but the incident convinced everyone, except a few sticklers, that the regulation under which they had been imposed was obsolete. Within a year the ascama imposing such fines had been removed from the statute book and not long after fines for refusal of office followed them into limbo. In 1884 the office of Vice-President of the Elders was created, the first to be elected being Abraham Mocatta, well entitled to the highest offices in the Congregation, both by his devoted service to it and by heredity. The office of President of the Elders had been instituted in 1733, David Lopes Pereira being the first to be chosen. In 1882, as in 1884, the qualification for the office of Elder was again under consideration, but the Yehidim decided to make no change and the office continued to be reserved for ex-members of the Mahamad and for representatives of the Congregation on the Board of Deputies.

One other matter had long demanded consideration. That was the position of women in the administration of the Congregation. Until 1884 widows and unmarried daughters of Yehidim might be elected as Yehidot, but not the wives. These last mentioned enjoyed the advantages of membership through their husbands. In the administration of the Congregation they had, either in their own right or as the wives of Yehidim, no part. The Girls' and Infants' School was, however, managed by a committee of women, under the nominal direction of the Mahamad, but this committee seems to have grown up unofficially outside of the constitution. The women also took their part in such minor matters as the decoration of the Tabernacle for the Feast of Succot and of the Synagogue on that of Shebuot. Inevitably this status was not accepted by all the women of the Congregation, and as time passed, the number of the dissatisfied grew. The earliest hint of dissatisfaction is given in a minute of the Yehidim for 8 January 1843. The perennial question of Ascama No. 1 regarding the holding of services elsewhere than at Bevis Marks was under consideration when a letter from 'the undersigned members of your Body, and ratepayers to the Synagogue, not being able personally to attend your meetings, beg to express our approbation of the report of the Committee and the proposed alterations and request that our opinions be entered on your books'. This letter was signed by twenty women and three men, bearing some of the best-known names in the Congregation. The men were either strong sympathizers with the women, or in their own persons compulsory absentees from the meeting, who would have liked to have been able to vote by proxy. Thirty years had, however, to pass before any positive step in the direction of the goal was taken, and then it was on a side-issue. In May 1874 the Yehidot made a formal claim on the Elders for participation in the election of representatives of the Congregation on the Board of Deputies. The claim was inevitably rejected, but it was the beginning of a campaign which in the end gave to the women of the congregation a full share in all spheres outside of participation in the services. It was not until 1920, however, that all women, whether married or single, were eligible for admission as Yehidot and to vote at meetings. As late as that year the wives of Yehidim were still refused admission as Yehidot, although in 1917 a Sephardi lady whose husband was not a Yahid was accepted. Women were also made eligible to represent the Congregation on the Board of Deputies, while on the charitable and educational committees of the Congregation they were elected in the proportion that their numbers entitled. The change, gradual as it was, did not take place without protest. When in 1907 the Board of Guardians, as it was entitled to do without reference to any other body, decided to co-opt women members,[1] one of the Elders, José de Sola Pinto, who had previously served as Parnas, was so shocked that in protest he resigned his membership of the Congregation. It is true that after an interval for reflexion he applied to be reinstated. De Sola Pinto was, however, of a somewhat eccentric disposition. On another occasion, being dissatisfied with his assessment for finta, he appealed against it and informed the Mahamad that he proposed to assess himself at a higher figure, the maximum. Finally he resigned from the Congregation. In the end, in February 1946, the bar was removed from women on membership even of the Elders, no longer limited to ex-members of the Mahamad. The Elders themselves in that year adopted a new ascama to the effect that 'notwithstanding the provisions of any other ascama, no woman otherwise qualified shall be disqualified by reason of her sex from election to any honorary office in the Congregation, except those of Parnas, Gabay and Levantador, but no women shall be entitled to perform any duties in the Synagogue of the Congregation'. (The three offices named involved such duties.) The first wife of a Yahid to be accepted as a Yehida was Mrs. Oliver Sebag-Montefiore. But it was not until early in 1948 that a Yahida was nominated for election as an Elder by the Mahamad. Two years later a Yahida for the first time secured election. This was Mrs. Pamela Mocatta, the wife of Mr. Alan Mocatta, a descendant of that Moses Mocatta whose name appears in one of the earliest lists of the governing members of Bevis Marks.

A decision, more important perhaps in principle than it became in practice, was taken in 1888, whereby it became no longer possible to elect a Yahid to office without his knowledge or consent.

[1] Women could not be directly elected to the Board until 1929.

The power to do so had ceased to serve any purpose since there was no longer any penalty for refusal of office. In 1891 the Yehidim recommended to the Elders that payment of finta and offerings amounting in all to £6 per annum for the two immediately preceding years should be made a qualification for election as parnas or gabay. In 1893 the method of appointment of Elders came up again, and it was at length decided that while the existing elders should remain undisturbed for life, future ex-members of the Mahamad should be Elders for three years only but be eligible for re-election by the Yehidim. A further step was taken in 1905 when it was laid down that the Elders could co-opt three Yehidim to serve as Elders for three years. The new ascamot were approved in the following year and the first Yahid to be so co-opted was Charles de Pass. He, however, refused the office. The first Yehidim to accept co-option were Michael John Garcia and Mr. Charles Edward Sebag-Montefiore, the present President of the Elders. In 1922 the number to be co-opted by the Elders was increased to four, but to serve only for two years, and the Yehidim were entitled to elect two others for a similar period.

There were a few other constitutional matters of interest on which decisions were taken during this period. Occasional lack of unanimity in the Mahamad necessitated a definition of what was in law the Mahamad. It was decided that when a decision of that body was required it was sufficient if the decision was by a majority. The question of opening the meetings of the Elders and Yehidim to the press was also finally settled. The Yehidim met the request without hesitation as early as 1881, and at the same time by resolution recommended the Elders to follow their example. But the latter refused the invitation. The subject was not taken up again until late in 1896 when the Elders again refused to adopt the suggestion of the Yehidim. But the latter were this time more in earnest. At the first opportunity they confirmed their recommendation, and this step also proving ineffectual, in the following year they once more called on the Elders to follow the example they had set with no untoward results sixteen years earlier and to admit representatives of the Jewish press to their meetings. When the Mahamad came forward to the reinforcement of the Yehidim, the Elders found themselves unable further to resist and at length, on 16 January 1898, they gave way.

By 1901 the time was again ripe for a new revision of the Ascamot, and on this occasion a joint committee of the Elders and the Yehidim was appointed to carry out the work. The result appeared in 1905, and the new version was approved in the following year.

The amendments accepted were not of great importance. More interesting were those that were rejected by the Elders. The committee recommended that the Hazan should be permitted to commence the service in synagogue without first asking the permission of the presiding warden. This was refused. The proposal to increase the maximum finta for any Yahid to £50 and to reassess the finta triennially instead of biennially was also rejected. It was agreed, however, that salaried officials were no longer to be liable for finta. While the shape of the central organ of the Community was being moulded and new patterns were appearing, the subsidiary organizations of the Community were also undergoing changes. The relief of the poor, it will be remembered, was, after the provision of facilities for worship, the first work undertaken by the Community on its organization in the middle of the seventeenth century. This was at first a function of the Mahamad, and no separate institution was created for the purpose. From time to time pious donors created trusts, which the Mahamad directly or indirectly administered for the assistance of specific classes of Sephardim in need. By this means a group of organizations, all with related functions, came into existence. The creation in 1837 of a Board of Guardians to some extent reduced the state of disorder that had been a consequence, but there were still too many organizations doing very closely related work. At length, in 1878, the entire subject of poor relief was put on a satisfactory footing. As a preliminary, however, at the end of 1876 a minor reform was effected in a neighbouring field. 'Considering that the ancient charity known in our Congregation under the name of Cautivos[1] had long ceased to have any practical application and that it is unlikely again to have any legitimate call upon its fund, resolved that the funds allocated for its purposes be transferred to the General funds of the Congregation.' The *Honen Dalim*, established in 1724 as a combination of four existing societies for aiding poor women in child-bed, for helping the bereaved during their week of mourning and consequent absence from employment, and for granting dowries to fatherless girls, continued independent, but the administration of the *Mehil Sedaca*, established in 1720 for granting marriage portions, and the *Mahasim Tobim*, instituted in 1749 for apprenticing boys, lending money without interest, rewarding employés for their zeal, and assisting boys to emigrate, and of other similar institutions established later, was transferred to the Board of Guardians. So was also the large surplus income of the Lara Trust, with the proviso, however, that in accordance with

[1] For the ransom of captives.

the terms of the trust the beneficiaries should be limited to those whose parents were of Spanish or Portuguese origin on both sides, although it remained to some extent under the control of the Mahamad.[1] It was at the same time decided that the Board of Guardians should be given its independence, together with a handsome annual subsidy from congregational funds. This annual vote, which was supplemented by contributions from the members of the Congregation as individuals, did not represent the whole of the Congregation's contributions to relief and assistance. For the poor and dependent of its own Community there were still the Mahamad's payments to its pensioners.

From outside the country, appeals for assistance in periods of chronic or exceptional distress, for the relief of suffering, for the building or rebuilding of synagogues in all the four corners of the world were continuous. The Jews of Monastir in Serbia suffered severely from a widespread fire: not only was a grant made from the congregational funds, but there was an appeal from the pulpit to members of the Congregation to supplement the grant. The Sephardi Community in Montreal asked for assistance which had to be refused, but with an expression of 'the deep sympathy of the Elders at the position in which that congregation is placed and their regret at being unable to comply with his request'. Montreal had to be again refused a grant towards the cost of rebuilding their synagogue some years later, in 1884. They were, however, very persistent, for they appealed again in 1886 and 1887. In the year 1883 the synagogue of the Spanish and Portuguese Jewish Community in Kingston, Jamaica, was destroyed by fire. An appeal for a grant was at once sent to London. It was refused with the advice that the numbers of the Jewish Community of Jamaica had so greatly declined that it would be well if the applicants were to unite with the local Ashkenazi Community. The Kingston Sephardi Community took this advice and then asked for guidance in the preparation of a book of ritual for the United Congregation. But Bevis Marks was not yet finished with Jamaica, for two years later, in February 1886, came a renewed request for a grant, for the purchase of furniture. Again in 1907 there was another appeal for a grant for assistance after the earthquake and fire from which the Community had suffered in that year. In 1882 when the whole of world Jewry was deeply moved by the sufferings of the Jews in

[1] The distribution of the funds of this trust with the fulfilment of this condition was becoming more difficult every year. Inter-marriage between Sephardim and Ashkenazim and also with spouses, especially but not in every case wives, of non-Jewish origin, was becoming so prevalent that among the longer settled families it had become usual for a member to be of mixed parentage.

Russia, the Congregation made a grant of £200 to the Mansion House Fund that was being raised for their relief. In 1886 there was even an appeal from the Russian Zionist enthusiast, Leo Pinsker, who seems to have recently heard of the death of Sir Moses Montefiore and of the 'unnumbered millions' that he had bequeathed to the London Sephardi Community, asking for the means of establishing an agricultural settlement in Palestine. He was referred to Montefiore's executors. In 1890 came an appeal for assistance from the Jewish Community of Sefrow in Morocco; in 1893 there was one from the Jewish Community of Aberdeen to share the cost of providing them with a synagogue, and in the following year a similar one from Leeds. Early in 1895 a young gentleman, ambitious to qualify as a physician, asked the Mahamad to help him to do so, although he was not even a member of the Sephardi Community. In 1902 there came a request with a very strong sentimental support. The Jews of Lisbon, a remnant that had returned after centuries of exile, appealed for assistance to build themselves a synagogue. Even this appeal had to be refused. Financial conditions were too difficult at the time. An appeal from the Sephardi Community of the Dutch colony of Curaçao in 1881 was of a different character. It was for assistance in obtaining an Assistant Hazan. The London Community did its best and advertised for candidates, but there was no response. A curious application came late in 1885 when a 'Sephardi Congregation' in Dublin wrote to the authorities of Bevis Marks to inform them that they had recently been formed and comprised about one hundred members. They had appointed as their teacher Philip Wolfers, an Ashkenazi, but he had been immediately recalled by the Ashkenazi Delegate Chief Rabbi, Hermann Adler, who had no jurisdiction over them. They asked the Mahamad to intervene on their behalf. Inquiries were made of the Ashkenazi authorities from whom it was learnt that the new congregation in Dublin did not consist of Sephardim, but for the most part of Polish Ashkenazim who had seceded from the main Dublin Community and had set up a congregation of their own. In these circumstances the Mahamad declined to take any steps in the matter and little more was heard of the Dublin 'Sephardi' Congregation. Twenty-four years later, in 1909, another Ashkenazi congregation, the Rumanian Synagogue in London, asked to be taken under the spiritual authority of Bevis Marks. The request was rejected, but there was no pretence on this occasion. The attraction may have been the Haham, Gaster, who was of Rumanian origin.

In the meanwhile the influence of the State in the education of the children of the nation was continuing to grow and as it increased, the powers of the voluntary associations, of which the Sephardi Congregation was one, were correspondingly reduced. Furthermore, the cost of education was rising and the voluntary organizations were beginning to find their burdens heavier than they could support. The alternative for the Jewish school authorities was of course to surrender their responsibility for secular education and to concentrate on the provision of instruction in Hebrew and Judaism. The adoption of this course was in fact sooner or later inevitable. It was taken in connexion with the boys' school, the Shaaré Tikva, as early as 1885, but with the Girls' National and Infant School not until 1923. When these schools were closed provision was made for the instruction in Hebrew and Judaism after school hours, but only in East London. This continued until well into the present century, but for the children living away from the City nothing was done. Ultimately the City classes fell away through lack of attendance—the Sephardi population of eastern London was continuously diminishing—and their place was later taken by similar classes centring on Shepherd's Bush and Lauderdale Road. The few Sephardi children not thus provided for and anxious to receive instruction attended the increasingly large number of classes organized by the Ashkenazi Community to the cost of which the Congregation had, as well as the West London Synagogue, contributed over a long period in the form of annual grants to the Jewish Religious Education Board, previously the Association for the Diffusion of Religious Knowledge. At the same time the Elders appealed to the Yehidim as individuals to supplement these grants. The institution of children's services came later, after a long period of ineffectual effort. Such occasional services in the premises of the Girls' School were determined on as long ago as 1900, but although agreed to in principle by all concerned, one difficulty or hindrance arose after another, and very many years had to pass before they became a regular part of the congregational activities. During a long period from the beginning of the century the most that could be attained was an occasional address suited for children, but these, like angels' visits, were few and far between.

The school of higher studies, the Beth Hamedrash or Heshaim, was a different matter. This was a sphere with which the secular authorities of the country had no concern. On the other hand, it was also not unaffected by the general movement and change which touched every phase of life in the nineteenth century. Founded in the seventeenth century, it may have moved in the course of the subsequent two hundred years, but not as rapidly or as far as the nation as a whole or Sephardi Jewry had moved. It had lost touch with the Community, and the need for reform was evident probably to everyone who gave consideration to this instrument of Jewish education. The Elders certainly realized the state of affairs, for on 12 February 1880 they appointed a committee to confer with the governing body of the Heshaim on the position and working of that institution. This action was, however, not spontaneous, for the criticisms and pressure of the Mahamad made it inevitable. The Mahamad was now beginning to recover some of its former influence and power. The education and clothing of boys, originally one of the purposes of the institution, had been transferred to the Shaaré Tikva school in 1830. In 1867 the Heshaim and the Mahané Raphael were amalgamated and the funds of the *Assifat Haberim* were also placed at the disposal of the Heshaim for the assistance of the students. The report of the committee of 1880 stated that the statement of accounts

> 'which are of a satisfactory character form an exception to the general tenor of the entries (in the books that were kept) which are a record of disorderly conduct, uncourteous behaviour, and irregular attendance of members. A visit paid to the Heshaim only lately to ascertain what its present arrangements were, elicited these facts: that during the month of Tebet 5639 (1879/80) no attendance whatever is registered and after the 15th Iyar 5639 (1879) a great number of leaves are torn out of the attendance books and lastly from 24th Nisan to the 15th Tamuz 5640 (April/July 1880) appear names of those signing but no detail is given of any proceedings; it is entirely left to imagination to infer what really has been done by the so-called Students, and that it appears two or three persons form the average number present.'

The committee recommended that a suitable head of the Heshaim should be appointed and the co-operation of scholars connected with 'the sister congregations' who should 'expound the law' occasionally in the Medrash should be obtained, that without affecting the position of the present students of the Medrash, in the case of future ones, payments to them should be made, not as a matter of course, but as the result of periodical examinations, that special courses of study should be provided for boys of the congregational schools, and that proper records of attendance should in future be kept. The report was adopted by the Elders on 13 February 1881 and confirmed a fortnight later.

The intentions were excellent, but unfortunately their results were quite inadequate. Very little improvement, if any, was evident as a consequence of them, for five years later the situation was not much altered. According to the annual report of the Mahamad of 17 January 1886

> 'For some years every Elder of this Congregation has desired to place the Medrash in a position worthy of its name, and in a way to accomplish the purposes for which such an Institution should exist; but unfortunately as each year has rolled on, so the working of the Medrash has become less and less efficient until it has arrived at such a point as to be no longer a source of honour and pride, as it should be, but rather a byword among its members, and those of other Congregations. No single instance can be brought forward of any good that has come from the classes or readings that are supposed to take place there twice a week during the year. No new scholar has of late years asked to be admitted to the religious readings, and only your three Hazanim are recorded as students on the books. There is no disguising the fact that this is most unsatisfactory; ill health compels one of these gentlemen to absent himself very frequently; distance from the Medrash no doubt at times interferes with another gentleman's attendance, and the third, having thrown upon him extra duties through the illness of his colleague, is frequently unable to attend. If you can accomplish this, you will be supplying a great want, which has long existed, and by sending forth to the world young men, renowned for piety and deep research, and worthy of any position to which they may aspire, you will, in the opinion of the Mahamad, be faithfully carrying out the wishes of the venerable Testator, whose one ambition in life was to see the Law of God and the teachings of our sages upheld in all their dignity and grandeur.'

This appeal to the Elders was not without effect. A new Haham had by now been appointed, one full of vigour, mental as well as physical, better aware than anyone in the Congregation of what a Medrash should be and anxious to raise the reputation of that of London to a level of which all connected with it might properly be proud. The recent death of Sir Moses Montefiore provided an opportunity for combining his ideals regarding the Judith Lady Montefiore College with those of Gaster and of the directors of the Community who were at his back. A scheme was drafted whereby the two institutions should in effect be merged and the joint institution become a college of the higher Jewish learning, the alumni to be able to pursue their studies in comfortable surroundings, freed from economic cares, under the direction of competent teachers. These proposals were accepted by the Elders, and the first student of the new class to be enrolled was Harry S. Lewis of St. John's College, Cambridge, a graduate of that university. Part of the scheme was to have been the retirement of Louis Loewe, who had been put in charge of the College long before by Sir Moses Montefiore. Loewe died two years later, and the Haham, Moses Gaster, was appointed Principal.

Lewis remained a collegiate for only a year and then resigned. His withdrawal gave a serious blow to the hopes of the reformers. A member of that class in the English Jewish Community from which there had been no previous recruits for the ministry, or even for Jewish scholarship for the greater part of a century, it was hoped that he would have created a precedent to be followed by others of his class. Lewis, on leaving the College, at first devoted himself—he was a man of independent means—to social work. Ultimately he entered the Ministry in Manchester and later in New York, returning to London after his retirement to die there in 1940. With Gaster as Principal—he of course retained his office of Haham—a new era opened in the history of Montefiore College, but it was of short duration. Difficulties arose which spread from Ramsgate to London. Long and deep controversies ensued as a consequence of which bitterness was displayed on both sides. In the end the experiment which had been so full of promise was terminated, and the College at Ramsgate returned to its earlier form, a home for retired Jewish scholars—in many cases officials of Ashkenazi congregations—who were given opportunities of continuing their studies if they wished to do so. For the five vacancies for collegiates there were sixty applicants. Gaster ceased to be Principal and was free to devote the whole of his energies to his office of Haham and to his other Jewish and scholarly interests. There was a project to combine Montefiore College with Jews' College, London, the theological seminary in the establishment of which the Congregation under the lead of Montefiore had shown some interest almost half a century earlier. The Elders were, however, advised that this could not be done without the sanction of the Charity Commissioners, for which sanction it was not at the time considered expedient to apply. Instead it was decided to make an annual grant of a thousand pounds, which amount had later, after the outbreak of the first World War, to be reduced, from the income of the Montefiore

College and Synagogue Endowment, amounting to about £5,500, and to place on loan at Jews' College the greater part of its library, which, under the direction of Gaster, had been greatly enriched. In return the Sephardi Community was given generous representation on the Council of the Jews' College.

The bitter feelings that were aroused by the secession in 1840 that led to the establishment of the West London Synagogue of British Jews had been soothed many years before the date now reached. Not only were the bitter strictures and severe penalties imposed on the seceders repealed and social intercourse, which had never been completely interrupted, fully restored, but it was not long before means of co-operation outside the field of the synagogue and religious worship were being employed on both sides. Leading members, clerical as well as lay, were soon accustomed to attend the lay functions of one another's communities. Members of the West London Synagogue readily gave support to the charitable and even educational institutions in the direction of which many of their ancestors had been so prominent. In the councils and work of such institutions as the Anglo-Jewish Association, Sephardi and Reform and also Ashkenazi sat side by side and worked together. When in 1895 it was realized that the historic cemetery in Mile End could not much longer be utilized and that a new one would very soon have to be found, large enough to serve the Congregation for at least a century and in a district, while within reach of Bevis Marks, was yet free from urban settlement, it was with the West London Synagogue authorities that the Sephardi Congregation co-operated in the joint purchase of land to serve both congregations, with the two cemeteries under joint management. It is interesting to note that of the first members of this committee of management the representatives of the West London Synagogue included Herbert G. Lousada, a collateral descendant of that Antonio Lousada, otherwise Moses Baruch, who was Gabay of the Spanish and Portuguese Congregation when it was first constituted in 1663, and that one of the Sephardi representatives was Arthur Lindo, a direct descendant of that Lorenço (in the Synagogue Isaac) Lindo who worshipped with his kinsmen in London even earlier, before Jews were permitted to have a cemetery in England. Each community appointed a Mocatta to the committee, Benjamin Elkin Mocatta from the West London Synagogue, Edward Lumbrozo Mocatta from Bevis Marks, distant cousins, both descended from Moses Mocatta, who, from his settlement in London when the Congregation was but a few years old until his death twenty years later, was

THE PENULTIMATE HALF-CENTURY 391

prominent in the counsels of Bevis Marks as he was, in another sphere, in the City.

Almost from the beginning there was an occasional return to the fold of Bevis Marks of a few of those who had at first joined the seceders. Prominent among these was Jacob Montefiore, who explained when withdrawing from the Burton Street Congregation that he could not withstand the pressure of his parents-in-law, of the Ashkenazi New Synagogue family of Gompertz. At first he joined no congregation in London being part of the time resident in Australia. But when he finally resettled in England he became again a Yahid. Of Joseph d'Aguilar Samuda, another of the original seceders, the story has already been told. The recruits from the West London Synagogue of a later generation were, however, not always of Sephardi origin. First among them was a member of the Goldsmid family. There was some grievance or objection on the part of ladies of this family, two or three of whom resigned from the West London Synagogue at this time. They were daughters of Sir Isaac Lyon Goldsmid and sisters of Sir Francis, the most prominent of the Ashkenazi founders. Rachel had married Count Salomon Henri d'Avigdor, son of Isaac Samuel Avigdor, a Sephardi from the south of France, one of the leading members of Napoleon's Paris Sanhedrin. Salomon d'Avigdor had settled in England, frequenting the circle in which the younger Napoleon and the Count d'Orsay and sometimes Benjamin Disraeli shone. In England he married a daughter of Sir Isaac Lyon Goldsmid and they later went to France in the wake of the Napoleon who was to become the Emperor Napoleon III. By Napoleon d'Avigdor was created Duke d'Acquaviva. The Countess d'Avigdor, as she was always known, did not, however, remain in France, but returned after a few years, in 1858, with her three young sons to England. In England she worshipped in the synagogue that her family had helped to found, but later, in 1884, first her two elder sons, Elim and Sergius, a few months later she herself, were admitted as Yehidim of the Spanish and Portuguese Community. Elim d'Avigdor in due course took a leading part in the work of the Congregation, occupying at one time or another most of the leading offices, until his death at the age of fifty-three, early in 1895. Elim d'Avigdor was a man of boundless energy, with wide interests. His profession of railway engineer he followed with ardour. At the same time he was a prolific writer and journalist, on the lighter side of journalism and literature. In a number of other communal activities he was almost equally prominent. He was one of the founders of the Maccabaeans. The Anglo-Jewish

Association owed much to him. Above all, his interest in the resettlement of Jews in Palestine made him one of the pillars of the *Chovevé Zion* (Lovers of Zion) Movement. His son, Osmond, later Sir Osmond d'Avigdor-Goldsmid, Bart., also became a Yahid, but resigned after nine years—at the end of 1908—to join the West London Synagogue.

Three years before the d'Avigdors joined the Sephardi Community there was another recruit from the West London Synagogue, one also who was to leave his imprint on the story of Anglo-Jewry. This was Oswald John Simon, whose father, Sergeant Simon, later Sir John Simon, M.P., although not a founder, was among the earliest of the prominent members of the Congregation that set up its house of worship in Burton Street. Oswald Simon was twenty-six at the time, but before the Elders would accept him, his father was asked whether he had any objection to their doing so. Mr. Sergeant Simon raised no objection, but the son remained in his new community for only two months. Of an entirely different character was the admission as a Yahid, in 1885, of Frederic David Mocatta. Not only was he a son of that Abraham Mocatta who had been among the founders of the West London Synagogue and a son-in-law of Frederick Goldsmid also prominent among the Ashkenazi founders: he had himself served as warden of the West London Synagogue of which he retained his membership and was to become eleven years later chairman of its Council and president, holding these offices until shortly before his death in 1905. He remained a Yahid until his death, thus being for a period of twenty years a member of both congregations. And in both he was honoured. In 1900, at a time when he was the lay head of he Reform Community, he was actually proposed and accepted as a warden of the Sephardi Congregation. The resolution was to hold him in reserve and if another candidate, who was considered to have a prior claim to the office, had not accepted, Mocatta would presumably have been elected Parnas. In these circumstances it is not altogether surprising that when Philip Magnus, previously a minister of the West London Synagogue and later to be chairman of its Council and its president, asked that his son, Laurie, should be allowed to read the portion of the Law in the Synagogue in Bryanston Street on the occasion of his *Bar-Mitzvah*, permission was given. 'Although not a member of your Synagogue, I should very much like my elder boy Laurie to be called up in the usual orthodox manner to read his portion on his thirteenth birthday. . . . Attaching some importance to the ancient Bar Mitzvah rule, I shall be glad if you are able to accede to my application.'

Permission was given by the Elders by a vote of nine to four, the minority arguing that Magnus should first seek admission as a Yahid. The future Sir Philip Magnus was at the time a warden of the West London Synagogue. When David Woolf Marks, the first minister of the same Synagogue to be appointed, whose prayer book brought down the solemn excommunication by the Sephardi authorities, died in 1909, the Elders formally passed a resolution of sympathy with the West London Synagogue in their loss.

On the other side of the account there was an incident that would have been unthinkable in the early eighteen-forties. Among the families that were split at the time of the great secession of 1842 was that of Montefiore. Sir Moses was a stalwart and determined supporter of the old order: his brother, Horatio, was one of the founders of the new congregation. The third brother, Abraham, had died eighteen years earlier, leaving two sons, Joseph Mayer and Nathaniel, both of whom remained in the older Community, taking in course of time a prominent part in its administration. Nathaniel was a parnas when he died in 1883, and a request was then made by his widow and surviving son that he should be buried in the cemetery of the West London Synagogue, near the grave of his elder son. Leonard Montefiore had died a young man, but already with a reputation to his credit and with the unfulfilled promise of an honourable and distinguished career before him. Although a Yahid, he had been buried in the cemetery of the West London Synagogue, perhaps for sentimental reasons since his mother, one of the Goldsmids, belonged to a family for which it was the last resting-place. The Mahamad not only acquiesced in the last wishes of their dead warden—they could not do otherwise. They attended the funeral, and during the week of mourning which was strictly observed, the Hazanim of the Congregation read prayers in the house of the mourners. Nathaniel Montefiore's younger son, Claude, later joined the West London Synagogue and ultimately founded the Liberal Jewish Synagogue. Claude Montefiore himself on occasions attended service in Lauderdale Road and was called to the Law just as if he were an ordinary Yahid. Half a generation later one of the ministers of the West London Synagogue, attending a service in Lauderdale Road, was similarly called to the Law. Almost seventy years earlier, in 1882, the question was put by the wardens of the Manchester Sephardi Synagogue to the authorities at Bevis Marks, whether a member of the Reform Community in that city could in similar circumstances be given a *mitzva* or honour in the synagogue. The reply came without hesitation that the Mahamad considered that 'any Jew attending our synagogue may have a mizvah given to him'.

There were at times other interesting questions put to the authorities of Bevis Marks. A Sephardi who had married civilly a Christian woman and had had by her a son, who had been circumcised, applied to the Ashkenazi Chief Rabbi for the admission of his wife and child to the Jewish community. A Sephardi being involved in the matter, the Chief Rabbi inquired the wishes of the Mahamad. The Mahamad displayed no interest. 'The Wardens have no wish to express in the matter but leave the Beth Din to deal with the question as they deem proper.' By now the bar to the reception of proselytes by the Sephardim had been completely demolished. The first exception was made by Artom. Gaster on his entry into office at once wholeheartedly followed the precedent, after asking the permission of the Mahamad. Henceforth the acceptance of proselytes was not sufficiently exceptional to arouse attention. Most of these were for marriage purposes, in many cases a civil marriage having preceded the conversion, but this was not always the case. The Mahamad authorized a religious remarriage following the acceptance of the proselyte, but in the records of these authorizations the absence of all enthusiasm was for long very obvious. On one occasion an entire family, father, mother, and children were received into the Community, the parents being remarried in the Synagogue and the new name of Moses Gaster being given to the head of the family. However, in 1915, the Mahamad did refuse permission for two marriages on the ground that the parties had neither legal nor moral claim on the Congregation. In both cases the bridegrooms were proselytes and the brides Ashkenazi girls. The Haham, who had accepted the bridegrooms as proselytes, protested against this decision. Any proselyte admitted by him he contended was *ipso facto* a member of the Sephardi Community. The Mahamad was compelled to give way. After much consideration it decided to give the required permission, provided that the bridegrooms became members of the Congregation and remained so, at least, until after their marriages, and that they attended at least four sabbath services. The Haham was at the same time informed that while the Mahamad admitted his right to receive proselytes, such admission 'does not constitute in any way whatsoever any claim on the Congregation'. One application for a marriage was emphatically rejected. Marriage between uncle and niece is permissible under Jewish law, and was legal in England until 1837, when the exceptions allowed to Jewish marriages were withdrawn by legislation. In August 1888 a request to authorize such a marriage—a religious one only—was refused, 'it being in direct contravention to the Law of this country'.

In 1891 the Haham, Moses Gaster, was married by the Ashkenazi Chief Rabbi, in the Bevis Marks Synagogue, and nine years afterwards the compliment was in a sense returned by permission being given to the Hazan, Joseph Piperno, to officiate at an Ashkenazi wedding in the Hampstead Synagogue. Half a century later on the occasion of an Ashkenazi bridegroom marrying in an Ashkenazi synagogue the daughter of a prominent Sephardi family, the Haham took a prominent part in the ceremony. Years earlier there had been drastic reforms in the arrangements for marriages under the auspices of the Community. In 1902 fees payable to the Synagogue were first introduced. Hitherto the bridegroom was accustomed to give the officiating minister whatever fee or douceur he might consider appropriate. A scale of fees, rising from five shillings to five guineas—later to ten and occasionally even higher —was laid down by the Elders, but this minimum was in suitable circumstances reduced or even no fee required. On the other hand, in cases that were considered appropriate, in which the bridegroom was not a Yahid, he was required to pay also an additional fee of five guineas for a grave, in anticipation of one being needed at some future date. In 1909 the third-class weddings, those agreed to most grudgingly at which the Haham and Hazanim were forbidden to officiate, were abolished. In 1896 the rule that it rested with the Mahamad to decide who should marry the bridal couple—the Haham, one of the Hazanim or the Samas—had also been abrogated. Henceforth the bridegroom was free to make his own choice. There was one incident, connected with a burial, not a wedding, that grates a little even after the lapse of half a century. The entry in the minutes of the Mahamad of 20 November 1899 runs as follows:

> 'Read a letter from Mr. Leslie I. Montefiore on the subject of the inscription to be placed on the tombstone of his late sister interred in our Hendon Cemetery, and pointing out the hardship to her children that her married name could not appear, since she had married out of the Jewish faith, though he had admitted that this was stipulated at the time of burial. Ordered that Mr. Montefiore be informed in reply that every consideration had been given to his representations, but the Mahamad regretted that it was not in their power to vary a rule, which, it is believed has existed for all time in the Congregation.'

The deceased lady was a daughter of Jacob Montefiore and Lydia

Gompertz, a niece of Sir Moses. She married Jacob Williams who later assumed the surname de Wilton. Her children appealed against the refusal. Inevitably the marriage was not recognized by the Synagogue authorities. Ten years later there was a similar case, also one of refusal, in which the non-Jewish husband begged for permission for his name to be included in the epitaph. However, the Mahamad did relent to some extent. When the subject arose once again, in 1914, it was referred to the Haham, who made the humane suggestion of a compromise. He ruled that the marriage could not be recognized by the Congregation, but there was no objection to the inscription on the tombstone of both the maiden and married names of the lady connected by a hyphen. The subject arose once again in 1920, and this time, the Haham having retired, there was a reversion to the earlier practice, only the unmarried name of the lady being permitted in the inscription.

New Yehidim were being admitted to the Congregation at almost every meeting of the Mahamad. The rule that both parents, that even one must be Sephardi had long since been abrogated and these admissions in very few instances call for comment. In only two or three instances over a long period of years need one stop for a moment. As long ago as 1860 one Mordecai Levy Lawson, who, judging by his name, should have been a member of the Levy family of which Lord Burnham is now the representative, was admitted a Yahid. That family was then connected with the West London Synagogue. He cannot, however, be identified. Some years later Benjamin Leopold Farjeon, the novelist who had lived for some years in New Zealand, applied for admission. A decision was deferred and the application was withdrawn. Two years later he married a non-Jewess. In 1892 Auguste van Biene, for half a century and more widely popular as a 'cellist, was admitted a Yahid. A new Yahid of a different character was Harold F. Aguilar, who was elected in 1898. He was a son of Emanuel Abraham Aguilar, himself the son of another Emanuel Aguilar who had been active in the congregation and had served as parnas for more than one term. The younger Emanuel Aguilar has been mentioned as a musician. While studying in Frankfurt he married Sarah, daughter of Elias Lindo, the eldest son of David Abarbanel Lindo, who had settled in Germany. Emanuel and Sarah Aguilar later returned to England where they lived as Christians and had their son, Harold, baptized as a child. It was this son who applied for readmission to the Community and was accepted. Other Yehidim of this period and the following years, better known without the Community than within it, were Solomon I. da Costa

(1825–1907), the conchologist; David James, born Belasco (1839–93), the actor, who left a legacy to the Congregation; Raphael Meldola (1839–1915), the chemist and F.R.S., a grandson of the Haham of the same name; Alfred Sutro (1863–1933), dramatist; Frederick George Aflalo (1870–1918), distinguished as a writer on sport and especially on angling, a son of Moses Aflalo, who served as Elder for fifty-six years; Sir Philip Sassoon, Bart., G.B.E. (1888–1939), a grandson of Sir Albert Sassoon, after being private secretary to Earl Haig, Commander-in-Chief in France from 1915 to 1918, successively Under-Secretary of State for Air and First Commissioner of Works. Sassoon was also eminent as a patron of the arts, a connoisseur and a social leader; Philip Guedalla (1889–1939), historian and man of letters who was also an Elder; Rudolph de Cordova (1859–1941), playwright and journalist, who had come from Jamaica many years before; and Moses Mordecai Simeon Gubbay (1876–1947), a distinguished Anglo-Indian civil servant who later turned to banking in London. Israel Solomons (1860–1923), the Jewish antiquary, was Ashkenazi in origin but became a Yahid some twenty years before his death. The Rt. Hon. Leslie Hore-Belisha was Secretary of State for War and a member of the War Cabinet for a time during the second World War, and at the same time one of the Elders of the Congregation and of its representatives on the Jewish Board of Deputies. Members of the de Pass family in successive generations took a prominent part in the direction of the Congregation. At the same time many of them and also members of the related family of Levy Bensusan—some intimately connected with the London Sephardi Community—were prominent in the early development—industrial and commercial—of South Africa. Members of this family also took their share in the establishment of a Jewish community there, Aaron de Pass (1815–77) being one of the first elders of the Cape Town Hebrew Congregation, and his brother, Elias (1829–1913), its honorary secretary.

By now the complexion of the Community had changed considerably. The names of the Yehidim were still for the most part Sephardi, whatever those of their mothers may have been, but the Lopezes, the Baruch Lousadas, the Gonzales, the Nunes, and others of the seventeenth and early eighteenth centuries, savouring of the peninsula, had become exceptional. Prominent in their place were not only Italian ones such as Montefiore, but also those reminiscent of oriental lands—Aloof, Abecasis, and above all Sassoon. The transition is marked by the names of the new Yehidim admitted on one day—3 January 1875—Edgar Lindo,

Jacob de Naphtali Pass, Haim Mendoza, Arthur J. Montefiore, Arthur Montefiore Sebag, and Sir Albert Sassoon, C.S.I. With two exceptions all the sons of David Sassoon of Bombay settled in England and became Yehidim, and in the case of one of these exceptions the widow did so. David Sassoon's widow, moreover, became a Yehida, and when she died and was buried in the communal cemetery her sons reserved twenty graves near hers for other members of the family. Later the related Gubbay family reserved ten. The first of the sons to settle in England, Sassoon D. Sassoon, was very active in the affairs of the Community, until his early death in 1867. Two of his brothers also, Reuben and Arthur, served their turns on the Mahamad and were Elders over a long period. The attractions of the Court, however, weaned them away from the communal service. In the next generation Sir Edward Sassoon, the son of Sir Albert Sassoon, Bart., served on the Mahamad for more than one term and was for a number of years President of the Elders. His cousin, David Solomon Sassoon, was more active in Jewish scholarship than in administration. This David Sassoon's mother, Flora (*née* Abraham, later Gubbay), the widow of Solomon David Sassoon, stood out in the record of Anglo-Sephardi womanhood. If women had gained admission to the ranks of the Elders in her day, she would certainly have been the first of them.

Seldom did a decade pass in which the clash of personalities among the group with whom the direction of the Congregation rested did not culminate in quarrels. Many of the Parnassim and Elders served the Community under a sense of *noblesse oblige*, for they were descendants of its founders and of those who supported the burden and enjoyed the happiness of its maintenance during the succeeding generations. The founders, coming from a land of hot tempers, were themselves hot-tempered, and for long their descendants inherited that characteristic, even though it was by the passage of time modified. Later immigration from the Arab lands brought with it the characteristics of their fellow nationals, and among these also was manifest the tendency easily to become excited, almost to lose control of oneself, to repent later for what was said or done in haste. Some Yehidim were of course more prone to this than others. Haim Guedalla had to some extent a gift for getting unduly excited, but in one of his fellow elders he seems to have met more than his match. It is only a couple of generations since Guedalla found himself compelled to appeal to the Elders for protection. Reminding them that he had been one of their number for forty-seven years, he begged them to intervene on his behalf. There had been a heated meeting of the Elders, and as a consequence of what passed there his colleague had instituted an action for libel against Guedalla. The Mahamad with its superior authority was asked to intervene. This it did, it is to be hoped, to the satisfaction of all parties. A year later the same gentleman appeared again in the minutes. On this occasion he had taken the first steps in legal proceedings against the Mahamad itself, whom he accused of breaking the laws of the Congregation by postponing the election of parnassim. The Elders came to the assistance of the Mahamad. The offender was severely censured, and the proceedings were stopped.

As a survival of the early days—a survival that continued in the mother community of Amsterdam even longer—the authorities of Bevis Marks were very jealous of their records. Very occasionally they relented somewhat, and it was partly as a consequence of the assistance they gave to James Picciotto that his pioneer and fascinating work on the Jews in England was able to appear in 1875. A far more distinguished historian than he, however, Lucien Wolf, was refused access to the records thirteen years later, although he had the influential support of the Anglo-Jewish Historical Exhibition which was then being organized. Even the offer to index the registers of births, deaths, and marriages was refused. Wolf was not a Yahid, not even a congregante. A later request by the Jewish Historical Society itself to be permitted to copy and publish the earliest minutes of the Congregation was also refused. Almost twenty years later when another Ashkenazi, with the support of the Jewish Historical Society, made a similar application, the matter was considered to be too weighty to be decided by an ordinary meeting of the Mahamad and was deferred for consideration by a complete Mahamad. The request seems to have been lost to sight or withdrawn, for there is no further reference to it in the minutes. An application two or three years later for a copy of the new edition of the Ascamot led to the reply that they were confidential and could not be given to any but Yehidim. However, almost immediately afterwards a copy was presented on request to the Library of Jews' College, of which the disappointed applicant was secretary. The Ashkenazi who had been refused in 1903 had to become a Yahid nine years later before he was given access to the records. Then everything was placed most generously at his disposal. Another Ashkenazi, Israel Solomons, already outstanding as a Jewish antiquary, was more wary. First he became a Yahid and then asked for access to the records. This request was readily granted, but the grant was little more than a gesture. Most of the records—and those the most interesting—were inaccessible. They were in a safe deposit, for there was no satisfactory accommodation at the offices of the Congregation. However, in 1900 all the records were at the disposal of the Haham, Moses Gaster, while he was engaged on his historical sketch, the publication of which formed part of the celebration of the bi-centenary of the opening of the Synagogue in Bevis Marks in 1701. The suggestion for this volume came in the first instance from Gaster, but the Elders were not sympathetic. Later, however, the Mahamad urged the Elders to reconsider their decision and they did so. Gaster wrote not only his history for the celebration of the bi-centenary. Contemporary with it also was a new edition of the Sephardi prayer book which he undertook and brought to a successful conclusion.

More recently the care of the Congregational records has been systematized. Not only are they accessible to students, but they are being put in order and catalogued, and the artistic treasures kept in good state. Gradually, also, the records are being edited and published. This work of care and publication has been placed under the charge of the Advisory Committee on Congregational Records which was instituted in February 1915.

In these last years of the nineteenth century there were a few incidents, trivial in themselves, yet perhaps worthy of mention in that they help to throw light on the life of the Community, and of its members, on its reaction to outside opinion, and perhaps on its fears. Over a long period of its history the Congregation was the owner of a public-house, 'The Old Three Mackerels' in the Mile End Road, the transfer of the lease of which to a succession of publicans runs almost like a continuous thread through the minutes of the Mahamad or Elders. How this property came into the possession of the Congregation there is no record. Probably it was the gift or legacy of some pious Yahid who when he retired from his activities knew of no better successor than Bevis Marks. The income from this property was enjoyed for a century or more, until in 1931 it was at length sold for a good price, after a number of previous offers had been refused. It may be that this long connexion of the Congregation with 'The Trade' was the reason why, in 1889, the lessee of a newly opened public-house at the corner of Heneage Lane—a neighbour of the Synagogue—appealed to the Mahamad for support for his application for an extension of his licence. Despite the similarity of their interests the Mahamad did not respond. An offer to lease part of their unoccupied land in Mile End for the accommodation of a circus was also declined.

Earlier unexpected entries in the minutes of the Mahamad relate to the damage caused by wanton boys to the Barrow almshouses, to prevent which one of the residences in the block was in the summer of 1882 placed at the disposal of a police constable at the nominal rental of five shillings a week. Many years later at the end of 1924 there was apparently a more serious request for protection or self-protection. The wife of the keeper of the Beth Haim in the Mile End Road, nervous of the possibility of being interviewed by a burglar, asked the Mahamad to support her application for a revolver licence. The request was not entertained. An entry in the minutes of a different character records how, in one instance, while steps were being taken to arrange the realization and transfer to the Congregation of a handsome legacy that had been bequeathed by one of its members, his widow suddenly came forward and claimed from the Congregation the dowry to which she said she was entitled. The Mahamad referred her to the executors, remarking, not inappropriately, that it was somewhat strange that she had waited sixty years for the dowry, which she claimed was due on her marriage.

One worry, that seemed to increase instead of diminishing as decade succeeded decade, was the difficulty in securing the interest of the members in the administration of the Congregation and also even in the synagogue services. Satisfied probably with the manner in which their affairs were managed, it was, when no topic of burning interest appeared on the agenda, often difficult to get a sufficient number of Yehidim to attend the statutory meetings. On one occasion, in the winter of 1891–2, three successive meetings of the Yehidim had to be called for the election of members of the Board of Guardians. At the first two of these the number of attendants fell short of a quorum, and since the work of the Board could not stand still, the retiring members had to be granted indemnity for acting after their term of office had expired. The Yehidim had grown tired of routine. When, however, a matter of wider interest was on the agenda they did not hesitate to come forward. Elections of representatives on the Board of Deputies, for instance, were not always perfunctory proceedings. Sometimes they were allied to subjects of controversy. They also afforded opportunities for inter-personal relations, always quick to arouse interest. There was one such fiercely contested election in 1901 when to fill a casual vacancy Joseph de Castro, one of the inner circle of the Elders, secured 107 votes as against 48 for his opponent, Abraham Lindo Henry. In the synagogue, habits had changed and also residences had spread over the whole of the metropolitan area. There had been a time when regular attendance at the synagogue, not only on sabbaths and the major festivals, but also on minor fasts and festivals and Monday and Thursday mornings, at least, had been the rule, an exception to which aroused attention. But this time was long past. A voluntary quorum on sabbaths and the major festivals was all that could be normally expected: occasionally at the end of the century this minimum number was not always available in Bevis Marks, even on a sabbath. To meet the difficulty recourse had for long been had to paid *minyanistas*. It must not, however, be deduced from these failings that the loyalty of the greater part of the Community and their pride in and love for their *alma mater* was in any way diminished. In some cases the relationship was even felt to be closer.

CHAPTER XX

THE LAST FIFTY YEARS

WE ARE NOW approaching the present day, when history merges into the narration of current events, in which the trees are inevitably more prominent than the wood. The appraisal of the events of yesterday is more difficult than of a century or even half a century ago. One is too close to them to be able to judge, especially when the whole of the material on which to base a judgment is not yet available. The historian ought never to deal or attempt to deal with events of which he has a personal knowledge. These should be left to his successor, who will have the advantage of being a student without the disadvantage of being a contemporary. Yet the story of the Sephardim in England cannot properly be allowed to end at the beginning of the twentieth century. An epilogue to cover the last fifty years is necessary, but it must not be taken as an attempt even at a full record of those fifty years. This period opened very appropriately with the celebration, in the old synagogue in Bevis Marks, on 26 June 1901, of the opening of that edifice to public worship. The celebration was fitting to the occasion. Not only did it mark the growth and development of the Community from the small group that met first in secret more than two centuries earlier in a small room in the city. By the presence at the service of representatives of the whole of the Anglo-Jewish Community, from the meticulously observant *Machzike Hadat* to the West London Synagogue, the sons and grandsons of those whose secession from the parent congregation sixty years earlier, had almost endangered its continuous existence, all were made aware, if anyone still doubted, that in essentials Anglo-Jewry was one. A link with its children beyond the seas was the presence of Henry Pereira Mendes, whose father had as a boy come to it and its service from the West Indies, and had after a long interval returned to the new world to minister to some of the descendants of Bevis Marks who had settled there. The presence of the Lord Mayor and Sheriffs touched on the relations in earlier times between the Congregation and the State and in particular the City of London. This attendance of the Lord Mayor at a service in Bevis Marks was, however, not a precedent, for thirty-five years earlier, in February 1866, a predecessor had attended a sabbath service.

This celebration, marking an historic date in the story of the

Community, was followed some eighteen months later by the death of its civil head, whose term of service, linked with that of his famous kinsman, covered almost a century. Sir Joseph Sebag-Montefiore had been born and bred for the service of the Sephardim of England. When he died he had for many years been its titular head, but this was and is to a large extent an honorary post. In addition, in early manhood and middle age and beyond, he had taken to himself a large part of the direction and day-to-day work of Bevis Marks. Although he had resigned the presidency of the Elders not very long before his death, he died in harness. He remained the representative of the Mahamad and Elders at Ramsgate, and the administration of the Congregation's affairs there was in his hands. Only ten days before his death he presided at a meeting called to deal with those affairs. Sir Joseph's heir, in public as in private life, was his eldest son, Arthur, but he had died seven years earlier, while still in early manhood. In his few years he also had thrown himself wholeheartedly into the work of the Community and had attained to a position of authority and influence that marked him out as the successor of his father and to some extent also of his great-uncle. His brothers, Edmund and Cecil, took their share, but never aspired to take their father's place. The mantle fell or rather was about to be donned by one of the next generation, Robert, the eldest son of Arthur. He took the place, to which he may be said to have been born, in the Community and also his share in English public life. Unfortunately he was one of the national and communal sacrifices of the first World War, dying of wounds sustained in action in 1915. In his devotion to public service he was, however, not solitary either in his family or in his generation. His brothers have taken their share in public service, and the eldest of them, Mr. Charles Sebag-Montefiore, in due course succeeded to the lay headship of the Community, previously held by their grandfather.

Sir Joseph Sebag-Montefiore was not the only heavy loss the Congregation suffered during the first years of the twentieth century. In April 1908 Gabriel Lindo died, and in the following year Joseph de Castro. Both had given a lifetime of service to the Community, succeeding in that their fathers and their grandfathers. Lindo had risen to the position of vice-president of the Elders in 1904 in succession to Sir Francis Montefiore on his election as president in place of Sir Edward Sassoon. Lindo was also for many years solicitor to the Congregation in succession to his father, Nathaneel. De Castro was the only son of Hananel de Castro, and as he had no sons himself, with him the family died out of the annals of Anglo-Jewry. Joseph de Castro was identified with the history of the Sephardi Community for half a century. He also was vice-president of the Elders at the time of his death. For more than fifty years he had been an Elder and had filled almost every honorary office in the Congregation. These few names have been selected for mention as outstanding. They represent a far larger number of Yehidim who, conscious of the duty imposed on them by their ancestry and at the same time harkening to the call of their Community, spent wholeheartedly their time and thought in its service. Many another name will be found in the list of the Mahamad at the end of this volume. So long as that list continues to extend no one need fear for the future and welfare of *Sahar Asamaim*.

The mutual approach of Sephardi and Ashkenazi, which had been apparent for a century and longer continued to gain strength until, while retaining each its individuality, the two communities had become, and realized that they had become, one. In all communal work and interests outside of the synagogue there was no difference between their members. There was a time when some sort of proportional representation was observed in the different forms of co-operation, but that also passed and in this common field a man or woman was no longer chosen by or for the Community of which he or she was a member, but solely on the basis of suitability. Each Community readily placed its synagogues at the disposal of the other when—for instance, on the occasion of a largely attended wedding—greater accommodation was required. At first the hospitality was always on the part of the Ashkenazim, but after the destruction of the Ashkenazi Great Synagogue in an air raid in May 1941 the Sephardim were able to some extent to repay the debt. Fifty years earlier, in 1890, the Bevis Marks Synagogue was lent to the Federation of Synagogues for the inauguration of their newly appointed rabbi. There was also an occasional interchange of pulpit, and ministers were invited to take part in marriages in one another's congregations. When, in 1919, the synagogue which the Ashkenazi Chief Rabbi was accustomed to attend, was closed for redecoration and repair, a suitable seat was immediately placed at his disposal at the neighbouring Lauderdale Road. Still earlier, in 1897, when the almshouses of the (Ashkenazi) Jewish Board of Guardians were temporarily not available, the inmates were received in those of the Sephardi Community.

Between the Orthodox and the Reformed congregations there was no interchange of pulpits, and the need for the loan of a synagogue from one to the other never arose, but when the Communal Centre of the West London Synagogue was consecrated in 1934 the Sephardi Congregation was represented by one of its ministers and later, when the West London Synagogue needed *sepharim* for its overflow services on the principal Holy Days, the Sephardi Congregation readily lent some of its own. In the year 1890 Lord Rothschild, as President of the United Synagogue, put forward a far-seeing scheme for dealing with all aspects of the problem of the large population of poorer Jews—almost entirely Ashkenazim—in East London and the Elders were invited to send representatives to a conference, convened to consider the proposals. This was, however, a matter that not only in effect concerned Ashkenazim alone, but was also in part concerned with provision of synagogue facilities. The Elders considered that the proposals were outside their province and declined the invitation, although 'most desirous to co-operate in any efforts to improve the social and religious condition of the Jews in East London'. There were occasional joint Ashkenazi and Sephardi services on special occasions, although as a rule each Community arranged its own. Such was, for instance, that in 1910 in celebration of the formation a century and a half earlier of the Jewish Board of Deputies. Since the Board, although almost from the beginning representative of both branches of the Jewish Community, was originally a committee of the Sephardi congregation the use of the Bevis Marks Synagogue for the service was especially appropriate. For a century and more after the establishment of the Board of Deputies the arrangements for the periodical elections of its members from all congregations were still made by the secretary of Bevis Marks, and the first meeting of the newly elected Board was convened by him. In May 1933, at the opening of the Nazi persecution of the Jews of Germany, there was a similar joint service for intercession, and in 1942, in a happier connexion, Ashkenazim and Sephardim joined together to celebrate by a special service in the Bevis Marks Synagogue the election of a Jewish Lord Mayor, Sir Samuel Joseph. The Sephardi Community took advantage of the opportunity to present the Lord Mayor with a silver salver which had been given by the Congregation to one of his predecessors in 1728, when it was still the custom to make annually a similar gift. The salver had been bought by the Congregation a few years earlier and placed among its treasures. There were a number of other special services in these years, arranged for members of the Sephardi Community alone, on the occasion of the coronation, the jubilee, or the funeral of a monarch, for instance. In January 1892 there was a special service on the occasion of the very severe influenza epidemic, one of whose victims was the Heir Presumptive to the Throne. In the previous year there had been special prayers on the Day of Atonement on behalf of 'our oppressed brethren in Russia'. The two world wars brought a succession of special services and special prayers. Within a month of the outbreak of war in 1914 a prayer was drawn up for recital every sabbath and holy day until the end of the war, and this was followed three months later by a special service for Humiliation and Prayer. In the following year there was another service of intercession 'for the Success of our Arms', and after the war had reached a successful conclusion, there was a Day of Thanksgiving 'on signing the Treaty of Peace'. Finally, in 1945, at the end of the second World War, a service of Thanksgiving was held and followed a few months later by a similar service on the capitulation of Japan.

Three special services during the latter half of this period were outside the ordinary course. On 27 May 1935 the eight hundredth anniversary of the birth of Moses Maimonides, the outstanding Spanish Jewish philosopher and teacher of the Middle Ages, was commemorated by the Sephardim and Ashkenazim in the Bevis Marks Synagogue in the presence of a representative of the Spanish Government and prominent members of all sections of the Jewish Community. Two years later there was a service in commemoration of the five hundredth anniversary of the birth of Don Isaac Abarbanel, the Spanish-Jewish statesman who led the exodus of the Jews on their expulsion from Spain and a few years later from Portugal. On this occasion the Ashkenazi Chief Rabbi, Joseph Herman Hertz, took part in the service in Bevis Marks. The 31 August 1940 was the turn for a more recent historical event. On that day the Queen of Holland, then an exile in England, completed her sixtieth year. Most of the founders of the English Sephardi Community had previously been sheltered in her country, and later many of the new-comers to the Congregation had come from the same land. It was a happy idea to celebrate the birthday also by a service in Bevis Marks and this was done. Two of the Queen's ministers were present.

The invitation to representatives of the Spanish Government at the Maimonides service was not the first approach to the Government of the State from which the ancestors of the worshippers in Bevis Marks had been exiled 450 years before. A year earlier, on 11 May 1934, the Spanish Ambassador in London and a former Foreign Minister who happened to be in England visited the

Synagogue. This visit may be said to have sealed the reconciliation between the English Sephardim and their former country. Earlier, in 1905, when the King of Spain was in England, the Elders presented an address to him and invited him to visit the Synagogue, an invitation he was unable to accept. A few months before, when the King and Queen of Portugal were in England, they also had been similarly invited, and when King Manuel came in 1909 an address was presented to him. There was another interesting connexion with Portugal and its Jews in these later years. Early in the year 1925 the story began to spread of the survival in the north of Portugal of a community of secret Jews, descendants of Marranos of the end of the fifteenth century. The discovery was due to Samuel Schwarz, a Polish-Jewish mining engineer whose interests took him to northern Portugal, where he found among the population not only distinct traces of Judaism but avowals of their secret faith. He communicated his discovery to the Jewish Community of Lisbon, which had come into existence during the preceding century, and by them it was made public with an appeal to their fellow Jews to help them to reintegrate this hitherto unknown Jewry in the greater Jewry of the twentieth century. In Paris the *Alliance Israélite* and in London the Sephardi Congregation and the Anglo-Jewish Association at once became interested. By them Lucien Wolf was sent to Portugal to make further inquiries. On his return he confirmed in detail the accounts that had reached London.[1] There was undoubtedly in the north of Portugal a community descended directly from the Marranos of the fifteenth century still practising Judaism, within their very limited knowledge, and anxious to be connected again after the lapse of centuries with their lost kinsmen. Wolf's report completely satisfied those who had commissioned him. The London Sephardi Community admitted their moral and historic responsibility for succouring, spiritually more than materially, their lost brethren. Paul Goodman, instinctively deeply interested in the cause, went on a mission to Portugal, got into contact with members of the secret Community and in particular with Captain Arthur Carlos de Barros Basto, who became President of the Oporto Jewish Congregation which was established, to which congregation two of the sepharim that had been inherited by Bevis Marks from the defunct Community of Barbados were presented. The interest of the Kadoorie family of Shanghai and London was in particular

[1] See *Report on the 'Marranos' or Crypto-Jews of Portugal* by Lucien Wolf (London, Anglo-Jewish Association, 1926), and Samuel Schwarz, *Os Cristraos-Novos em Portugal no Século XX* (Lisbon, 1925).

aroused, and through their generosity a synagogue, bearing the name of this family, was erected in Oporto. At its consecration in 1938 the London Community was represented by Goodman and Arthur de Caceres. The gift of Bevis Marks on the occasion of the celebration consisted of a pair of bells, also from Barbados, a sepher mantel and a gown for the Hazan. In all the Sephardi synagogues in England a *misheberach* was offered in honour of the newly founded community. The Oporto Community on its part, mindful of its moral debt to Bevis Marks, vested its property in the Elders as trustees for the London Congregation, who had made an annual grant of £50 to its funds from the year 1931. As it was put in the formal deed, the Israelite Community of Oporto recognizes the Spanish and Portuguese Jewish Congregation of London as owners of their synagogue and its land, the Israelite Community of Oporto acting as their trustees and administrators.

Although the most interesting and arresting of the contacts between Bevis Marks and foreign Sephardi communities during these years, that with the Marranos of Portugal was not the only one. The resuscitation of a community was most exceptional: assistance to survive was far more usual. For instance, when, in 1921, the Jewish quarter of Salonica, inhabited almost entirely by Sephardim, was devastated by fire, Bevis Marks as a first measure of assistance sent four of its sepharim so that public worship might at once be resumed. A more ordinary method of support was the provision of prayer books of the Sephardi ritual to small and outlying communities such as those of India and China, books which were and are also in use in the larger and wealthier Sephardi communities of the New World. Out of these activities on behalf of Sephardi communities beyond the seas developed naturally the movement, in which London took the lead, for the co-operation of Sephardi communities in all lands. This movement became noticeable late in 1933 when the Mahamad had under consideration the formation of a Confederation of Sephardi Jews. Two years later a World Sephardi Conference was held in London and out of this came the Union of Sephardi Communities. The outbreak of war a few years later necessarily led to the suspension of the activities of this organization, but it is only quiescent, and its recent stirrings point to an approaching period of activity.

Palestine, as the reader will have noticed, had always been close to the heart of Bevis Marks: the assistance of poor co-religionists in the Holy Land was one of the first duties it accepted as soon as a community had been organized in London. This service soon became formally organized and with the aid of generous gifts and bequests by pious Yehidim adequate means for performing this function, in normal circumstances, were available. Several of the leading Yehidim, especially in the nineteenth century, were prominent among the Lovers of Zion. Thus when in November 1917 the Balfour Declaration recording the sympathy of the British Government with the ideal of 'the establishment in Palestine of a national home for the Jewish people' was made, the Mahamad promptly expressed its appreciation. The successive funds raised for the furtherance of this ideal received support from individual Yehidim, although the Congregation as a body made no contribution. After a few years these appeals—in some cases direct to the Congregation—became more insistent and some of them were specifically Sephardi to Sephardi. For instance, in March 1925 the Federation of Sephardi Jews of Jerusalem invited the co-operation of the London Community in the establishment of a group of Sephardi settlers, and five years later there came an appeal for the provision of *matzot* for the Sephardi poor of the same city. The Mahamad did not look on these specific appeals with favour.

In the first half of the twentieth century the country and the world suffered from two devastating wars, and inevitably Anglo-Jewry, as a part of the British nation, did not pass through them unscathed. So far as Britain and Anglo-Jewry were concerned there was also a third, relatively a minor war, although one that loomed somewhat large at the time. In both the South African War of the beginning of the century and the first World War, the young men of the Community vied with their fellow citizens in giving their services to the country. In the second World War all were equally subject to conscription, so there was little claim to fame in volunteering for active service. In the South African War the Elders were active in securing contributions to the National Fund that was raised for the benefit of its victims. The two world wars touched the nation and the Jewish Community far more closely. The earlier brought a large number of Jewish and other refugees to England, and the men and women of the Community threw themselves into the work of caring for them. Provision was made for many of these refugees in hostels and one such hostel was established and maintained by members of the Sephardi Community. Among the Sephardi volunteers who gave their lives for their country two, perhaps three, names stand out. Lieutenant Frank Alexander de Pass of the 34th Poona Horse was awarded the Victoria Cross, the first Jew to gain that coveted distinction, for outstanding heroism in the battle of Festubert on 25 November 1914. He did not live to learn of the award, for it was posthumous.

The act that gained it cost him his life. The second hero whom Bevis Marks gave to England was Lieutenant Solomon Benzecry, who was killed on 19 March 1918 in circumstances of great bravery, at the battle of Bourlon Woods. These young men were not yet old enough to follow in the footsteps of their fathers and give service to their community. Captain Robert Sebag-Montefiore, who died of wounds suffered at Gallipoli in November 1915, had already given it valuable service with the promise of far more to follow. After the end of the war, tablets containing thirty-eight names of members and sons of members who had given their lives were placed outside the two synagogues. Similarly, after the end of the second World War, the names of those members and their sons who had died for their country were recorded.

The second World War fell even more heavily on the Community psychologically and materially, though its toll of lives was smaller. Early in the war, on the threat of hostile air raids, the historic and artistic treasures of the Congregation—sepharim and their accoutrements, precious on account of their age or associations, portraits of the fathers of the Community, much of the synagogue silver, the records of the Congregation, were sent out of London to places of security. The handsome candelabra which form such a striking ornament to Bevis Marks were dismantled and removed by the Central Council for the Care of Churches to Somerset, where they remained under their care until, after the end of the war, they could be restored to their normal home. The fixed property of the Congregation suffered severely in these air raids. The Lauderdale Road Synagogue and the neighbouring communal buildings were all damaged. The congregational almshouses in Mile End were entirely demolished, and some of the properties of which the Congregation was the ground landlord also destroyed. The war necessarily imposed additional expenditure on the Congregation: by this last-mentioned damage its revenues were reduced. Bombs fell even on the old cemeteries in the Mile End Road, leaving their mark in craters replacing obliterated graves. After the entry into the war, in 1940, of Italy, Gibraltar came into the forefront and the authorities considered it desirable to evacuate all non-combatants from the fortress. Of the refugees an appreciable proportion were Jews, in many cases connected with families long resident in London. Unconsciously a precedent set on the occasion of an earlier siege at the end of the eighteenth century was followed. The majority of the uprooted, all Sephardim, were sent to England, where their needs were met by the Ministry of Health. There were some comforts, however, only a Jewish organization could supply, and the Sephardi Community readily came forward to provide them. Their offer was gladly accepted by the Ministry of Health, and the two organizations co-operated until, after the end of the war, the refugees returned to their homes. Earlier, before the outbreak of the war, there had been another immigration of Sephardi refugees into England, from Italy, under the pressure of Fascist persecution. The British Government had, of course, no responsibility for these refugees, and the support of most of them fell on the Jewish Community, with the assistance of non-Jewish sympathizers. The Sephardi Community made these Italian refugees their special care. After their return to Italy, the Congregation made a grant of some £300 for the repair and reconstitution of the Home for Aged Sephardim in Venice. At the same time the Congregation took its full part in dealing with the larger problem of Jewish refugees from Europe. In human service on behalf of these victims and in providing the means of giving them assistance, Sephardi vied with Ashkenazi and to neither can be given the foremost place.

The Sephardi refugees from Italy and from Gibraltar were for the most part but temporary visitors to England. With few exceptions, as soon as they were free to return to their own countries, they did so. Earlier, however, in the twentieth century, there were two waves of immigration which seem to have set their permanent mark on the London Sephardi Community. One of the consequences of the Balkan wars that ended in 1913 was the destruction of the great Sephardi Community of Salonica. The severance of this great port from its hinterland was an economic disaster which involved the Jewish section of the population comprising more than a third. Many of the Jews, established in the city for more than four centuries, left for other lands: of those who remained few survived the second World War. Some of the dispersed came to England, and keeping together so far as they could formed a small Sephardi Community in the Shepherds Bush district of London. Another group settled in Shoreditch. The latter was near enough to Bevis Marks to be absorbed into the Congregation there. The Shepherd's Bush group, however, felt itself too small to live by itself. It approached the Mahamad with the request to be taken under its jurisdiction. It received a ready welcome. The greatest need of the small community was synagogue accommodation. Hitherto they had had to worship in temporary premises liable to frequent change. They had not even the necessary appurtenances of public worship. The first step taken by the Mahamad was to lend the Sephardim of Shepherd's Bush four sepharim. Very shortly afterwards a recommendation was made to the Elders that a sum of £1,000 should be granted towards the cost of the erection or adaptation of a synagogue provided the new Community accepted the jurisdiction in ecclesiastical matters of Bevis Marks. This was at the end of 1925. This gift from the parent congregation was later almost doubled, after the Congregants in Shepherd's Bush had themselves subscribed almost £2,000 and Yehidim as individuals £2,352. In addition, two years later, a windfall came in a gift of £10,000 from the Sir Sassoon David Charity Fund. By this gift all difficulties in the way of the little congregation were smoothed away, and in December 1928 a newly built and adequately endowed synagogue in St. James's Square, Holland Park, was consecrated.

A little later than the settlement of Sephardim from Salonica in Shepherd's Bush, a similar settlement of Jews from Persia and Bokhara, not strictly Sephardim but akin to the Sephardim in ritual, began in North London, in Stamford Hill. These, however, did not find a benefactor such as the Sassoon David Trustees, and had to rely more on themselves. The Bevis Marks authorities looked on this group also with sympathy, but the mutual relations were never as close as those with the Holland Park Congregation. However, a number of the worshippers in Stamford Hill became Yehidim of the parent congregation, while continuing to attend service in their own synagogue.

In 1932 it was agreed that a representative of the Holland Park Synagogue should be co-opted on the Board of Elders of the Parent Congregation. Seven years earlier, in 1925, a Conjoint Board, representative of the London and Manchester Boards of Elders, had been appointed to consider matters affecting the Sephardim of England as a whole, and these representatives were *ex-officio* members of the Board of Elders of one another. In 1950 all three were given two representatives each, without limitation of rights, on the London Board of Elders. At the same time the Haham, who had been appointed in the previous year, was given the title of Haham of the Spanish and Portuguese Jews of Great Britain.

But to turn to the internal history of the Congregation. During these last years events happened, but those of consequence were not numerous. Perhaps the most noteworthy change the Congregation underwent—hardly perceptible at the time—was the expansion of the influence of the Mahamad. There had been a time—as the reader will have noticed—when the whole of the power among the Sephardim rested with that body. Gradually this position of limited omnipotence had been undermined by the Elders, who, as their numbers grew and with the incorporation in them of all the Yehidim experienced in administration came more and more to be consulted and relied on in all matters of moment. Later, in the period of an expanding democracy, external influences could not be kept outside of the gates of Bevis Marks. Year by year the Yehidim, once with no other function but that of listening to what the Mahamad troubled to tell them, secured greater power. That power is not diminished, but much discretion is necessarily entrusted to the executive body, which the Yehidim as a whole cannot be. The body of Elders also no longer consists solely of those who have had direct contact with the administration of the Congregation. The knowledge and experience lie largely among the gentlemen of the Mahamad, and although they cannot again become an uncontrolled oligarchy their influence has expanded and with it their power.

The Haham, Moses Gaster, retired at the end of 1918, to die in 1939, at the age of eighty-two. No successor was appointed for many years, but Rabbi Shemtob Gaguin, of the Withington Sephardi Congregation, Manchester, later to become Principal of the Judith Lady Montefiore College at Ramsgate, was appointed Ab Beth Din, holding the two offices simultaneously. Born in Jerusalem, Rabbi Gaguin had been Dayan in Cairo before coming to England in 1919. The office of Haham remained vacant until 1949, when the Senior Hazan, Rabbi Solomon Gaon, was appointed to it. Rabbi Gaon and his colleague as Hazan, the Rev. Eliezer Abinun, had been trained for service in the Community, having both come to England from Serajevo in Yugoslavia as very young men. Under the influence of the new Haham, both before and after his appointment there were several welcome developments in the activities of the Congregation. Before his appointment to the new office, the Orphanage next to the Lauderdale Road Synagogue, no longer needed for the purpose for which it was built, was transformed into a centre for the intellectual and social life of the Community. At the same time, even the provision of Hebrew and religious education was transformed. There had been many attempts to provide this for the children who lived in all parts of Greater London. At first classes were held in Golders Green as well as in Lauderdale Road, and instruction had also been given by post. Later the teaching was concentrated in Lauderdale Road, the children being brought to the classes every Sunday from all parts of West and North-west London. Monthly talks to children had been introduced by Mr. Bueno de Mesquita in 1938:

THE LAST FIFTY YEARS 415

these developed nine years later into regular children's services in
'The Little Synagogue' which was set up in the Communal Centre.
In the conduct of the services—in a modified form—in this synagogue boys take a leading part. At the same time the practice of
sermons in the main synagogue at short intervals was instituted.
In 1950 an innovation that attracted wider attention was the
Confirmation of girls, but at a special Sunday service. The
previous year a hostel under the control of the Congregation had
been opened for young men studying for the Sephardi ministry.

The appointment of Rabbi Gaon as Haham was followed by his
formal induction into office. The whole of Anglo-Jewry, through
its representatives, participated in the function, at which were
present also, to mark the position Bevis Marks had reached in the
nation, the Lord Mayor and Sheriffs, a representative of the Bishop
of London, who was unable to attend in person, the Dean of St.
Paul's, the Master of the Temple, and a representative of the Dutch
Ambassador, to underline again the historic connexion between
Bevis Marks and Holland. The wide interest the function aroused
was illustrated by the broadcasting of a portion of the service by
the British Broadcasting Corporation. The general public showed
itself sufficiently interested to justify the broadcasting five months
later of a Hanucca service. A Passover service had been previously
broadcast in the spring of 1946. The appointment of a Haham
also drew closer the ties between Bevis Marks and the other
Sephardi congregations in Manchester and London. He was
accepted as the ecclesiastical head of all the Sephardim of England,
and to show that his title was not intended to be an empty one, the
three Manchester congregations and that of Holland Park agreed
to contribute towards the cost of upholding the office. The
presence at the induction of the Haham of representatives of the
Church was not the only manifestation of the recognition by Jew
and Christian that they were equally parts of the British nation.
When William Temple, that great Liberal Churchman, was
appointed Archbishop of Canterbury in 1942, the Sephardim
joined with the other religious communities in offering him their
congratulations. Three years earlier the Mahamad, in the name
of the Congregation, offered to the Cardinal Archbishop of
Westminster an expression of their sympathy on the occasion of
the death of the Pope, Pius XI.

The two and a half centuries since the Consecration of the
Synagogue in Bevis Marks are now ended and their story has been
told. The foregoing pages will tell their own tale and point their
own moral. These may be left to the reader.

APPENDIX I

CHANGES IN RITUAL AND ORDER OF SERVICES
By the Very Rev. The Haham, Dr. Solomon Gaon

LIVING IN THE Iberian peninsula under both Arabic and non-Arabic influences for well over a thousand years, the Sephardim developed some characteristics of their own, which are reflected in their religious and lay literature as well as in their liturgy.

The prayers which in Spain enhanced the joy of the House of Israel on happy occasions and brought them solace in their sorrows have survived almost intact in the present liturgy of the Congregations of the Spanish and Portuguese Jews. Few changes have been introduced in the order of service in London: and these on the whole are of such minor significance that they have in no way affected the essential character of the ancient Castilian liturgy.[1] This is confirmed by a comparison of the present prayer book of the Spanish and Portuguese Jews of London with the prayer book of the Spanish rite printed in Venice in 1546 (about fifty years after the expulsion from Spain) and the Spanish translation of this prayer book printed in Ferrara in 1552.

The order of service as found in these two prayer books is almost identical with that of the Spanish and Portuguese Congregation of London, most of the changes which have taken place being in decorum, music, and incidental matters, such as announcements in Portuguese and translations of prayers. The evidence of these changes is to be found in records made by outside visitors and in the minutes of the Mahamad and the Elders. These also show that there have indeed been attempts to introduce more sweeping innovations in the prayers and their traditional rendering, which, however, were always tenaciously resisted by the majority of the members of the congregation, who would permit only such alterations as were intended to improve decorum in the Synagogue and enhance the dignity and solemnity of the service.

One of the earliest references to the service of the Spanish and Portuguese Jews in London is found in the diary of Samuel Pepys, when he visited the Synagogue for the second time on the afternoon of 14 October 1663, which happened to be the last day of Tabernacles (the Rejoicing of the Law). He was not very edified by the spectacle of the service, because, on this day, the Jews—and the custom even now continues in some synagogues—allowed themselves some licence by singing and dancing in honour of the Law, as did David in the days of old when the Sanctuary was brought to Jerusalem.[2] Pepys writes: 'And

[1] There were other liturgies in Spain, e.g. those of Aragon, Catalonia, etc.

[2] It is interesting to note that by 1765, when the Frenchman Grosely visited the Synagogue, a great advance in decorum had already been made: 'The psalmody of the English synagogue surprised me, by the sweetness as well as

416

anon their laws that they take out of the press are carried by several men, four or five burthens in all, and they do relieve one another, and whether it is that every one desires to have the carrying of it, thus they carried it round about the room while such a service is singing.'

The custom of carrying the scrolls of the Law round the Synagogue on the eve and on the day of *Simhhat Torah*[1] was not introduced until the beginning of the sixteenth century, and consequently could not have been performed in Spain; it was eventually accepted, however, by many Sephardi communities of the East. In the prayer books printed in Venice and Ferrara no trace of this custom is to be found. Had it been generally accepted by the Spanish exiles, it would no doubt have been included in these prayer books.

In 1674, 'considering the tumult and disorder which the decorations made on Simhat Torah and Sabatt Beresitt cause', the Mahamad 'suppressed the picturesque custom in pursuance of which the Bridegrooms of the Law were wont to adorn the Synagogue with wreaths of myrtle and the like, permitting only decorations of tapestries, gilded leather, and flowers in the candelabra'. In this decision, there is again no mention whatsoever of any circuits with the scrolls of the Law taking place in the Synagogue. It must be concluded, therefore, that this ceremony was never officially carried out in the Spanish and Portuguese Synagogue of London. Pepys' statement can only be explained if we presume that he witnessed an unofficial ceremony, organized probably by some society, as was the custom in Amsterdam until just before the last war. There a study circle arranged *Minha*[2] in a hall on the afternoon of Simhhat Torah, and during this service the ceremony of the circuits took place. That the same was the case in London, except that the ceremony was carried out in the Synagogue itself, is borne out by the entry in the diary. The visit there recorded took place 'after dinner', that is, in the afternoon, and the 14 October was the day of Simhhat Torah itself, so the reference cannot have been to the customary circuits on the eve of the Festival. Apparently, even this unofficial ceremony was dropped early in the history of the Congregation—perhaps immediately after the visit of Pepys. It is known that the leaders of the community were sensitive to any outside criticism, and it was for this reason that they also discouraged members from bringing non-Jewish visitors to the services.

The service on the eve of Simhhat Torah for a long time remained the same as that of all other festivals. It was not until the nineteenth century that the community, in a desire to make the service more attractive, commissioned Matthew Moss (1795–1868), who was choirmaster at Bevis Marks, to compose for the services on the eve of

the agreeable simplicity of its modulation. My astonishment was caused by a comparison of this symphony, with the vociferation of the German synagogue, and even with the Church music which I had heard in England.' (*Trans. Jew. Hist. Soc. of Eng.*, vol. XIII, p. 325.)

[1] The day of the Rejoicing of the Law.   [2] Afternoon service.

Simhhat Torah and *Shabbat Beresheet* new tunes, some of which are still in use. It was no doubt the fear that the compositions of Moss for these two occasions might lead to demands for the introduction of new tunes in the other services, that gave rise to the following resolution by the Elders on 24 January 1869: 'Proposed that the ancient tunes hitherto in use at the Synagogue be maintained and that no departure thereof be permitted without the previous consent of the Mahamad except on the days of Simhhat Torah and Shabbat Beresheet.' When the first Sephardi synagogue was built in Manchester in 1873, the Haham of the Spanish and Portuguese Jews in London—Benjamin Artom—gave special permission for circuits to be introduced there in the evening service for Simhhat Torah, because most of the members came from Eastern and African communities which had adopted this custom. It is for the same reason that they were also performed at the Holland Park Synagogue.

As the excessive decorations on Simhhat Torah and Shabbat Beresheet tended to disturb the decorum of the Congregation, so also on the Feast of Purim did the conduct of unruly boys and men, who, during the reading of the Book of Esther, knocked loudly against the synagogue benches at the mention of the names of Haman and his sons. In March 1783 the authorities of the Synagogue issued strict orders forbidding such irreverent conduct within the precincts of the House of God.[1] Some congregants, disregarding these orders, continued this indecorous practice, but, on being summoned before the Mahamad, acknowledged their fault. Nevertheless, the practice of gently knocking on the floor with the feet at the mention of the names of Haman and his sons continues to the present day.

In the year 1827 Haham Meldola suggested that the prayer for the dew on Passover and for the rain on Tabernacles should be rearranged, so that the repetition of the *Ngamidah* for *Musaph* would be unnecessary. According to Meldola's suggestion, these prayers (which consist mostly of hymns) were to be chanted immediately after the return of the *Sepher* to the Ark, after which Musaph was to be recited as on ordinary festivals. He insisted that this was not just a suggestion, but that it should be made a point of the *Din*, because the practice which he wished to introduce was observed throughout all the congregations of Sephardi Jewry, except those in the London and Amsterdam synagogues. He believed that the practice of these congregations was entirely due to a mistake which must have crept into the order of service, and the time had come for it to be rectified. He also contended that he was animated in his decision by the otherwise unnecessary lengthening of the service. This suggestion being made just before Passover, the Mahamad decided to have the innovation introduced for that Festival as an experiment. It was probably due to the popular outcry against this departure from the accepted *Minhag* that, after Passover, the decision was rescinded. The former practice was thereupon reintroduced, despite the indignation of the Haham as expressed in his letters to the Mahamad.

[1] See M. Gaster, *History of the Ancient Synagogue*, p. 58.

There is no doubt that Meldola was correct when he claimed that the order of service which he wished to introduce was practised by most Sephardi communities; but, on the other hand, the manner in which the prayers for the dew and for the rain are offered in the Spanish and Portuguese congregations is in keeping with the ancient tradition of the Jews in Spain. In the previously mentioned prayer books of Venice and Ferrara, these prayers are to be found in the same places as in our present prayer book, so it must be assumed that the rabbis did not then consider this an infringement of religious law, as was held by Meldola. It is interesting to note that, in 1946, the same suggestion was made in order to shorten the service on the first day of Passover and the eighth day of Tabernacles, but this was again rejected by the Yehidim.

Both on the sabbath and the festivals, the length of the service has from time to time caused considerable worry to the authorities of the Congregation, and measures for shortening it have more than once been considered. In July 1880 the Elders agreed that the reading of *Zemirot*[1] should last 55 minutes instead of an hour, and that there should be an interval of 5 minutes between the ending of the Zemirot and the beginning of *Shahrit*. This change could not have lasted very long, for the earlier custom now persists; the reading of Zemirot takes one hour and is immediately followed by Shahrit. At this meeting, in 1880, it was also decided that the *Kaddeesh* before *Yotser*[2] should be simply 'intoned', not sung. We can gather from this that the present tune this Kaddeesh on sabbaths and festivals is not of very ancient for origin, and that, prior to that date, it was sung to one of the festival tunes.

The mode of announcing the *Mitzvot* was also changed in 1880.[3] It was once the custom that for each man given the privilege of opening the Ark, carrying the Scroll, or of performing any other Mitzva, a separate *Misheberach* was offered. At the same meeting of the Elders it was decided that one general Misheberach should be said for all who had Mitzvot. It was probably for the same reason that in April 1829 the singing of *Hodu* (1 Chronicles XVI, 8-36) on sabbath morning was discontinued. The melody in which this passage was intoned has in London fallen into desuetude, but it is still preserved in Amsterdam, and is also used for the circuits on the eve of Simhhat Torah in the Manchester Synagogue of *Shaare Tefilla*.

In December 1866 the Mahamad agreed with the suggestion of Haham Artom that the prayers for the Royal Family and for the Congregation should be recited by the Haham while holding the Sepher Torah, and not by the minister, as was previously the custom. In February of the following year Artom wrote to the Mahamad concerning the

[1] Introductory psalms, supplications, and hymns.
[2] Second part of the morning prayers.
[3] Originally the Mitzvot were distributed by lot on *Rosh Hashana* and *Kippur*, as stated in Ascama 11, and in 1673 the Mahamad decreed that Mitzvot generally should be assigned by lot. Now the Mitzvot are given away by the Mahamad.

Barmitzvah ceremony. Having expressed the view that the Barmitzvah day is for the boy 'the realization of the finest dream of youth', he proceeded to urge that the preparations for this ceremony were not commensurate with its significance. He considered that the boy should receive, prior to the Barmitzvah, 'such a religious training as to render him efficient to undergo at least a private examination'. He also suggested that a prayer, which he would compose, should be introduced and recited by the boy either when he was called to the Sepher or at the end of the service, when, after a short address, the Haham would invoke a blessing on him. The result of this letter was the beautiful prayer which every boy now recites on his Barmitzvah day before reading his portion from the Law. This prayer was later adopted by the Ashkenazim and is included in Singer's Prayer Book.

From the old Sephardi books as well as from those printed in Amsterdam, even up to modern times, it can be seen that the prayer books begin with certain hymns which were sung on sabbaths and weekday mornings before the beginning of the service. There is every probability that as the first prayer books used in London came from Amsterdam, or even perhaps from Venice, these hymns were chanted prior to the beginning of the morning service.[1] Since, however, the services in this country on sabbaths and weekdays never begin as early as in other countries, the singing of these hymns was discontinued, and they were not printed in the Hebrew Sephardi prayer books published in England. It is also interesting to note that the prayer *Mode Ani* on page 1 of our present prayer book is not found in any earlier editions, or in the editions of Venice and Amsterdam. It is included in the liturgy of the Ashkenazim and of the oriental Sephardi congregations, and was introduced by Haham Gaster into the existing edition of our prayer book.

It was customary in earlier days for candles to be lit in honour of the dead.[2] Some benefactors, who left legacies to the Synagogue, stipulated that lamps should be lit for them during the first year after their death.

Gaster mentions also in his *History of the Ancient Synagogue* that in the early days of the Congregation the members used to go to the Thames to perform the ancient ceremony of *Vetashlih*. 'This signified, throwing their sins into the water, in order that they might sink deep to the bottom, in accordance with the biblical passage recited on the occasion.' The prayer for this ceremony is not found either in the old or the new prayer books of the Congregation, but there is every

---

[1] This view is confirmed by the fact that in the first translation of the Sephardi prayer book made by Joseph Messias and published in London in 1720–1, these hymns are found preceding the daily prayers.

[2] Ascama 39, of 5424. *El Libro de los Acuerdos*, p. 13: 'On the days of the completions of the Abelim there shall be kindled, in addition to the regular candles of the Ehal and the Teba, six candles placed in their candelabra above the Teba, three in one group and three in the other, and not more; and the Abelim shall sit with the Parnasim, who shall bear them company on the bench which stands behind the Hazan.'

likelihood that it was performed at some time in England, and it is still practised by many Sephardi communities.

Until the beginning of the last century, it was customary to read on sabbath afternoons three verses from the coming week's *Parasha* and *Haphtara* in Hebrew and Spanish. These verses are now read only in Hebrew. The reading in Spanish was discontinued, as a natural consequence of the decrease in numbers of Spanish-speaking members; but the Haphtara on *Tishnga' beab*[1] is still read verse by verse in Hebrew with a Spanish paraphrase. To the Jews exiled from Spain the Spanish language remained the means of their daily intercourse as well as the only language, apart from Hebrew, in which they offered their prayers. In time it became second in sanctity to Hebrew, especially in the Moroccan and Balkan communities. Considering the part played by the Sephardi Jews in the development, both economic and political, of the Balkan states, it is remarkable that until the destruction of these Sephardi communities during the last war, very few of them would allow their rabbis—who in many cases were educated in the centres of Western culture—to preach sermons in any language but Judaeo-Spanish, and the only translation of the prayers permitted was into that language. The same was apparently the case with London until the nineteenth century. It was only in 1839 that the boys who had assisted the Hazanim in chanting prayers were formed into a permanent choir, which was placed under the direction of Moss.

[1] The 9th of Ab: the fast commemorating the destruction of both the first and second Temple of Jerusalem.

APPENDIX II

THE FOUNDERS OF THE CONGREGATION

Signatures to the first Code of Ascamot (1664)

Dauid Abrabanel Dormido
Eliau de Lima
Moseh Baruh Louzada
Abraham Roïz da Costa
Samuel da ueiga
Jahacob Berahel
Jahacob Gomez Serra
Yssache Barçillay
Isha dazeuedo (d'Azevedo)

Dr. Mendes Brauo
Jahacob de Chaues
Imanuel Mussaphia
Jacob Sasportas
Abraham Coen Gonsales
Jacob Netto
Jacob Pardo
Aron Vega
Benjamin Nunes

Signatures to the Ascamot of 1677

Abraham Roiz Pinhel
Isaque Roiz Francia
Jahacob Jeserun Alvares, Gabai
Abraham de Siqra (Sequevia)
Josua Lopes Arias
Ishac Tellez da Costa
Abraham Do Porto
Abraham de Morais
Mosseh Mocatta
Josseph Dasilua (da Silva)
Joseph Frances
Dr. Abraham Perez Galuã
Abraham Lopez
Binyamin Leuy
P. Henriques, el Moço (junior)
Abraham Baruh Rosa
Jacob Abenacar
Dauid Abarbanel
Joshua da Silva

Isaac Israel Avila
Issack Barçilay
Moseh Baruh Louzada
Abraham de o Livera (Oliveira)
Izaque de Paiva
Abram de Francia
Jacob Gomes Serra
Abraham Roiz da Costa
Ishac Israel Nunes
Selomoh de Medina
Ishack Suarez Dorta (d'Orta)
Moshe Nunes Xaues (Chaves)
Abraham de Sosa Mendes
Isack dandrade (Andrade)
Samuel Dias
Joseph Cohen d'Azeuedo
Ben. Nunez
Jacob Franco Mendes
Ishac Semah de Valençia

APPENDIX III

SEATHOLDERS in 5442 (1682)

PAUTA DOS LUGARES DE CADA SU NA SNOGA AMĀO SQUERDA DO HECHAL SÃO OS DE ENCOSTO[1]

NO.
1. Abraham Mz. Henriquez
2. Mosseh Baruh Louzada
3. Aharon Levy Recio
4. Abraham Roiz de Morais
5. Aharon Abarbanel Dormido
6. Solomoh Arari
7. Don Abraham Perez Galuão
8. Ishac Israel Correa
9.
10. Mosseh Israel Nunez
11. Jossep Coen de Azevedo
12. Abraham Roiz de Paiva
13. Jahacob Abenjacar
14. David Abarbanel
15. Ishac Aboab Cardoso
16. Benjamin Franco de Paiva
17. Benjamin Levy
18. Mosseh Nunez Xaves
19. Jahacob de Sequeira
20.
21. Samuel Elbot (Heilbut)
22. Samuel Samas

NO.
1. Jaacob Gomez Serra
2. Abraham de Porto
3. Ishac Israel de Sequeira

1. Abraham Berahel
2. Jahacob Gonzales
3. Jahacob Jesurun Alvarez
4. Jaacob Franco Mendez
5. Jaacob Israel Henriquez
6. Ishac Zemah de Valença
7. Benjamin Israel Nunez
8. Daniel Peçoa

1. David de Francia
2. Joseph Henriquez o Moco (junior)
3. Mahir Levy
4. Mosseh de Francia
5. Eliau Abenacar

[1] List of places of each gentleman in the Synagogue. At the left side of the Hechal are those with backs.

5442 (1682)

PAUTA DOS LUGARES DE CADA SU NA SNOGA AMÃO DEREITA DO HECHAL SÃO OS DE ENCOTTO[1]

NO.
1. Ishack Barzilay
2. Ishack de Francia
3. Abraham Mendes da Costa
4. Ishac Is. Nunez
5.
6. Josseph frances
7. Jaacob frasão
8. Jaacob Bueno Henriquez
9. Imanuel de Caceres
10. David de Silva
11. Menasseh Mendez
12. David Is. Nunez
13. Ishac de Ramos
14. Daniel Lopez Ris
15. Eliau de oliveira
16.
17. Abraham Zusarte
18. Jaacob Suares Munhão
19. Aharon Pacheco
20. Abraham da Silva
21. Abraham de leão Templo
22. Imanuel Mocata
23. Selomoh de la faya
24. Jaacob de Paz
25.   Israel
26. David Israel Seu irmão (his brother)
27. Jaacob Roiz
28. Abraham Rosa
29. Samuel Sapertas (Sasportas)
30. Selomoh Dormido

NO.
1. Abraham Roiz Pinhel
2. Abraham de oliveira
3. Abraham Israel Henriquez

1. Josseph Henriquez de Sequeira
2. Ishac de Paiva
3. Selomoh de Medina
4. Abraham Lopez Brito
5. Abraham Baruh Lousada
6. Moses Mocata
7. Jahacob cohen Ariaz
8. Ishac Lopez Pereira

1. Daniel Soares Munhão
2. Daniel Mz. Henriquez
3. Samuel de Caceres
4. Jaacob Fernandez Carvajal
5. Abraham Bueno Henriquez
6. Samuel Bueno
7. Abraham Nunez Paiva
8.

[2]el Lugar del Semuel Bueno sedis allo Jahacob Rodrigues
[3]y el Lugar de Abraham Nunez paiva A Moseh Baruh Bueno

---

[1] List of places of each gentleman in the Synagogue. At the right side of the Hechal are those with backs.
[2] The seat of Samuel Bueno they gave to Jahacob Rodrigues.
[3] The seat of Abraham Nunes paiva to Moseh Baruh Bueno.

APPENDIX IV

THE EARLIEST LIST OF ELDERS

LISTA DOS NOMES
DOS SES. VELHOS DA NACAO 5481[1]

Abm. Lopes de Britto
Joseph Mendes Crasto
Joseph Israel Henriques
Moseh Mendes da Costa
Jacob Jesurun Alvares
~~Rohiel Abudiente~~ (died 5483)
~~Jacob Gonzales~~ (died 5487)
~~Ishac De Avila~~
Moseh de Medina
David Mendes da Costa
Jacob Jesurun Roiz
Ishac fez Nunes
Rephael Penso
Ishac da Costa Alvarenga
~~Joseph Mendes da Costa~~
~~Selomoh Israel Pereira~~ (died 5485)
Joseph Telles da Costa
~~Abm. Bernal~~ (died 5482)
~~Abm. da Costa~~ (died 5488)
Abm. Haim Mendes
Aaron Lamego
Joseph Rodr. Sequeira
Ishac Vaz Martines

~~Ishac Cohen Peixoto~~ (died 5486)
~~Moseh Dias Arias~~ (died ....)
Abm. de Mos: m. da Costa
Moseh Levy Ximenes
Daniel Jesurun Rodrigues
Ishac de Selomoh Mendes
Moseh da Costa
Abm. de Moseh Franco
Abm. Levy Ximenes
Jacob Fern. Nunes
Abm. Dias Fern.z. (elec. 5482)
Abm. Franco Nunes
Moseh Lopes Dias (elec. 5483)
Jacob Alvares Per.a
David Lopes Per.a (elec. 5484)
Jacob Mos: m'Costa (elec. 5485)
Jacob Israel Suasso (elec. 5486)
Abm. de Mos: Mendes
Jacob de David Da Costa
               (elec. 5487)
Jahacob do Abm. M. da Costa
               (elec. 5488)
Jahacob de Mos: Franco

[1] List of the names of the Elders of the Nation in 1721.

APPENDIX V

LIST OF MEMBERS OF THE MAHAMAD
(1663–1951)

The following is a complete list, so far as can be ascertained, of the Mahamad, from the adoption of the first *Ascamot* in 1663 until the present day. All who were elected, whether they accepted office or not, are included, those who refused office being indicated by an asterisk (*). At first the Mahamad consisted of two *parnassim* or wardens, and a *gabay* or treasurer. These were chosen in September or October, immediately before the beginning of the Jewish New Year. In 5460 (1699–1700) the number of wardens was increased to four, two of them and the treasurer being chosen as previously and the remaining two six months later. Thus the new Mahamad was never devoid of members with experience, there being after every election at least two members who had already been six months in office. A gap in the annual list of names separates the earlier and later elections of the year. Election was for one year except in 5434 (1673–4) when the period was extended for a further six months for reasons that are explained in the text. Members of the Mahamad were, however, eligible for re-election.

5424 (1663–4)
David Abarbanel Dormido
Eliau de Lima
Moses Baruh Lousada, *Gabay*

5425
Isaac Barzilay
Isaac de Azevedo
Isaac Israel Nunes, *Gabay*

5426

5427
Jacob Beruhiel
Samuel da Vega
Jacob Gomes Serra, *Gabay*

5428
Isaac Alvarez (Israel) Nunes
Moses Baruh Lousada
Abraham de Oliveira, *Gabay*

5429
Abraham Rodrigues de Francia
Dr. Joseph Mendes Bravo
Joseph Henriques, *Gabay*

5430
Jacob Gomes Serra
Isaac Lopes Pereira

5431
Isaac Israel de Francia
Abraham de Oliveira
Abraham do Porto, *Gabay*

5432
Jacob Beruhiel
Abraham Rodrigues Pinhel
Isaac de Paiva, *Gabay*

5433
Joshua Lopes Arias
*Joseph Henriques

APPENDIX V

Abraham de Sequeira, otherwise Gomes Rodrigues
Jacob Franco Mendes, *Gabay*

5434
Isaac Israel Nunes
Abraham do Porto
Jacob Gomes Serra, *Gabay*
(term of office of the three extended for a further period of six months)

5435
Isaac Barzilay
Abraham de Oliveira
Isaac Soares Dorta, *Gabay*

5436
Abraham Rodrigues de Francia
Isaac de Paiva
Solomon de Medina, *Gabay*

5437
Abraham Rodrigues Pinhel
Isaac Rodrigues de Francia
Jacob Jesurun Alvarez, *Gabay*

5438
Isaac Rodrigues de Francia
Abraham de Sequeira
Jacob Jesurun Alvarez, *Gabay*

5439
Isaac Soares Dortha
Abraham de Francia
Moses Mocatta (at first gabay)
Abraham do Porto, *Gabay*

5440
Isaac Barzilay
Isaac Alvares
Jacob Gonzalez, *Gabay*

5441
Isaac Barzilay
Abraham Israel Henriques
Jacob Gonzalez, *Gabay*

5442
Abraham Israel Henriques
Aaron Abarbanel Dormido
Abraham Berahel, *Gabay*

5443
Moses Baruh Lousada
Isaac de Francia
Isaac Semah de Valencia, *Gabay* (resigned)
David Pessoa, *Gabay*

5444
Isaac Barzilay
Aaron Levi Recio
David Pessoa, *Gabay*

5445
Benjamin Franco, *Gabay*

5446

5447
Jacob Coen Arias, *Gabay*

5448
Abraham Lopes de Britto, *Gabay*

5449
Joseph Bernal
Isaac Semah de Valencia
Moses Henriques de Mesquita, *Gabay*

5450
†Moses Henriques de Mesquita
†Moses Israel Nunes
David Penso, *Gabay*
†Isaac Semah de Valencia
Jacob Gonzales
Abraham Fernandes Nunes

† Retired after three months.

5451
Jacob Gomes Serra
Aaron Pacheco
Menasseh Mendes, *Gabay*

5452
Aaron Pacheco
Benjamin Franco
Abraham Vaz Martinez, *Gabay*

5453
Moses Henriques de Mesquita
Moses Israel Nunes, *Gabay*

5454
Isaac Israel Henriques
Abraham Lopes de Britto
Joseph Mendes de Castro, *Gabay*

5455
Abraham Vaz Martines
Isaac Telles da Costa
Jacob Nunes Miranda, *Gabay*

5456
Isaac Israel Correa
Isaac Lopes Pereira
Joseph Henriques, *Gabay*

5457
Jacob Gomes Serra
Isaac Israel de Sequeira
Isaac Rodrigues Mogadouro, *Gabay*

5458
Moses Henriques de Mesquita
Menasseh Mendes
Phineas Gomes Serra, *Gabay*

5459
Aaron Franco Pacheco
Jacob Nunes Miranda
Moses Mendes da Costa, *Gabay*

5460 (1699–1700)
Jacob Gomes Serra
Isaac Israel de Sequeira
Abraham Mendes Machado, *Gabay*

Jacob Mendes de Britto
David Penso

5461
Isaac Lopes Pereira
Isaac Israel Correa
Moses de Francia, *Gabay*

Abraham Vaz Martines
Isaac Israel Henriques

5462
Selomoh de Medina
Jacob Jessurun Alvares
Rohiel Abudiente, *Gabay*

Isaac Telles da Costa
David Israel Penso

5463
Moses Mendes da Costa
Joseph Mendes de Castro
Jacob Haim Gabay, *Gabay*

Jacob Gonzales
Isaac Rodrigues Mogadouro

5464
Menasseh Mendes
Aaron Franco Pacheco
Isaac Rodrigues Portello, *Gabay*

Isaac Israel de Sequeira
Jacob Nunes Miranda

5465
Dr. Isaac de Avila
Selomoh Mendes
Moses de Medina, *Gabay*

David Mendes da Costa
Joseph Israel Henriques

APPENDIX V

5466
Abraham Vaz Martines
Rohiel Abudiente
Isaac Jessurun Mendes, *Gabay*

Jacob Jessurun Rodrigues
Isaac Israel Henriques

5467
David Israel Penso
Pinhas Gomes Serra
Isaac Fernandes Nunes, *Gabay*

Jacob Jessurun Alvares
Jacob Haim Gabay

5468
Menasseh Mendes
Isaac Rodrigues Portello
Moses da Silva, *Gabay*

Joseph Mendes de Castro
Jacob Israel Bravo

5469
Jacob Mendes de Britto
Raphael Penso
Jacob da Veiga, *Gabay*

Selomoh Mendes
Moses de Medina

5470
Abraham Vaz Martinez
Moses Mendes da Costa
Isaac da Costa Alvarenga, *Gabay*

Rohiel Abudiente
Joseph Israel Henriques

5471
David Mendes da Costa
Aaron Israel Pereira
Moses da Costa, *Gabay*

Jacob Haim Gabay
Isaac Vaz Nunes

5472
Jacob Jesurun Alvares
Pinhas Gomes Serra
Samuel da Costa Alvarenga, *Gabay*

Menasseh Mendes
Moses da Silva

5473
Joseph Mendes de Castro
Jacob da Veiga
Abraham de Moseh Franco, *Gabay*

Joseph Mendes da Costa
Isaac Roizh Portello

5474
Jacob Rodrigues Silva
Abraham Levi Ximenes
*Selomoh Israel Pereira, *Gabay*
Joseph Telles da Costa, *Gabay*

Isaac da Costa Alvarenga
Moses de Medina

5475
Aaron Israel Pereira
Abraham Bernal
Abraham de David Mendes da Costa, *Gabay*

Isaac de Avila
Abraham Haim Mendes

5476
Jacob Jessurun Alvares
Aaron Lamego
*Joseph Rodrigues Sequeira, *Gabay*
*Isaac Vaz Martinez, *Gabay*

Isaac Fernandes Nunes
Samuel da Costa Alvarenga

5477
David Mendes da Costa
Moses da Costa
*Isaac Cohen Peixotto, *Gabay*
*Isaac de Selomoh Mendes, *Gabay*
Moses Dias Arias, *Gabay*

Joseph Mendes Crasto
Abraham de Moses Franco

5478
Abraham Levi Ximenes
Solomon Israel Pereira
Abraham de Moses Mendes da Costa, *Gabay*

Isaac Portello
Moses de Medina

5479
Abraham Bernal
Joseph Telles da Costa
Joseph da Costa, *Gabay*

Moses Levi Ximenes
Abraham Haim Mendes

5480
Jacob Jessurun Alvares
Isaac Vaz Martinez
*Daniel Jessurun Rodrigues, *Gabay*
Aaron Pereira, *Gabay*

*Samuel da Costa Alvarenga
Abraham da Costa

5481
Joseph Israel Henriques
Isaac de Selomoh Mendes
Jacob Fernandes Nunes, *Gabay*

Moses da Costa
Abraham Moses Franco

5482
Aaron Lamego
Abraham Fernandes Dias
Abraham Franco Nunes, *Gabay*

Solomon Israel Pereira
Abraham Moses Mendes da Costa

5483
Isaac Fernandes Nunes
Moses Lopes Dias
Jacob Alvares Pereira, *Gabay*

Joseph Telles da Costa
*Joseph Jacob da Costa
Jacob Gonzales

5484
Moses de Medina
Isaac Cohen Peixotto
David Lopes Pereira, *Gabay*

Joseph Mendes de Crasto
Isaac Vaz Martines

5485
Abraham Levi Ximenes
Jacob Fernandes Nunes
Jacob Moses Mendes da Costa, *Gabay*

Aaron Israel Pereira
Abraham Haim Mendes

5486
Aaron Lamego
Abraham Dias Fernandes
*Abraham Moses Mendes, *Gabay*
Jacob Israel Suasso, *Gabay*

Jacob Jessurun Alvares
Abraham Franco Nunes

5487
Abraham Moses Franco
Jacob Alvares Pereira

APPENDIX V

Jacob de David da Costa, *Gabay*

Moses Lopes Dias
Joseph Rodrigues Sequeira

5488
Joseph Telles da Costa
Jacob Mendes da Costa
*David Lopes Pereira
Jacob de Moses Franco, *Gabay*

*Joseph Israel Henriques
Isaac Fernandes Nunes
Joseph de Jacob da Costa

5489
Joseph Mendes de Crasto
Isaac Vaz Martines
Daniel Dias Fernandes, *Gabay*

*Daniel Jessurun Rodrigues
Isaac da Costa Villareal
Jacob Fernandes Nunes

5490
*Aaron Israel Pereira
*Jacob de Moses Mendes da Costa
*Moses Lopes Pereira, *Gabay*
Aaron Lamego
Abraham Dias Fernandes
Jacob Gomes Serra, *Gabay*

Moses da Costa
Abraham Mendes Seixas

5491
*Jacob Jessurun Alvarez
*Moses de Medina
*Benjamin de Menasseh Mendes, *Gabay*
*Abraham de Moses Franco
*Abraham Franco Nunes
*Benjamin Mendes da Costa, *Gabay*
David Mendes da Costa
*Jacob Alvarez Pereira

*Moses Lamego, *Gabay*
Eliau de la Faya
Selomoh Hisquiahu Mendes, *Gabay*

Moses Haim Espinoza
Jacob Israel Suasso

5492
Jacob de Abraham Mendes da Costa
Jacob de Moses Franco
*Jacob Abenatar Pimentel, *Gabay*
Jacob Israel Bernal, *Gabay*

Abraham Alvarez Corcho
Jacob de David Mendes da Costa

5493
David Lopes Pereira
Moses Lopes Dias
*Abraham Joseph Capadoce, *Gabay*
Benjamin Mendes Pacheco, *Gabay*

Daniel Jessurun Rodrigues
Isaac Israel Suasso

5494
Aaron Israel Pereira
*Jacob Fernandes Nunes
Jacob Isaac Jessurun Alvarez, *Gabay*
Abraham Dias Fernandes

*Isaac de Moses Mendes
Jacob Belmonte Ergas
Abraham de Moses Mendes da Costa

5495
†Benjamin de Manasseh Mendes
†Moses Lamego
Abraham da Fonseca, *Gabay*
Moses Lopes Dias

Abraham Mendes Seixas
Benjamin Mendes da Costa

† One of these refused office.

5496
Jacob Abenatar Pimentel
Selomoh de Moses Hisquiahu Mendes
*Abraham Aboab Osorio, *Gabay*
Benjamin Mendes da Costa, *Gabay*

Isaac de Abraham Dias Fernandes
Jacob Israel Bernal

5497
Abraham de Moses Franco
Abraham de Joseph Capadoce
Daniel Mendes Seixas, *Gabay*

Jacob Alvarez Pereira
Jacob de Moses Mendes da Costa

5498
Benjamin Mendes Pacheco
Jacob Israel Suasso
*Moses Haim Gomes Serra, *Gabay*
Abraham da Fonseca, *Gabay*

*Jacob de Abraham Mendes da Costa
*Jacob de Moses Franco
Aaron Israel Pereira
Daniel Jessurun Rodrigues

5499
Abraham Alvarez Corcho
Daniel Dias Fernandes
Haim Supino, *Gabay*

*Moses da Costa
*Abraham da Fonseca
Jacob Jessurun Alvarez

5500
*Jacob Nunes Fernandes
*Moses Lamego
*Aaron Israel Pereira, *Gabay*
Benjamin Mendes da Costa

Benjamin de Manasseh Mendes
Joseph Dias Fernandes, *Gabay*

Abraham Aboab Osorio
Jacob Israel Bernal

5501
Abraham Dias Fernandes
Daniel Mendes Seixas
*Joseph Jessurun Rodrigues, *Gabay*
David Franco, *Gabay*

Abraham Mendes Campos
Abraham de Joseph Capadoce

5502
Jacob Alvarez Pereira
Moses Haim Gomes Serra
Moses de Abraham Pereira, *Gabay*

†Benjamin Mendes Pacheco
†Jacob de Moses Mendes da Costa
Jacob Israel Suasso

5503
Abraham de Moses Franco
Moses Lopes Dias
*David Aboab Cardozo, *Gabay*
Jacob Alvarez Pereira, *Gabay*

Isaac de Abraham Dias Fernandes
Abraham da Fonseca

5504
Isaac Lamego
Benjamin Mendes da Costa
*Jacob Alvarez Corcho, *Gabay*
Jacob Israel Bernal, *Gabay*

Jacob de Moses Franco
Joseph Dias Fernandes

† One of these refused office.

APPENDIX V

5505

5506
*Jacob de Abraham Mendes da Costa
Joseph Jessurun Rodrigues
*Moses Abraham Corcho, *Gabay*
Jacob de David da Costa
Jacob Brandon, *Gabay*

Moses Lamego
Daniel Mendes Seixas
Abraham Aboab Osorio (in place of Jacob de David da Costa, retired)

5507
Daniel Jessurun Rodrigues
Benjamin de Manasseh Mendes
Naphtali Levi Sonsino, *Gabay*

Jacob Gomes Serra
Abraham da Fonseca

5508
†Jacob de Mose Mendes da Costa
†David Aboab Cardozo
Jacob Alvarez Pereira
Jacob Baruh Lousada, *Gabay*

†Benjamin Mendes Pacheco
†Jacob Alvarez Corcho
Jacob Brandon

5509
*Jacob Israel Suasso
Abraham de Joseph Capadoce
Jacob Jessurun Rodrigues, *Gabay*
*Benjamin Mendes da Costa
Joseph Dias Fernandes

*Isaac Lamego
Moses Haim Gomes Serra
*Daniel Mendes Seixas
Jacob Baruh Lousada

5510
Jacob de David da Costa
Moses de Jacob Mendes da Costa
Joseph Hisquiau de Chaves, *Gabay*

†Moses Alvares Corcho
†Jacob Nunes Gonzales
Abraham da Fonseca

5511
*Abraham de Moses Franco
*Jacob de Abraham Mendes da Costa
Jacob Gomes Serra
Joseph Jessurun Rodrigues
Isaac Rebello de Mendoza, *Gabay*

*Moses Lamego
*Abraham Aboab Ozorio
Jacob Alvares Corcho

5512
Jacob de Moses Franco
Moses de Joseph da Costa
*Abraham del Prado, *Gabay*
David Abenatar Pimentel, *Gabay*

Daniel Jessurun Rodrigues
Jacob Alvares Pereira

5513
David Aboab Cardozo
*Jacob Fernandez Nunes
David Franco
Jacob Levi Sonsino, *Gabay*

*Isaac Lamego
Daniel Mendes Seixas
Joseph Dias Fernandes

5514
Moses Haim Gomes Serra
*Joseph Hizquiau de Chaves
Isaac Rebello de Mendoza

† One of these refused office.

Moses de Jacob Franco, *Gabay*

Daniel Dias Fernandes
Jacob Nunes Gonzales

5515
Abraham de Moses Franco
*Moses Alvares Corcho
Joseph Jessurun Rodrigues
Isaac Jacob Jessurun Alvares, *Gabay*

*Moses Lamego
Abraham Aboab Osorio
Jacob Nunes Gonzales

5516
Abraham da Fonseca
David Abarbanel
*Abraham del Prado
Judah de Selomoh Supino, *Gabay*

Jacob de Moses Franco
Moses de Jacob Mendes da Costa

5517
*Jacob Fernandes Nunes
*David Abenatar Pimentel
Isaac de Daniel Mendes da Costa, *Gabay*
Semania Nunes
David Aboab Cardozo

Moses Lopes Pereira
Daniel Mendes Seixas

5518
Moses Gomes Serra
*Isaac Lamego
Moses de Jacob Franco
Hananel Mendes da Costa, *Gabay*

Joseph Dias Fernandes
*Joseph Hisquiau de Chaves
Isaac Rebello de Mendoza

5519
Moses Alvares Corcho
Joseph Abraham Franco
Isaac Fernandes Nunes, *Gabay*

*Moses Lamego
Abraham Aboab Osorio
Daniel Dias Fernandes

5520
Jacob Nunes Gonzales
David Abraham Franco
Ephraim Lopes Pereira
 (Ephraim de Aguilar), *Gabay*

David Abarbanel
Abraham de Jacob Fernandes Nunes

5521
Abraham del Prado
*Joseph Jessurun Rodrigues
Isaac de Jacob Jessurun Alvares
Jacob Abraham Aboab Osorio, *Gabay*

Jacob de Moses Franco
Isaac de Daniel Mendes da Costa

5522
David Aboab Cardozo
Moses de Joseph da Costa
Isaac de Jacob Mendes da Costa, *Gabay*

Daniel Mendes Seixas
Semania Nunes

5523
Benjamin Mendes da Costa
Moses de Jacob Franco
Moses de Isaac a Levi, *Gabay*

Moses Haim Gomes Serra
*Joseph Hisquiau de Chaves
Isaac Rebello de Mendoza

APPENDIX V

5524
Joseph Fernandes Dias
Aaron Haim Lousada
Jeosuah Mendes da Costa, *Gabay*

Abraham Aboab Osorio
Jacob Nunes Gonzales

5525
†David Abarbanel
†Hananel Mendes da Costa
†Raphael Jacob Franco, *Gabay*

Joseph Abraham Franco
Ephraim Lopes Pereira
*Abraham de Jacob Fernandez Nunes
Jacob de Abraham Aboab Osorio
Joseph Jessurun Rodrigues

5526
Selomoh Henriques Fereira
*David de Abraham Franco
Isaac de Jacob Jessurun Alvares
David Ximenes Cardozo, *Gabay*

Jacob de Moses Franco
Semania Nunes

5527
Abraham Rodrigues Brandão
Isaac de Jacob Mendes da Costa
David de Haim Supino, *Gabay*

*Moses Haim Gomes Serra
*Joseph Hisquiau de Chaves
Isaac Rebello de Mendoza

5528
*Abraham del Prado
*Moses de Isaac a Levi
*Judah Supino
*Aaron Haim Lousada
Jacob Nunes Gonzales
Moses de Jacob Franco

Samuel de Solomon de Crasto, *Gabay*

Abraham Aboab Osorio
Joseph Dias Fernandes

5529
David Abarbanel
Hananel Mendes da Costa
Isaac Israel Nunes, *Gabay*

*Moses de Joseph da Costa
Raphael Jacob Franco
Gabriel Lopes de Britto
Phineas Gomes Serra

5530
*Abraham Fernandes Nunes
*Joshua Mendes da Costa
Abraham Levi Ximenes, *Gabay*
*Selomoh Henriques Fereira
*Jacob Mendes Pereira
Moses Haim da Costa Alvarenga
Isaac Fernandes Valencia
*Abraham Alvares Correa

*Joseph de Abraham Franco
*Abraham Jessurun Mendes
Jacob Aboab Osorio
Ephraim Lopes Pereira

5531
*Abraham Alvarez Correa
David Ximenes Cardozo
*Immanuel Fernandes Marques, *Gabay*
*Jacob de Moses Franco
Daniel Brandon Seixas, *Gabay*
Semania Nunes

*David de Abraham Franco
*Joseph Jessurun Rodrigues
*Isaac de Jacob Jessurun Alvarenga
*David de Haim Supino
*Moses Haim Gomes Serra

† Retired from office.

*Isaac de Jacob Mendes da Costa
Joseph Hisquiau de Chaves
Isaac Rebello de Mendoza

5532
Abraham Aboab Osorio
Moses de Isaac aLevy
Eliau Lindo, *Gabay*

*Jacob Nunes Gonzales
*Abraham del Prado
Abraham Lindo
Moses de Jacob Franco

5533
Abraham Aboab Osorio
Isaac Israel Nunes
Isaac Gomes Serra, *Gabay*

David Abarbanel
*Joseph Dias Fernandes
*Raphael de Jacob Franco
Pinhas Gomes Serra

5534
*Abraham Fernandes Nunes
Abraham Levi Ximenes
*Abraham de Mattos Mocatta, *Gabay*
Moses Haim da Costa Alvarenga
David Alves Rebello, *Gabay*

Joseph de Abraham Franco
*Abraham Jessurun Mendes
Ephraim Lopes Pereira

5535
*Imanuel Fernandes Marques
David Ximenes Cardozo
Jacob Rodrigues Peynado, *Gabay*
Daniel Brandon Seixas

Moses Israel da Fonseca
Daniel de Selomoh de Castro

5536
Abraham Alves Correa
Eliau Lindo
David Lopes Pereira, *Gabay*

*Jacob de Moses Franco
Mordecai Rodrigues Lopes
Semania Nunes

5537
Joseph de Isaac Capadose
Isaac Gomes Serra
Emanuel de Jacob Baruh Lousada, *Gabay*

*David de Abraham Franco
*Isaac de Jacob Jessurun Alvares
Samuel de Selomoh de Castro
Moses de Isaac aLevy

5538
*Moses Haim Gomes Serra
*Abraham del Prado
Abraham Haim Franco, *Gabay*
Jacob Aboab Osorio
David Alves Rebello
Isaac Israel Nunes

*Abraham de Mattos Mocatta
*Abraham Fernandes Nunes
Abraham Levi Ximenes

5539
Abraham Jessurun Mendes
Jacob Rodrigues Peynado
Israel de Jacob Baruh Lousada, *Gabay*

*Emanuel Fernandes Marques
Daniel Selomoh de Castro
Eliau Lindo

5540
*Moses de Joshua Macharro
David Lopes Pereira

APPENDIX V 437

Raphael Rodrigues Brandon, *Gabay*
Moses Haim Montefiore

*Abraham Lopes Pereira
*Mordecai Rodrigues Lopes
Jacob Israel Brandon
David Samuda

5541
Raphael de Jacob Franco
Emanuel de Jacob Baruh Lousada
Isaac Henriques Moron, *Gabay*

Joseph de Isaac Capadose
*Jacob Jessurun Barzilay
Abraham Israel Ricardo

5542
*Moses de Isaac aLevy
*Abraham Haim Franco
*Hananael Lopes Pereira, *Gabay*
Eliau Lindo
Raphael Rodrigues Brandon
Joseph de Jacob Baruh Lousada, *Gabay*

*Moses Haim Gomes Serra
*Abraham del Prado
Jacob Aboab Osorio
David Alves Rebello

5543
Isaac Israel Nunes
Ephraim Lopes Pereira
Benjamin Nunes de Lara, *Gabay*

*Emanuel Fernandes Marques
*Abraham de Mattos Mocatta
*Abraham Jessurun Mendes
Daniel de Selomo de Castro
Jacob Rodrigues Peinado

5544
*Moses de Joshua Machorro
*Eliau de David Lindo
*Jacob de Moses Franco, *Gabay*
*Isaac de Jacob Jessurun Alvares
*Isaac Mendes Pereira
*Jacob de Hananel Mendes da Costa, *Gabay*
*Raphael Vaz da Silva
Eliau Lindo (for six months)
Jacob Israel Brandon
Isaac Henriques Moron, *Gabay*

*Benjamin Dias Fernandes
Abraham Lopes Pereira
*Mordecai Rodrigues Lopes
David Samuda

5545
Samuel Mendes Pereira
Abraham Aguilar
Jacob Samuda, *Gabay*

Joseph Israel Capadose
Abraham Israel Ricardo

5546
*Isaac Gomes Serra
Emanuel de Jacob Baruh Lousada
Gabriel Israel Brandon, *Gabay*
*Moses de Isaac Levy
Raphael Rodrigues Brandon

*Abraham Alves Correa
*Moses Haim Montefiore
Jacob Aboab Osorio
David Alves Rebello

5547
Benjamin Nunes Lara
David de Leon
Benjamin Mendes Pereira, *Gabay*

Abraham Lopes Pereira
*Isaac de Jacob Baruh Lousada
Isaac Israel Nunes

5548
*Moses de Joshua Machorro
*Abraham de Mattos Mocatta
Moses de David Ximenes, *Gabay*
Isaac Israel Brandon
Isaac de Jacob Jessurun Alvares

*Raphael Vaz da Silva
*Benjamin Dias Fernandes
David Samuda
Mordecai Rodrigues Lopes

5549
Jacob Samuda
*Abraham Aguilar
*Jacob de Benjamin Dias Fernandes, *Gabay*
Eliau Lopes Pereira
Isaac de Jacob Mendes Pereira, *Gabay*

*Joseph de Isaac Capadose
Emanuel de Jacob Baruh Lousada
Abraham Israel Ricardo

5550
*Isaac Gomes Serra
Gabriel Israel Brandon
*Jacob Abenatar Pimentel, *Gabay*
*Moses de Isaac Levy
Menasseh Rodrigues Lopes, *Gabay*
Raphael Rodrigues Brandon

David Alves Rebello
Benjamin Mendes Pereira

5551
Benjamin Nunes Lara
David de Leon
Isaac H. Aguilar, *Gabay*

Abraham Lopes Pereira
Isaac de Jacob Mendes Pereira

5552
*Isaac de Jacob Baruh Lousada
*Moses de David Ximenes
Moses de Eliau Lindo, *Gabay*
Naphtali Basevi
Moses de Joshua Machorro

Jacob Israel Brandon
Isaac de Jacob Jessurun Alvares

5553
*David Samuda
*Jacob Dias Fernandes
Samuel Haim Montefiore, *Gabay*
Mordecai Rodrigues Lopes
Jacob Samuda

*Eliau Lopes Pereira
*Abraham de David Texeira
Joseph de Isaac Capadose
Abraham Israel Ricardo

5554
*Abraham Mocatta
*Jacob Abenatar Pimentel
*Isaac Saportas, *Gabay*
Emanuel de Jacob Baruh Lousada
Gabriel Israel Brandon
Isaac de Aaron Capadoce, *Gabay*

*Isaac Gomes Serra
*Menasseh Rodrigues Lopes
Moseh de Isaac Levy
Rephael Rodrigues Brandon

5555
Benjamin Mendes Pereira
Isaac Haim Aguilar
Jacob Baruh (Barrow), *Gabay*

*Abraham Lopes Pereira
*Joseph Saportas
Jacob Israel Brandon
Isaac de Jacob Mendes Pereira

APPENDIX V

5556
*Moses Norsa
*Isaac de Jacob Baruh Lousada
Ephraim Lindo, *Gabay*
Jacob Samuda
Moses de David Ximenes

*Joseph Bendalack
*Isaac de Jacob Jessurun Alvares
Emanuel de Jacob Baruh Lousada
Gabriel Israel Brandon

5557
Naphtali Basevi
Moses de Eliau Lindo
Isaac Rebello de Mendoza, *Gabay*

David Samuda
*Jacob Dias Fernandez
Eliau Lopes Pereira

5558
Abraham Israel Ricardo
Isaac Saportas
Abraham Mendes Pereira, *Gabay*

*Abraham de David Teixeira
*Isaac de Aaron Capadose
Abraham Mocatta
Jacob Abenatar Pimentel

5559
*Isaac Gomes Serra
Jacob Baruh (Barrow)
Isaac Ribeiro Furtado, *Gabay*
Menasseh Rodrigues Lopes
Raphael Rodrigues Brandon
Moses de Isaac Levy

*Benjamin Mendes Pereira
Isaac Haim Aguilar
Joseph Saportas

5560
Jacob Israel Brandon
Elisha (Alexander) Lindo
*Jacob Aboab Osorio, *Gabay*
Jacob Mocatta, *Gabay*

Jacob Samuda
Moses Haim Norsa

5561
*Isaac de Jacob Baruh Lousada
Isaac Rebello de Mendoza
*Joshua Basevi, *Gabay*
Gabriel Israel Brandon
Joseph Aguilar, *Gabay*

Emanuel Baruh Lousada
Ephraim Lindo

5562
*Eliau Lopes Pereira
*Jacob Dias Fernandes
*Abraham Israel Bravo, *Gabay*
Abraham Israel Ricardo
Isaac Saportas
Jacob da Fonseca Brandon, *Gabay*

*Naphtali Basevi
Moses de Eliau Lindo
Abraham de David Teixeira

5563
*Isaac Gomes Serra
*Jacob Abenatar Pimentel
David de Jacob Israel Brandon, *Gabay*
Moses de Isaac Levy
Raphael Rodrigues Brandon

Joseph Saportas
Emanuel Israel de Piza

5564
*Isaac Haim Aguilar
Jacob Aboab Osorio
*Moses Mocatta, *Gabay*

Jacob Mocatta
Gabriel Israel Brandon, *Gabay*

Jacob Samuda
Elisha Lindo

5565
*Abraham Lopes Pereira
Moses Haim Norsa
David Abarbanel Lindo, *Gabay*
Isaac Jessurun Alvares

Jacob Samuda
Elisha Lindo

5566
*Isaac de Jacob Baruh Lousada
*Joshua Basevi
Masahod de Levante, *Gabay*
Emanuel de Jacob Baruh Lousada
Abraham Israel Bravo

*Joseph Baruch (Barrow)
Jacob da Fonseca Brandon
Ephraim Lindo

5567
Isaac Saportas
*Jacob Dias Fernandez
David Samuda, *Gabay*
Abraham Teixeira

*Isaac Gomes Serra
Jacob Abenatar Pimentel
Emanuel Israel de Piza

5568
David Berlandina
*Isaac Haim Aguilar
Daniel Mocatta, *Gabay*
Jacob Aboab Osorio

Rephael Rodrigues Brandon
*David de Isaac Lindo
Eliau Lopes Pereira

5569
Joseph Benhacok
Moses Mocatta
Joseph de Gabriel Israel Brandon, *Gabay*

Moses de Rephael Franco
Abraham de Zachariah Jalfon

5570
*David Lopes Pereira
David Abarbanel Lindo
Judah Guedalla, *Gabay*
Abraham Israel Bravo

*Judah Cohen
Jacob da Fonseca Brandon
Menahem Levy Bensusan

5571
Moses de Eliau Lindo
Masahod de Levante
Moses de Isaac Baruh Lousada, *Gabay*

*Jacob Abenatar Pimentel
*David Samuda
Joseph Benhacok
Joseph de Gabriel Israel Brandon

5572
Jacob de Hananel Mendes da Costa
*Joshua Basevi
Emanuel Lousada, *Gabay*
Selomoh Israel

David de Isaac Lindo
Moses de Aaron Gomes da Costa

5573
*Rephael Rodrigues Brandon
Jacob Mocatta
*Moses de Benjamin Nunes Lara, *Gabay*
Israel A. Levy

Simon Baruh (Barrow), *Gabay*

*Abraham Z. Jalfon
*Joshua Levy Bensusan
Jacob Attias
Selomoh Gomes da Costa

5574
*Eliezer Montefiore
Daniel Mocatta
*Isaac de Emanuel Baruh Lousada, *Gabay*
*Isaac de Israeli
Joshua Rodrigues Brandon, *Gabay*

*Judah Cohen
Meir Cohen Macnin
Jacob da Fonseca Brandon

5575
*Isaac de Jacob Baruh Lousada
*Ephraim Lindo
Moseh de Joseph Eliau Montefiore, *Gabay*
Emanuel de Jacob Baruh Lousada
Menahem Levy Bensusan

Moseh de Eliau Lindo
*Jacob Abenatar Pimentel
David Samuda

5576
Judah Guedalla
Moseh de Isaac Baruh Lousada
Jacob de Gabriel Israel Brandon, *Gabay*

*Selomoh Israel
*Jacob de Hananel Mendes da Costa
Masahod de Levante
*David de Eliau Lopes Pereira

5577
Moses Nunes Lara
Joseph de Gabriel Israel Brandon
Abraham de Joseph Eliau Montefiore, *Gabay*

Emanuel Lousada
Simon Baruh (Barrow)

5578
*Moses Mocatta
Moses Gomes da Costa
*David Rodrigues Brandon, *Gabay*
David Abarbanel Lindo
*David Cohen, *Gabay*

*Abraham de Z. Jalfon
*Isaac de Emanuel Baruh Lousada
*Joshua Levy Bensusan
*Joshua Rodrigues Brandon
*Judah Cohen
*Jacob Attias

5579
David de Isaac Lindo
*Jacob Mocatta
Moses da Costa Lindo, *Gabay*
*Selomoh Gomes da Costa
*Eliezer Montefiore
*Daniel Mocatta

*Menahem Levy Bensusan
*Moses de Joseph Eliau Montefiore
*Jacob Abenatar Pimentel
*David Samuda

5580
Moses de Joseph Eliau Montefiore (six months)
Joseph de Gabriel Israel Brandon
Moses de Eliau Lindo
Moses Baruh Lousada

Semuel de Menahem Levy
  Bensusan *Gabay*

*Judah Guedalla
*Abraham Q. Henriques
*Selomoh Israel
 Jacob de Hananel Mendes da
  Costa
 David de Eliau Lopes Pereira

5581
*Ephraim Lindo
 Abraham de Joseph E. Montefiore
 Baruh Norsa, *Gabay*
 Jacob Mendes Belisario

*Isaac de Jacob Baruh Lousada
*David de Jacob Israel Brandon
*Isaac Haim Aguilar
 Emanuel Lousada

5582
Jacob Aboab Osorio
Aron Mocatta
Benjamin Lindo, *Gabay*

Moseh Gomes da Costa
*David Rodrigues Brandon
 Moses de Benjamin Nunes Lara

5583
*Emanuel de Jacob Baruh
  Lousada
 Simon Baruh (Barrow)
 Abraham de Isaac Mocatta,
  Gabay
 Isaac de Emanuel Baruh Lousada

*Abraham D. Z. Jalfon
*Joshua Rodrigues Brandon
 Solomon Gomes da Costa
*Moses da Costa Lindo
*Eleazar Montefiore

5584
*Moses Mocatta
*David Samuda
*Jacob de Menahem Levy Bensusan, *Gabay*
 Jacob Mocatta
 Joseph de Gabriel Israel Brandon
 Emanuel de Joseph Aguilar,
  Gabay

*Menahem L. Bensusan
 Selomoh Israel
*Jacob de Hananel Mendes da
  Costa
*David Lopes Pereira

5585
Moses de Eliau Lindo
*Moses Baruh Lousada
 Abraham de Jacob Mocatta,
  Gabay
*Abraham Quixano Henriques

David Cohen
Samuel Levy Bensusan

5586
*Ephraim Lindo
 Baruh Norsa
 Solomon Sebag, *Gabay*
*Jacob Mendes Belisario

*Judah Guedalla
*Emanuel Lousada
*Moses Franco
*Benjamin de Pinhas Nunes

5587
Moses de Joseph E. Montefiore
Simon Baruh (Barrow)
*Jacob Bonfil, *Gabay*
 Rephael Bonfil, *Gabay*

Moses Nunes Lara
Moses Gomes da Costa

APPENDIX V

5588
*Abraham Jalfon
*David Abarbanel Lindo
*Jacob de Eliezer Montefiore, *Gabay*
Moses da Costa Lindo
Joshua Israel Brandon
Moses de Samuel H. Montefiore, *Gabay*

Solomon Gomes da Costa
Joseph Israel Brandon

5589
Meir Cohen Macnin
*Jacob Levy Bensusan
Abraham Lindo Mocatta, *Gabay*
*Jacob Mendes da Costa, senior

*Abraham Q. Henriques
*David Rodrigues Brandon
Samuel Levy Bensusan
Joshua Mendes da Costa

5590
*David Cohen
*Abraham de Isaac Mocatta
*Emanuel Brandon, *Gabay*
David Lopes Pereira
Moses Mocatta
Isaac Foligno, *Gabay*

Menachem Levy Bensusan
Joshua Rodrigues Brandon

5591
Moses Mendes da Costa
Benjamin Nunes
Joseph de Joseph E. Montefiore, *Gabay*

Solomon Aloof
Moses Gomes da Costa

5592
Moses da Costa Lindo
Abraham de Jacob Mocatta
Hananel de Castro, *Gabay*

Abraham Jalfon
Jacob Montefiore

5593
Judah Guedalla
Daniel Melhado
*Gabriel de Joseph Israel Brandon, *Gabay*
Yedidya Foligno, *Gabay*

Joseph Israel Brandon
Moses de Joseph Eliau Montefiore

5594
Emanuel Lousada
Samuel Levy Bensusan
*Isaac de Jacob Mendes da Costa, *Gabay*
Elias Mendes Pereira, *Gabay*

Moses de Samuel H. Montefiore
Isaac Foligno

5595
*David Lopes Pereira
Moses Mendes da Costa
Abraham de Daniel Mocatta, *Gabay*
Jacob de M. L. Bensusan

Solomon Aloof
Abraham Lindo Mocatta

5596
Moses Gomes da Costa
*David R. Brandon
Emanuel de Jacob Mocatta, *Gabay*
Elias Henriques Valentine

Hananel de Castro
Horatio Joseph Montefiore

5597
*Judah Guedalla
Jacob Israel Brandon
Judah Aloof, *Gabay*
Yedidya Foligno

*Moses da Costa Lindo
Solomon Zagury
Jacob de Eliezer Montefiore

5598
David Abarbanel Lindo
Solomon Abecasis
David Q. Henriques, *Gabay*

Joshua Mendes da Costa, junior
Jacob Hassan

5599
Abraham de Jacob Mocatta
Joseph Gutteres Henriques
*Elias de Daniel Mocatta, *Gabay*
Aaron Valentine, *Gabay*

Samuel Levy Bensusan
Jacob de Joseph Pariente

5600
*Moses de Samuel Montefiore
Isaac Foligno
*David de Moses Mocatta, *Gabay*
Isaac Aflalo
Elias Lindo, *Gabay*

Moses Mendes da Costa
Joseph Israel Brandon

5601
*Isaac de Jacob Mendes da Costa
*Abraham de Daniel Mocatta
Joshua de M. L. Bensusan,
  Gabay
Judah Guedalla
Horatio Joseph Montefiore

Sir Moses Montefiore, F.R.S.
Abraham Lindo Mocatta

5602
Judah Guedalla
Hananel de Castro
Isaac Jalfon, *Gabay*

*Jacob Levy Bensusan
Judah Aloof
Yedidya Foligno

5603
Jacob Israel Brandon
Moses da Costa Lindo
Judah de Jacob Pariente, *Gabay*

Solomon Abecasis
Moses Gomes Silva

5604
*Samuel Levy Bensusan
Isaac Foligno
Haim Guedalla, *Gabay*
Elias Haim Lindo

Samuel Levy Bensusan
Emanuel Aguilar

5605
Joseph Israel Brandon
*Moses de Samuel Montefiore
Nathaniel Lindo, *Gabay*
Emanuel Lousada

*Jacob Pariente
Isaac Aflalo
Moses Gomes Silva

5606
Joshua Levy Bensusan
Isaac Jalfon
Joseph Mayer Montefiore, *Gabay*

Judah Aloof
Daniel de Pass

APPENDIX V

5607
Yedidya Foligno
Isaac Jalfon
Joseph Mayer Montefiore, *Gabay*

*Moses da Costa Lindo
Jacob Hassan
Solomon Abecasis

5608
Isaac Foligno
Haim Guedalla
Nathaniel Montefiore, *Gabay*

Elias Haim Lindo
Naphtali Hart Lyon

5609
*Judah Guedalla
Sir Moses Montefiore, Bart.
Judah Varicas, *Gabay*
Moses de Samuel H. Montefiore, junior

Solomon Abecasis
Yedidya Foligno

5610
Joseph Israel Brandon
Nathaneel Lindo
David de Daniel de Pass, *Gabay*

*Abraham Lindo Mocatta
Isaac Aflalo
Emanuel Lousada

5611
Judah Aloof
Daniel de Pass
Joseph d'Aguilar Samuda, *Gabay*

Joshua Benoliel
Joseph Mayer Montefiore

5612
Moses da Costa Lindo
Isaac Jalfon
Moses Picciotto, *Gabay*

*Isaac Foligno
Nathaniel Montefiore
Naphtali Hart Lyon

5613
*Moses de Samuel H. Montefiore, junior
Abrm. Levy Bensusan
Joseph Sebag, *Gabay*
Elias Haim Lindo

*Isaac Benoliel
Nathaniel Montefiore
Solomon Abecasis

5614
David Rodrigues Brandon
Alexander Israel Montefiore
Samuel Zagury, *Gabay*

Sir Moses Montefiore
Yedidya Foligno

5615
David R. Brandon
Judah Aloof
Isaac de Abraham Mocatta, *Gabay*

Joseph Mayer Montefiore
David de Daniel de Pass

5616
Isaac Aflalo
Solomon Sequerra
*Moses Benoliel, *Gabay*
Jacob E. Henriques Valentine, *Gabay*

Nathaneel Lindo
Haim Guedalla

5617
Isaac Jalfon
Solomon Sequerra
Michael de Daniel de Pass, *Gabay*

Moses H. Picciotto
Joseph d'Aguilar Samuda

5618
Nathaniel Montefiore
Joseph Sebag
Michael de Pass, *Gabay*

Solomon Abecasis
Alexander Israel Montefiore

5619
Abraham Levy Bensusan
Abraham D. de Pass
Abraham A. Mocatta, *Gabay*

Yedidya Foligno
Joseph M. Montefiore

5620
Joshua Benoliel
Isaac Mocatta, junior
Joseph de Castro, *Gabay*

David de Pass
Manuel Castello

5621
Solomon Aloof
Joseph de Castro
Benjamin Colaço, *Gabay*

Haim Guedalla
Michael de Pass

5622
Nathaniel Montefiore
Solomon Aloof

Benjamin Colaço, *Gabay*

Solomon H. Andrade
Joseph Sebag

5623
Nathaniel Montefiore
Benjamin Colaço
Abraham Hakim, *Gabay*

Alexander I. Montefiore
Abraham A. Mocatta

5624
Abraham D. De Pass
Moses de Joshua Levy
Baruch Castello, *Gabay*

Nathaneel Lindo
*Moses da Costa Andrade
Joseph Mayer Montefiore

5625
David De Pass
Manuel Castello
Solomon Pool, *Gabay*

Mordecai Adutt
Nathaniel Montefiore

5626
Michael de Pass
Solomon Pool
Daniel Castello, *Gabay*

Nathaniel Montefiore
*Aaron Abecasis
Benjamin Colaço

5627
Abraham Levy Bensusan
Joseph Sebag
Daniel Castello, *Gabay*

Alexander I. Montefiore
Sassoon D. Sassoon

APPENDIX V

5628
Joseph Mayer Montefiore
Abraham A. Mocatta
Daniel Lindo, *Gabay*

Haim Guedalla
Moses Aflalo

5629
Abrm. A. Mocatta
Joseph M. Montefiore
Joseph Norsa Lindo, *Gabay*

Manuel Castello
Isaac Abitbol

5630
David De Pass
Solomon Pool
Joseph Norsa Lindo, *Gabay*

Nathaniel Montefiore
Reuben D. Sassoon

5631
Benjamin Colaço
Daniel Castello
Haim Pinto, *Gabay*

Nathaniel Montefiore
Joseph Sebag

5632
Manuel Castello
Judah Nahon
Haim Pinto, *Gabay*

Alexander I. Montefiore
Abrm. D. De Pass

5633
Abrm. A. Mocatta
Manuel Castello
Saml. N. Carvalho, *Gabay*

Fredk. B. Halford
Moses Aflalo

5634
Joseph M. Montefiore
Solomon Pool
Gabriel Lindo, *Gabay*

Gabriel S. Brandon
Joseph de Castro

5635
Elias De Pass
Daniel Castello
Jacob de Abrm. Brandon, *Gabay*

Gabriel S. Brandon
Arthur D. Sassoon

5636
Haim Guedalla
Daniel Castello
Moses L. Bensusan, *Gabay*

Isaac Pariente
Haim Pinto

5637
Alexander Kursheedt
Joseph Sebag
Daniel De Pass, *Gabay*

*Charles Lindo
Manuel Castello
Daniel Lindo

5638
Joseph Sebag
David Goldsmith
Eugenio Arbib, *Gabay*

Alexander I. Montefiore
Manuel Castello

5639
*Joseph Mayer Montefiore
Joseph de Castro
Gabriel Lindo

Eugenio Arbib, *Gabay*

Alexander I. Montefiore
Fredk. B. Halford

5640
Joseph de Castro
Gabriel Lindo
Phineas Paiba, *Gabay*

Fredk. B. Halford
Saml. N. Carvalho, junior

5641
John P. Paiba
Gabriel S. Brandon
*David Lindo, *Gabay*
Enrico Arbib, *Gabay*

Abraham Mocatta
Daniel Castello

5642
Isaac Pariente
Solomon Ezekiel
Arthur Montefiore Sebag, *Gabay*

Nathaniel Montefiore (died in office)
Daniel Castello

5643
Gabriel Lindo
Daniel De Pass
Philip B. Goldsmith, *Gabay*

Solomon Ezekiel
Manuel Castello

5644
Joseph de Castro
Gabriel Lindo
Philip B. Goldsmith, *Gabay*

Haim Guedalla
Lazare Allatini

5645
Alexander I. Montefiore
Joseph de Castro
Jacob N. Castello, *Gabay*

Gabriel S. Brandon
Abraham Mocatta

5646
Alexander I. Montefiore
Joseph de Castro
Jacob N. Castello, *Gabay*

Gabriel S. Brandon
Abraham Mocatta

5647
Haim Pinto
Manuel Castello
Arthur Lindo, *Gabay*

Abraham Mocatta
Philip B. Goldsmith

5648
Manuel Castello
Eugenio Arbib
Abraham H. Pinto, *Gabay*

Abraham De Pass
Philip B. Goldsmith

5649
Gabriel Lindo
Abraham H. Pinto
Charles A. Mocatta, *Gabay*

Abraham D. De Pass
Joseph de Castro

5650
Gabriel Lindo
Charles A. Mocatta
Elim H. d'Avigdor, *Gabay*

Abraham D. De Pass
Enrico Arbib

APPENDIX V

5651
Gabriel Lindo
Elim H. d'Avigdor
Edward Sassoon, *Gabay*

Abraham D. De Pass
Sir Francis A. Montefiore, Bart.

5652
Gabriel Lindo
Elim H. d'Avigdor
James Castello, *Gabay*

Abraham D. De Pass
Sir Francis A. Montefiore, Bart.

5653
Arthur Lindo
James Castello
Edward L. Mocatta, *Gabay*

Abraham D. De Pass
Sir Francis A. Montefiore, Bart.

5654
Manuel Castello
Arthur Lindo
Edward L. Mocatta, *Gabay*

Abraham D. De Pass
Eugenio Arbib

5655
Manuel Castello
Arthur Lindo
Edward L. Mocatta, *Gabay*

Eustace A. Lindo
Joshua M. Levy

5656
Edward Sassoon
Edward L. Mocatta
M. A. N. Lindo, *Gabay*

Joshua M. Levy
Eustace A. Lindo

5657
Isaac Genese
Edward Sassoon
M. A. N. Lindo, *Gabay*

Joshua M. Levy
Eustace A. Lindo

5658
Isaac Genese
Sir Edward Sassoon, Bart.
Eliot A. De Pass, *Gabay*

Edward H. Pinto
Eustace A. Lindo

5659
Gabriel Lindo
Sir Edward Sassoon, Bart.
Percy M. Castello, *Gabay*

Edward H. Pinto
Eustace A. Lindo

5660
Gabriel Lindo
Sir Edward Sassoon, Bart.
Edmund Sebag-Montefiore,
   Gabay

Joseph de Castro
Isaac Genese

5661
Gabriel Lindo
Sir Edward Sassoon, Bart.
Edmund Sebag-Montefiore

Joseph de Castro
Isaac Genese

5662
Gabriel Lindo
Sir Francis A. Montefiore, Bart.
Edmund Sebag-Montefiore,
   Gabay

Isaac Genese
Joshua M. Levy

5663
Gabriel Lindo
Aaron E. J. Abraham (Ronnie Gubbay)
Cecil Sebag-Montefiore, *Gabay*

Frederick B. Halford
Joshua M. Levy

5664
Ronnie Gubbay
Edward L. Mocatta
Cecil Sebag-Montefiore, *Gabay*

Frederick B. Halford
Joshua M. Levy

5665
Edward L. Mocatta
Cecil Sebag-Montefiore
José de Sola Pinto, *Gabay*

Judah Benoliel
Eustace A. Lindo

5666
José de Sola Pinto
Edward L. Mocatta
Joseph de Castro, *Gabay*

Judah Benoliel (died in office)
Eustace A. Lindo
Isaac Genese

5667
Joseph de Castro
James Castello
Judah D. Israel, *Gabay*

Isaac Genese
Eustace A. Lindo

5668
Joseph de Castro
James Castello

Judah D. Israel, *Gabay* (resigned)

Robert M. Sebag-Montefiore, *Gabay*
Isaac Genese
Judah D. Israel

5669
Joshua M. Levy
David A. Romain
Robert M. Sebag-Montefiore, *Gabay*

Isaac Genese
Judah D. Israel

5670
Joshua M. Levy
David A. Romain
Robert M. Sebag-Montefiore, *Gabay*

Bertram H. Pinto, *Gabay*
Percy M. Castello
Robert M. Sebag-Montefiore

5671
Joshua M. Levy (resigned)
David A. Romain
Bertram H. Pinto, *Gabay*

Raphael Nahon
Percy M. Castello
Edward L. Mocatta

5672
Bertram H. Pinto
Raphael Nahon
Charles E. Sebag-Montefiore, *Gabay*

Percy M. Castello
Edward L. Mocatta

5673
Eustace A. Lindo
Raphael Nahon
Charles E. Sebag-Montefiore, *Gabay*

Edward L. Mocatta
Dr. Lionel D. Barnett

5674
Isaac A. Shamasch (died in office)
Eustace A. Lindo
David Gubbay, *Gabay*

Judah D. Israel
Dr. Lionel D. Barnett
Ronnie Gubbay

5675
Ronnie Gubbay
Harold M. Wiener
David Gubbay, *Gabay*

M. A. N. Lindo
Dr. Lionel D. Barnett

5676
Ronnie Gubbay
Frederick N. Martinez
David Gubbay, *Gabay*

M. A. N. Lindo
Dr. Lionel D. Barnett

5677
Ronnie Gubbay
Frederick N. Martinez
David Vaz Nunes da Costa, *Gabay*

M. A. N. Lindo
Dr. Lionel D. Barnett

5678
Aubrey J. David
Frederick N. Martinez
David V. N. da Costa, *Gabay* (resigned)
Bertram Pinto (in place of M. A. N. Lindo, resigned)

Bertram Pinto
David V. N. da Costa
John Sebag-Montefiore, *Gabay*

5679
Eustace A. Lindo
Aubrey J. David
John Sebag-Montefiore, *Gabay*

Bertram H. Pinto
David V. N. da Costa

5680
Eustace A. Lindo
Alfred A. Isaacs
John Sebag-Montefiore, *Gabay*

David V. N. da Costa
Gershom Delgado

5681
Eustace A. Lindo
Alfred A. Isaacs
Joseph S. Elmaleh, *Gabay*

Gershom Delgado
M. A. N. Lindo

5682
Eustace A. Lindo
Alfred A. Isaacs
Joseph S. Elmaleh, *Gabay*

Gershom Delgado
Judah D. Israel

5683
Eustace A. Lindo
Alfred A. Isaacs
Joseph S. Elmaleh, *Gabay*

Gershom Delgado
Judah D. Israel

5684
Jonathan Pinto
Edward L. Mocatta
Joseph S. Elmaleh, *Gabay*

Judah D. Israel
Ellis S. Manasseh

5685
Jonathan Pinto
Edward L. Mocatta (resigned)
Major T. H. Sebag-Montefiore, *Gabay*
Frank I. Afriat

Edward L. Mocatta
Ellis S. Manasseh

5686
Jonathan Pinto
Frank I. Afriat
Leon B. Castello, *Gabay*

Edward L. Mocatta
Ellis S. Manasseh

5687
Ronnie Gubbay
Frank I. Afriat
Leon B. Castello, *Gabay*

M. A. N. Lindo
Charles E. Sebag-Montefiore

5688
Ronnie Gubbay
Gershom Delgado
Leon B. Castello, *Gabay*

M. A. N. Lindo
Charles E. Sebag-Montefiore

5689
Ronnie Gubbay
Gershom Delgado
Leon B. Castello, *Gabay*

Dr. Lionel D. Barnett
Charles E. Sebag-Montefiore

5690
Ronnie Gubbay
Gershom Delgado
Joseph S. Elmaleh, *Gabay*

Dr. Lionel D. Barnett
Charles E. Sebag-Montefiore

5691
Ronnie Gubbay (died in office)
Joseph S. Elmaleh
Joseph N. Nabarro, *Gabay*

Dr. Lionel D. Barnett
John Sebag-Montefiore
Edward L. Mocatta

5692
Edward L. Mocatta
David V. N. da Costa
Joseph N. Nabarro, *Gabay*

David Beriro
John Sebag-Montefiore

5693
Edward L. Mocatta
David V. N. da Costa
Joseph N. Nabarro, *Gabay*

David Beriro
John Sebag-Montefiore

APPENDIX V

5694
David V. N. da Costa
Arthur de Casseres
Judah S. Benzecry, *Gabay*

David Beriro
Judah S. Benzecry
Denis D. G. Israel, *Gabay*

5695
Arthur de Casseres
Artom A. Romain
Denis D. G. Israel, *Gabay*

Neville J. Laski, K.C.
Judah S. Benzecry

5696
Arthur de Casseres
Artom A. Romain
Denis D. G. Israel, *Gabay*

Neville J. Laski, K.C.
Judah S. Benzecry

5697
Artom A. Romain
Joseph S. Elmaleh
Denis D. G. Israel, *Gabay*

David V. N. da Costa
Neville J. Laski, K.C.

5698
Joseph S. Elmaleh
John Sebag-Montefiore
Harold W. E. Lindo, *Gabay*

David V. N. da Costa
Neville J. Laski, K.C.

5699
Joseph S. Elmaleh
John Sebag-Montefiore

Harold W. E. Lindo, *Gabay*

Alfred A. Isaacs
Alan A. Mocatta

5700
David Beriro
John Sebag-Montefiore
Harold W. E. Lindo, *Gabay*

Alfred A. Isaacs
Joseph I. Mendes

5701
Joseph N. Nabarro
Neville J. Laski, K.C.
Asher Benroy, *Gabay* (resigned)

Alfred A. Isaacs
Asher Benroy
James M. Sebag-Montefiore, *Gabay*

5702
Joseph N. Nabarro
Neville J. Laski, K.C.
James M. Sebag-Montefiore, *Gabay*

Artom A. Romain
Asher Benroy

5703
Joseph N. Nabarro
Neville J. Laski, K.C.
James M. Sebag-Montefiore, *Gabay*

Artom A. Romain
Asher Benroy

5704
Ralph Pinto (in place of A. A. Romain, resigned)
Joseph N. Nabarro
Neville J. Laski, K.C.

Robert N. Carvalho, *Gabay*

Ralph Pinto
Asher Benroy

5705
Joseph N. Nabarro
Neville J. Laski, K.C.
Robert N. Carvalho, *Gabay*

Artom A. Romain
Ralph Pinto

5706
Robert N. Carvalho
Lt.-Col. Alan A. Mocatta, O.B.E.
Henry de Casseres, *Gabay*
Col. T. H. Sebag-Montefiore. D.S.O., M.C. (in place of A. A, Romain, resigned)

Col. T. H. Sebag-Montefiore, D.S.O., M.C.
Ralph Pinto

5707
Henry de Casseres
Alan A. Mocatta, O.B.E.
Samuel I. Mendoza (in place of Ralph Pinto, resigned)
Richard D. Barnett, *Gabay*

Col. T. H. Sebag-Montefiore, D.S.O., M.C.
Samuel I. Mendoza

5708
Henry de Casseres
Alan A. Mocatta, O.B.E.
Richard D. Barnett, *Gabay*

Sigmund G. da Costa (in place of H. de Casseres, resigned)
Neville J. Laski, K.C.
Samuel I. Mendoza

5709
Sigmund G. da Costa
Richard D. Barnett
Felix J. N. Nabarro, *Gabay*

Asher Benroy
Neville J. Laski, K.C.

5710
Sigmund G. da Costa
Felix J. N. Nabarro
H. Manuel Cansino, *Gabay*

Neville J. Laski, K.C.
J. H. Bueno de Mesquita

5711
Ralph Pinto
Felix J. N. Nabarro
H. Manuel Cansino, *Gabay*

J. H. Bueno de Mesquita
Geoffrey Whitehill

5712
Ralph Pinto
H. Manuel Cansino
Denzil Sebag-Montefiore, *Gabay*

APPENDIX VI

GLOSSARY

ADJUNTO	Co-opted member either of the Mahamad or of the Board of Elders.
ASCABA	Memorial prayer.
ASCAMA (*pl.* ASCAMOT)	One of the civil laws of the Congregation.
ASHKENAZI	Jew originating in northern or central Europe.
BARMITZVAH	A boy, who on attaining the age of thirteen years, becomes a full member of the Jewish Community: the service of initiation of such a boy.
BETH DIN (*pl.* BOTAI DIN)	Ecclesiastical court: Bench of rabbis.
BETH HAIM	Cemetery (lit. House of Life).
BETH HAMEDRASH	Theological College.
BETH HOLIM	Hospital.
BODEK	Examiner of cattle after slaughter, to ascertain whether it is fit for human consumption.
CAUTIVOS	Captives.
COHEN	A member of the Priestly Caste among the Jews (a reputed descendant of Aaron, who, in view of his ancestry, enjoys certain privileges in the synagogue).
CONGREGANTE	A regular worshipper in the Synagogue, who has, however, not been elected a member of the Congregation.
DAYAN	Ecclesiastical judge.
DIN	Jewish ecclesiastical law.
EHAL	Ark in the synagogue, containing the Scrolls of the Law.
ESNOGA	Synagogue.
FINTA	Originally a loan to the Congregation, later a tax.
FINTADORE	Assessor of the Finta.
GABAY	Treasurer of the Congregation.
GEMARA	The Talmud: the body of early Rabbinical discussions on Jewish law and observance and a variety of other matters.
GUER (*fem.* GUERA)	A proselyte to Judaism.
HAHAM	Sephardi Chief Rabbi.
HAPHTARA	Portion from the Prophets read in synagogue.
HAZAN	Leader in prayer in the synagogue.
HEBRA	Burial society.
HEREM	Form of excommunication.

HESHAIM	Theological College.
IMPOSTA	Tax on income.
KAAL	Congregation.
KADDEESH	Prayer recited by mourners.
KASHER	Ritually approved (of food).
KIPPUR	Day of Atonement.
LADINO	Judaeo-Spanish.
LEVANTADOR	Member of the congregation entrusted with the raising of the scroll of the Law in synagogue.
MAHAMAD	The governing body of a Sephardi Congregation.
MARRANO	A forced convert from Judaism or his descendant, who in secret practises Judaism so far as he understands it.
MATZA (*pl.* MATZOT)	Unleavened bread.
MEDRASH	See Beth Hamedrash.
MEDRASISTA	Student at the Medrash or theological college.
MINHAG	Religious custom.
MINYAN	A quorum of ten males necessary for public worship.
MINYANISTA	A man hired to complete a quorum for public service.
MISHEBERACH	Prayer in honour of an individual or institution.
MISHNAH	The oldest collection, apart from the Pentateuch, of Jewish legislative writings.
MITZVA (*pl.* MITZVOT)	An honour involving participation in the Synagogue service.
MUSAPH	Additional service.
NEDABOT	Offerings in the Synagogue.
PARNAS	Warden.
PARNAS PRESIDENTE	Presiding warden.
PURIM	Feast of Mordecai and Esther.
RUBI	Rabbi or teacher.
SAMAS (SHAMASH)	Official responsible for the care and management of the synagogue etc.
SEDACA	General communal fund (properly, charitable fund)
SEPHARDI	Jew originating from Spain or Portugal.
SEPHER: SEPHER TORAH (*pl.* SEPHARIM: SIPHRE TORAH)	Scroll of the Law.
SHALIACH (*pl.* SHILUCHIM)	Messenger, as a rule one sent from the Holy Land to collect money.
SHEBUOT	Pentecost or Feast of Weeks.
SHECHITA	The ritual slaughter and preparation of meat for consumption by Jews.
SHOCHET	Ritual slaughterer.
SHULCHAN ARUCH	A code of Jewish law, compiled by Joseph Caro in the sixteenth century.
SIMHHAT TORAH	Festival of the Rejoicing of the Law.
SOFER	A scribe.

TALMUD TORAH	Religious school (lit. Study of the Law).
TEBA	Reading platform in the synagogue.
TERRA SANTA	The Holy Land.
TUDESCO (*fem.* TUDESCA)	An Ashkenazi.
VELHO	An Elder.
YAHID (*fem.* YAHIDA: *pl.* YEHIDIM, YEHIDOT)	A member of the Sephardi Congregation.
YESHIBA	Religious school.

INDEX

Abarbanel, Don Isaac, 407
Abecasis, Solomon, 233, 234, 235–7, 247, 318
Abendana: Hazan, 154; Isaac, 60; Haham Jacob, 33, 59–60, 68; Hazan Moses, 155
Abendanon, Joseph, 51, 78, 79, 87, 93, 111
Aberle, Reb (Abraham Nathan), 93
Abinun, Hazan Eliezer, 414
Abrahams: Dayan Barnett, 304–5, 312, 340; Israel, 340; Joseph, 340, 357, 360–1; Mordecai, 340; Moses, 340
Abudiente, Rehuel (Rowland Gideon), 129, 130, 142
Abulafia—*see* Bolaffi: Bolaffy
Adler: Chief Rabbi Hermann, 355, 357, 366; Chief Rabbi Nathan, 292, 306, 308, 343
Aflalo, Frederick George, 397
Africa, North, Immigration from, 248
Aga, Israel, 215
Aguilar, d': family, 31, 102; Diego Lopes Pereira, Baron d', 31, 102; Emanuel, 259, 261, 367, 396; Ephraim Lopes Pereira, Baron d', 102–3; Grace, 261–2
Alexander: Alexander, 226; Levy, 226
Alien Import Duties, 99
Almeida: Abraham Nunez de, 79; Joseph d', 113; Manuela Nunez de, 110; Mordecai Nunez de, 110
Almosnino: Hasdai, 136n., 220; Hazan Isaac, 194, 230–2, 340; Solomon, 194, 230–1, 367
Almshouses, Communal, 241, 242, 268, 319, 322, 371, 375, 411
Aloof: Judah, 235, 237, 294, 318; Solomon, 233, 234–6, 237, 260, 336
Alvarenga, Rear-Admiral Isaac da Costa, 206
Alvares: Duarte Henriques (Daniel Cohen Henriques), 11; Isaac Jessurun, 135; Jacob, 143
Alvarez, Isaac—*see* Nunez, Isaac Israel
America, Sephardi settlement in South and Central, 2
Amsterdam, Sephardi Community of, 8, 28, 93, 145, 164, 292, 324
Andrada (Andrade), Antonio Rodrigues, 5

Andrade, Solomon Haim, 343–4
Añes or Ames family, 5, 6, 7, 9
Anne, Queen, 60–1
Annuities, sale of, 186
Anriques (Henriques), Simão, 6
Antonio, Don, 9
Antwerp: Jewish Community of, 164; Jewish Conference at, 6
Appeals: from abroad for assistance, 86, 163–6, 250–1, 347, 384; for non-Jewish charities, 251, 347; from Provincial Communities, 249–50
Arditti, Ephraim Abraham, 255
Arias, Diego Rodrigues, 11
Artom, Haham Benjamin, 342–3, 345, 347, 357, 358
Army contractors, 12, 68, 100, 101, 103
Artists, Jewish, 114–15, 214, 262
Ascamot: The, 27–32, 33, 50, 64n., 86–7; amendment of, 38, 49, 196, 290; revision of, 188–90, 221, 272, 332–9, 343, 378–80, 382–3
Ashkenazi Community of London, 67, 71, 138, 169; Community, relations with the, 137n., 143–4, 165, 171, 172, 174–5, 178–9, 223, 225–6, 227–8, 302, 305–9, 326, 405; contributions to the Congregation, 54–5, 58, 71, 327–8; officials of, origin, 303, 305—*see also* Levy, Benjamin; Purim, Isaac; preachers, 137n., 261, 304, 366
Ashkenazi, Rabbi Zevi, 93–4
Ashkenazim: The, 1; to Congregation, admission of, 169–71, 303, 391, 396; co-operation with, 406
Assifat Haberim, 95, 387
Association for the Promotion of Jewish Literature—*see* Sussex Hall
'Astley's Jews', 115
Athias: Moses Israel, 20, 34; Solomon da Costa, 112–13
Attendance at Synagogue, 344
Australia: emigration to, 251, 322; Sephardim in, 251
Avigdor: Elim H. d', 391–2; Count Salamon Henri d', 391; Countess d', 391
Avila: Hannah de, 85; Isaac Israel d', 51, 79
Ayllon, Haham Solomon, 68–9, 70, 81, 91, 93

Azevedo: Benjamin Cohen d': 160; Hazan Daniel Cohen d', 220; Isaac d', 40; Joseph Cohen d', 93, 100; Moses Cohen d', 136n., 182, 183, 194
Azores, Jewish Community of, 165, 250
Azulay, Isaac Leonini (Joseph), 209

Banco, Asser del, 170
Bank of England, 99, 129; foundation of, 100, 200
Barbados Jewish Community, 151-4
Barmitzvah Prayer, 345, 358
Barros Basto, Capt. A. C. de, 408
Barrow family, 22, 27, 130, 265, 330: Joseph, 152, 241; (Baruh), Moses, 22, 27, 54, 63; Simon, 152, 265, 330
Baruch (Baruh), Lousada family, 22, 27; Abigail, 213; Emanuel, 296
Barzilai, Isaac, 40
Basevi: George (Elias), 245, 246; Naphtali, 114, 245, 246
Beaconsfield, Lord, 114, 245, 296
Beaumont, the brothers, 56
Belais, Abraham, 208-9, 291
Belasco brothers, 216; Hazan George, 366
Belilios, Jacob, 164
Belisha, Isaac D., 359
Belgrade, 51, 164
Belisario: Isaac Mendes, 136n., 262; Jacob Mendes, 233-4; Miriam Mendes, 262
Belmonte: Bienvenida Cohen, 111; Francisco (Jacob) de, 104
Benguegui, Joseph, 255
Benider, Jacob, 206-7
Bennett, Solomon, 227, 228
Benrimoh, Samuel, 236-7
Bensusan: family, 336, 397; Samuel Levy, 247
Benzecry, Lieutenant Solomon, 411
Berahel (Baruhiel), Jacob, 54, 57-8, 212
Bergson, Michael, 345
Berkshire, Earl of, 37
Bernal: family, 197-8; Jacob Israel, 170, 171, 197; Ralph, 198
Bernal-Osborne, Ralph, 198
Beth Din, the, 194
Beth Haim—see Cemeteries
Beth Holim (hospital), 59, 83-4, 226, 238, 302, 320, 326
Bevis Marks: origin of name, 75-8; Synagogue, proposed demolition of, 263, 373-5
Birmingham Jewish Community, 306
Bitton, Isaac, 216-17
Bland, Maria Theresa (*née* Romanzini), 215
Board of Deputies, Jewish, 123, 124, 125, 126-7, 128, 134-9, 152, 194, 294-5, 339, 351, 406
Board of Deputies and Jewish Emancipation, 296-8
Board of Guardians, Sephardi, 271, 322, 326, 383
Bohemia, 165-6
Bolaffi (Abulafia), Michael, 214
Bolaffy, Hayim Vita (Hananiah), 214-215, 235
Books, Control of Publication of, 29, 184-5, 221
Bossy (Garcia), Dr., 116
Boyno, Dr.—*see* Bueno
Brampton, Sir Edward, 3
Branch Synagogue, Sephardi, 279-81, 288-9, 305, 312-15, 342
Brandon: David (Rodriguez), 255, 289
Bravo, Abraham, 111
Breach of Promise actions, 118-19, 185
Brent (Pinto), Charlotte, 114
Bristol, Marrano settlement in, 2, 6-7
British Museum Library, 112
Brito: Abraham Israel de, 21, 88, 96; Abraham Lopes de, 87-8, Gabriel Lopes de, 143, 187; Jacob Mendes de, 87, 96, 124
Brokers, Sworn, 14, 142-3
Bryanston Street Synagogue, 315-16, 344, 373, 375-6
Buckingham, Duchess of, 47-8
Bueno: Dr. Joseph Mendes, 23, 49; de Mesquita, Benjamin, 146; de Mesquita, Hazan David, 364, 414
Bulama Expedition, the, 201
Burglaries, 63, 169
Burials, 338, 395-6; Prae Resettlement, Jewish, 8
Burton Street Synagogue, 285
Buzaglo, Abraham, 116

Caceres: Samuel de, 50-1; Simon (Jacob) de, 12, 14, 21, 24, 33
Canary Islands, 10
Cano, Moses del, 87
Cape Town, 250, 397
Carvajal, Antonio Fernandez (Abraham Israel), 10, 11, 12, 14, 21, 24
Carvalho, Hazan Emanuel Nunes, 153-4, 160-2
Casseres, James, 5
Castro: Mrs. (artist), 115; Abraham de, 194; Daniel Jacob de, 220; (Crasto) Hazan David Isaac de,

Castro—*contd.*
 115, 195; Hananel de, 259, 287, 291, 293, 295; General Henry de, 108; Jacob de (surgeon), 83, 109; Jacob de (comedian), 113, 115; Joseph de, 375, 401, 404–5; Moses Pereyra de, 83; Samuel de, 264; Sarmento, Dr. Jacob de, 83, 84, 88, 106–9, 167, 184, 185–6
Catherine of Braganza, 21
Cautivos (captives,) 32, 81, 326, 383
Cemeteries: Jewish, in London, 14, 24, 319–22, 390; protection of, 58, 195–6
Cemetery administration, 39, 390
Census of Jews, 34, 62, 70, 222, 330–1
Cervetto (Basevi): Giacobbe, 114, 246; James, 114
Chacon, Augustin Coronel—*see* Coronel
Charity, dissatisfied applicants for, 339
Charles II, King, 21, 23, 37, 46, 56, 63, 298
Charleston (Charles Town), South Carolina, 153, 154, 159, 162
Chaves: Dr. David de, 84, 111; Hazan Isaac de, 78, 258
Chavez, Aaron de, 55, 149, 258
Chief Rabbi, proposal to appoint a joint, 306–7, 361–2
Children, maintenance of baptized, 124
Children's services, 415
Chile, proposed conquest of, 13–14
Chillon, Isaac Lopes, 21
Choir, The, 271, 272, 275, 276, 345, 366–7
Cholera epidemics, 249, 251, 254–5, 326, 346
Chumaceiro, Abraham Mendes, 167
Church: charities, contributions to, 62; office, compulsory, 62; rates, 143
City Corporation, 56, 139, 143, 180, 355
Cohan, Eve, 56
Cohen: Hazan Jacob Raphael, 150; Levi Barent, 348; Louis, 315, 327; Rubi Salomon, 220; Samuel Isaac, 367
Colquhoun, Patrick, 222
Communal Centre, the, 376, 415
Confederation of Sephardi Jews, 409
Confirmation of girls, 415
Conquy, Hazan Solomon, 364
Conventicle Act of 1664, 37, 46
Converts: to Christianity, 45, 56; the House of, 2–3
Cordova: Francisco de, 68; Rudolph de, 397

Corfu Community, 251
Cork Community, 146, 358
Cormano, Solomon, 8
Coronel (Chacon), Sir Augustin, 21–22, 58
Correa, Isaac Israel, 75, 96
Cortissos, Joseph, 101
Coryate, Thomas, 9
Cos, Jewish Community of, 165
Costa: da—*see* also Gomez da Costa, Mendes da Costa; Abraham (John) da, 99; Alvaro da, 21, 33, 34, 62, 99; Benjamin da, 119 n., 120 n., 177; Bento de la—*see* Costa, Alvaro da; Catherine (Rachel Mendes) da, 114–15; David da, 21; Hazan Isaac da, 159; Sergeant Isaac da, 266; Isaac, 232; Joseph da, 118; Moses (Anthony) da, 99, 110, 115, 143, 156, 187–8; Moses de Joseph da, 135; Solomon da, 158; Solomon I. da, 396–7; da v. Villa Real, 118–19
Cour, Dr. Philip de la (Abraham Gomes Ergas), 83, 84, 105, 213
Creechurch Lane Synagogue, the, 14–21, 78
Crewe, Marquess of, 119
Crime, Jews and, 193
Cromwell, Oliver, 13, 26, 131
Cuming (Cumming), Sir Alexander, 159

Damascus Blood Accusation, 152, 251, 349
David: Aubrey J., 377; Sir Sassoon, Charity Fund, 413
Davidson, Sir William, 60
Declaration of Indulgence, the (1673), 46
Decorum in the Synagogue, 30, 49–51, 52, 78, 86, 87, 89, 90, 196, 233–4, 272, 273, 288, 318–19
Delpini, Carlo Antonio, 215
Desertion of families, 253–4
Disraeli: Benjamin—*see* Beaconsfield, Earl of; Coningsby, 246
D'Israeli, Isaac, 204, 214, 242–6
Distribution of London Jewry, 70, 120–2, 217, 273, 344, 372, 376
Divorces, Regulation of, 30, 238
Domingo: Dr. Jacob, 9
Dormido: David Abrabanel, 21, 24–6, 40; Solomon, 14, 26, 142
Dowry Charities, 57, 83 n., 242
Dublin Jewish Community, 31, 67–8, 145–6, 250, 358, 385
Duque, Abraham, 88–9
Dury, John, 32

Eardley, Lord, 130
East End Scheme, 406
Edinburgh Jewish Community, 153
Edrehi, Moses, 263
Education, Jewish Religious, 38–9, 50, 94–5, 376, 386, 414
Elders: election of, 334–5, 380, 382, 413; status of, 32, 33, 86–7, 188, 275, 332–3, 414
Elegies in Hebrew, 137n.
Elizabeth, Queen, 7, 8
Elkin, Benjamin, 259
Elmaleh, Joseph, 363
Elopements, 191–3
Emancipation, political, 296–8
Emanuel, Moses, legacy from, 328
Emigration to North America, 156–9
English substituted for Portuguese, 195, 224, 241, 260, 269, 270, 272
Ergas, Abraham Gomez—see Cour, Philip de la
Essex, Earl of, 7
Estevens, David, 115
Esteves, Haim and Rachel, 85
Excommunication—see Herem
Expulsion of the Jews from England, 2

Falk, Chaim Samuel (Jacob), 328
Families, size of, 218n.
Fano, Alessandro da, 362
Farjeon, Benjamin Leopold, 396
Faro, Jacomo, 31
Fernandes, Beatriz—see Nunez, Beatrice
Fernandez, Joseph Dias, 133
Fidanque: Abraham, 69, 70n.; Jacob, 51, 69–70
Finances, Synagogue, 30, 31, 32, 36, 40, 41, 58, 168, 180–1, 188, 223, 240–2, 248–9, 316–18, 369–71, 372
Fines, 29, 87, 88, 89, 95, 96, 186, 189, 222, 242–8, 278, 332, 339, 343, 379
Finta, 33, 40, 55, 168, 188–9, 241, 251, 316–18, 369–70, 383
Fintadores, 278, 316–17
Fire: danger of, 168–9; the Great, 36
Foligno: Edward, 336, 346; Isaac, 233, 294; Isaac—in memoriam gift, 327–8; John, 114
Fonseca: Isaac de, 147; Manuel da, 21
'Forty-Five' Panic, the, 129, 133–4
Foundlings, 36
France, immigration from, 2
Francia: Abraham de, 40, 55; Domingo (Israel) Rodriguez, 21; Isaac (Domingo Rodriguez) de, 22, 40, 55; Francis, 41, 104; Francisco Rodriguez, 22; Moses, 75

Franco: Jacob de Moses, 125, 135, 252; Solomon, 22, 44–5
Franks: family, 147; Aaron, 139, 144, 147, 165, 327; Jacob, 146–7; Moses, 148
Freedom of the City, 32, 129, 141–2
Freehold Lands Scheme, 371–2, 372–5
Furtado—see Mendes Furtado: Orobio Furtado

Gabay, office of, 26, 27, 28, 33, 194, 247, 332, 337
Gaguin, Rabbi Shemtob, 414
Gaon, Haham Solomon, 414, 415
Galvano, Dr. Abraham Perez, 49
Galway, Sarah (Elizabeth) Viscountess, 119
Garcia, Christopher, 5
Gaster, Haham Moses, 360, 362–3, 389, 394, 395, 400, 414
Gates of Hope School, 85, 94, 257, 270–1, 287, 386, 387
George I, King, 124
George II, King, 165–6
George III, King, 100, 115, 135, 137n.
George IV, King, 137n., 211, 216
Georgia, colonization of, 99, 156–8
Germany, persecution of Jews in, 14, 165, 406
Gibraltar, immigration from, 97, 411–12
Gideon: Rowland—see Abudiente, Rehuel; Sampson, 84, 111, 128–33, 142
Glückstadt, Jewish Community of, 163
Goldsmid: Abraham, 223; Asher, 200; Sir Francis, Bart., 286, 391; Sir Isaac Lyon, Bart., 296, 391
Gomez da Costa, Benjamin, 220
Gomes de Mesquita: Hazan Joseph, 364–5; Haham Moses, 115, 165, 167, 183, 214
Gomes Serra, Isaac, 265
Gomes Serra, Pinhas, 187
Gomez Serra, Jacob (Antonio), 32, 53, 74
Gonzales: Jacob, 124; Jacob Nunes, 135, 137
Gonzalez, Abraham Cohen, 21, 32
Goodman: Paul, 367–8, 408, 409; Tobias, 260
Gracia, Dona—see Luna, Beatrice de
Great Synagogue, London, 139, 144, 167, 186, 224, 298, 301–2, 307, 328
Green, Aaron Levy, 366
Greenberg, Leopold J., 374

INDEX 463

Greenhalgh, visit of John to the Synagogue, 15–20
Gubbay, Mordecai Simeon, 397
Guedalla: Haim, 263–4, 291, 293, 294, 295, 374, 398–9; Judah, 287, 327; Judah, Trust, 327; Philip, 397

Haliva, Abraham, 256, 285, 291, 305, 311–12
Hambro: Baron Joseph, 327; Synagogue, 139; Establishment of the 144
Hamburg Sephardi Community, 163, 164, 250
Hamilton, John, 158
Handel, George Frederick, 114
Hardwicke, Lord Chancellor, 126, 127
Hart: Rabbi Aaron, 167; Moses, 165, 324, 327
Head: Sir Francis Bond, 111; Sir George, 111
Hebra de Bikur Holim e Guemilut Hasadim, 39, 59, 82–3
Heilbut: Reuben, 300, 315; Samuel, 43, 71
Heneage: Lane—origin of name, 75; Sir Thomas, 75
Henrietta Maria, Queen, visits a synagogue, 61
Henriques—*see also* Anriques
Henriques: family, 63, 280; Abraham Lopes, 79; Daniel Cohen—*see* Alvares, Duarte Henriques; Isaac Israel, 75; Jacob, 100–1
Henry VII, King, 3
Henry VIII, King, 4, 6
Herem: Legality of, 92; Punishment of, 28, 40, 185, 289, 291–3
Hirschel, Chief Rabbi Solomon, 226, 227, 238, 239, 252, 256, 283, 285, 306
Holland Park Synagogue, 413, 415
Holy Land: 31–2, 165, 251–3, 353–5, 356, 409–10; emissaries from the—*see Shiluchim*
Honen Dalim, Menahem Abelim, Hebrat Yetomot e Hebrat Moalim, 83, 383
Honourable Artillery Company, 266
Hore-Belisha, Mr. Leslie, 397
Hospitals Sunday Fund, Metropolitan, 347

Immigration: of Jews, 67, 96–7, 177, 179–80, 223, 269; of Poor, 39, 44, 48, 71–2, 82, 179–80, 248
Imposta, 30, 33, 40, 190, 241, 248, 318
India, commercial interests in, 68 n., 97

Inquisition, the, 23, 176
'Intelligencers', Jewish, 7, 12
Ireland, naturalization of Jews in, 124, 125
Israel, Debora, 58
Italy: immigration from, 96–7, 164, 348, 412; Sephardim in, 163

Jalfon, Isaac, 287
Jamaica, 12, 136–8, 146, 155, 250, 384
James II, King, 56, 181
James (Belasco), David, 397
Janathus (Jonathan) of Spain, 3
Jerusalem, 327
Jessey, Henry, 32
Jessurun: Elias Robert, 367; Jessurun Rodrigues—*see* Salvador
'Jew Bill, The', 127–8
Jewish Chronicle, The, 259
Jewish Orphanage, The, 223
Jews' College, 305, 308, 389–90
John of Castile, 3
Joseph, Morris, 366
Julian, Hazan Moses Henriques, 154, 220

Kadoorie family, the, 408
Kennicott, Bishop Benjamin, 194
Keyser, Jacob, 71, 74
Kimhi, Jacob, 179, 215–16
King, John, 209–11, 270
Kirk, visit to Synagogue by Robert (1689), 73

Laguna, Daniel Israel Lopez, 110
Lamego, Moses, 85, 95 n.
Landor, Walter Savage, 214
Lara. D. E. Cohen de, 261; Joshua, elopement of, 191–2; Moses Nunes, 228–30, 242; Moses, Trust, 242, 326, 383–4; Sara Nunes, 271
Lauderdale Road Synagogue, 376–7, 411
Lazarus, Solomon, 280
Lee, Rachel Fanny Antonina ('Baroness Despenser'), 215
Legacies: to the Congregation, 57, 241, 327–8; for advancement of Judaism disallowed, 126
Leon: Abraham de, 51; Abraham Judah, 79
Levi or Levy, Samuel—rabbi or *samas*, 20, 42, 71, 79
Levy: Benjamin—Hazan, 41–2, 49, 54; Benjamin—Ashkenazi worthy, 42–4, 67, 71, 74, 143, 169; Isaac, 143; Isaac de David, 95; Judith (Judy), 43; Mayer (Michael), 54, 56, 64, 71; Samuel—*see* Levi

Lewis, Harry S., 389
Lima, Elias de, 26–7
Lindo: Abigail, 261; Abraham Alexander, 137n., 260–1, 278; David Abarbanel, 246, 256–7, 274, 279, 286, 346; Elias Haim—Historian and Parnas, 261; Elias Haim—Secretary, 367; Ephraim, 245, 246; Gabriel, 375, 404; Lorenco (Isaac), 11, 33; Manuel, 11; Moses, 160; Nathaneel, 294, 298; Dr. Zachariah, 298; v. Belisario, 192–3
Lipton, Mr. Marcus, 104
Lisbon, Jewish Community of, 385
'Little Synagogue, The', 344, 415
Liverpool, Sephardim in, 358
Liz: Francisco de—*see also* Berahel, Jacob; Francisco (Abraham) de, 61, 212; Francisco (Jacob) de (3), 212–13
Loewe, Louis, 137n., 261, 304, 305, 349
London: Hospital, The, 226, 324–6; Marrano settlement in, 2, 4–5
Lopes: family, 5, 203; Alves, 5; Gaspar, 5; Sir Manasseh, 201–4; (Franco) Sir Ralph, 203
Lopes Pereira family, 31, 102—*see also* Aguilar, d'; Abraham, 241–2; David, 380; Elias, 194; Isaac, 75, 96
Lopez: Mordecai Rodriguez, 186, 202–3; Dr. Rodrigo, 7–8, 75; Solomon, 42;
Lopez Pereira: family, 11; Elian, 31; Manoel (Isaac), 8, 31
Lord Mayor, The Congregation and the, 46–7, 56, 139–41, 403, 406, 415
Lorenço, Benjamin Dias, 195
Lowry, Mrs. Rebecca, 213
Lucena, John Charles, 205
Luna, Beatrice de, 4
Luzzatto, Dr. Ephraim, 109
Lyon: Rabbi Hart, 179; Naphtali Hart, 303, 314, 330

Machado: David, 111; and Pereira, 68
Macnin: Abraham Cohen, 207; David Cohen, 207–8; Masahod, 207
Madras, 68 n.
Magnus, Sir Philip, Bart., 392–3
Mahamad: election of, 26–7, 28, 33, 53, 189, 275, 334–6; powers of, 33, 65, 275; qualifications for membership of, 189, 335, 337
Mahatim Tobim, 84–5, 383
Maimonides celebration, 407

Manasseh ben Israel, 13, 60, 61
Manchester, Sephardim of, 358–60, 413, 415
Marchant, Mr. Michael, 368
Marchina, Anthony de, 5, 200
Marks, David Woolf, 285, 393
Marques: Antonio Rodrigues, 34; Abraham Hezekiah (Diego Rodriquez), 34, 57, 68 n.
Marquez, Isabel, 11
Marranos, The, 2, 4, 23, 175–6, 408
Marriage Act of 1836, 299, 328
Marriages, Jewish, 127, 175, 191–3, 227, 234, 300–2, 328–9, 395
Marriages: with Ashkenazim, 170–1, 190, 228, 299–300; with non-Jews, 66, 176–7, 190, 396
Marriage Regulations, 30, 171, 190, 192, 299, 302, 339, 394–5
Marriages, validity of Jewish, 192–3, 299
Martinez: Abraham Vaes, 75; Isaac N., 154
Mary, Queen, 7
Mattos: Joshua de, 79; Moses Lumbrozo de, 199, 200
Meat, supply of, 49, 67, 178—*see also* Shechita questions
Medina: Moses de, 91; Sir Solomon de, 54, 55, 68, 96, 103, 242, 350
Medrash of *Heshaim*, 81, 94–5, 224, 270, 346, 386–9
Mehil Sadaca, 383
Meldola: Abraham, 228–9, 329; David 228–32, 233, 234–5, 255, 256–7, 259, 283, 285, 291, 293, 309–11; Haham Raphael, 151, 224, 227–30, 235, 236, 238–9, 255, 271; Raphael, F.R.S., 397
Mellish, William, M.P., 119
Mello, Samuel Abenatar, 79
Men and Women of Letters, Jewish, 110–11, 261–2
Mendes: Abraham, 115–16, 144; Abraham Pereira, 155, 341, 342, 357, 365, 366; Harry Pereira, 359–360, 365, 403; Dr. Fernando, 34, 62–3, 105, 110; Frederick de Sola, 365; Francisco and Diogo, 4; (Pye) Jael Henrietta, 111; Solomon, 111; Moses, 111
Mendes da Costa: family, 99; Benjamin, 95, 102, 116–17, 125, 135, 143, 147, 158, 169, 252, 320, 328; David, 103; Emanuel, 103, 110; Fernando, 23; George, 23; Jacob, 103, 147; John, 99, 124; Moses (Philip), 99; Philip (Jacob), 118
Mendes Furtado, Isaac, 197

INDEX

Mendoza: Aaron (engraver), 115; Daniel, 216; Israel, *Samas*, 314
Mesquita—*see* Bueno de Mesquita; Gomes de Mesquita
Messias, Joseph, 184
Meza, Alonzo da Fonseca, 21
Michalki, Jacob, 227
Mildmay Park Synagogue, 344
Minyan, a paid, 316, 344–5, 402
Miranda, Jacob de, 55
Missionary work among Jews, 224–5
Mocatta: family, 199–200, 280; Abraham (d. 1751), 147, 199; Abraham (1798–1880), 273, 286, 314, 336; Abraham (1831–1900), 380; Abraham (Lumbroso de Mattos) (1730–1780), 200; Abraham Lindo (1796–1891), 287; Daniel (1774–1865), 271–2, 274, 276, 286; David (1806–1882), 264; Frederic David (1828–1905), 392; Isaac (*c.* 1700), 71, 200; Isaac (1765–1801), 214; Isaac Lindo 1818–79, 261; Jacob (1770–1825), 223–4, 270; Manuel (Immanuel), 55, 199; Moses (d. 1693), 5, 55, 199, 390–1; Moses (1768–1857), 224, 258, 261, 264, 296, 348; and Goldsmid, 200; Mr. Owen, 200
Mombach, Julius (Israel), 344
Montagu,—*see* Swaythling, Lord
Montefiore: family, 200–2, 329; Abraham, 171, 248, 329; Claude, 393; Charlotte, 259; College, Judith Lady, 308, 356, 388–9; Eliezer, 201; Sir Francis, 329n.; Horatio Joseph, 258, 393; Jacob, 201, 280, 322, 391, 395; Joseph Mayer, 307, 329, 336, 349, 393; Joseph Barrow, 201, 213, 281, 286, 322; Joshua, 201–2; Lady (Judith), 352, 353; Leonard, 393; Sir Moses, 146, 152, 171, 242, 273, 287, 294–5, 296, 303, 307, 308, 347–56, 359, 393; Sir Moses, bequests of, 355–6; Sir Moses, missions of, 264, 349–51; Sir Moses, Testimonial Fund, 355; Nathaniel, 393
Montreal Jewish Community, 150–1, 250, 304, 384
Moraes, Sabbathai, 261, 341
Moroccan envoys, 34, 206–9
Moses, Marcus, 144
Motteux, Timothy, legacy from, 327
Mozart, 113, 114
Mudahy: Elimelech, 255, 256; Moses Judah, 154, 341
Myers: Hazan Isaac Henry, 303–4; Hazan Emanuel, 303–4; Dr. Joseph Hart, 220

Names, 130, 217–18
Nasi, Joseph, Duke of Naxos, 4, 354
National and Infant School, 94, 271, 327, 345, 375, 386
Naturalization of Jews, 124, 125, 127–8, 130
Nedabot, 55
Netto (Nieto), Jacob, 32, 248
Nevis, 154
Newman, Alfred Alvarez, 374
Newport, R.I., 148–9, 366
New York Sephardi Community, 146–8, 151, 360
Nieto: Abraham, 304; Abraham Haim, 363–4; (Nietto) Haham David, 79–81, 85–6, 94, 106, 110, 115, 167; Haham David—charge of heresy against, 90–4; Moses, 86, 184–5; Haham Isaac, 86, 136n., 167, 168, 182–4
Noah, Mordecai Manuel, 161
Norsa: Hannah, 115; Laura (Lady Walpole), 115
North, Christopher, 263
Northey's, Sir Edward, opinion, 92
Nunes: Isaac Fernandes, 135; Jacob Fernandes, 125; Manuel Rodriguez, 21
Nunez: Dr. Hector, 6, 7; Henrique and Beatriz, 6, 7; Isaac Israel, 40, 47, 53, 54; Isaac Rodriquez, 88; Maria, 8

Oath on admission to office, 28, 238, 278
Offerings in the Synagogue, 55, 316, 331, 338, 368, 369, 378, 404
Office, refusal of, 28–9
Officers of the Congregation, appointment of, 337–8
Oglethorpe, James Edward, 157
Oliveira: Abraham (Polycarp) de, 41; Abraham Lopes de, 110, 114; Jacob de, 160
Orobio Furtado family, 206
Orphan Charities, 57–8, 248, 256
Orphanage, Sephardi, 85–6, 376, 414
Osborne charge against the Jews of murder, 125–6
Osorio, Abraham, 214

Pacheco, Benjamin Mendes, 125, 143
Pacifico: Don David, 266–8; Emanuel, 268
Paine, Tom, 210–11
Palestine—*see* Holy Land; Jewish settlement in, 354–5, 385
Palmerston, Viscount, 267–8
Pardo: Hazan David, 51, 78–9, 258; Hazan Joseph, 78–9

Pass: Aaron de, 294, 397; Abraham de, 314, 336; Lieutenant Frank Alexander de, V.C., 410–11
Paul of Burgos (de Santa Maria), 3
Paz, Elias de, 126
Penha, Mordecai de la, 83
Penso, David (Alexander Felix), 68
Pepys, Samuel—visit to the Synagogue, 20–1, 135 n.
Perceval, John, Viscount (Earl of Egmont), 156, 157
Pereira—*see also* Lopez Pereira; Aaron Israel, 147; Isaac, 68; Dr. Jonathan, 264; Moses de Morais, 88, 185
Peres, Daniel, 70, 79
Peterborough, Henry Mordant, 2nd Earl of, 57
Phila, the name, 130
Philadelphia Sephardi Congregation, 149–50, 153, 159
Phillimore, Joseph, 299
Physicians, Communal, 22, 40, 49, 220, 227, 368–9
Picciotto: Moses, 294, 353; James, 353, 399
Pina y Pimentel, Sara de Fonseca, 111
Pinsker, Leo, 385
Pinto: Charles, 114; G. F., 114; José de Sola, 381; Joseph Jessurun, 148; Thomas, 114
Piperno, Hazan Joseph, 314, 340, 364
Piza, Hazan David, 150–1, 340, 341, 359, 365
Plague, The Great, 34, 36, 45
Poland, Jews of, 86, 164
Political Rights, 199, 296–8
Pool, Solomon, 344
Poor: legal liability to support, 45, 180; relief of the, 39, 44, 48, 71, 72, 82, 85, 169–70, 222–3, 249, 271, 322, 324
Popes, The, 23, 415
Porto: Abraham (Antonio) do, 53, 54, 68; Jacob do, 68
Portugal: expulsion of the Jews from, 3–4; Marranos of, 408–9; prohibition of return to, 175–6; refugees from, 324
Prado: Abraham, 103; Samuel, 103
Prayer Book, translation of the, 183, 184, 221, 226–7, 258, 400
Prayers, special, 81, 135 n., 255, 353; for the Royal Family, 20, 135 n.
Press—admission to meetings, 382
Proselytes, 19, 22, 45, 54, 58, 66, 173–7, 181, 329, 358, 394
Proselytization, prohibition of, 29, 65–7, 173–7, 221

Publications to receive the authorization of the Mahamad, 29, 184–5, 221
Pugilists, Jewish, 216
Purim: celebration of, 3n, 19, 31, 196–7, 221; Isaac, 79

Rabbis, powers of, 87
Ramsgate Synagogue, 264, 303–4, 343, 358, 366
Ranelagh Gardens, 115
Raphall, Morris J., 258, 259
Rathom: Abraham, 142; Isaac, 142
Rawlinson, Daniel, 21
Rebello, David Alves, 113–14, 186
Records, Congregational, 399–400
Refusal of office, 95, 96, 186, 202, 242–4, 246–7
Resettlement of the Jews in England, 13
Rey, Jacob—*see* King, John
Rhodes Blood Accusation, 152, 251
Ricardo: David, 204–5, 213, 296; John Lewis, 205, 213
Rieti, Solomon, 115
Robles: Antonio Rodrigues, 11–12, 13; Joseph, 142
Roco, Hazan Simson Jechiel, 363, 365
Rodriguez, Affonso and Gomez—*see* Sequeira
Rogna, Antonio della, 5
Romain, Abraham Anidjar, 374
Romondo (Raymondo), George, 215
Roth, Mr. Cecil, 3, 13
Rothschild: Sir Anthony de, 294, 352; Baron Lionel de, 294, 297; Nathan Meyer, 348; Mrs. N. M.—gift from, 328
Rowlanda, the name, 130
Royal Marriages Act, 115
Royal Society, The, 105, 106, 109–10
Ruiz, Simon, 7
Rumanian Synagogue in London, 385
Russia, persecution of Jews in, 385, 407
Rycaut, Paul, 37

Saa Silveira, Aaron de, 220
Saare Orah Veabi Yetomim—see Orphanage
Sabbathaian Heresy, The, 69, 81
St. Paul's Cathedral, Jewish contributions to rebuilding of, 61–2
St. Thomas, W.I., 154
Salaries of officers of the Congregation, 220, 341, 342–3, 364, 368
Salom, Hazan Mordecai, 221, 258
Salomon, Dr. Berendt, 366

INDEX 467

Salomons: Sir David, 294–5, 298, 349–50; Sir David—legacy from, 328; Levy, 139
Salonica, Jewish Community of, 164, 250, 409, 412
Salvador: (Jessurun Rodrigues) family, 117; Francis (1), 125, 143, 156, 158, 327; Francis (2), 117; Jacob, 118, 124; Joseph, 110, 117–18, 135
Samuda: Jacob, 264; Joseph d'Aguilar, 264–5, 280, 329–30, 391; Sequeira—*see* Sequeira Samuda
Samuel, Mr. Wilfred, 14, 15, 24
Saraval, Jacob, 164
Sarfaty, Joshua, 91
Sarmento—*see* Castro Sarmento
Sasportas: Haham Jacob, 32, 34–5, 51, 206; Samuel, 38, 54
Sassoon: family, 330, 398; Sir Albert, 359; David Solomon, 398; Sir Edward, 398, 404; Mrs. Flora, 398; Sir Philip, 397; Reuben, 344, 398; Sassoon David, 330
Schomberg: family, 105; Meyer Löw, 105
Schools—*see* Education
Schoonenberg, Franz van, 104
Scottish East India Company, 100
Sebag: Isaac, 255; Solomon, 207; Solomon (junior), 304, 314
Sebag-Montefiore: Arthur, 404; Mr. Charles, 382, 404; Sir Joseph, 294, 295, 361–2, 404; Robert, 404, 411
Séches, Edgar, 366
Secretaries of the Congregation, 194
Seixas, Gershom Mendes, 149, 150, 162
Semon, Sir Felix, 105 n.
Sephardim, The, 1
Sequeira: Abraham Israel de (Gomez Rodriguez), 54, 55, 68; David Machado de, 68; Isaac Henriques, 213; Isaac Israel (Affonso Rodriguez) de, 68, 74; Joseph Rodriguez, 156; Samuda, Isaac de, 105–6, 167
Sermons, 59 n, 85, 108–9, 135 n., 183, 255, 258–261, 272–3, 306, 365
Serrão, Manuel, 6
Service: description of Synagogue, 15–20, 20–1, 72–3
Services: religious, outside of Bevis Marks, 28, 49, 188, 235–8, 241, 277, 279–80, 290, 336, 343, 379; special, 135 n., 271, 352, 355, 406–7
Shaare Tikva—*see* Gates of Hope School
Shandel, Hermann, 366
Shechita Questions, 67, 178–9, 182, 225–6, 234

Shepherd's Bush, Sephardi Settlement in, 386, 412–13
Shiluchim, 31–2, 68, 149, 238, 252–3
Shomere Mishmeret Hakodesh, 274
Shoreditch, New Sephardi Settlement in, 412
Sick, care of the—*see Hebra*
Sierra, Moses, 177
Silva: Duarte and Francisco da, 23; Dr. Joseph Vaz de, 83; Haham Joshua da, 41, 59; Samuel da, 115
Simeon of Treves, Rabbi, 212
Simhhat Torah, 49–50
Simon: Sir John, 206, 392; Oswald John, 392
Singer, Simeon, 366
Smyrna, 149, 251
Sola: Hazan Abraham de, 151, 258, 304, 341; Hazan David Aaron de, 151, 226, 255, 258–9, 260, 261, 305–6, 341, 346–7, 365, 367, 368; Hazan Isaac de, 258; Hazan Joseph Mendes de, 258; Hazan Samuel de, 308–9, 340, 341, 342
Soldiers, Anglo-Jewish, 265–6
Solla, Henri de, 292, 345, 366, 367
Solomons, Israel, 106, 397, 399
South Carolina, 158—*see also* Charleston
Souza, Antonio da, Portuguese Ambassador, 12
Spain, expulsion of the Jews from, 3
Spanish Government, visits to Synagogue by representatives of the, 407–8
Spira, Rabbi Nathan, 32
Stamford Hill Congregation, 413
Suasso: Alvaro (Jacob Israel), 110, 143, 156; Francisco Lopez, 1st Baron d'Avernas le Gras, 67
Sumbel, Joseph, 207
Surinam, 164–5
Sussex, Duke of, 137 n., 208, 259
Sussex Hall, 259, 295
Sutro, Alfred, 397
Swaythling, Samuel Montagu, Lord, 315, 375, 379
Sweden, invitation to Sephardim to settle in, 166–7
Synagogue: Bevis Marks—purchase of lease, 169; enlargement of the, 49, 53–6; erection of new (Bevis Marks), 74–8

Talmud Torah—*see Medrash*
Taxation, threat of special, 64
Terra Santa or Holy Land, gifts for, 32, 81
Theobald (from Turkey), 3

Tiberias, 251, 354
Tobago, 154
Toledo (Toledano), Chayim ben Daniel de, 206
Torres, Abraham, 88
Touro, Judah, 355
Treves: Joseph, 211; Pellegrin (Gershom) (1), 211–12; Pellegrin (2), 212
Trinidad Community, 154
Tryphena, the name, 130
Tudesco: Tudesca—*see* Ashkenazim
Turner, Sharon, 245

Union of Sephardi Communities, 409
Uzzielli, David, 266

Van Biene, Auguste, 396
Van Oven, Joshua, 222
Varicas, Judah, 330
Vaz, Hazan Aaron Nunes, 365
Veiga: Aaron, 26, 32; Rodrigo da, 6; Samuel da, 32
Velhos—*see* Elders
Venice, Sephardi Community of, 28, 163–4, 412
Victoria, Queen, 137n., 346, 349
Villa Real: Catharine da Costa (Mrs. Mellish), 118–19, 120n.; Catharine da Costa (widow of Jacob), 88, 119n., 185; Joseph (Isaac) (John) da Costa, 85, 94, 118; School, 85, 94, 271, 345–6, 375
Visits of non-Jews to Synagogue, 15, 21, 38, 60, 61, 73
Vitoria, Gaspar de, 31
Voice of Jacob, The, 259

Walpole, Sir Robert 141
Wars, the two World, 372, 375, 404, 405, 407, 411–12
Watchmen, 58, 181, 195–6, 322

Wealth of Sephardim, 54, 122, 168
Webb, Philip Carteret, 128
Wedding celebrations, 89–90
Wells, Mrs. Mary, 207
West Indian trade, 97
West Indies: Sephardi settlement in the—*see* Barbados, Jamaica, Nevis, Tobago, Trinidad; immigration from, 177
West London Synagogue, 204, 245, 263, 264, 280–2, 309, 390, 406
Western (Westminster) Synagogue, The, 227, 260, 330
Whitehall Conference, The, 13
Wigmore Street Synagogue, 305, 313–14, 343
Wild, Jonathan, 116
William III, King, 67, 68, 81, 103, 104
William IV, King, 137n., 260, 322, 353
Wolf, Lucien, 10, 13, 21, 99, 374, 399, 408
Women, the status of, in the Congregation, 190, 337, 380–1

Ximenes: Lieutenant-General Sir David, 202; Haham Isaac, 193; Sir Morris, 201, 202; Sarah, elopement of, 191–2

Yehidim: acceptance of Askerazim as, 303; compulsory recruitment of, 48, 247, 337, 343, 381–2; definition of, 32, 33, 190, 337, 379; meetings of, 240–1, 275–80, 333–4
Yeshiba, bequest for a, disallowed, 127
Yeshiba Mahané Raphael, 95, 346, 387

Zevi, Haham—*see* Ashkenazi, Rabbi Zevi

For Product Safety Concerns and Information please contact our EU representative GPSR@taylorandfrancis.com
Taylor & Francis Verlag GmbH, Kaufingerstraße 24, 80331 München, Germany

www.ingramcontent.com/pod-product-compliance
Lightning Source LLC
Chambersburg PA
CBHW070722020526
44116CB00031B/999